LETTERS OF NICHIREN

Translated by
Burton Watson and others

Edited by
Philip B. Yampolsky

Columbia University Press
New York

Columbia University Press
New York   Chichester, West Sussex
Copyright © 1996 NSIC and Soka Gakkai

Nichiren, 1222–1282.
    [Correspondence. English. Selections]
    Letters of Nichiren / translated by Burton Watson and others˜:
edited by Philip B. Yampolsky.
    p.   cm. — (Translations from the Asian classics)   (The
Columbia Asian studies series)
    Includes bibliographical references and index.
    ISBN 0-231-10384-0
    1. Nichiren, 1222–1282—Correspondence.   2. Priests, Nichichen—
Japan—Correspondence.   I. Watson, Burton, 1925–   .
II. Yampolsky, Philip B. (Philip Boas), 1920–   .   III. Title.
IV. Series.   V. Series: The Columbia Asian studies series.
BQ8349.N577A4   1996
294.3'928'092— dc20
    [B]
                                                    95-46774
                                                    CIP

Printed in the United States of America

c 10 9 8 7 6 5 4 3 2 1
p 10 9 8 7 6 5 4 3 2 1

CONTENTS

PREFACE

Nichiren (1222–1282) was one of a remarkable group of dedicated and creative Buddhist leaders who worked to make Mahayana Buddhism more readily available to the population as a whole by simplifying its practices in various ways and by stressing its message of universal salvation. To assist him in propagating his ideas, Nichiren produced a large body of writings in both Chinese and Japanese, known collectively as the *Gosho*. Some of these were lengthy doctrinal treatises; some were exhortations addressed to government officials; some dealt with doctrinal topics and expositions of his teachings; others were informal letters of advice, consolation, and encouragement directed toward his followers. Nichiren is of particular importance in the history of thought and religion because, although he may not have originally intended that result, his teachings came to constitute a separate sect of Buddhism, known as the Nichiren sect, the only major Buddhist sect to have its origin in Japan.

The present work serves as a companion volume to the *Selected Writings of Nichiren*, published in 1990. Its purpose is to introduce to readers of English a sampling of the voluminous correspondence that Nichiren produced during his lifetime. Contained here are some seventy-three letters, written between the years 1255 and 1282. They are addressed to his followers in various parts of eastern Japan, where Nichiren's teaching efforts were centered. The letters, although addressed to a particular follower, were frequently meant to be shared with other believers who lived in the same general area as did the person to whom the letter was addressed. Here the letters have been arranged under the provinces in which the addressee lived. Letters 1 to 7, although sent to a particular believer, were meant for Nichiren's followers in general; letters 8 through 13 were directed to his followers in Awa Province (the southern part of what is now Chiba Prefecture); letters 14 to 25 to his followers in Shimōsa Province (northern Chiba Prefecture and a part of Ibaraki Prefecture); letters 26 to 27 to his followers in Musashi Province (Tokyo, Saitama Prefecture, and a part of Kanagawa Prefecture); letters 28 to 45 to his followers in the city of Kamakura (Bakufu headquarters in Sagami Province, at present the southeastern part of Kanagawa Prefecture); letters 46 to 52 to followers in Sado Province, the island of Nichiren's second exile (now under the administration of Niigata Prefecture); and letters 53 to 73 to his followers in Suruga Province (eastern part of present-day Shizuoka Prefecture).

In the late 1970s the Nichiren Shoshu International Center (NSIC) in Tokyo, which is allied with the Soka Gakkai,* began preparing English translations of Nichiren's writings, mainly for the use of its overseas followers. The translations were prepared by Burton Watson and the members of the Gosho Translation Committee of the Center, and have been published by the Center under the title *The Major Writings of Nichiren Daishonin*. So far seven volumes of translations have appeared, and further volumes are in preparation. The longer pieces in the present volume were translated by Burton Watson, but a number of the shorter ones are the work of other members of the Gosho Translation Committee. In the case of these letters, efforts were made to determine just which translator or translators were responsible for which piece. But because the translations were done a number of years ago, often by persons no longer associated with the Committee, it proved impossible to assign a translator's name to each piece. Thus, as in the case of *Selected Writings of Nichiren*, we have had to resort to the rather evasive-sounding "Burton Watson and others."

The translations in the present volume were drawn from the first six volumes of the *Major Writings of Nichiren Daishonin*. But in order to adapt them to the needs of general readers, certain changes have been made by Philip Yampolsky in the translations, the explanatory material accompanying them, and in the annotations to the texts.

To a large extent the translations as found in the original texts of the *Major Writings* have been followed. These translations are based on the texts found in the *Nichiren Daishōnin Gosho Zenshū*, published in 1952. Numerous variant texts for Nichiren's writings exist, but no attempt has been made either to reconcile them or to note the textual variants. In the translations, however, in several instances, changes have

---

*The name Nichiren Shoshu means the "Orthodox School of Nichiren Buddhism," whose tradition originated with Nikkō, one of Nichiren's disciples.

been made to conform with what has been the generally accepted rendition of a term by writers and translators of Buddhist materials. Thus the terms for the Ten Worlds, Three Bodies, and so forth have been given in the conventional rendition. These changes and their alternative forms are given in both the notes to each letter and in the Glossary. In some instances the form used in the *Major Writings* has been maintained: for example Former, Middle, and Latter Day of the Law, in place of the conventional Three Periods of the Law, i.e., the True, Simulated, and Degenerate periods (*shōbō, zōbō,* and *mappō*). Nichiren is himself referred to by the honorary title, *shōnin,* sage, in most Nichiren schools, and by the title *daishōnin,* great sage, in *Nichiren Shoshu* and the *Soka Gakkai.* These titles have been dropped in the present work.

The aim of this work is to present, in translation, the major thought and teachings of Nichiren, as well as his concern for his followers, as reflected in his letters. Thus the Introduction is intentionally brief and avoids mention and discussion of the many problems and intricacies of Kamakura Buddhism. Much scholarly work has been done in this area in the West and Japan, but the inclusion of this material would make for a cumbersome and weighty introduction not in consonance with the aims of this work. Thus the reader will find little reference to contemporary academic scholarship. The notes, too, are in general confined to an explanation of terms and an identification of sources. As it developed, the Nichiren sect divided into several schools descended from Nichiren's major disciples. Divergent interpretations of Nichiren's writings gave rise to certain doctrinal differences among the various schools. No attempt is made here to reconcile these differences; they center largely on the relative importance of different sections of the Lotus Sutra, interpretations of the concept of the Three Bodies of the Buddha, and the Three Great Secret Laws, and so forth. The bibliography is confined to an identification of the Buddhist materials of which Nichiren made use.

In most instances the conventions established by the original translations have been followed. Inasmuch as these translations were made over a period of years, variations in these conventions have at times occurred, so that occasional inconsistencies are present. All personal names are given in accordance with the nationality of the individual, with the exception of Sanskrit names where the original is unknown, and figures in the sutras who have no historical existence. Nichiren frequently refers to priests and lay officials by posthumous names and titles and these have for the most part been maintained, even though Western works generally use the more common name. Thus Chih-i is always T'ien-t'ai. Chan-jan is Miao-lo, Saichō is Dengyō, and so forth. Book titles for Buddhist works are always given their Japanese readings, even when the work is Chinese in origin, again with the exception of those works that are conventionally rendered in English. Diacritical marks have been entered for words in all languages, despite the awkward appearance of some Sanskrit words. For certain often-repeated names that are fairly familiar to readers of Buddhist materials, the diacritical marks have been omitted: thus Hinayana, Mahayana, Tathagata, etc., appear without marks. By convention Shakyamuni always appears as such. Sutra names are italicized with the exception of those that have English titles and those that use proper names (i.e., Vimalakirti) or widely known terms in their titles (i.e., Nirvana).

On the assumption that this book will not be read through at one sitting, endnotes are very often repeated under each specific letter, and little attempt is made to cross reference similar notes that appear in different letters. A glossary is provided for the various names, technical terms, and more frequently encountered book titles. Appendixes give the Japanese equivalent of Sanskrit and Chinese names, as well as the Japanese names of the various letters.

In compiling the notes and introductory materials, much use was made of the *Dictionary of Buddhist Terms and Concepts* (1983) and the *Nichiren Daishōnin Gosho jiten* (1977) as well as materials in the *Major Writings* itself.

ABBREVIATIONS
USED IN THE NOTES

DDZ   *Dengyō Daishi Zenshū*. 5 vols. Reprint edition.
DNBZ   *Dai-Nihon Bukkyo Zenshō*. 150 vols. Original edition.
T   *Taishō Shinshū Daizōkyō*. 100 vols.
ZZ   *Zoku Zōkyō*. 150 cases.

LETTERS OF NICHIREN

INTRODUCTION

BY BURTON WATSON

Nichiren, who lived from 1222 to 1282, was a figure of prime importance in the history of Japanese Buddhism. Through his forceful preaching and voluminous writings, he attempted single-handedly to change the direction and focus of Japanese Buddhism, for he believed that its erroneous practices were calling down destruction on the nation. His efforts laid the groundwork for a new sect of Buddhism, which now bears his name, the only major Buddhist sect to originate in Japan.

An earlier volume edited by Philip B. Yampolsky, *Selected Writings of Nichiren* (Columbia University Press, 1990), presented translations of some of Nichiren's major doctrinal writings, along with a few of his letters. The present volume is devoted to translations of the longer and more important of Nichiren's letters to his disciples and lay followers, some dealing with doctrinal matters, others more personal in nature. The two volumes of translations are so designed that they may be read either separately or in conjunction.

Background

According to traditional accounts, Buddhism was introduced into Japan from the Korean kingdom of Paekche in the middle of the sixth century. Initially the new creed met with strong opposition from supporters of Shinto, the indigenous religion of Japan. In time, however, it was taken up and patronized by the rulers and high ministerial families, who saw it as an important and prestigious part of the continental culture they were endeavoring to foster in Japan. With government encouragement, numerous temples were established in the capital area, Buddhist clerics from Korea and China were welcomed to the country, and Japanese monk-students, dispatched by the government, journeyed to the mainland to deepen their knowledge of the religion.

In 741 Emperor Shōmu ordered the establishment of an officially sponsored temple and nunnery in each of the provinces in order to encourage the spread of Buddhist teachings throughout the country. And in the succeeding centuries, the rulers and high court officials frequently patronized one or another of the new schools of Buddhism introduced from the continent and lent it prestige and material support. Buddhism was seen as a vital force for the protection of the nation and its people and for the promotion of social harmony. The Japanese thus became accustomed to look to their political leaders for guidance and sanction in religious matters, a point to be kept in mind when approaching the writings of Nichiren, since his appeals for reform are often addressed primarily to the government officials of his time.

As Nichiren remarks in one of his letters, Japan is "a tiny island country in the east separated by two thousand *ri* of mountains and seas from the country of the Buddha's birth" ("The Recitation of the *Hōben* and *Juryō* Chapters," Letter 28). As a result, the Japanese had virtually no direct contact with Indian Buddhists, but depended for their understanding of the religion upon Chinese translations of Indian sutras and exegetical works or on works composed in China. The volume of such works is staggering, and those attempting to make their way through them will find themselves baffled by seeming inconsistencies and contradictions at every turn.

The two major divisions of Indian Buddhism, the Hinayana or Lesser Vehicle and the Mahayana or Great Vehicle, though both represent themselves as the teaching of the Buddha, very often appear to differ greatly in their practices and the overall bent of their doctrines. And even among the Mahayana teachings, which were the ones dominant in Japanese Buddhism, different sutras and schools of interpretation seem to impart a quite different tone and intention to the Buddha's message. How was one to establish some sort of order in this chaos, to determine which teachings and which texts were to be viewed as authoritative?

Chinese Buddhist scholars in the centuries following the introduction of Buddhism to China had earlier grappled with this problem, coming up with a variety of answers. Chih-i (538–597) or the Great Teacher T'ien-t'ai, one of the most creative thinkers to address the issue, worked out an elaborate system of interpretation that endeavored to explain and surmount the apparent contradictions in the sacred texts. Proceeding on the pious premise that all the sutras represent the words of the Buddha, and that the Buddha would not or could not speak untruthfully, he classified the sutras into various categories depending upon the type of persons to whom they were addressed or the period in the Buddha's preaching life when they were delivered. (See Glossary under "five periods" and "eight teachings.")

According to this system, the Buddha, adapting the content of his teachings to the capacity of his hearers and employing various expedient devices or temporary and partial revelations of the truth, gradually prepared them for the full and final revelation that he delivered in the last period of his life. The sutras are thus arranged in ascending order of importance, culminating, according to Chih-i, in the Lotus Sutra, the highest and most authoritative embodiment of the Buddha's enlightenment.

This was the interpretation followed by the T'ien-t'ai school founded in China by Chih-i and his disciples and by its Japanese counterpart, the Tendai sect, founded by Saichō (767–822) or the Great Teacher Dengyō. And, as we will see when we come to discuss Nichiren's life in greater detail, it is the interpretation upon which Nichiren founds his own assertion of the absolute superiority of the Lotus Sutra. It was, however, only one of a number of different theories regarding the relative superiority of the various sutras and, as Nichiren's writings reveal, was disputed or rejected outright by many of his contemporaries, a fact that was a source of unending distress to him.

Nichiren in his writings refers often to the "six sects of Nara." These were the earliest sects or schools of Japanese Buddhism, those associated with the great temples of Nara, the capital of Japan from 710 to 794. Some were allied with the Hinayana branch of Buddhism, others were Mahayana in nature; their doctrines were for the most part highly abstruse or philosophical and probably had little popular appeal. Despite the magnificent temples that adorned the capital and the impressive Buddhist ceremonies conducted under government auspices, it is doubtful that at this early period Buddhism had penetrated very deeply into Japanese life as a whole or was very widely and correctly understood. In the few instances where its doctrines did extend to the popular level, they tended to fuse with native Shinto or shamanistic beliefs and to find expression as semimagical practices for the relief of illness or the acquisition of material benefits.

Early in the succeeding Heian period (794–1185), two new Mahayana schools of Buddhism were introduced from China. One, the T'ien-t'ai or Tendai sect, which venerated the Lotus Sutra as the highest expression of Buddhist truth, has already been mentioned. The other was the Shingon sect, also referred to as Esoteric Buddhism, which was introduced by Kūkai (774–835) or the Great Teacher Kōbō. Both sects stressed that the attainment of Buddhahood was a possibility open to all individuals, regardless of sex or social status. Moreover, they asserted that, rather than requiring successive lifetimes of earnest devotion, as earlier teachings had implied, the goal of enlightenment could be attained in one's present form or existence provided one relied on proper beliefs and practices.

Both sects attracted many adherents among court and aristocratic circles, whose members had the wealth, learning, and leisure required to master their doctrines and participate in their elaborate and costly ceremonies. But, despite their message of universal salvation, neither developed, or attempted to develop, the kind of simple, direct approach needed to win the understanding and acceptance of the populace as a whole. Moreover, by this time a new factor had arisen to complicate the religious scene: belief in the concept known as *mappō* or the End of the Law.

The mutability or impermanence of all things is a basic tenet in Buddhism, and the Buddhist teachings themselves are held to be no exception to this rule. Thus, according to Mahayana belief, after the passing of Shakyamuni Buddha, his Law or doctrine is destined to pass through three distinct periods or phases of change. First is the era of the Correct Law, called in the translations in this volume the Former Day of the Law, when the Buddha's teachings flourish in the world and many persons readily gain enlightenment through them. Then follows the era of the Simulated Law or the Middle Day of the Law, customarily believed to last a thousand years. During this period, the religion is beset by increasing formalism and fewer and fewer people find salvation in its doctrines. Finally the world enters the period known as *mappō* or the End of the Law, translated here as the Latter Day of the Law, which will last many thousands of years. Japanese Buddhists generally calculated that this fateful era, when Shakyamuni's teachings will lose all power to confer enlightenment, had begun in the year 1052.

Buddhism originated in India as a monastic religion, and though the state and lay community as a whole were believed to play a very important role by supporting and protecting the monastic order, there was a strong tendency to view full enlightenment as something that could be attained only by those who had abandoned the secular world and could observe the numerous precepts that governed the life and conduct of Buddhist monks and nuns. Mahayana texts such as the Lotus Sutra insisted that all persons, members of the monastic order and lay believers alike, possessed the inherent Buddha nature and were capable of gaining enlightenment. But such texts themselves were couched in difficult and highly technical language, making them far beyond the comprehension of the semiliterate or illiterate masses. And what of those groups in society such as hunters, fisherfolk, or members of the warrior class, whose occupation or profession obliged them to violate the most basic of all Buddhist precepts, that against the taking of life? Moreover, if the time had come when Shakyamuni's teachings were no longer effectual, where was one to look for aid and guidance in realizing one's potential for salvation?

These were some of the problems that vexed the world of Japanese Buddhism in the late Heian and the succeeding Kamakura period (1185–1333), when alarming social and political upheavals and a series of natural disasters lent credence to the view that the world had entered upon an era of moral decline. Compassion, or the determination to lead as many living beings to salvation as possible, is a keynote of Mahayana Buddhism. And in keeping with its demands, the more thoughtful leaders in the centers of Mahayana belief such as the Tendai headquarters on Mount Hiei began casting about for some solution to these religious dilemmas of the time.

The first such solution to be put forth, borrowed from Chinese Buddhist thinkers who had faced similar dilemmas, counseled faith in a Buddha known as Amida, who was said to have taken a vow to save all those who called on him with true sincerity and to lead them to his Pure Land or Western Paradise. Adherents of this belief were urged to practice the *nembutsu*, a term that originally referred to meditation on Amida but later came to mean recitation of the invocation of his name, the formula pronounced in Japanese as *Namu Amida Butsu*. Such Pure Land or Amidist beliefs and practices, as they are termed, at first flourished alongside other forms of Buddhism at the older centers of the religion such as Mount Hiei or among lay devotees. But later a Tendai priest named Hōnen (1133–1212) founded a new sect, the Jōdo or Pure Land sect, that called for exclusive reliance on faith in Amida and the *nembutsu*. Believers thus no longer needed to master complex philosophical doctrines, observe exacting precepts, or rely upon the efficacy of costly religious rites. Absolute faith and the recitation of one simple formula were the only requisites for salvation.

The Ch'an or Zen Sect, which enjoyed great popularity in China at this time and was introduced into Japan in the late twelfth and early thirteenth century, represented another sort of solution to the problem. It set little store by scriptural learning or subtleties of doctrine, but called on its believers to discover enlightenment for themselves, as Shakyamuni had, by looking within. This was to be achieved through the practice of *zazen* or Zen-style meditation, usually under the guidance of a Zen master. Unlike the Pure Land teachings, Zen held out no promise of help from external agents. But the practice it enjoined was simple, not at all costly, required no particular learning or mental acumen, and could be pursued equally effectively by women or men, clerics or lay believers. In this sense, therefore, like the Pure Land doctrine, it made the quest for enlightenment far more accessible to ordinary persons than it had been under the older forms of Buddhism.

Nichiren, as we will see, was deeply troubled by the question of how best to reform the Buddhism of his time and make its message meaningful to all persons in society. After some years of intense youthful study, he announced his conclusions to the world. Following Tendai teaching, he accorded highest honor to the Lotus Sutra, declaring it to be the supreme embodiment of the Dharma or truth of Buddhism and the agent by which all beings may attain Buddhahood. But whereas the Lotus Sutra itself repeatedly calls on believers to "embrace, read, recite, expound, and copy" the sutra, practices that are for the most part far beyond the capacity of unlettered persons, Nichiren declared that in the troubled times of the Latter Day of the Law, simply embracing the sutra with utter sincerity of faith is all that is required. Moreover, he went a step further by announcing that the *daimoku* or Chinese title of the sutra, pronounced *Myōhō-renge-kyō* in Japanese, sums up and embodies the entire truth expounded in the sutra. Therefore, by chanting the devotional formula Nam-myoho-renge-kyo, believers could summon forth all the salvational power of the sutra and bring it to bear on their individual lives.

These new and revolutionary doctrines propounded by Nichiren or by the Pure Land and Zen sects met with strong opposition from the older centers of Buddhism. Steps were taken to hinder or prohibit their propagation and, as we will see in the case of Nichiren, their proponents often faced persecution or physical assault. These were turbulent times, when the newly risen warrior class was in the process of wresting political power from the hands of the old court nobility, and an air of militancy is reflected in the religious debates and controversies of the period.

Whereas earlier Buddhism such as that of the Nara period had often been characterized by a kind of benign plurality of approaches, the stress now was upon one single doctrine or devotional practice to replace all others. Hōnen, founder of the Pure Land sect, in a passage that Nichiren frequently quotes with great disapprobation, urged believers to "discard, close, ignore, and abandon" all sutras and practices other than those relating to Amida, since they were no longer relevant in the Latter Day of the Law. The Zen proponents, on the other hand, insisted that meditation was the only path to true enlightenment. Nichiren put forth his own views with equal conviction and finality, condemning all other approaches as not merely futile and erroneous, but as constituting in their rejection of the supremacy of the Lotus Sutra a kind of slander of the Dharma itself. Like the Christian divines of earlier centuries, these Buddhist reformers, in the depth and fervor of their religious zeal, often thundered at the times and at one another, for they were convinced that they were dealing with questions of surpassing import and gravity. The rumble of such thunder resounds again and again in the letters of Nichiren that follow.

Nichiren

As is true of the biographies of so many renowned religious leaders, accounts of Nichiren's life have been much embellished by later legend, and it is not always easy to separate fact from pious fiction. Below is a summary of the main events in his life. The annotated translations of his letters that follow will throw further light on many of the episodes touched on here.

Nichiren was born on the sixteenth day of the second month of 1222 in the village of Kominato, on the eastern coast of the province of Awa in present-day Chiba Prefecture; his parents made their living by fishing. In one of the letters in this volume, he describes himself as "born poor and lowly to a *caṇḍāla* family" ("Letter from Sado," Letter 3), the *caṇḍāla* being the lowest class in traditional Indian society, comprising those whose means of livelihood obliged them to kill living beings. In an age when many of the higher clergy of the older sects of

Buddhism were imperial princes or members of the great aristocratic families, Nichiren chose to stress the humbleness of his own origin.

At the age of twelve he entered Seichō-ji, a nearby temple belonging to the Tendai sect, where he learned to read Chinese and studied the Tendai and Shingon doctrines. The main object of worship at the temple was a statue of Bodhisattva Kokūzō, and Nichiren tells us that he prayed to the statue to become "the wisest man in Japan."

In 1237, at the age of sixteen, he was ordained by Dōzen-bō, his teacher and the chief priest of the temple. Later he left the temple and went to Kamakura, the seat of the shogunal government and a cultural center of eastern Japan, where he spent four years studying various forms of Buddhism, among them the recently established Pure Land and Zen sects. He returned to Seichō-ji briefly in 1242 but then set off for western Japan.

There he went to Mount Hiei, the center of the Tendai sect, and later to Mount Kōya, headquarters of the Shingon sect, as well as to other important temples in the area. After extensive study of the sutras and their commentaries at these centers, he concluded, as stated earlier, that the Lotus Sutra represents the highest and most authoritative statement of the Buddhist truth, all other sutras being merely expedient or provisional statements leading up to it.

Nichiren returned to Seichō-ji early in 1253. There, on the twenty-eighth day of the fourth month, he made public the conclusions drawn from his long years of study and spiritual questing. Preaching before his teacher and other priests, he chanted his devotional formula, Nam-myoho-renge-kyo, and declared that the Lotus Sutra is superior to all other sutras. He also took the name Nichiren at this time, his earlier religious name having been Renchō. His bold pronouncements aroused the ire of the steward in charge of the region, a devotee of Pure Land doctrines, who attempted to have him arrested. With the help of his teacher, he was able to escape, but soon left the area and moved to Kamakura.

There he set about making converts, preaching in the streets of the city, legend says, or visiting Pure Land temples to debate with the priests. He openly attacked the Pure Land and Zen sects for failing to pay due honor to the Lotus Sutra, thus angering not only religious leaders but government officials who supported these doctrines. Soon he was faced with widespread opposition, though he continued his efforts to win converts. It was in these early years of propagation that such major lay disciples as Shijō Kingo and Toki Jōnin, to whom many of the letters translated in this volume are addressed, were converted to his teachings.

Around this time a series of disasters struck the nation. Storms, floods, drought, earthquakes, epidemics, and unusual astronomical portents such as comets and eclipses terrified the population and inflicted great suffering. Nichiren believed that such portents and disasters were caused by the nation's failure to uphold the "correct Law" as it was expounded in the Lotus Sutra. In 1258 he went to Jissō-ji, a temple in Iwamoto in present day Shizuoka Prefecture, to consult its copy of the Buddhist canon and compile scriptural evidence to support his contentions.

The most powerful man in the country at this time was Hōjō Tokiyori (1227–1263), a former regent of the Kamakura shogunate who had retired to a Zen temple. In the seventh month of 1260, Nichiren presented to him a treatise entitled *Risshō Ankoku Ron* or "Establishment of the Legitimate Teaching for the Protection of the Country," which has been translated in the *Selected Writings of Nichiren* volume mentioned earlier. In it, he attributes the cause of the recent calamities to slander against the Lotus Sutra and to reliance on the erroneous teachings of the Pure Land sect. He cites various sutras that describe the disasters that will befall any nation that turns against true Buddhism. They are usually listed as seven in number, and of these seven, only two, foreign invasion and internal disorder, had so far failed to strike Japan. Nichiren predicted that unless the authorities took steps to remedy the situation, these disasters too were certain to occur.

In effect, Nichiren was calling on the government to recognize the Lotus Sutra as the supreme embodiment of the Buddhist Law and to suppress all doctrines that are at variance with it. Japanese rulers in earlier centuries had at times patronized Buddhism and adopted various measures to regulate the ordination of its clergy. But no government had ever attempted to implement the kind of drastic steps urged by Nichiren. To have done so would have implied a whole new interpretation of the relationship between religion and the state. Not surprisingly, Hōjō Tokiyori and the shogunal officials made no response to Nichiren's treatise.

The Pure Land believers, however, learning of its contents, were incensed. A band of them stormed the hut in Kamakura where Nichiren was staying and he barely managed to escape from the city with a few followers. But in 1261 he returned to Kamakura and resumed his preaching. The Pure Land priests thereupon persuaded the government to have him banished to an isolated area of the Izu Peninsula in the fifth month of 1261.

In a letter translated below under the title "The Izu Exile" (Letter 54), Nichiren describes his banishment there and the unexpected kindness shown him by a boat-manager and his wife. Sometime later the shogunate issued a pardon and Nichiren returned to Kamakura early in 1263.

In the eighth month of 1264, he visited his birthplace in Kominato, his first trip there in ten years. Both his parents had earlier converted to his teachings; his father had died in the interim, but his mother was still alive, though seriously ill. Nichiren's prayers for her recovery appear to have been efficacious, for she regained her health and lived four years more. Unfortunately, word of his return reached Tōjō Kagenobu, the steward of the region who had earlier attempted to arrest him. Tōjō and his armed attendants attacked Nichiren and a group of his followers at a place called Komatsubara, killing two of the followers and wounding several others. Nichiren, though he escaped with his life, suffered a broken hand and a sword wound on the forehead.

After spending several years in nearby provinces, Nichiren returned to Kamakura in 1268. The same year, the Mongols sent a letter to the Japanese authorities in Kamakura demanding that they acknowledge fealty to the Mongol leader, Khubilai Khan. Nichiren, convinced that the foreign invasion he had earlier predicted was about to take place, wrote letters to eleven high officials and religious leaders in Kamakura, repeating his prediction and calling on the government to heed his teachings. All these went unanswered. Meanwhile the government, though making no reply to the Mongol demands, set about strengthening its defenses in northern Kyushu where an attack was expected. When the Mongols renewed their demands, Nichiren submitted another copy of his *Risshō Ankoku Ron* to the government, but again it elicited no response.

In the spring and summer of 1271 the nation was troubled by severe drought. The shogunate ordered Ryōkan (1217–1303), an eminent Shingon-Ritsu priest, to pray for rain. Hearing of this, Nichiren challenged Ryōkan to a contest to see who could prove more effective in producing rain, the loser to become the disciple of the winner. Ryōkan, ignoring the challenge, proceeded with his rain-making supplications, aided by a large number of assistant priests, but the drought continued worse than ever.

By this time Nichiren's repeated attacks on the teaching of the Pure

Land, Zen, and other sects had aroused much hostility among the clergy and government officials of Kamakura. Finally charges were brought against him and his followers accusing them of condemning all forms of Buddhism other than their own and of building up secret stores of arms.

Nichiren was summoned to answer the charges, but his replies failed to satisfy the authorities. On the twelfth day of the ninth month he was arrested, subjected to brief questioning, and ordered exiled to the distant island province of Sado.

He was escorted out of Kamakura, bound for the town of Echi, the first stop on the journey. As the party approached the execution ground at Tatsunokuchi, however, Nichiren became aware that he was about to be put to death. Evidently his arch enemies in the government had decided to do away with him in this manner before the sentence of exile could be carried out. In the long autobiographical piece entitled "On Various Actions of the Priest Nichiren," translated in *Selected Writings of Nichiren*, which describes these events in dramatic detail, he relates how, as the beheading was about to take place, a strange meteorological phenomenon lit up the night sky and so terrified the soldiers escorting him that they were unable to perform their grim task. In his letters, however, he sometimes speaks as though the beheading had actually taken place, for the crisis marked a turning point in his life, a moment when in a sense he took on a whole new identity.

His "Letter from Teradomari" and "Aspiration for the Buddha Land" (Letters 16 and 17) tell of his journey north to Sado and of the harsh life he faced there. On Sado he was housed in a dilapidated Buddhist hall at a place called Tsukahara, where the corpses of criminals and paupers were abandoned. He suffered greatly from lack of food, clothing, and heat, but somehow managed to survive the severe winter.

In the second month of 1272, internal dissention broke out within the ruling Hōjō family, thus fulfilling Nichiren's prediction that disaster would strike the country. Meanwhile he was able to move to more comfortable quarters and to go about making converts and writing letters and doctrinal works in greater ease. Finally, in the second month of 1274 he was pardoned and allowed to return to Kamakura after an exile of almost two and a half years.

The government authorities, faced with the continued threat of Mongol invasion and impressed perhaps with the accuracy of

Nichiren's predictions, summoned him to express his views. He predicted that a Mongol attack would come within the year, and added that the government should not ask the Shingon priests to pray for the destruction of the Mongols, since their prayers would only aggravate the situation.

An old Chinese maxim states that a sage withdraws if his warnings go unheeded for the third time. Nichiren saw this occasion as his third remonstrance, the previous two being the submission of the *Rissho Ankoku Ron* and his declarations at the time of his questioning and arrest. He accordingly left Kamakura in the fifth month of 1274 to take up a life of retirement.

He settled at Mount Minobu in the province of Kai in present-day Yamanashi Prefecture, a site chosen for him by one of his disciples who was friendly with the lord of the region. In the letter translated below under the title "Fourteen Slanders" (Letter 59), he describes the remoteness of the site, and elsewhere refers to the privation that he and his disciples suffered there.

Despite the difficulty of access, many of his followers visited him at Mount Minobu, as will be evident from his letters, and helped to supply him and his disciples with food and clothing. He continued writing letters and important doctrinal works, as well as lecturing to his disciples on the Lotus Sutra, and kept in contact with followers in other parts of the country.

Meanwhile, the long-feared Mongol attack took place late in 1274 when enemy forces landed in northern Kyushu. But a typhoon destroyed much of the Mongol fleet and the remainder went back to Korea to prepare for another attempt. The second invasion, much more formidable in size than the first, came in the late spring of 1281. The Japanese were better prepared to meet it this time, however, and once more a fortuitous typhoon wrecked many of the enemy ships. This ended the threat of Mongol invasion, but the cost of building fortifications and combating the invaders significantly weakened the finances and morale of the Kamakura shogunate, contributing to its eventual collapse in 1333.

Though these late years were peaceful ones for Nichiren, his followers, as will be apparent from his letters, encountered frequent harassment because of their beliefs. A particularly nasty incident known as the Atsuhara Persecution occurred in 1279, when twenty of Nichiren's lay followers were arrested and subjected to torture by the government authorities; three were eventually beheaded. Impressed by the courage and steadfastness these men displayed in the face of oppression, Nichiren at this time inscribed the Dai-Gohonzon, the mandala that he "bestowed upon all the world" as a universal object of worship.

By this time Nichiren's health, undermined by years of exile and privation, was failing rapidly. In the ninth month of 1282 he left Minobu for a hot spring in the province of Hitachi that he hoped would prove beneficial. He died in mid-journey at the home of followers in Ikegami in present day Tokyo.

The Letters

Well over four hundred writings attributed to Nichiren have been preserved in the various temples affiliated with the sect that bears his name. Known as *Gosho* or "Writings," they range in nature from formal documents of remonstrance submitted to government officials, such as the *Risshō Ankoku Ron*, to doctrinal treatises, graphs, and personal letters addressed to disciples and lay followers. A few, such as the *Risshō Ankoku Ron*, are in classical Chinese, but the vast majority, in keeping with Nichiren's policy of making his ideas as easily accessible as possible, are in the colloquial Japanese style of the period, albeit one often adorned with allusions to Chinese and Japanese history and literature or to the lore of Indian Buddhism. Some of the writings are preserved in manuscripts from Nichiren's own hand, others in copies made by later priests of the sect. Doubts concerning their authenticity surround some of them, but none of the works presented here in translation appear to be open to serious question.

Anyone wishing to gain a clear understanding of Nichiren's teachings, particularly as they were evolved and refined over the years of his life, must of course consult his doctrinal works such as the five major treatises translated in *Selected Writings of Nichiren*. The letters presented in the present volume are of a less formal nature, though they often contain discussions of doctrinal matters as these pertain to the background and spiritual needs of the particular recipient. They reveal the warmer, more intimate side of Nichiren's personality, as we observe him offering his supporters counsel in their daily affairs, comforting them in their trials, or thanking them for gifts they have sent or visits they have made to him, often at considerable cost and hardship to themselves.

Because we lack full information concerning the private matters referred to, we sometimes have difficulty making out the exact meaning in such letters. Some letters are of uncertain date, or the identity of the recipient is unknown, while others appear to be fragmentary. Yet through these letters we gain invaluable information on the daily life and customs of the Japanese of the Kamakura period and acquire a remarkably lively picture of the relationships that existed between Nichiren and his various disciples and lay followers.

Despite the diversity of content one would naturally expect in letters addressed to men and women of highly varied social position and livelihood, there are certain dominant themes that keep recurring. One is the theme of Nichiren's identity and of his sense of mission. As we have seen, he was of very humble birth, a fact that he often calls attention to. Thus, for example, in the letters that follow he declares that "I am nothing but a lowly and ignorant monk" ("The Four Debts of Gratitude," Letter 8), or says that people reject his advice "because of my low social position" ("The Supremacy of the Law," Letter 38).

But, as mentioned previously, early in his life he became convinced of the absolute superiority of the Lotus Sutra, and thereafter he believed it was his mission in life to act as a "votary of the Lotus Sutra," vigorously propagating its teachings and reprimanding all those who reject them. In so doing, he sees himself as following in the footsteps of the two earlier champions of the Lotus, Chih-i or the Great Teacher T'ien-t'ai, founder of the T'ien-t'ai school of Chinese Buddhism, and Saichō or the Great Teacher Dengyō, who introduced the T'ien-t'ai doctrines into Japan. But Nichiren, as he often points out, is the first to proclaim the message of the Lotus in the difficult era of the Latter Day of the Law, and the hardships he faces are thus far greater than those encountered by his distinguished predecessors.

There are two factors that reinforce Nichiren in his conviction that this is his destined role in life. One is the fact that his prophecies of internal strife and of invasion from abroad, voiced first in 1260 in his *Risshō Ankoku Ron*, have in time been dramatically fulfilled. The second, paradoxically enough, is the very hostility and opposition that his assertions arouse. The Lotus Sutra states emphatically that in the ages that follow the Buddha's passing, those who sincerely attempt to uphold and propagate its teachings will encounter great difficulties and persecution. Pointing to such passages in the sutra, Nichiren declares that the persecutions he himself faces are irrefutable proof that he is propagating its teachings just as the sutra directs. The greater the animosity his preaching incites, therefore, the stronger is his certainty that he is fulfilling his mission as votary of the sutra in the Latter Day of the Law.

This mission, to save the ruler of Japan and its people from their errors of belief, endows him with new potential, lifts him to a new level of authority. The calamities befalling Japan in his time, he declares, "do not occur because I myself am respectworthy but because the power of the Lotus Sutra is supreme." ("A Sage Perceives the Three Existences of Life," Letter 21). He is acutely aware that his role of perpetual admonisher rouses great hostility against himself and his followers, and his letters dwell on the dangers and tribulations he and they must endure as a result. But if he is to be faithful to his mission to propagate "this secret Law, the one great reason for which all the Buddhas made their advent" ("Aspiration for the Buddha Land," Letter 17), he cannot remain silent. For, as a true votary of the Lotus, the son of a lowly fisherman now feels himself in a position to declare, "I, Nichiren, am parent to all the people of Japan, I am their sovereign, I am their enlightened teacher!" ("Letter to Ichinosawa," Letter 50).

A second important theme in his letters is that of just how the intricacies of Buddhist doctrine and the manifold Buddha and bodhisattva figures who appear in the Lotus Sutra relate to the individual believer. The T'ien-t'ai school of Buddhism, in its doctrine of *ichinen sanzen* or "three thousand realms in one instant of thought," had worked out a highly sophisticated philosophical explanation of how all beings in all the Ten Worlds or realms of existence could at any given moment be capable of experiencing any of the ten conditions of life—in other words, how persons even in the lowest realms of existence could possess the potential to attain Buddhahood. Nichiren in his doctrinal writings and letters often refers to these and other concepts of the T'ien-t'ai philosophy and interpretation of the Lotus Sutra. He no doubt hoped that his followers, even ordinary lay believers, could to some extent grasp these difficult doctrines and appreciate their significance.

But again and again in the letters that follow we see him abruptly setting aside the many numerical categories so beloved in Buddhist doctrine or the mythic figures and metaphorical language of the sutras to stress the underlying unity of all existence and the Buddha nature inherent in all persons. Thus, when a believer named Abutsu-bō writes asking him to explain the symbolism of the Treasure Tower that miraculously rises up out of the ground in chapter eleven of the Lotus Sutra,

Nichiren replies with startling directness, "Abutsu-bō is the Treasure Tower itself, and the Treasure Tower is Abutsu-bō himself. No other knowledge is purposeful" ("On the Treasure Tower," Letter 47). And in a letter translated here under the title "The Izu Exile" (Letter 54), he states, "The Lord Shakyamuni . . . is none other than each of us. . . . Let it be known that the Buddha of *ichinen sanzen* is anyone in any of the Ten Worlds who manifests his inherent Buddha nature."

In discussing the Gohonzon, the mandala that he inscribed for his followers, he emphasizes this need to internalize the symbols and tenets of the faith. "Never seek the Gohonzon outside yourself," he writes. "The Gohonzon exists only within the mortal flesh of us ordinary people who embrace the Lotus Sutra and chant Nam-myoho-renge-kyo" ("The Real Aspect of the Gohonzon," Letter 40). Thus he directs the believer's attention to the principle of nondualism that lies at the core of Mahayana Buddhist belief. All the various mythical realms depicted so vividly in the sutras are in fact a part of our own makeup. "Neither the pure land nor hell exists outside ourselves; both lie within our own hearts," he declares ("Hell Is the Land of Tranquil Light," Letter 56). To the question of exactly where hell and the Buddha are located, he replies emphatically, "both exist in our five-foot body" ("New Year's Gosho," Letter 72).

In statements such as these, Nichiren is endeavoring to convey the Lotus Sutra's message of universal salvation to his followers in terms that will be meaningful to them here and now. Other sacred writings of Buddhism had stated that women are incapable of attaining Buddhahood, at least until they are reborn in male form in some future existence. But the Lotus Sutra rejects this idea, illustrating its rejection with the surprising story of the dragon king's daughter in chapter twelve. In letters to women followers, Nichiren takes pains to point out this fact and otherwise to counsel them on how the sutra's teachings apply to their own lives. One woman had written him asking whether she should modify her regular devotional practices during her menstrual period, a quite understandable question when we recall that the native Shinto religion regarded menstruation as a source of ritual defilement. Nichiren, after trying without success to think of some scriptural passage that touches on the problem, concludes that menstruation "is simply a characteristic of the female sex" and is not to be regarded as in any way polluting" ("The *Hōben* and *Juryō* Chapters," Letter 28). Thus in his letters we see Nichiren not only making doctrinal pronouncements but advising his followers on how the principles of Buddhist teaching and practice relate to their particular problems and mode of life.

In addition to its view regarding the attainment of Buddhahood by women, the Lotus Sutra is famous for asserting that even the greatest of evildoers can hope to attain Buddhahood, as illustrated by the example of Devadatta in chapter twelve. Earlier Buddhism had envisioned the search for enlightenment as a long and arduous process, requiring many successive lifetimes of devotion to the observance of strict rules of conduct. Mahayana doctrine pictured enlightenment as more readily accessible and tended to play down the importance of the precepts, particularly those that could not be observed by persons living the household life. Nichiren went a step further by declaring that, in the Latter Day of the Law, it is faith in the power of the Lotus Sutra alone that insures salvation, and that the only "precept" to be observed is the chanting of the devotional formula, Nam-myoho-renge-kyo. Thus, in the letter entitled "The Treasure of a Filial Child," he states, "One's acts of great good are nothing to rely on. If one fails to encounter the Lotus Sutra, what can they avail? Nor should one lament that he has committed acts of evil. For if only he practices the one vehicle, then he can follow in the footsteps of Devadatta [in attaining Buddhahood]" (Letter 52).

Faith alone, then, is all that is required. Writing to a woman of advanced years who had recently accepted his teachings, Nichiren assures her that simply chanting the title of the Lotus Sutra, even though she may have no understanding of the sutra as a whole, is sufficient to insure that she will gain great spiritual advancement ("Daimoku of the Lotus Sutra," Letter 2). Though Nichiren wrote tirelessly and at great length on doctrinal matters, he repeatedly stresses that it is not knowledge of the scriptures or the grasp of subtle philosophical concepts, but simple faith, that leads one to nirvana. Hence, in a letter here entitled "Three Tripitaka Masters Pray for Rain," he concludes by reminding the recipient that "Śuddhipanthaka was unable to memorize a teaching of fourteen characters even in the space of three years, yet he attained Buddhahood. Devadatta, on the other hand, had committed to memory sixty thousand sacred texts but fell into the hell of incessant suffering" (Letter 57).

These letters, then, at times highly intellectual in tone, at others charged with emotion, some conveying sympathy and gratitude, others delivering a scolding, reveal to us the many varied facets of Nichiren's personality, and it would seem to have been that unusual personality, perhaps more than his ideas themselves, that made such a deep impression on his contemporaries.

Nichiren was a man of passionate conviction. Unlike some of the other influential Buddhist leaders of the period, who favored a life of reclusion or viewed salvation as something to be attained in another world and time, he called for concrete and immediate action to relieve the ills that afflicted the nation. Living in a highly class-conscious society, he made no attempt to hide his humble origin, and he did not hesitate to address his proposals to the highest government officials or the most eminent Buddhist prelates, admonishing them in outspoken language or challenging them to public debate. He was ready at all times to fight for his ideas, even in the face of repeated harassment and exile. In an age dominated by the warrior ideal, it is hardly surprising that such courage and dedication should have attracted to him followers who were fiercely loyal to his cause. The letters that follow vividly reflect these qualities of leadership, and the devotion they inspired.

1 THE TEACHING, CAPACITY, TIME, AND COUNTRY

NICHIREN, THE ŚRAMAṆA OF JAPAN[1]

In the seventh month of 1260, Nichiren submitted his treatise *Risshō Ankoku Ron* (Establishment of the Legitimate Teaching for the Protection of the Country) to the former regent Hōjō Tokiyori, who, though retired from office, was still the most influential member of the ruling Hōjō clan.

Infuriated by Nichiren's criticism of the Pure Land sect set forth in this treatise, a group of Pure Land believers attacked his dwelling at Matsubagayatsu in an attempt to do away with him. Nichiren narrowly escaped and fled to Toki Jōnin's residence in the neighboring province of Shimōsa. When he returned to Kamakura in the spring of 1261 and resumed his propagation activities, Nichiren was summarily exiled to Itō on the Izu Peninsula. He remained in Izu from the twelfth day of the fifth month until he was pardoned and returned to Kamakura on the twenty-second day of the second month, 1263. The precise dating of this letter remains unclear since it is given only as the tenth day of the second month. Internal evidence would indicate, however, that the year of composition was, in all likelihood, the tenth day of the second month, 1272.

With regard to the first item, the teaching consists of all the sutras, rules of monastic discipline, and treatises expounded by Shakyamuni Buddha, comprising 5,048 volumes contained in 480 scroll cases. These teachings, after circulating throughout India for a thousand years, were introduced to China 1,015 years after the Buddha's passing. During the 664-year period beginning with the tenth year of the Yung-p'ing era, the year with the cyclical sign *hinoto-u* (A.D. 67), in the reign of Emperor Ming of the Later Han, and ending with the eighteenth year of the K'ai-yüan era, the year with the cyclical sign *kanoe-uma* (A.D. 730), in the reign of Emperor Hsüan-tsung of the T'ang, all of these teachings were introduced to China.

The contents of these sutras, rules of monastic discipline and treatises, can be divided into the categories of Hinayana and Mahayana teachings, provisional and true sutras, and exoteric and esoteric sutras, and one should carefully distinguish between them. Such designations did not originate with the later scholars and teachers of Buddhism, but derive from the preaching of the Buddha himself. Therefore they must be used without exception by all the people of the worlds of the ten directions, and anyone who fails to do so should be regarded as non-Buddhist.

The custom of referring to the teachings of the *Agon* sutras as Hinayana derives from the various Mahayana sutras such as the *Hōdō*, *Hannya*, Lotus, and Nirvana sutras. In the Lotus Sutra the Buddha says that had he preached only the Hinayana teachings without preaching the Lotus Sutra, he would have been guilty of concealing the truth. Moreover, the Nirvana Sutra states that those who accept only the Hinayana sutras, declaring that the Buddha is characterized by impermanence, will have their tongues fester in their mouths.[2]

Second is the matter of capacity. Anyone who attempts to propagate the teachings of Buddhism must understand the capacity and basic nature of the persons he is addressing.[3] The Venerable Śāriputra attempted to instruct a blacksmith by teaching him to meditate on the vileness of the body, and to instruct a washerman by teaching him to count his breaths in meditation. Even though he spent over ninety days with them, these pupils of his did not gain the slightest understanding of the Buddha's Law. On the contrary, they took on erroneous views and ended by becoming *icchantika* or persons of incorrigible disbelief.

The Buddha, on the other hand, instructed the blacksmith in the counting-of-breath meditation, and the washer of clothes in the meditation on the vileness of the body, and as a result both were able to obtain understanding in no time at all. If even Śāriputra, who was counted foremost in wisdom among the major disciples of the Buddha, failed in understanding the capacity of the persons he was instructing, then how much more difficult must it be for ordinary teachers in this, the Latter Day of the Law, to have such an understanding! Ordinary teachers who lack an understanding of capacity should teach only the Lotus Sutra to those who are under their instruction.

Question: What about the passage in the Lotus Sutra that says one should not preach this sutra among the ignorant?[4]

Answer: When I speak of understanding capacity, I am referring to the preaching of the Law done by a man of wisdom. Yet, [even though one understands the capacity of one's listeners,] one should preach only the Lotus Sutra to those who slander the Law, so that they may establish a so-called "poison-drum relationship"[5] with it. In this respect, one should proceed as Bodhisattva Fukyō did.[6]

However, if one is speaking to persons who one knows have the capacity to become wise, then one should first give them instruction in Hinayana teachings, then introduce them to the provisional Mahayana teachings, and finally instruct them in the true Mahayana. But if one knows that one is dealing with ignorant persons of lesser capacity, then one should first give them instruction in the true Mahayana teaching. In that way, whether they choose to believe in the teaching or to slander it, they will still receive the seed of enlightenment.

Third is the consideration of time. Anyone who hopes to spread the Buddhist teachings must make certain that he understands the time. For example, if a farmer should plant his fields in autumn and winter, then, even though the seed and the land and the farmer's efforts were the same as ever, this planting would not result in the slightest gain but rather would end in loss. If the farmer planted one small plot in that way, he would suffer a minor loss, and if he planted acres and acres, he would suffer a major loss. But if he plows and plants in the spring and summer, then, whether the fields are of superior, medium, or inferior quality, each will bring forth its corresponding share of crops.

The preaching of the Buddhist Law is similar to this. If one propagates the Law without understanding the time, one will reap no benefit but on the contrary will fall into the evil paths of existence. When Shakyamuni Buddha made his appearance in this world, he was determined to preach the Lotus Sutra. But though the capacities of his listeners may have been right, the proper time had not yet come. Therefore he spent a period of more than forty years without preaching the Lotus Sutra, explaining, as he says in the Lotus Sutra itself, that this was "because the time to preach so had not yet come."[7]

The day after the Buddha's passing begins the thousand-year period known as the Former Day of the Law, when those who uphold the precepts are many while those who break them are few. The day after the end of the Former Day of the Law marks the beginning of the thousand-year period known as the Middle Day of the Law, when those who break the precepts are many while those without precepts are few. And the day after the ending of the Middle Day of the Law begins the ten-thousand-year period known as the Latter Day of the Law, when those who break the precepts are few while those without precepts are many.

During the Former Day of the Law, one should cast aside those who break the precepts or who have no precepts at all, giving alms only to those who uphold the precepts. During the Middle Day of the Law, one should cast aside those without precepts and give alms only to those who break them. And during the Latter Day of the Law, one should give alms to those without precepts, treating them in the same way as if they were the Buddha.

However, whether in the Former, the Middle, or the Latter Day of the Law, one should never in any of these three periods give alms to those who slander the Lotus Sutra, whether they keep the precepts, break the precepts, or do not receive them at all. If alms are given to those who slander the Lotus Sutra, then the land in which this happens will invariably be visited by the three calamities and seven disasters,[8] and the persons who give such alms will surely fall into the great citadel of the hell of incessant suffering.

When the votary of the Lotus Sutra speaks words of condemnation against the provisional sutras, it is like a ruler meting out punishment to his followers, a father punishing his sons, or a teacher, his disciples. But when the votaries of the provisional sutras speak words of condemnation and slander against the Lotus Sutra, it is like followers attempting to mete out punishment to their ruler, sons attempting to punish their father, or disciples to punish their teacher.

At present, it has been more than 210 years since we entered the Latter Day of the Law. One should consider very carefully whether now is the time when the provisional sutras or the Nembutsu teachings should be propagated, or whether it is the time when the Lotus Sutra should be spread!

Fourth is the consideration of the country. In spreading the Buddhist teachings, one must not fail to take into account the kind of country involved. There are cold countries, hot countries, poor countries, rich countries, central countries and peripheral countries, big countries and small countries, countries wholly given over to thieving, countries wholly given over to the killing of living creatures, and countries known for their utter lack of filial piety. In addition, there are countries wholly devoted to the Hinayana teachings, countries wholly devoted to the Mahayana teachings, and countries in which both Hinayana and Mahayana are pursued. In the case of Japan, therefore, we must carefully consider whether it is a country suited exclusively to Hinayana, a country suited exclusively to Mahayana, or a country in which both Hinayana and Mahayana should be pursued.

Fifth is the sequence of propagation. In a country where the Buddhist teachings have never been introduced, there of course will be no inhabitants who are familiar with Buddhism. But in a country where Buddhism has already been introduced, there will be inhabitants who are believers in the Buddhist Law. Therefore one must first learn what kind of Buddhist doctrines have already spread in a particular country before attempting to propagate Buddhism there oneself.

If the Hinayana and provisional Mahayana teachings have already spread, then one should by all means propagate the true Mahayana teaching. But if the true Mahayana teaching has already spread, then one must not propagate the Hinayana or provisional Mahayana teachings. One throws aside rubble and broken tiles in order to pick up gold and gems, but one must not throw aside gold and gems in order to pick up tiles and rubble.

If one takes the five considerations outlined above into account when propagating the Buddhist Law, then one can surely become a teacher to the entire nation of Japan. To understand that the Lotus Sutra is the king, the first among all the various sutras, is to have a correct understanding of the teaching. Yet Fa-yün[9] of Kuang-che-ssu and Hui-kuan[10] of Tao-ch'ang-ssu claimed that the Nirvana Sutra is superior to the Lotus Sutra. Ch'eng-kuan[11] of Mount Ch'ing-liang and Kōbō[12] of Mount Kōya claimed that the *Kegon* and *Dainichi* sutras are superior to the Lotus Sutra. Chi-tsang[13] of Chia-hsiang-ssu and the priest K'uei-chi[14] of Tz'u-en-ssu claimed that the two sutras known as the *Hannya* and the *Jimmitsu* are superior to the Lotus Sutra. One man alone, the Great Teacher Chih-che of Mount T'ien-t'ai,[15] not only asserted that the Lotus Sutra is superior to all the other sutras, but urged that anyone claiming there is a sutra superior to the Lotus should be admonished and made to see the light; he said that if such a person persists in his false claim, his tongue will surely fester in his mouth during his present existence, and after his death he will fall into the Avīci Hell. One who is able to distinguish right from wrong among all these different opinions may be said to have a correct understanding of the teaching.

Of all the thousand or ten thousand scholars of the present age, surely each and every one is confused as to this point. And if so, then there must be very few who have a correct understanding of the teaching. If there are none with a correct understanding of the teaching, there will be none to read the Lotus Sutra. And if there are none who read the Lotus Sutra, there will be none who can act as a teacher to the nation. If there is no one to act as a teacher to the nation, then everyone within the nation will be confused as to the distinctions within the body of sutras, such as those between the Hinayana and the Mahayana, the provisional and the true, and the exoteric and the esoteric sutras. Not a single person will be able to escape from the sufferings of birth and death, and in the end they will all become slanderers of the Law. Those who, because of slandering the Law, fall into the Avīci Hell, will be more numerous than the dust particles of the earth, while those who, by embracing the Law, are freed from the sufferings of birth and death, will amount to less than the quantity of soil that can be placed on top of a fingernail. How fearful it is to contemplate!

During the four hundred or more years since the time of Emperor Kammu, all the people in Japan have had the capacity to attain enlightenment solely through the Lotus Sutra. They are like those persons who for a period of eight years listened to the preaching of the Lotus Sutra on Eagle Peak, with capacities suited to the pure and perfect teaching. (Confirmation of this may be found in the records of the Great Teacher T'ien-t'ai, Crown Prince Shōtoku, the Eminent Priest Ganjin, the Great Teacher Dengyō, the Eminent Priest Annen, and Eshin.)[16] To understand this is to have an understanding of the people's capacity.

Yet the Buddhist scholars of our time say that the people of Japan all have capacities fit only for the recitation of Amida Buddha's name, the Nembutsu. They are like Śāriputra in the incident I mentioned earlier who, because he was misled as to the capacity of the persons under his instruction, in the end turned them into *icchantika* or persons of incorrigible disbelief.

At present in Japan, some 2,210 years after the demise of Shakyamuni Buddha, in the last of the five five-hundred-year periods after his death,[17] the hour has come for the widespread propagation of Myōhō-renge-kyō. To understand this is to have an understanding of the time.

Yet there are Buddhist scholars in Japan today who cast aside the Lotus Sutra and instead devote themselves exclusively to the practice of the invocation of Amida Buddha's name. And there are others who teach the Hinayana precepts and speak contemptuously of the high-ranking priests of Mount Hiei, as well as those who present what they describe as a special transmission outside the sutras,[18] disparaging the True Law of the Lotus Sutra. Such persons may surely be said to misunderstand the time! They are like the monk Shōi,[19] who slandered Bodhisattva Kikon, or the scholar Guṇaprabha,[20] who behaved with contempt toward Bodhisattva Miroku, and thus invited the terrible sufferings of the Avīci Hell.

Japan is a country related exclusively to the teaching of the Lotus Sutra, just as the country of Śrāvastī in India[21] was related solely to the Mahayana teachings. In India there were countries that were wholly devoted to Hinayana teachings, those that were wholly devoted to Mahayana teachings, and those that were devoted to both Hinayana and Mahayana teachings. Japan is a country that is exclusively suited to Mahayana teachings, and among those teachings it should be dedicated solely to the Lotus Sutra. (The above statement is attested to in the *Yuga Ron*,[22] the writings of Seng-chao,[23] and the records of Crown Prince Shōtoku, the Great Teacher Dengyō, and Annen.)[24] To understand this is to understand the country.

Yet there are Buddhist teachers in our present age who address the people of Japan and instruct them only in the precepts of the Hinayana, or who attempt to make them all into followers of the Nembutsu. This is like "putting rotten food in a precious vessel." (This simile of the precious vessel is taken from the *Shugo Kokkai Shō* by the Great Teacher Dengyō.)[25]

In Japan during the 240 or more years from the time when Buddhism was first introduced from the Korean kingdom of Paekche in the reign of Emperor Kimmei to the reign of Emperor Kammu, only the Hinayana and provisional Mahayana teachings were propagated throughout the country. Though the Lotus Sutra existed in Japan, its significance had not yet been made clear. This was similar to the situation years before in China, where the Lotus Sutra had existed for more than three hundred years before its significance was clarified.

In the time of Emperor Kammu, the Great Teacher Dengyō refuted the Hinayana and provisional Mahayana teachings and made clear the true significance of the Lotus Sutra. From that time on, opposing opinions ceased to prevail, and everyone single-mindedly put faith in the Lotus Sutra. Even those scholars of the earlier six sects[26] of Buddhism who studied Hinayana and Mahayana teachings such as the *Kegon, Hannya, Jimmitsu*, and *Agon* sutras regarded the Lotus Sutra as the ultimate authority. Needless to say, this was even more so with scholars of the Tendai and Shingon sects, and of course with the lay believers of Buddhism who had no special knowledge of the subject. In its relation to the Lotus Sutra, the country was like the K'un-lun Mountains,[27] where not a single worthless stone is to be found, or the mountain island of P'eng-lai,[28] where no harmful potion is known.

However, during the fifty or more years since the Kennin era (1201–03), the priests Dainichi and Kakuan[29] have spread the teachings of the Zen sect, casting aside all the various sutras and postulating a doctrine that is transmitted outside the scriptures, while Hōnen and Ryūkan[30] have established the Jōdo or Pure Land sect, contradicting the teachings of the true Mahayana and setting up sects based on the provisional teachings. They are in effect casting aside gems and gathering stones instead, abandoning the solid earth and endeavoring to climb up into the air. Men such as this know nothing about the order in which the various doctrines should be propagated. The Buddha warned of such men when he said, "Better to encounter a mad elephant than an evil friend!"[31]

In the *Kanji* chapter of the Lotus Sutra it is recorded that, in the last five-hundred-year period or two thousand or so years after the Buddha's passing, there will be three types of enemies[32] of the Lotus Sutra. Our present age corresponds to this last five-hundred-year period. And as I, Nichiren, ponder the truth of these words of the Buddha, I realize that these three types of enemies are indeed a reality. If I do not cause them to come forth, then I will not be a true votary of the Lotus Sutra. Yet if I cause them to appear, then I am almost certain to bring death and destruction upon myself.

In the fourth volume of the Lotus Sutra, it is stated, "Since hatred and jealousy toward this sutra abound even during the lifetime of the Buddha, how much more will this be so after his passing?"[33] In the fifth volume it says, "The people will be full of hostility, and it will be extremely difficult to believe."[34] The same volume also reads, "We do not hold our own lives dear. We value only the supreme Way."[35] And the sixth volume says, "Not begrudging their lives."[36]

In the ninth volume of the Nirvana Sutra, we read: "For example, if an envoy who is skilled in discussion and knows how to employ clever expedients should be sent to a foreign country to carry out a mission for his sovereign, it is proper that he should relate the words of his ruler without holding back any of them, even though it may cost him his life. And a wise man should do the same in teaching Buddhism, going out among the common run of people, willing to give up his life, and proclaim without fail . . . the Mahayana sutras."[37] The Great Teacher Chang-an, commenting on the words "without holding back any of them, even though it may cost him his life," says, "One's body is insignificant while the Law is supreme. One should give his life in order to propagate the Law."[38]

When I examine these passages, I know that if I do not call forth these three enemies of the Lotus Sutra, then I will not be a true votary of the Lotus Sutra. Only by making them appear can I be a true votary. And yet if I do so, I am almost certain to lose my life. I will be like the Venerable Āryasiṃha[39] or Bodhisattva Āryadeva.[40]

Nichiren

The tenth day of the second month

Notes

1. "One who endeavors to seek the Way." Originally in India, any ascetic, recluse, mendicant, or other religious practitioner who has renounced the world to seek the Way. Later, it came to mean chiefly one who has renounced the world to practice Buddhism.

2. Reference is to a passage in the *Hokke Gengi* (T33, 704b) commenting on the passage in the Nirvana Sutra (T12, 391b) that condemns those who claim that the Buddha is characterized by impermanence.

3. The following story is found in the Nirvana Sutra (T12, 520a). Mentioned are the five meditations (Jap: *go jōshinkan*), mastery of which enables one to attain a certain stage of *shōmon* in the Hinayana teachings. They are: meditations on the vileness of the body; compassion for all; dependent origination; right discrimination; and breath control. They remove attachments to transient phenomena: anger, stupidity, attachment to the self, and thoughts that distract.

4. Reference to a passage in the Lotus Sutra (T9, 16a) in which Shakyamuni enjoins Śāriputra from expounding this sutra to those with a shallow, self-satisfied understanding or strong attachment to earthly desires.

5. Poison-drum relationship (Jap: *dokko no en*) is another term for reverse relationship (Jap: *gyakuen*), i.e., a bond formed with the Lotus Sutra by opposing or slandering it. That is, even though one should fall into hell for slandering the Lotus Sutra, because of the relationship, albeit a negative or reverse one, that one forms with the

sutra, one will eventually be able to obtain Buddhahood. The expression "poison drum" comes from the Nirvana Sutra (T12, 120a), which states, "Once the poison drum is beaten, all the people who hear it will die, regardless of whether or not they have a mind to listen." Similarly, when one preaches the Lotus Sutra, both those who embrace it and those who oppose it will equally receive the seed of Buddhahood.

6. Reference is to the bodhisattva Fukyō, described in the *Jōfukkyō* chapter (20th) of the Lotus Sutra.

7. T9, 8a.

8. Three calamities and seven disasters; *see* Glossary.

9. Fa-yün (467–529) was a famed lecturer on the Lotus Sutra and the Vimalakīrti Sutra. He was appointed chief priest of the Kuang-che-ssu by Emperor Wu of the Liang. In 523 to 525 he became General Administrator of Monks.

10. Hui-kuan (368–438) was a priest during the Northern and Southern Dynasties period. In 401 he became a disciple of Kumārajīva and joined in the master's translation work. It is said that after Kumārajīva's death he assisted Buddhabhadra with his translation of the *Kegon* Sutra. He also revised the two existing translations of the Nirvana Sutra and produced the *Nambon Nehangyō*, or "southern version" of the sutra.

11. Ch'eng-kuan (738–839) was the fourth patriarch of the Hua-yen (Kegon) school in T'ang China. In 775 he practiced the T'ien-t'ai meditation under Miao-lo and later studied under many teachers of the various schools. He eventually succeeded the third Kegon patriarch, Fa-tsang, and propagated the Kegon doctrines. He lectured on the *Kegon* Sutra at Ta-hua-yen-ssu and produced a number of commentaries, including the *Kegongyō Shō*.

12. Kōbō (774–835), founder of the Shingon Sect in Japan; *see* Glossary.

13. Chi-tsang (549–623) was a teacher of the San-lun (Sanron) school in China and is sometimes regarded as the first patriarch of the school. He was also called Chiahsiang after the name of the temple at which he lived.

14. K'uei-chi (632–682) was the founder of the Chinese Fa-hsiang (Hossō) school. He is also called Tz'u-en after the name of the temple at which he lived. He was one of the outstanding disciples of Hsüan-tsang and worked with him on the translation of many important texts.

15. The Great Teacher Chih-che is the title of Chih-i (538–597), the founder of the T'ien-t'ai school. Nichiren most frequently refers to him as the Great Teacher T'ien-t'ai; *see* T'ien-t'ai in Glossary.

16. This passage is given as a note in the text. It is difficult to determine to which texts Nichiren is referring. Shōtoku (574–622), the second son of Emperor Yōmei and the regent during the reign of Empress Suiko, carried out important reforms and contributed greatly to the spread of Buddhism. Ganjin (Chin Chien-chen, 688–763) was a celebrated Chinese monk who was invited to Japan to perform orthodox ordination ceremonies. After five failed attempts, he finally arrived in Japan in 754, where he conducted ceremonies conferring the precepts on the emperor, high court officials, and numerous Buddhist priests. The Great Teacher Dengyō (767–822), known also as Saichō, was the founder of the Tendai Sect in Japan. Nichiren refers to him here as Kompon Daishi, the basic teacher. Annen (841–899?) was a noted Tendai monk who studied both the exoteric and the esoteric doctrines. Eshin (942–1017), more commonly known as Genshin, was a Tendai monk who is noted for his advocacy of Pure Land teachings.

17. *See* Fifth five-hundred-year period in Glossary.

18. A reference to the Zen sect.

19. Shōi is a monk mentioned in the *Shohō Mugyō* Sutra who lived in the Latter Day of the Buddha Shinshionnō. He slandered Bodhisattva Kikon who taught the doctrine of the true aspect of reality, and was therefore said to have fallen into hell.

20. Guṇaprabha was a scholar of India who first studied the Mahayana but converted to Hinayana after reading the *Daibibasha Ron*, and wrote scores of commentaries. According to the *Daitō Saiiki Ki* (T51, 891b-c), he ascended to heaven in order to resolve his doubts concerning the Hinayana and the Mahayana. There he met Bodhisattva Miroku but did not respect him because Miroku was not an ordained monk. Thus he failed to learn from Miroku because of his arrogance.

21. The kingdom of Kośala in central India in ancient times. Śrāvasti was properly the name of the capital, but the kingdom itself was also called Śrāvasti.

22. *Yuga Ron* is an abbreviation of *Yuga Shiji Ron* (T30, no. 1579), a work attributed to Maitreya or Asanga, which was translated into Chinese by Hsüan-tsang.

23. Seng-chao (384–414) was a priest of the Later Ch'in dynasty and one of Kumārajīva's major disciples.

24. Textual note. Here again it is difficult to determine precisely to which texts Nichiren is referring.

25. Note in original text. The passage is found in DBZ 2, 349.

26. The six schools of Buddhism that flourished in the Nara period (710–794). They are the Kegon, Sanron, and Hossō sects, which are based on Mahayana sutras—the *Kegon* Sutra, the *Hannya* sutras and the *Jimmitsu* Sutra, respectively; as well as the Kusha, Jōjitsu, and Ritsu sects, which are based upon Hinayana teachings—the *Agon* sutras, the *Jōjitsu Ron*, and *Shibun Ritsu*, respectively.

27. The name of a mountainous region including the Pamirs, Tibet, and the plateaus of Mongolia. According to the *Shih Chi* (Records of the Historian), it was traditionally believed that jewels could be found there.

28. A legendary mountainous island off the eastern coast of China, where, according to the *Shih Chi* and other sources, an immortal possessing the elixir of perennial youth and eternal life dwells in a palace made of gold and jewels.

29. Reference is to Dainichi Nōnin and his disciple Kakuan. Dainichi Nōnin (d. 1196?) was a self-enlightened Zen priest who established temples in Settsu and Kyoto. Because he was criticized for not having received his teachings from a master, in 1189 he sent two disciples to China to have his teachings authenticated by a prominent Lin-chi (Jap: Rinzai) Zen master, Cho-an Te-kuang (1121–1203). His school, known as the Nihon Daruma-shū, or Japanese Bodhidharma school, flourished for some time during the early Kamakura period. Little is known of Kakuan. The text here reads Dainichi Buddha. A variant text gives Dainichi Butchi. Since Butchi-bō was the name of Kakuan's residence, it is assumed that reference is to him. Kakuan had a temple at Tōnomine in present-day Nara Prefecture. The temple is said to have been destroyed by monks from the Kōfuku-ji. Many of Kakuan's disciples later studied under Dōgen (1200–1253), honored as the founder of Sōtō Zen.

30. Hōnen (1133–1212) was the founder of the Pure Land (Jōdo) sect in Japan; *see* Glossary. Ryūkan (1148–1227) was the founder of the Chōraku-ji of the Pure Land sect. He first studied the Tendai doctrine, but, attracted by the Pure Land teachings, he became a disciple of Hōnen. He advocated the doctrine of many-time recitation, the belief that one should recite the Nembutsu as many times as possible in order to ensure birth in the Pure Land.

31. Nirvana Sutra. T12, 497a.

32. *See* Three powerful enemies in Glossary.

33. T9, 31b.

34. T9, 39a.

35. T9, 36c.

36. T9, 43b.

37. T12, 660a.

38. *Nehangyō Shō*, T38, 114b.

39. Āryasiṃha (Shishi biku) is the last of Shakyamuni's twenty-four successors. He was born to a Brahman family in central India in the sixth century. Tradition has it that, when he was propagating Buddhism in Kashmir in northern India, King Dammira (Sanskrit unknown), an enemy of Buddhism, destroyed many Buddhist temples and stupas and murdered a number of priests. He finally beheaded Āryasiṃha, but it is said that instead of blood, pure white milk gushed from his neck. *Fu Hōzō Innen Den* (T50, 321c).

40. Āryadeva is the fifteenth of Shakyamuni's twenty-four successors. He was born in a Brahman family in southern India in the third century and studied under Nāgārjuna. He was also called Kāṇadeva because of the loss of an eye (*kāṇa* means "one eye"). He refuted teachers of Brahmanism at Pāṭaliputra in a religious debate and was killed by one of their disciples. *Fu Hōzō Innen Den* (T50, 318c–319b).

2 THE DAIMOKU OF THE LOTUS SUTRA

NICHIREN, FOLLOWER OF THE GREAT TEACHER DENGYŌ

This letter was written in 1260 for a woman of advanced years. Nothing is known about her other than that she was a new believer in Nichiren's Buddhism and lived in Amatsu of Awa Province.

In the fall of 1264, one year after he had been pardoned from his exile in Izu, Nichiren returned to his birthplace in Awa Province. News of his mother's grave illness and the lessening of official pressures prompted his decision to return home. However, Tojo Kagenobu, the steward of this district, a passionate follower of the Nembutsu teaching, was incensed at Nichiren's propagation activities and was determined to put a halt to them.

On his return Nichiren's primary concern was to visit his mother, and their reunion seems to have had a great effect upon her and she quickly recovered. Meanwhile Kudō Yoshitaka and the other disciples in the area were anxious to see him and urged Nichiren to visit Kudō's manor. On the eleventh day of the eleventh month, 1264, accompanied by messengers sent to guide them, the group set out. When they reached a place known as Komatsubara, they were ambushed by Tōjō Kagenobu and his Nembutsu followers. Two of Nichiren's group lost their lives and Nichiren suffered a sword slash to his forehead and a broken hand.

Nichiren remained in Awa from 1264 through 1267 at considerable personal risk and was highly successful in gaining converts in his native province and adjoining areas. He resided at his old temple, the Seichō-ji, and it was here that he wrote several doctrinal treatises, including the present letter.

Nam-myoho-renge-kyo

Question: Is it possible, without understanding the meaning of the Lotus Sutra, but merely by chanting the five or seven characters[1] of Nam–myoho–renge–kyo once a day, once a month, or simply once a

31

year, once a decade, or once in a lifetime, to avoid being drawn into trivial or serious acts of evil, to escape falling into the four evil paths, and instead to eventually reach the stage of nonregression?[2]

Answer: Yes, it is.

Question: You may talk about fire, but unless you put your hand in a flame, you will never burn yourself. You may say "water, water!" but unless you actually drink it, you will never satisfy your thirst. Then how, just by chanting the daimoku of Nam-myoho-renge-kyo without understanding what it means, can you escape from the evil paths of existence?

Answer: They say that if you play a koto strung with a lion's sinews, then all the other kinds of strings will snap. And if you so much as hear the words "pickled plum," your mouth will begin to water. Even in everyday life there are such wonders, so how much greater are the wonders of the Lotus Sutra!

We are told that parrots, simply by twittering the Four Noble Truths[3] of the Hinayana teachings, were able to be reborn in heaven,[4] and that men, simply by respecting the Three Treasures, were able to escape being swallowed by a huge fish.[5] How much more effective, then, is the daimoku of the Lotus Sutra, which is the very heart of all the eight thousand sacred teachings[6] of Buddhism and the eye of the countless Buddhas! How can you doubt that, by chanting it, you can escape from the four evil paths?

The Lotus Sutra, wherein the Buddha honestly discarded all provisional teachings, says that one may "gain entrance through faith."[7] And the Nirvana Sutra, which the Buddha preached in the grove of sāla trees on the last day of his life, states, "Although there are innumerable practices which lead to enlightenment, if one teaches faith, then that includes all those practices."[8]

Thus faith is the basic requirement for entering the way of the Buddha. In the fifty-two stages of bodhisattva practice, the first ten stages, dealing with faith, are basic, and the first of these ten stages is that of arousing pure faith. Though a person has no knowledge of Buddhism, if he has pure faith, then even though he may be dull-witted, he is to be reckoned as a man of correct views. But even though one has some knowledge of Buddhism, if he is without faith, then he is to be considered a slanderer and an *icchantika* or person of incorrigible disbelief.

The monk Sunakṣatra[9] observed the two hundred and fifty precepts,[10] mastered the four stages of meditation,[11] and was versed in all the twelve divisions of the scriptures, while Devadatta learned the sixty thousand non-Buddhist teachings and the eighty thousand Buddhist teachings and could manifest eighteen miraculous powers[12] with his body. And yet it is said that these men, because they had knowledge but no faith, are now in the great citadel of the Avīci Hell. Mahākāśyapa and Śāriputra on the other hand lacked knowledge but had faith, and the Buddha accordingly predicted that they would become the Buddhas Light Bright and Flower Light respectively. The Buddha stated, "One who gives way to doubt and does not have faith will surely fall into the evil paths."[13] These words refer to those who have knowledge but are without faith.

And yet contemporary scholars ask, "How is it possible simply by chanting Nam-myoho-renge-kyo, with faith but no understanding, to avoid the evil paths of existence?" If we accept the words of the sutras, these scholars themselves can hardly avoid falling into the great citadel of the Avīci Hell.

Thus as we have seen, even if a person lacks understanding, so long as he chants Nam-myoho-renge-kyo, he can avoid the evil paths. This is like the lotus blossom that turns in the direction of the sun, though the lotus has no mind to direct it,[14] or like the plantain that grows with the rumbling of thunder, though this plant has no ears to hear it.[15] Now we are like the lotus or the plantain, and the daimoku of the Lotus Sutra is like the sun or the thunder.

People say that if you tie a piece of living rhinoceros horn[16] to your body and enter the water, the water will not come within five feet of you. They also say that if one leaf of the sandalwood tree unfurls, it can eradicate the foul odor of the *eraṇḍa* trees for a distance of forty *yojana*.[17] In this case, our evil karma may be likened to the *eraṇḍa* trees or the water, and the daimoku of the Lotus Sutra may be likened to the living horn of the rhinoceros or the leaf of the sandalwood tree.

Diamonds are so hard that almost no substance will cut them, and yet they can be cut by a sheep's horn or a turtle's shell.[18] The limbs of the *nyagrodha*[19] tree are so stout that the largest birds can perch on them without breaking them, and yet they are vulnerable to the tailorbird,[20] which is so tiny it could almost build its nest on the eyelashes of a mosquito. Here, our evil karma is analogous to the diamond or the *nyagrodha* tree, and the daimoku of the Lotus Sutra, to the sheep's horn or the tailorbird. Amber draws dust and a loadstone attracts iron particles; here our evil karma is like the dust or iron, and the daimoku of the Lotus Sutra is like the amber or the loadstone. If we consider these analogies, we can see why we should always chant Nam-myoho-renge-kyo.

The first volume of the Lotus Sutra states, "Throughout numberless and incalculable kalpas it will be a difficult thing to hear this Law."[21] And the fifth volume says, "As for this Lotus Sutra, throughout countless numbers of countries one cannot even hear the name of it."[22] Thus it is an extremely rare thing to hear the name of the Lotus Sutra. Though the Buddhas Shusenda[23] and Tahō made their appearance in the world, they did not utter so much as the name of the Lotus Sutra. And though Shakyamuni Buddha made his advent expressly for the purpose of preaching the Lotus Sutra, during a period of forty-two years, he kept the name of that sutra a secret and never referred to it. It was only when he reached the age of seventy-two that he first began to intone the title of the sutra, *Myōhō-renge-kyō*. However, the people of faraway countries such as China and Japan were unable to hear of it at that time. It was over a thousand years before China heard so much as the name of the sutra, and another three hundred fifty years or more before it was heard in Japan.

Thus, encountering this sutra is as rare as the blossoming of the *udumbara*[24] flower, which occurs but once in three thousand years, or the one-eyed turtle[25] finding a floating piece of sandalwood, which happens only once in innumerable kalpas.

Suppose one were to stick a needle in the earth point up and throw down tiny mustard seeds at it from the palace of King Bonten in the sky. One could sooner impale a mustard seen on the point of the needle than encounter the daimoku of the Lotus Sutra.[26] Or suppose one were to place a needle upright on top of the Mount Sumeru in one world and then, standing atop the Mount Sumeru of another world on a very windy day, were to try to cast a thread so that it reached the other mountain and passed through the eye of the needle.[27] One could sooner thread a needle in this way than encounter the daimoku of the Lotus Sutra.

Therefore, when you chant the daimoku of the Lotus Sutra, you should be aware that it is a more joyful thing than for one who was born blind to gain his eyesight and see his father and mother, and a rarer thing than for one who has been seized by a powerful enemy to be released and reunited with his wife and children.

Question: What passages of proof can be cited to show that one should chant only the daimoku?

Answer: The eighth volume of the *Myōhō-renge-kyō*[28] states, "One who receives and embraces the name of the Lotus Sutra will enjoy good fortune beyond measure."[29] The *Shō-hokke-kyō* says, "If one hears this sutra and proclaims and embraces its title, he will enjoy blessings beyond measure."[30] And the *Tembon-hoke-kyō* says "One who receives and embraces the name of the Lotus Sutra will enjoy good fortune beyond measure."[31] These passages indicate that the good fortune one receives from simply chanting the daimoku is beyond measure.

To embrace, read, recite, take delight in, and protect all the eight volumes and twenty-eight chapters of the Lotus Sutra is called the comprehensive practice. To receive and protect the *Hōben* and *Juryō* chapters is called the abbreviated practice. And simply to chant one four-phrase verse or the daimoku, and to protect those who do so, is called the essential practice. Hence among these three kinds of practice, the comprehensive, the abbreviated, and the essential, the daimoku is defined as the essential practice.

Question: How great are the blessings contained within the five characters of Myōhō-renge-kyō?

Answer: The great ocean contains all the numerous rivers that flow into it, the great earth contains all sentient and insentient beings, the wish-granting jewel[32] is capable of showering down innumerable treasures, and the heavenly king Bonten rules over all the threefold world. The five characters of Myōhō-renge-kyō are comparable to all these. All beings of the nine worlds, as well as those in the world of Buddhahood, are contained within them. And since all beings of the Ten Worlds are contained within them, so are their environments.

Let us first examine the fact that the five characters, Myōhō-renge-kyō, contain within them all teachings. The single character *kyō* or "sutra" is the king of all sutras, and all the various other sutras are encompassed by it. The Buddha appeared in the world and over a period of fifty years and more preached eighty thousand sacred teachings. At that time the life span of human beings is said to have been one hundred years.[33] The Buddha passed away in the middle of the night on the fifteenth day of the second month of the year with the cyclical sign *mizunoe-saru* (949 B.C.).[34] Thereafter, during some ninety days of summer, or the period from the eighth day of the fourth month until the fifteenth day of the seventh month of the same year, one thousand arhats gathered at the Chamber of the First Council and set down all the sutras.

After that, during the one thousand years of the Former Day of the Law, all these various sutras spread throughout the five regions of

India,[35] but they did not reach as far as China. It was only in the fifteenth year of the Middle Day of the Law, or 1,015 years after the
Buddha's death, that Buddhist statues and sutras were first introduced
to China. This was in the year with the cyclical sign *hinoto-u* (A.D. 67),
the tenth year of the Yung-p'ing era in the reign of Emperor Ming the
Filial of the Later Han dynasty. From that time until the year with the
cyclical sign *kanoe-uma* (A.D. 730), the eighteenth year of the K'ai-yüan
era of the reign of Emperor Hsüan-tsung of the T'ang dynasty, a total
of 176 translators went to China, taking with them 1,076 sutras, works
on discipline, and treatises comprising 5,048 volumes contained in 480
scroll-cases. All of these sacred writings are followers of the single character *kyō*, or sutra, of the Lotus Sutra.

Among the sutras that the Buddha preached during the forty or
more years before he expounded *Myōhō-renge-kyō*, there is one called
the *Daihōkōbutsu Kegon* Sutra. This sutra is preserved in the dragon
king's palace in three versions.[36] The first version contains as many
chapters as there are dust particles in ten major world systems. The second version contains 498,800 verses, and the third version contains
100,000 verses in forty-eight chapters. Outside of these three versions,
only the eighty-volume and sixty-volume versions[37] are preserved in
China and Japan.

In addition, there are the Hinayana sutras such as the *Agon* sutras,
and the various Mahayana sutras of the *Hōdō* and *Hannya* categories.
Among the latter, the Sanskrit text of the *Dainichi* Sutra devotes a total
of 3,500 verses simply to the explanation of the five characters of the
mantra *Avarahakha*,[38] to say nothing of the countless verses it uses to
describe the "seeds,"[39] august forms, and *samayas*[40] of the various
Buddhas. In China, however, the text exists in a mere six- or seven-
volume form. The Nirvana Sutra, which the Buddha preached in the
sāla grove on his last day, is preserved in China in a version that is only
forty volumes long, though in this case, too, the Sanskrit versions of
the text have many more volumes. All these various sutras are followers of the Lotus Sutra, the heart of Shakyamuni Buddha's teachings. In
addition, all the sutras expounded by the seven Buddhas of the past,[41]
the thousand Buddhas, or the Buddhas of countless kalpas ago, as well
as those expounded by the Buddhas presently living in the ten directions, are all followers of the single character *kyō* of the Lotus Sutra.

Thus, in the *Yakuō* chapter of the Lotus Sutra, the Buddha addresses
the bodhisattva named Shukuōke, saying in essence, "It [the Lotus
Sutra] is like the ocean, which is foremost among all bodies of water

such as rivers and streams; like Mount Sumeru, which is foremost among all mountains, or like the god of the moon, which is foremost among all the heavenly bodies [shining in the night sky]."[42] The Great Teacher Miao-lo comments on this by saying, "[It] is foremost among all the sutras the Buddha has preached, now preaches and will preach."[43]

Within this single character *kyō* are contained all the sutras in the entire universe. It is like the wish-granting jewel that contains within it all manner of treasures, or the vastness of space that encompasses all phenomena. And because this single character *kyō* of Myōhō-renge-kyō is the supreme achievement of the Buddha's lifetime of teaching, the other four characters, Myōhō-ren-ge, likewise surpass all the other eighty thousand doctrines that the Buddha taught.

Coming now to the character *myō* [meaning "mystic" or "wonderful"], the Lotus Sutra says, "This sutra opens the door of expedient teachings and reveals the true aspect of reality."[44] The Great Teacher Chang-an comments on this as follows: "*Myō* means to reveal the depths of the secret storehouse."[45] And the Great Teacher Miao-lo says of this, "To reveal means to open."[46] Hence the character *myō* means to open.

If there is a storehouse full of treasures but no key, then it cannot be opened, and if it cannot be opened, then the treasures inside cannot be seen. The Buddha preached the *Kegon* Sutra, but he did not give the kind of explanation that would be a key to open this sutra. Likewise, in the forty or more years that followed, he preached other sutras such as the *Agon*, *Hōdō*, *Hannya*, and *Kammuryōju* sutras, but he did not reveal their meaning. Their doors remained closed, and therefore no one could understand these sutras. Even though people thought they understood, they in fact had only a distorted view.

But then the Buddha preached the Lotus Sutra and in this way opened the storehouses of the sutras. And for the first time in more than forty years, all the people of the nine worlds were able to view the treasures that lay within. To give an analogy, even though there are people and animals, plants and trees on the earth, without the light of the sun or moon, even those who have eyes cannot make out their shapes and colors. Only when the sun or moon rises can one discern for the first time what they are really like. The sutras that preceded the Lotus Sutra were shrouded in the darkness of a long night, and the essential and theoretical teachings of the Lotus Sutra were like the sun and the moon.

Among the bodhisattvas with their two good eyes, the cross-eyed men of the two vehicles, common mortals with their blind eyes, or those of incorrigible disbelief who have been blind since birth, there were none who could make out the true color or shape of things by means of the earlier sutras. But when the Lotus Sutra was preached and the moon of the theoretical teaching came forth, then the bodhisattvas with their two good eyes first gained enlightenment, to be followed by the cross-eyed men of the two vehicles. Next the blind eyes of the common mortals were opened, and then even the persons of incorrigible disbelief, who had been blind from birth, were able to establish a relationship with the Lotus Sutra that assured them that their eyes would one day open. All this was due entirely to the virtue of the single character *myō*.

There are two *myō* or mystic principles[47] expounded in the Lotus Sutra, one in the first fourteen chapters, which constitute the theoretical teaching, and one in the latter fourteen chapters, which constitute the essential teaching. From another point of view there are twenty mystic principles,[48] ten in the theoretical teaching and ten in the essential teaching, or there are sixty mystic principles, thirty in the theoretical teaching and thirty in the essential teaching. From yet other points of view, forty mystic principles[49] may be discerned in each half of the Lotus Sutra. By adding these to the forty mystic principles concerning the observation of the mind,[50] the single character *myō* will be found to contain fully one hundred and twenty *myō* or mystic principles.[51]

One fundamental *myō* or mystic principle underlies every one of the 69,384 characters that make up the Lotus Sutra. Hence the Lotus Sutra comprises a total of 69,384 mystic principles.

The character *myō* is rendered in Sanskrit by the word *sad*, and in Chinese is pronounced *miao*. *Myō* means "fully endowed," which in turn has the meaning of "perfection." Each word and each character of the Lotus Sutra contains within it all the 69,384 characters that compose the sutra. To illustrate, one drop of the great ocean contains within it the waters of all the various rivers that flow into the ocean, and the wish-granting jewel, though no bigger than a mustard seed, is capable of showering down all the treasures that one could wish for.

To give another analogy, plants and trees are withered and bare in autumn and winter, but when the sun of spring and summer shines on them, they put forth branches and leaves, and then flowers and fruit. Before the preaching of the Lotus Sutra, the people in the nine worlds were like plants and trees in autumn and winter. But when the single character *myō* of the Lotus Sutra shone on them like the spring and summer sun, then the flower of the aspiration for enlightenment blossomed and the fruit of Buddhahood emerged.

Bodhisattva Nāgārjuna in his *Daichido Ron* says, "[The Lotus Sutra is] like a great physician who changes poison into medicine."[52] This quotation occurs in a passage in the *Daichido Ron* that explains the virtues inherent in the character *myō* of the Lotus Sutra. The Great Teacher Miao-lo comments on this as follows: "Because it can cure that which is thought to be incurable, it is called *myō* or mystic."[53]

In general, there are four kinds of people who have great difficulty in attaining Buddhahood. First are those predestined for the realms of *shōmōn* and *engaku*,[54] second are those of incorrigible disbelief (*icchantika*), third are those who cling to the doctrine of void,[55] and fourth are those who slander the True Law. But through the Lotus Sutra, all of these people are able to attain Buddhahood. That is why the Lotus Sutra is called *myō*.

Devadatta was the eldest son of King Droṇodana and a nephew of King Śuddhodana,[the father of the Buddha Shakyamuni,] which made him the Buddha's cousin. He was also the elder brother of the Buddha's disciple, the Venerable Ānanda. He was thus by no means a person of low station in the continent of Jambudvīpa. He became a disciple of the monk Sudāya[56] and entered the religious life. From Ānanda he learned the eighteen miraculous powers,[57] and he committed to memory the sixty thousand teachings of the non-Buddhist schools and the eighty thousand teachings of Buddhism. He observed the five practices[58] and appeared almost more saintly than the Buddha himself. Thinking to make himself a leader like the Buddha, he dared to commit the crime of disrupting the Buddhist Order by establishing his own ordination platform on Mount Gayā[59] and inviting the Buddha's disciples over to his side. He confided to Crown Prince Ajātaśatru, "I intend to kill the Buddha and become the new Buddha. You must kill your father, King Bimbisāra, and become the new king in his place!"

After Crown Prince Ajātaśatru had in fact killed his father, Devadatta kept watch on the Buddha's activities and with a large stone succeeded in wounding him to the extent that blood flowed. He also struck and killed the nun Utpalavarṇā[60] who had reached the state of arhat. Thus he committed three of the five cardinal sins.[61]

In addition, with Kokālika[62] as his disciple and King Ajātaśatru as his patron, Devadatta began to attract followers from everywhere, until, throughout the five regions of India with its sixteen great states and five hundred medium-sized states, every soul guilty of one, two or three of the cardinal sins was a member of his group. They gathered about him as the various rivers gather in the great ocean, or as plants and trees gather on a great mountain. As wise men gathered about Śāriputra, and those of occult powers flocked to Maudgalyāyana, so did men of evil bent throw in their lot with Devadatta.

As a result, the great earth, which is 168,000 *yojana* thick and rests on a windy circle[63] as hard as a diamond, nevertheless split open, plunging Devadatta alive into the hell of incessant suffering. His leading disciple Kokālika also fell into hell alive, as did the female Brahman Ciñcāmānavika,[64] King Virūḍhāka[65] and Sunakṣatra the monk.[66] Moreover, the people of the five regions of India with its sixteen great states, five hundred medium-sized states, and ten thousand small states all observed this. Those in the six heavens of the world of desire and in the four meditation heavens,[67] all beings in both the worlds of form and formlessness,[68] including Bonten, Taishaku, the Devil of the Sixth Heaven, and King Emma, likewise witnessed their fate.

All the beings throughout the major world system and the entire universe heard about this, and unanimously concluded that, even though as many kalpas should pass as there are dust particles on the earth, Devadatta and the others would never escape from the hell of incessant suffering, and though the stone that marks the duration of a kalpa might be worn completely away, they would continue to suffer in the great citadel of the Avīci Hell. How astounding, then, that in the Devadatta chapter of the Lotus Sutra, Shakyamuni should reveal that Devadatta was his teacher in a past existence and should predict that he would attain enlightenment in the future as a Buddha called Heavenly King! If the sutras preached before the Lotus Sutra are true, then the Lotus Sutra must be an outrageous lie. But if the Lotus Sutra is true, then the previous sutras must be guilty of perpetrating the wildest deceptions.

If Devadatta, who committed three of the five cardinal sins, and in addition was guilty of countless other grave offenses, could become the Buddha Heavenly King, then there can be no doubt that the other evildoers who committed only one or two of the cardinal sins will surely attain enlightenment as well. For if something is capable of overturning the great earth itself, then it can surely overturn mere plants and trees. And if something can crush the hardest stone, it can certainly bend the pliant grasses. Therefore the Lotus Sutra is called *myō*.

Coming now to the subject of women, we find that they are strongly condemned in both the Buddhist and non-Buddhist writings. The works known as the *Three Records* and *Five Canons*[69] of the Three Rulers and Five Emperors of ancient China depict them as fawning and perverse. For this reason, disaster is said to have come about because of the three evil women of antiquity.[70] Thus women are identified as the cause of the downfall of a nation and its people.

The *Kegon* Sutra, the first great Buddhist doctrine that the Buddha preached following his enlightenment, states, "Women are messengers of hell who can destroy the seeds of Buddhahood. They may look like bodhisattvas, but at heart they are like *yaksa*[71] demons."[72] And the Nirvana Sutra, the Buddha's last teaching which he delivered in the grove of sāla trees, says, "All rivers and streams are invariably winding and devious, and all women are invariably fawning and perverse." And it also says, "If all the desires and delusions of all the men throughout the major world system were lumped together, they would be no greater than the karmic impediment of one single woman."[73]

When the *Kegon* Sutra says that women "can destroy the seeds of Buddhahood," it means that they scorch and burn up the seeds that would otherwise allow them to attain Buddhahood. When cloud masses form in the sky during a time of great drought and heavy rain falls on the earth, then countless withered plants and trees everywhere will put forth blossoms and bear fruit. But this is not true of seeds that have been scorched. They will never sprout; rather the heavy rain makes them rot.

Now the Buddha is like the masses of clouds, his teachings are like the heavy rain, and the withered plants and trees are like all living beings. When they are watered by the rain of the Buddhist teachings and observe the five precepts, the ten good precepts[74] and the meditational practices, all of which bring merit, then they will put forth blossoms and bear fruit. But the scorched seeds never sprout even though the rain falls on them, but instead rot. They are comparable to women who, though they encounter the Buddhist teachings, cannot free themselves from the sufferings of birth and death but instead turn away from the truth of Buddhism and fall into the evil paths. This is what the sutra means when it says that women "can destroy the seeds of Buddhahood."

The passage in the Nirvana Sutra cited above says that, just as all rivers and streams twist and wind, so too are women perverse and devious. Because water is a fluid substance, block its path with some hard object such as a rock or a mountain, and it will split into two streams or turn aside, flowing now this way, now that. Women are the same; their minds are soft and weak. Though they may believe that a certain course is right, if they come up against the strong will of a man and find their way blocked, then they will turn in some direction quite different from the one they originally intended.

Again, though you may trace pictures on the surface of the water, nothing of what you have drawn will remain. Women are the same, for lack of steadfastness is their basic character. Hence they will think a certain way at one moment, and then a moment later have quite a different view. But the basic character of a Buddha is honesty and straightforwardness. Hence women, with their devious ways, can never become Buddhas.

Women are doomed to the five obstacles and the three types of obedience.[75] Hence the *Gonjikinyo* Sutra says, "Though the eyes of all the Buddhas of the past, present and future were to fall to the ground, a woman could still never become a Buddha."[76] And the *Daichido Ron* says, "You could sooner catch the wind than grasp the mind of a woman."[77]

Yet though all female beings were so despised in the various sutras, when Bodhisattva Monjushiri spoke the single character *myō*, a woman was instantly able to become a Buddha. So extraordinary was this occurrence that Bodhisattva Chishaku, the foremost disciple of Tahō Buddha in the world of Treasure Purity, and Śāriputra, who was known among Shakyamuni Buddha's disciples as the foremost in wisdom, protested. They said that according to all the Mahayana and Hinayana sutras that the Buddha had preached in the previous forty years and more, the dragon king's daughter could not possibly become a Buddha. And yet in the end their arguments were of no avail and in fact she did become a Buddha.

Thus the passage in the Buddha's first sutra declaring that women "can destroy the seeds of Buddhahood," and that in his final sermon in the sāla grove about how "all rivers and streams are invariably winding and devious," were utterly contradicted, and the mirror or diviner's tortoise shell[78] of the *Gonjikinyo* Sutra and the *Daichido Ron* were proven to be nonsense. Chishaku and Śāriputra were obliged to still their tongues and shut their mouths, while all the human and heavenly beings present at the great gathering where the Lotus Sutra was preached pressed their palms together in an excess of joy. All this was due entirely to the virtue of the single character *myō*.

In the continent of Jambudvīpa in the southern region of the world, there are 2,500 rivers, and every single one of them is winding. They are devious like the minds of the women of Jambudvīpa. And yet there is one river called the Shabaya[79] that follows a course as straight as a taut rope, flowing directly into the western sea. A woman who has faith in the Lotus Sutra will be like this river, proceeding directly to the Pure Land in the west.[80] Such is the virtue inherent in the single character *myō*.

Myō means to revive, that is, to return to life. This is like the yellow crane's chick. It is said that though the chick may die, if the mother crane calls the name of Tzu-an, then the dead chick will come back to life again. Or it is like the case of the fish and shellfish that have been killed because a poisonous secretary bird has entered the water. If they are touched with a rhinoceros horn,[81] we are told, they will all be brought back to life. Similarly, persons of the two vehicles, those of incorrigible disbelief (*icchantika*) and women were described in the sutras that preceded the Lotus Sutra as having scorched and killed the seeds that would have allowed them to attain Buddhahood. But by holding fast to this single character *myō*, they can revive the scorched seeds of Buddhahood.

T'ien-t'ai says, "The *icchantika* nevertheless have minds, and so it is still possible for them to attain Buddhahood. But persons of the two vehicles have annihilated consciousness, and therefore cannot arouse the mind which aspires to enlightenment. And yet the Lotus Sutra can cure them, which is why it is called *myō*."[82] Miao-lo comments on this as follows: "The reason that the other sutras are called *dai* or 'great' but not *myō* is simply that it is easy to cure those who have a mind, but difficult to cure those who are without a mind. Because it [the Lotus Sutra] can cure that which is thought to be incurable, it is called *myo* or mystic."[83]

These passages refer to the fact that sutras such as the *Daihōkōbutsu Kegon* Sutra, *Daijuku* Sutra, *Daibon Hannya* Sutra, and *Dainehan* Sutra all have the character *dai* in their titles but not the character *myō*. This is because they can cure only the living but cannot cure the dead. The Lotus Sutra, however, can cure the dead as well as the living, and therefore it has the character *myō* in its title.

Thus, with the other sutras, persons who should become Buddhas are unable to do so. But with the Lotus Sutra, even those who would ordinarily find it impossible to do so can attain Buddhahood, not to mention those for whom it is relatively easy. This being the case, in the time since the Lotus Sutra was preached, there ought not to be a single person who puts faith in the other sutras.

Now the two thousand years of the Former and Middle Days of the Law have passed, and we have entered the Latter Day of the Law. In such an age, it is ten billion times more difficult for ordinary people to attain Buddhahood than it was for even the persons of the two vehicles or those of incorrigible disbelief who lived when the Buddha was alive. And yet people nowadays think that by relying on the *Kammuryōju* Sutra or some other of the sutras preached in the forty-odd years before the Lotus Sutra, they can escape the sufferings of birth and death. How futile, how utterly futile!

Women, whether they live at the time of the Buddha or in the Former, Middle, or Latter Day of the Law, cannot attain Buddhahood through any teaching but the Lotus Sutra. None of the other sutras expounded by any of the Buddhas anywhere can help them. The Great Teacher T'ien-t'ai, who heard the Buddha's teachings at Eagle Peak[84] and later attained an awakening in the place of meditation, has stated unequivocally: "The other sutras predict Buddhahood for men only and not for women. Only this sutra predicts Buddhahood for all."[85]

Shakyamuni Buddha, in the presence of Tahō Buddha and the other Buddhas of the ten directions, preached the Lotus Sutra over a period of eight years at the place called Eagle Peak northeast of Rājagṛha, the capital of the kingdom of Magadha. The Great Teacher T'ien-t'ai was present and heard him preach. "During my fifty or more years of teaching," said the Buddha, "I have preached various sacred doctrines, all in order to bring benefit to living beings. In the sutras of the first forty-two years, I taught that it was not possible for women to attain Buddhahood. But now with the Lotus Sutra I declare that women can become Buddhas."

Northeast of Eagle Peak, at a distance of some 108,000 *ri*[86] beyond the mountains and seas, there is a country called Mahācina [in Sanskrit]. We know it as China. Some fifteen hundred years after the Buddha's passing, there appeared in this country a messenger of the Buddha called the Great Teacher T'ien-t'ai, who declared that women could never attain Buddhahood through any teaching other than the Lotus Sutra.

Three thousand *ri* to the east of China there is a country called Japan. Some two hundred years after the Great Teacher T'ien-t'ai passed away, he was reborn in this country and bore the name of the Great Teacher Dengyō.[87] He then wrote a work entitled *Hokke Shūku* in which he stated: "Neither teachers nor disciples need undergo countless kalpas of austere practice in order to attain Buddhahood. Through the power of the Lotus Sutra they can do so in their present form."[88] Thus he made clear why the dragon king's daughter was able to become a Buddha.

It may seem somewhat difficult for women of the age we live in to attain Buddhahood without changing their present form. But if they put their trust in the Lotus Sutra, there is no doubt that they will be reborn in the Pure Land of Perfect Bliss when they die. They will reach it more readily than the rivers and streams flowing into the great ocean, or more swiftly than the rain falling from the sky.

And yet we find that the women throughout Japan do not chant Nam-myoho-renge-kyo. Instead they put their faith in works such as the *Muryōju* Sutra or the *Kammuryōju* Sutra, which can never lead women to the Pure Land or to Buddhahood. They intone the name of the Buddha Amida sixty thousand or a hundred thousand times a day. Amida is indeed the name of a Buddha, and to invoke it would seem to be a laudable practice. But because the women who do so are relying upon sutras that deny that women can ever attain Buddhahood, they are in effect merely counting other people's riches. And this comes about solely because they are led astray by evil teachers. The women throughout Japan face an enemy more fearful than tigers or wolves, mountain bandits or pirates at sea, their parents' foes or their husbands' concubines. Their real enemies are the persons who, instead of teaching them to rely on the Lotus Sutra, teach them the Nembutsu!

Women who put their faith in the Lotus Sutra should chant Nam-myoho-renge-kyo sixty thousand, a hundred thousand, or even ten million times a day, and after that, if they still have some time to spare, they may now and then murmur to themselves the name of Amida or one of the other Buddhas. But women these days spend their whole lives constantly reciting the name of Amida and busying themselves with matters that concern the Nembutsu. They never recite the Lotus Sutra or give alms for its sake. True, there are a few of them who have the Lotus Sutra read by priests who follow its teachings. But they look up to the Nembutsu priests as though they were their parents or brothers, and treat the practitioners of the Lotus Sutra with less respect than they would their retainers or followers. And yet they claim that they are believers in the Lotus Sutra!

By contrast, Lady Jōtoku[89] gave permission for her sons, the two princes, to enter the Buddhist Order and encouraged them to propagate the Lotus Sutra. Moreover, the dragon king's daughter took a vow, saying, "I will reveal the teachings of the Great Vehicle and bring release to suffering beings."[90] These women surely took no vow to practice only the teachings of the other sutras and to neglect the practice of the Lotus Sutra. Nevertheless, that is what the women of today do, paying all their attention to the practice of other sutras and none to that of the Lotus Sutra. You must change your ways immediately. Nam-myoho-renge-kyo, Nam-myoho-renge-kyo.

Nichiren

Completed at the Hour of the Sheep (2:00 P.M.) at Seichō-ji[91] on the sixth day of the first month of the third year of Bun'ei (1266), the year with the cyclical sign hinoe-tora.

Notes

1. The five characters are *myō, hō, ren, ge,* and *kyō,* the title of the Lotus Sutra. The seven characters are the above five plus *na* and *mu* (read here as *nam*); *nam* is the transliteration of the Sanskrit *namas,* devotion.

2. The eleventh of the fifty-two stages of bodhisattva practice and the first of the ten stages of security. One who reaches this stage can no longer backslide and is certain to attain Buddhahood. The four evil paths are the worlds of hell, hungry ghosts, animals, and asura. *See* Ten Worlds in Glossary.

3. A fundamental doctrine of Buddhism, clarifying the cause of suffering and the way of emancipation. They are (1) all existence is suffering; (2) suffering is caused by selfish craving; (3) the eradication of selfish craving brings about the cessation of suffering and enables one to obtain nirvana; and (4) this eradication can be achieved by following the eightfold path: (1) right views, (2) right thinking, (3) right speech, (4) right action, (5) right way of life, (6) right endeavor, (7) right mindfulness, and (8) right meditation.

4. This story appears in the *Kengu* Sutra (T4, 436c). According to the sutra, when Shakyamuni lived in Śrāvastī, his disciple Ānanda made pets of two parrots kept at the house of the Buddha's patron Sudatta and taught them the four noble truths. One evening, a raccoon dog attacked and ate them, but they were said to have been reborn in the Heaven of the Four Heavenly Kings because of the benefit obtained by repeating the Four Noble Truths.

5. This story appears in the *Daihi* Sutra (T12, 957b). The Three Treasures are the Buddha, the Law, and the Priesthood. According to this sutra, once when a merchant was sailing the ocean, a huge fish named *makara* was about to swallow up his ship. Although the other people aboard were in despair, he fixed his mind upon the Three

Treasures and called upon the mercy of all the Buddhas. Seeing him, the others joined him in sincere prayers with their palms joined, and the huge fish ceased attacking them.

6. All of Shakyamuni's teachings.

7. T9, 15b.

8. T12, 573c.

9. A son whom, according to some sources, Shakyamuni sired before he renounced the world. He entered the Buddhist Order but, influenced by evil friends, he lost his mastery of the four stages of meditation and became attached to the mistaken view that there is no Buddha, no Law, and no attainment of nirvana. He is said to have eventually fallen into hell alive. His story appears in the Nirvana Sutra (T12, 561c).

10. The two hundred and fifty precepts are the rules of discipline to be observed by fully ordained monks of Hinayana Buddhism.

11. Four levels of meditation that enable those in the world of desire to throw off illusions and be reborn in the four meditation heavens in the world of form. The first meditation leads one to the first heaven, and so on.

12. A variety of actions and appearances which Buddhas and bodhisattvas manifest in order to lead people to enlightenment. Explanations vary depending on the sutra. *See also* note 57.

13. Lotus Sutra (T9, 42a).

14. Simile drawn from the Nirvana Sutra (T12, 419b).

15. Simile drawn from the Nirvana Sutra (T12, 418b).

16. The rhinoceros horn is mentioned in a textual note in the *Daijuku* Sutra (T13, 388a). The source of the accompanying story has not been traced.

17. The *eraṇḍa* is a tall, noxious-smelling tree said to have grown in India. *Yojana* is a unit of measurement in ancient India, equal to the distance the royal army was thought to march in a day. Approximations vary as widely as 9.6, 18, and 24 km.

18. Simile drawn from Nirvana Sutra (T12, 418b).

19. Banyan trees found in tropical and subtropical regions, usually from thirty to forty feet tall. Their abundant foliage offers cool shade from the sun.

20. The tailorbird (Jap: *shōryōchō*) is an imaginary bird. It is also said to be the name of a kind of worm. The source of this passage has not been traced.

21. T9, 10a.

22. T9, 38c.

23. Shusenda (Skt: Suśānta) is the name of a Buddha mentioned in the *Daibon Hannya* Sutra (T8, 374c) and other sources. He is said to have manifested a transient aspect in the world in order to lead his disciples to the path of bodhisattva practice. After preaching for half a kalpa and completing his mission, he entered nirvana.

24. The *udumbara* is an imaginary plant said to bloom once every three thousand years to herald the advent of a gold-wheel-turning king or a Buddha. Often mentioned in Buddhist writings as a metaphor for something of exceptional rarity.

25. A reference to a story mentioned briefly in the *Myōshōgonnō* (17th) chapter of the Lotus Sutra. The story behind this reference appears in the *Zō-agon* Sutra (T2, 108c). A blind turtle, whose lifespan is immeasurable kalpas, lives at the bottom of the sea. Once every hundred years it rises to the surface. There is only one log floating in the sea with a hollow in it suitable to the turtle's size. Since the turtle is blind and the log is tossed about by wind and waves, the likelihood of the turtle finding the log is extremely remote.

26. Similar stories are found in the *Nehan Gyō Sho* (T38, 60a) and the *Shikan Bugyōden Guketsu* (T46, 303a).

27. The source of this story has not been traced.

28. The *Myōhō-renge-kyō* is one of the three extant versions of the Lotus Sutra, consisting of eight volumes or rolls and twenty-eight chapters, translated by Kumārajīva in 406. The other two are the *Shō-hokke-kyō* in ten volumes and twenty-seven chapters, translated by Dharmarakṣa in 286, and the *Tembon-hoke-kyō* in seven volumes and twenty-seven chapters, translated by Jñānagupta and Dharmagupta in 601. Among them, Kumārajīva's *Myōhō-renge-kyō* has been the most popular. Therefore, in China and Japan, the name Lotus Sutra usually indicates Kumārajīva's *Myōhō-renge-kyō*.

29. T9, 59b.

30. T9, 130c.

31. T9, 1187c.

32. A jewel said to possess the power of producing whatever one desires. It symbolizes the greatness and virtue of the Buddha and the Buddhist scriptures. It is described in the *Daichido Ron* (T25, 134a; 478b) and elsewhere.

33. According to the *Kusha Ron*, in the Kalpa of Continuance—the second of the four-stage cycle of formation, continuance, decline, and disintegration—the lifetime of human beings repeats a cycle of change, decreasing by a factor of one year every hundred years until it reaches ten years, and then increases at the same rate until it reaches eighty thousand years. Then it begins to decrease again until it reaches ten years, and so on. It is said that Shakyamuni appeared in the present Kalpa of Continuance, in the ninth period of decrease, when the lifespan of human beings was one hundred years long.

34. According to the *Shōsho no iki*, or Record of the Wonders of the Book of Chou, a work that is no longer extant, as cited in the *Benshō Ron* (T52, 530a), Shakyamuni died on the fifteenth day of the second month, in the fifty-second year of the reign of King Mu (949 B.C.).

35. East, west, south, north, and central India, indicating the entire country of India.

36. A legendary palace located under the sea, filled with great treasures and beautiful ornaments. It is said that Bodhisattva Nāgārjuna obtained the *Kegon* Sutra at this palace. The source for the story relating to the three versions kept in the Dragon Palace is the *Hokke Gengi Shakusen* (T33, 956c).

37. The eighty-volume *Kegon* Sutra, called the new translation, was translated by Śikṣānanda in the T'ang dynasty, and the sixty-volume *Kegon* Sutra, called the old translation, was translated by Buddhabhadra in the Eastern Chin dynasty.

38. The five characters of *a, va, ra, ha*, and *kha* indicate respectively the five universal elements of earth, water, fire, wind, and space. The Shingon sect holds this to be one of the secret truths revealed by Dainichi (Skt: Mahavairocana) Buddha. This one word was used as a mantra and was said to express the Buddha's quality, wisdom, appearance, and practice.

39. Seed characters (Skt: *bija*; Jap: *shuji*) are characters of the Sanskrit alphabet, written in the calligraphic Siddham script. They are used in dharani and to represent various Buddhas and bodhisattvas.

40. Various attributes of Buddhas and bodhisattvas, in particular, their vows to lead all people to the supreme enlightenment. The term is often used in a variety of meanings in the esoteric teachings.

41. The Seven Buddhas of the Past are Shakyamuni and the six Buddhas who pre-

ceded him. The first three appeared in the Glorious Kalpa and other four, including Shakyamuni, in the present Wise Kalpa. They are described in the *Agon* Sutra (T1, 1b-c) and the *Shichibutsu* Sutra (T2, 150c). The thousand Buddhas are described in the *Sankō Sanzenbutsu Engi* (T14, 364c) where a thousand Buddhas are said to be born in each of the three major kalpas: the past Glorious Kalpa (Jap: *Shōgonkō*), the present Wise Kalpa (Jap: *Kengō*), and the future Constellation Kalpa (Jap: *Seishukukō*). These major kalpas are each divided into four periods. *See* Kalpa in the Glossary.

42. T9, 52a.

43. *Hokke Mongu Ki* (T34, 280b).

44. T9, 31c.

45. Preface to the *Hokke Gengi* (T33, 681c).

46. *Hokke Gengi Shakusen* (T33, 818b).

47. The mystic principle of the theoretical teaching is that the Buddha discards the provisional teaching and reveals the true teaching, the Lotus Sutra, which allows people of the two vehicles (*shōmon* and *engaku*) to attain Buddhahood. The mystic principle of the essential teaching is that the Buddha discards his transient status and reveals his true identity as the Buddha who attained enlightenment countless kalpas ago.

48. Principles set forth by T'ien-t'ai in the *Hokke Gengi* (T33, 697b). The ten mystic principles of the theoretical teaching are based on the concepts of the true entity of all phenomena and the replacement of the three vehicles (*shōmon, engaku*, and bodhisattva) with the one vehicle of Buddhahood. The ten mystic principles of the essential teaching are set forth on the basis of the revelation of the Buddha's original enlightenment in the remote past of *gohyaku-jintengō*, as expounded in the *Juryō* (16th) chapter.

49. Thirty mystic principles related to the life of sentient beings, the Buddhist Law and the nature of one's mind, or the Law within, plus ten in either the theoretical teaching or the essential teaching. *Hokke Gengi* (T33, 697b).

50. Observation of the mind is to perceive or awaken to the ultimate reality inherent in one's own life. This is particularly stressed in T'ien-t'ai practice, in which meditation is focused on the true nature of one's mind rather than some exterior object.

51. The above discussions of *myō* are based largely on a passage in the *Hokke Gengi* (T33, 697b).

52. T25, 754b.

53. *Maka Shikan Bugyōden Guketsu* (T33, 818b).

54. This refers to two of the five groups into which people are by nature divided according to the Hossō sect. People in these two groups can eventually attain the state of arhat (*shōmon*) and that of *pratyekabuddha* respectively.

55. This refers to those who deny the law of cause and effect.

56. Sudāya was a Brahman master who taught Devadatta occult powers, according to the *Zōichi-agon* Sutra (T2, 802c). His name appears in the sutra as Shurada.

57. Eighteen miraculous manifestations that Buddhas and bodhisattvas use to educate and convert sentient beings. These are variously given in the canonical literature; they are detailed in the *Maka Shikan Bugyōden Guketsu* (T46, 442a-b).

58. Here, austerities established and practiced by Devadatta. According to the *Daibibasha Ron* (T17, 602c), they were: (1) wearing only clothing discarded by others after washing and mending it; (2) obtaining food only by begging; (3) eating only once a day; (4) always seating oneself outside under a tree; and (5) never eating salt or other food possessing the five tastes.

59. A mountain whose summit resembled an elephant's head, located about 1.6 km west of Gayā in Magadha. It is described in *Kusha Ron Ki* (T41, 278a). According to one legend, Devadatta dropped a boulder from this peak when Shakyamuni's party passed by the foot of the mountain.

60. A follower of Shakyamuni Buddha. She is said to have attained the state of arhat under the guidance of the nun Mahāprajāpatī. According to the *Daichido Ron* (T25, 165a) she was beaten to death by Devadatta when she reproached him for his evil deeds.

61. *See* Glossary.

62. Kokālika was a member of the Shakya tribe and an enemy of Shakyamuni. He fell under Devadatta's influence and slandered Śāriputra and Maudgalyāyana. He is said to have fallen into hell alive. This story appears in several sources; which one Nichiren used cannot be identified.

63. The windy circle in Buddhist cosmology is the circle first formed when a world takes shape and living beings appear in it in the Kalpa of Formation. According to the *Kusha Ron* (T29, 57ff) the power of the karma of living beings first causes a small wind to arise in space. This wind grows and forms the windy circle thought to lie at the base of a world. Upon this circle a watery circle and then a gold circle take shape, and upon them the land itself is formed, with its Mount Sumeru, seas, and mountains.

64. A woman who slandered Shakyamuni by tying a pot to her belly under her robe and publicly declaring that she was pregnant by him. Her falsehood was exposed by Taishaku, who assumed the form of a rat and gnawed through the string holding the pot in place. The story appears in the *Kōkigyō* Sutra (T4, 170c ff).

65. Virūḍhaka was a king of Kosala in the days of Shakyamuni. His father was Prasenajit and his mother was originally a servant of a lord of the Shakya tribe. When he discovered that he was the son of a servant and then was humiliated by the Shakyas because of his lowly birth, he decided to take revenge. Seizing the throne from Prasenajit, he led an army against the Shakya kingdom, killing about five hundred people. It is said that seven days later, in accordance with the Buddha's prediction, he burned to death and fell into the hell of incessant suffering. His story is found in the *Binaya Zōji* (T24, 240a).

66. Sunakṣatra was a monk who devoted himself to Buddhist austerities and attained a limited form of enlightenment. He was arrogant, however, and believed he had mastered Buddhism. Later he turned to non-Buddhist teachings and discarded his faith in Buddhism. He is said to have fallen into hell alive. His story is found in the Nirvana Sutra (T12, 560b).

67. Heavens located in the worlds of desire and form. The six heavens referred to in the *Daichido Ron* and the *Kusha Ron*, are said to exist between the earth and the Brahma heaven. They are the Heaven of the Four Heavenly Kings, the Heaven of the Thirty-three Gods, the Yama Heaven, the Tuṣita Heaven, the Joy-born Heaven (Skt: Nirmāṇarati), and the Heaven of Mara, the devil king. The four meditation heavens constitute the world of form. They are further subdivided into eighteen heavens. When, by practicing the four stages of meditation, persons can free themselves from the illusions of the world of desire, they can be reborn in these four meditation heavens.

68. The two divisions of the threefold world, the realm where unenlightened beings transmigrate within the six paths. Beings in the world of form have material form but are free from desires, those in the world of formlessness are free from both desire and the restrictions of matter.

69. The *Three Records* are said to record the deeds of the three legendary rulers of ancient China (Fu Hsi, Shen Nung, and Huang Ti) who realized model governments. The *Five Canons* are the writings of the Five Emperors (Shao Hao, Chuan Hsü, Ti Kao, T'ang Yao, and Yü Shun) who reigned after the Three Rulers. These works do not exist.

70. Mo Hsi of the Hsia dynasty, Ta Chi of the Yin dynasty, and Pao Ssu of the Chou dynasty. All were favorites of the ruler and helped bring about the downfall of the state.

71. *Yakṣa* were originally beings who served Kubera, the god of wealth in Hindu mythology. They were later incorporated into Buddhism as one of the eight kinds of nonhuman beings who work to protect Buddhism. In some sutras, however, they are depicted as ugly and fierce beings who eat human flesh. *See* Eight kinds of nonhuman beings in the Glossary.

72. This passage is not found in any extant version of the *Kegon* Sutra.

73. The first quotation is excerpted from a verse in the Nirvana Sutra (Northern text, T12, 425b). The second quotation does not appear in the text.

74. The five precepts are the basic precepts to be observed by lay people. They are not to kill, not to steal, not to commit unlawful sexual intercourse, not to lie, and not to drink intoxicants. The ten precepts for lay believers are: prohibitions against the ten evils of killing, stealing, unlawful sexual intercourse, lying, flattery or random irresponsible speech, defaming, duplicity, greed, anger, and the holding of mistaken views.

75. The limitations imposed on women in Buddhist and secular thought. The five obstacles as set forth in some Buddhist teachings are: a woman cannot become a Bonten, a Taishaku, a Mara (devil) king, a wheel-turning king, or a Buddha. They are mentioned in the Lotus Sutra (T9, 35c). Three types of obedience derive from Confucianism and demand that a woman obey her parents in childhood, her husband after marriage, and her sons in old age. They are mentioned as well in Buddhist literature: *Kengu* Sutra (T4, 374c) and *Kegon* Sutra (T10, 790b); they are not, however, characterized as three types of obedience.

76. The *Gonjikinyo* Sutra is a brief text, translated into Chinese by Buddhaśānta, expounding the benefits of the practice of almsgiving (T3, no.179). The quoted passage does not appear in the text.

77. T25, 166a.

78. Metaphors for the Buddhist teachings. The tortoise shell was used as a divining tool to tell fortunes. The "mirror or diviner's tortoise shell" means criteria used for judgment, or the paragon on which everything is based.

79. A legendary river in the continent of Aparagodānīya located to the west of Mount Sumeru. Described in the Nirvana Sutra (T12, 426a).

80. Although Nichiren's Buddhism teaches that faith in the Lotus Sutra will enable anyone, man or woman, to attain Buddhahood in his or her present form as a common mortal, because the recipient of this letter was still strongly attached to the views of the Pure Land sect, Nichiren explained his teaching in a way that she could readily understand.

81. This appears to be an elaboration of a passage in Genshin's *Ōjō Yōshū* (DBZ 31, 135) that is based on Tao-an's *Anraku Shū* (T47, 10a). The yellow crane is an imaginary bird that is said to be able to fly a thousand miles carrying a hermit on its back. Tzu-an is a figure described in Chinese legend. When he saw a yellow crane being sold on the road, he felt pity for it, offered his clothes in exchange for it, and set it free.

When he died the crane flew down to his grave and continued calling his name for three years. As a result he came back to life again. The story has it that if the wing of the secretary bird (*chen*) touches water, anyone who drinks of it will die. The horn of the rhinoceros has been highly esteemed in China for its medicinal properties since ancient times.

82. *Maka Shikan* (T46, 79b).

83. *Maka Shikan Bugyōden Guketsu* (T46, 345b).

84. T'ien-t'ai is said to have been the reincarnation of Bodhisattva Yakuō, who was present at the assembly on Eagle Peak, because he attained awakening through the *Yakuō* (23d) chapter of the Lotus Sutra.

85. Adapted from a passage in the *Hokke Mongu* (T34, 97a).

86. Unit of linear measurement. A *ri* was defined as 6 *cho* (0.65 km), but from the Heian period (794–1183) onward, it was commonly understood as 36 *cho* (3.03 km).

87. In the early ninth century Dengyō (also known as Saichō, 767–822) went to T'ang China and received the transmission of the T'ien-t'ai teachings. After returning to Japan, he established the Tendai sect and devoted himself to upholding T'ien-t'ai Buddhism. It is said that Tao-sui, one of Dengyō's masters, identified him as the reincarnation of T'ien-t'ai, referring to T'ien-t'ai's prediction.

88. DDZ3, 265–266.

89. Jōtoku (Skt: Vimaladattā) was the wife of King Myōshōgon whose story appears in the *Myōshōgonnō* (27th) chapter of the Lotus Sutra. Her sons, Jōzō and Jōgen, were taught the Lotus Sutra by the Buddha Unraionnō and begged their mother to meet him. Jōtoku urged them to take along their father, who was a devout believer in Brahmanism, as well, and to convince him of the righteousness of Buddhism. At her suggestion, the two princes displayed various occult powers and thus aroused a desire for Buddhism in the king's heart. They all went to see the Buddha and later attained enlightenment.

90. Lotus Sutra (T9, 35c).

91. The temple, located on Mount Kiyosumi in Kominato, Awa Province, where Nichiren studied Buddhism in his boyhood. On the twenty-fourth day of the fourth month, 1253, he declared the establishment of his Buddhism there with his first invocation of Nam-myoho-renge-kyo.

3 LETTER FROM SADO

This letter was written on the twentieth day of the third month, 1272, some six months after Nichiren had arrived on the island of Sado to begin his exile. Nichiren had been banished on the tenth day of the tenth month, 1271. Charges of treason had been brought against him by Ryōkan, a priest of the Gokuraku-ji in Kamakura and Hei no Saemon, deputy chief of the Office of Military and Police Affairs. Hei no Saemon determined to execute Nichiren at Tatsunokuchi before he could be delivered to the custody of Homma Shigetsura, the deputy constable of Sado. The attempt at execution failed and after a delay of almost a month Homma's troops escorted him to Teradomari on the Sea of Japan. After a delay occasioned by bad weather, Nichiren finally arrived on Sado on the twenty-eighth day of the tenth month.

Nichiren was at first housed in a dilapidated building known as Sammai-dō, where he lived for six months, exposed to the wind and snow that blew through the gaps in the roof. After six months he was able to move to more comfortable quarters at Ichinosawa. Nichiren engaged in debates with Pure Land followers and actively propagated his own teachings. While on Sado he wrote two major treatises, *Kaimoku Shō* (The Opening of the Eyes) and *Kanjin no Honzon Shō* (The True Object of Worship). Finally, on the eighth day of the third month, 1274, Nichiren was pardoned and was able to return to Kamakura on the twenty-sixth day of the same month.

This letter is addressed to Toki Jōnin and other disciples. An alternative title is *Toki Dono Tō Gohenji* (In Reply to Lord Toki and Others).

＊＊＊

This letter is addressed to Toki Jōnin. It should also be shown to Shijō Kingo, Tōnotsuji Jūrō, Sajiki no Ama,[1] and my other disciples. Send me the names of those killed in the battles at Kyoto and Kamakura. Also please have those who are coming here bring me the *Geten Shō*,[2] volume two of the *Hokke Mongu*, and volume four of the *Hokke Gengi*, as well as the collected Imperial edicts and reports from the court and shogunate.[3]

The most dreadful things in the world are the pain of fire, the shadow of swords, and the intimation of death. Even horses and cattle fear being killed; no wonder human beings are afraid of death. Even a leper clings to life; how much more so a healthy person. The Buddha taught that offering one's little finger for the sutra is more rewarding than covering an entire galaxy with the seven treasures.[4] Sessen Dōji offered his life, and Gyōbō Bonji ripped off his own skin to seek the truth of Buddhism.[5] Since nothing is more precious than life itself, those who dedicate their lives to the Buddhist practice are certain to attain Buddhahood. If they are prepared to offer their lives, why should they begrudge any other treasure for the sake of Buddhism? On the other hand, if one is loath to part with his material possessions, how can he possibly give away his life, which is far more valuable?

Society dictates that one should repay a great obligation to another, even at the cost of his life. Many warriors die for their lords, perhaps many more than one would imagine. A man will die to defend his honor; a woman will die for a man. Fish want to survive; they deplore their pond's shallowness and dig holes in the bottom to hide in, yet tricked by bait, they take the hook. Birds in a tree fear that they are too low and perch in the top branches, yet bewitched by bait, they too are caught in snares. Human beings are equally vulnerable. They give their lives for shallow, worldly matters but rarely for the noble cause of Buddhism. Small wonder they do not attain Buddhahood.

Buddhism should be spread by the method of either *shōju* or *shakubuku*, depending upon the age. These are analogous to the two worldly arts of the pen and the sword. The bodhisattvas of old practiced the Law as befitted the times. Sessen Dōji offered his own body when told that he would be taught the Law in return. Prince Satta gave his own flesh and blood to carry out his bodhisattva practice.[6] But should one sacrifice his life at a time when it is not required? In an age when there is no paper, one should use his own skin. In an age when there are no pens, one should use his own bones. In an age when society accepts the True Law and honors the precepts while denouncing those who break or ignore them, one should strictly follow all the precepts. In an age when Confucianism or Taoism is used to assail Buddhism, one should risk his life to debate with the emperor, as did the priests Tao-an, Hui-yüan, and Fa-tao.[7] In an age when people confuse Hinayana and Mahayana, provisional and true teachings, or exoteric and esoteric doctrines, as though unable to distinguish gems from tiles and pebbles or cow's milk from asses' milk,[8] one should strictly differentiate between them, following the example of the Great Teachers T'icn-t'ai and Dengyō.

It is the nature of beasts to threaten the weak and fear the strong. Our contemporary scholars are just like them. They despise a wise man without power but fear the evil rulers. They are merely sycophantic retainers. Only by defeating a powerful enemy can one prove his real strength. When an evil ruler in consort with heretical priests tries to destroy true Buddhism and banish a man of wisdom, those with the heart of a lion will surely attain Buddhahood as will Nichiren. I say this not out of arrogance but because I am committed to true Buddhism. An arrogant man will be overcome with fear when he meets a strong enemy, just like the haughty asura who shrank in size and hid himself in a lotus flower blossoming in Munetchi Lake when reproached by Taishaku.[9] Even a word or phrase of true Buddhism will lead one to the path of enlightenment, if it suits the times and the capacity of the people. But even though one may study a thousand sutras and ten thousand doctrines, he cannot attain Buddhahood, if these teachings do not fit the times and the people's capacity.

Now, twenty-six years have passed since the battle of Hōji,[10] and fighting has already broken out twice on the eleventh and the seventeenth day of the second month of this year (1272).[11] Neither non-Buddhists nor the enemies of Buddhism can destroy the Buddha's True Law, but the Buddha's disciples definitely can. As the sutra says, a parasite in the lion's body will devour the lion.[12] A man of great fortune cannot be ruined by his enemies but only by those close to him. The current rebellion is what the *Yakushi* Sutra means by "the disaster of internal strife."[13] The *Ninnō* Sutra states, "When the sage departs, the seven disasters will invariably arise."[14] The *Konkōmyō* Sutra states, "The thirty-three heavenly gods become furious because the king permits evil to run rampant."[15] Although Nichiren is not a sage, he is equal to one, for he embraces the Lotus Sutra exactly as the Buddha taught. Furthermore, since he has long understood the ways of the world, all the prophecies he wrote have come true without exception. Therefore you should not doubt what he has told you concerning your future existence.

On the twelfth day of the ninth month past, when I was about to be punished, I called out in a loud voice: I, Nichiren, am the ridgepole, sun, moon, mirror, and eyes of the ruling clan of Kanto.[16] On the twelfth day of the ninth month of last year when I was arrested, I boldly declared that if the country should lose Nichiren, the seven disasters would occur without fail. Didn't this prophecy come true just sixty and then one hundred fifty days later? And those battles were only the first signs. What lamenting there will be when the full effect appears! People foolishly wonder why Nichiren is persecuted by the government if he is truly a wise man. Yet it is all just as I expected. King Ajātaśatru killed his father and nearly murdered his mother, for which he was hailed by the six royal ministers.[17] When Devadatta killed an arhat and shed the Buddha's blood, Kokālika and others were delighted.[18] Nichiren is father and mother to the ruling house and is like a Buddha or an arhat to this age. The sovereign and his subjects who rejoice at his exile are truly the most shameless of all. Those heretical priests who have been bewailing the exposure of their errors may be overjoyed for the moment, but eventually they will suffer no less than Nichiren and his disciples. Their joy is like Fujiwara no Yasuhira's when he killed his brother and Minamoto no Yoshitsune.[19] The devil who shall destroy the ruling clan has already entered the country. This is the meaning of the passage from the Lotus Sutra which reads, "The devil enters one's body."[20]

The persecutions Nichiren has faced are the result of karma formed in previous lifetimes. The *Fukyō* chapter states, "after expiating his sins," indicating that Bodhisattva Fukyō was vilified and beaten by countless slanderers because of his past karma.[21] So, too, it is with Nichiren, who in this life was born poor and lowly to a *caṇḍāla*[22] family. In my heart I cherish some faith in the Lotus Sutra, but my body, while outwardly human, is fundamentally that of an animal, which once subsisted on fish and fowl and was born from two fluids, the blood of the mother and the semen of the father. My spirit dwells in this body like the moon reflected in a muddy pond or gold wrapped in a bag of excrement. Since my heart believes in the Lotus Sutra, I do not fear even Bonten or Taishaku, but my body is still that of an animal. With such disparity between my body and my mind, no wonder the foolish despise me. Without doubt, when compared to my body, my mind shines like the moon or like gold. Who knows what slander I may have committed in the past? I may possess the soul of Priest Shōi[23] or the spirit of Mahādeva.[24] Maybe I am descended from those who contemptuously persecuted Bodhisattva Fukyō or am among those who forgot their original faith in the Lotus Sutra. I may even be related to the five thousand arrogant people who would not remain to hear the sutra, or belong to the third and lowest group of Daitsū Buddha's disciples.[25] It is impossible to fathom one's karma. Iron, when heated in the flames and pounded, becomes a fine sword. Wise men and sages are tested by abuse. My present exile is not because of any crime. It is solely so that I may expiate in this lifetime my past heavy slanders and be freed from the three evil paths in the next.

The *Hatsunaion* Sutra states, "In the coming age, there will be those who enter the priesthood, don clerical robes and make a show of studying my teachings. However, being neither diligent nor serious about their practice, they will slander the Mahayana sutras. You should be aware that these people are the ones who are following the heretical religions of today."[26] Those who read this passage should reflect deeply on their own practice. The Buddha is saying that those of our contemporary priests who are lazy and remiss were disciples of the six non-Buddhist teachers[27] in Shakyamuni's day. On the one hand you have Hōnen, on the other Dainichi[28]; they call their schools the Nembutsu and the Zen sects. Hōnen applies the four characters "discard, close, ignore, and abandon" to the Lotus Sutra, and calls for its rejection, and advocates the exclusive calling of the name of the Buddha Amida, a Buddha who appears in the provisional sutras. The followers of Dainichi speak of a separate teaching outside the scriptures and deride the Lotus Sutra, saying that it is no more than a finger pointing at the moon, a pointless conglomeration of words. These priests must both be followers of the six non-Buddhist teachers, who only now have entered the stream of Buddhism.

The Nirvana Sutra states that the Buddha emitted a radiance that illumined the one hundred and thirty-six hells[29] and found that there were no sinners there.[30] This was because they had all achieved Buddhahood on the basis of the *Juryō* chapter of the Lotus Sutra. Instead the hell wardens were found to be detaining the people of incorrigible disbelief (*icchantika*) who had slandered the True Law. They proliferated until they became the people of Japan today.

Since Nichiren himself committed slander in the past, he became a Nembutsu priest in this lifetime, and for several years he also laughed at those who practiced the Lotus Sutra, saying, "Not a single person has ever attained Buddhahood through that sutra"[31] or "Not one person in a thousand can reach enlightenment through its teachings."[32] Awakening from my slanderous condition, I feel like a drunken son who, in his stupor, strikes his parents but thinks nothing of it. When he returns to his senses, he regrets it bitterly but to no avail. His offense is extremely difficult to erase. Even more so are past slanders of the Law that stain the depth of one's heart. A sutra[33] states that both the crow's blackness and the heron's whiteness are actually the deep stains of their past karma. The Brahmans and other non-Buddhists refused to recognize this causality and claimed it was the work of nature, and today, when I expose people's slanders in an effort to save them, they deny it with every excuse possible and argue back with Hōnen's words about barring the gates to the Lotus Sutra. From Nembutsu believers this is scarcely surprising, but even the Tendai and Shingon priests actively support them.

On the sixteenth and the seventeenth day of the first month of this year, hundreds of priests and believers from the Nembutsu and other sects here in the province of Sado came to debate with me. A leader of the Nembutsu sect, Inshō-bō[34] said, "Saint Hōnen did not instruct us to discard the Lotus Sutra. He simply wrote that everyone should chant the Nembutsu, and its great blessings would assure birth in the Pure Land. Even the Tendai priests of Onjō-ji and Enryaku-ji,[35] exiled to this island, praise Saint Hōnen and say how excellent his teaching is. How do you dare try to refute it?" The local priests are even more ignorant than the Nembutsu priests in Kamakura. They are absolutely pitiful.

How terrible are the slanders Nichiren committed in his past and present existences! Since you have been born into this evil country and become the disciples of such a man, there is no telling what you may have to endure. The *Hatsunaion* Sutra reads, "Men of devout faith, because you committed countless sins and accumulated much evil karma in the past, you must expect to suffer retribution for everything you have done. You may be reviled, cursed with an ugly appearance, be poorly clad and poorly fed, seek wealth in vain, be born to an impoverished or heretical family, or be persecuted by your sovereign." It goes on to say, "It is due to the blessings obtained by protecting the Law that one can diminish in this lifetime his suffering and retribution."[36] Were it not for Nichiren, these passages from the sutra would virtually make the Buddha a liar. For none, save Nichiren, have experienced all eight sufferings described in the sutra: (1) to be slighted; (2) to possess an ugly physical form; (3) to lack clothing; (4) to lack food; (5) to seek wealth in vain; (6) to be born to a poor family; (7) to be born to a heretical family; and (8) to be persecuted by one's sovereign. One who climbs a high mountain must eventually descend. One who slights another will in turn be despised. One who deprecates those of handsome appearance will be born ugly. One who robs another of food and clothing is sure to fall into the realm of hungry ghosts. One who mocks noble men or anyone who observes the precepts will be born to a poor family. One who slanders a family that embraces the True Law will be born to a heretical family. One who laughs at those who cherish the precepts will be born a commoner and meet with persecution from his sovereign. This is the general law of cause and effect.

Nichiren's sufferings, however, are not ascribable to this causal law. In the past he despised the votaries of the Lotus Sutra and ridiculed the sutra itself, sometimes with exaggerated praise and other times with contempt. He has met all eight of these terrible sufferings for such acts against the Lotus Sutra, that sutra which is as magnificent as two jewels combined, two moons shining side by side, two stars conjoined or one Mount Hua[37] placed atop another. Usually these sufferings would torment a person over many lifetimes, appearing one at a time, but Nichiren has denounced the enemies of the Lotus Sutra so severely that all eight descended upon him at once.[38] His situation is like that of a peasant heavily in debt to his lord and others. As long as he remains on the estate, they are likely to defer his debts from one year to the next, rather than mercilessly hounding him. But as soon as he tries to leave, everyone will rush over and demand that he repay everything at once. Thus the sutra states, "It is due to the blessings obtained by protecting the Law that one can diminish . . . his suffering and retribution."[39]

The Lotus Sutra reads, "There are many ignorant people who will vilify and attack us, the votaries of the Lotus Sutra, with swords, staves, and stones . . . they will denounce us to the sovereign, ministers, Brahmans, and other influential men . . . we will be banished again and again."[40] If hell wardens did not torment the sinners, the sinners never would be able to pay for their sins and escape from hell. Were it not for the authorities who now persecute Nichiren, he could not expiate his past sin of slandering the Law. Nichiren is like Bodhisattva Fukyō,[41] who lived in ages past, and the people of this day are like the priests, nuns, and lay men and women who disdained and persecuted Fukyō. The people are different, yet the cause is the same. Different people may kill their parents, but they all fall into the same hell of incessant suffering. Since Nichiren is making the same cause as Fukyō, he is certain to become a Buddha equal to Shakyamuni. Moreover, those who now persecute him are like Bhadrapāla[42] and the others who persecuted Fukyō. They will be tortured in the depths of hell for a thousand kalpas. I therefore pity them deeply and wonder what can be done for them. Those who at first disdained and persecuted Fukyō later took faith in his teachings and became his followers. The greater part of their slander was thus expiated, but even the small part which remained caused them to suffer as terribly as one who had killed his parents a thousand times over. The people of this age refuse to repent at all and must therefore suffer for interminable kalpas as described in the *Hiyu* chapter, perhaps even for the duration of *sanzen-* or *gohyaku-jintengō*.[43]

There are also those who appeared to believe in Nichiren but began doubting when they saw him persecuted. They have not only forsaken the Lotus Sutra but actually think themselves wise enough to instruct Nichiren. The pitiful thing is that these perverse people must suffer in the depths of hell even longer than the Nembutsu believers. An *asura* contended that the Buddha had only eighteen sensory functions but that he himself had nineteen.[44] Brahmans claimed that the Buddha offered only one way to enlightenment but that they had ninety-five.[45] In the same way, the renegade disciples say that although Priest Nichiren is their teacher, he is too rigid, and they will spread the Lotus Sutra in a more flexible way. In so asserting, they are being as ridiculous as fireflies laughing at the sun and moon, an anthill belittling Mount Hua, small inlets despising the boundless sea, or a magpie mocking the Chinese phoenix. Nam-myoho-renge-kyo.

Nichiren

The twentieth day of the third month in the ninth year of Bun'ei (1272)

TO MY DISCIPLES AND PARISHIONERS

There is very little writing paper here in the province of Sado, and to write to you individually would take too long. However, if even one person fails to hear from me, it will cause resentment. Therefore, I want all sincere believers to meet and read this letter together for encouragement. When disaster strikes, our personal troubles seem insignificant. I do not know how accurate the reports reaching me are, but there must surely be intense grieving over those killed in the recent battles. What has become of Izawa no Nyūdō and Sakabe no Nyūdō?[46] Send me news of Kawanobe, Yamashiro, Tokugyō-ji[47] and the others. Also, please be kind enough to send me the *Essentials of Government in the Chen-kuan Era*,[48] the *Anthology of Tales*,[49] and the *Teachings of the Eight Sects*.[50] Without these, I cannot even write letters.

Notes

1. Toki Jōnin (1216–1299) and Saburōzaemon Shijō Kingo (1230–1300) were devoted followers of Nichiren. Both Okura Tōnotsuji and Sajiki are place names in Kamakura. Presumably they refer to followers who lived in these areas. Sajiki no ama is also known as Myōichi no ama and Bendono no ama.

2. This is presumably a collection of non-Buddhist writings. The specific work to which Nichiren refers is not known.

3. This and the concluding paragraph are marginal notes, added presumably after the letter was completed.

4. Paraphrase of a passage in the *Yakuō* (23d) chapter of the Lotus Sutra. The seven treasures are mentioned in the *Tahō* (11th) chapter of the Lotus Sutra; they are gold, silver, lapis lazuli, crystal, agate, pearl, and carnelian.

5. Sessen dōji was the name under which Shakyamuni, in a past life, practiced the bodhisattva way. He was prepared to sacrifice his life to hear the second half of a verse that a demon recited (Nirvana Sutra, T12, 450a). Gyōbō Bonji ripped his own skin to provide writing paper, used his own bone as a writing brush, and his blood for ink in order to learn the Buddha's teachings. *Daichido Ron* (T25, 412a).

6. Prince Satta sacrificed his body to feed a starving tiger with seven cubs. *Konkōmyō* Sutra (T16, 354a-b).

7. Tao-an (?–580?), Hui-yüan (523–592), and Fa-tao (1086–1147) all dedicated themselves to the defense of Buddhism against persecution and attack by antagonistic rulers.

8. Cows' milk, purified, becomes ghee (Buddhism); asses' milk, purified, becomes urine (non-Buddhist teachings). *Daichido Ron* (T25, 191c).

9. This story appears in the *Kambutsu Zammai* Sutra (T15, 647b). Munetchi, an imaginary lake the source of the rivers of Jambudvīpa, is described in the *Kusha Ron* (T29, 58a).

10. The battle of 1247 in which Hōjō Tokiyori and his allies destroyed Miura Yasumura and his family, forcing some five hundred family members and retainers to commit suicide.

11. Hōjō Tokisuke (d. 1272), a commissioner in Kyoto, attempted unsuccessfully to overthrow his half-brother Hōjō Tokimune (1251–1284).

12. *Rengemon* Sutra (T12, 1072c).

13. One of the seven disasters enumerated in the *Yakushi* Sutra (T14, 407c). They are: (1) pestilence, (2) foreign invasion, (3) internal strife, (4) unnatural changes in the heavens, (5) solar and lunar eclipses, (6) unseasonable storms and typhoons, and (7) drought.

14. The seven disasters enumerated in the *Ninnō* Sutra (T8, 833a) are: (1) unnatural changes in the sun and moon, including eclipses, (2) foreign invasion, (3) internal strife, (4) great floods, (5) typhoons and damaging wind storms, (6) droughts, and (7) attack by bandits from outside and within the nation.

15. T16, 429c.

16. Reference is to the Kamakura government.

17. Stories relating to Ajātaśatru are found in various sources. The Nirvana Sutra (T12, 480b–c) details his activities. The six ministers are described in detail at T12, 474 ff.

18. Kokālika, a clansman of Shakyamuni, entered the Buddhist order but later fell under Devadatta's influence and slandered Shakyamuni's close disciples, Śāriputra and Ānanda. Nirvana Sutra (T12, 560b).

19. Fujiwara Yasuhira (1135–1189) was the son of Fujiwara Hidehira, lord of the province of Mutsu in northeastern Japan. He killed his brother and usurped power for himself. Minamoto no Yoritomo, the Kamakura shogun, ordered him to kill Yoshitsune, Yoritomo's brother, which he did to prove his loyalty. Later, however, Yoritomo had him executed to consolidate his own power in the northern part of Japan.

20. T9, 36c.

21. The *Fukyō* (20th) chapter of the Lotus Sutra details the story of this bodhisattva.

22. *Caṇḍāla* is a general name in India for many kinds of individuals or outcasts who engage in professions considered menial or unclean. Among them were those who made their living as hunters, fishermen, or leather workers. Nichiren was born to a family of fishermen.

23. Shōi biku appeared in the Latter Day of Shishionnō Buddha. He is said to have fallen into hell alive for slandering Bodhisattva Kikon, who propagated Buddhism. *Shohō Mugyō* Sutra (T15, 759b).

24. Mahādeva is said to have appeared about a hundred years after Shakyamuni. He is said to have committed three of the five cardinal sins, killing his father, his mother, and an arhat. Later he repented, became a monk, and set forth five new opinions concerning the state of arhatship, precipitating the first schism in the Buddhist community. *Daibibasha Ron* (T27, 510c).

25. Reference is to those who vilified the Bodhisattva Fukyō in the *Fukyō* (20th) chapter; those in the *Juryō* (16th) chapter who lost faith; the five thousand arrogant people in the *Hōben* (2d) chapter who thought they had already mastered Buddhism; and the third group of Daitsū's disciples who heard the Lotus Sutra in the remote past but did not take faith in it and could not gain enlightenment during Shakyamuni's lifetime, as described in the *Kejōyu* (7th) chapter of the Lotus Sutra.

26. T12, 877c.

27. The six most influential teachers (Jap: *rokushi gedō*) who lived in central India at the time of Shakyamuni and who challenged the old Vedic traditions and advocated philosophical and religious concepts of their own.

28. For Dainichi Nōnin, *see* Letter 1, note 29.

29. There are eight hot hells, one above the other, each with sixteen subsidiary hells. They are described in the *Shōbō Nenshō* Sutra (T17, no. 721). In addition, there are eight cold hells; Nichiren does not mention them here.

30. Not a direct quotation. Based on a passage at T12, 431c–432a.

31. Quotation from Tao-ch'o's *Anraku Shū* (T47, 13c).

32. Quotation from Shan-tao's *Ōjō Raisan* (T47, 439c).

33. Based on a passage in the *Shuryōgon* Sutra (T19, 125b).

34. Unidentified. Presumably a high-ranking Pure Land priest on Sado.

35. Onjō-ji, also known as Miidera, is located in Ōtsu, near Kyoto. It became the headquarters temple of the Jimon school of Tendai in 993 when Chishō Daishi's disciples left Enryaku-ji on Mt. Hiei, the main temple of the Sammon branch of the Tendai sect. Here Nichiren refers to the Enryaku-ji priests as *sansō* and the Onjō-ji priests as *ji-hōshi*.

36. T12, 877c.

37. This passage has been rearranged somewhat for the sake of clarity. Mount Hua is celebrated as one of the five highest mountains in China.

38. The practitioner who severely denounces the slanderer of the Lotus Sutra has endless kalpas worth of births and deaths subsumed into the births and deaths of his present existence and, because he has transcended successive births and deaths in the three worlds, the karmic obstructions from the beginningless beginning burst forth at one time.

39. *Hatsunaion* Sutra (T12, 877c). The translation has been expanded for clarity.

40. Three phrases excerpted from the concluding verse in the *Kanji* (13th) chapter of the Lotus Sutra (T9, 36b–c).

41. The *Fukyō* (20th) chapter of the Lotus Sutra details the persecutions of the Bodhisattva Fukyō.

42. The Bodhisattva Bhadrapāla was the leader of the five hundred bodhisattvas involved in the persecution of Fukyō (T9, 51b).

43. *See* Glossary under *sanzen-jintengō* and *gohyaku-jintengō*.

44. Based on a passage in the Nirvana Sutra (Northern text, T12, 825b).

45. Based on a passage in the *Daichido Ron* (T25, 195c) where Brahmans claim that where Buddhism has only one way to enlightenment, non-Buddhist teachings have ninety-five ways. The original text here gives the number as ninety-six.

46. Little is known about these followers of Nichiren.

47. Followers of Nichiren, said to have been imprisoned in an underground cell following the Tatsunokuchi Persecution.

48. The *Chen-kuan Cheng-yao*, a work written by Wu Ching during the T'ang dynasty. Chen-kuan is an era name (627–646); the work discusses political matters between the emperor and his subjects.

49. It is unknown to which non-Buddhist work this refers.

50. Presumably a work detailing the basic doctrines of the eight Buddhist sects of the Heian period: Kusha, Jōjitsu, Ritsu, Hossō, Sanron, Kegon, Shingon, and Tendai.

4 ON PRACTICING THE BUDDHA'S TEACHINGS

This letter was written for the sake of his disciples in general from his place of exile at Ichinosawa on Sado island. It was written in the fifth month, 1273, shortly after he had completed his treatise *Kanjin no Honzon Shō* (The True Object of Worship).

It is now clear that those who are born in this land and believe in this sutra, when its propagation is undertaken in the Latter Day of the Law, will suffer persecutions even more severe than those that occurred in the Buddha's lifetime. In that age the master was a Buddha, and his disciples were great bodhisattvas and arhats. Moreover, the Buddha expounded the Lotus Sutra only after he had thoroughly taught and trained everyone who was to hear it, including gods, humans both lay and ordained, and the eight kinds of nonhuman beings.[1] Still, some of his followers rejected it.

Now in the Latter Day of the Law, even though the teaching, the people's capacity, and the time for propagation are in accord, we must expect all the more hostility. "For this is the age of conflict in which the Pure Law has been lost."[2] Moreover, the teacher is but a common person, and his disciples come from among impious men defiled by the three poisons.[3] For this reason, people reject the virtuous teacher and seek out evil priests instead.

What is more, once you become a follower of the Lotus Sutra's true votary whose practice accords with the Buddha's teachings, you are bound to face the three powerful enemies.[4] Therefore, from the very day you take faith in this teaching, you should be fully prepared to face the three kinds of persecutions,[5] which are certain to be more terrible now after the Buddha's passing. Although my disciples had already heard this, some became so terrified when both great and small persecutions confronted us that they even forsook their faith. Did I not warn you in advance? I have been teaching you day and night directly from the sutra, which says, "Since hatred and jealousy abound even during the lifetime of the Buddha, how much worse will it be in the world after his passing?"[6] You have no reason to be suddenly frightened when you witness me driven from my home, wounded, or officially censured and exiled twice—this time to a distant province.

Question: The votary who practices according to the Buddha's teachings should live a peaceful life in this world. Why then are you beset by the three powerful enemies?

Answer: Shakyamuni faced the nine great persecutions[7] for the sake of the Lotus Sutra. In the distant past, Bodhisattva Fukyō was attacked with sticks and stones. Chu Tao-sheng was exiled to Mount Su, Priest Fa-tao was branded on the face, and Āryasiṁha was beheaded.[8] The Great Teacher T'ien-tai was opposed by the seven schools of the north and the three schools of the south, and the Great Teacher Dengyō was vilified by the six sects of the old capital of Nara. The Buddha and these bodhisattvas and great saints were all votaries of the Lotus Sutra, yet they suffered great persecutions. If you deny that they practiced according to the Buddha's teachings, then where can you find those who did? "This is the age of conflict in which the Pure Law has been lost." Moreover, in this evil country, the ruler, his ministers, and even the common people are without exception tainted by slander. They have opposed the true teaching and revered heretical doctrines and priests instead. Therefore, demons have poured into the country and the three calamities and seven disasters[9] strike again and again.

However, the Buddha has commanded me to be born in this age, inauspicious though it is, and it would be impossible to go against his decree. And so, I have put complete faith in the sutra and launched the battle of the provisional and true teachings. Donning the armor of endurance and girding myself with the sword of the true teaching, I have raised the banner of the five characters, Myōhō-renge-kyō, the essence of the entire eight volumes of the Lotus Sutra. Then, drawing the bow of the Buddha's declaration, "I have not yet revealed the truth"[10] and notching the arrow of "honestly discarding the provisional teachings,"[11] I have mounted the cart[12] drawn by the great white ox and battered down the gates of the provisional teachings.

Attacking first one and then another, I have refuted the Nembutsu, Shingon, Zen, Ritsu, and other sects. Some of my adversaries have fled headlong while others have retreated, and still others have been captured to become my disciples. I continue to repulse the attacks of my enemies and to defeat them, but there are legions of enemies opposing the single king of the Law and the handful who follow him. So the battle goes on even today.

"The practice of the Lotus Sutra is *shakubuku*, the refutation of the provisional doctrines."[13] True to the letter of this golden saying, the believers of all provisional teachings and sects will ultimately be defeated and join the followers of the king of the Law. The time will come when all people, including those of *shomon*, *engaku*, and bodhisattva, will enter on the path to Buddhahood, and the Mystic Law alone will flourish throughout the land. In that time because all people chant Nam-Myoho-renge-kyo together, the wind will not buffet the branches or boughs, nor will the rain fall hard enough to break a clod. The world will become as it was in the ages of Fu Hsi and Shen Nung[14] in ancient China. Disasters will be driven from the land, and the people will be rid of misfortune. They will also learn the art of living long lives. Realize that the time will come when the truth will be revealed that both the Person and the Law are unaging and eternal. There cannot be the slightest doubt about the sutra's solemn promise of a peaceful life in this world.[15]

Question: How should one practice if he is to be faithful to the Buddha's teachings?

Answer: The Japanese people of this age are one in their opinion of what practice accords with the Buddha's teachings. They believe that since all vehicles are incorporated in the one supreme vehicle, no teaching is superior or inferior, shallow or profound, but that all are equal to the Lotus Sutra. Hence the belief that repeating the Nembutsu chant, embracing Shingon esotericism, practicing Zen meditation, or professing and chanting any sutra or the name of any Buddha or bodhisattva equals following the Lotus Sutra.

But I insist that this is wrong. The most important thing in practicing Buddhism is to follow and uphold the Buddha's golden teachings, not the opinions of others. Our master, Shakyamuni Buddha, wished to reveal the Lotus Sutra from the moment of his enlightenment. However, because the people were not yet mature enough to understand, he had to employ provisional teachings for some forty years before he could expound the true teaching of the Lotus Sutra. In the

Muryōgi Sutra, which served as an introduction to the Lotus Sutra, the Buddha clearly distinguished the provisional teachings from the true teaching. He declared, "I have preached the Law in many ways, devising many means. But in these more than forty years, I have not yet revealed the truth."[16] The eighty thousand bodhisattvas, including Bodhisattva Daishōgon, fully understood why Shakyamuni had preached the provisional teachings, demonstrated that they were nothing more than means, and finally discarded them entirely. They expressed their understanding by declaring that no one can attain supreme enlightenment by embracing any of the provisional sutras, which expound bodhisattva austerities spanning millions of kalpas. Finally the Buddha came to reveal the Lotus Sutra and stated, "The World-Honored One has long expounded his doctrines and now must reveal the truth."[17] He also warned, "In all the Buddha's lands of the universe there is but one supreme vehicle, not two or three, and it excludes the provisional teachings of the Buddha,"[18] and "Honestly discarding the provisional teachings, I will expound the Supreme Law,"[19] and "Never accept even a single phrase from the other sutras."[20] Thus, ever since that time, the supreme vehicle of the Mystic Law has been the only teaching profound enough to enable all people to attain Buddhahood. Even though no sutra other than the Lotus Sutra can provide even the slightest benefit, the Buddhist scholars of the Latter Day claim that all sutras must lead to enlightenment because they were expounded by the Buddha. Therefore, they arbitrarily profess faith in any sutra and follow whatever sect they choose, whether Shingon, Nembutsu, Zen, Sanron, Hossō, Kusha, Jōjitsu, or Ritsu. The Lotus Sutra says of such people, "One who refuses to take faith in this sutra and instead slanders it immediately destroys the seeds for becoming a Buddha in this world. . . . After he dies, he will fall into the hell of incessant suffering."[21] Thus the Buddha himself concluded that one's practice accords with the Buddha's teachings only when he bases his faith precisely on the standard of the sutra, believing that there is but one Supreme Law.

Question: Then it would be wrong to say that faith in any sutra or any Buddha of the provisional teachings equals faith in the Lotus Sutra. But what of one who believes only in the Lotus Sutra and carries out the five practices[22] of the *Hosshi* chapter or follows the easy practices of the *Anrakugyō* chapter? Could we not say that his practice accords with the Buddha's teachings?

Answer: Anyone who practices Buddhism should first understand the two types of practice—*shōju* and *shakubuku*. Any sutra or treatise must be practiced in one of these two ways. Although scholars in this country may have studied Buddhism extensively, they do not know which practice accords with the time. The four seasons continually repeat themselves, each in turn manifesting its own characteristics. In summer it is hot; in winter, cold. Flowers blossom in spring, and fruit ripens in autumn. Therefore, it is only natural to sow seeds in spring and reap the harvest in fall. If one sowed in autumn, could he harvest in spring? Heavy clothing is useful in bitter cold, but of what use is it in sweltering heat? A cool breeze is pleasant in summer, but what good is it in winter? Buddhism works in the same way. There are times when Hinayana Buddhism should be disseminated for the benefit of humanity, times when the provisional Mahayana doctrines are necessary, and times when the true Mahayana teaching must spread to lead people to Buddhahood. The two millennia of the Former and Middle Days of the Law required the spread of Hinayana and provisional Mahayana Buddhism, while the first five hundred years of the Latter Day call for the *kōsen-rufu* of the perfect, supreme teaching of the Lotus Sutra. As predicted by the Buddha, now is the age of conflict when the Pure Law has been lost, and the provisional and true teachings of Buddhism are hopelessly confused.

When one must face enemies, he needs a sword, a stick, or a bow and arrows. However, when he has no enemies, such weapons are of no use at all. In this age the provisional teachings have turned into enemies of the true teaching. When the time is right to propagate the supreme teaching, the provisional teachings become enemies. If they are a source of confusion, they must be thoroughly refuted from the standpoint of the true teaching. Of the two types of practice, this is *shakubuku*, the practice of the Lotus Sutra. With good reason T'ien-t'ai stated: "The practice of the Lotus Sutra is *shakubuku*, the refutation of the provisional doctrines."[23] The four easy practices[24] in the *Anrakugyō* chapter are *shōju*. To carry them out in this day would be as foolish as sowing seeds in winter and expecting to reap the harvest in spring. It is natural for a rooster to crow in the morning but strange for him to crow at dusk. Now when the true and provisional teachings are utterly confused, it would be equally unnatural for one to seclude himself in the mountains, carrying out the easy practice of *shōju*, and avoid refuting the enemies of the Lotus Sutra. He would lose all chance to practice the Lotus Sutra. Now in the Latter Day of the Law, who is carrying out the practice of *shakubuku* in strict accordance with the Lotus

Sutra? Suppose someone, no matter who, should loudly proclaim that the Lotus Sutra alone can lead people to Buddhahood and that all other sutras, far from enabling them to attain enlightenment, only drive them into hell. Observe what happens should he thus try to refute the teachers and doctrines of all the other sects. The three powerful enemies will arise without fail.

The true master, Shakyamuni Buddha, practiced *shakubuku* during the last eight years of his lifetime, the Great Teacher T'ien-t'ai for more than thirty years, and the Great Teacher Dengyō for more than twenty. Nichiren has been refuting the provisional teachings for more than twenty years, and the great persecutions he has suffered during this period are beyond number. I do not know whether they are equal to the nine great persecutions suffered by the Buddha, but surely neither T'ien-t'ai nor Dengyō ever faced persecutions as great as Nichiren's for the sake of the Lotus Sutra. They encountered only envy and slander, whereas I was twice exiled by the regent, this time to a remote province. Furthermore, I was nearly beheaded at Tatsunokuchi, wounded on the forehead at Komatsubara, and slandered time and again. My disciples have also been exiled and thrown into prison, while my lay followers have been evicted and had their property confiscated. How can the persecutions faced by Nāgārjuna, T'ien-t'ai or Dengyō possibly compare with these? Understand then that the votary who practices the Lotus Sutra exactly as the Buddha teaches will without fail be attacked by the three powerful enemies. Shakyamuni himself, T'ien-t'ai, and Dengyō were the only three who perfectly carried out the Buddha's teachings in these more than two thousand years. Now in the Latter Day of the Law, the only such votaries are Nichiren and his disciples. If we cannot be called votaries faithful to the Buddha's teachings, then neither can Shakyamuni, T'ien-t'ai, nor Dengyō. Could Devadatta, Kokālika, Sunakṣatra,[25] Kōbō, Jikaku, Chishō, Shan-tao, Hōnen, Ryōkan, and others like them be called votaries of the Lotus Sutra? Could Shakyamuni Buddha, T'ien-t'ai, Dengyō, or Nichiren and his disciples be followers of the Nembutsu, Shingon, Zen, Ritsu, or other sects? Could the Lotus Sutra be called a provisional teaching, and the *Amida* Sutra and others be the Lotus Sutra? None of this could ever be possible, even if east were to become west and west become east; even if the earth and all its trees and plants were to fly up and become the heavens, while the sun, the moon, and the stars tumbled down and became the earth.

What a great pity it is that all the Japanese people are delighted to see Nichiren and his disciples suffer at the hands of the three powerful enemies! What befell another yesterday may befall oneself today. Nichiren and his disciples have but a short time to endure, the time it takes for frost or dew to vanish in the morning sun. When our prayers for Buddhahood are answered and we dwell in the land of eternal enlightenment where we will experience the boundless joy of the Law, what pity we will feel for those suffering incessantly in the depths of hell! How they will envy us then!

Life flashes by in but a moment. No matter how many terrible enemies we may encounter, banish all fears and never think of backsliding. Even if someone were to cut off our heads with a saw, impale us with lances, or shackle our feet and bore them through with a gimlet, as long as we are alive, we must keep chanting Nam-Myoho-renge-kyo, Nam-Myoho-renge-kyo.

Then, if we chant until the very moment of death, Shakyamuni, Tahō, and all other Buddhas in the universe will come to us instantly, exactly as they promised during the ceremony at Eagle Peak. Taking our hands and bearing us upon their shoulders, they will carry us to Eagle Peak. The two saints,[26] the two heavenly gods,[27] and the Ten Goddesses[28] will guard us, while all the Buddhist gods raise a canopy over our heads and unfurl banners on high. They will escort us under their protection to the Buddha's jeweled land of Tranquil Light. How can such joy possibly be described! Nam-Myoho-renge-kyo, Nam-Myoho-renge-kyo.

The fifth month of the tenth year of Bun'ei (1273)

POSTSCRIPT: KEEP THIS LETTER WITH YOU AT ALL TIMES AND READ IT OVER AND OVER.

Notes

1. Beings that protect Buddhism; they are described in the *Hiyu* (3d) chapter of the Lotus Sutra. They are: (1) heavenly beings, (2) dragons, (3) *yasha* (Skt: *yakṣa*), demons, sometimes described as fierce, who are followers of Bishamonten, one of the Four Heavenly Kings, (4) *kendatsuba* (Skt: *gandharva*), gods of music, (5) *ashura* (Skt: *asura*), fighting demons, said to live at the bottom of the seas surrounding Mt. Sumeru and who inhabit the fourth of the Ten Worlds, (6) *karura* (Skt: *garuda*), birds that devour

dragons, (7) *kinnara* (Skt: *kiṃnara*), gods with beautiful voices, and (8) *magoraka* (Skt: *mahoraga*), gods in the form of snakes.

2. *Daijuku* Sutra, T13, 363b.

3. The three poisons (Jap: *sandoku*) are: greed, anger, stupidity. *Daichido Ron* (T25, 286c).

4. The three powerful enemies are the three types of heretics detailed in Miao-lo's *Hokke Mongu Ki* (T34, 315a): (1) arrogant laymen who, in their ignorance, slander the practitioner of the Lotus Sutra and beat and stab him; (2) arrogant priests who advocate heterodox teachings; and (3) people who behave as saints and inspire respect, but are jealous of practitioners of the Lotus Sutra and use their position to have them exiled, harmed, or killed.

5. These are the same as the three powerful enemies, mentioned above.

6. T9, 31c.

7. The nine great persecutions or ordeals that Shakyamuni suffered are listed in the *Daichido Ron* (T25, 121c) and elsewhere. They are: (1) At the instigation of a group of Brahmans, a beautiful woman named Sudari spread rumors to the effect that she was having an affair with Shakyamuni; (2) Brahmans mocked Shakyamuni when a maid-servant gave him an offering of stinking rice gruel; (3) King Ajita invited Shakyamuni and five hundred disciples to his kingdom but neglected to make any offerings, so that, for a period of ninety days, they had nothing to eat but horse fodder; (4) A great many members of the Shakya clan were killed by King Virūdhaka of Kosala; (5) When Shakyamuni entered a Brahman city, the king forbade the people to make offerings or listen to him; thus he was unable to receive alms; (6) A Brahman woman, Ciñcāmānavika, tied a bowl to her belly under her robe and claimed to be pregnant by Shakyamuni; (7) Devadatta dropped a boulder on Shakyamuni from the top of Eagle Peak, but it missed and only injured his toe; (8) Once, around the time of the winter solstice, an icy wind arose that continued for eight days; Shakyamuni protected himself by wearing three robes; and (9) At the instigation of Devadatta, King Ajātaśatru made some wild elephants drunk and let them loose among Shakyamuni and his disciples, but he failed in his attempt to kill the Buddha.

8. Chu Tao-sheng (d. 434) mentioned that even an *icchantika* possessed the Buddha nature; for this assertion he was banished, but he was later vindicated when the translation of the Nirvana Sutra verified his assertion. His biography is in *Kōsō Den* (T50, 366b-367a). Fa-tao (1086–1147) was a Sung dynasty monk who opposed the emperor's change of allegiance from Buddhism to Taoism. He wrote a memorial in protest, enraging the emperor, who had his face branded and sent him into exile. His story is in *Busso Tōki* (T49, 420c–421b). Āryasimha (Shishi Sonja) was the twenty-fourth successor to Shakyamuni and lived in central India during the sixth century. He was executed by King Dammira for propagating Buddhism. *Fu Hōzō Innen Den* (T50, 321c).

9. The three calamities and seven disasters (Jap: *sansai shichinan*) are variously described in the sutras. There are two kinds of the three calamities: the greater calamities of fire, water, and wind that destroy a world at the end of the Kalpa of Destruction, and the three lesser calamities of higher grain prices or inflation (especially that caused by famine), warfare, and pestilence. The seven disasters differ with the sutra. The *Yakushi* Sutra lists them as pestilence, foreign invasion, internal strife, unnatural changes in the heavens, solar and lunar eclipses, unseasonable storms and typhoons, and drought.

10. *Muryōgi* Sutra (T9, 386b).

11. Lotus Sutra (T9, 10a). Not a precise quotation.

12. The cart of the great white ox is one of the three carts described in the *Hiyu* (3d) chapter of the Lotus Sutra. The ox cart signifies the Lotus Sutra.

13. *Hokke Gengi* (T33, 792b).

14. Legendary kings who reigned over ideal societies in ancient China.

15. Reference is to a passage in the *Yakusōyu* (5th) chapter in the Lotus Sutra (T9, 19b).

16. *Muryōgi* Sutra (T9, 386b).

17. T9, 6a.

18. T9, 8a.

19. T9, 10a.

20. T9, 16a.

21. T9, 15b.

22. To embrace, read, recite, teach, and transcribe the Lotus Sutra.

23. Previously cited, see note 13.

24. Practice by peaceful deeds, words, thoughts, and vows.

25. Kokālika, a clansman of Shakyamuni, originally entered the Buddhist Order but, influenced by Devadatta, slandered Shakyamuni's disciples. He is frequently mentioned by Nichiren. Sunakṣatra was a monk who was said to have been a son of Shakyamuni while the latter was still a prince.

26. Bishamonten and Jikokuten, two of the Four Heavenly Kings.

27. The Bodhisattvas Yakuō and Yuze.

28. The Jūrasetsu, the ten daughters of Kishimojin (Skt: Hāritī), described in the *Darani* (26th) chapter of the Lotus Sutra. The mother and daughters vow to protect the votaries of the Lotus Sutra.

5 ON THE BUDDHA'S PROPHECY
NICHIREN, THE ŚRAMAṆA OF JAPAN

Nichiren wrote this letter in his fifty-second year while in exile at Ichinosawa on the island of Sado. It is dated the eleventh day of the fifth intercalary month, 1273, and is not addressed to any specific person; thus it is assumed that it was meant for all of his followers. The location of the original manuscript of this letter is not known.

The seventh volume of the Lotus Sutra states, "In the fifth five hundred years after my death, accomplish worldwide *kōsen-rufu* and never allow its flow to cease."[1] On the one hand, it is deplorable to me that more than twenty-two hundred and twenty years have already passed since the Buddha's death. What evil karma prevented me from being born in his lifetime? Why couldn't I have seen the four ranks of saints in the Former Day of the Law,[2] or T'ien-t'ai and Dengyō in the Middle Day? On the other hand, I rejoice at whatever good fortune enabled me to be born in the fifth five hundred years and read these words of the Buddha.

Even if I had been born in the Buddha's lifetime, it would have served no purpose, for those who embraced the first four tastes[3] of teachings had not yet heard of the Lotus Sutra. Again, my being born in either the Former or Middle Day of the Law would have been meaningless, for neither the scholars of the three schools of the south or the seven schools of the north, nor those of the Kegon, Shingon, or any other sects, believed in the Lotus Sutra.

The Great Teacher T'ien-t'ai said, "In the fifth five hundred years, the Mystic Way shall spread and benefit mankind far into the future."[4]

Doesn't this describe the time of *kōsen-rufu*? The Great Teacher Dengyō said, "The Former and Middle Days are almost over, and the Latter Day is near at hand."[5] These words reveal how he longed to live at the beginning of the Latter Day of the Law. When one compares the rewards of living in the three different periods, it is clear that mine surpass not only those of Nāgārjuna and Vasubandhu, but those of T'ien-t'ai and Dengyō.

Question: You are not the only person living in this five-hundred-year period; why are you in particular so overjoyed to be living now?

Answer: The fourth volume of the Lotus Sutra reads, "Since hatred and jealousy abound even during the lifetime of the Buddha, how much worse will it be in the world after his passing?"[6] The Great Teacher T'ien-t'ai stated, "It will be 'much worse' in the future because the Lotus Sutra is so hard to teach."[7] The Great Teacher Miao-lo explained, "T'ien-t'ai calls the Lotus Sutra 'hard to teach' to let us know how hard it is to enable people to understand it."[8] Priest Chih-tu[9] stated, "It is said that good medicine tastes bitter. Similarly, this sutra dispels attachments to the five vehicles and establishes the one supreme teaching. It reproaches common mortals and censures saints, denies Mahayana and refutes Hinayana . . . All those who are repudiated persecute the believers in the Lotus Sutra."[10] The Great Teacher Dengyō said, "The propagation of the true teaching will begin in the age when the Middle Day of the Law ends and the Latter Day opens, in a land to the east of T'ang and to the west of Katsu,[11] among people stained by the five impurities who live in a time of conflict. The sutra says, 'Since hatred and jealousy abound even during the lifetime of the Buddha, how much worse will it be in the world after his passing?' There is good reason for this statement."[12] The Great Teacher Dengyō wrote as though describing his own day, but actually, he was referring to the present time. That is what gives such profound meaning to his words, "The Former and Middle Days are almost over, and the Latter Day is near at hand."

The sutra states, "Devils, people under their influence, heavenly beings, *yakṣas* and *kumbhandas*, and others will seize the advantage."[13] Another portion of the sutra details these "others": Yakṣa, rākṣasa, hungry ghosts, stinking demons, vengeful demons, *bidara*, reddish-yellow, black, and blue demons, and so on."[14] These passages explain that those who in previous lifetimes embraced the four tastes or the three teachings, Brahmanism, or the doctrines of Humanity and Heaven appear in this life as devils, spirits, or human beings who persecute the votary of the true and perfect teaching when they see or hear of him.

Question: In comparing the Former and Middle Days with the Latter Day of the Law, it seems to me that the first two periods were far superior in terms of both time and the people's inborn capacity.[15] Why are these factors of time and capacity ignored in the Lotus Sutra which refers exclusively to this age?

Answer: The Buddha's thoughts are difficult to fathom. Indeed, even I am still unable to do so. We may attempt to understand, however, by taking Hinayana Buddhism as a point of clarification. During the thousand years of the Former Day of the Law, Hinayana was fully endowed with teaching, practice and proof. In the subsequent thousand years of the Middle Day, teaching and practice still remained, but no longer was there any proof. Now in the Latter Day of the Law, the teaching remains, but there is neither practice nor proof. To examine this from the standpoint of the Lotus Sutra: In the thousand years of the Former Day of the Law, those who possessed all three had most probably formed a bond of faith with the Lotus Sutra during the Buddha's lifetime. They were born again in the Former Day and were able to obtain the proof of Hinayana through its teaching and practice. Those born in the Middle Day had not developed strong ties to the Lotus Sutra during the Buddha's lifetime and were therefore unable to attain proof through Hinayana. They turned instead to provisional Mahayana and were thus able to be born in pure lands throughout the universe. In the Latter Day of the Law, there is no longer any benefit to be gained from either Mahayana or Hinayana. Hinayana retains nothing but its teaching; it has neither practice nor proof. Mahayana still has its teaching and practice but no longer provides any benefit whatsoever, either conspicuous or inconspicuous.

Furthermore, the sects of Hinayana and provisional Mahayana established during the Former and Middle Days of the Law cling all the more stubbornly to their doctrines as they enter the Latter Day. Those who espouse Hinayana reject Mahayana, and those who espouse provisional teachings attack the true teachings, until the country is overrun with people who slander. Those who fall into the evil paths because of their mistaken practice of Buddhism outnumber the dust particles that comprise the earth, while those who attain Buddhahood by practicing the true teachings are fewer than the dust specks you can hold on a fingernail. The gods have now abandoned the country, and only demons remain, possessing the minds and bodies of the ruler, his subjects, priests and nuns, and causing them to vilify and humiliate the votary of the Lotus Sutra.

If, however, in this time period after the Buddha's death, one renounces his attachments to the four tastes and three teachings and converts to faith in the Lotus Sutra which is true Mahayana, all the gods and countless Bodhisattvas of the Earth will protect him as the votary of the Lotus Sutra. Under their protection, he will establish the true object of worship represented by the five characters of Myōhō-renge-kyō and bring it to the entire world.

It was the same with Bodhisattva Fukyō, who lived in the Middle Day of the Buddha Ionnō's Law. He propagated the teaching of twenty-four characters which begins, "I deeply respect . . . ,"[16] and was persecuted and attacked with staves. The words of the twenty-four characters of Fukyō are different from the five characters of Nichiren, but their spirit is the same. The method of propagation is also exactly the same both at the end of the Buddha Ionnō's Middle Day and now at the beginning of the Latter Day. Bodhisattva Fukyō was a person of *shozuiki* and Nichiren is a common mortal of *myōji-soku*.[17]

Question: How can you be certain that you are the votary of the Lotus Sutra prophesied to appear at the beginning of the Latter Day of the Law?

Answer: A passage from the Lotus Sutra states, ". . . how much worse will it be in the world after his passing?"[18] Another passage reads, "There are many ignorant people who will vilify and attack us, the votaries of the Lotus Sutra, with swords and staves."[19] A third passage says, "We will be banished again and again."[20] A fourth reads, "The people will be full of hostility, and it will be extremely difficult to believe."[21] A fifth reads, "They will stone him and beat him with staves."[22] A sixth reads, "Devils, people under their influence, spirits of the heavens and seas, sinister demons called Yasha, demons that drain human vitality, and others will seize the advantage."[23]

That the people might believe in the Buddha's words, I have sought throughout Japan, among the sovereign and his subjects, among priests and nuns, lay men and women, for one who has fulfilled these explicit predictions, but I can find none other than myself. Now is most certainly the beginning of the Latter Day of the Law, but had Nichiren not appeared, the Buddha's predictions would be false.

Question: You are an extremely arrogant priest—even more arrogant than Mahādeva or Sunakṣatra.[24] Is this not so?-

Answer: Slandering Nichiren is a sin even graver than those of Devadatta or Vimalamitra.[25] My words may sound arrogant, but my sole purpose is to fulfill the Buddha's predictions and reveal the truth of his teachings. In all Japan, who but Nichiren can be called the votary of the Lotus Sutra? By denouncing Nichiren, you would make lies of the Buddha's prophecies. Are you not then an extremely evil man?

Question: You certainly fit the Buddha's prophecies. But are there perhaps not other votaries of the Lotus Sutra in India or China?

Answer: Throughout the four continents of the world there are surely not two suns. So, throughout the four seas, how can there be two rulers?

Question: On what basis do you say that?

Answer: The moon appears in the west[26] and gradually shines eastward, while the sun rises in the east and casts its rays to the west. The same is true of Buddhism. It spread from west to east in the Former and Middle Days of the Law, but will travel from east to west in the Latter Day. The Great Teacher Miao-lo said, "Buddhism has been lost in India, and they are seeking it abroad."[27] Thus, there is no Buddhism in India anymore. One hundred fifty years ago in China, during the reign of Emperor Kao-tsung, barbarians from the north invaded the Eastern Capital[28] and put an end to what little was left of both Buddhism and the political order there. Now, not one Hinayana sutra remains in China and most Mahayana sutras have also been lost. Even when Jakushō[29] and other priests set out from Japan to take some sutras to China, there was no one there to whom these sutras could be taught. Their efforts were as meaningless as trying to teach Buddhism to wooden or stone statues garbed in priests' robes and carrying mendicants' bowls. That is why Tsun-shih[30] said, "Buddhism was first transmitted from the west, just as the moon first appears in the west. Now Buddhism returns from the east like the sun rising in the east."[31] The words of Miao-lo and Tsun-shih make it clear that Buddhism is lost in both India and China.

Question: Now I can see there is no Buddhism in either India or China, but how do you know there is no Buddhism in the other three continents—to the east, west, and north?[32]

Answer: The eighth volume of the Lotus Sutra states, "After the Buddha's death, I will spread this sutra within Jambudvīpa and never allow it to perish."[33] The word "within" indicates that the other three continents were excluded.

Question: You have fulfilled the Buddha's prophecy; now what do you yourself predict?

Answer: There can be no doubt that the fifth five-hundred-year period has already begun as prophesied by the Buddha. I say that, without fail, Buddhism shall arise and flow forth from the east, from the land of Japan. Omens will occur in the form of natural disasters of a magnitude greater than ever before witnessed in the Former or Middle Day of the Law. When the Buddha was born, when he turned the wheel of doctrine, and also when he entered nirvana, the omens, both auspicious and inauspicious, were greater than any ever observed. The Buddha is the teacher of all saints. The sutras describe how, at the time of his birth, five colors of light shone forth in all directions, and the night became as bright as noon. At the time of his death, twelve white arcs crossed the sky from north to south, the sun's light was extinguished, and the day became as dark as midnight. There followed the two thousand years of the Former and Middle Days of the Law; saints, some Buddhist and some not, were born and died, but never were there any omens of such magnitude.

However, from the beginning of the Shōka period through this year[34] there have been tremendous earthquakes and extraordinary phenomena in the heavens, exactly like the signs which marked the Buddha's birth and death. You should know from this that a saint like the Buddha has been born. A great comet crossed the sky, but for which sovereign or subject did this omen come? The earth tilted, and gaping fissures opened three times, but for which saint or sage did this occur? You should realize that these great omens, both good and bad, are of no ordinary significance. They are signs that the Great Pure Law is ascending and the Pure Law is in decline. T'ien-t'ai stated, "By observing the fury of the rain, we can tell the greatness of the dragon that caused it, and by observing the flourishing of the lotus flowers, we can tell the depth of the pond in which they grow."[35] Miao-lo said, "Wise men can see omens and what they foretell, as snakes know the way of snakes."[36]

Twenty-one years ago[37] I, Nichiren, understood what was to come. Since then I have suffered persecution day after day and month after month. In the last two or three years, among other things, I was almost put to death. The chances are one in ten thousand that I will survive the year or even the month. If anyone questions these things, let him ask my disciples for details. What joy is ours to expiate in one lifetime our slanders from the eternal past! How fortunate to serve Shakyamuni, lord of the teachings, who has never been known until now! I pray that before anything else I can guide to the truth the sovereign and those others who persecuted me. I will tell the Buddha about all the disciples who have aided me, and before they die, I will share the great blessings of this faith with my parents who gave me life. Now as if in a dream I understand the heart of the *Hōtō* chapter, which reads, "To hurl Mount Sumeru into countless Buddha lands would not be difficult . . . but to spread this sutra in the evil age after the Buddha's death is difficult."[38] The Great Teacher Dengyō stated, "Shakyamuni taught that the shallow is easy to embrace, but the profound is difficult. To discard the shallow and seek the profound requires courage. The Great Teacher T'ien-t'ai practiced in a manner true to Shakyamuni's teachings and spread the Hokke sect[39] throughout China. Dengyō and his followers received the doctrine from T'ien-t'ai and disseminated it throughout Japan."[40] Nichiren of Awa Province inherited the lineage of Buddhism from these three teachers and propagated the Lotus Sutra in the Latter Day of Law. Together they should be called "the four masters of Buddhism in the three countries." Nam-myoho-renge-kyo, Nam-myoho-renge-kyo.

The eleventh day of the fifth intercalary month in the tenth year of Bun'ei (1273)

Notes

1. T9, 54b.
2. Reference is to such figures as Nāgārjuna, Vasubandhu, etc.
3. Reference is to the four tastes or flavors: fresh milk, cream, curdled milk, and butter, associated with *Kegon*, *Āgamas*, *Hōdō*, and *Hannya* teachings. The fifth taste, ghee, is likened to the Lotus teaching.
4. *Hokke Mongu* (T34, 2c).
5. *Shugo Kokkai Shō* (DDZ 2, 349).
6. T9, 31b.
7. *Hokke Mongu* (T34, 110b).
8. *Hokke Mongu Ki* (T34, 306C).
9. Chih-tu (n.d.) was a disciple of Miao-lo.
10. *Hokekyō Shogisan* (ZZI, 45, 3, 273a). The five vehicles are: humanity, heaven, *shōmon*, *engaku*, and bodhisattva.
11. T'ang refers to China, Katsu to a Tungusic nation in northeastern China that flourished for about one hundred years from the mid-sixth century. Thus, east of T'ang and west of Katsu refers to Japan.
12. *Hokke Shūku* (DDZ 3, 251).
13. T9, 54c. *Yakṣas* (Jap: *Yasha*) are fierce demons, followers of Bishamonten. *Kumbhandas* (Jap: *Kuhanda*) are demons that drain the vitality from humans.

14. T9, 59b. *Rākṣasa* (fem: *rākṣāsī*; Jap: *rasetsu*) are demons that eat human flesh; stinking demons (Jap: *futanna*; Skt: *pūtana*) are a kind of hungry ghost; vengeful demons (Jap: *kissha*; Skt: *kṛtya*) are demons that can raise corpses and wreak harm on their enemies; *bidara* (Skt: *vetāla*) are demons that can raise a corpse to kill someone; the various colored demons are reddish-yellow (Jap: *kenda*; Skt: *skanda*), black (Jap: *umaraogyu*; Skt: *umāraka*), and blue (Jap: *abutsumara*; Skt: *apasmāraka*). The last two are varieties of *yasha kissha* and human *kissha*.

15. Two of the five conditions (Jap: *gokō*) necessary for a religion to spread. The other three are the teaching, the place, and the sequence of propagation. They are described in the first letter: "The Teaching, Capacity, Time, and Country."

16. The passage appears in the *Fukyō* (20th) chapter of the Lotus Sutra (T9, 50a).

17. T'ien-t'ai, in his *Hokke Mongu* (T34, 137), lists four stages of faith and five methods of practice (Jap: shishin gohon). The stages of faith apply to those who embraced the Lotus Sutra during Shakyamuni's lifetime; the five methods of practice are for believers who came after Shakyamuni's death. *Shozuiki*, to rejoice on hearing the Lotus Sutra, is the first of these five methods of practice. In the *Maka Shikan* (T46, 10b) T'ien-t'ai describes the six stages of practice (Jap: rokusoku) of the Lotus Sutra. The second stage is *myōji-soku*, the stage in which one hears the name (*myō*) of the truth or reads the words (*ji*) of the sutras.

18. T9, 31b.

19. T9, 36b.

20. T9, 36c.

21. T9, 39a.

22. T9, 50c.

23. T9, 54c.

24. For Mahādeva, see Letter 3, note 24; for Sunakṣatra, see Letter 2, note 66.

25. Devadatta, while continuing to slander the Buddha's teachings, falsely asserted that he had attained Buddhahood. He is an archvillain, frequently mentioned by Nichiren. Vimalamitra (Muku Ronji) was an Indian monk, a native of Kashmir, who vowed to destroy the reputation of Vasubandhu and of Mahayana Buddhism. He is described in *Daitō Saiiki Ki* (T51, 892b).

26. This refers to the fact that the new moon is first seen in the west just after sunset. On successive nights as the moon grows fuller, it appears to move a little further toward the east. Of course, the direction of the moon's movement is the same as that of the sun and stars, east to west, but because of its orbital motion, it appears to move slightly in retrograde, from west to east, each day.

27. *Hokke Mongu Ki* (T34, 359c).

28. Kao-tsung was the first emperor of the Southern Sung. The eastern capital, K'ai-feng, was captured by barbarians from the north in 1127, forcing Kao-tsung to establish a new capital south of the Yangtze River.

29. Jakushō (d. 1034) was a disciple of Genshin (942–1017); he went to China to study the T'ien-t'ai teaching. He brought with him a copy of Nan-yüeh's writing that had been lost in China. Jakushō died on the mainland without returning to Japan.

30. Tsun-shih (964–1032) was a Chinese priest who upheld T'ien-t'ai's teachings.

31. From Tsun-shih's preface to an edition of Hui-ssu's *Daijō Shikan Hōmon* (T46, 641c).

32. In Buddhist cosmology there are four continents surrounding Mt. Sumeru. Jambudvīpa is the only one in which Buddhism can spread.

33. T9, 61c.

34. The first year of Shōka (1257) until the present year, 1273.

35. *Hokke Mongu* (T34, 125b).

36. *Hokke Mongu Ki* (T34, 326b).

37. The year 1253, when Nichiren first proclaimed his teachings.

38. T9, 34a.

39. Reference is to T'ien-t'ai's teaching, based on the Lotus Sutra, as well as to Nichiren's teachings.

40. *Hokke Shūku* (DDZ 3, 273).

6 TEACHING, PRACTICE, AND PROOF

In the fifth month of 1274 Nichiren, feeling that his remonstrations had three times failed to gain acceptance, withdrew from Kamakura and retired to a small hermitage amidst the wilderness of Mount Minobu. Here he continued to write letters and other documents in an effort to encourage his disciples to increase their propagation efforts. He lectured on the Lotus Sutra but himself remained apart from active proselytizing.

This letter presents several problems: the date of its composition is in dispute. The letter is dated the twenty-first day of the third month; the year is probably 1275, although some hold it to be 1277. Sammi-bō, to whom the letter is addressed, was a follower of Nichiren who was noted for his eloquence and learning. He had studied on Mount Hiei, delivered lectures for the aristocracy in Kyoto, and was for a while active in helping to spread Nichiren's teachings. Nichiren, however, chided him on several occasions for his arrogance. He eventually abandoned his faith and is said to have met an extremely unpleasant death, probably in 1279, although the precise details are not known.

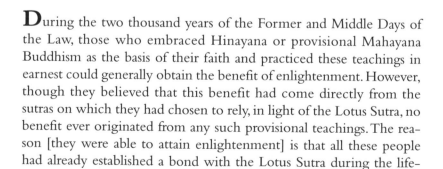

During the two thousand years of the Former and Middle Days of the Law, those who embraced Hinayana or provisional Mahayana Buddhism as the basis of their faith and practiced these teachings in earnest could generally obtain the benefit of enlightenment. However, though they believed that this benefit had come directly from the sutras on which they had chosen to rely, in light of the Lotus Sutra, no benefit ever originated from any such provisional teachings. The reason [they were able to attain enlightenment] is that all these people had already established a bond with the Lotus Sutra during the lifetime of the Buddha, though the results they gained varied according to whether or not their receptivity had fully matured. Those whose capacity to understand the Lotus Sutra was fully mature attained enlightenment during the lifetime of the Buddha, while those whose capacity was inferior and immature [could not attain enlightenment at that time. However, they] reappeared in the Former Day of the Law, and, by embracing provisional Mahayana teachings such as the Vimalakīirti, *Shiyaku*, *Kammuryōju*, *Ninnō*, and *Hannya* sutras, they were able to gain the same proof of enlightenment obtained by those of higher capacity during the Buddha's lifetime.

Thus the Former Day of the Law possessed all three: teaching, practice and proof, whereas in the Middle Day of the Law, there were teaching and practice but no longer any proof. Now in the Latter Day of the Law, only the teaching remains; there is neither practice nor proof. There is no longer a single person who has formed a relationship with Shakyamuni Buddha. Those who possessed the capacity to gain enlightenment through either the provisional or true Mahayana sutras have long since disappeared. In this impure and evil age, Nammyoho-renge-kyo of the *Juryō* chapter, the heart of the essential teaching, should be planted as the seed of Buddhahood for the first time in the hearts of all those who commit the five cardinal sins and slander the True Law. This is what is indicated in the *Juryō* chapter where it states: "I leave this good medicine here for you now. You should take it and not worry that it will not cure you."[1]

In the distant past, in the Middle Day of the Law of the Buddha Ionnō, not a single person knew of the Three Treasures. However, Bodhisattva Fukyō appeared, and to all people he declared the teaching of twenty-four characters which Ionnō Buddha had expounded. Not one of them listened to this twenty-four-character teaching, but they were later reborn with Bodhisattva Fukyō, and were at last able to obtain the benefit of enlightenment. This was solely because they had already received the seed of Buddhahood when they first heard the teaching. The same thing occurs in our present era. Bodhisattva Fukyō's age was the Middle Day of the Law, whereas this age is the defiled Latter Day of the Law. He was a practitioner of *shozuiki*, and I, Nichiren, am a common mortal of *myōji-soku*,[2] [both indicating the initial stages of practice]. He sowed the seed of Buddhahood with the twenty-four characters, while I do so with only the five characters of Myōhō-renge-kyo. Although the age is different, the process of attaining Buddhahood is exactly the same.[3]

Question: You have mentioned above that the teaching, practice, and proof are not all present in each of the three periods of the Former, Middle, and Latter Days of the Law. If so, how do you explain the Great Teacher Miao-lo's statement, "The beginning of the Latter Day of the Law will not be without inconspicuous benefit, for it is the time when the great teaching will be propagated?"[4]

Answer: The essence of this passage is that those who obtained benefit during the Former and Middle Days of the Law received "conspicuous" benefit, because the relationship they formed with the Lotus Sutra during the lifetime of the Buddha had finally matured. On the other hand, those born today in the Latter Day of the Law receive the seed of Buddhahood for the first time, and their benefit is therefore inconspicuous. The teaching, practice and proof of this age differ greatly from those of Hinayana, provisional Mahayana, the pre-Lotus Sutra teachings or the theoretical teaching of the Lotus Sutra. There is no one now who can gain benefits like those of the Former and Middle Days of the Law. According to Miao-lo's interpretation, the benefits in the Latter Day are inconspicuous, and people can therefore neither perceive nor understand them.

Question: Is there any sutra passage which says that inconspicuous benefits are limited to the Latter Day of the Law?

Answer: A passage from the *Yakuō* chapter in the seventh volume of the Lotus Sutra reads: "This sutra is beneficial medicine for the illnesses of all mankind. If one is ill and can hear of this sutra, his illness will vanish immediately, and he will find perpetual youth and eternal life."[5] The Great Teacher Miao-lo says: "To regard the last five-hundred-year period after the Buddha's passing as the time when no one can attain benefit is a superficial viewpoint. The beginning of the Latter Day of the Law will not be without inconspicuous benefit, for it is the time when the great teaching will be propagated. The last five-hundred-year period corresponds to that time."[6]

Question: The passages you have quoted indicate that the propagation of the Lotus Sutra is limited to the first five hundred years of the Latter Day of the Law. Yet the provisional Mahayana sutras say that their practices will still be appropriate throughout the ten thousand years[7] of the Latter Day of the Law. How do you reply to this?

Answer: Miao-lo states in the above-mentioned commentary that such an interpretaion of the last five-hundred-year period is "superficial." From a more profound viewpoint, the Lotus Sutra will spread throughout the ten thousand years of the Latter Day. The Great

Teacher T'ien-t'ai comments on the previously quoted passage from the *Yakuō* chapter, stating: "It is not only the people who live during the lifetime of the Buddha who obtain great benefits. In the fifth five hundred years, the Mystic Way shall spread and benefit mankind far into the future."[8] Does this annotation suggest anything other than the ten thousand years of the Latter Day of the Law? The *Fumbetsu Kudoku* chapter in the sixth volume of the Lotus Sutra refers to "one who is able to uphold this sutra in the evil age of the Latter Day of the Law."[9] Also the *Anrakugyō* chapter reads, "In the Latter Day of the Law, one who desires to teach this sutra . . ."[10] These quotations refer to the ten thousand years of the Latter Day of the Law. All the Buddha's teachings other than the Lotus Sutra are covered by his declaration: "In these more than forty years, I have not yet revealed the truth."[11] Moreover, there are some cases where the sutras have been revised according to the understanding of those who compiled them and therefore cannot be trusted.

The scholars of the various sects remain oblivious to the fact that the Buddha sowed the seed of enlightenment when he expounded the Lotus Sutra in the past. How foolish they are! Quite unaware of the distant past of *sanzen-jintengō* and of *gohyaku-jintengō*,[12] they abandon the mystic teaching which is pure and perfect, and sink again into the sea of the sufferings of birth and death. It is pitiful beyond description that, though born in a land where the people's capacity to receive the perfect teaching is fully mature, they vainly fall back into the great citadel of the hell of incessant suffering. They are no different from a person who arrives at the bejeweled K'un-lun Mountains[13] only to return to his impoverished country without a single gem, or one who enters a forest of sandalwood trees, yet goes back to the barren rubble of his own land without ever plucking the *champaka*'s [14] blossom. The third volume of the Lotus Sutra reads, "It is as if one came from a famished land and suddenly encountered a great king's feast."[15] And the sixth volume reads, "This, my land, remains safe and unharmed. . . . My pure land is indestructible."[16]

In your letter you mentioned a difficult question put to you, as to the assertion that people are able to achieve enlightenment through their practice of the pre-Lotus Sutra teachings. In reply, you should quote the third volume of the Nirvana Sutra which reads, "Men of devout faith! Study and practice [until you learn that the Three Treasures are one and eternal]."[17] Further, quote the third volume of the *Guketsu* which comments on this passage where it states, "Only those who have heard the Mahayana teachings in the remote past [are able to attain enlightenment through the practice of the Hinayana teachings]," and, "Those who achieved Buddhahood through the practice of the pre–Lotus Sutra teachings were able to do so only because of their initial practice in the remote past."[18] You should make clear that the pre–Lotus Sutra teachings provide no benefit of enlightenment whatsoever. Then explain that the same principle holds true in the time of propagation following the Buddha's death. All who obtained the proof of enlightenment in the Former and Middle Days of the Law were able to do so solely because of the relationship they had formed with the Lotus Sutra during the Buddha's lifetime.

Should your opponents repeatedly insist that the pre–Lotus Sutra teachings provide a path to enlightenment, cite to them the Buddha's own declaration in the *Muryōgi* Sutra: "In these more than forty years, I have not yet revealed the truth." Common mortals like ourselves at the initial stage of practice can expect to attain Buddhahood by relying on the teachings of the Buddha. The words of the various teachers are in themselves of no use at all. The Buddha gave strict counsel against following them with his statement in the Nirvana Sutra, "Rely on the Law and not upon persons."[19] Remind your opponents of this and repeatedly cite the passage, "I have not yet revealed the truth," to refute their arguments. However, do not carelessly cite such passages [of the Lotus Sutra] as "Honestly discarding the provisional teachings, [I will expound only the supreme Way]"[20] or "The World-Honored One has long expounded his doctrines [and now must reveal the truth]."[21] Rather, keep these teachings deep in your heart.

Another difficult question you mentioned concerns the assertion that the enlightenment indicated in the pre–Lotus Sutra teachings and that of the Lotus Sutra are ultimately the same. This question arises because the *Kammuryōju* Sutra says that those who rely upon it are able to ascend to the Pure Land [where they will eventually attain enlightenment], or because of similar assertions in other sutras. Explain this and cite again the teaching, "In these more than forty years, I have not yet revealed the truth," and others, such as "Merely by provisional names and words, [I have led and instructed all living beings in order to reveal the Buddha wisdom]."[22] If they further contend that the *Kammuryōju* Sutra and the Lotus Sutra were expounded during the same period of time, you should deal with this by quoting the passage from the *Hosshi* chapter in which the Buddha says: "Among all those [sutras] I have preached, now preach and will preach, this Lotus Sutra is the most difficult to believe and the most difficult to understand."[23] In addition, you can quote the relevant passages from the third volume of the *Hokke Gengi*[24] or the third volume of the *Shakusen*.[25] Be sure, however, that you consider these sutras and annotations well, and do not quote them haphazardly.

In your letter, you also asked how to reply to the claims of the Shingon sect. First, ask upon which scriptural passage Kōbō Daishi based his denunciation of the Lotus Sutra as a doctrine of childish theory and of Shakyamuni as being still in the region of darkness. If they reply by citing some sutra, ask them which of the Buddhas of the past, present or future is represented by Dainichi Buddha. Then ask them if they are aware of the deceit perpetrated by such priests as Shan-wu-wei and Chin-kang-chih.[26] Tell them how Shan-wu-wei deceived the priest I-hsing[27] when he dictated to him his commentary on the *Dainichi* Sutra, [making it seem as though that sutra contained the principle of *ichinen sanzen*]. Although not the slightest indication of *ichinen sanzen* is to be found in the *Dainichi* Sutra, this false interpretaion was put forth when the sutra was introduced to China. As regards the most perverted of their distortions, ask them if there is documentary proof in the teachings of any of the Buddhas of the three existences which permits them to tread on the head of Vairocana Buddha.[28] If they retort in some way or other, then tell them about the Great Arrogant Brahman[29] who used statues [of the three deities of Brahmanism[30] and of the Buddha Shakyamuni] as the legs of his preaching platform. On other points, ask them in the same way just which sutra or treatise they can provide as proof of their assertions, and for the rest, debate with them as I have always taught you. No matter which sect you may debate, if the teachings of the Shingon sect are mentioned, clearly refute that sect's distorted views.

Next, as to the assertions of the Nembutsu sect: The priest T'an-luan[31] defines the Nembutsu as the easy-to-practice way and the practices of the other sects as the difficult-to-practice way. Tao-ch'o defines the Nembutsu teachings as the Pure Land teachings and all the other teachings as the Sacred Way teachings.[32] Shan-tao distinguishes between correct and incorrect practices, while Hōnen enjoins people to "discard, close, ignore and abandon"[33] all sutras other than those relating to Amida's Pure Land. Have those who cite these statements identify the exact sutra or treatise from which they are derived. Of sutras there are of course two types—true and provisional. Treatises can also be divided into two types—those which discuss Hinayana,

Mahayana or Buddhism in general, and those dealing with specific sutras or chapters. Moreover, there are those treatises that are faithful to the sutras and those that distort the sutras. One should clearly master these distinctions. Ask them if they can point out any passage from among the three Pure Land sutras[34] verifying the above-mentioned assertions. Everyone reveres the Nembutsu of Amida Buddha, but ask your opponents as before if there exists any teaching which affords a solid basis for this. In short, let them cite the sutra or treatise on which the adherents of the Nembutsu sect in both China and Japan base their denunciation of the Lotus Sutra as an incorrect practice, and urge people to discard, close, ignore and abandon it. When they fail to cite any passage which clearly validates these statements, tell them that, just as expounded in the *Hiyu* chapter of the Lotus Sutra, the grave offense which they commit by slandering the true teaching on the basis of provisional teachings will surely plunge them into the great citadel of the Avīci Hell, where they will be reborn again and again for kalpas without number. Let the audience judge for themselves the seriousness of the offense which derives from following the perverted doctrines of their sect and forsaking the very teaching which all the Buddhas of the three existences verified with the words: "All that you [Shakyamuni Buddha] have expounded is the truth."[35] Could any thinking person fail to discern which is true and which is false? Then, strictly denounce the teachers of their sect.

How naive are those who cling only to the stump[36] of one sutra without knowing which are superior and which inferior among all the sutras! Even if one cannot discern this for himself, there can be no mistaking that the Lotus Sutra is the only sutra whose truth was attested to by Shakyamuni, Tahō and all the other Buddhas. Should one nonetheless view the Lotus Sutra as false and misread the Buddha's words, "I have not yet revealed the truth," as "I have already revealed the truth," his distorted vision would be inferior even to that of cattle or sheep. Exactly what is meant by the passage in the *Hosshi* chapter: "Among all those I have preached, now preach and will preach, this Lotus Sutra is the most difficult to believe and the most difficult to understand. [Yakuō! This sutra is the mystic, essential treasury of all Buddhas . . .]"?[37] Does the *Muryōgi* Sutra not make it clear that Shakyamuni taught the practice of Buddhist austerities spanning myriads of kalpas before declaring, "In these more than forty years, I have not yet revealed the truth"? These passages are nothing less than the Buddha's own statements of the relative superiority of the various sutras expounded during his fifty years of teaching. In turn, the relative superiority of the sutras is determined by whether or not they lead to Buddhahood.

Jikaku and Chishō[38] held the view that, although the Lotus Sutra and the *Dainichi* Sutra are equal in terms of principle, the latter is superior in terms of practice. Shan-tao and Hōnen maintained that no practice other than the Nembutsu suits the capacity of the people in the Latter Day. The Zen sect claims to represent a special transmission apart from the sutras. Their views are as distorted as the eyesight of a person who mistakes east for west or who cannot tell north from south. Their understanding is inferior to that of cattle or sheep, and their teachings are as ambiguous as a bat, [which is neither animal nor bird]. How could they not feel terror at defying the Buddha's words: "Rely on the Law and not upon persons" and "One who slanders this sutra [immediately destroys the seeds for becoming a Buddha in this world]?"[39] They must have been possessed by devils or become drunk on the evil wine of delusion.

Nothing is more certain than actual proof. Look at the horrible fates of Shan-wu-wei and I-hsing in China or of Kōbō and Jikaku in Japan. Could they have met such fates if they were actually votaries of the True Law? How do you read the *Kambutsu Sōkai*[40] and other sutras or Bodhisattva Nāgārjuna's treatise[41] which describes the state of death? The priest I-hsing incorporated Shan-wu-wei's deceptions into his explanation of the *Dainichi* Sutra. Kōbō denounced the Lotus Sutra as a doctrine of childish theory. Jikaku contended that the *Dainichi* Sutra was equal to the Lotus Sutra in terms of principle but superior in terms of practice. T'an-luan and Tao-ch'o proclaimed that the Nembutsu alone suits the people's capacity in the Latter Day. Such views are commonplace in the false teachings of sects founded on provisional sutras. No one would wish to die as these people did. Say these things mildly but firmly in a quiet voice with a calm gaze and an even expression.

In your letter you asked how to treat questions regarding the difference between the benefits of the Lotus Sutra and those of the other sutras. First of all, state that the benefit of the pre-Lotus Sutra doctrines is incomplete. Then, ask your opponents if any of the sutras upon which their sects are based were confirmed as true and valid by Shakyamuni Buddha, Tahō Buddha and all other Buddhas of the ten directions. Say that you have never heard of such. Tahō and all the other Buddhas who were Shakyamuni's emanations assembled to testify to the truth of the Lotus Sutra; how could they possibly attest to any other sutra? A Buddha never states two contrary things. Next, ask if there is any other sutra which mentions the six difficult and nine easy acts.[42] With the possible exception of the sutras fabricated by people after the Buddha's passing, there is not a single word or phrase in any other of the Buddha's entire fifty years of teachings which describes them. You should make all this clear.

Do the other sutras reveal that the Buddha originally attained enlightenment uncountable kalpas ago, in *gohyaku-jintengō*? Do they tell how the people formed a bond with the Lotus Sutra when he expounded it in the remote past of *sanzen-jintengō*? What other sutra teaches that one can gain immeasurable benefit by arousing even a single moment of faith in it,[43] or that incalculable benefits will accrue even to the fiftieth person who rejoices upon hearing of it?[44] The other sutras do not claim that such great benefit can be obtained by even the first, second, third or tenth listener, let alone by the fiftieth. Moreover, they do not speak of even one or two dust-particle kalpas, let alone of such vast reaches of time as *gohyaku-jintengō* or *sanzen-jin-tengō*. Only through the Lotus Sutra was Buddhahood opened to the people of the two vehicles, and the lowly dragon king's daughter enabled to attain enlightenment in her present form. Neither the *Kegon* or *Hannya* sutras nor any other provisional Mahayana teaching expounds such wonders. [T'ien-t'ai made this quite clear when he declared that] the capacity of people of the two vehicles to attain Buddhahood was first revealed in the Lotus Sutra. We may be certain that, unlike Kōbō or Jikaku, a philosopher as enlightened as the Great Teacher T'ien-t'ai could not have fabricated any theories that were not based on the words or meaning of the sutras. The Lotus Sutra predicts Devadatta's future enlightenment in the land called Heavenly Way, but what other sutra asserts that such an evil man can attain Buddhahood? Even leaving all such questions aside, what other sutra reveals the mutual possession of the Ten Worlds or teaches that even plants and trees can attain Buddhahood? T'ien-t'ai explains the enlightenment of plants, saying that all things having color or fragrance are manifestations of the Middle Way, and Miao-lo adds that this marvelous teaching will surely shock and cause doubts in those who hear it for the first time.[45] Can their interpretations be classed with the distorted views of Jikaku and Chishō, who claim that the *Dainichi* Sutra is equal to the Lotus Sutra in terms of principle but superior in terms of practice? T'ien-t'ai is one of the teachers who kept the torch of Buddhism burning as it passed through India and China to Japan. He is the saint who gained an awakening at the P'u-hsien Monastery;[46] he is also the reincarnation of a bodhisattva and attained enlightenment by means of his inherent wisdom. How could he possibly have formulated any interpretations not based on the sutras or treatises?

Is any single great matter to be found in the other sutras? The Lotus Sutra contains twenty outstanding principles.[47] Among those twenty, the most vital is the *Juryō* chapter's revelation that Shakyamuni first attained Buddhahood in *gohyaku-jintengō*. The people may well wonder what the Buddha meant by this. Through this revelation he taught that common mortals like ourselves, who have been submerged in the sufferings of birth and death since time without beginning and who never so much as dreamed of reaching the shore of enlightenment, are in essence Buddhas originally endowed with the three bodies.[48] That is, he taught the ultimate doctrine of *ichinen sanzen*. From this perspective, you should assert the supremacy of the Lotus Sutra among all the Buddha's teachings.

Such a profound teaching may be brought forth in an official debate, but not during personal discussions. Should you indiscriminately mention it to whomever you meet, on any occasion or at any time, you will certainly incur punishment from all the Buddhas of the three existences. This is the principle that I have always referred to as my own inner realization.

Can even the slightest indication of this principle be found in the *Dainichi* Sutra? The three Pure Land sutras state that about ten kalpas have passed since Amida Buddha attained enlightenment. Can this possibly compare with the Lotus Sutra's revelation of Shakyamuni's original enlightenment in *gohyaku-jintengō*? Meet each argument with rebuttals such as these, citing each quotation in its proper context. Then, tell your opponents to stop and consider this: It is precisely because the Lotus Sutra is so lofty that Tahō Buddha came from far away to testify to its truth and that all the other Buddhas assembled to join him. Then Shakyamuni, Tahō, and all the other Buddhas attested that the sutra is free from falsehood, extending their tongues all the way to the Brahma Heaven.[49] Innumerable bodhisattvas appeared from beneath the earth and were specifically entrusted with the transmission of Myōhō-renge-kyō to all the people throughout the world in this impure and evil latter age. Was it not precisely because these bodhisattvas were the Buddha's envoys that he denied all of the other eighty myriads of millions of nayutas of bodhisattvas, saying, "Desist, men of devout faith"?[50] If, as is the way with the adherents of misleading sects, they demand that you cite documentary evidence for these statements, quote the *Yujutsu* chapter of the Lotus Sutra,[51] as well as the ninth volume of the *Hokke Mongu* and the ninth volume of the *Hokke Mongu Ki* which clarify the three reasons for the rejection of the bodhisattvas from other worlds and the three reasons for the emergence of the bodhisattvas of the essential teaching.[52] Herein lies the matter of utmost importance for Nichiren and his followers.

Your opponents may attempt to attack you by citing the passage from the *Daichido Ron* which states: "If one denounces the teachings others follow out of love for his own, then even if he observes the precepts, he will be destined to fall into the path of evil."[53] Ask them whether they know why Nāgārjuna wrote this admonition, and if Nāgārjuna could possibly have been ignorant of how serious an offense it is to slander the true teaching by clinging to provisional teachings. He stated, "The various sutras are not secret teachings; only the Lotus Sutra is secret."[54] He declared that the Lotus Sutra alone is the seed of enlightenment, likening it to a great physician. Is it possible that he later had misgivings about this, and therefore wrote the above admonition? If so, he would have been directly contradicting the Buddha's own words, for the Lotus Sutra states, "Honestly discarding the provisional teachings," and, "Never accept even a single phrase from the other sutras."[55] It is hardly conceivable. Nāgārjuna was a great bodhisattva who appeared in accordance with the Buddha's prediction, as well as a scholar in the direct lineage of Shakyamuni's teaching. He may well have written this admonition in his treatise because he foresaw that such priests as Kōbō and T'an-luan would slander the Lotus Sutra, the teaching which befits this age of the Latter Day of the Law. Reproach your opponents for not knowing the meaning of the words they cite. Tell them: "Are not you yourselves followers of those 'destined to fall into the path of evil'? Are you not to be counted among those who will suffer for numberless kalpas to come? How pitiful!"

In his appeal to Regent Hōjō Tokimune,[56] Ryōkan[57] of the Ritsu sect stated as follows: "Of late I am most vexed by the priest called Nichiren who proclaims that those observing the precepts are destined to fall into hell. What sutra or treatise states such a thing? Moreover, even though there is scarcely anyone in Japan today, whether of high or low rank, who does not chant the Nembutsu, he asserts that the Nembutsu forms the karmic cause for falling into the hell of incessant suffering. On what sutra is this based? I would like to ask Nichiren what reliable proof he has to justify these statements." He sent the government six such questions concerning in general whether or not enlightenment can be achieved through the practice of the pre-Lotus Sutra teachings. If Ryōkan of the Gokuraku-ji again lets it be known, as he claims in his petition, that he desires to meet and debate with me, submit a petition to the government to meet with Ryōkan, and say to him: "My teacher Nichiren incurred the displeasure of the government and was exiled to the province of Sado in the eighth year of Bun'ei (1271). In the first month[58] of the eleventh year of Bun'ei(1274), he was pardoned and returned to Kamakura. On his return he remonstrated with Hei no Saemon[59] about various matters and then secluded himself deep in the mountains of Kai Province. He has stated that even if he were to be summoned by the emperor or empress, he will never emerge from his retirement to debate his teachings with the scholars of other sects. Therefore, although I, his disciple, am a mere novice and my knowledge of his teachings is less than a hair from the hides of nine head of cattle, if anyone comes forth to state the doubts he has about the Lotus Sutra, I will do my best to reply to them." During the subsequent debate, explain my teachings in direct response to your opponent's questions.

Moreover, when you must reply to the six difficult questions posed in Ryōkan's appeal, bear in mind, as I have always said, that Nichiren's disciples cannot accomplish anything if they are cowardly. As you debate the relative superiority and depth of the Lotus Sutra and other sutras and whether or not they lead to enlightenment, remember that the Shakyamuni Buddha described in the pre-Lotus Sutra teachings and even in the theoretical teaching of the Lotus Sutra is no one to be in awe of; even less so are bodhisattvas at the stage of *tōgaku*.[60] Followers of sects based on the provisional teachings are of still less account. As you debate, bear in mind that because we embrace the Lotus Sutra, our position is like that of the heavenly king Daibonten,[61] and it is not at all wrong to regard those who hold to lesser teachings as our subjects or even as barbarians.

The adherents of the Ritsu sect do violence to the precepts which exceeds even that of a crumbling mountain or a flooding river. Far from attaining Buddhahood, they will not even be able to be reborn in the world of Humanity or Heaven. The Great Teacher Miao-lo states, "If one observes but a single precept, he will be born as a human being. But if he breaks even a single precept, he will instead fall into the three evil paths."[62] Who, among Ryōkan's followers in the Ritsu sect, embraces even one of the precepts set forth in the *Saihō*, the *Shōbōnen*,[63] and other sutras, or truly observes the rules of conduct expounded in the *Agon* and other Hinayana or Mahayana sutras? Without doubt they are all destined to fall into the three evil paths, or even sink into the hell of incessant suffering. How pitiful they are! You should tell them so and reproach them by citing the *Hōtō* chapter's explanation of what "one who observes the precepts" truly means.[64] Then, pausing briefly, tell them that the five characters of Myōhō-renge-kyō, the heart of the essential teaching of the Lotus Sutra, contain all the benefits amassed by the beneficial practices and meritorious deeds of all the Buddhas throughout the past, present and future. Then, how can this phrase not include the benefits obtained by observing all of the Buddha's precepts? Once the practitioner embraces this perfectly endowed mystic precept, he cannot break it, even if he should try. It is therefore called the precept of the diamond chalice.[65] Only by observing this very precept have the Buddhas of the three existences obtained the properties of the Law, wisdom and action, which are each without beginning or end. The Great Teacher T'ien-t'ai wrote of this precept, "The Buddha kept it secret and did not transmit it in any other sutra."[66] Now in the Latter Day of the Law, if any person embraces Myōhō-renge-kyō and practices it in accordance with the Buddha's teaching—whether he be wise or foolish, priest or lay believer, or of high or low position—he cannot fail to attain Buddhahood. For precisely this reason, Shakyamuni declared, in reference to the votary of the Lotus Sutra in the impure and evil age after the Buddha's passing, that "[concerning this man's attainment of Buddhahood,] there can assuredly be no doubt."[67] On the other hand, those who practice the provisional teachings against the admonition of Shakyamuni, Tahō and all the other Buddhas will definitely fall into the hell of incessant suffering. Now that so wondrous a precept has been revealed, none of the precepts expounded in the pre-Lotus Sutra teachings, or in the theoretical teaching itself, have the slightest power to benefit people. Since they provide not the slightest benefit, it is totally useless to observe them, even for a single day.

At the time when the mystic precept of the essential teaching is to spread, there will doubtless be omens never witnessed in any previous age. The great earthquake of the Shōka era and the huge comet of the Bun'ei era[68] were two such signs. But who among our contemporaries, what sect of Buddhism, is actually propagating the teaching of the true object of worship and the high sanctuary of the essential teaching? Not a single person carried out this task during the 2,220 years and more following the Buddha's passing. Now, more than 700 years after Buddhism was introduced to Japan in the reign of the thirtieth emperor Kimmei,[69] the Great Law never heard of in previous ages is spreading throughout Japan. How reassuring it is that not only the people here but those of India, China and the entire world shall attain Buddhahood!

Concerning the teaching, practice and proof which I stressed earlier, [if we speak with respect to the Great Law,] then the Latter Day of the Law possesses all three, just like the Former Day of the Law with respect to Shakyamuni's teaching. Jōgyō, the leader of the Bodhisattvas of the Earth, has already made his advent in this world, so the Great Law, the essence of the Lotus Sutra, will spread without fail. For the people of Japan and China as well as the people of all other countries of the world, it will be an event as rare as seeing the *udumbara* flower[70] blossom to herald the advent of a gold-wheel-turning king. In the first forty-two years of the Buddha's teachings, as well as in the theoretical teaching or the first fourteen chapters of the Lotus Sutra, he kept this Great Law secret and did not preach it, expounding it only in the revelation portion of the essential teaching[71] of the Lotus Sutra.

I have heard that when the priest Ryōkan knew I was far away in a distant province, he told everyone how he wished I would hasten to Kamakura so that he might debate with me and dispel the people's doubts. Demand to know if praising oneself and disparaging others[72] in this fashion is one of the precepts followed by the Ritsu sect. What is more, when I actually did return to Kamakura, Ryōkan shut his gates and forbade anyone to enter. At times, he even feigned illness, saying that he had caught a chill. Tell him, "I am not Nichiren but merely one of his disciples. Though I am poor at debating and my understanding of his teachings is incomplete, I fully agree with his assertion that the Ritsu sect is traitorous." When in public debate, although the teachings that you advocate are perfectly consistent with the truth, you should never on that account be impolite or abusive, or display a conceited attitude. Such conduct would be disgraceful. Order your thoughts, words, and actions carefully and be prudent when you meet with others in debate.

Nichiren

The twenty-first day of the third month
To the priest Sammi Ajari[73]

Notes

1. T9, 43a.

2. For *shōzuiki* and *myōjisoku*, *see* Letter 5, note 17.

3. That is, in both Bodhisattva Fukyō's time and Nichiren's as well, people received the seed of Buddhahood, and, though they proceed to slander the True Law, they are eventually able to attain Buddhahood by virtue of the bond they have thereby formed with it.

4. *Hokke Mongu Ki* (T34, 157b).

5. T9, 54c.

6. *Hokke Mongu Ki* (T34, 157b). A fuller quotation of the passage cited above.

7. The ten thousand years is an indefinite period of time from the beginning of the Latter Day onward.

8. *Hokke Mongu* (T34, 2c).

9. T9, 46a.

10. T9, 37c–48a.

11. *Muryōgi* Sutra (T9, 386b).

12. *See* Glossary for these terms.

13. The mountainous region that includes the Pamirs, Tibet, and the plateaus of Mongolia.

14. A large tree with leaves about twenty centimeters long and golden blossoms whose aroma can be smelled from a distance.

15. T9, 21a.

16. T9, 43c.

17. T12, 382c.

18. A rephrasing of a passage in the *Maka Shikan Bugyōden Guketsu* (T46, 252a).

19. T12, 642b.

20. T9, 10a.

21. T9, 6a.

22. T9, 8a.

23. T9, 31b.

24. The *Hokke Gengi* (T33, 713b) reads: "Whether one rejects or accepts [the Buddha's teachings], one should in all cases do so from the standpoint of the Lotus Sutra."

25. The *Hokke Gengi Shakusen* (T33, 866b) reads: "In evaluating the Buddhist sutras, one should judge on the basis of the Lotus Sutra whether to reject or accept them, because the Lotus Sutra is the single source from which all the other teachings come and to which they return."

26. Shan-wu-wei (683–727) and Chin-kang-chih (671–641) were priests from India who introduced the esoteric teachings to China. *See* Glossary under each name.

27. I-hsing (683–727), a disciple of Shan-wu-wei, translated numerous esoteric works and was responsible for compiling his teacher's commentary on the *Dainichi* Sutra. He was famed also as a mathematician and astronomer.

28. This refers apparently to the initiation rituals conducted in esoteric Buddhism in which candidates toss flowers on a mandala depicting various Buddhas, bodhisattvas, and other figures to determine with which figure they have a special relationship. The reference to walking on the head of the figures is unclear.

In the *Selection of the Time* (*Selected Writings of Nichiren*, 225) there is a very similar passage in which Nichiren refers to Shingon mandalas and Zen priests who declare that their teachings represent a great law that steps upon the head of the Buddha. The same passage also alludes to the Great Arrogant Brahman. It should be noted that, whereas Vairocana is the main Buddha in the *Kegon* Sutra and in the esoteric sutras, there are instances in Chinese Buddhist texts in which Vairocana is used to indicate the Law Body of the Buddha, the true body of the Buddha, or Shakyamuni Buddha himself.

29. The story of the Great Arrogant Brahman, based on a notice in the *Daitō Saiiki Ki* (T51, 935c–936a), is described in detail by Nichiren in his *Senji Shō* (Selection of the Time) (*Selected Writings of Nichiren*, 225–226). This Brahman was overly proud of his erudition and boasted that he surpassed all other scholars in his wisdom. However, he was defeated in debate by a Mahayana monk, Bhadraruci, and was sentenced to death. The Arrogant Brahman was spared at Bhadraruci's request, but was so consumed by rancor that he slandered Bhadraruci and as a result fell into hell while still alive.

30. The three deities of Brahmanism are: Makeishara (Skt: Maheśvara), Bichūten (Viṣṇu), and Naraten (Nārāyaṇa).

31. T'an luan (476–542), the founder of the Pure Land school in China, advocated in his *Ōjō Raisan* (T40, no. 1819), calling on the name of Amida Buddha as the "easy to-practice way" that enables all people to attain salvation, and rejected all other practices as the "difficult-to-practice way."

32. Tao-ch'o (562–645), known as the second patriarch of the Pure Land school, in his *Anraku Shū* (T47, 13c) divided Buddhist teachings into those that advocated rebirth in the Pure Land through the invocation of the Nembutsu, and the Sacred Way that required practice in this world through one's own efforts.

33. Shan-tao (613–681) is the third patriarch of the Chinese Pure Land school. In his *Kammuryōjubutsu Kyō Sho* (T37, 272a) he distinguishes between the correct and incorrect practices. Hōnen, the founder of the Pure Land school in Japan, urges people to "discard, close, ignore, and abandon" all other practices other than those of the Pure Land in his *Senchaku Shū* (T83, 2, 17–19).

34. The three basic scriptures of the Pure Land school: the *Amida*, *Muryōju*, and *Kammuryōju* Sutras.

35. T9, 32c.

36. Reference is to a story in the *Han Fei Tzu* in which a farmer, planting his field, saw a rabbit run into a stump and break its neck. He abandoned his farming and stood guard by the stump, expecting to catch other rabbits. Here Nichiren uses the "stump" to signify attachment to the provisional teaching, without being able to distinguish superior and inferior sutras.

37. T9, 31b.

38. Jikaku (794–866), also called Ennin or Jikaku Daishi, was the third chief priest of the Enryaku-ji, the chief temple on Mount Hiei. Chishō (814–891), also called Enchin or Chishō Daishi, was the fifth chief priest of the Enryaku-ji. Nichiren frequently condemns these two priests for having introduced esoteric teachings into the Tendai doctrines.

39. The first quotation, seen previously is from the Nirvana Sutra (T12, 642a); the second is from the Lotus Sutra (T9, 15b).

40. There is no extant sutra by this name. It is possible that Nichiren is referring to

the *Kambutsu Zammaikai* Sutra (T15, no. 643) which tells of a monk who fell into the Avīci Hell for confusing correct and incorrect teachings.

41. The treatise to which Nichiren is referring has not been identified.

42. *See* Glossary for six difficult and nine easy acts.

43. As expounded in the *Fumbetsu Kudoku* (17th) chapter of the Lotus Sutra.

44. As expounded in the *Zuiki Kudoku* (18th) chapter of the Lotus Sutra.

45. The above passage is expanded somewhat for clarity. T'ien-t'ai in the *Maka Shikan* (T46, 1c, 9a, 27a, 42b, 75b) states that "all things having color and fragrance are manifestations of the Middle Way." Miao-lo in his *Shikan Bugyōden Guketsu* (T46, 151c) underscores this by adding that this will "shock and cause doubts."

46. The monastery on Mount Ta-su where T'ien-t'ai studied the Lotus *samadhi* and gained awakening.

47. Twenty principles in which the Lotus Sutra is superior to other teachings. They are described by Miao-lo in the *Hokke Mongu Ki* (T34, 234a).

48. Also called the three properties or three enlightened properties: (1) Law or Dharma body (Jap: *hosshin*; Skt: *dharmakāya*), the body of ultimate reality; (2) the Reward or Bliss body (Jap: *hōjin* or *hōshin*; Skt: *sambhogakāya*), the Buddha body received for meritorious actions; and (3) the Manifested body (Jap: *ōjin*; Skt: *nirmānakāya*), the body in which a Buddha appears to correspond to the needs and capacities of sentient beings.

49. As described in the *Jinriki* (21st) chapter of the Lotus Sutra (T9, 51c).

50. T9, 39c.

51. In the *Yujutsu* (15th) chapter of the Lotus Sutra, declining the offer from the bodhisattvas from other worlds, Shakyamuni says that the *sahā* world already has bodhisattvas who will carry on the task of propagating the Lotus Sutra after the Buddha's death. At this point the earth trembles, and bodhisattvas equal in number to the sands of sixty thousand Ganges Rivers emerge, each with his own retinue of followers. The *Yujutsu* chapter says that these people will embrace, read, recite, and propagate this sutra widely after the Buddha's passing.

52. The translation has been somewhat amplified for clarity. The passages alluded to are in the *Hokke Mongu* (T34, 124c) and the *Hokke Mongu Ki* (T34, 323b). The three reasons for the rejection of bodhisattvas from other worlds are: first, bodhisattvas from other worlds have their own tasks to fulfill in their respective worlds; second, they have little connection with the people in the *sahā* world; third, if Shakyamuni had allowed them to carry out the mission of propagation, he would have had no reason to summon the bodhisattvas of the essential teaching. And unless these bodhisattvas had appeared from beneath the earth, he would neither have cast off his provisional status nor revealed his true identity. The three reasons for the emergence of the bodhisattvas are: first, the Bodhisattvas of the Earth are the Buddha's original disciples; second, they have a deep relationship with the people of the *sahā* world; third, by summoning and entrusting them with the propagation of his teachings, Shakyamuni was able to reveal his original enlightenment which had been achieved in the remote past.

53. T25, 63c.

54. T25, 749b.

55. T9, 10a, 16a. A combination of two passages from the *Hiyu* (3d) chapter of the Lotus Sutra.

56. Hōjō Tokimune (1251–1284), the Hōjō regent to whom Nichiren addressed

his letter warning of the imminent invasion by Mongols. He is referred to here as Hōkōji-dono.

57. Ryōkan (1217–1303) was a prominent priest of the Shingon-Ritsu sect who entered the priesthood at seventeen and received the precepts from Eizon (1202–1290), and is considered the restorer of the Ritsu sect. In 1261 he went to Kamakura where he was named chief priest of Kōsen-ji, founded by a Hōjō regent. Later he was named chief priest of the Gokuraku-ji, founded by Hōjō Shigetoki. Nichiren considered him an archenemy and writes disparagingly of his talents.

58. In actuality, Nichiren returned to Kamakura in the third month, 1274.

59. Hei no Saemon (d. 1293) was an official of the Hōjō regency, known also as Taira no Yoritsuna (by which name he is called here). He served two successive regents, Hōjō Tokimune (1251–1284) and Hōjō Sadatoki (1271–1311) and wielded tremendous influence in political and military affairs as deputy chief (the chief being the Regent himself) of the Office of Police and Military Affairs. He took an active part in persecuting Nichiren and his followers.

60. The fifty-first of the fifty-two stages of bodhisattva practice.

61. Daibonten is Mahābrahman (or Bonten, Brahma). A god said to live in the first of the four meditation heavens in the world of form above Mount Sumeru and to rule the *sahā* world. In Buddhism he was adopted as one of the two tutelary gods, together with Taishaku. Bonten is also the Japanese name for the Brahma Heaven.

62. Quotation not identified.

63. It is unclear as to which sutra Nichiren is referring when he mentions the *Saihō* Sutra; it can be any of four sutras devoted to the Hinayana precepts. The *Shōbōnen* Sutra (full title *Shōbō Nenjo* Sutra (T17, no. 721) details life in the six lower realms of existence.

64. A passage in the *Hōtō* (11th) chapter of the Lotus Sutra reads: "It is difficult to sustain faith in this sutra. One who embraces it only for a short time will delight me and all other Buddhas. . . . Such a person deserves to be called an observer of the precepts and a performer of the *dhuta*, or ascetic, practices."

65. The precept that is impossible to break, like the diamond chalice. It is mentioned in the *Bommō* Sutra (T24, 1003c) and Dengyō interprets the Buddha nature or the true aspect of all phenomena as the diamond chalice. (*Isshin Kongō Kaitai Hiketsu*, DDZ 1, 471).

66. *Hokke Mongu*, T34, 129c.

67. T9, 52c.

68. Reference is to the great earthquake that flattened the Kamakura area in the eighth month of 1257, and the huge comet that appeared in the seventh month of 1264.

69. Emperor Kimmei is now regarded as the twenty-ninth emperor because the administration of the fifteenth ruler, Empress Jingu, is no longer considered a formal reign. In Nichiren's time, however, she was included in the lineage, thus accounting for the designation of Emperor Kimmei as the thirtieth emperor.

70. An imaginary plant said to bloom once every three thousand years to herald the advent of a Buddha or a gold-wheel-turning king, who was said to rule all the four continents surrounding Mount Sumeru.

71. The second half of the *Yujutsu* (15th), the *Juryō* (16th), and the first half of the *Fumbetsu Kudoku* (17th) chapters of the Lotus Sutra. Here the reference is specifically to the *Juryō* chapter. In a formulation attributed to the fourth-century monk Tao-an,

a sutra is divided into three sections: preparation (introductory remarks), revelation (main subject), and transmission (setting forth of benefits and urging transmission to posterity).

72. One of the ten major prohibitions, together with twenty-eight lesser rules of conduct, described in the *Bommō* Sutra (T24, 1004a).

73. An honorific title meaning "teacher," given to a monk of virtue who guides the conduct of other disciples and serves as an example to them.

7 ON PERSECUTIONS BEFALLING THE SAGE

This letter to his parishioners in general, dated the first day of the tenth month, 1279, was composed at Minobu, where Nichiren had retired after leaving Kamakura. Nichiren speaks of the twenty-seven years of persecution he had endured until he gained the ultimate goal of his teachings, and compares them with the sufferings that Shakyamuni and his predecessors had undergone.

The letter makes special reference to the persecutions at Atsuhara, a village in the Fuji district of Suruga Province. Here, priests associated with a local temple antagonistic to Nichiren's teachings, aligning themselves with officials in Kamakura, persecuted a group of Nichiren's followers, with the result that several lost their lives. Apparently Sammi-bō, a promising disciple who had defected, lost his life in the altercations that took place at Atsuhara.

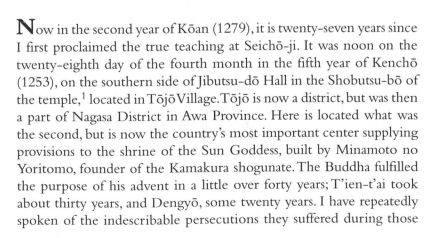

Now in the second year of Kōan (1279), it is twenty-seven years since I first proclaimed the true teaching at Seichō-ji. It was noon on the twenty-eighth day of the fourth month in the fifth year of Kenchō (1253), on the southern side of Jibutsu-dō Hall in the Shobutsu-bō of the temple,[1] located in Tōjō Village. Tōjō is now a district, but was then a part of Nagasa District in Awa Province. Here is located what was the second, but is now the country's most important center supplying provisions to the shrine of the Sun Goddess, built by Minamoto no Yoritomo, founder of the Kamakura shogunate. The Buddha fulfilled the purpose of his advent in a little over forty years; T'ien-t'ai took about thirty years, and Dengyō, some twenty years. I have repeatedly spoken of the indescribable persecutions they suffered during those years. For me it took twenty-seven years, and the persecutions I faced during this peiod are well known to you all.

The Lotus Sutra reads, "Since hatred and jealousy abound even during the lifetime of the Buddha, how much worse will it be in the world after his passing?"[2] Shakyamuni Buddha suffered innumerable persecutions: For ninety days he was forced to eat horse fodder; a huge boulder was dropped on him, and though it missed him, his foot was injured and bled; a group of eight priests led by Sunakṣatra,[3] outwardly acting as the Buddha's disciples but in spirit siding with Brahmans, watched every moment of the day and night for a chance to kill him; King Virūḍhaka[4] killed great numbers of the Shakya clan; King Ajātaśatru[5] had many of Shakyamuni's disciples trampled to death by wild elephants and subjected the Buddha to a series of severe tribulations. Such were the persecutions that took place "in the Buddha's lifetime."

In the more than two thousand years "after his passing," no one, not even Nāgārjuna, Vasubandhu, T'ien-t'ai, or Dengyō, encountered any of the still greater persecutions predicted to occur. No one can say they were not votaries of the Lotus Sutra, but if they were, why did none shed even a drop of blood, as did the Buddha, nor suffer even greater trials? Could the sutra's predictions be false and the Buddha's teachings nothing but great lies?

However, in these twenty-seven years, Nichiren was exiled to the province of Izu on the twelfth day of the fifth month in the first year of Kōchō (1261), was wounded on the forehead and had his left hand broken on the eleventh day of the eleventh month in the first year of Bun'ei (1264).[6] He was to be executed on the twelfth day of the ninth month in the eighth year of Bun'ei (1271), but was instead exiled to the province of Sado. In addition, many of his disciples were murdered or executed, banished, or heavily fined. I do not know whether these trials equal or surpass those of the Buddha. Nāgārjuna, Vasubandhu, T'ien-t'ai, and Dengyō came nowhere near me in what they endured. Had it not been for the advent of Nichiren in the Latter Day of the Law, the Buddha would have been a great liar and the testimony given by Tahō and all the other Buddhas would have been false. In the twenty-two hundred and thirty years since the Buddha's death, Nichiren is the only person in the whole world to fulfill the Buddha's prophecy.

In the Latter Day of the Law of both Shakyamuni and the Buddhas before him, the rulers and people who despised the votaries of the

Lotus Sutra seemed to be free from punishment at first, but eventually they were all doomed to fall. Among those who attacked Nichiren, there were at first no signs of punishment. During these twenty-seven years, the Buddhist gods who vowed to protect the votary of the Lotus Sutra—Bonten, Taishaku, the gods of the sun and moon, and the Four Heavenly Kings—did little to help Nichiren. But by now they have realized in terror that unless they fulfill the oath they swore before the Buddha, they will fall into the hell of incessant suffering. Consequently they are now earnestly carrying out their vow by punishing those who attacked the votary of the Lotus Sutra. The deaths of Ōta Chikamasa, Nagasaki Tokitsuna, and Daishin-bō,[7] for example, who were all thrown from their horses, can be seen as punishment for their treachery against the Lotus Sutra. There are four kinds of punishment: general and individual, patent and covert. The massive epidemics, nationwide famines, insurrections and foreign invasion suffered by Japan are general punishment. Epidemics are a form of covert punishment. The deaths of Ōta and the others are both patent and individual.

Each of you should summon up the courage of a lion and never succumb to threats from anyone. The lion fears no other beast, nor do its cubs. Slanderers are like howling jackals, but Nichiren's followers are like roaring lions. Hōjō Tokiyori and Hōjō Tokimune, the past and present regents, pardoned me when they found I was innocent of the accusations against me. The regent will no longer take action on any charge without confirming its validity. You may rest assured that nothing, not even a person possessed by a powerful demon, can harm Nichiren, because Bonten, Taishaku, the gods of the sun and moon, the Four Heavenly Kings, Tenshō Daijin and Hachiman are safeguarding him. Strengthen your faith day by day and month after month. Should you slacken even a bit, demons will take advantage.

We common mortals are so foolish that we do not fear the warnings in the sutras or treatises so long as they do not concern us directly. But you must be fully prepared for the havoc Hei no Saemon and Adachi Yasumori,[8] in their outrage, will wreak upon us. People are now being sent to Tsukushi[9] to fight the Mongols; consider yourself in the same position as those who are on their way or who are already at the battlefield. So far our believers have not experienced anything so terrible. The warriors in Tsukushi, however, now face a dreadful fate, and if they are killed in battle, they will be doomed to fall into hell. Even if we too should meet such severe trials, we will attain

Buddhahood in the future. Our present tribulations are like moxa cautery, minor pain necessary to remove greater pain.

You need not frighten those peasant believers from Atsuhara, but you should encourage them in every way possible. Tell them to be prepared for the worst. Do not expect good times, but take the bad times for granted. If they complain of hunger, tell them about the hell of starvation. If they grumble that they are cold, tell them of the eight freezing hells. If they say they are frightened, explain to them that a pheasant sighted by a hawk, or a mouse stalked by a cat, is as desperate as they are. I have repeated the foregoing almost daily for the past twenty-seven years. Yet with Nagoe no Ama, Shōfu-bō, Noto-bō, Sammi-bō,[10] and others, who are so cowardly, closed-minded, greedy, and filled with doubt, my words have no more effect than water poured over lacquerware or an attempt to slice up the air.

There was something very strange about Sammi-bō. However, I was afraid that any admonition would be taken by the ignorant as mere jealousy of his wisdom, and therefore I refrained from speaking out. In time his wicked ambition led to treachery, and finally to his doom during the Atsuhara Persecution. If I had scolded him more strictly, he might have been saved. I did not mention this before because no one could understand it. Even now the ignorant will say that I am speaking ill of the deceased. Nevertheless, I mention this for the benefit of other believers. I am sure that those who persecuted the believers at Atsuhara were frightened by the fate of Sammi-bō.

Even if others take up arms and make troubles, my disciples should never do the same. If there are any who do, please write to me immediately.

With my deep respect,

Nichiren

The first day of the tenth month
This letter should be kept by Shijō Kingo.

Notes

1. Buildings in the compound of Seichō-ji, the temple where Nichiren first proclaimed his teachings. Jibutsu-dō was the main hall where the object of worship was enshrined. Shobutsu-bō was the priest's lodging quarters.

2. T9, 31b.

3. Sunakṣatra was a monk who devoted himself to Buddhist austerities and attained a limited form of enlightenment. He later discarded his faith in Buddhism and fell into hell while alive. Nirvana Sutra (T12, 560b).

4. The story of King Virūḍhaka appears in *Binaya Zōji* (T24, 240a).

5. Ajātaśatru was a king of Magadha who was converted to Buddhism by Shakyamuni. His story appears in the Nirvana Sutra (T12, 480b-c) and elsewhere.

6. This was the date of the Komatsubara persecution, the day when Nichiren barely escaped execution before his exile to Sado.

7. Once followers of Nichiren, they renounced their faith and plotted against other believers during the Atsuhara persecution.

8. Hei no Saemon (d.1293) was an official in the Hōjō regency who was Nichiren's archenemy. Here Nichiren refers to him as Heira, meaning Hei no Saemon and his entire family. Adachi Yasumori (1231–1285) was the leader of an influential clan under the Hōjō regency who vied with Hei no Saemon for power. Nichiren refers to him here as Jōra, meaning the position as head of the Akita castle (*jō*) and his family. The Akita family had succeeded to the title "Akita Jōsuke" in 1218.

9. The ancient name for Kyushu.

10. These are all disciples who renounced their faith.

8 THE FOUR DEBTS OF GRATITUDE

This letter was written by Nichiren on the sixteenth day of the first month in 1262 from Itō on the Izu Peninsula. It is addressed to Kudō Sakan no jō Yoshitaka (d.1264), known also as Kudō Yoshitaka, the lord of Amatsu in Awa Province. Kudō is said to have been converted to Nichiren's teachings around 1256, about the same time that Shijō Kingo and Ikegami Munenaka became followers. Kudō was killed defending his teacher at the time of the Komatsubara persecution when Nichiren barely managed to avoid execution. This is the only letter still extant that Nichiren addressed to Kudō·

The alternative title for this letter is *Izu Gokanki Shō* (The Izu Dishonor).

Concerning my present exile,[1] there are two important matters that I must mention. One is that I feel immense joy. As for the reason, this world is called the *sahā* world, *sahā* meaning "endurance." This is why the Buddha [who appears in this world] is also called Nōnin, "He Who Can Forbear." In the *sahā* world system, there are ten million Mount Sumerus, ten million suns and moons, and ten million groups of four continents. Among all these worlds, it was in the world at the center—with its Mount Sumeru, sun and moon, and four continents—that the Buddha made his advent. This country of Japan is an islet situated in a remote corner to the northeast of the country in which the Buddha appeared. Since all the lands in the ten directions, with the exception of those in the *sahā* world system, are pure lands, their people, being gentlehearted, neither abuse nor hate the worthies and sages. In contrast, this world is inhabited by people who were rejected from the pure lands in the ten directions. They have committed the ten evil acts[2]

or the five cardinal sins, slandered the worthies and sages, and been unfilial to their fathers and mothers or disrespectful to the priests. For these offenses they fell into the three evil paths, and only after dwelling there for countless kalpas were they reborn in this world. Yet the residue of the evil karma formed in their previous existences has not yet been eradicated, and they still tend to perpetrate the ten evil acts or the five cardinal sins, to revile the worthies and sages, and to be undutiful to their fathers and mothers or irreverent toward the priests.

For these reasons, when Shakyamuni Buddha made his advent in this world, some people offered him food into which they had mixed poison. Others tried to harm him by means of swords and staves, mad elephants, lions, fierce bulls or savage dogs. Still others charged him with violating women, condemned him as a man of lowly status, or accused him of killing. Again, some, when they encountered him, covered their eyes to avoid seeing him, and others closed their doors and shuttered their windows. Still others reported to the kings and ministers that he held erroneous views and was given to slandering exalted personages. These incidents are described in the *Daijuku* Sutra, the Nirvana Sutra and other scriptures. The Buddha was innocent of all such evil deeds. Yet this world is peculiar or deficient in that those with bad karma are born into it and inhabit it in great numbers. Moreover, the Devil of the Sixth Heaven,[3] scheming to prevent the people of this world from going to the pure lands elsewhere, seizes every opportunity to carry out his perverse acts.

It appears that his scheming is ultimately intended to prevent the Buddha from expounding the Lotus Sutra. The reason is that the nature of this devil king is to rejoice at those who create the karma of the three evil paths and to grieve at those who form the karma of the three good paths.[4] He does not lament so greatly over those who form the karma of the three good paths, but he sorrows indeed at those who aspire to the three vehicles.[5] Again, he may not sorrow that much over those who seek to attain the three vehicles, but he grieves bitterly at those who form the karma to become Buddhas, and avails himself of every opportunity to obstruct them. He knows that those who hear even a single sentence or phrase of the Lotus Sutra will attain Buddhahood without fail, and, exceedingly distressed by this, contrives various plots and restrains and persecutes believers, in an attempt to make them abandon their faith.

Although the age in which the Buddha lived was certainly a defiled one, the five impurities[6] had only just begun to manifest themselves, and, in addition, the devil stood in awe of the Buddha's powers. Yet even in a time when the people's greed, anger, stupidity and false views were still not rampant, a group of Brahmans of the Bamboo Staff school killed the Venerable Maudgalyāyana, who was known as the foremost in occult powers; and King Ajātaśatru, by releasing a mad elephant, threatened the life of him who alone in all the threefold world is worthy of honor. Devadatta killed the nun Utpalavarṇā, who had attained the state of arhat; and the Venerable Kokālika spread evil rumors about Śāriputra, who was renowned for his unsurpassed wisdom.[7] How much worse matters became in the world as the five impurities steadily increased! And now, in the latter age, there will be all the more tremendous hatred and jealousy toward those who believe even slightly in the Lotus Sutra! Thus the Lotus Sutra states, "Since hatred and jealousy abound even during the lifetime of the Buddha, how much worse will it be in the world after his passing!"[8] When I read this passage for the first time, I did not think that the situation would be as bad as it predicts. Now I am struck by the unfailing accuracy of the Buddha's words, especially in light of my present circumstances.

I, Nichiren, do not observe the precepts with my body. Nor is my heart free from the three poisons.[9] But since I myself believe in the Lotus Sutra and also enable others to form a relationship with it, I had thought that perhaps society would treat me rather gently. Probably because the world has entered into the latter age, even monks who have a wife and children have followers, as do priests who eat fish and fowl. I, Nichiren, have neither wife nor children, nor do I eat fish or fowl. I have been blamed merely for trying to propagate the Lotus Sutra. Though I have neither wife nor child, I am known throughout the country as a monk who transgresses the code of conduct, and though I have never killed even a single ant or mole cricket, my bad reputation has spread throughout the realm. This may well resemble the situation of Shakyamuni Buddha, who was slandered by a multitude of Brahmans during his lifetime. It seems that, solely because my faith in the Lotus Sutra accords slightly more with its teachings than does the faith of others, evil demons must have entered their bodies and be causing them to feel hatred toward me. I am nothing but a lowly and ignorant monk without precepts. Yet, when I think that such a person should be mentioned in the Lotus Sutra, which was expounded more than two thousand years ago, and that the Buddha prophesied that that person would encounter persecution, I cannot possibly express my joy.

It is already twenty-four or twenty-five years since I began studying Buddhism. Yet, as for the Lotus Sutra, I have believed in it wholeheartedly only for the past six or seven years. Moreover, although I had faith in the sutra, because I was negligent, and because of my studies and the interruptions of mundane affairs, each day I would recite only a single scroll, a chapter or the title. Now, however, for a period of more than 240 days—from the twelfth day of the fifth month of last year to the sixteenth day of the first month of this year—I think I have practiced the Lotus Sutra twenty-four hours each day and night. I say so because, having been exiled on the Lotus Sutra's account, I now read and practice it continuously, whether I am walking, standing, sitting or lying down. For anyone born human, what greater joy could there be?

It is the way of common mortals that, even though they spur themselves on to arouse the aspiration for enlightenment and wish for happiness in the next life, they exert themselves no more than one or two out of all the hours of the day, and this only after reminding themselves to do so. As for myself, I read the Lotus Sutra without having to remember to, and practice it even when I do not read its words aloud. During the course of countless kalpas, while transmigrating through the six paths and the four forms of birth,[10] I may at times have risen in revolt, committed theft or broken into others' homes at night, and, on account of these offenses, been convicted by the ruler and condemned to exile or death. This time, however, it is because I am so firmly resolved to propagate the Lotus Sutra that people with evil karma have brought false charges against me; hence my exile. Surely this will work in my favor in future lifetimes. In this latter age, there cannot be anyone else who upholds the Lotus Sutra twenty-four hours of the day and night without making a conscious effort to do so.

There is one other thing for which I am most grateful. While transmigrating in the six paths for the duration of countless kalpas, I may have encountered a number of sovereigns and become their favorite minister or regent. If so, I must have been granted fiefs and accorded treasures and stipends. Never once, however, did I encounter a sovereign in whose country the Lotus Sutra had spread, so that I could hear its name, practice it, and, on that very account, be slandered by other people and have the ruler send me into exile. The Lotus Sutra states, "As for this Lotus Sutra, throughout countless numbers of countries one cannot even hear the name of it, let alone behold it, receive and keep it or read and recite it!"[11] Thus those people who slandered me and the ruler [who had me banished] are the very persons to whom I owe the most profound debt of gratitude.

One who studies the teachings of Buddhism must not fail to repay the four debts of gratitude. According to the *Shinjikan* Sutra,[12] the first of the four debts is that owed to all living beings. Were it not for them, one would find it impossible to make the vow to save innumerable living beings. Moreover, but for the evil people who persecute bodhisattvas, how could those bodhisattvas accumulate benefit?

The second of the four debts is that owed to one's father and mother. To be born into the six paths one must have parents. If one is born into the family of a murderer, a thief, a violator of the rules of proper conduct or a slanderer of the Law, then even though he may not commit these offenses himself, he in effect forms the same karma as the persons who do. As for my parents in this lifetime, however, they not only gave me birth, but made me a believer in the Lotus Sutra as well. Thus I owe my present father and mother a debt far greater than I would had I been born into the family of Bonten, Taishaku, one of the Four Heavenly Kings or a wheel-turning king,[13] and so inherited the threefold world or the four continents, and been revered by the four kinds of believers[14] in the worlds of Humanity and Heaven.

The third is the debt owed to one's sovereign. It is thanks to one's sovereign that one is able to warm his body in the three kinds of heavenly light[15] and sustain his life with the five kinds of grain[16] that grow on earth. Moreover, in this lifetime, I have been able to take faith in the Lotus Sutra and to encounter a ruler who will enable me to free myself in my present existence from the sufferings of birth and death. Thus how can I dwell on the insignificant harm that he has done me and overlook my debt to him?

The fourth is the debt owed to the Three Treasures. When Shakyamuni Buddha was engaged in bodhisattva practices for countless kalpas, he accumulated all manner of good fortune and virtue in himself. This he divided into sixty-four parts, of which he reserved only one part for himself. The remaining sixty-three parts he left behind in this world, making a vow as follows:[17] "There will be an age when the five impurities will become rampant, heresies will flourish, and slanderers will fill the land. At that time, because the innumerable benevolent guardian deities will be unable to taste the flavor of the Dharma, their majesty and strength will diminish. The sun and the moon will lose their brightness, the heavenly dragons will not send down rain, and the earthly deities will decrease the fertility of the soil.

The roots and stalks, branches and leaves, flowers and fruit will all lose their medicinal properties as well as the seven flavors.[18] Even kings who have observed the ten good precepts[19] will grow in greed, anger and stupidity. The people will cease to be dutiful to their parents, and the six kinds of relatives[20] will fall out with one another. My disciples will consist of unlearned people without precepts. For this reason, even though they shave their heads, they will be forsaken by the tutelary deities and left without any means of subsistence. It is in order to sustain these monks and nuns [that I now leave these sixty-three parts behind]."

Moreover, as for the benefits that the Buddha had attained as a result of his practices, he divided them into three parts, of which he himself expended only two. For this reason, although he was to have lived in this world until the age of 120, he passed away after 80 years, bequeathing the remaining 40 years of his life span to us.[21]

Even if we should gather all the water of the four great oceans[22] to wet inkstones, burn all the trees and plants to cinders to make ink, collect the hairs of all beasts for writing brushes, employ all the surfaces of the worlds in the ten directions for paper, and, with these, set down expressions of gratitude, how could we possibly repay our debt to the Buddha?

Concerning the debt owed to the Law, the Law is the teacher of all Buddhas. It is because of the Law that the Buddhas are worthy of respect. Therefore, one who wishes to repay his debt to the Buddha must first repay the debt he owes to the Law.

As for the debt owed to the Priesthood, both the treasure of the Buddha and the treasure of the Law are invariably perpetuated by priests. To illustrate, without firewood, there can be no fire, and if there is no earth, trees and plants cannot grow. Likewise, even though Buddhism existed, without the priests who studied it and passed it on, it would never have been transmitted throughout the two thousand years of the Former and Middle Days into the Latter Day of the Law. Therefore the *Daijuku* Sutra states, "Suppose that, in the fifth five-hundred-year period, there should be someone who harasses unlearned monks without precepts by accusing them of some offense. You should know that this person is extinguishing the great torch of Buddhism."[23] Difficult to recompense indeed is the debt we owe to the Priesthood!

Thus it is imperative that one repay one's debt of gratitude to the Three Treasures. In ancient times, there were sages such as Sessen Dōji, Bodhisattva Jōtai, Bodhisattva Yakuō, and King Fumyō,[24] all of whom [offered their lives in order to make such repayment]. The first offered himself as food to a demon. The second sold his own blood and marrow. The third burned his arms, and the fourth was ready to part with his head. Common mortals in the Latter Day, however, though receiving the benefits of the Three Treasures, completely neglect to repay them. How, then, can they attain the Buddha Way? The *Shinjikan*, *Bommō* and other sutras state that those who study Buddhism and receive the precepts of perfect and immediate enlightenment must repay the four debts of gratitude without fail. I am but an ignorant common mortal made of flesh and blood; I have not rid myself of even a fraction of the three categories of illusion.[25] Yet, for the sake of the Lotus Sutra, I have been reviled, slandered, attacked with swords and staves, and sent into exile. In light of these persecutions, I believe I may be likened to the great sages who burned their arms, crushed their marrow, or did not begrudge being beheaded. This is why I feel immense joy.

The second of the two important matters is that I feel intense grief. The fourth volume of the Lotus Sutra states, "If there is an evil person who, with unwholesome thought, shall appear before the Buddha and for an entire kalpa constantly malign him, his offense will be comparatively light. But if there is a person who, with a single malicious word, shall denigrate the monks or laity who read and recite the Lotus Sutra, his offense will be very grave."[26] When I read this and similar passages, my belief is aroused, sweat breaks out from my body, and tears fall from my eyes like rain. I grieve that, by being born in this country, I have caused so many of its people to create the worst karma possible in a lifetime. Those who struck Bodhisattva Fukyō came to repent of it while they were alive; yet even so, their offense was so difficult to expiate that they fell into the Avīci Hell and remained there for a thousand kalpas. But those who have done me harm have not yet repented of it even in the slightest.

Describing the karmic retribution which such people must receive, the *Daijuku* Sutra states, "[The Buddha asked,]'If there should be a person who draws blood from the bodies of a thousand, ten thousand, or a hundred thousand Buddhas, in your thinking, how is it? Will he have committed a grave sin or not?' King Bonten replied, 'If a person causes the body of even a single Buddha to bleed, he will have committed an offense so serious that he will fall into the hell of incessant suffering. His sin will be unfathomably grave, and he will have to remain in the great Avīci Hell for so many kalpas that their number cannot be calculated even by means of counting sticks. Graver still is the offense a person would commit by causing the bodies of ten thousand or a hundred thousand Buddhas to bleed. No one could possibly explain in full either that person's offense or its karmic retribution—no one, that is, except the Buddha himself.' The Buddha said, 'King Bonten, suppose there should be a person who, for my sake, takes the tonsure and wears a surplice. Even though he has not at any time received the precepts and therefore observes none, if someone harasses him, abuses him, or strikes him with a staff, then that persecutor's offense will be even graver than that [of injuring a hundred thousand Buddhas].' "[27]

Nichiren

The sixteenth day of the first month in the second year of Kōchō (1262), cyclical sign mizunoe-inu.

Notes

1. Reference is to Nichiren's exile to the Izu Peninsula, from the tenth day of the fifth month, 1261, to the second day of the second month, 1263.

2. Described in the *Kusha Ron* (T29, 25a–b) they are: killing, stealing, unlawful sexual intercourse, lying, flattery (or random and irresponsible speech), defaming, duplicity, greed, anger, and stupidity, or the holding of mistaken views.

3. The Devil of the Sixth Heaven (Jap: *Dairokuten no Maō*) is Takejizaiten, who resides in the sixth of the six heavens of the world of desire. He works to obstruct Buddhist practice and delights in sapping the life force of other beings. He is described in *Daichido Ron* (T25, 1223a).

4. The three good paths are the realms of Asura, Humanity, and Heaven, areas where beings can influence their own karma. The three evil paths are the realms of hell, hungry ghosts, and animals. *See also* Ten Worlds in Glossary.

5. The worlds of *shōmon*, *engaku*, and bodhisattva.

6. The five impurities or defilements (Jap: *gojoku*) are listed in the *Hōben* (2d) chapter of the Lotus Sutra (T9, 7b). They are: impurities of the age (kalpa), of desire, of the people, of thought, and of life itself.

7. All the above enemies of Shakymuni Buddha are frequently referred to by Nichiren throughout his writings. The story about Maudgalyāyana appears in the *Binaya Zōji* (T24, 287c); the story of Ajātaśatru (Nirvana Sutra, T12, 457b) is included as one of the nine ordeals suffered by Shakyamuni; Utpalavarṇā, a nun said to have attained the state of arhat, was beaten to death by Devadatta when she reproached him for his evil deeds (*Daichido Ron* T25, 165a); Kokālika is said to have falsely accused

Śāriputra and Maudgalyāyana of great evil acts and to have fallen into hell for his slander. (Nirvana Sutra, T12, 560b). The above stories are found in several works; the precise source Nichiren used often cannot be identified.

8. T9, 31b.

9. The three poisons (Jap: *sandoku*) are greed, anger, and stupidity.

10. Birth from the womb (mammals), from eggs (birds), from moisture (the supposed method of generation of worms), and by transformation (deities and beings in the various hells, who are reborn spontaneously because of their karma).

11. T9, 38c.

12. T3, 297a.

13. Brahma, Indra, the lords of the four quarters, and the four kings who rule the world by turning the wheel of the Law. These wheels are of four kinds: gold, silver, copper, and iron. The gold-wheel-turning king rules the lands in all directions; the silver-wheel-turning king the eastern, western, and southern lands; the copper-wheel-turning king, the eastern and southern lands; and the iron-wheel-turning king, the southern land. They are described in the *Kusha Ron* (T29, 64b-c).

14. Monks, nuns, laymen, and laywomen.

15. The light of the sun, moon, and stars.

16. A general term for all grains; specifically wheat, rice, beans, and two types of millet.

17. The division of good fortune and virtue is described in the *Daijuku* Sutra (T13, 333a). The following quotation is a summary of passages from this sutra.

18. The seven flavors are: sweet, pungent, sour, bitter, salty, astringent, and subtle.

19. The ten good precepts are precepts for lay believers of Mahayana. They are prohibitions against the ten evils described in note 2. One was said to be born a king as a result of the good fortune accumulated by keeping the ten good precepts in prior lives.

20. The six kinds of relatives are: father, mother, elder brother, younger brother, wife, and son or daughter. Another classification gives father, son or daughter, elder brother, younger brother, husband, and wife.

21. The source of this statement has not been traced; presumably it is based on a passage in the *Daijuku* Sutra.

22. The seas surrounding the four continents to the east, west, north and south of Mount Sumeru.

23. Not a direct quotation. Presumably based on a passage in the *Daijuku* Sutra (T13, 363b).

24. Sessen Dōji was the name under which Shakyamuni, in a past life, practiced the bodhisattva way. He met a demon in the Himalaya who recited the first half of a four-line verse. Sessen Dōji was prepared to sacrifice his life to the demon in order to hear the second part of the verse (Nirvana Sutra, T12, 450a). The Bodhisattva Jōtai sought the teaching of the perfection of wisdom from Bodhisattva Dommukatsu. Having nothing to offer him, Jōtai attempted to sell himself to obtain money for alms. The god Taishaku, determined to test his resolve, assumed the form of a Brahman and told Jōtai that he needed a heart, human blood, and marrow in order to perform a certain ritual. Jōtai agreed to provide them and voluntarily drew blood from his arm with a knife. Just as he was about to cut his thigh to obtain marrow, the daughter of a wealthy householder offered to provide for what he might need. Taishaku then assumed his

true form and praised Jōtai for his devotion (*Daibon Hannya* Sutra, T6, 1059c; *Daichido Ron*, T25, 732a). The story of Yakuō appears in the *Yakuō* (23d) chapter of the Lotus Sutra. Fumyō was the name of Shakyamuni in a past existence when he was a king engaged in the *pāramitā* of observing the precepts. He and ninety-nine other kings were captured by King Rokusoku and were about to be beheaded. Fumyō asked Rokusoku to first let him carry out a promise he had made to give offerings to a certain monk. Rokusoku granted him seven days' grace to fulfill his promise, and Fumyō returned to his own country, where he gave the monk offerings and transferred the throne to his son. After proclaiming to his people that keeping one's promise is the most important precept, he returned to King Rokusoku; the latter was so impressed by Fumyō's sincerity that he released him and the other kings and converted to Buddhism. *Kengu* Sutra (T4, 406a); *Daichido Ron* (T25, 88c–89a).

25. The three categories of illusion (Jap: *sanwaku*) are: (1) illusions of thought and desire possessed by persons in the six paths; (2) illusions preventing bodhisattvas from saving others; and (3) the forty-two illusions that prevent bodhisattvas from attaining enlightenment. They are described in *Maka Shikan* (T46, 37c).

26. T9, 31a.

27. T13, 359b.

9 THE TRIPITAKA MASTER
SHAN-WU-WEI

Nichiren wrote this letter from his residence in Matsubagayatsu in Kamakura to Jōken-bō and Gijō-bō, two priests who had been his seniors at the Seichō-ji in Awa, where he had first entered Buddhism. The letter was written at some time in the year 1270; the precise month and day are not known. The motivation for this letter is not quite clear. The Seichō-ji was originally a temple of the Tendai sect, but later had fallen under Shingon and Pure Land influences. The head priest of the temple, Dōzen-bō, had been Nichiren's original teacher, one to whom he felt a sincere obligation. It is possible that because Dōzen-bō had begun to embrace the Lotus teachings, Nichiren wished to express his gratitude.

The title of the letter,"The Tripitaka Master Shan-wu-wei" is accounted for by the lengthy discussion of the activities of this esoteric Buddhist master. Shan-wu-wei (Skt: Śubhākarasimha; Jap: Zemmui, 637–735), born as a prince in India, introduced the esoteric teachings to China. He arrived in 716 and engaged in the translation of a large number of sutras.

An alternative title for this letter is *Shion Hōshū Shō* (On Fulfilling Obligations to My Teacher).

The Lotus Sutra is the heart and core of the teachings expounded by Shakyamuni Buddha during the course of his lifetime, the foundation of all the eighty thousand doctrines[1] of Buddhism. The various exoteric and esoteric sutras such as the *Dainichi*, the *Kegon*, the *Hannya*, and the *Jimmitsu* sutras spread in China, India, the palaces of the dragon kings, and the heavens above. In addition, there exist the teachings expounded by the various Buddhas throughout the lands of the ten directions, which are as numerous as the sands of the Ganges. Even if one were to use all the water of the oceans to mix his ink and fashion all the trees and bushes of the major world system into writing brushes, he could never finish writing them all. Yet when I examine them and weigh their contents, I see that among all these sutras, the Lotus Sutra occupies the highest place.

Nevertheless, among the various schools of India and in Buddhist circles in Japan, there were many scholars and teachers who failed to understand the Buddha's true intention. Some of them declared that the *Dainichi* Sutra is superior to the Lotus Sutra. Others said that the Lotus Sutra is inferior not only to the *Dainichi* Sutra but to the *Kegon* Sutra as well, or that the Lotus Sutra is inferior to the Nirvana, *Hannya*, and *Jimmitsu* sutras. Still others maintained that the sutras each have their distinctive character, and therefore possess various superior or inferior aspects. Some said that the worth of a particular sutra depends upon whether or not it accords with the capacities of the people; sutras that fit the capacities of the people of the time are superior, while those that do not are inferior.[2] Similarly, some persons claimed that if people had the capacity to gain enlightenment through the teaching that phenomena have real existence, then one should condemn the teaching that phenomena are without substance, praising only the teaching that phenomena actually exist.[3] And the same principle, they said, should be applied to all other situations.

Because no one among the people of the time refuted such doctrines, the rulers and leaders of the various states, ignorant as they were, began to put great faith in them, donating cultivated fields for the support of those who taught them, until their followers grew to be numerous. And as time passed, because such doctrines had been prevalent for an extended period, people came to be firmly convinced that they were correct teachings and no longer even dreamed of questioning them.

But then, with the arrival of the latter age, there appeared one wiser than the scholars and teachers whom the people of the time had followed.[4] He began to question one by one the doctrines upheld by the early scholars and teachers and to criticize them, pointing out that they differed from the sutras on which they were based, or clarifying solely in the light of the various sutras that, in formulating their doctrines, the scholars and teachers had failed to distinguish which sutras had been preached early in the Buddha's teaching life and which later, and which were shallow and which profound. Thus attacked, the adherents of these doctrines found themselves unable to defend the erroneous teachings of the founders of their various sects, and were at a loss how to answer. Some in their doubt declared that the scholars and teachers whom they followed must surely have had their passages of proof in the sutras and treatises to support such doctrines, but that they themselves, lacking the requisite wisdom, could not defend these doctrines effectively. Others, likewise doubtful, decided that, while their masters had been wise men and sages of high antiquity, they themselves were ignorant men of the latter age. In this way, they convinced virtuous and high-placed men to ally with them and totally opposed the one who challenged their beliefs.

But I have discarded prejudice—whether against the opinions of others or in favor of my own—and set aside the views propounded by the scholars and teachers. Instead, relying solely on the passages of the sutras themselves, I have come to understand that the Lotus Sutra deserves to occupy first place. If there are persons who assert that some other sutra surpasses the Lotus Sutra, we must suppose it is for one or another of the following reasons. First, they may have been deceived by passages in other scriptures that resemble those of the Lotus Sutra.[5] Or they may have been deceived by spurious sutras that have been fabricated by men of later times and passed off as the words of the Buddha. Lacking the wisdom to distinguish true from false, they may have consequently accepted such texts as the Buddha's actual words. Beginning with Hui-neng[6] and his Platform Sutra or Shan-tao[7] and his *Kannen Hōmon* Sutra, there have been numerous false teachers in India, China, and Japan who have simply made up their own "sutras" and preached them to the world. In addition, there are many others who have made up what they claim to be scriptural passages, or who have interpolated their own words into passages of the scriptures.

Unfortunately, there are ignorant people who accept these spurious texts as genuine. They are like sightless persons who, if told that there are stars in the sky that shine more brightly than the sun or moon, will accept that assertion as fact. When someone says that his own teacher was a worthy man or sage of high antiquity while Nichiren is a mere foolish man of the latter age, ignorant persons will tend to agree.

This is by no means the first time that doubts of this kind have been raised. In the time of the Ch'en and Sui dynasties (557–617) in China there was a lowly priest called Chih-i, who later became the teacher of the emperors of two dynasties and was honored with the title of the Great Teacher T'ien-t'ai Chih-che.[8] Before he rose to honor, this man not only refuted the doctrines of the various learned doctors and teachers who had lived in China in the preceding five hundred years or more, but he also refuted those of the scholars who had taught in India over the course of a thousand years. As a result, the wise men of northern and southern China rose up like clouds in opposition, while the worthy men and sages from east and west came forth like ranks of stars. Criticisms fell on him like rain, while his doctrines were attacked as though by strong winds. Yet in the end he succeeded in refuting the one-sided and erroneous doctrines of the scholars and teachers, and established the correct doctrines of the T'ien-t'ai school.

Likewise, in Japan during the reign of Emperor Kammu there was a humble priest named Saichō, who later was honored with the title of the Great Teacher Dengyō. He refuted the doctrines that had been taught by the Buddhist teachers of the various sects in Japan during the two hundred and some years following [the introduction of Buddhism in] the reign of Emperor Kimmei. At first people were infuriated with him, but later they all joined in becoming his disciples.

These people had criticized T'ien-t'ai and Dengyō by saying, "The founders of our sects were scholars of the four ranks of saints,[9] worthy men and sages of high antiquity, while you are no more than an ordinary, foolish man of the end of the Middle Day of the Law!" The question, however, is not whether a person lives in the Former, the Middle or the Latter Day of the Law, but whether he bases himself upon the text of the true sutra. Again, the point is not who preaches a doctrine, but whether it accords with truth.

The believers of Brahmanism criticized the Buddha, saying, "You are a foolish man living at the end of the Kalpa of Formation and the beginning of the Kalpa of Continuance,[10] while the original teachers of our doctrines were wise men of ancient times, the two deities[11] and the three ascetics!"[12] In the end, however, all the ninety five different types of Brahman teachings came to be discarded.

On considering the eight sects[13] of Buddhism, I, Nichiren, have discovered the following. The Hossō, Kegon, and Sanron sects, based upon the provisional sutras, declare that the provisional sutras are equal to the true sutra, or even that the true sutra is inferior to the provisional sutras. These are obviously errors originating with the scholars and teachers who founded these sects. The Kusha and Jōjitsu sects are a special case,[14] while the Ritsu sect represents the very lowest level of the Hinayana teachings.

The scholars excel the ordinary teachers, and the true Mahayana sutra excels the provisional Mahayana sutras. Thus the *Dainichi* Sutra of the Shingon sect cannot equal the *Kegon* Sutra, much less the Nirvana and Lotus sutras. Yet when the Tripitaka Master Shan-wu-wei came to judge the relative merits of the *Kegon*, Lotus, and *Dainichi* sutras, he erred in his interpretation by declaring that, though the Lotus Sutra and the *Dainichi* Sutra are equal in terms of principle, the latter is superior in terms of practice. Ever since that time, the Shingon followers have arrogantly asserted that the Lotus Sutra cannot even compare to the *Kegon* Sutra, much less to the Shingon sutras,[15] or that, because it fails to mention mudras and mantras, the Lotus Sutra cannot begin to compete with the *Dainichi* Sutra. Or they point out that many of the teachers and patriarchs of the Tendai sect have acknowledged the superiority of the Shingon sect, and that popular opinion likewise holds the Shingon to be superior.

Since so many people hold mistaken opinions on this point, I have examined it in considerable detail. I have outlined my findings in other writings,[16] which I hope you will consult. And I hope that people who seek the Way will take advantage of the time while they are alive to learn the truth of the matter and pass it on to others.

One should not be intimidated by the fact that so many people hold such beliefs. Nor does the truth of a belief depend on whether it has been held for a long or short time. The point is simply whether or not it conforms with the text of the scriptures and with reason.

In the case of the Jōdo sect, the Chinese priests T'an-luan,[17] Tao-ch'o[18] and Shan-tao made numerous errors and led a great many people to embrace false views. In Japan, Hōnen adopted the teachings of these men and not only taught everyone to believe in the Nembutsu but also attempted to wipe out all the other sects of Buddhism in the empire. Because the three thousand priests of Mount Hiei,[19] as well as the priests of Kōfuku-ji, Tōdai-ji, and the other temples of Nara— indeed, of all the eight sects of Buddhism—strove to put a stop to this, emperor after emperor issued edicts, and directives went out from the shogunate, all in an attempt to prevent the spread of this teaching, but in vain. On the contrary, it flourished all the more, until the emperor, the retired emperor, and the populace as a whole all came to believe in it.

I, Nichiren, am the son of a humble family, born along the shore in Kataumi of Tōjō village in the province of Awa, a person who has neither authority nor virtue. If the censures of the temples of Nara and Mount Hiei and the powerful prohibitions of emperors, the Sons of Heaven, could not put a stop to the Nembutsu teachings, then I wondered what I could do. But, employing the passages of the sutras as my mirror and divining tool and the teachings of T'ien-t'ai and Dengyō as my compass, I have attacked these teachings for the past seventeen years, from the fifth year of the Kenchō era (1253)[20] to the present, the seventh year of the Bun'ei era (1270). And, as may be seen by the evidence before one's eyes, the spread of the Nembutsu in Japan has been largely brought to a halt. Even though there are people who do not cease chanting the Nembutsu with their mouths, I believe they have come to realize in their hearts that the Nembutsu is not the path by which to free themselves from the sufferings of birth and death.

The Zen sect likewise is guilty of doctrinal errors. By observing one thing, you can surmise ten thousand. I can bring an end to the errors of the Shingon and all the other sects at will. The "wisdom" of the Shingon teachers and other eminent priests of the present time cannot compare to that of an ox or a horse, and their "light" is less than that given off by a firefly. To expect anything from them is like placing a bow and arrows in the hands of a dead man, or asking questions of one who is talking in his sleep. Their hands form the mudra gestures, their mouths repeat the mantras, but their hearts do not understand the principles of Buddhism. In effect, their arrogant minds tower like mountains, and the greed in their hearts is deeper than the seas. And all these mistaken opinions mentioned above have come about because they are confused as to the relative superiority of the various sutras and treatises and because none of them has corrected the errors originally propounded by the founders of these sects.

Men of wisdom should of course devote themselves to the study of all the eighty thousand doctrines of Buddhism, and should become familiar with all the twelve divisions of the scriptures.[21] But ignorant persons living in this latter age of ours, a time of evil and confusion, should discard the so-called "difficult-to-practice way" and "easy-to-practice way"[22] that the Nembutsu believers talk of, and devote themselves solely to chanting Nam-myoho-renge-kyo, the daimoku of the Lotus Sutra.

When the sun rises in the eastern sector of the sky, then all the skies over the great continent of Jambudvīpa in the south will be illuminated, because of the vast light that the sun possesses. But the feeble glow of the firefly can never shed light on a whole nation. A man who carries a wish-granting jewel in his bosom can produce whatever he desires, but mere tiles and stones can confer no treasures upon him. The Nembutsu and other practices, when compared to the daimoku of the Lotus Sutra, are like tiles and stones compared to a precious jewel, or like the flicker of a firefly compared to the light of the sun.

How can we, whose eyes are darkened, ever distinguish the true color of things by the mere glow of a firefly? The fact is that the lesser, provisional sutras of the Nembutsu and Shingon sects are not teachings that enable common mortals to attain Buddhahood.

Our teacher, Shakyamuni Buddha, in the course of his lifetime of teaching, expounded eighty thousand sacred doctrines. He was the first Buddha to appear in this *sahā* world of ours, which previously had not known any Buddha, and he opened the eyes of all living beings. All the other Buddhas and bodhisattvas from east and west, from the lands of the ten directions, received instruction from him.

The period prior to his advent was like the time before the appearance of the rulers and emperors[23] of ancient China, when men did not know who their own fathers were and lived like beasts. In the time before Emperor Yao, people knew nothing about the duties to be performed in the four seasons, and were as ignorant as horses or oxen.

In the period before the appearance of Shakyamuni Buddha in the world, there were no orders of monks and nuns; there were only the two categories of men and women. But now we have monks and nuns who, because of the teachers of the Shingon sect, have decided to look upon *Dainichi* Buddha as the supreme object of veneration and have demoted Shakyamuni Buddha to an inferior position, or who, because they believe in the Nembutsu, pay honor to Amida Buddha and thrust Shakyamuni Buddha aside. They are monks and nuns by virtue of the Lord Shakyamuni, but because of the erroneous teachings handed down from the founders of these various sects, they have been led to behave in this way.

There are three reasons why Shakyamuni Buddha, rather than any of the other Buddhas, has a relationship with all the people of this *sahā* world. First of all, he is the World-Honored One, the sovereign of all the people of this *sahā* world. Amida Buddha is not the monarch of this world. In this respect, Shakyamuni Buddha is like the ruler of the country in which we live. We pay respect first of all to the ruler of our own country, and only then do we go on to pay respect to the rulers of other countries. The Sun Goddess Tenshō Daijin and the Great Bodhisattva Hachiman are the original rulers of our country, provisional manifestations of Shakyamuni Buddha who appeared in the form of local deities. No person who turns his back on these deities can become the ruler of Japan. Thus the Sun Goddess is embodied in the form of the sacred mirror known as Naishidokoro,[24] and imperial messengers are sent to the Bodhisattva Hachiman to report to him and receive his oracle. Shakyamuni, the World-Honored One, is our august sovereign. It is he who is to be regarded as the supreme object of veneration.

The second reason is that Shakyamuni Buddha is the father and mother of all the persons in this *saha* world. It is proper that we should first of all pay filial respect to our own father and mother, and only then extend the same kind of respect to the fathers and mothers of other people. In ancient times we have the example of King Wu of the Chou dynasty in China, who carved a wooden image of his deceased father and placed it in a carriage, designating it as the general who would lead his troops into battle.[25] Heaven, moved by such conduct, lent him protection, and thus he succeeded in overthrowing his enemy, Chou,[26] the ruler of the Yin dynasty.

The ancient ruler Shun, grieved because his father had gone blind, shed tears, but when he wiped his hands, wet with those tears, on his father's eyes, his father's eyesight was restored.[27] Now Shakyamuni Buddha does the same for all of us, opening our eyes so as to "awaken the Buddha wisdom"[28] innate within us. No other Buddha has ever yet opened our eyes in such a way.

The third reason is that Shakyamuni is the original teacher of all persons in this *saha* world. He was born in central India as the son of King Śuddhodana during the ninth kalpa of decrease in the present Wise Kalpa,[29] when the life span of human beings measured a hundred years. He left family life at the age of nineteen, achieved enlightenment at thirty, and spent the remaining fifty or more years of his life expounding the sacred teachings. He passed away at the age of eighty, leaving behind his relics[30] to provide the means of salvation for all the persons of the Former, Middle and Latter Days of the Law. Amida, Yakushi, Dainichi and the others, on the other hand, are the Buddhas of other realms; they are not the World-Honored One of this world of ours.

This *saha* world occupies the lowest position among all the worlds of the ten directions. Among these worlds, it holds a place like that of a prison within a nation. All the persons in the worlds of the ten directions who have committed any of the ten evil acts, the five cardinal sins,[31] the grave offense of slandering the True Law or other terrible crimes and have been driven out by the Buddhas of those worlds have been brought together here in this *saha* land by Shakyamuni Buddha. These people, having fallen into the three evil paths or the great citadel of the hell of incessant suffering and there duly suffered for their offense, have been reborn in the realm of Humanity or Heaven. But, because they still retain certain vestiges of their former evil behavior, they are inclined to easily commit some further offense by slandering the True Law or speaking contemptuously of men of wisdom. Thus, for example, Śāriputra, though he had attained the status of an arhat, at times gave way to anger. Pilindavatsa,[32] though he had freed himself from the illusions of thought and desire,[33] displayed an arrogant mind, while Nandā,[34] though he had renounced all sexual attachment, continued to dwell on the thought of sleeping with a woman. Even these disciples of the Buddha, though they had done away with delusions, still retained their vestiges. How much more so must this be the case, therefore, with ordinary mortals? Yet Shakyamuni Buddha entered this *sahā* world of ours with the title *Nōnin*, "He Who Can Forbear." He is so called because he does not berate its people for the slanders they all commit but shows forbearance toward them.

These, then, are the special qualities possessed by Shakyamuni Buddha, qualities that the other Buddhas lack.

Amida Buddha and the other various Buddhas were determined to make compassionate vows. For this reason, though they felt ashamed to do so,[35] they made their appearance in this, the *sahā* world, Amida Buddha proclaiming his forty-eight vows,[36] and Yakushi Buddha, his twelve great vows.[37] Kanzeon and the other bodhisattvas who live in other lands also did likewise.

When the Buddhas are viewed in terms of the unchanging equality of their enlightenment, there are no distinctions to be made among them. But when they are viewed in terms of the ever-present differences among their preaching, then one should understand that each of them has his own realm among the worlds of the ten directions, and that they distinguish between those with whom they have already had some connection, and those with whom they have no such connection.

The sixteen royal sons of Daitsūchishō Buddha[38] each took up his residence in a different one of the lands of the ten directions and there led their respective disciples to salvation. Shakyamuni Buddha, who was a reincarnation of one of these sons, appeared in this *sahā* world of ours. We people, too, have been born into the *sahā* world. Therefore, we must not in any way turn away from the teachings of Shakyamuni Buddha. But people all fail to realize this. If they would look carefully into the matter, they would understand that, as the Lotus Sutra says, "I [Shakyamuni] alone can save them,"[39] and that they must not cut themselves off from the helping hand of Shakyamuni Buddha.

For this reason, all the persons in this *sahā* world of ours, if they detest the sufferings of birth and death and wish to have an object of veneration to which they can pay respect, should first of all fashion images of Shakyamuni Buddha in the form of wooden statues and paintings, and make these their object of worship. Then, if they still have strength left over, they may go on to fashion images of Amida and the other Buddhas.

Yet when the people of this world today, being unpracticed in the sacred way,[40] come to fashion or paint images of a Buddha, they give priority to those of Buddhas other than Shakyamuni. This does not accord either with the intentions of those other Buddhas, or with the intentions of Shakyamuni Buddha himself, and is moreover at variance with secular propriety.

The great king Udayana,[41] when he carved his image of red sandalwood, made it of none other than Shakyamuni Buddha, and the painting offered to the King of a Thousand Stupas[42] was likewise of Shakyamuni Buddha. But people nowadays base themselves upon the various Mahayana sutras, and because they believe that the particular sutra they rely on is superior to all others, they accordingly relegate the Lord Buddha Shakyamuni to a secondary position.

Thus all the masters of the Shingon sect, convinced that the *Dainichi* Sutra surpasses all other sutras, regard Dainichi Buddha, who is described therein as the supreme Buddha, as the one with whom they have a special connection. The Nembutsu believers, on the other hand, putting all their faith in the *Kammuryōju* Sutra, look upon Amida Buddha as the one who has some special connection with this *sahā* world of ours.

Because the people of our time in particular have mistaken the erroneous doctrines of Shan-tao and Hōnen for orthodox teachings and taken the three Pure Land sutras[43] as their guide, eight or nine out of every ten temples that they build have Amida Buddha enshrined as the principal object of worship. And in the dwellings of both lay believers and priests, in houses by the tens, the hundreds or the thousands, the image hall attached to the residence is dedicated to Amida Buddha. Moreover, among the thousand or ten thousand paintings and images of Buddhas to be found in a single household today, the great majority are of Amida Buddha.

Yet people who are supposed to be wise in such matters see these things happening and do not regard them as a calamity. On the contrary, they find such proceedings quite in accord with their own views and consequently greet them with nothing but praise and admiration. Paradoxical as it may seem, men of wholly evil character who have not the least understanding of the principle of cause and effect and who are not dedicated to any Buddha whatsoever would appear to be the ones free from error with respect to Buddhism.

Shakyamuni Buddha, our father and mother, who is endowed with the three virtues of sovereign, teacher and parent, is the very one who encourages us, the people driven out by all other Buddhas, saying,"I alone can save them." The debt of gratitude we owe him is deeper than the ocean, weightier than the earth, vaster than the sky. Though we were to pluck out our two eyes and place them before him as an offering until there were more eyes there than stars in the sky, though we were to strip off our skins and spread them out by the hundreds of thousands of ten thousands until they blanketed the ceiling of heaven, though we were to give him our tears as offerings of water and present him with flowers for the space of a hundred billion kalpas, though we were to offer him our flesh and blood for innumerable kalpas, until our flesh piled up like mountains and our blood overflowed like vast seas, we could never repay a fraction of the debt we owe to this Buddha!

But the scholars of our time cling to distorted views. Even though they may be wise men who have mastered all the eighty thousand doctrines of Buddhism and committed to memory the twelve divisions of the scriptures, and who strictly observe all the rules of discipline of the Mahayana and Hinayana texts, if they turn their backs upon this principle, then one should know that they cannot avoid falling into the evil paths.

As an example of what I mean, let us look at the Tripitaka Master Shan-wu-wei, the founder of the Shingon school in China. He was a son of King Busshu,[44] the monarch of the kingdom of Udyāna in India. The Lord Buddha Shakyamuni left his father's palace at the age of nineteen to take up the religious life. But this Tripitaka Master abdicated the throne at the age of thirteen, and thereafter traveled through the more than seventy states of India, journeying ninety thousand ri[45] on foot and acquainting himself with all the various sutras, treatises and schools of Buddhism. In a kingdom in northern India, he stood at the foot of the stupa erected by King Konzoku,[46] gazed up at the heavens and uttered prayers, whereupon there appeared in midair the Womb Realm mandala,[47] with the Buddha Dainichi seated in its center.

Shan-wu-wei, out of his compassion, determined to spread the knowledge of this teaching to outlying regions, and thereupon traveled to China, where he transmitted his secret doctrines to Emperor Hsüan-tsung. At the time of a great drought, he offered up prayers for rain, and within three days, rain fell from the sky. This tripitaka master was thoroughly familiar with the seed characters[48] representing the twelve hundred and more honored ones,[49] their august forms, and their *samayas*.[50] Today all the followers of the Shingon sect belonging to Tō-ji[51] and the other Shingon temples in Japan look upon themselves as disciples of the Tripitaka Master Shan-wu-wei.

But the time came when the tripitaka master suddenly died. Thereupon a number of guardians from hell appeared, bound him with seven iron cords, and led him off to the palace of Emma, the king of hell. This was a very strange thing to happen.

For what fault did he deserve to be censured in this way? Perhaps in the life he had just lived, he might have committed some of the ten evil acts, but surely he had not been guilty of any of the five cardinal sins. And as for his past existences, in view of the fact that he had become the ruler of a great kingdom, he must have strictly observed the ten good precepts[52] and dutifully served five hundred Buddhas.[53] What fault, then, could he have committed?

Moreover, at the age of thirteen he had voluntarily relinquished his position as king and entered the religious life. His aspiration for enlightenment was unequaled throughout the entire world. Surely such virtue should have canceled out any major or minor offenses that he might have committed in his present or previous lives. In addition, he had made a thorough study of all the various sutras, treatises and schools that were propagated in India at that time, and that fact too should have served to atone for any possible faults.

In addition to all this, the esoteric doctrines of Shingon are different from the other teachings of Buddhism. They declare that, though one may make no more than a single mudra with the hands or utter no more than a single mantra with the mouth, even the gravest offenses accumulated throughout the three existences of past, present and future will thereby without fail be eradicated. Moreover, they say that all the offenses and karmic hindrances that one may have created during the space of innumerable kotis[54] of kalpas will all be extinguished the moment one looks upon the esoteric mandalas. How much more should this be true, therefore, in the case of the Tripitaka Master Shan-wu-wei, who had memorized all the mudras and mantras pertaining to the twelve hundred and more honored ones, who had understood as clearly as though it were reflected in a mirror the practice of contemplation for "attaining Buddhahood in one's present form," and who, when he underwent the ceremony of anointment[55] in the Diamond Realm and Womb Realm mandalas, had become in effect the Enlightened King Dainichi or Dainichi Buddha himself! Why, then, should such a man be summoned before Emma, the king of hell, and subjected to censure?

I, Nichiren, had resolved to embrace that teaching which is supreme among the two divisions of Buddhism, the exoteric and the esoteric, and which allows us to free ourselves from the sufferings of birth and death with the greatest ease. Therefore, I acquainted myself in general with the esoteric doctrines of Shingon and made inquiries concerning this matter of Shan-wu-wei. But no one was able to give a satisfactory answer to the question I have posed above. If this man could not escape the evil paths of existence, then how could any of the Shingon teachers of our time, let alone the priests and lay believers who had performed no more than a single mudra or uttered no more than a single mantra, hope to avoid them?

Having examined the matter in detail, I concluded that there were two errors for which Shan-wu-wei was summoned before King Emma for censure.

First of all, the *Dainichi* Sutra is not only inferior to the Lotus Sutra, but cannot even compare to the Nirvana, *Kegon* or *Hannya* sutras. And yet Shan-wu-wei maintained that it is superior to the Lotus Sutra, thus committing the error of slandering the Law.

Second, although Dainichi Buddha is an emanation of Shakyamuni Buddha, Shan-wu-wei held to the biased view that Dainichi is in fact superior to the Lord Shakyamuni. The offense of such slanders is so grave that no one who commits them could avoid falling into the evil paths, even though he should carry out the practices pertaining to the twelve hundred and more honored ones over a period of innumerable kalpas.

Shan-wu-wei committed these errors, the retribution for which is very difficult to escape, and therefore, although he performed mudras and mantras peculiar to the various honored ones, it was to no avail. But when he merely recited those words from the *Hiyu* chapter in the second volume of the Lotus Sutra that read: "Now this threefold world is all my domain. The living beings in it are all my children. Yet this world has many cares and troubles from which I alone can save them,"[56] he escaped from the iron cords that bound him.

Be that as it may, the Shingon teachers who came after Shan-wu-wei have all maintained that the *Dainichi* Sutra is not only superior to the various other sutras, but surpasses even the Lotus Sutra. In addition, there were other persons who have declared that the Lotus Sutra is also inferior to the *Kegon* Sutra. Though these groups differ in what they maintain, they are alike in being guilty of slandering the Law.

The Tripitaka Master Shan-wu-wei held the prejudiced opinion that both the Lotus Sutra and the *Dainichi* Sutra should be regarded with great respect, since they agree in the profound principles that they embody, but that because the Lotus Sutra says nothing about mudras and mantras, it is inferior to the *Dainichi* Sutra. The Shingon teachers who came after him, moreover, were of the opinion that even with respect to the important principles expressed, the Lotus Sutra is inferior to the *Dainichi* Sutra, to say nothing of being inferior with respect to the matter of mudras and mantras. Thus they went much farther in their slander of the Law, piling up offense upon offense. It is impossible to believe that they can long avoid being censured by King Emma and consigned to the sufferings of hell. Indeed, they will immediately call down upon themselves the flames of the Avīci Hell.

The *Dainichi* Sutra does not originally contain any mention of the profound principle of *ichinen sanzen*. This principle is confined to the Lotus Sutra alone. But Shan-wu-wei proceeded to steal and appropriate this profound principle that the Great Teacher T'ien-t'ai had put forth on the basis of his reading of the Lotus Sutra, incorporating it into his own interpretation of the *Dainichi* Sutra. He then asserted that the mudras and mantras of the *Dainichi* Sutra, which were originally expounded merely to lend adornment to the Lotus Sutra, are the very elements that make the *Dainichi* Sutra superior to the Lotus. Shan-wu-wei was putting forth a distorted view when he stated that the Lotus and *Dainichi* sutras are equal in principle, and he was likewise stating an erroneous view when he claimed that the *Dainichi* Sutra is superior by reason of its mantras and mudras.

This is like a foolish and lowly person who looks upon his six sense organs as his personal treasures, though in fact they belong to his feudal lord.[57] Consequently, he is led into all manner of erroneous conduct. We should keep such a case in mind when interpreting the sutras, because the doctrines set forth in inferior sutras serve only to adorn the sutra which is truly superior.

I, Nichiren, was a resident of [Seichō-ji on] Mount Kiyosumi in

Tōjō Village in the province of Awa. From the time I was a small child, I prayed to Bodhisattva Kokūzō,[58] asking that I might become the wisest person in all Japan. The bodhisattva transformed himself into a venerable priest before my very eyes and bestowed upon me a jewel of wisdom as bright as the morning star. No doubt as a result, I was able to gain a general mastery of the principal teachings of the eight older sects of Buddhism in Japan, as well as of those of the Zen and Nembutsu sects.

During the sixteen or seventeen years since the fifth year or so of the Kenchō era until the present, the seventh year of the Bun'ei era, I have leveled many criticisms against the Zen and Nembutsu sects. For this reason, the scholars of those sects have risen up like hornets and flocked together like clouds, though as a matter of fact their arguments can be demolished with hardly more than a word or two.

Even the scholars of the Tendai and Shingon sects, losing sight of the principles laid down by their own sects concerning which teachings are to be adopted and which discarded, have come to hold opinions identical to those of the Zen or Nembutsu sect. Because the lay members of their communities hold to such beliefs, they themselves have thought it best to lend support to these sects and their erroneous views by declaring that the Tendai and Shingon teachings are the same as those of the Nembutsu and Zen sects. As a result, they join the others in attempting to refute me. But although it might appear as though they are indeed refuting me, in fact they are simply destroying their own Tendai and Shingon teachings. It is a shameful, shameful thing they are doing!

The fact that I have in this way been able to discern the errors of the various sutras, treatises, and sects is due to the benefit of Bodhisattva Kokūzō, and is owed to my former teacher, Dōzen-bō.[59]

Even a turtle, we are told, knows how to repay a debt of gratitude,[60] so how much more so should human beings? In order to repay the debt that I owe to my former teacher Dōzen-bō, I desired to spread the teachings of the Buddha on Mount Kiyosumi and lead my teacher to enlightenment. But he is a rather foolish and ignorant man, and in addition he is a believer in the Nembutsu, so I did not see how he could escape falling into the three evil paths. Moreover, he is not the kind of person who would listen to my words of instruction.

Nevertheless, in the first year of the Bun'ei era (1264), on the fourteenth day of the eleventh month, I had an interview with him at the priests' lodgings[61] of Saijō in Hanabusa. At that time, he said to me, "I have neither wisdom nor any hope for advancement to important position. I am an old man with no desire for fame, and I claim no eminent priest of Nembutsu as my teacher. But because this practice has become so widespread in our time, I simply repeat like others the words Namu Amida Butsu. In addition, though it was not my idea originally, I have had occasion to fashion five images of Amida Buddha. This perhaps is due to some karmic habit that I formed in a past existence. Do you suppose that as a result of these faults I will fall into hell?"

At that time I certainly had no thought in mind of quarreling with him. But because of the earlier incident with Tōjō Saemon Nyūdō Renchi,[62] I had not seen my teacher for more than ten years, and thus it was in a way as though we had become estranged and were at odds. I thought that the proper and courteous thing would be to reason with him in mild terms and to speak in a gentle manner. On the other hand, when it comes to the realm of birth and death, there is no telling how either young or old may fare, and it occurred to me that I might never again have another opportunity to meet with him. I had already warned Dōzen-bō's elder brother, the priest Dōgi-bō Gishō,[63] that he was destined to fall into the hell of incessant suffering if he did not change his ways, and they say that his death was as miserable as I had foretold. When I considered that my teacher Dōzen-bō might meet a similar fate, I was filled with pity for him and therefore made up my mind to speak to him in very strong terms.

I explained to him that, by making five images of Amida Buddha, he was condemning himself to fall five times into the hell of incessant suffering. The reason for this, I told him, was that the Lotus Sutra— wherein the Buddha says that he will now "honestly discard the provisional teachings"[64]—states that Shakyamuni Buddha is our father, while Amida Buddha is our uncle. Anyone who would fashion no less than five images of his uncle and make offerings to them, and yet not fashion a single image of his own father—how could he be regarded as anything but unfilial? Even hunters in the mountains or fishermen, who cannot tell east from west and do not perform a single pious act, are guilty of less offense than such a person!

Nowadays those who have set their minds upon the Way no doubt hope for a better existence in their future lives. Yet they cast aside the Lotus Sutra and Shakyamuni Buddha, while never failing even for an instant to revere Amida Buddha and call upon his name. What kind of behavior is this? Though they may appear to the eye to be pious people, I do not see how they can escape the charge of rejecting their own parent and devoting themselves to a relative stranger. A completely evil person, on the other hand, has never given his allegiance to any Buddhist teaching at all, and so has not committed the fault of rejecting Shakyamuni Buddha. Therefore, if the proper circumstances should arise, he might very well in time come to take faith in Shakyamuni.

Those men who follow the heretical doctrines of Shan-tao, Hōnen, and the Buddhist teachers of our time, making Amida Buddha their object of worship and devoting themselves entirely to the practice of calling upon his name—I do not believe that they will ever renounce their erroneous views and give their allegiance to Shakyamuni Buddha and the Lotus Sutra, even though lifetime after lifetime throughout countless kalpas should pass. Accordingly, the Nirvana Sutra that was preached just before Shakyamuni Buddha's death in the grove of sāla trees states that there will appear frightful persons whose offenses are graver than the ten evil acts or the five cardinal sins—*icchantika* or men of incorrigible disbelief and those who slander the Law. We also read there that such persons will be found nowhere else but among the company of wise men who observe the two hundred and fifty precepts,[65] wrap their bodies in the three robes[66] of a Buddhist monk and carry a mendicant's bowl.

I explained all this in detail to Dōzen-bō at the time of our interview, though it did not appear that he completely understood what I was saying. Nor did the other persons present on that occasion seem to understand. Later, however, I received word that Dōzen-bō had come to take faith in the Lotus Sutra. I concluded that he must have renounced his earlier heretical views and had hence become a person of sound belief, a thought that filled me with joy. When I also heard that he had fashioned an image of Shakyamuni Buddha, I could not find words to express my emotion. It may seem as though I spoke to him very harshly at the time of our interview. But I simply explained things as they are set forth in the Lotus Sutra, and that is no doubt why he has now taken such action. They say that words of good advice often grate on the ears, just as good medicine tastes bitter.

Now I, Nichiren, have repaid the debt of gratitude that I owe to my teacher, and I am quite certain that both the Buddhas and the gods will approve what I have done. I would like to ask that all I have said here be reported to Dōzen-bō.

Even though one may resort to harsh words, if such words help the person to whom they are addressed, then they are worthy to be regarded as truthful words and gentle words. Similarly, though one may use gentle words, if they harm the person to whom they are addressed, they are in fact deceptive words, harsh words.

The Buddhist doctrines preached by scholars these days are regarded by most people as gentle words, truthful words, but in fact they are all harsh words and deceptive words. I say this because they are at variance with the Lotus Sutra, which embodies the Buddha's true intention.

On the other hand, when I proclaim that the practitioners of the Nembutsu will fall into the hell of incessant suffering or declare that the Zen and Shingon sects are likewise in error, people may think I am uttering harsh words, but in fact I am speaking truthful and gentle words. As an example, I may point to the fact that Dōzen-bō has embraced the Lotus Sutra and fashioned an image of Shakyamuni Buddha, actions that came about because I spoke harsh words to him. And the same thing holds true for numerous other persons throughout Japan. Ten or more years ago, virtually everyone was reciting the Nembutsu. But now, out of ten persons, you will find that one or two chant only Nam-myoho-renge-kyo, while two or three recite it along with the Nembutsu. And even among those who recite the Nembutsu exclusively, there are those who have begun to have doubts and who in their hearts put their faith in the Lotus Sutra and have even begun to paint or carve images of Shakyamuni Buddha. All this, too, has come about because I, Nichiren, have spoken harsh words.

This response is like the fragrant sandalwood trees that grow among the groves of foul-smelling *eraṇḍa* trees,[67] or the lotus blossoms that rise out of the muddy water. Thus, when I proclaim that the followers of the Nembutsu will fall into the hell of incessant suffering, the "wise men" of our day, who are in fact no wiser than cows or horses, may venture to attack my doctrines. But in truth they are like scavenger dogs barking at the lion, the king of beasts, or foolish monkeys laughing at the god Taishaku.

Nichiren

The seventh year of Bun'ei (1270)

Notes

1. Said to be all the teachings that Shakyamuni expounded during his lifetime. The figure eighty thousand is not intended literally but simply indicates a large number.

2. A reference to the assertion of Hōnen and other followers of the Jōdo (Pure Land) sect that calling upon the name of Amida Buddha, relying on his power of salvation as taught in the three Pure Land sutras, is the practice most suitable for people in the Latter Day of the Law, who are of inferior capacity.

3. This controversy was exemplified by a debate held in southern India around the sixth century between Dharmapāla of the Consciousness-Only school and Bhāvaviveka who followed Nāgārjuna's teachings. Dharmapāla asserted that all phenomena that arise from the ālaya consciousness have actual existence, while Bhāvaviveka took the position that all things have nonsubstantiality (kū) as their true nature.

4. Nichiren is referring to himself.

5. That is, passages that assert, in words similar to those of the Lotus Sutra, that the sutra in which they appear is supreme among the Buddha's teachings.

6. Hui-neng (638–713) is known as the sixth patriarch of Zen Buddhism in China. The *Rokuso Dankyō* or Platform Sutra of the Sixth Patriarch is attributed to him.

7. Shan-tao (613–681) is an early patriarch of Pure Land Buddhism. The original text of the *Kannen Hōmon* (T47, no.1959) does not include the character for "sutra" in its title.

8. Chih-i is usually referred to by Nichiren as the Great Teacher T'ien-t'ai.

9. The four ranks of saints are Buddhist teachers upon whom people can rely. According to the Nirvana Sutra (T12, 637a-c) they are: (1) *shōmon* people who have yet to attain any of the four stages of Hinayana enlightenment; (2) those who have attained either the first stage, at which one enters the stream leading to nirvana, or the second stage, at which one must undergo only one more rebirth in the human world before entering nirvana; (3) those who have attained the third stage, at which one will never be reborn in the world; and (4) those who have eliminated the illusions of thought and desire and attained the fourth stage, that of arhat.

10. The time of transition between the first two stages of the four-stage cycle, described as the four kalpas of formation, continuance, decline, and disintegration, which a world is said to undergo repeatedly. During these first two stages a world takes shape and living beings appear and continue to exist.

11. Śiva and Viṣṇu.

12. The three ascetics are Kapila, Ulūka, and Ṛṣabha. Kapila was a legendary figure, said to have been the founder of the Samkhya school, one of the six schools of Brahmanism in ancient India. Ulūka (or Kanāda) was a founder of the Vaiśesika school, another of the six schools. Ṛṣabha's teachings are said to have paved the way for Jainism.

13. The major sects in Japan, which fall into two categories: the Kusha, Jōjitsu, Ritsu, Hossō, Sanron, and Kegon sects, which flourished in the Nara period (710–794), and the Tendai and Shingon sects, which appeared during the Heian period (794–1185).

14. The Kusha and Jōjitsu were studied in conjunction, respectively, with Hossō and Sanron; thus presumably Nichiren did not regard them as independent religious sects.

15. *Dainichi, Kongōchō,* and *Soshitsuji* sutras.

16. Presumably the *Hokke Shingon Shōretsu Ji* (The Relative Superiority of the Hokke and Shingon Sects), dated the seventh month, 1254, and the *Shingon Tendai Shōretsu Ji* (The Relative Superiority of the Shingon and Tendai Sects), dated 1270, and other letters.

17. T'an-luan (476–542) is traditionally held to be the founder of the Pure Land school in China. He received the *Kammuryōju* Sutra from Bodhiruci at Lo-yang and devoted himself to the Pure Land teachings, stressing the practice of calling on the name of Amida Buddha, as the "easy-to-practice way" which enables all people to attain salvation and rejecting all other practices as the "difficult-to-practice way." These "ways" were earlier described by Nāgārjuna. See note 22, below.

18. Tao-ch'o (562–645) is the second patriarch of the Pure Land school. In his *Anraku Shū* (T47, 13c) he divided Buddhist teachings into the Sacred Way, those teachings that required practice in the world through one's own efforts, and those who advocated birth in the Pure Land, relying on the powers of Amida Buddha.

19. Reference is to the Enryaku-ji, the head temple of the Tendai sect, located on Mount Hiei, between Kyoto and Lake Biwa.

20. On the twenty-eighth day of the fourth month, 1253, at the Seichō-ji in Awa, Nichiren proclaimed that Nam-myoho-renge-kyo was the only teaching in the Latter Day that enabled all persons to attain Buddhahood in this lifetime.

21. A classification of Buddhist teachings according to their content and style of presentation. The expression indicates all Buddhist teachings.

22. Two categories of Buddhist practice mentioned by Nāgārjuna in his *Jūjū Bibasha Ron* (T26, 41a–b). The "difficult-to-practice way" means the exertion of strenuous effort in austere practices for countless kalpas in order to attain enlightenment, while the "easy-to-practice way" means calling upon the names of Buddhas and bodhisattvas, relying on their power of salvation.

23. A reference to the Three Rulers, Fu Hsi, Shen Nung, and Huang Ti, legendary rulers of ancient China said to have established model governments, and the Five Emperors, Shao Hao, Chuan Hsü, Ti Kao, T'ang Yao, and Yü Shun, said to have reigned after them.

24. Originally the palace which enshrined the mirror, one of the three sacred treasures of the imperial court, and which was guarded by court ladies of honor called *naishi*. Later, *naishidokoro* came to mean the sacred mirror itself.

25. King Wu, carrying out the will of his father, King Wen, defeated Chou, the last ruler of the Yin dynasty, who was a virtual slave to his consort, Ta Chi, and totally misgoverned the country. The story of Wu carving his father's image is found in the *Shih Chi* (Records of the Historian), chapter 4.

26. Chou, along with King Chieh of the Hsia dynasty, are the traditional evil rulers whose excesses brought their dynasties to an end.

27. Shun was one of the Five Emperors. Although his father, a commoner, treated him cruelly, being partial to his younger half-brother Hsiang, Shun practiced filial piety toward his parent. The Buddhist textual source for the story of Shun restoring his father's eyesight is found in the *Hōon Jurin* (T53, 658c).

28. A reference to the reason that all Buddhas appear in the world, as expounded in the *Hōben* (2d) chapter of the Lotus Sutra. The full passage reads: "to awaken in all beings the Buddha wisdom, to reveal it, to let all beings know about it, and enter into it" (T9, 8a).

29. The Wise Kalpa (Jap: *kengō*) is the present major kalpa, during which, it is said, a thousand Buddhas of great wisdom will appear in order to save the people. Specifically, Shakyamuni was born in the present Kalpa of Continuance, one of the four kalpas that comprise this major kalpa. During the Kalpa of Continuance, the human life span is said to repeat a cycle of change, decreasing by a factor of one year every hundred years until it reaches ten years, and then increasing at the same rate until it reaches eighty-thousand years. Then it begins to decrease again until it reaches ten years, and so on. Shakyamuni is said to have appeared during the ninth cycle of decrease.

30. Here the relics (Jap: *shari*) of the Dharma Body, namely the teachings that Shakyamuni expounded.

31. The ten evil acts are: the three physical evils of killing, stealing, and unlawful sexual intercourse; the four verbal evils of lying, flattery, (or irresponsible speech), defaming, and duplicity, and the three evils of greed, anger, and stupidity or the holding of mistaken views. They are described in the *Kusha Ron* (T29, 85a) and elsewhere. The five cardinal sins are killing one's father, killing one's mother, killing an arhat, injuring a Buddha, and causing disunity in the Buddhist Order. Explanations vary with the various sutras and treatises.

32. Pilindavatsa, one of the Buddha's disciples, was born to a Brahman family in Śrāvasti, India. He was arrogant and held others in contempt and had won renown for the practice of magic. He lost his powers when he met Shakyamuni and instead became the Buddha's disciple (*Daichido Ron*, T25, 71a). Shakyamuni's prediction of his future enlightenment appears in the *Gohyaku Deshi Juki* (8th) chapter of the Lotus Sutra.

33. The first of the three categories of illusion (Jap: *sanwaku*). The illusions of thought are distorted perceptions of the truth. The illusions of desire mean base inclinations such as greed and anger which arise from the contact of the sense organs with their respective objects. The other two illusions are: illusions preventing bodhisattvas from saving others, and the forty-two basic illusions that prevent a bodhisattva from attaining enlightenment. They are described in the *Maka Shikan* (T46, 37c).

34. Nandā was Shakyamuni's younger half-brother and disciple. He had a graceful figure and was known as Sundarananda (Beautiful Nandā). Just when he was about to marry the beautiful Sundarī, Shakyamuni returned to Kapilavastu to spread his teaching, and Nandā was persuaded to join the Buddhist order. His story appears in *Zappō Zōkyō* (T4, 485c).

35. For example, Amida Buddha lives in the Pure Land of Perfect Bliss, located ten billion Buddha lands to the west of the *sahā* world, and Yakushi Buddha lives in the Pure Emerald World said to lie in the eastern part of the universe. As these names suggest, the living beings in these lands experience only pleasure; consequently there is no one there to be freed from suffering. For this reason, Nichiren says, the Buddhas of these worlds, though embarrassed to appear in another Buddha's realm, came down to this *sahā* world, which is full of suffering, in order to fulfill their vows of compassion.

36. The vows which Amida Buddha is said to have made while he was still engaged in practice under Sejizaiō Buddha as the monk Hōzō. They are listed in the *Muryōju* Sutra (T12, 267b ff). Hōzō is said to have studied the characteristics of twenty-one million Buddha lands and then, after five kalpas of meditation, to have made forty-eight vows concerning the Buddha land he himself would establish after attaining enlightenment.

37. The vows which Yakushi Buddha of the Pure Emerald World in the east made while still engaged in bodhisattva practice. They are vows to cure all illnesses and lead all people to enlightenment. They are found in the *Yakushi Rurikō Nyorai Hongan Kudoku* Sutra (T14, 405a-b).

38. As described in the *Kejōyu* (7th) chapter of the Lotus Sutra (T9, 26a ff).

39. T9, 14c.

40. The sacred way of practice (Jap: *shōgyō*) is the first of the five forms of practice or conduct into which the bodhisattva enters, as described in the Nirvana Sutra (T12, 432a ff). It is the true bodhisattva practice of the three learnings (Jap: *sangaku*), precepts, meditation, and wisdom. The second is pure practice (Jap: *bongyō*), in which the bodhisattva, with a pure mind free of attachments, releases sentient beings from suffering and brings them ease. The third is the marvelous activity perfected by the bodhisattva through the principles of nature (Jap: *tengyō*). Fourth is the so-called activity of children (Jap: *yōnigyō*), in which the bodhisattva, with a compassionate heart, conducts himself to accord with the good activities of humankind and heavenly beings (who are likened to children). Fifth is the activity that indicates that the bodhisattva is himself incurring the sufferings and passions that afflict humankind (Jap: *byōgyō*).

41. Udayana was a king of Kauśāmbī in India. He converted to Buddhism at the urging of his wife and became a patron of Shakyamuni Buddha. According to the *Zōichi-agon* Sutra (T2, 703b), when Shakyamuni ascended to the Heaven of the Thirty-three Gods to preach the Law to his mother Māyā, King Udayana lamented that he could no longer worship the Buddha and fell ill. He ordered his retainers to make a five-foot image of the Buddha out of aromatic sandalwood from Mt. Goshira. As a result of this virtuous deed, he recovered from his illness. It is said that this was the first image of the Buddha ever made.

42. The reference is unclear but this may refer to King Sentō in ancient India who is mentioned in the *Kompon Setsu Issaiubu Binaya* (Monastic rules of the Sarvāstivāda School; T23, 873c-874a). According to this work, Sentō gave five treasures to one Keishō (Sanskrit unknown), king of Rājagṛha in Magadha, but King Keishō had no gift to offer him in return and was at a loss. At the suggestion of his chief minister, however, he had an image of Shakyamuni Buddha painted and presented it as the most precious of all treasures in the world. King Sentō at first became angry, but, on realizing that it was an image of the Buddha, he came to have deep faith and converted to Buddhism.

43. The three basic scriptures of the Pure Land sect: the *Amida*, *Muryōju*, and *Kammuryōju* sutras.

44. King Busshu (Sanskrit unknown) was king of Udyāna who lived around the seventh century, was a descendant of King Amṛtodana, Shakyamuni's uncle. He is mentioned in Li Hua's *Gensōchō Hongyō Sanzō Zammai Zemmui Zō Kōryokyo Gyōi* (T50, 290b).

45. A *ri* was a unit of linear measurement, defined as 6 *chō* (0.65 km) but from the Heian period, it was commonly understood to be 36 *chō*.

46. Konzoku (Sanskrit unknown) was a king who built a great stupa in Gandhara. Little else is known about him. It is said that at the beginning of the eighth century Shan-wu-wei offered prayers at the foot of the stupa and achieved sudden understanding of the *Dainichi* Sutra. He is mentioned in the *Daibirushana Kyō Kuyō Shidaihō Sho* (T39, 790b). The text differs somewhat from Nichiren's description.

47. The Womb Realm (Jap: *Taizōkai*) mandala is one of the two mandalas of the

Shingon teaching, and is based on the *Dainichi* Sutra. It represents the fundamental principle of the universe, that is the Dharma body of Dainichi Buddha. The other mandala is the Diamond Realm (Jap: *Kongōkai*) mandala, based on the *Kongōchō* Sutra. It depicts the Diamond Realm, which represents Dainichi Buddha's wisdom.

48. Characters written in Siddham, a variety of the Brāhmi script. Initially the characters were written with a wooden stylus, a wedge-shaped piece of thin flat wood, but later came to be written also with a writing brush. In China and Japan a distinctive calligraphic style of the Siddham script developed.

49. The Buddhas, bodhisattvas, and other figures that appear in the mandalas. They are either pictorially represented, or in some instances, the "seed" characters are used in place of the pictorial representations.

50. Here *samaya* is used to refer to the mudras as well as the objects held by the various figures in the mandalas. The term is also used to signify the vows.

51. The Tōji, located in Kyoto, is one of the major Shingon temples in Japan.

52. Precepts for lay believers of Mahayana, which are prohibitions against the ten evil acts.

53. According to the *Ninnō* Sutra (T8, 833a) kings are born to their high position as the karmic reward of having served five hundred Buddhas in prior lifetimes.

54. A very large number, variously rendered as ten million, one hundred million, etc.

55. The ceremony of anointment (Skt: *abhiṣeka*; Jap: *Kanjō*) is a ceremony commonly performed in esoteric Buddhism, in which one is invested with a certain position. The name derives from the practice of pouring water on the heads of rulers in ancient India upon their ascending the throne. Broadly speaking, there are three kinds of esoteric anointment ceremonies: those designed to establish a relationship between the individual and the Buddha, those to confer the status of practitioner of the esoteric teaching, and those to invest a person with the rank of *ajari*, qualifying him to teach the esoteric doctrine.

56. T9, 14c.

57. In feudal Japan a vassal was regarded as so heavily indebted to his lord for providing him with his sole means of livelihood that he was expected to dedicate his entire being to loyal service in return. The six sense organs are the eyes, ears, nose, tongue, body, and mind — that is, the physical and mental components of a human being. This is another way of saying that a retainer's life belongs to his lord.

58. Kokūzō, the "Bodhisattva of Space" is so called because his wisdom and good fortune are said to be as vast and boundless as the universe itself (*kokūzō* means "space repository"). Kokūzō was the original object of worship at the Seichō-ji where Nichiren first studied Buddhism, since the time of the priest Fushigi, who in 771 carved an image of the bodhisattva and enshrined it there.

59. Dōzen-bō (d. 1276) was the chief priest of Seichō-ji.

60. This story appears in the *Shih-wen Lei-chü* (Collection of Stories and Poems) and other sources. When the young Mao Pao, who later became a general of the Chin dynasty, was walking along the Yangtze River, he saw a fisherman catch a turtle and prepare to kill it. Moved to pity, he gave the fisherman his clothes in exchange for the turtle and thus saved its life. Later, Mao Pao was attacked by enemies. When he fled in retreat to the Yangtze River, the turtle he had saved in his childhood appeared and carried him on its back to the opposite shore.

61. Probably part of the compound of Renge-ji, located in Hanabusa, Awa Province. Renge-ji is said to have been a branch temple of Seichō-ji.

62. Tōjō Saemon Nyūdō Renchi, also called Tōjō Kagenobu (n.d.), was the steward of Tōjō Village in Awa and a strong believer in the Nembutsu. When Nichiren first declared the establishment of his Buddhism at the Seichō-ji on the twenty-eighth day of the fourth month, 1253, Tōjō Kagenobu was so infuriated by his harsh criticism of Nembutsu that he attempted to have Nichiren killed. Nichiren escaped with Dōzenbō's aid, but was not able to return to his native province for many years.

63. Dōgi-bō Gishō (n.d.) was a priest at Seichō-ji, thought to have been Dōzenbō's elder brother or a priest senior to him. He opposed Nichiren's teachings.

64. T9, 10a.

65. Rules of discipline to be observed by fully ordained monks of Hinayana Buddhism.

66. Reference to three kinds of robes worn according to the time or the occasion. Together with a mendicant's bowl, these are all that a monk was permitted to possess.

67. According to Indian tradition, tall trees whose noxious odor, similar to that of a rotting corpse, was said to reach a distance of forty *yojana* (one *yojana* measures 9.6, 18, or 24 km, depending on the source). A single leaf of a sandalwood tree was thought to dispel the stench of the *eraṇḍā*.

10 REPLY TO NII-AMA

This letter was written on the sixteenth day of the second month, 1275, the year after Nichiren had returned from his exile to Sado and had retired to Mount Minobu. The letter is in response to a letter from Nii-ama Gozen and her husband's grandmother, Ō-ama Gozen, requesting that Nichiren inscribe the Gohonzon for them. She was referred to as Nii-ama (younger nun) in contrast to Ō-ama (elder nun).

The Gohonzon is the object of worship, in this instance the mandala, inscribed on paper in *sumi* ink or on wood in gilded characters. Down the center is inscribed "Nam-myo-ho-renge-kyo, Nichiren" and on either side, running down along the central inscription, are characters that represent each of the Ten Worlds. At the top, to the left and right of the character *namu*, are the characters for Shakyamuni and Tahō Buddha. Below them are the four bodhisattvas of the earth, and below them representative figures for the other ten worlds, ending with Devadatta, representing hell. (See Glossary for a more detailed description.)

Ō-ama had been the wife of Hōjō Tomotoki, a younger brother of the third regent Yasutoki and the lord of the Nagasa district in Awa Province where Nichiren was born. Nii-ama is said to have been the wife of either Tomotoki's son or grandson. Both nuns were widows and lived together in the village of Tōjō.

Ō-ama had been a follower of Nichiren since the time that he had first proclaimed the establishment of his Buddhism, but she later wavered in her faith. For this reason, as Nichiren explains at the end of his letter, he was unable to inscribe a Gohonzon for her, whereas he felt confidence in providing one for Nii-ama.

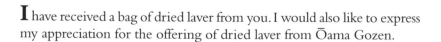

I have received a bag of dried laver from you. I would also like to express my appreciation for the offering of dried laver from Ōama Gozen.

This area is called Mount Minobu. Suruga Province lies to the south, and it is more than a hundred *ri* from the seaside of Ukishimagahara[1] in that province to this mountain at Hakiri village[2] in Kai Province. The way is more difficult than ten times the distance on an ordinary path. The Fuji River,[3] the swiftest in all Japan, runs from north to south. High mountains rise to the east and west of this river, forming deep valleys where huge rocks stand about everywhere like tall folding-screens. The waters of the river rush through the valley like an arrow shot through a tube by a powerful archer. The river is so swift and rocky that sometimes a boat will be smashed against the rapids as it travels along the riverbanks or attempts to cross the stream. Coming through this dangerous pass, one arrives at a large mountain called the peak of Minobu.

To the east stands the peak of Tenshi, to the south, Takatori, to the west, Shichimen, and to the north, Minobu, and they all tower as though four giant folding-screens had been set up. Climbing these peaks, you will see a vast stretch of forest below, while going down to the valleys, you will find huge rocks lined up side by side. The howls of wolves fill the mountains, the chatter of monkeys echoes through the valleys, stags call plaintively to their does, and the voices of cicadas sound shrilly. Here spring flowers bloom in summer, while trees bear autumn fruit in winter. Occasionally one sees a woodcutter gathering firewood, and my rare visitors are only friends of old. Mount Shang[4] in China where the four white-haired recluses[5] retired from the world, and the deep recesses in the mountains where the Seven Worthies of the Bamboo Grove[6] secluded themselves, must have been like this place.

As you climb the peak, it looks as if kelp were growing there, but instead you find only an expanse of bracken. Going down to the valleys, you think surely it must be laver growing there, but it is only a dense growth of parsley.

Though I had long since ceased to think about my home, this laver brings back trivial nostalgic memories, making me feel sad. It is the same kind of laver I saw long ago on the shore at Kataumi, Ichikawa, and Kominato.[7] I feel an unwarranted resentment that the color, shape and taste of this laver should remain unchanged while my parents have passed away, and I cannot restrain my tears.

Enough of this. Ō-ama has asked me to inscribe the Gohonzon for her, but I am troubled by her request. The reason is as follows. This Gohonzon was never mentioned in the writings of the many Buddhist scholars who traveled from India to China or in those of the priests who journeyed from China to India. All the objects of worship ever enshrined in the temples throughout India are described without exception in the *Daitō Saiiki Ki*,[8] the *Jion Den*,[9] and the *Dentō Roku*,[10] [and this Gohonzon is not among them]. Nor have I found it mentioned among the objects of worship of the various temples which were described by those sages who traveled from China to Japan or by those wise men who went from Japan to China. Since all the records of the first temples in Japan such as Gangō-ji,[11] Shitennō-ji[12] and other temples as well as many histories, beginning with the *Nihon Shoki*,[13] name them without omission, the objects of worship in these temples are clearly known, but this Gohonzon has never been listed among them.

People may say in doubt: "It was probably not expounded in the sutras or treatises. That is why the many wise men have neither painted nor carved images of it." I say that, because the sutras lie before their eyes, those who so doubt should examine whether or not it is revealed in the sutras. It is wrong to denounce this object of worship merely because it was never painted or carved in previous ages.

For example, Shakyamuni Buddha once ascended to the Trāyastriṃśa Heaven to fulfill his obligations to his [deceased] mother. But because of the Buddha's supernatural powers, no one in the entire world, except for the Venerable Maudgalyāyana, was aware of it.[14] Thus even though Buddhism may exist before their eyes, people will not realize it if they lack the proper capacity, nor will it spread unless the time is right. This is in accordance with the natural law, just as the tides of the ocean ebb and flow and the moon in the sky wanes and waxes according to the time.

Lord Shakyamuni treasured this Gohonzon in mind since the remote past of *gohyaku-jintengō*, but even after he appeared in this world, he did not expound it for more than forty years following his first preaching. Even in the Lotus Sutra he did not allude to it in the earlier chapters of the theoretical teaching. Only in the *Hōtō* chapter[15] did he begin to suggest it. He revealed it in the *Juryō* chapter, and concluded his explanation in the *Jinriki* and *Zokurui* chapters.[16]

Bodhisattvas such as Monjushiri living in the Golden World, Miroku in the palace of the Tuṣita Heaven, Kannon on Mount Potalaka,[17] and Yakuō, who had served the Buddha Nichigatsu Jōmyōtoku,[18] all vied with one another in asking [the Buddha's permission to propagate faith in the Gohonzon in the Latter Day of the

Law], but the Buddha refused. Those bodhisattvas were known to possess excellent wisdom and profound learning, but since they had only recently begun to hear the Lotus Sutra, their understanding was still limited. Thus they would not be able to endure great difficulties in the Latter Day.

Then the Buddha declared, "There are my true disciples whom I have hidden at the bottom of the earth since *gohyaku-jintengō*. I will entrust it to them." So saying, the Buddha summoned those bodhisattvas led by Jōgyō in the *Yujutsu* chapter and entrusted them with the five characters of Myōhō-renge-kyō, the heart of the essential teaching of the sutra, [in the *Jinriki* chapter].

Then the Buddha stated: "You must not propagate it in the first millennium of the Former Day of the Law or in the second millennium of the Middle Day following my death. In the beginning of the Latter Day of the Law, slanderous priests will fill the entire world, so that all heavenly gods will be enraged and comets will appear in the sky and the earth will shake like the movement of huge waves. Innumerable disasters and calamities such as drought, fires, floods, gales, epidemics, famine and war will all occur at once. The people throughout the world will don armor and take up bows and staves, and since none of the Buddhas, bodhisattvas or benevolent deities will be able to help them, they will all die and fall like rain into the hell of incessant suffering. At this very time, kings can save their countries and the people will escape calamities if they embrace and believe in this great mandala of the five characters, and in their next life they will not fall into the great fires of hell."

Now I, Nichiren, am not Bodhisattva Jōgyō, but perhaps by his design I have already attained a general understanding of this teaching, and I have been expounding it for these more than twenty years. When one resolves to propagate it, he will meet difficulties, as the sutra states: "Since hatred and jealousy [toward this sutra] abound even during the lifetime of the Buddha, how much worse will it be in the world after his passing?"[19] and, "The people will be full of hostility, and it will be extremely difficult to believe."[20] Of the three types of powerful enemies[21] predicted in the sutra, the first indicates the sovereign, district and village stewards, and lords of manors as well as the ordinary populace. Believing the charges leveled by the second and third types of enemies, who are priests, they will vilify or slander the votary of the Lotus Sutra, or attack him with swords and staves.

Tōjō village in Awa Province, though it is a remote place, may well be called the center of Japan because the Sun Goddess resides there. In ancient times she lived in Ise Province.[22] Later on, the emperor came to take deep faith in Bodhisattva Hachiman and in the Kamo Shrine,[23] and neglected the Sun Goddess, so that she became enraged. At that time, Minamoto no Yoritomo[24] wrote a pledge and ordered Aoka no Kodayū[25] to enshrine her in the outer shrine of Ise. Probably because Yoritomo thus satisfied the goddess's desire, he became the shogun and ruled the whole of Japan. He then decided on Tōjō district as the residence of the Sun Goddess, and so she no longer lives in Ise Province but in Tōjō district in Awa Province. This is similar to Bodhisattva Hachiman who, in ancient times, resided at Dazaifu in Chikuzen Province but later dwelt at Otokoyama in Yamashiro Province and now lives at Tsurugaoka[26] in Kamakura in Sagami Province.

Nichiren began to propagate this true teaching in Tōjō district in Awa Province in Japan, out of all places in the entire world. Accordingly, the Tōjō steward became my enemy, but his clan has now been half destroyed.

Ō-ama Gozen is insincere and foolish. She was also irresolute, believing at one time, while renouncing her belief at another. When Nichiren incurred the displeasure of the government authorities,[27] she quickly discarded the Lotus Sutra. This is why, even before, I told her the Lotus Sutra is "the most difficult to believe and the most difficult to understand,"[28] whenever we met.

If I give her the Gohonzon because I am indebted to her, then the Ten Goddesses[29] will certainly think I am a very partial priest. On the other hand, if I follow the sutra and do not give her a Gohonzon because of her lack of faith, I will not be partial, but she may well harbor a grudge against me because she does not realize her fault. I have explained the reasons for my refusal in detail in a letter to Suke no Ajari.[30] Please send for the letter and show it to her.

You are of the same family as Ō-ama Gozen, but you have demonstrated the sincerity of your faith. Because you have often sent offerings to me, both to Sado and here to Minobu, and because your resolve does not seem to wane, I have inscribed a Gohonzon for you. But I still worry whether you will maintain your faith to the end and feel as if I were treading on thin ice or facing a drawn sword. I will write to you again in more detail.

When I incurred the displeasure of the government, even in Kamakura 999 out of 1,000 discarded their faith, but since popular feeling toward me has now softened, some of them seem to regret. I do not class Ō-ama Gozen with those people and I feel deeply sorry for her, but I can no more bestow the Gohonzon upon someone who goes against the Lotus Sutra than flesh can replace bone. Please explain to her thoroughly why I cannot grant her request.

With my deep respect,
Nichiren

The sixteenth day of the second month

Notes

1. An area in eastern Suruga Province (present-day Shizuoka Prefecture) extending from the southern foot of Mount Ashitaka near Numazu to Suzukawa in Fuji-shi.

2. One of three villages included in the southern part of Kai Province. When Nichiren resolved to leave Kamakura, his disciple Nikkō Shonin (1246–1333) chose a place in this village, which had been offered by the steward of the area, Hakiri Sanenaga (1222–1297), an earlier convert to Nichiren's Buddhism.

3. A river to the west of Mount Fuji flowing south into Suruga Bay. It is some 140 km long.

4. A mountain in Shensi Province in northern China.

5. Master Tung Yüan, Scholar Lu-li, Ch'i Li-chi, and Master Hsia-huang. Emperor Kao-tsu (247–195 B.C.), founder of the Han dynasty, tried to disown his son, the future Emperor Hui. At that time, Hui's mother, Empress Lü, persuaded these four eminent recluses living on Mount Shang to become the son's advisers. On seeing these recluses, the emperor was so impressed with their dignity that he finally accepted Hui as his successor.

6. The seven Worthies of the Bamboo Grove were Shan T'ao, Hsi K'ang, Juan Chi, Juan Hsien, Wang Jung, Hsiang Hsiu, and Liu Ling. Toward the end of the Wei dynasty (220–265), when the government was corrupt and chaotic, they are said to have retired to a bamboo grove and pursued the philosophy of Lao Tzu and Chuang Tzu.

7. Places along the Pacific coast in Awa. The precise location of Kataumi is difficult to identify clearly.

8. The *Daitō Saiiki Ki* (Record of the Western Regions; T51, no. 2087) is a twelve-volume account by Hsüan-tsang of the T'ang dynasty, that records his travels in Central Asia and India between 629 and 645 in search of Buddhist scriptures.

9. The *Jion Den* (full title: *Daitō Daionji Sanzō Hōshi Den*; T50, no. 2053) is the biography of Hsüan-tsang, the patriarch of the temple Tz'u-en-ssu (Jap: *Jion-ji*), recording his travels in Central Asia and India, and also dealing with his translation of Buddhist scriptures and lectures he gave after his return.

10. The *Dentō Roku* has the full title *Keitoku Dentō Roku* (The Ching-te Era Record of the Transmission of the Lamp; T51, no. 2076). It is a thirty-volume work

written by Tao-yüan in 1004 during the Sung dynasty. It traditionally is said to contain biographies of 1,701 Zen monks; in actuality nine hundred and sixty men are given biographies and seven hundred and forty are listed by name only.

11. A temple of the Kegon sect; one of the seven major temples of Nara. The construction of this temple was begun in 588 by the court official Soga no Umako and was completed in 596.

12. The oldest extant Japanese Buddhist temple, it was founded by Prince Shōtoku in 587 and is located in what is now Osaka. It is said that Shōtoku built it in gratitude for his victory together with Soga no Umako over Mononobe no Moriya, and that he enshrined there statues of the Four Heavenly Kings (Jap: Shitennō).

13. "Chronicles of Japan," a thirty-fascicle history of Japan written in 720 and, along with the *Kojiki* (Records of Ancient Matters) written in 712, one of the two oldest extant histories. Both were compiled by imperial command.

14. The Trāyastriṃśa Heaven, or the Heaven of the Thirty-three Gods is the second of the six heavens of the world of desire. It is located on a plateau on top of Mount Sumeru, where thirty-three gods, including Taishaku, are said to live. Taishaku rules from his palace in the center and the other thirty-two gods live on four peaks, eight gods to a peak, in each of the four corners of the plateau. Shakyamuni ascended to this heaven after the death of his mother Māyā and expounded the Māyā Sutra for her here. Maudgalyāyana was the only one who knew of this. The story appears in the *Zō Agon* Sutra (T2, 223a-b) and the *Zappōzō* Sutra (T4, 450b) and elsewhere.

15. The eleventh chapter of the Lotus Sutra, which describes the Treasure Tower of Tahō Buddha, who comes to bear witness to the truth of the Lotus Sutra. After Shakyamuni's proclamations in the previous chapters that the *shōmon* and *engaku* will attain Buddhahood in the future, a magnificent tower emerges from beneath the earth and hangs suspended in midair. This marks the beginning of the Ceremony in the Air, which symbolizes the Buddha's enlightenment.

16. The twenty-first and twenty-second chapters of the Lotus Sutra. In the *Jinriki* chapter, Shakyamuni Buddha transfers the essence of the sutra specifically to the Bodhisattvas of the Earth led by Jōgyō. Then in the *Zokurui* chapter, he makes a general transfer of the sutra to all the bodhisattvas. Thereafter all the Buddhas who have gathered from throughout the universe return to their respective lands; the Treasure Tower returns to its original place; and the location of the assembly shifts from midair back to Eagle Peak.

17. Monjushiri's Golden World is described in the sixty-volume *Kegon* Sutra (T9, 418c). The Tuṣita Heaven is the fourth of the six heavens in the world of desire. It is said that bodhisattvas are reborn there just before their last rebirth in the world when they attain Buddhahood. Bodhisattva Miroku is said to reside in the inner court of this heaven. Tuṣita Heaven is described in numerous texts. Mount Potalaka, said to be located on the southern coast of India, is regarded as the home of the Bodhisattva Kannon. The mountain is mentioned in the eighty-volume *Kegon* Sutra (T10, 366c).

18. A Buddha who expounded the Lotus Sutra to Bodhisattva Yakuō when the latter was practicing austerities in a past existence as a bodhisattva called Kiken. This Buddha is referred to in the *Yakuō* (23d) chapter of the Lotus Sutra.

19. Lotus Sutra (T9, 31b).

20. Lotus Sutra (T9, 39a).

21. The three types of powerful enemies (Jap: *sanrui no gōteki*) are the three types of people described in the *Kanji* (13th) chapter of the Lotus Sutra (T9, 36b-c) who

will persecute those people who propagate the Lotus Sutra in the evil age after the Buddha's passing. *See* Three Powerful Enemies in Glossary.

22. Ise Province is presently in Mie Prefecture; it is the site of the Grand Shrines of Ise, dedicated to the Sun Goddess, Amaterasu Ōmikami, or Tenshō Daijin.

23. Hachiman is a major Shinto deity, adopted into the Buddhist pantheon as a protective deity during the Heian period. The Kamo shrines (Kamigamo and Shimogamo) are located in Kyoto.

24. Minamoto no Yoritomo (1147–1199) was the first shogun of the Kamakura government, who initiated a state administration by samurai and shifted the virtual power in government from the imperial court in Kyoto to Kamakura.

25. Aoka no Kodayū (no dates) was the first attendant of the shrine to the Sun Goddess, erected in Tōjō village by Minamoto no Yoritomo. Aoka is mentioned in *Azuma Kagami* (vol. 3).

26. The original shrine to Hachiman was near Dazaifu in Kyushu, where government headquarters were established to regulate contact with the mainland and to provide defensive positions. Later a shrine, the Iwashimizu Hachiman, was established on Otokoyama south of Kyoto. In 1063 Minamoto no Yoriyoshi (988–1075) established a Hachiman shrine at Tsurugaoka in Sagami. Even after Minamoto no Yoritomo relocated the shrine in 1180 to Kitayama in Kamakura, it still retained the name Tsurugaoka.

27. Reference is to the Tatsunokuchi Persecution, an unsuccessful attempt to execute Nichiren on the twelfth day of the ninth month, 1271. Shortly after this incident he was exiled to Sado Island.

28. T9, 31b.

29. The Ten Goddesses (Skt: *Rākṣasī*; Jap: *Jurasetsu-nyo*) are the ten demon daughters of Kishimojin (Skt: Hārītī). In the *Darani* (26th) chapter of the Lotus Sutra this mother and her daughters pledge to protect the votaries of the Lotus Sutra.

30. Believed to have been a follower of Nichiren who was very close to the local lord in the Tōjō district. According to another view, he may have been among the priests of Seichō-ji where Nichiren entered the priesthood.

11 *LETTER TO THE PRIESTS OF SEICHŌ-JI*

This letter was written on the eleventh day of the first month, 1276, after Nichiren had retired to Mount Minobu. As the title indicates, it was written to the priests at Seichō-ji, the temple to which he had been sent as a child of twelve to study under Dōzen-bō.

Seichō-ji had a history typical of many temples of Nichiren's time. The temple had been founded in 771 by a Buddhist priest named Fushigi, who had chopped down an oak tree, carved it into an image of the Bodhisattva Kokūzō and placed it in a shrine he had constructed. The shrine suffered from complete neglect, however, until Jikaku Daishi (Ennin, 794–866), the third chief priest of the Enryaku-ji on Mount Hiei, visited there in the next century, after which it developed into a prestigious institution in that region.

Seichō-ji became a center for the study of the Lotus Sutra, since it belonged to the Tendai sect. After that it fell under Shingon influence with its esoteric rituals and later adopted Pure Land teachings with their reliance on Amida Buddha. Nichiren had taken his vows in 1237 and later left the temple to visit and study at various centers of Buddhist learning. Eventually in 1253, twenty years after he had entered Seichō-ji for the first time, he proclaimed his new Buddhism.

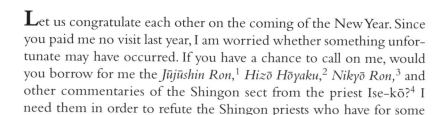

Let us congratulate each other on the coming of the New Year. Since you paid me no visit last year, I am worried whether something unfortunate may have occurred. If you have a chance to call on me, would you borrow for me the *Jūjūshin Ron,*[1] *Hizō Hōyaku,*[2] *Nikyō Ron,*[3] and other commentaries of the Shingon sect from the priest Ise-kō?[4] I need them in order to refute the Shingon priests who have for some time been clamoring against me. Bring with you also volumes one and two of the *Maka Shikan*. I would also appreciate the *Tōshun*[5] and the *Fushō Ki*[6] if they are available. Borrow the *Shūyō Shū*,[7] which is owned by Kanchi-bō, the disciple of Enchi-bō.[8] Moreover, I have heard people say that he is in possession of other relevant writings. Please borrow them as well, and tell him that I will return them as soon as possible. This year the question of which Buddhist teachings are right and which are wrong will definitely be resolved.

Tell Jōken-bō, Gijō-bō,[9] and other priests on my behalf: "Nichiren has often been on the verge of being killed. Twice he was exiled and once almost beheaded. This is not because of any worldly wrongs on his part. [As a youth,] he received supreme wisdom from the living Bodhisattva Kokūzō. He had been praying to the bodhisattva to become the wisest person in Japan. The bodhisattva must have taken pity on him, for he presented him with a great jewel as brilliant as the morning star, which Nichiren tucked away in his right sleeve. Thereafter, on perusing the entire body of sutras, he was able to discern in essence the relative worth of the eight sects as well as of all the scriptures."

The Shingon sect is especially blameworthy, because it violates the Lotus Sutra. However, it is no easy matter to refute Shingon, so in preparation I first attacked the errors of the Zen and Nembutsu sects. I have good reason for my accusation. I will reserve discussion of the rights or wrongs of Buddhist sects in India and China for some other time, but for Japan, all the people have discarded the righteous teaching of the Lotus Sutra and are therefore without exception destined to fall into the evil states of existence. This is because, at each and every temple, the Shingon sect invariably exists side by side with the Hokke sect[10] just as a shadow follows the body. Thus, to the correct practice of the Lotus Sutra is added the Shingon practice of the eighteen paths,[11] and to its performance of penitence is joined that based on the *Amida* Sutra. And in conferring titles upon eminent monks of the Tendai sect, the Shingon procedure predominates, while that of the Lotus Sutra is relegated to a secondary position.

In reality, the sutras of Shingon belong to the provisional teachings and are inferior even to the *Kegon* or the *Hannya* sutras. Yet Jikaku and Kōbō were confused on this point and held that the Shingon sutras are equal or even superior to the Lotus Sutra. The ceremony for "opening the eyes"[12] of a newly made image of the Buddha is therefore conducted with the mudra of the Buddha-eye Goddess and the mantra of Dainichi

Buddha. As a result, all the wooden and painted images of the Buddha in Japan have been rendered soulless and sightless, and in consequence, have been possessed by the Devil of the Sixth Heaven,[13] bringing ruin upon their own worshipers. This is why the Imperial court [in Kyoto] is about to perish. Now the evil teaching of Shingon has made its appearance in Kamakura and threatens to destroy all of Japan.

The Zen and Jōdo sects also hold extremely perverted views. I knew that if I declared this, it would certainly cost me my life. Yet I was determined to requite the favor of Bodhisattva Kokūzō. With this in mind, on the twenty-eighth day of the fourth month in the fifth year of Kenchō (1253), I pointed out the errors of the various sects for the first time to a small audience including Jōen-bō[14] on the southern side of the image hall in Dōzen-bō's[15] quarters in Seichō-ji, located in Tōjō village in Awa Province. For more than twenty years since then, I have persisted in my declaration without retreating a step. For this reason, I was at times driven from my dwelling and at other times exiled. In former days Bodhisattva Fukyō was beaten with staves; now Nichiren must face the sword.

All the people in Japan, both wise and foolish, from the sovereign down to the common people, say that the priest Nichiren is no match for the scholars, teachers, great masters, and sages of old. I waited for the right time to dispel their distrust of me. The time finally came when great earthquakes occurred in the Shōka era (1257), followed by the appearance of a huge comet in the Bun'ei era (1264). Observing these, I made this prediction: "Our country will suffer two terrible disasters, internal strife and foreign invasion. The former will take place in Kamakura, in the form of internecine strife[16] among the descendants of Hōjō Yoshitoki.[17] The latter may come from any direction, but that from the west[18] would be the most violent. This latter will occur solely because of the fact that all the Buddhist sects in Japan are heretical, and Bonten and Taishaku will therefore command other countries to attack us. So long as the country refuses to heed me, it will certainly be defeated, no matter whether it has a hundred, a thousand or even ten thousand generals as brave as Masakado,[19] Sumitomo,[20] Sadatō,[21] Toshihito,[22] or Tamura.[23] If these words of mine prove false, then the people are free to believe in the distorted views of the Shingon, Nembutsu and other sects." This is the prediction that I made known far and wide.

I especially warn the priests on Mount Kiyosumi. If they treat me with less respect than they show their own parents or the Three Treasures, they will become wretched beggars in this life and will fall into the hell of incessant suffering in the next. I will explain why. The villainous Tōjō Saemon Kagenobu[24] once hunted the deer and other animals kept by Seichō-ji and tried to force the priests in the various lodging temples to become Nembutsu believers. At that time I pitted myself against Tōjō and supported the lord of the manor.[25] I composed a fervent oath which read, "If the two temples at Kiyosumi and Futama should come into Tōjō's possession, I will discard the Lotus Sutra!" Then I tied it to the hand of the object of worship,[26] to which I prayed continuously. Within a year, both temples were freed from Tōjō's grasp. Certainly Bodhisattva Kokūzō will never forget this, so how can those priests who make light of me avoid being forsaken by the heavens? Hearing me say this, the more foolish of you may think that I am invoking a curse upon you. That is not so, however. I am warning you simply because it would be a pity if you should fall into the hell of incessant suffering after your death.

Let me say a few words about the nun in the family of the lord of the manor. Being a woman, and a foolish one at that, she must have been turned against me by threats from others. I pity her, for, having forgotten her debt of gratitude, she will fall into one of the evil states of existence in her next life. Despite that, however, she extended great favor to my parents, so I am praying that I may somehow be able to save her from that fate.

The Lotus Sutra is nothing other than a scripture that reveals that Shakyamuni Buddha attained enlightenment at a time even more distant than *gohyaku-jintengō*. It also predicts that Śāriputra and the other disciples will become Buddhas in the future. Those who do not believe the sutra will fall into the hell of incessant suffering. Not only did Shakyamuni himself declare all this, but Tahō Buddha also testified to its truth and the Buddhas from the ten directions extended their tongues by way of verification. Furthermore, the Lotus Sutra states that the votary of this sutra will receive the protection of the innumerable Bodhisattvas of the Earth, Bodhisattvas Monju and Kannon, Bonten, Taishaku, the gods of the sun and the moon, the Four Heavenly Kings, and the Ten Goddesses. Therefore, there is no other way to attain Buddhahood than by practicing the Lotus Sutra, for it is the only scripture that reveals all things past and future.

I have never seen Tsukushi,[27] nor do I know anything about the Mongol empire. Yet, because my prediction concerning the Mongols derived from my understanding of all the sutras, it has already come true. Hence, when I say that you will all fall into the hell of incessant suffering because of your ingratitude, how can my words prove false? You may be safe for the time being, but wait and see what happens later. All of Japan will be reduced to the same miserable state in which the islands of Iki and Tsushima now find themselves. When vast numbers of Mongol hordes close in on the province of Awa, those of you priests who cling to heretical teachings will cringe in terror and finally fall into the hell of incessant suffering, saying, "Now I know that the priest Nichiren was right." What a pity! What a shame!

Nichiren

The eleventh day of the first month
To the priests of Seichō-ji in the province of Awa

This letter is to be read aloud by the priests Sado and Suke Ajari[28] before the statue of Bodhisattva Kokūzo for all the priests of Seichō-ji to hear.

Notes

1. The *Jūjūshin Ron* (Treatise on the Ten Stages of Mind; T77, no.2425) was written about 830 by Kūkai (Kōbō Daishi, 774–835), founder of the Japanese Shingon sect. In this work he defined ten stages of the mind's development. He placed a follower of the Lotus Sutra in the eighth stage, and a follower of the *Kegon* Sutra in the upper ninth. Ultimately he placed a follower of the Shingon teaching in the upper tenth stage, because such a person had obtained the secret teaching. The treatise consists of ten volumes and asserts the supremacy of the *Dainichi* Sutra, the basic sutra of the Shingon sect.

2. The *Hizō Hōyaku* (T77, no. 2426) is a three-volume commentary on the *Jūjūshin Ron*, also composed by Kōbō.

3. The *Nikyō Ron* (full title: *Ben Kemmitsu Nikyō Ron* (A Comparison of Exoteric and Esoteric Buddhism), T77, no. 2427); also by Kōbō Daishi is a comparison of the esoteric and exoteric teachings, asserting the supremacy of the former over the latter. This work also explains each of the ten stages of mind.

4. Said to have been a priest of a sub-temple of Seichō-ji; nothing is known of him.

5. *Tōshun* is an alternative title of the *Hoke Kyō Shogisan* (ZZ1, 45, 3), a commentary on T'ien-t'ai's *Hokke Mongu*, by Chih-tu (no dates).

6. The *Fushō Ki* is the abbreviated title of Tao-hsien's *Hokke Mongu Fushō Ki*; ZZ1, 45, 1), a commentary on Miao-lo's *Hokke Mongu Ki*.

7. Generally, a collection of the fundamental teachings of a Buddhist sect. Here it means a collection of Tendai documents.

8. The biographies of these two priests are not known.

9. Nichiren's senior priests at Seichō-ji. When, on the twenty-eighth day of the fourth month, 1253, at the Seichō-ji, Nichiren denounced the established sects and proclaimed the founding of his Buddhism, thus incurring the wrath of Tōjō Kagenobu, the local lord of the district, Jōken-bō and Gijō-bō protected Nichiren, helping him to leave the temple safely and escape arrest by Tōjō's warriors.

10. Here the Tendai sect.

11. The Womb and Diamond Realm mandalas each contain nine central objects of worship. Shingon practitioners join their fingers in eighteen specific ways (mudras) when they meditate on these eighteen objects of worship.

12. Ceremony for imbuing a newly made Buddha image with a spiritual property, thus making it an object of worship.

13. The Devil of the Sixth Heaven (Jap: *Dairokuten no Maō*) is the king of the devils who dwells in the highest of the six heavens of the World of Desire. He works to obstruct Buddhist practice and delights in sapping the life force of other beings. Here Nichiren refers to him simply as Temma, heavenly demon.

14. Jōen-bō was a priest at Renge-ji at Hanabusa in Tōjō village. Renge-ji is thought to have been a branch temple of Seichō-ji.

15. Dozen-bō (d.1276) was the chief priest of Seichō-ji, under whom Nichiren first studied Buddhism. Nichiren never forgot his first teacher, and after the latter's death wrote "Repaying Debts of Gratitude," (*Selected Writings of Nichiren*, 250–318) as an expression of his gratitude.

16. Reference is to the uprising of the second month of 1272 when Hōjō Tokisuke (1247–1272) staged an ill-fated rebellion against his younger half brother, the regent Hōjō Tokimune (1251–1284).

17. Hōjō Yoshitoki (1163–1224) was the second regent of the Kamakura government. Nichiren refers to him here as Gon no Tayū.

18. Mongol forces from the west attacked southwestern Japan in 1274 and 1281.

19. Taira no Masakado (d.940) was a distinguished warrior who wielded power in eastern Japan.

20. Fujiwara no Sumitomo (d.941) was a military commander, celebrated for subduing a band of pirates in 936.

21. Abe no Sadatō (1019–1062) was head of a powerful family in eastern Japan.

22. Fujiwara no Toshihito was a distinguished warrior of the Fujiwara family in the Heian period. Little is known about him.

23. Sakanoue no Tamuramaro (758–811) was a military leader who obtained the Imperial commission of Sei-i Tai Shōgun (Generalissimo for Subjugation of the Barbarians) and established the authority of the Imperial court in the northeastern area of Japan around the early ninth century.

24. Tōjō Saemon Kagenobu was the local lord of the Tōjō district in Awa and an ardent believer in the Nembutsu. His dates are not known.

25. "The lord of the manor" refers to Hōjō Tomotoki (1193–1245), the younger brother of Hōjō Yasutoki (1183–1242), the third regent of the Kamakura government. The nun, his wife, was called Nagoe no Ama or Ō-ama. After the Tatsunokuchi Persecution she chose to abandon her faith in Nichiren's Buddhism. The previous letter, "Reply to Nii-ama," makes reference to her.

26. A statue of Shakyamuni Buddha.

27. The ancient name for Kyushu where Mongol forces attacked after sweeping

across the islands of Iki and Tsushima. It may also refer to the two provinces, Chikuzen and Chikugo.

28. Sado is another name for Nikō (1253–1314). He was one of the six closest disciples of Nichiren, known as the six senior priests. Details concerning Suke Ajari are unknown.

12 *REPLY TO A BELIEVER*

This brief letter is thought to have been written at Minobu in the fourth month of 1278, when Nichiren was fifty-seven. It is possible that this letter was addressed to Shijō Kingo, one of Nichiren's staunch followers in Kamakura. Shijō Kingo was in a precarious situation. His lord and fellow warriors at the manor showed open resentment toward his belief in Nichiren's teachings. Nevertheless, he maintained his faith steadfastly in spite of the great dangers involved.

In this letter Nichiren refers to his two exiles at the hands of the Kamakura government, alludes to the textual passages in the sutras that foretell the disasters that afflict a country that does not honor the True Law, and expresses his desire to share in the suffering of votaries of the past.

I have just received your letter. Considering how disasters have struck one after another in the wake of Nichiren's exile, would they dare attempt to harass us any further? I feel they will do no more, but people on the brink of ruin are capable of anything. Should some persecution be about to occur, there will certainly be signs. Even if I were to be exiled again, it would bring ten billion times greater good fortune than if my teachings were to be accepted. The next exile would be my third. Should it happen, the Lotus Sutra could never accuse me of being a fainthearted votary. I might well become heir to the blessings of Shakyamuni, Tahō, and all the other Buddhas of the ten directions, as well as those of the countless bodhisattvas of the Earth. How wonderful if that were to come about!

I will follow in the path of Sessen Dōji and live as did Bodhisattva Fukyō. In comparison to such a life, how wretched and meaningless it would be to fall victim to an epidemic or simply to die of old age! I would far rather suffer persecution from this country's ruler for the sake of the Lotus Sutra and thereby free myself from the sufferings of birth and death. Then I could test the vows that the Sun Goddess, Hachiman, the gods of the sun and the moon, Taishaku and Bonten made in the presence of the Buddha. Above all, I will urge them to protect every one of you.

If you continue living as you are now, there can be no doubt that you are practicing the Lotus Sutra twenty-four hours each day. Regard your service to your lord as the practice of the Lotus Sutra. [The *Hokke Gengi* makes precisely this point when it says:] "No affairs of life or work are in any way different from the ultimate reality."[1]

I fully understand what you have said in your letter.

With my deep respect,
Nichiren

The eleventh day of the fourth month

Note

1. Reference is to a passage in T'ien-t'ai's *Hokke Gengi* (T33, 683a) that comments on a passage in the *Hosshi Kudoku* (19th) chapter of the Lotus Sutra that reads, "And whatever he preaches according to his understanding will never contradict the truth. All matters that he preaches pertaining to learning, government, language, and daily living will accord with the True Law" (T9, 50a).

13 GREAT EVIL AND GREAT GOOD

It is not certain whether this letter is a self-contained statement or a fragment of a longer piece. Neither date nor recipient is known, although one theory has it that the letter was written in the second month, 1275.

❧

Great events do not have small omens. When great evil occurs, great good will follow. Since the worst slander already prevails throughout the country, the supreme True Law will spread without fail. What have any of you to regret? Although you are not the Venerable Mahā-kāśyapa, you should leap for joy! Although you are not Śāriputra, you should rise and dance! When Bodhisattva Jōgyō emerged from the earth, he leapt forth joyfully, and when Bodhisattva Fugen arrived, the ground trembled in six directions. There are many things I wish to tell you, but as they are too numerous, I shall stop here. I will write to you again.

14 ON ATTAINING BUDDHAHOOD

Two years after proclaiming his Buddhism, Nichiren was living in Kamakura; the year was 1255. This letter was written to Toki Jōnin (1216–1299?), a staunch follower of Nichiren throughout his life. Some thirty letters, including the "Letter from Sado" and the major treatise "The True Object of Worship," were entrusted to his care. He was a retainer of a certain Lord Chiba in Wakamiya in Shimōsa Province and had become a lay priest in 1251 and a follower of Nichiren in 1254. Nichiren stayed briefly at his family temple in 1260 and when Nichiren was in exile in Sado, Toki played an important role in rallying the believers in the Shimōsa area.

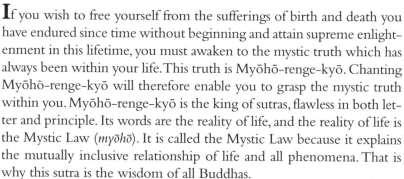

If you wish to free yourself from the sufferings of birth and death you have endured since time without beginning and attain supreme enlightenment in this lifetime, you must awaken to the mystic truth which has always been within your life. This truth is Myōhō-renge-kyō. Chanting Myōhō-renge-kyō will therefore enable you to grasp the mystic truth within you. Myōhō-renge-kyō is the king of sutras, flawless in both letter and principle. Its words are the reality of life, and the reality of life is the Mystic Law (*myōhō*). It is called the Mystic Law because it explains the mutually inclusive relationship of life and all phenomena. That is why this sutra is the wisdom of all Buddhas.

Life at each moment encompasses both body and spirit and both self and environment of all sentient beings in every condition of life,[1] as well as insentient beings—plants, sky and earth, on down to the most minute particles of dust. Life at each moment permeates the universe and is revealed in all phenomena. One awakened to this truth himself embodies this relationship. However, even though you chant and believe in

Myōhō-renge-kyō, if you think the Law is outside yourself, you are embracing not the Mystic Law but some inferior teaching.

"Inferior teachings" means those other than this sutra, which are all provisional and transient. No provisional teaching leads directly to enlightenment, and without the direct path to enlightenment you cannot attain Buddhahood, even if you practice lifetime after lifetime for countless kalpas. Attaining Buddhahood in this lifetime is then impossible. Therefore, when you chant the Mystic Law and recite the Lotus Sutra, you must summon up deep conviction that Myōhō-renge-kyō is your life itself.

You must never seek any of Shakyamuni's teachings of the Buddhas and bodhisattvas of the universe outside yourself. Your mastery of the Buddhist teachings will not relieve you of the sufferings of birth and death in the least unless you perceive the nature of your own life. If you seek enlightenment outside yourself, any discipline or good deed you do will be meaningless, just as a poor man cannot earn a penny just by counting his neighbor's wealth, even if he does so night and day. That is why Miao-lo states, "Unless one perceives the nature of his life, he cannot eradicate his heavy crimes.[2] He means here that unless one perceives the nature of his life, his practice will become an endless, painful austerity. Miao-lo therefore condemns such students of Buddhism as non-Buddhist. He refers to the passage in the *Maka Shikan*, "Although they study Buddhism, their views revert to those of non-Buddhists."[3]

Whether you chant the Buddha's name,[4] recite the sutra, or merely offer flowers and incense, all your virtuous acts will implant benefits and good fortune in your life. With this conviction you should put your faith into practice. For example, the *Jōmyō* Sutra[5] says the Buddha's enlightenment is to be found in human life, thus showing that common mortals can attain Buddhahood and that the sufferings of birth and death can be transformed into nirvana. It further states that if the minds of the people are impure, their land is also impure, but if their minds are pure, so is their land. There are not two lands, pure or impure in themselves. The difference lies solely in the good or evil of our minds.

It is the same with a Buddha and a common mortal. While deluded, one is called a common mortal, but once enlightened, he is called a Buddha. Even a tarnished mirror will shine like a jewel if it is polished. A mind which presently is clouded by illusions originating from the innate darkness of life is like a tarnished mirror, but once it is polished it will become clear, reflecting the enlightenment of immutable truth. Arouse deep faith and polish your mirror night and day. How should you polish it? Only by chanting Nam-myoho-renge-kyo.

What then does *myō* signify? It is simply the mysterious nature of our lives from moment to moment, which the mind cannot comprehend nor words express. When you look into your own mind at any moment, you perceive neither color nor form to verify that it exists. Yet you still cannot say it does not exist, for many differing thoughts continually occur to you. Life is indeed an elusive reality that transcends both the words and concepts of existence and nonexistence. It is neither existence nor nonexistence, yet exhibits the qualities of both. It is the mystic entity of the Middle Way that is the reality of all things. *Myō* is the name given to the mystic nature of life, and *hō* to its manifestations.

Renge, the lotus flower, symbolizes the wonder of this Law. Once you realize that your own life is the Mystic Law, you will realize that so are the lives of all others. That realization is the mystic *kyō*, or sutra. It is the king of sutras, the direct path to enlightenment, for it explains that the entity of our minds, from which spring both good and evil, is in fact the entity of the Mystic Law. If you have deep faith in this truth and chant Myōhō-renge-kyō, you are certain to attain Buddhahood in this lifetime. That is why the sutra states, "After my death, you must embrace this sutra. Those who do so shall travel the straight road to Buddhahood."[6] Never doubt in the slightest, but keep your faith and attain enlightenment in this lifetime. Nam-myoho-renge-kyo, Nam-myoho-renge-kyo.

Respectfully,
Nichiren

Notes

1. In any of the ten worlds.
2. *Maka Shikan Bugyōden Guketsu* (T46, 258c).
3. Based on a passage in the *Maka Shikan* (T46, 132b).
4. As used here, it denotes Nam-myoho-renge-kyo.
5. *Jōmyō* is another name for the Vimalakīrti Sutra. The following text is not found in the present version of the Vimalakīrti Sutra itself, but is based on a passage in the *Maka Shikan* (T46, 9a).
6. T9, 52c.

15 LESSENING ONE'S KARMIC RETRIBUTION

Nichiren drafted this letter on the fifth day of the tenth month, 1271, only three weeks after he was on the verge of being executed at Tatsunokuchi. It was sent to three of his leading disciples. Ōta Saemon, Soya Nyūdō, and Kimbara Hokkyō. At the time Nichiren was being held in custody at the residence of Lord Homma, deputy constable of Sado Island, in Echi in the northern part of what is now Atsugi-shi, Kanagawa Prefecture. Since these disciples lived in the area it is quite possible that they visited Nichiren at Echi. The government had difficulty in determining what to do with Nichiren, but eventually it was decided to send him into exile on Sado.

There were two brothers called Suri and Handoku.[1] Both of them answered to the name Suri Handoku. You three believers are like them. When any one of you comes, I feel as though all three of you were here with me.

The Nirvana Sutra teaches the principle of lessening karmic retribution. If one's heavy karma from the past is not expiated within this lifetime, he must undergo the sufferings of hell in the future, but if he experiences extreme hardship in this life, the sufferings of hell will vanish instantly. When he dies, he will obtain the blessings of Humanity and Heaven, as well as those of the three vehicles and the supreme vehicle. Bodhisattva Fukyō was not abused and vilified, stoned and beaten with staves without reason. He had probably slandered the True Law in the past. The phrase "after expiating his sins"[2] indicates that because Bodhisattva Fukyō met persecution, he could eradicate his sins from previous lifetimes.

161

The twenty-five successors[3] were all emissaries from the Buddha, who had predicted their advent. Of these, the fifteenth, Bodhisattva Kāṇadeva, was killed by a heretic, and the twenty-fifth, Āryasiṃha, was beheaded by King Dammira.[4] Buddhamitra and Bodhisattva Nāgārjuna[5] also suffered many persecutuions. Yet others propagated Buddhism under the protection of devout kings, without encountering persecution. This would seem to show that there are both good and evil countries in the world, and accordingly there are two ways of propagation, *shōju* and *shakubuku*.[6] Persecutions occurred even in the Former and Middle Days of the Law—even in India, the center of Buddhism. Now is the beginning of the Latter Day, and this country is far away from India. I therefore expected that persecutions would arise, and I have long been awaiting them.

I expounded this principle a long time ago, so it should not be new to you. *Kangyō-soku* is one of the six stages of practice[7] in the perfect teaching. It means that one acts as he speaks and speaks as he acts. Those at the stages of *ri-soku* and *myōji-soku* believe in the perfect teaching, but even though they praise it, their actions fail to reflect their words. For example, many people study the books of the Three Great Rulers and the Five Emperors,[8] but there is not one case in ten million where society is governed as those ancient Chinese sages taught. Thus it is very difficult to establish peace in society. One may be letter-perfect in reciting the Lotus Sutra, but it is far more difficult to practice as it teaches. The *Hiyu* chapter states, "They will despise, hate, envy and bear grudges against those who read, recite, transcribe and embrace this sutra."[9] The *Hosshi* chapter reads, "Since hatred and jealousy abound even during the lifetime of the Buddha, how much worse will it be in the world after his passing?"[10] The *Kanji* chapter reads, "They will attack us with swords and staves . . . we will be banished again and again."[11] The *Anrakugyō* chapter states, "The people will be full of hostility, and it will be extremely difficult to believe."[12] These quotations are from the sutra, but there is no way of knowing when these prophecies will be fulfilled. In the past, Bodhisattva Fukyō and Priest Kakutoku read and lived these passages. But leaving aside the two thousand years of the Former and Middle Days of the Law, now in the Latter Day, in all Japan only Nichiren seems to have done so. From my present situation, I can well imagine how followers, relatives, disciples and believers must have grieved when so many of their holy priests met persecution in the ancient days of evil kings.

Nichiren has now read the entirety of the Lotus Sutra. Even a single phrase or passage will assure one's enlightenment; since I have read the entire sutra, my benefits will be far greater. Though I may sound presumptuous, my most fervent wish is to enable the whole nation to attain enlightenment. However, in an age when none will heed me, it is beyond my power. I will close now to keep this brief.

Nichiren

The fifth day of the tenth month in the eighth year of Bun'ei (1271)

Notes

1. Suri and Handoku were brothers, sons of a Brahman family and disciples of Shakyamuni. Sources differ: some say both were stupid, others that the older brother alone was wise, and still others that the two were actually one person. At any rate, the stupid brother practiced assiduously for three years and eventually became an arhat. They are described in the *Zōichi-Agon* Sutra (T2, 601a-b), the *Honyaku Myōgi Shū* (T54, 1065a), and elsewhere. Nichiren compares their closeness to the staunch unity of the three believers from Shimōsa to whom this letter is addressed.

2. T9, 51a.

3. The numbering and order of listing of the Buddha's successors (often referred to as the twenty-four Indian patriarchs) varies slightly according to different documents. The translation here is based on Nichiren's full list that appears in a letter of 1280 (*Tayū no Sakan Gohenji*), which follows the list found in *Maka Shikan* (T46, 1a-b), and lists the traditional twenty-four successors. The present text writes twenty-five successors; Shakyamuni is added at the head of the list. Thus, Āryasiṃha, below in the text, is given as the twenty-fifth successor.

4. Kāṇadeva (also known as Āryadeva; given here in the text as Daiba bosatsu) studied under Nāgārjuna and was killed by an antagonist during a religious debate. He is described in the *Fu Hōzō Innen Den* (T50, 318c-319b). Āryasiṃha (Shishi sonja) was beheaded by King Dammira, an enemy of Buddhism. The story has it that, instead of blood, white milk flowed from his veins. His biography is in the *Fu Hōzō Innen Den* (T50, 321a).

5. Buddhamitra is the ninth and Nāgārjuna the fourteenth in the order of succession.

6. *See shōju and shakubuku in Glossary.*

7. The six stages of practice of the Lotus Sutra (Jap: *rokusoku*) are described in the *Maka Shikan* (T46, 10b ff.). They are: (1) *ri-soku*, the stage in which one has not heard the True Law and is ignorant of Buddhism; (2) *myōji-soku*, the stage at which one hears the name (*myō*) of the truth; (3) *kangyō-soku*, the stage at which one perceives the truth within one's self; (4) *sōji-soku*, the stage at which one attains the purification of the six sense organs and outwardly resembles (soku) a Buddha; (5) *bunshin-soku*, the stage at

which one eradicates all illusions except fundamental darkness; and (6) *kukyō-soku*, the stage at which one eliminates fundamental darkness and manifests the Buddha nature.

8. Writings popularly ascribed to eight legendary rulers of ancient China.

9. T9, 15b.

10. T9, 31b.

11. T9, 36b–c.

12. T9, 39a.

16 LETTER FROM TERADOMARI

After failing in his attempt to execute Nichiren, Hei no Saemon, deputy chief of the Office of Military and Police Affairs, had no choice other than to follow government instructions and deliver Nichiren into the custody of Homma Shigetsura, the deputy commissioner of Sado. Nichiren was confined for almost a month at Homma's residence in Echi, Sagami Province.

Determination was finally made that Nichiren be sent into exile on Sado Island. On the tenth day of the tenth month, 1271, Nichiren, escorted by Homma's warriors set out for Teradomari in Echigo (present-day Niigata Prefecture). Arriving on the twenty-first day of the same month, they were obliged to wait for a storm to abate before crossing to Sado Island. The day after reaching Teradomari, Nichiren wrote this letter, entrusting it to a lay priest whom Toki Jōnin had sent to accompany him.

The group reached Sado on the twenty-eighth day of the tenth month and arrived on the first day of the eleventh month at Tsukahara, the cold and desolate place that had been designated as Nichiren's place of banishment. Nichiren remained on Sado for nearly two and a half years, writing prolifically, and gaining many converts to his teaching.

I have received the string of coins that you sent. Those resolved to seek the Way should all gather and listen to the contents of this letter.

This month (the tenth month), on the tenth day, we left the village of Echi in Aikō District of the province of Sagami. Along the way we stopped at Kumegawa in the province of Musashi, and, after traveling for twelve days, arrived here at the harbor of Teradomari in the province of Echigo. From here we are going to cross the sea to the island province of Sado, but at the moment the winds are not favorable, so I do not know when we will depart.

The hardships along the way were worse than I could have imagined, and indeed more than I can put down in writing. I will leave you to surmise what I endured. But I have been prepared for such difficulties from the outset, so there is no point in starting to complain about them now. I shall accordingly say no more of the matter.

The fourth volume of the Lotus Sutra states: "Since hatred and jealousy toward this sutra abound even during the lifetime of the Buddha, how much worse will it be in the world after his passing?"[1] The fifth volume says: "The people will be full of hostility, and it will be extremely difficult to believe."[2] And the thirty-eighth volume[3] of the Nirvana Sutra states: "At that time all the heretics spoke to [King Ajātaśatru], saying, 'O Great King, at present there is a man of incomparable wickedness, a monk called Gautama.[4] All sorts of evil persons, hoping to gain profit and alms, have flocked to him and become his followers. They do not practice goodness, but instead use the power of spells and magic to win over men like Mahākāśyapa, Śāriputra, and Maudgalyāyana.' "

This passage from the Nirvana Sutra recounts the evil words that the various Brahman heretics spoke against Shakyamuni Buddha because he refuted the scriptures preached by their original teachers, the two deities, and the three ascetics.[5]

In the above passages from the Lotus Sutra, however, it is not the Buddha himself who is being looked upon as an enemy. Rather, as T'ien-t'ai explains, it is [the Lotus Sutra which is being opposed by] "the various *śrāvakas* and *pratyekabuddhas* and the bodhisattvas who seek only the Buddha of recent enlightenment."[6] In other words, persons who show no desire to hear or believe in the Lotus Sutra or who say that it does not match their capacity, though they may not actually slander the Law in so many words, are all to be regarded as envious and hostile enemies.

Observing the situation when the Buddha was in the world and comparing it with the situation since his passing, we may say that the scholars of the various sects in the world today are like the heretics of the Buddha's time. They too speak of "a man of incomparable wickedness," by which they mean me, Nichiren. They speak of "all sorts of evil persons who have flocked to him," by which they mean my disciples and followers. The heretic believers, having incorrectly received and transmitted the teachings of the earlier Buddhas, displayed hostility toward the later Buddha, Shakyamuni. The scholars of the various sects today are doing the same sort of thing. In effect, they have let their own way of understanding the Buddha's teachings lead them into heretical views. They are like persons who, dizzy from drink, think that the huge mountain in front of them is spinning round and round. And so we now have these eight sects or ten sects[7] all disputing with one another over their various doctrines.

The eighteenth volume of the Nirvana Sutra sets forth the doctrine of "the precious jewels that ransom life."[8] The Great Teacher T'ien-t'ai, after studying and pondering this passage, concluded that "life" refers to the Lotus Sutra, and the "precious jewels," to the first three [of the four] teachings[9] expounded in the Nirvana Sutra. But what then of the fourth or perfect teaching, which the Nirvana Sutra also expounds? This teaching represents a reiteration of the doctrine already expounded in the Lotus Sutra concerning the eternally inherent Buddha nature, and was preached to lead people to the Lotus Sutra from which it originated. The Nirvana Sutra's perfect teaching of the eternally inherent Buddha nature in fact belongs to the Lotus Sutra. The merits unique to the Nirvana Sutra are consequently limited to the first three of the four teachings [and do not include the fourth].

The third volume of T'ien-t'ai's *Hokke Gengi* states, "The Nirvana Sutra offers precious jewels to ransom the life [of the Lotus Sutra], and thus the hands are clapped and the bargain concluded."[10] The third volume of the *Hokke Gengi Shakusen* explains this by saying: "The Tendai school cites this metaphor to indicate that the contents of the Nirvana Sutra are to be regarded as precious jewels [that ransom the life of the Lotus Sutra]."[11]

The Great Teacher T'ien-t'ai, in his work entitled *Shi'nenjo*, cites the passage in the Lotus Sutra that reads, "Though they may set forth various paths . . ."[12] and declares that the four flavors[13] [of the *Kegon*, *Agon*, *Hōdō*, and *Hannya* sutras] are also to be regarded as precious jewels. If so, then both the Nirvana Sutra, which was preached after the Lotus Sutra, and the other sutras that were preached before, are all to be regarded as precious jewels offered for the sake of the Lotus Sutra.

But the Buddhist scholars in the world today are of the opinion that this interpretation represents a doctrine put forward by the Tendai sect alone, and that none of the other sects accepts it. When I, Nichiren, consider the matter, however, I have this to say. The eight or ten sects we are speaking of all came into existence after the death of the Buddha and are the creation of the various scholars and teachers of the time. But we should not evaluate the sutras that the Buddha preached during his lifetime on the basis of the doctrines of sects established after his death. The judgments put forward by T'ien-t'ai, however, completely accord with the teachings of the various sutras. It is wrong to discard them on the grounds that they represent no more than the opinions of a single sect.

The scholars of the various sects continue to cling to the mistaken opinions of their respective teachers. Therefore, they declare that religious practices must be accommodated to the people's capacities, or they defer to the opinions of their founders or try to persuade the worthy rulers of the time to be their allies. The upshot of all this is that in the end they give themselves up wholly to evil intentions, engage in wrangling and doctrinal disputes, and take delight in inflicting injury upon persons who are guilty of no fault.

Among the various sects, the opinions of the Shingon are particularly distorted. Its founders, Shan-wu-wei and Chin-kang-chih,[14] maintained: "The concept of *ichinen sanzen* is the most important of all T'ien-t'ai's principles and the heart and core of the teachings put forward by the Buddha in the course of his lifetime. But setting aside the doctrine that the three thousand realms are encompassed by the mind, which constitutes the foundation of both the exoteric and the esoteric teachings, the mudras and mantras form the most crucial part of the Buddhist teachings." The Shingon leaders in later times have used this pronouncement as a pretext to declare that all sutras which do not mention mudras and mantras are to be regarded as inferior and, in fact, as no different from non-Buddhist teachings.

Some of the esoteric teachers assert that the *Dainichi* Sutra was preached by [Dainichi Buddha,] a Buddha other than Shakyamuni Buddha, others declare that it is the highest of all the teachings put forth by the Lord Shakyamuni, while still others say that the same Buddha manifested himself once in the form of Shakyamuni Buddha to preach the exoteric sutras, and on another occasion appeared in the form of Dainichi Buddha to preach the esoteric sutras. Thus, misunderstanding the underlying principles of Buddhism, they produce an endless array of erroneous opinions. They are like a group of people who, unaware of the true color of milk, venture various speculations as to what the color might be, though none are able to surmise it correctly.[15] Or, they are like the blind men in the parable who try to guess the true shape of the elephant.[16] In this connection, the scholars of the various sects should understand that the *Dainichi* Sutra, if preached before the Lotus Sutra, is on a level with the *Kegon* Sutra, and if preached after the Lotus Sutra, is on a level with the Nirvana Sutra, [both of which serve only as precious jewels to ransom the life of the Lotus Sutra].

Is it not possible that the Lotus Sutra in India contained descriptions of mudras and mantras, but that those who translated the text into Chinese omitted those sections—Kumārajīva calling his version *Myōhō-renge-kyō*? And is it also not possible that Shan-wu-wei added mudras and mantras and called his version the *Dainichi* Sutra? For example, there were other versions of the Lotus Sutra, such as the *Shō-hokke-kyō*, the *Tembon-hoke-kyō*, the *Hokke-zammai-kyō*, and the *Satsuun Fundari-kyō*.[17]

In India after the Buddha's passing, Bodhisattva Nāgārjuna was the one who truly understood the relationship between the Lotus Sutra and the other sutras, while in China, the Great Teacher T'ien-t'ai Chih-che was the first to grasp it correctly. Men like Shan-wu-wei of the Shingon school, Ch'eng-kuan[18] of the Kegon school, Chia-hsiang[19] of the Sanron school and Tz'u-en[20] of the Hossō school each publicly upheld the doctrines of the school they had established, but in their hearts they were all won over to the teachings of the T'ien-t'ai school. Yet their disciples were ignorant of this fact [and hence developed erroneous opinions]. How can they avoid being guilty of slandering the Law?

Some people criticize me, saying, "Nichiren does not understand the capacities of the people of the time but goes around preaching in a harsh manner—that's why he meets with difficulties." Other people say, "The *shakubuku* practices described in the *Kanji* chapter are for bodhisattvas who are far advanced in practice, [not for someone like Nichiren. He ought to follow the *shōju* methods of] the *Anrakugyō* chapter, yet he fails to do so." Others say, "I, too, know the Lotus Sutra is supreme, but I say nothing about it." Still others complain that I give all my attention to doctrinal teachings [and say nothing about the observation of the mind].[21]

I am well aware of all these criticisms against me. But I recall the case of Pien Ho,[22] who had his feet cut off, and of Kiyomaro[23] [literally, Pure Man], who was dubbed Kegaremaro [Filthy Man] and almost put to death. All the people of the time laughed at them with scorn, but unlike those two men, those who laughed left no good name behind them. And all the people who level unjust criticisms at me will meet with a similar fate.

The *Kanji* chapter says: "There will be many ignorant people who will curse and speak ill of us." I observe my own situation in this passage. Why should it not apply to all of you as well? "They will attack us with swords and staves," the passage continues. I have experienced this passage from the sutra with my own body. Why do my disciples not do likewise? Further on, the passage says, "Constantly they will go about among the populace, seeking in this way to slander us." And, "They will address the rulers, high ministers, Brahmans and great patrons of Buddhism [. . . slandering and speaking evil of us]." And, "They will confront us with foul language and angry frowns; again and again we will be banished."[24] "Again and again" means time after time. And I, Nichiren, have been repeatedly driven away, and have twice been condemned to exile.[25]

The Lotus Sutra invariably concludes the Dharma preaching of all Buddhas of the three existences.[26] The past events described in the *Fukyō* chapter[27] I am now experiencing as predicted in the *Kanji* chapter; thus the present foretold in the *Kanji* chapter corresponds to the past of the *Fukyō* chapter. The *Kanji* chapter of the present will be the *Fukyō* chapter of the future, and at that time, I, Nichiren, will be its Bodhisattva Fukyō.

The Lotus Sutra consists of a single work in eight volumes and twenty-eight chapters, but I have heard that the sutra as it existed in India was long enough to stretch over a whole *yojana*.[28] In other words, there must have been many more chapters to it. The twenty-eight–chapter version used today in China and Japan represents the most essential portion of an abbreviated version.

Let us set aside for now the revelation section[29] of the sutra. In the following, transmission, section, the three pronouncements[30] of the *Hōtō* chapter are delivered to the assembly gathered at Eagle Peak and present at the Ceremony in the Air. As to the vow made in the *Kanji* chapter by the twenty thousand, the eighty thousand, and the eighty myriads of millions of nayutas[31] of great bodhisattvas, a man of shallow wisdom like myself cannot comprehend it. But I would note that the phrase "in an age of fear and evil" which appears in this chapter indicates the beginning of the Latter Day of the Law. This "age of fear and evil" is later referred to in the *Anrakugyō* chapter as "in the latter age." And looking at other translations of the sutra, we find that in the *Shō-hokke-kyō* it appears as "in the latter age hereafter" or "in the latter age to come," while in the *Tembon-hoke-kyō* it appears as "in an age of fear and evil."

In this latter age that corresponds to our own time, the three types of enemies[32] have appeared, but not a single one of the eighty myriads of millions of nayutas of bodhisattvas is anywhere to be seen. It is like a dried-up lake missing its full share of water, or a waning moon that is far from full. If the water is clear, the image of the moon will be reflected on it, and if trees are planted, then birds can nest in them. Therefore I, Nichiren, propagate this sutra in place of the eighty myriads of millions of nayutas of bodhisattvas. I ask that those bodhisattvas grant me their aid and protection.

The lay priest[33] who bears this letter tells me that you instructed him to accompany me to the province of Sado. But in view of the expenses of the trip and other difficulties, I am sending him back to you. I already know the depths of your consideration. Please explain to the others what I have written here. I am very much concerned about the priests who are in prison,[34] and I hope you will inform me of their situation at your earliest convenience.

Respectfully,
Nichiren

The Hour of the Cock (5:00–7:00P.M.), the twenty-second day of the tenth month

Notes

1. T9, 31b.
2. T9, 39a.
3. The following passage is actually from volume thirty-nine of this sutra (T12, 592c).
4. The family name of Shakyamuni, meaning "best cow." Early texts frequently refer to Gautama Buddha.
5. The two deities are Maheśvara and Viṣṇu; the three ascetics are Kapila, Ulūka, and Ṛṣabha.
6. This quotation is a rephrasing of a passage by Miao-lo in his *Hokke Mongu Ki* (T34, 306c), commenting on a passage in T'ien-t'ai's *Hokke Mongu* in reference to the passage in the *Hosshi* (10th) chapter of the Lotus Sutra that reads: "Since hatred and jealousy toward this sutra abound during the lifetime of the Buddha, how much worse will it be after his passing?" (T9, 31b). A *śrāvaka* (Jap: *shōmon*) is a disciple who listens to the Buddha's teaching and strives for enlightenment. A *pratyekabuddha* (Jap: *engaku*) is one who attains awakening by himself. The Buddha of recent enlightenment refers to Shakyamuni in his provisional capacity as the historical Buddha who first attained enlightenment under the Bodhi tree.
7. The eight sects are the Nara (710–794) sects: Kegon, Hossō, Sanron, Ritsu,

Kusha, and Jōjitsu, plus the Tendai and Shingon sects that were established in the Heian period (794–1185), to which are added the Jōdo (Pure Land) and Zen schools of the Kamakura period (1185–1333) to make ten.

8. This quotation actually appears in the *Hokke Gengi* (T33, 704c) and the *Hokke Gengi Shakusen* (T33, 858b). See notes 11 and 12 below. The Nirvana Sutra states that the store of seven gems can ransom one's life when threatened by famine, bandits, or an evil king (T12, 472b). The expression "precious jewel that ransoms life" is based on this passage.

9. The four teachings of doctrine is a part of the eight teachings (Jap: *hakkyō*) by which T'ien-t'ai classified the sutras. *See* Eight Teachings in Glossary. The fourth, or perfect teaching, or True Mahayana, teaches the mutually inclusive relationship of the ultimate reality with all phenomena.

10. This quotation appears in the second volume of the *Hokke Gengi* (T33, 704c). The statement, "the hands are clapped and the bargain concluded," indicates that after Shakyamuni expounded the perfect teaching in the Lotus Sutra, he reiterated it in the Nirvana Sutra.

11. T33, 858b.

12. The *Shi'nenjo* (Four Meditations; T46, no. 1918) was narrated by T'ien-t'ai and recorded by Chang-an. It does not cite the passage from the *Hōben* (2d) chapter of the Lotus Sutra given here (T9, 9b), although it does cite a passage of similar import.

13. The first four of the five flavors: fresh milk, cream, curdled milk, butter, and ghee. T'ien-t'ai used them as metaphors for the teachings of the five periods: Kegon, Agon, Hōdō, Hannya, and Hokke-Nehan. The four flavors indicate all the sutras expounded before the Lotus Sutra.

14. *See* Glossary for these early founders of esoteric Buddhism in China.

15. The Nirvana Sutra (T12, 446c–447a) states that Brahmans, being ignorant of Shakyamuni's teachings of eternity, happiness, true self, and purity, fall into erroneous views, like blind men who do not know the true color of milk.

16. This parable appears in the Nirvana Sutra (T12, 556a). A king had his high minister bring an elephant to a group of blind men, let them touch it, and then asked them to describe it to him. One blind man who pressed his hands against the elephant's stomach said that it was like a pot; another who touched the elephant's tail said that it resembled a rope; still another who stroked the elephant's trunk insisted that the animal resembled a pestle; and so on. In this parable, Shakyamuni likened the king who knows the truth to the Buddha's wisdom, the high minister to the Nirvana Sutra, the elephant to the Buddha nature, and the blind men, ignorant of the Buddha nature, to deluded common mortals.

17. The *Shō-hokke-kyō* (T9, no. 263) and the *Tembon-hoke-kyō* (T9, no. 264) are two of the three extant translations of the Lotus Sutra, done by Dharmarakṣa in 286, and by Jñānagupta and Dharmagupta in 601, respectively. The *Hokke-zammai-kyō* (T9, no. 260) was translated by Chih-yen in 427. The translator of the *Satsuun Fundari-kyō*, also known as the *Satsudon Fundari-kyō*, is unknown. These latter two versions have both been lost.

18. Ch'eng-kuan (738–839) was the fourth patriarch of the Hua-yen (Kegon) school, known also by the title Ch'ing-liang. He studied various schools under different masters but concentrated his teachings on the *Kegon* Sutra, participating in the translation of the forty-volume version of this sutra. He was greatly honored by several emperors and was awarded numerous titles and high rank.

19. Chia-hsiang (549–643) is more commonly known as Chi-tsang; Chia-hsiang is the name of the temple at which he lived. He is often regarded as the first patriarch of San-lun (Sanron) in China. He studied the three teachings of the San-lun: *Chūron, Jūnimon Ron,* and *Hyaku Ron,* and organized the teachings of this school.

20. Tz'u-en (632–692) was the founder of the Fa-hsiang (Hossō) school. He is also known as K'uei-chi. One of the outstanding disciples of Hsüan-tsang, he collaborated with him on the translation of important texts, and wrote several commentaries on the Consciousness-Only doctrines.

21. The translation of the above passage has been expanded for clarity. The *Kanji* (13th) chapter of the Lotus Sutra describes how the eighty myriads of millions of nayutas of bodhisattvas vow to teach the sutra in the frightful, evil age after the Buddha's passing, and enumerates the types of persecutions that will be met with in the degenerate age to come. The *Anrakugyō* (14th) chapter details the four peaceful means of practice, by peaceful deeds, words, thoughts, and vows. The observation of the mind is the perception through meditation of the ultimate reality inherent in one's life. This, along with the doctrinal study of the sutras, are the two integral aspects of practice taught in the Tendai sect. Nichiren gives emphasis to the meditational aspect (the intonation of the daimoku) but feels that criticism is leveled against him because, in doing *shakubuku,* he emphasized scriptural comparison to establish the superiority of the Lotus Sutra.

22. Pien Ho was a native of Ch'u in China during the Chou dynasty. According to the *Han Fei Tzu,* he found a precious gem at Mount Ch'u and presented it to King Li. When the king had it appraised, the appraiser identified it as a mere stone. So the king had Pien Ho's left foot cut off. After the king's death, Pien Ho again presented the precious stone, this time to King Wu, but had his right foot cut off on a second charge of deception. Later, when King Wen had ascended the throne, Pien Ho wept for three days at the foot of Mount Ch'u, holding the precious stone, and finally shed tears of blood. Hearing this, King Wen obtained the stone from Pien Ho and had it polished. It was then finally identified as being genuine.

23. Wake no Kiyomaro (733–799) was a high-ranking court official who thwarted the attempts of the priest Dōkyō, Empress Shōtoku's favorite, to ascend the throne and was persecuted as a result. After the death of the empress, however, Dōkyō was stripped of power, and Kiyomaro was pardoned from his sentence of exile and recalled to service at court.

24. T9, 36b-c.

25. Nichiren was exiled by government authorities to Izu from the fifth month, 1261 to the second month, 1263 and to Sado Island from the tenth month, 1271 to the third month, 1274.

26. The translation here is based on a passage in the *Hōben* (2d) chapter of the Lotus Sutra which reads: "As has been the manner in which all the Buddhas of the three existences preach the Law, so I, too, now preach the Law without distinctions." (T9, 10a). The five categories of Buddhas—all Buddhas in general, past Buddhas, present Buddhas, future Buddhas, and Shakyamuni Buddha—invariably follow the same method of preaching, expounding their various teachings in order to lead people to the one Buddha vehicle, to the Lotus Sutra.

27. The twentieth chapter of the Lotus Sutra, which describes the practices of Bodhisattva Fukyō, who lived in the Middle Day of the Law of the Buddha Ionnō and persevered in the face of persecution for the sake of the True Law.

28. A *yojana* was a unit of measurement in ancient India, equal to the distance which the royal army was thought to march in a day. Approximations vary as widely as 9.6, 18, and 24 km.

29. One of the three divisions of a sutra—preparation, revelation, and transmission—used in interpreting the Buddhist teachings. Nichiren applies these divisions solely to the theoretical teaching (former half) of the Lotus Sutra. From this viewpoint, preparation consists of the *Muryōgi* Sutra and the *Jo* (1st) chapter; revelation, the *Hōben* (2d) through *Ninki* (9th) chapters; and transmission, the *Hosshi* (10th) through *Anrakugyō* (14th) chapters.

30. The three pronouncements (Jap; *sanka no chokusen*) are exhortations by Shakyamuni in the *Hōtō* (11th) chapter, three times urging the assembly before him to propagate the Lotus Sutra after his death.

31. *Nayuta* is an Indian numerical unit of immense size; explanations differ according to the source. The *Kusha Ron* defines it as one hundred billion.

32. Also referred to as the three powerful enemies. They are defined by Miao-lo in the *Hokke Mongu Ki* (T34, 315a) on the basis of descriptions in the twenty-line verse that concludes the *Kanji* (13th) chapter of the Lotus Sutra. They are: (1) lay people ignorant of Buddhism who denounce the votaries of the Lotus Sutra and attack them with swords and staves; (2) arrogant and cunning priests who think they have attained what they have not yet attained and slander the votaries; and (3) priests revered as saints and respected by the general public who, in fear of losing fame or profit, induce the secular authorities to persecute the votaries of the Lotus Sutra.

33. One who is tonsured as a priest but continues to live as a layman. In Japan, from the Heian period (794–1185) on, a distinction was made between lay priests (*nyūdō*) and those who had formally renounced the world and lived in temples.

34. After the Tatsunokuchi persecution, five of Nichiren's disciples, including Nichirō (1245–1320), were imprisoned.

17 ASPIRATION FOR THE BUDDHA LAND

Nichiren arrived on Sado on the twenty-eighth day of the tenth month, reaching Tsukahara, a desolate field used as a graveyard, that was to be his home, on the first day of the eleventh month, 1271. His lodging was a dilapidated shrine known as Sammai-dō; wind and snow poured through the gaping holes in the roof and walls. Lacking for both food and shelter, he sent back to the mainland some of the young priests who had accompanied him. With them he sent this letter to his loyal disciple, the lay priest Toki Jōnin. This was the first letter that he wrote from Sado Island. The present letter, entitled "Aspiration for the Buddha Land" (*Gambō Bukkoku no Koto*), also bears the title *Toki Nyūdō Dono Gohenji* (In reply to the Lay Priest Toki).

⁓

It is now the last ten-day period of the eleventh month. While I was living in Kamakura in Sagami province, I thought that the changing of the four seasons was the same in all provinces, but in the two months[1] that have passed since I arrived in this northern province of Sado, the icy winds have been blowing without pause, and although there are times when the frost and snow stop falling, one never sees the sunlight. I feel the eight cold hells[2] in my present body. The hearts of the people here are like those of birds and beasts; they recognize neither sovereign, teacher, nor parent. Even less do they distinguish between truth and error in Buddhism, or between good and evil teachers. But I will say no more of this.

When I sent back from Teradomari the lay priest whom you had dispatched on the tenth day of the tenth month to accompany me, I wrote and entrusted to him certain teachings for you.[3] As you have probably surmised from these, the advent of the Great Law is already before our very eyes. In the two thousand two hundred years and more since the Buddha's passing, in all of India, China, Japan, and the entire world, [as the Great Teacher T'ien-t'ai states:] "Vasubandhu and Nāgārjuna clearly perceived the truth in their hearts, but they did not teach it. Instead, they preached the provisional Mahayana teachings, which were suited to their times."[4] T'ien-t'ai and Dengyō gave a general indication of it but left its propagation for the future. Now this secret Law, the one great reason for which all Buddhas make their advent, will be spread for the first time in this country. And is not Nichiren the very person who propagates it?

The portents of its rise have already appeared. The great earthquake of the past Shōka era[5] was a major omen of a kind never before witnessed in previous ages, one totally unprecedented in the twelve generations of divine rule,[6] the ninety reigns of human emperors,[7] and the two thousand two hundred years and more since the Buddha's passing. The *Jinriki* chapter [of the Lotus Sutra] states, "Because [there will be those who] faithfully uphold this sutra after the Buddha's passing, all the Buddhas rejoice and display their limitless mystic powers."[8] It also refers to "all the laws of the Buddha."[9] Once this great Law spreads, the pre-Lotus Sutra teachings as well as the theoretical teaching of the Lotus Sutra will no longer provide even the slightest benefit. The Great Teacher Dengyō states, "When the sun rises, the stars go into hiding."[10] And the preface written by the priest Tsun-shih reads, "At the beginning of the Latter Day of the Law, [Buddhism rises in the east and] illuminates the west."[11] This great Law has already appeared. The signs heralding its advent far surpass those of previous ages. In pondering the significance of this, I realize it is because the time [for propagation] has arrived. The sutra states: "[Among these bodhisattvas] were four who led the entire multitude. The first was called Jōgyō...."[12] It also reads, "One who is able to uphold this sutra in the evil age of the Latter Day of the Law ... ,"[13] and "To seize Mount Sumeru and fling it far off."[14]

I would like you to gather and keep together in one place the five notebooks I mentioned to you, which contain essential passages from the various sutras and from the *Daichido Ron*. Please make sure that the essential passages from the treatises and commentaries as well do not become scattered and lost. Tell the young priests not to neglect their studies. You must not lament too bitterly over my exile. The *Kanji* and *Fukyō* chapters[15] clearly state [that the votary of the Lotus Sutra will

meet persecution]. Life is limited, and we must not begrudge it. What
we should aspire to, after all, is the Buddha land.

Nichiren

*The twenty-third day of the eleventh month in the eighth year of
Bun'ei (1271)*

I AM SENDING BACK SOME OF THE YOUNG PRIESTS [WHO ACCOMPANIED
ME HERE TO SADO]. YOU CAN ASK THEM WHAT THIS PROVINCE IS LIKE
AND ABOUT THE CIRCUMSTANCES UNDER WHICH I LIVE. IT IS IMPOSSIBLE
TO DESCRIBE THESE MATTERS IN WRITING.

Notes

1. Nichiren arrived on Sado on the twenty-eighth day of the tenth month. In referring to the "two months that have passed," he means that his stay on the island, which
began in the tenth month, had now also gone through most of the eleventh month.

2. The eight cold hells lie beneath the continent of Jambudvīpa. According to the
Nirvana Sutra (T12, 430a) they are: (1) the hell of Hahava, (2) the hell of Atata, (3) the
hell of Alalā, (4) the hell of Ababa, (5) the hell of the blue lotus, (6) the hell of the
blood-red lotus, (7) the hell of the scarlet lotus, and (8) the hell of the white lotus. The
first four are named for the cries that sufferers are said to utter because of the terrible
cold. The second four are named for the changes that come about in the appearance
of their flesh when the cold causes it to break open.

3. This refers to the "Letter from Teradomari," which Nichiren wrote to Toki Jōnin
on the twenty-second day of the twelfth month, 1271.

4. *Maka Shikan* (T45, 55a).

5. A major earthquake that occurred on the twenty third day of the eighth month,
1257, in the vicinity of Kamakura, causing great havoc and destroying almost all of the
temples and shrines in the city.

6. The seven generations of heavenly gods and the five generations of earthly
deities said to have reigned in Japan before the first human emperor, Jimmu. The first
of the earthly deities was Amaterasu Ōmikami, or the Sun Goddess, revered as the pro-
genetrix of the imperial clan.

7. The successive emperors from the first emperor Jimmu through the ninetieth
emperor, Kameyama (r. 1259–1274).

8. T9, 52b.

9. In the *Jinriki* (21st) chapter, in transferring the Mystic Law to Bodhisattva Jōgyō,
Shakyamuni states, "I have briefly described in this sutra all the laws of the Buddha, all
the invincible mystic powers of the Buddha, all the secret storehouses of the Buddhas,
and all the profound practices of the Buddha" (T9, 52a).

10. A rephrasing of Dengyō's *Tendai Hokkeshū Dembōge* (DDZ 5, 12). In the original Dengyō uses the sun to represent the Lotus Sutra and the stars to represent the provisional teachings. Nichiren here places the first part of the Lotus Sutra (the theoretical teaching) in a category that includes the provisional teachings.

11. Tsun-shih (964–1032), a Sung dynasty T'ien-t'ai priest, wrote a preface or introduction to the *Daijō Shikan Hōmon* (T46, 641a-c) by T'ien-t'ai's teacher Nan-yüeh (515–577). Nan-yüeh's work had been lost for centuries in China; but a copy was brought from Japan by Jakushō, a priest of the Tendai sect, when he traveled to China in the beginning of the eleventh century. Tsun-shih therefore says that Buddhism "rises in the east." Nichiren paraphrases his expression.

12. Lotus Sutra (T9, 40a).

13. T9, 46a.

14. This passage is a part of the verse section of the *Hōtō* (11th) chapter of the Lotus Sutra that explains the six difficult and nine easy acts (Jap: *rokunan kui*). The sentence reads: "to seize Mt. Sumeru and fling it far off to the measureless Buddha lands—this is not difficult," followed later by the statement, "But in the evil times after the Buddha's passing, to be able to preach this sutra—that is difficult indeed!" *See* Six difficult and nine easy acts in Glossary.

15. The thirteenth and twentieth chapters of the Lotus Sutra. In the *Kanji* chapter, eighty myriads of millions of nayutas of bodhisattvas make a vow to teach the Lotus Sutra in the frightful evil age after the Buddha's passing. Their vow is stated in verse and enumerates the types of persecutions that will be met in propagating the sutra in the latter age. The *Fukyō* chapter tells of a bodhisattva of the same name who persevered in his practice despite slander and abuse, finally attaining supreme enlightenment through the benefit of the Lotus Sutra.

18 THE VOTARY OF THE LOTUS SUTRA WILL MEET PERSECUTION

Nichiren wrote this letter from Sado to all his priest disciples and lay followers, including Toki Jōnin, Shijō Kingo, Kawanobe, and Yamato Ajari. The date was the fourteenth day of the first month, 1274. Although the government issued a pardon a month later, Nichiren was still being treated as a criminal, a fact evident from the orders issued by Hōjō Nobutoki, quoted toward the end of this letter. Throughout his stay on Sado Nichiren suffered from the hostility of the authorities as well as from cold and hunger.

To Kawanobe and his people, Priest Yamato Ajari and
the others, and all of my disciples, and my followers Saburō
Zaemon-no-jō and Toki.[1]
Respectfully, Nichiren.

❧

Postscript:[2] Nāgārjuna and Vasubandhu were both scholars of a thousand works.[3] However, they expounded only the provisional Mahayana teachings. Though they understood [the meaning of] the Lotus Sutra in their hearts, they did not declare it in words. (An oral transmission exists concerning this.)[4] T'ien-t'ai and Dengyō went so far as to expound it, but they left unrevealed the object of worship of the essential teaching, the four bodhisattvas,[5] the high sanctuary and the five characters of Nam-myoho-renge-kyo.[6] Their reasons were, first, because the Buddha had not transferred these teachings to any of them, and second, because the time was not ripe and the people's capacity had not yet matured. Now the time has arrived, and the four bodhisattvas will surely make their advent. I, Nichiren, was the first to

179

understand this. It is said that the flight of a bluebird heralds the appearance of the Queen Mother of the West, and that the singing of a magpie foretells the arrival of a guest.[7] [In the same way, there are omens announcing the advent of the four bodhisattva.] All those who consider themselves my disciples should know that now is the time for the four bodhisattvas to appear. Therefore, even if it should cost your lives, you must never discard your faith.

Toki, Saburō Zaemon-no-jō, Kawanobe, Yamato Ajari, and the rest of you, gentlemen and priests, should read this letter to one another and listen. In this defiled age, you should always talk together and never cease to pray for your next life.

The fourth volume of the Lotus Sutra states: "Since hatred and jealousy [toward this sutra] abound even during the lifetime of the Buddha, how much worse will it be in the world after his passing!"[8] The fifth volume says: "The people will resent [the Lotus Sutra] and find it extremely difficult to believe."[9] The thirty-eighth volume[10] of the Nirvana Sutra states, "At that time there were countless Brahmans.... Their hearts gave rise to fury." It also says, "At that time there were a countless number of Brahmans who plotted together and went in a body to King Ajātaśatru of Magadha and said, 'At present there is a man of incomparable wickedness, a monk called Gautama. O King, you have never examined him, and this arouses much fear in us. All sorts of evil persons, hoping to gain profit and alms, have flocked to him and become his followers. [They do not practice goodness, but instead use the power of spells and magic to win over men like] Mahākaśyapa, Śāriputra, and Maudgalyāyana.'" This well illustrates the meaning of the passage: "Since hatred and jealousy abound even during the lifetime of the Buddha."

The Monk of Great Virtue Tokuitsu reviled the Great Teacher T'ien-t'ai Chih-che, saying: "See here, Chih-i, whose disciple are you? With a tongue less than three inches long you slander the teachings that come from the Buddha's long, broad tongue."[11] Tokuitsu also said, "Surely he [T'ien-t'ai] must be perverse and insane." More than three hundred priests, including the high-ranking prelates of the seven major temples[12] in Nara such as the Supervisor of Monks Gōmyō[13] and the Discipline Master Keishin,[14] hurled abuse at the Great Teacher Dengyō, saying, "Just as in the Western Hsia land of Central Asia there was an evil Brahman named Devil Eloquence[15] who deceived people, now in this eastern realm of Japan there is a shave-pated monk who spits out crafty words. Demons like this will attract to themselves those who are of like mind and will deceive and mislead the world."[16]

However, Dengyō states in his *Hokke Shūku*: "Shakyamuni taught that the shallow is easy to embrace, but the profound is difficult. To discard the shallow and seek the profound requires courage. The Great Teacher T'ien-t'ai trusted and obeyed Shakyamuni Buddha and worked to uphold the Hokke [Lotus] school, spreading its teachings throughout China. We of Mount Hiei inherited the doctrine from T'ien-t'ai and work to uphold the Hokke school and to disseminate its teachings throughout Japan."[17]

During the entire lifetime of the Buddha as well as the two thousand years of the Former and Middle Days of the Law that followed after his death, there were only three votaries of the Lotus Sutra. They were Shakyamuni Buddha himself, T'ien-t'ai, and Dengyō. By contrast, Shan-wu-wei and Pu-k'ung[18] of the Shingon school, Tu-shun and Chih-yen[19] of the Kegon school, and the teachers of the Sanron and Hossō schools all interpreted the sentences of the sutra of the true teaching so that they accorded with the meaning of the provisional sutras. Scholars such as Nāgārjuna and Vasubandhu inwardly grasped [the meaning of] the Lotus Sutra but did not outwardly speak of it. Not even the four ranks of saints[20] in the Former Day of the Law could compare with T'ien-t'ai and Dengyō when it came to propagating the Lotus Sutra just as it teaches.

If the Buddha's prediction is true, there must be a votary of the Lotus Sutra in the Latter Day of the Law, and the great difficulties that he encounters will surpass those that occurred during the Buddha's lifetime. The Buddha himself underwent nine great ordeals.[21] He was slandered by Sundarī; he was offered stinking rice gruel; he was forced to eat horse fodder; King Virūḍhaka massacred the greater part of the Shakya clan; he went begging but his bowl remained empty; Ciñcāmāṇavika slandered him; Devadatta dropped a boulder from atop a hill [in an attempt to kill him]; and the cold wind forced him to seek robes for protection. And in addition, he was denounced by all the Brahmans, as I mentioned earlier. If we go by the prediction in the sutra [that hatred and jealousy will be "much worse" after the Buddha's passing], then T'ien-t'ai and Dengyō did not fulfill the Buddha's prophecy. In view of all this, it must be that a votary of the Lotus Sutra will appear at the beginning of the Latter Day of the Law, just as the Buddha predicted.

In any event, on the seventh day of the twelfth month in the tenth year of Bun'ei (1273), a letter from [Hōjō Nobutoki] the former governor of Musashi Province reached the province of Sado. The letter, to which he had set his seal, read:

> We have heard a rumor that Nichiren, the priest exiled to Sado, is leading his disciples in plotting some evil action. His scheme is nothing short of outrageous. From now on, those who follow that priest are to be severely punished. Should there be those who nevertheless still violate this prohibition, their names are to be reported. This is an official order.
> Priest Kan'e[22]
> The seventh day of the twelfth month in the tenth year of Bun'ei
> To Echi-no Rokurō Zaemon-no-jō[23]

This letter reads that I am "plotting some evil action." Brahmans slandered the Buddha, saying that Gautama was an evil man. I, Nichiren, have personally suffered each of the nine great ordeals. Among them, Virūdhaka massacring the Shākya clan, going begging but being left with an empty bowl, and being forced to seek robes for protection from the cold wind have been great trials far surpassing those that occurred during the Buddha's lifetime.[24] These are hardships that T'ien-t'ai and Dengyō never met. Truly you should know that, adding Nichiren to the other three, there is now a fourth votary of the Lotus Sutra, who has appeared in the Latter Day of the Law. How glad I am to fulfill the words of prophecy from the sutra: "How much worse will it be in the world after his passing!" How sad I feel that all the people of this country will fall into the Avīci Hell! I will not go into detail here, or this letter will become too involved. You should think this through seriously for yourselves.

Nichiren

The fourteenth day of the first month in the eleventh year of Bun'ei (1274), cyclical sign kinoe-inu.

ALL MY DISCIPLES AND FOLLOWERS SHOULD READ AND LISTEN TO THIS LETTER. THOSE WHO ARE IN EARNEST SHOULD DISCUSS IT WITH ONE ANOTHER.

Notes

1. Toki Jōnin (1216–1299) was one of Nichiren's leading disciples and Saburō Zaemon-no-jō is another name for Shijō Kingo (c.1230–1300), a samurai follower who lived in Kamakura. Little is known about Kawanobe and Yamato Ajari. Kawanobe, a lay believer, is thought to have been arrested and imprisoned at the time of the Tatsunokuchi Persecution. One opinion identifies Yamato Ajari with Ben Ajari Nisshō (1221–1323), one of Nichiren's six senior disciples.

2. Judging from the word "postscript," this entire opening section of the letter, up through "never cease to pray for your next life," may have appeared at the end of the letter. Nichiren wrote many of his letters on several separate sheets of paper, and, in later ages, his followers pasted these sheets together in their proper order, to prevent them from getting scattered. In the case of this letter, this section may for some reason have been pasted at the beginning. Another possibility is that Nichiren ran out of paper as he neared the end of this letter and therefore added the postscript at the letter's head. In any event, we have preserved this order in translation, though the first two paragraphs are probably better understood as a concluding postscript.

3. Both Nagarjuna and Vasubandhu were so called because of the great number of works either written by or later attributed to them.

4. This note is in the original text. It probably refers to a passage from the *Maka Shikan* (T46, 55a), which reads, "Vasubandhu and Nāgārjuna perceived the truth in their hearts, but they did not teach it. Instead they preached the provisional Mahayana teachings, which were suited to their times."

5. Reference is to the four leaders of the Bodhisattvas of the Earth. *See* Glossary.

6. The five characters are *myō*, *hō*, *ren*, *ge*, and *kyō*. In Nichiren's writings Myōhō-renge-kyō is often used synonymously with Nam-myoho-renge-kyo, which consists of seven Chinese characters.

7. The Queen Mother of the West is a legendary goddess who dwells on a mountain in the western part of China. A similar statement is found in the *Shih-wen Lei-chü*. The *Hokke Gengi Shakusen* (T33, 905a) states, "A magpie sings, foretelling the coming of a guest."

8. T9, 31b.

9. T9, 39a.

10. This and the following text appear in the thirty-ninth volume of the Nirvana Sutra (T12, 591b–592a). Gautama is the family name of Shakyamuni; he is frequently referred to by this name in early scriptures.

11. Tokuitsu (also read Tokuichi, 780?–842?) was a famous Hossō priest who carried on a long-standing controversy with Dengyō. The *Shugo Kokkai Shō* contains details of the controversy, including many quotations (of which this is one) from Tokuitsu's *Chūhen Gikyō* (Mirror on Orthodox and Heterodox Doctrines), the original of which is no longer extant. Chih-i is another name for T'ien-t'ai. The long, broad tongue is one of the distinguishing marks of a Buddha. The citation is from Dengyō's *Shugo Kokkai Shō* (DDZ 2, 186), as is the subsequent quotation.

12. The principle temples of Buddhism in Nara, the capital of Japan during the Nara period (710–794). They are: Tōdai-ji, Kōfuku-ji, Gangō-ji, Daian-ji, Yakushi-ji, Saidai-ji, and Hōryū-ji.

13. Gōmyō (750–834) was a priest of the Hossō sect. When Dengyō sought permission from the emperor in 818 to construct a Mahayana ordination platform on Mount Hiei, Gōmyō condemned the project as slanderous in a petition submitted to the throne the following year.

14. Keishin (n.d.) was a priest at Tōdai-ji in the early Heian period. He opposed Dengyō's project of constructing a Mahayana ordination platform.

15. Devil Eloquence was an Indian Brahman whose story appears in the *Daitō Saiiki ki* (T51, 913a-b). Extremely conceited, he amused himself with paradoxical theories and worshiped demons. Because he conducted debates from behind a curtain, nobody had seen his true form. One day Aśvaghoṣa confronted him in debate and argued him into silence. Then Aśvaghoṣa lifted the curtain, exposing his demonic appearance.

16. Cited in the *Kenkai Ron* (DDZ 1, 195).

17. DDZ 3, 273.

18. Shan-wu-wei (Jap: Zemmui; Skt: Śubhākarasiṃha, 637–735) was the first to introduce esoteric teachings to T'ang China. He is frequently criticized by Nichiren. Pu-k'ung (Jap: Fukū; Skt: Amoghavajra, 705–774) is considered the sixth patriarch in the Shingon tradition. A native of India, he arrived in China in 720 and was active in the translation of esoteric texts. He was greatly honored by Hsüan-tsung and other T'ang emperors.

19. Tu-shun (557–640) and Chih-yen (602–668) were the founder and the second patriarch, respectively, of the Chinese Hua-yen (Jap: Kegon) school.

20. The four ranks of saints (Jap: *shie*) refers to Buddhist teachers upon whom people could rely. Such scholars as Nāgārjuna and Vasubandhu are indicated.

21. Also known as the nine great persecutions (Jap: *Kuō no dainan*), the major hardships that Shakyamuni Buddha suffered. Nichiren lists most of them in the following text. They are described in *Daichido Ron* (T25, 121c).

22. It is not certain whether Kan'e refers to Hōjō Nobutoki himself or to someone who functioned as his secretary.

23. Echi-no Rokurō Zaemon-no-jō is Homma Rokurō Zaemon, a retainer of Hōjō Nobutoki. He was so called because his fief was at Echi in Sagami Province. He was also steward of Niiho on Sado Island and deputy constable of the island itself, and in the latter capacity had official custody of Nichiren.

24. Here Nichiren interprets his own experiences in terms of Shakyamuni Buddha's nine ordeals.

19 *THE PROBLEM TO BE PONDERED NIGHT AND DAY*

Nichiren wrote this letter to Toki Jōnin, his learned and dedicated disciple in Shimōsa Province. The letter is dated simply the twenty-third day of the eighth month; the year is not indicated. The general consensus is that it was written in 1275 at Minobu, although there is room for doubt; there is some support for theories giving the date as 1276 or even 1273, when Nichiren was still on Sado Island.

The title, "The Problem to Be Pondered Night and Day" (*Shika Dammin Gosho*) is an alternative title. The letter is also known simply as *Toki Dono Gosho* (Letter to Lord Toki).

The second volume of *Myōhō-renge-kyō* states, "One who refuses to take faith in this sutra and instead slanders it [immediately destroys the seeds for becoming a Buddha in this world]. . . . [There will be those who slander a sutra such as this in the Buddha's lifetime or in the age after his death.] They will despise, hate, envy, and bear grudges against those who read, recite, transcribe, and embrace this sutra. . . . After they die, they will fall into the Avīci Hell. . . . In this way they will be reborn there again and again for kalpas without number."[1] The seventh volume reads, "For a thousand kalpas in the Avīci Hell, [they underwent great pain and torment]."[2] The third volume mentions [those who wandered in the evil paths for the duration of] *sanzen-jintengō*,[3] and the sixth volume refers to [those who were submerged in the realm of suffering for the span of] *gohyaku-jintengō*.[4] The Nirvana Sutra states, "Even if you are killed by a mad elephant, you will not fall into the three evil paths. But if you are killed by an evil friend, you are certain to fall into them."[5]

The *Hōshō Ron* of Bodhisattva Sāramati reads, "Those who are ignorant and unable to believe in the True Law, who hold false views and are arrogant, suffer such hindrances in retribution for the slanders of their former lives. They cling to incomplete doctrines and are attached to receiving alms and humble respect; they recognize only false doctrines, distance themselves from good friends, approach with familiarity such slanderers of the Law who delight in attachment to the teachings of the lesser vehicle, and do not believe in the great vehicle. Therefore they slander the Dharma of the Buddhas.

"A wise man should not fear enemy households, snakes, fire, poison, the thunderbolts of Indra,[6] attacks by swords and staves, or the various wild beasts such as tigers, wolves, and lions. For these can only destory one's life, but cannot cause him to fall into the Avīci Hell, which is truly terrifying. What he should fear is slander of the profound Dharma as well as companions who are slanderers, for these will surely cause him to fall into the frightful Avīci Hell. Even if one befriends evil companions and with evil intent spills the Buddha's blood, kills his own father and mother, takes the lives of many sages, disrupts the unity of the Buddhist Order, and destroys all his roots of goodness, if he fixes his mind on the True Law, he can free himself from that place. But if there is another who slanders the inconceivably profound Law, that person will for immeasurable kalpas be unable to obtain release. However, if there is one who can cause others to awaken to and take faith in a teaching such as this, then he is their father and mother, and also their good friend. This man is a person of wisdom. Because, after the Buddha's passing, he corrects false views and perverse thoughts and causes people to enter the true Way, he shows himself to have pure faith in the three treasures, and performs beneficial deeds which bring enlightenment."[7]

Bodhisattva Nāgārjuna states in his *Bodai Shiryō Ron,* "The World-Honored One expounded five causes[8] leading to the hell of incessant suffering. . . . But if, with respect to the profound Law that one has yet to comprehend, one were to remain attached [to lesser teachings, and declare that this is not the Buddha's teaching] then the accumulated sins of all the above-mentioned five acts would not amount to even a hundredth part of this offense."[9]

A worthy man, while dwelling in security, anticipates danger; a deceitful flatterer, while dwelling amid danger, takes security for granted. A great fire fears even a small quantity of water, and a large tree can have its branches broken by even a small bird. What a wise man fears is slander of the great vehicle. It was on this account that Bodhisattva Vasubandhu declared that he would cut out his tongue,[10] Bodhisattva Aśvaghoṣa implored that his own head be cut off,[11] and the Great Teacher Chi-tsang[12] made a bridge of his own body. The Learned Doctor Hsüan-tsang went to the sacred land of India to divine [which teaching represents the truth],[13] the Learned Doctor Pu-k'ung likewise went to India to resolve his doubts,[14] and the Great Teacher Dengyō sought confirmation in China.[15] Did not all these men act as they did in order to protect the true meaning of the sutras and treatises?

In Japan today, among the four kinds of believers[16] of the eight sects[17] as well as of the Pure Land and Zen sects, from the emperor and the retired emperor on down to their vassals and the common people, there is not a single person who is not a disciple or supporter of one of the three great teachers: Kōbō, Jikaku, and Chishō. Ennin, the Great Teacher Jikaku, stated: "[Even though the *Kegon* and other sutras are termed 'esoteric,' they do not fully expound the secret teaching of the Tathagata]; therefore, they differ [from the Shingon teachings]."[18] Enchin, the Great Teacher Chishō, said: "When compared with the *Dainichi* Sutra, the *Kegon* and the Lotus are mere childish theory."[19] And Kūkai, the Great Teacher Kōbō, remarked: "[Each vehicle that is put forward is claimed to be the true vehicle, but] when examined from a later stage, they are all seen to be mere childish theory."[20]

Thus all three of these great teachers held that, though the Lotus Sutra is foremost among all the teachings that Shakyamuni Buddha has preached, now preaches or will preach in the future,[21] when compared with the *Dainichi* Sutra [expounded by Dainichi Buddha], it is a doctrine of childish theory. Should any thinking person place credence in this assertion? A hundred, a thousand, ten thousand, a hundred thousand times more than mad elephants, vicious horses, fierce bulls, savage dogs, poisonous snakes, poisonous thorns, treacherous bluffs, steep cliffs, floods, evil men, evil countries, evil towns, evil dwellings, bad wives, wicked children, and malicious retainers, the people of Japan today should fear those eminent priests who keep the precepts and yet hold distorted views!

Question: Are you suggesting that the three great teachers mentioned above were slanderers of the Law? Enchō,[22] the Great Teacher Jakkō, the second chief priest of Mount Hiei; the Great Teacher Kōjō,[23] superintendent of the temple; Anne,[24] the Great Teacher Daigyō; Priest Eryō;[25] Priest Annen;[26] the Supervisor of Monks

Jōkan;[27] the Administrator of Monks Danna;[28] the Virtuous Monk Eshin,[29] and several hundred others [of the Tendai sect], as well as several hundred of Kōbō's disciples including Jitsue,[30] Shinzei[31] and Shinga,[32] and also the other great teachers and virtuous monks of the eight sects and ten sects[33] were like so many suns, moons, and stars all appearing in succession. During the passage of four hundred years and more, not a single person among these men has ever questioned the teachings of the three great teachers you mentioned above. What sort of wisdom do you base yourself on that you presume to criticize them?

Considering this in light of the points I have made above, I hope my disciples will ponder this matter, cutting short their sleep by night and curtailing their leisure by day. Do not spend this life in vain and regret it for ten thousand years to come.

With my deep respect,
Nichiren

The twenty-third day of the eighth month

I HAVE RECEIVED ONE STRING OF COINS. I HOPE ALL THOSE WHO SEEK THE TRUTH WILL GATHER IN ONE PLACE AND LISTEN TO THIS LETTER.

Notes

1. T9,15b-c. Nichiren quotes only a portion of this well-known passage from the *Hiyu* (3d) chapter of the Lotus Sutra.

2. T9,51a. Reference is to the karmic retribution suffered by those who persecuted Bodhisattva Fukyō.

3. The *Kejōyū* (7th) chapter of the Lotus Sutra explains that in the remote past of what Nichiren refers to as *sanzen-jintengō* (*see* Glossary), Shakyamuni preached the Lotus Sutra as the sixteenth son of a Buddha called Daitsū. Among those who received the seed of Buddhahood from him at that time, some later abandoned the Lotus Sutra in favor of lesser teachings and sank back to the level of *shōmon*. Not until they were reborn in India with Shakyamuni and heard the Lotus Sutra from him again were they able to receive the Buddha's prediction that they would attain Buddhahood in the future. This is interpreted to mean that they suffered in the evil paths for the duration of *sanzen-jintengō*.

4. The *Nyorai juryō* (16th) chapter of the Lotus Sutra reveals that Shakyamuni first attained Buddhahood in the inconceivably remote past of *gohyaku-jintengō* (*see* Glossary), a time more distant even than *sanzen-jintengō*. The interpretation is that

there were some who received the seed of Buddhahood from Shakyamuni at that time but later abandoned the Lotus Sutra and wandered in the realm of suffering for the duration of *gohyaku-jintengō*, until they were reborn in India with Shakyamuni and heard him preach the Lotus Sutra again.

5. T12, 497c.

6. Indra (Jap: Taishaku) was originally a god of thunder in Indian mythology. He was later incorporated into Buddhism as a major tutelary deity.

7. The *Hōshō Ron* has the full title *Kukyō Ichijō Hōshō Ron*. A treatise in four fascicles, translated by Ratnamati (c.500) of the Northern Wei dynasty, it repudiates Hinayana doctrines from the viewpoint of Mahayana, and argues that because all people possess the Matrix of the Tathagata or Buddha nature, even those of the two vehicles or *icchantika* can attain Buddhahood. The *Hōshō Ron* is generally thought to be the work of Sāramati, an Indian scholar who lived sometime during the peirod from the fifth century through the beginning of the sixth, though there are differing opinions. Tibetan tradition attributes the *Hōshō Ron* to Maitreya. The present quotation is from T31, 820b-c.

8. The five causes are the five cardinal sins. *See* Glossary.

9. The *Bodai Shiryō Ron* is a treatise is six fascicles consisting of original verses attributed to Nagarjuna, with prose commentary added later. Translated into Chinese by Dharmagupta during the Sui dynasty, it sets forth various bodhisattva practices for attaining Buddhahood. The quotation is found at T32, 532a.

10. According to the *Basubanzu Hosshi Den* (T50, 191a) and other sources, when Vasubandhu, originally a Hinayana scholar, was awakened to the greatness of the Mahayana by his brother Asanga, he wanted to cut out his tongue to expiate the slander he felt he had committed in preaching the Hinayana teachings and criticizing those of the Mahayana. However, Asanga persuaded him that he could better eradicate his offense by using the same tongue to praise the Mahayana.

11. No mention of this incident appears in the biography of Aśvaghoṣa. Possibly, after his conversion to Mahayana by Pārśva, he felt regret similar to that of Vasubandhu for having previously condemned the Buddhist teachings.

12. Chi-tsang (549–623) is also called Chia-hsiang. A priest of the San-lun (Sanron) school in China, he is sometimes regarded as the founder of the school. He wrote commentaries on the three treatises on which the school's doctrines are based, and upheld the supremacy of the *Hannya* sutras. In 597 he corresponded with T'ien t'ai concerning the Lotus Sutra and was won over by his teachings. According to the *Hokke Mongu Fushō Ki* (ZZ1 45, 1) he personally served T'ien-t'ai as his master in reparation for his previously shallow understanding. "Made a bridge of his own body" means that he lifted T'ien-t'ai on his back whenever the latter mounted the elevated lecture platform.

13. Perplexed by apparent contradictions, the Chinese priest Hsüan-tsang made a seventeen-year journey though central Asia and India, where he studied Buddhism in the original Sanskrit.

14. According to his biography in the *Sō Kōsō Den* (T50, 719b ff.) Pu-k'ung returned to India to obtain a copy of the *Kongōchō* Sutra and so resolve doubts he had about the Diamond Realm mandala.

15. Dengyō went to China in 804 to master T'ien-t'ai teachings.

16. Monks, nuns, laymen, laywomen.

17. *See* Letter 16, note 7.

18. This quotation is from the *Soshitsuji Kyō Ryakusho* (T61, 393b).

10. The precise source for this quotation is not certain. However, the *Hokke Gengi Shiki* (DBZ (new ed.) 4, 215) by Shōshin, a priest living between the twelfth and thirteenth centuries, quotes Chishō to this effect.

20. *Hizō Hōyaku* (T77, 374c). This statement means that each of the many sects claims to be the vehicle of Buddhahood, but that their doctrines prove to be shallow when compared to those of the Shingon sect.

21. Reference is to a passage in the *Hosshi* (10th) chapter of the Lotus Sutra in which Shakyamuni declares, "The scriptures I preach number in the countless millions. Among all those I have preached, now preach, and will preach, this Lotus Sutra is the most difficult to believe, and the most difficult to understand" (T9, 31b).

22. Enchō (771–837) was the second chief priest of the Enryaku-ji, the head temple of the Tendai sect located on Mount Hiei. According to Nichiren's writings, he was among the first to begin incorporating Shingon elements into the Tendai sect. His posthumous title is Jakkō.

23. Kōjō (779–858) was a priest of the Tendai sect. He became Dengyō's disciple in 808 and also studied the esoteric teachings under Kōbō. He exerted himself to realize Dengyō's dream of establishing a Mahayana ordination platform on Mount Hiei and received the imperial permission seven days after Dengyō's death in 822. The efforts to establish this ordination platform are recorded in his *Isshin Kaimon* (T74, no. 2379). He was appointed superintendent of the Enryaku-ji in 854.

24. Anne (794–868) was the fourth chief priest of Enryaku-ji. He studied under Dengyō and Jikaku, learning both the Tendai and the esoteric teachings. He wrote the *Ken Hokke Gi Shō*, a work that is no longer extant. His posthumous name is Daigyō.

25. Eryō (801–859) was a priest of the Tendai sect. He studied under Enchō and Jikaku, the second and third chief priests of Enryaku-ji, and learned both exoteric and esoteric doctrines. He was supervisor of a temple on Mount Hiei called Hōdō-in.

26. Annen (841–889?) was a Tendai priest who helped establish both the doctrine and practice of Tendai esotericism. He studied the exoteric and esoteric teachings under Jikaku and also received the doctrine of the Womb Realm from Henjō of the Genkyō-ji in Kyoto. Annen became chief priest of this temple in 884.

27. Jōkan (834–927), also known as Zōmyō, was initiated into the esoteric teachings by Chishō and in 906 became chief priest of Enryaku-ji. He was named Lesser Supervisor of Monks (*shō-sōzu*) in 915, and Greater Supervisor of Monks (*dai-sōzu*) the year after. He is said to have excelled in conducting prayer rituals to avert calamities and was appointed Administrator of Monks (*sōjō*) in 923 after his prayers had allegedly cured the emperor of illness.

28. Danna (953–1007), known also as Kakuun, is considered the founder of the Danna school of the Tendai sect. This school takes its name from a temple called Danna-in on Mount Hiei, where Kakuun lived. His lineage became known as the Danna school and, together with the Eshin school, formed one of the two branches of the Tendai sect. He was posthumously granted the title Administrator of Monks by the imperial court.

29. Eshin (942–1017), known also as Genshin, practiced at a temple called Eshin-in on Mount Hiei, and his lineage later became known as the Eshin school of the Tendai sect. His *Ōjō Yōshū* (T84, no. 2682), completed in 985, lent tremendous influence to the rise of Japanese Pure Land Buddhism.

30. Jitsue (780–847) was originally a priest of the Hossō sect who became Kōbō's

disciple after the latter returned from China in 806. Jitsue helped Kōbō establish the Kongōbu-ji on Mount Kōya; then in 823 he moved to the Tō-ji in Kyoto. Regarded as the foremost among Kōbō's ten major disciples, he was instrumental in spreading the esoteric teachings.

31. Shinzei (800–860) was a disciple of Kōbō who lived at the Jingo-ji on Mount Takao. In 856 he was appointed Administrator of Monks, the first Shingon priest to receive this title. He wrote a biography of Kōbō and also collected his writings.

32. Shinga (801–879) was a disciple and younger brother of Kōbō. He served as chief priest of both Tōdai-ji and Tō-ji and was appointed Administrator of Monks in 864. After Kōbō's death, he became an influential leader in the Shingon sect and often performed esoteric rituals for the protection of the country.

33. The eight Nara and Heian sects plus the Pure Land and Zen sects.

20 *CURING KARMIC DISEASE*

This letter is in reply to a communication from Ōta Jōmyō reporting that he was suffering from illness. The letter is dated the third day of the eleventh month, 1275, and was sent from Nichiren's place of retirement on Mount Minobu. Ōta, one of Nichiren's most devout believers, was a government official who had been introduced to Nichiren's teachings by Toki Jōnin, and the two worked together in the Shimōsa area to promote Nichiren and his teachings. Around 1278 Ōta received the tonsure and was given the religious name Myōnichi and is also known as Ōta Nyūdō, *nyūdō* meaning one who is tonsured but does not live within the temple.

The title of this letter, "Curing Karmic Disease" (*Gōbyō Nōji no Koto*) is an alternative title. The letter is also known as *Ōta Nyūdō Dono Gohenji* (A Reply to Lord Ōta).

～✦～

I see from your letter that you have been stricken with a painful affliction. Knowing you are in agony grieves me, but, on the other hand, it is cause for delight. The Vimalakīrti Sutra states, "Once the wealthy Vimalakīrti of his own volition became ill. . . . At that time the Buddha told Bodhisattva Monju to go and visit him and inquire after his illness."[1] The Nirvana Sutra says, "At that time the Tathagata . . . assumed the appearance of one who is ill in body, and lay on his right side like a sick man."[2] The Lotus Sutra states, "[The Tathagata is at ease,] with few ailments and few troubles."[3] The eighth volume of the *Maka Shikan* explains, "Vimalakīrti utilized his sickbed in Vaiśālī[4] to expound his teachings. . . . The Tathagata used his death to teach the eternity of life and clarified the power of Buddhism through sickness."[5] Another passage from the *Maka Shikan* says, "There are six causes of illness: (1) disharmony of the four elements; (2) immoderate eating or drinking;

(3) poor posture; (4) an attack by demons from without; (5) the work of devils from within, and (6) the effects of karma."[6]

The Nirvana Sutra reads, "There are three types of people whose illness is extremely difficult to cure. They are: (1) those who slander Mahayana Buddhism, (2) those who commit the five cardinal sins, and (3) those of incorrigible disbelief (*icchantika*). People in these categories suffer the worst known maladies."[7]

Another passage from the Nirvana Sutra states, "One who creates evil karma in this life will surely suffer the torments of hell in the next. However, by serving the Three Treasures, one can avoid falling into hell in the next life, but will instead suffer afflictions of the head, eye or back in this one."[8] The *Maka Shikan* states, "Even if one has committed heavy slanders . . . their retribution can be lessened in this life. Thus, illness occurs when evil karma is about to be dissipated."[9] In his *Daichido Ron*, Bodhisattva Nāgārjuna writes, "Question: If that is so, then none of the sutras from the *Kegon* to the *Hannya* is a secret teaching, but the Lotus Sutra is secret. . . . The Lotus Sutra is like a great physician who changes poison into medicine."[10] T'ien-t'ai explained the quotation further, saying, "This sutra enables the people of the two vehicles to attain enlightenment in the same way that a skilled physician can change poison into medicine."[11] Therefore, the *Daichido Ron* reads, "No other sutras are secret, but the Lotus Sutra is secret." The *Maka Shikan* says, "Since the Lotus Sutra can cure [illness], it is also called *myō* or mystic."[12] Miao-lo said, "Because it can cure that which is very difficult to cure, it is called *myō* or mystic."[13]

The Nirvana Sutra relates the following story: "King Ajātaśatru of Rājagṛha was wicked by nature . . . He killed his father, but later, in a fit of remorse, he developed a high fever and boils broke out over his entire body. They were foul and evil-smelling, repelling all who came near. His mother, Vaidehi, tried to help by applying various medicines, but this only made the boils worse; there appeared to be no hope of recovery. The king explained to his mother that the boils had a spiritual cause and did not arise from a disharmony of the four elements, and that therefore ordinary physicians could not cure them. Then the World-Honored One, the compassionate and merciful teacher, entered into a special 'moon-loving' meditation[14] for the king's sake. When he had reached the deepest stage of his meditation, a brilliant ray of light shone forth from the Buddha and fell upon the body of the king. In that instant the boils were healed."[15]

The seventh volume of the Lotus Sutra, the sutra of universal wisdom, says, "This sutra is beneficial medicine for the illnesses of all mankind. If one is ill and can hear of this sutra, his illness will vanish immediately, and he will find perpetual youth and eternal life."[16]

In light of the above quotations, it would seem that your illness cannot have originated anywhere outside the six causes of disease. I will set aside the first five causes for the moment. Illnesses of the sixth, which result from karma, are the most difficult to cure. They vary in severity and one cannot make any fixed pronouncements, but we know that the gravest illnesses result from slandering the Lotus Sutra. Even Shen Nung, Huang Ti,[17] Hua T'o[18] and Pien Ch'üeh[19] threw up their hands, and Jisui, Rusui,[20] Jīvaka,[21] and Vimalakīrti likewise kept silent. Such illnesses can only be cured by the beneficial medicine of Shakyamuni Buddha's Lotus Sutra, as that sutra itself explains.

The Nirvana Sutra, referring to the Lotus Sutra, states: "Even slander of the True Law will be eradicated if one repents and professes faith in the True Law. . . . He should devote himself to the True Law, because no other teaching can save or protect him."[22] The Great Teacher Miao-lo says, "Shakyamuni himself in the Nirvana Sutra says that the Lotus Sutra is the highest of his teachings." He further says, "One who falls to the ground rises by pushing himself up from the ground. In the same way, one with an evil heart who is destined for hell can, by slandering the True Law, be saved by it."[23]

Bodhisattva Vasubandhu was originally a scholar of Hinayana Buddhism. In an effort to prevent Mahayana Buddhism from spreading throughout Inida, he wrote five hundred treatises on Hinayana Buddhism. He awoke to the error of his views, however, when he talked with Bodhisattva Asaṅga.[24] Vasubandhu told Asaṅga that he wanted to cut out his tongue in order to eradicate the error of his former preaching. Asaṅga restrained him, saying, "Instead, use your tongue to praise Mahayana Buddhism." Then Vasubandhu immediately wrote five hundred treatises on Mahayana Buddhism in order to refute Hinayana Buddhism. He also vowed that he would never preach another word of Hinayana Buddhism for the rest of his life. In this way he eradicated his slander and was later reborn in the heaven where Bodhisattva Miroku lives.[25]

Bodhisattva Aśvaghoṣa, a native of eastern India, was thirteenth among Shakyamuni's successors.[26] At one time Aśvaghoṣa had been a leader of Brahmanism. However, when he debated with the Buddhist monk Puṇyayaśas[27] over the validity of their respective teachings, he quickly realized the superiority of Buddhism. Aśvaghoṣa was prepared to behead himself in order to pay for his past offense, saying,"I have been my own worst enemy, leading myself to hell." But Puṇyayaśas admonished him, saying, "Do not behead yourself! Instead, use your mind and your mouth to praise Mahayana Buddhism." Aśvaghoṣa soon thereafter wrote the *Daijō Kishin Ron* (Awakening of Faith in the Mahayana),[28] in which he refuted all Brahman teachings as well as Hinayana Buddhism. This marked the beginning of the spread of Mahayana Buddhism in India.

The Great Teacher Chi-tsang[29] of Chia-hsiang temple was among the most outstanding scholar-priests in China. He was the founder of the Sanron sect, and lived in Hui in Wu. Believing that none could equal him in knowledge, he was very haughty. He challenged the Great Teacher T'ien-t'ai to discuss the meaning of the phrase in the Lotus Sutra which states: "Of all the innumerable sutras I have taught, now teach, or will teach in the future, the Lotus Sutra is the most difficult to believe and the most difficult to understand."[30] In the debate, Chi-tsang was soundly defeated, and thereupon renounced his misguided beliefs. In order to expiate his heavy slander of the True Law and those who practiced it, he gathered more than one hundred eminent scholars and begged T'ien-t'ai to lecture to them. Chi-tsang used his body as a bridge for the Great Teacher T'ien-t'ai to walk on and supported T'ien-t'ai's feet with his head. Moreover, he served T'ien-t'ai for seven years, cutting firewood and drawing water for him. He ceased giving lectures of his own, dispersed his followers and, in order to purge himself of his great conceit, refrained from reciting the Lotus Sutra. After T'ien-t'ai's death, Chi-tsang had an audience with the emperor of the Sui dynasty to pay his respects. As he was leaving, he clutched His Majesty's knees and tearfully bade him farewell. Sometime later, Chi-tsang looked into an old mirror and, seeing his reflection, condemned himself for his past errors. All these many acts of penitence were done to eradicate his evil karma.

The Lotus Sutra, the supreme vehicle, is the golden teaching of the three sages.[32] Likened to an unsurpassed gem, it ranks highest among all the teachings of the past, present and future. There are passages in the Lotus Sutra which say, "This sutra is superior to all other sutras," and "The Lotus Sutra is the foremost of all teachings."[33] The Great Teacher Dengyō said that [of all the sects in Japan] the Hokke (Lotus) sect is the very one "founded by Shakyamuni Buddha himself."[34]

I have made a thorough study of the *Dainichi*, *Kongōchō*, *Soshitsuji*, and other sutras upon which the Shingon sect is based, but have found nothing written in them to justify the claim that these sutras are superior to the Lotus Sutra. This claim appears to be no more than the prejudiced view held by Shan-wu-wei, Chin-kang-chih, Pu-k'ung, Kōbō, Jikaku, Chishō, and others. Now, more than ever, I realize that it is the real intent of the Buddhas Shakyamuni and Dainichi to place the Lotus Sutra above all other sutras. When Kōbō Daishi, founder of the Shingon sect in Japan, Jikaku Daishi, and Chishō Daishi went to China during the T'ang dynasty, they inherited from Hui-kuo[35] and Fa-ch'üan[36] the distorted doctrines originally held by Shan-wu-wei, Chin-kang-chih, and Pu-k'ung. Returning to Japan, they propagated the Lotus Sutra and the Shingon teachings in such a way as to make it seem that the dim light of fireflies—the two Shingon mandalas—outshone the full moon of the Lotus Sutra, the supreme vehicle that surpasses all other sutras of the past, present, and future. Not only that, they slandered the Lotus Sutra, saying that it was a work of "childish theory" and that the Buddha of the Lotus Sutra was still in the region of darkness. However, these comments were like a dagger turned against those who made them. It is not the Lotus Sutra but the *Dainichi* Sutra that is filled with childish theory, and it was Dainichi himself who was in the region of darkness. The roots of the Shingon sect were its founders, and they were warped, to begin with. So how could its branches, their disciples and followers, be otherwise? Contamination at the source of a river will pollute its entire length. Because of this, the tree of Japan has had a long, dark night and is now about to be blighted by an alien frost. Although you were not in the mainstream of Shingon, you were still a retainer of a patron of that sect. You lived for many years in a house whose family was dedicated to an erroneous sect, and month after month your mind was infected by the teachers of error. Though huge mountains may crumble and the great seas dry up, this offense of yours will not easily pass away. However, because of the influence of past karma and the mercy that the Buddha bestows on you in this lifetime, you have met me and have determined to reform your ways. Therefore you will be spared worse suffering, though at the moment your offense has brought on these boils from which you suffer.

King Ajātaśatru[37] suffered from severe boils because he committed the five cardinal sins and slandered the Lotus Sutra. But his boils disappeared instantly when the light produced by the Buddha's "moon-loving" meditation illuminated his body. And, though it had been predicted that the king had only twenty-one days left to live, his life span was extended forty years. In deep appreciation, he rendered full support to one thousand arhats so that they could record the golden teachings of the Buddha,[38] thus enabling the spread of Buddhism in the ages of the Former, Middle, and Latter Days of the Law.

Your boils have resulted from only one offense—slandering the Lotus Sutra. The healing power of the Mystic Law you now embrace is superior to that of the Buddha's "moon-loving" meditation. There is no reason why your boils cannot be healed and your life extended. If these words of mine do not prove to be true, you should shout, "The Buddha, the eye of the entire world, is a great liar, and the Lotus Sutra of the supreme vehicle is filled with falsehood! The World-Honored One should give me proof if he cares about his good name! All the saints and sages should come to protect me if they do not want to be untrue to their vows!"

A letter cannot convey all that one would like to say, and words cannot fully express what is in the heart. The rest will have to wait until the next time we meet.

Respectfully,
Nichiren

The third day of the eleventh month

Notes

1. Vimalakīrti Sutra (T14, 539c; 544a).

2. T12, 672c.

3. This is the answer to a question addressed to Shakyamuni Buddha by the Bodhisattvas of the Earth, "Is the World-Honored One in comfort, with few ailments and few troubles?" in the *Yushutsu* (15th) chapter of the Lotus Sutra (T9, 40a).

4. Vaiśālī was one of the sixteen major countries in India. The Licchavi clan, to which Vimalakīrti belonged, lived here. Shakyamuni often visited Vaiśālī to preach Buddhism, and after the Buddha's passing, the second assembly for compiling the Buddha's teaching was held here.

5. T46, 106a–b.

6. T46, 106c.

7. T12, 431b.

8. T12, 462b.

9. T46, 107c.

10. T25, 754b.

11. *Hokke Gengi* (T33, 755a).

12. T46, 79b.

13. *Shikan Bugyōden Guketsu* (T46, 345b).

14. Here the boundless compassion of the Buddha is compared to the moonlight that releases one from uneasiness and brings peace of mind.

15. T12, 474a-b; 480c.

16. T9, 54c.

17. Shen Nung and Huang Ti were two of the Three Rulers, legendary ideal rulers of ancient China, who were skilled in medical matters.

18. Hua T'o was a physician of the Later Han, said to have been especially skillful in surgical operations. When acupuncture and medicines proved ineffectual, he performed operations under anesthesia. He invented a system of physical exercise which he himself practiced. As a result he is said to have been still vigorous even at the age of one hundred.

19. Pien Ch'üeh was a physician of the Spring and Autumn period (722–481 B.C.) in China. In his boyhood he learned medical arts and is said to have been skilled in treating almost all kinds of diseases.

20. Jisui and Rusui (Sanskrit unknown) were father and son, both excellent physicians, who are described in the *Konkōmyō* Sutra (T16, 351c). According to this sutra, they lived countless kalpas in the past. At one time an epidemic broke out and spread through their country. Jisui was too old to perform medical treatment, but Rusui mastered his medical art and, in his father's place saved the people from the epidemic.

21. Jīvaka (Jap: Giba) was an Indian physician in Shakyamuni's time. Immediately after birth he is said to have seized hold of the acupuncture needle and medicine bag. He had devout faith in Buddhism and also served as minister to King Ajātaśatru. His story is found in the Nirvana Sutra (T12, 477a-b).

22. T12, 425b.

23. *Hokke Mongu Ki* (T34, 212c; 349c).

24. Asaṅga was the younger brother of Vasubandhu. According to tradition, Vasubandhu heard that his elder brother was ill and went to visit him. Asaṅga explained that he had become ill with grief thinking of the suffering his younger brother would incur from slandering Mahayana, and persuaded him to renounce his faith in Mahayana. *Basubanzu Hosshi Den* (T50, 191a).

25. The story is detailed in Chi-tsang's *Hyaku Ron Sho* (T42, 234a). The heaven where Bodhisattva Miroku (Maitreya) lives is the Tuṣita Heaven, fourth in the six heavens of the world of desire.

26. *See* Twenty-four successors in Glossary.

27. Punyayaśas was twelfth of the twenty-four successors. Nichiren refers to him as Roku biku.

28. The *Daijō Kishin Ron* (T32, nos. 1666 and 1667) is attributed to Aśvaghoṣa, but is very likely of Chinese origin. The source of the above quotation has not been traced.

29. *See* Letter 19, note 12.

30. Famous passage in the *Hosshi* (10th) chapter of the Lotus Sutra (T9, 31b). Nichiren cites it only as *ikontō*, past, present, and future.

31. The stories relating to T'ien-t'ai and Chi-tsang are frequently mentioned by Nichiren. Their precise source is not known.

32. The three sages are Shakyamuni Buddha, Tahō Buddha, and all the other Buddhas of the ten directions.

33. The above quotations from the Lotus Sutra are at T9, 39a and 31b.

34. Adapted from a passage in the *Hokke Shūku* (DDZ 3, 253).

35. Hui-kuo (746–805) was the seventh master in the lineage of esoteric Buddhism in China. He studied esoteric teachings under Pu-k'ung. When Kōbō came to China from Japan, Hui-kuo transferred the doctrines of the Womb Realm mandala of the *Dainichi* Sutra and the Diamond Realm mandala of the *Kongōchō* Sutra to him.

36. Fa-ch'üan was a Chinese priest of the esoteric teachings. He transferred the doctrines of these teachings to Jikaku and Chishō when they journeyed to China in 838 and in 853, respectively. He wrote many treatises on the esoteric teachings.

37. The story of King Ajātaśatru appears in the Nirvana Sutra (T12, 480b ff.).

38. Reference is to the first council, which began the task of compiling the Buddha's teachings. In the year when Shakyamuni died, this council was convened, with the support of King Ajātaśatru, in Pippala Cave at Rājagṛha in Magadha.

21 A SAGE PERCEIVES THE THREE EXISTENCES OF LIFE

This letter was sent to Toki Jōnin, one of Nichiren's staunchest disciples and himself a lay priest, from Nichiren's place of retirement on Mount Minobu. The letter was written in the twelfth month of 1275. By the three existences of life Nichiren means the past, present, and future, all of which are known to the sage, or the Buddha.

A sage is one who fully understands the three existences of life—past, present, and future. The Three Rulers and the Five Emperors[1] referred to in Confucianism, as well as the Three Sages[2] of ancient China, comprehended only the present; they knew neither the past nor the future. Brahmans, however, were able to see eighty thousand kalpas into the past and the future, thus in a small way resembling sages. People of the two vehicles, as mentioned in the Hinayana teachings, were aware of the law of cause and effect working throughout the past, present, and future. Hence they were superior to the Brahmans.

The Hinayana bodhisattvas could see three *asōgi*[3] kalpas into the past, whereas the bodhisattvas of the lowest Mahayana teachings (*tsūgyō*) spent as many kalpas practicing Buddhism as there are dust particles in a world, and the bodhisattvas of the intermediate Mahayana teachings (*bekkyō*) spent myriad kotis of kalpas to attain each of the fifty-two stages leading to enlightenment.[4]

In the theoretical teaching of the Lotus Sutra, Shakyamuni Buddha described the period of *sanzen-jintengō*, a time incomparably more distant than any that had been mentioned before. In the essential teaching of the sutra, Shakyamuni revealed the unimaginably remote past called *gohyaku-jintengō*, as well as matters pertaining to uncountable kalpas in the future.

From the above it is clear that a thorough understanding of both the past and the future is intrinsic to the nature of a sage. Shakyamuni Buddha accurately predicted the near future, saying that he would enter nirvana in three months' time. Can there then be any doubt about his prediction for the distant future, that *kōsen-rufu*[5] will be achieved in the last of the five-hundred-year periods after his passing? With such perception one can see the distant future by looking at what is close at hand. One can infer what will be from what exists in the present. This is the "consistency from beginning to end"[6] [mentioned in the Lotus Sutra].

Who should be acknowledged as the votary of the Lotus Sutra in the last five-hundred-year period? I did not trust my own wisdom, but because the rebellions and invasion that I had predicted have occurred, I can now trust it. These incidents happened solely to prove me correct.

My disciples should know that I, Nichiren, am the votary of the Lotus Sutra. Since I follow the same practice as Bodhisattva Fukyō, those who despise and slander me will have their heads broken into seven pieces,[7] whereas those who believe in me will amass good fortune as high as Mount Sumeru.

Question: Why is it that those who slander you have not yet had their heads broken into seven pieces?

Answer: Since ancient times, of all those who slandered saints and sages other than the Buddha, only one or two have suffered punishment by having their heads broken. The crime of abusing Nichiren is not by any means limited to only one or two persons. The entire Japanese nation has been punished simultaneously. What else do you think caused the great earthquake of the Shōka era and the huge comet[8] of the Bun'ei era? I am the foremost sage in the entire world.

Nevertheless, all people, from the ruler on down to the common people, have despised and slandered me, attacked me with sword and staff,[9] and even exiled me.[10] That is why Bonten, Taishaku, the gods of the sun and the moon, and the Four Heavenly Kings incited a neighboring country to punish our land. This was clearly prophesied in the *Daijuku* and *Ninnō* sutras, the Nirvana Sutra, and the Lotus Sutra. No matter what prayers may be offered, if the people fail to heed me, this country will suffer calamities such as those that occurred on Iki and Tsushima.[11]

My disciples, you should believe what I say and watch what happens. These things do not occur because I myself am respectworthy, but because the power of the Lotus Sutra is supreme. If I declare myself before the people, they will think that I am boastful, but if I humble myself before them, they will despise the sutra. The taller the pine tree, the longer the wisteria vine hanging from it. The deeper the source, the longer the stream. How fortunate, how joyful! In this impure land, I alone enjoy true happiness.

Notes

1. The Three Rulers are legendary rulers of ancient China said to have realized model governments. They are: Fu Hsi, Shen Nung, and Huang Ti. The Five Emperors, who reigned after the Three Rulers, are Shao Hao, Chuan Hsü, Ti Kao, T'ang Yao, and Yü Shun.

2. The Three Sages are Confucius, his disciple Yen Hui, and Lao Tzu.

3. *Asōgi* (Skt: *asaṃkhya*) indicates an immeasurable number in ancient India. According to one method of calculation, one *asōgi* is equal to 10^{51} and one kalpa is said to be 16 million minus 2,000 years. Altogether, three *asōgi* kalpas indicates an inconceivable span of time.

4. The text here has been expanded somewhat for clarity. Mentioned above are three of the four teachings (Jap: *kehō no shikyō*), formulated by Chegwan on the basis of T'ien-t'ai's writings. They are: (1) the tripitaka teaching (*zōkyō*), consisting of sutras, *vinayas*, and *abhidharma*, corresponding to Hinayana teaching; (2) the connecting or shared teaching (*tsūgyō*), which includes the *Hōdō* or *Vaipulya*, early Mahayana teachings; (3) the specific or distinctive teachings (*bekkyō*), which include *Hannya* or Wisdom sutras; and (4) the complete or perfect teaching (*engyō*), which includes the Lotus and Nirvana sutras. *Tendai Shikyō Gi* (T46, 774c ff.). The fifty-two stages are the stages of bodhisattva practice through which a bodhisattva progresses toward Buddhahood.

5. Literally, "to widely declare and spread [Buddhism]." See *Kōsen rufu* in Glossary.

6. A phrase found in the *Hōben* (2d) chapter of the Lotus Sutra indicating the last of the ten factors or suchnesses (Jap: *jūnyoze*). They are: (1) appearance or form (*nyozesō*), (2) nature or quality (*nyozeshō*), (3) substance or entity (*nyozetai*), (4) power (*nyozeriki*), (5) activity or substance (*nyozesa*), (6) cause (*nyozein*), (7) indirect cause or relation (*nyozeen*), (8) effect (*nyozekan*), (9) reward or retribution (*nyozechō*), and (10) the unifying factor that makes the above nine consistent from outset to end (*nyoze hommatsu ku kyōtō*).

7. Reference to a verse in the *Darani* (26th) chapter of the Lotus Sutra which reads: "Whoever resists our spell / And troubles a preacher of the Dharma, / May his head be split in seven pieces / Like the branches of an *arjaka* tree." (T9, 59b). It is also said that if one touches an *arjaka* flower its petals open and fall in seven pieces.

8. A great earthquake devastated Kamakura in 1257 and a huge comet, an ominous sign, appeared in 1264.

9. Reference is to the Komatsubara Persecution of the eleventh day of the eleventh month, 1264, when Nichiren and his followers were attacked by Tōjō Kagenobu and to the attempt to execute Nichiren at Tatsunokuchi on the twelfth day of the ninth month, 1271.

10. The exiles to Izu Peninsula and Sado Island.

11. These islands were overrun by the Mongol invaders.

22 ADMONITIONS AGAINST SLANDER

This letter was addressed to Lord Soya, an officer of the high court of the Kamakura shogunate. His full name is Soya Jirō Hyōe-no-jō Kyōshin. He lived in Shimōsa and had been converted to Nichiren's teachings by Ōta Jōmyō around 1260. In 1271 Soya became a lay priest and was given the Buddhist name Hōren. Hōren built two temples, living at one of them until he died in 1291 at the age of sixty-eight. The letter is dated the third day of the eighth month, 1276, and was sent from Minobu.

The usual title for this letter is *Soya Dono Gohenji* (In Reply to Lord Soya). The alternative title, *Jōbutsu Yōjin Shō* is rendered here as "Admonishments Against Slander," indicating the main topic of the letter. It could also be rendered more literally as "Cautionary Words on Attaining Buddhahood."

~~~~~~~

The *Hōben* chapter, in volume one of the Lotus Sutra, states, "The wisdom of all Buddhas is infinitely profound and immeasurable."[1] T'ien-t'ai explains, " 'Infinitely profound' indicates the reality attained by the Buddha, which is as vast as a wide and unfathomable riverbed. Because the riverbed is infinitely deep, the water of the Buddha wisdom is 'immeasurable.' "[2]

The sutra and its interpretation make clear that the path to enlightenment lies within the two elements of reality (*kyō*) and wisdom (*chi*). Reality means the entity of all phenomena in the universe, and wisdom means the perfect manifestation of this entity in the individual's life. When the reality is an infinitely broad and deep riverbed, the water of wisdom will flow ceaselessly. Enlightenment is the fusion of wisdom and reality.

All the sutras expounded prior to the Lotus Sutra are provisional teachings that cannot lead to enlightenment because they separate wisdom and reality. However, the Lotus Sutra joins the two. It expounds the purpose for which the Buddhas appear in this world: to open the door to the Buddha wisdom, to reveal it, to let all beings know it and enter into it. All people can attain enlightenment by realizing this wisdom of the Buddha.[3]

The *Hōben* chapter states that the Buddha wisdom is far beyond the understanding of the people of the two vehicles: "Neither *shōmon* nor *engaku* are able to comprehend it." What then are these two elements of reality and wisdom? They are simply the words Nam-myoho-renge-kyo. Shakyamuni called forth the Bodhisattvas of the Earth, his disciples from ages past, to give them these words, this Law that is the essence of his teachings.

The Lotus Sutra states that Bodhisattva Jōgyō and the other Bodhisattvas of the Earth will appear in the first five hundred years of the Latter Day of the Law to propagate these words, the Mystic Law, the crystallization of reality and wisdom. The sutra makes this perfectly clear. Who could possibly dispute it? I, Nichiren, am neither Bodhisattva Jōgyō nor his messenger, but I was the first to begin the propagation of the Mystic Law and have already taught it extensively. Bodhisattva Jōgyō received the water of wisdom of the Mystic Law from Shakyamuni Buddha to let it flow into the wasteland of the people's lives in the evil period of the Latter Day. This is the function of wisdom. Shakyamuni entrusted this teaching to Bodhisattva Jōgyō, and now Nichiren propagates it in Japan. In general, this transfer was made to the Bodhisattvas of the Earth, but specifically, to Bodhisattva Jōgyō himself. If you confuse the general with the specific even in the slightest,[4] you will never be able to attain enlightenment and will wander through endless lifetimes of suffering.

For example, the *shōmon* in Shakyamuni's time received the seed of enlightenment from Shakyamuni in the distant past when he was the sixteenth son of Daitsū Buddha. Therefore, they cannot attain enlightenment by following Amida, Yakushi, or any other Buddha. Or, to give another example, if someone brings home water from the ocean, his entire family can use it. But if they should refuse even a single drop of that water and instead go looking for water from some other ocean, they would be terribly misguided and foolish. In the same way, if one should forget the original teacher who brought him the water of wisdom from the great ocean of the Lotus Sutra and instead follow another, he is sure to sink into the endless sufferings of birth and death.

A disciple should abandon even his teacher if the teacher is misguided. However, this is not always necessary. He should decide according to the laws of both society and Buddhism. With no knowledge of Buddhist law, most priests in the Latter Day grow so conceited that they despise their original teacher and fawn on new-found patrons. Only honest priests who desire little and are happy with whatever they have can be called "priests" in the true sense of the word. Volume One of the *Hokke Mongu* states: "A priest who has yet to attain enlightenment should humble himself before the supreme law and all Buddhist saints. Then, he will have true modesty. When he manifests the Buddha wisdom, he will be a true priest."[5]

In the Nirvana Sutra Shakyamuni stated: "If even a good priest sees someone slandering the Law and disregards him, failing to reproach him, to oust him, or to punish him for his offense, then that priest is betraying Buddhism. But if he takes the slanderer severely to task, drives him off, or punishes him, then he is my disciple and one who truly understands my teachings."[6] Never forget this admonition against ignoring another's slander of Buddhism. Both master and disciple will surely fall into the hell of incessant suffering if they see enemies of the Lotus Sutra and fail to reproach them. The Great Teacher Nan-yüeh wrote: "They will fall into hell with evil men."[7] To seek enlightenment without repudiating slander is as futile as trying to find water in the midst of fire or fire in the midst of water. No matter how sincerely one believes in the Lotus Sutra, any violation of its teachings will surely cause him to fall into hell, just as one crab leg will ruin a thousand pots of lacquer. This is the meaning of the passage in the Lotus Sutra, "The poison has penetrated deeply, causing them to lose their true minds."[8]

The Lotus Sutra teaches us: "In lifetime after lifetime they were always born together with their masters in the Buddha lands throughout the universe,"[9] and "If one seeks out the teacher of the Law, he will soon attain the way of the bodhisattva. If he follows and studies under this teacher, he will be able to see Buddhas equal in number to the sands of the Ganges River."[10] T'ien-t'ai interprets this, saying: "One who first began to aspire for enlightenment when following this Buddha will follow him again and attain a stage of faith from which he can never backslide."[11] Miao-lo adds, "One who first hears about the Law from some Buddha or bodhisattva will return to the same Buddha or bodhisattva to attain enlightenment."[12] Above all, follow no one but your original teacher and go on to attain Buddhahood. Shakyamuni is the original teacher for all people, as well as their sovereign and their parent. Because I have expounded this teaching, I have been exiled and almost killed. As the saying goes: "Good advice grates on the ear." But still I am not discouraged. The Lotus Sutra is like the seed, the Buddha like the sower, and the people like the field. If you go against these principles, not even I, Nichiren, can save you from the consequences in your next lifetime.

With my deep respect,
Nichiren

The third day of the eighth month in the second year of Kenji (1276)

Notes

1. T9, 5b.
2. *Hokke Gengi* (T33, 710a).
3. The wording of the original has been expanded somewhat for clarity.
4. The general, or *sō*, means an overall or surface view, while the specific, *betsu*, means the individual aspect.
5. T34, 7a.
6. T12, 381a.
7. T46, 702a.
8. T9, 43a.
9. T9, 26c.
10. T9, 32b.
11. *Hokke Gengi* (T33, 756c).
12. *Hokke Mongu Ki* (T34, 324a).

23 ON PROLONGING LIFE

Nichiren sent this letter in 1279 to Myōjō, the wife of Toki Jōnin. After her first husband died, Myōjō married Toki Jōnin. Her son by her first marriage was later called Nitchō (1252–1317?); he became one of Nichiren's six elder priest-disciples. Myōjō had a second son, fathered by Toki Jōnin. This son also became one of Nichiren's disciples and assumed the name Nitchō (written with different Chinese characters than his half-brother). He lived from 1262 to 1310. Later, he was appointed by Nikkō Shonin to be the first chief priest of Omosu Dansho, the Buddhist school at Taiseki-ji.

There are two types of illness: minor and serious. Early treatment by a skilled physician can cure even serious illnesses, not to mention minor ones. Karma also may be divided into two categories: mutable and immutable. Sincere repentance will eradicate even immutable karma, to say nothing of karma that is mutable. The seventh volume of the Lotus Sutra states, "This sutra is beneficial medicine for the illness of all people."[1] These words can be found in no other sutra. All the Buddha's teachings are golden words of truth; for countless kalpas, they have never contained the slightest falsehood. The Lotus Sutra is the truth of all truths taught by the Buddha, for it includes his declaration that he would now honestly discard the provisional teachings.[2] Tahō Buddha confirmed the truth of the Lotus Sutra and all other Buddhas lent their tongues in testimony. How, then, could it be false? Moreover, this sutra contains the greatest of all secrets. Many women suffer from illness, and now in the fifth five-hundred-year period or a little more than twenty-five hundred years after the Buddha's death, the Lotus Sutra is "beneficial medicine" for them also.

King Ajātaśatru broke out in huge leprous sores all over his body on the fifteenth day of the second month of his fiftieth year. Not even the skills of his renowned physician Jīvaka were enough to cure him. It was foretold that he would die on the seventh day of the third month and fall into the hell of incessant suffering. All the pleasures of his more than fifty years suddenly vanished, and the sufferings of an entire lifetime were gathered into three short weeks. His death was predetermined by his immutable karma. But then the Buddha taught him the Lotus Sutra once more, through the teachings that became the Nirvana Sutra. The king immediately recovered from his illness, and the heavy sins which had burdened his heart vanished like dewdrops in the sun.[3]

More than fifteen hundred years after the Buddha passed away, there lived a man in China called Ch'en Ch'en.[4] It was prophesied that he would die at the age of fifty, but by following the precepts of the Great Teacher T'ien-t'ai, he was able to prolong his life by fifteen years, and lived to be sixty-five. The Buddha taught that Bodhisattva Fukyō also transformed his immutable karma and prolonged his life through his practice of the Lotus Sutra. Ajātaśatru, Ch'en Ch'en, and Fukyō were men, not women, but they prolonged their lives by practicing the Lotus Sutra. Ch'en Ch'en lived before the fifth five-hundred-year period, so his change of karma was as extraordinary as rice ripening in winter or chrysanthemums blossoming in summer. Today it is as natural for a woman to change her immutable karma by practicing the Lotus Sutra as it is for rice to ripen in fall or chrysanthemums to bloom in winter.

When I, Nichiren, prayed for my mother, not only was her illness cured, but her life was prolonged by four years. Now you too have fallen ill, and as a woman, it is all the more timely for you to try believing in the Lotus Sutra and see what it will do for you. In addition, you can go to Shijō Kingo,[5] who is not only an excellent physician but a votary of the Lotus Sutra.

Life is the most precious of all treasures. Even one extra day of life is worth more than ten million ryō of gold.[6] The Lotus Sutra surpasses all other teachings because of the Juryō chapter. The greatest prince in the world would be of less consequence than a blade of grass if he died in childhood. If he died young, even a man whose wisdom shone as brilliantly as the sun would be less than a living dog. So you must hasten to accumulate the treasure of faith and quickly conquer your illness.

I should speak to you frankly, but while some people will accept advice, others feel they are not being correctly understood. It is extremely difficult to fathom another person's mind. I have experienced such difficulties on many occasions. You do not readily accept advice, so I will not counsel you directly. Just pray to the Gohonzon frankly and sincerely, without help from anyone. When Shijō Kingo came to see me in the tenth month of last year, I told him how grieved I was about your illness. He replied that you were probably not overly concerned then because your illness was not yet serious, but that it would definitely become critical by the first or the second month of this year. His words saddened me deeply. Your husband also told me that he depends on you as a staff to lean on and a pillar for support. He is very worried about you. He is a man who never gives in to defeat and shows the greatest concern for his own kin.

If you are unwilling to take proper care of yourself, it will be very difficult to cure your illness. One day of life is more valuable than all the treasures of the universe, so first you must muster sincere faith. This is the meaning of the passage in the seventh volume of the Lotus Sutra which states that burning one's little finger as an offering to the Buddha and the Lotus Sutra is better than donating all the treasures of the universe.[7] A single life is worth more than the universe. You still have many years ahead of you, and moreover, you have found the Lotus Sutra. If you live even one day longer, you can accumulate that much more good fortune. How precious life is!

Write down your name and age in your own handwriting and send it to me quickly, so I can pray to the gods of the sun and moon. Your son Iyo-bō[8] is also extremely worried about you, so together we will offer the *jigage*[9] to those gods.

Respectfully,
Nichiren

Notes

1. T9, 54c.
2. T9, 10a.
3. Stories relating to King Ajātaśatru are frequently mentioned by Nichiren. The above story is from the Nirvana Sutra (T12, 477b).

4. Ch'en Ch'en was an elder brother of T'ien-t'ai and a general of the Ch'en dynasty. He is mentioned in *Busso Tōki* (T49, 353a-b).

5. Shijō Kingo (1230–1300) was a loyal disciple of Nichiren. Here he is referred to by the name Nakatsukasa Saburōsaemon no jō.

6. An old Japanese monetary unit. One *ryō* weighs about 37 gm.

7. T9, 54a.

8. Iyo-bō is another name for Nitchō (1252–1317?), Myōhō's son by her first husband.

9. The verse section that concludes the *Juryō* (16th) chapter of the Lotus Sutra.

24 A COMPARISON OF THE LOTUS SUTRA AND OTHER SUTRAS

This letter was sent from Minobu to Toki Jōnin in Shimōsa on the twenty-sixth day of the fifth month, 1280. It is unusual in that it is one of the few letters that uses the question and answer form, a device quite popular among Buddhist writers.

An alternative title for this letter is *Nanshin Nange Hōmon* (The Teaching That Is Difficult to Believe and Difficult to Understand).

~~~~~~~~

Question: The *Hosshi* chapter in the fourth volume of the Lotus Sutra reads, "[this Lotus Sutra is] the most difficult to believe and the most difficult to understand."[1] What is the meaning of this passage?

Answer: More than two thousand years have passed since the Buddha expounded the Lotus Sutra in India. It took a little more than twelve hundred years before this sutra was introduced to China, and two hundred more years before it was brought from China to Japan. Since then, more than seven hundred years have already passed.

After the death of the Buddha, there were only three persons who realized the true meaning of this passage of the Lotus Sutra. In India, Bodhisattva Nāgārjuna said in his *Daichido Ron*: "[The Lotus Sutra] is like a great physician who changes poison into medicine."[2] This is the way he explained the meaning of the passage, "the most difficult to believe and the most difficult to understand." In China, the Great Teacher T'ien-t'ai Chih-che[3] interpreted this phrase in light of its context: "Among all those [sutras] I have preached, now preach, and will preach, this Lotus Sutra is the most difficult to believe and the most difficult to understand."[4] And in Japan, the Great Teacher Dengyō elaborated on this phrase: "All the sutras of the first four of the five periods[5] preached in the past, the *Muryōgi* Sutra now being preached, and the Nirvana Sutra to be preached in the future, are easy to believe and easy to understand. This is because the Buddha taught these sutras in accordance with the capacity of his listeners. The Lotus Sutra is the most difficult to believe and to understand because in it the Buddha directly revealed what he had attained."[6]

Question: Can you explain what he meant by that?

Answer: The ease of believing and understanding in the one case is due to the fact that the Buddha taught in accordance with the capacity of the people. And the difficulty of believing and understanding in the other case is due to the fact that he taught in accordance with his own enlightenment.

Kōbō Daishi and his successors at the Tō-ji[7] in Japan hold that, of all the exoteric teachings, the Lotus Sutra is the most difficult to believe and the most difficult to understand. They assert, however, that in comparison to the esoteric teachings, the Lotus Sutra is easy to believe and easy to understand. Jikaku, Chishō, and their followers contend that both the Lotus Sutra and the *Dainichi* Sutra are among the most difficult to believe and the most difficult to understand, but that of these two, the *Dainichi* Sutra is by far the more difficult to believe and to understand.

All people in Japan agree with both of these contentions. However, in interpreting this passage ["the most difficult to believe and the most difficult to understand"], I, Nichiren, say that non-Buddhist scriptures are easier to believe and understand than Hinayana sutras, the Hinayana sutras are easier than the *Dainichi* and other [*Hōdō*] sutras, the *Dainichi* and other [*Hōdō*] sutras are easier than the *Hannya* sutras, the *Hannya* sutras are easier than the *Kegon* Sutra, the *Kegon* is easier than the Nirvana Sutra, the Nirvana is easier than the Lotus Sutra, and the theoretical teaching of the Lotus Sutra is easier than the essential teaching. Thus there are many levels of comparative ease and difficulty.

Question: What is the value of knowing them?

Answer: No other doctrine can surpass the Lotus Sutra, a great lantern that illuminates the long night of the sufferings of birth and death, a sharp sword that can sever the fundamental darkness inherent in life. The teachings of the Shingon, Kegon, and other sects are categorized as those expounded in accordance with the people's capacity. They are, therefore, easy to believe and understand. The teachings expounded in accordance with the people's capacity are those sutras which the Buddha preaches in response to the desires of the people of the nine worlds, just as a wise father instructs an ignorant son in a way suited to the child's understanding. On the other hand, the teaching expounded in accordance with the Buddha's enlightenment is the sutra that the Buddha preaches directly from the world of Buddhahood, just as a saintly father guides his ignorant son to his own understanding.

In the light of this principle, I have carefully considered the *Dainichi*, *Kegon*, Nirvana, and other [provisional] sutras, only to find that all of them are sutras expounded in accordance with the people's capacity.

Question: Is there any evidence to support this contention?

Answer: The Śrīmālā Sutra says: "The Buddha brings to maturity those who have only practiced non-Buddhist teachings by enabling them to make good causes leading to the states of Humanity and Heaven. For those seeking the state of *shōmon*, the Buddha imparts the vehicle that leads them to that state. To those seeking the state of *engaku*, the Buddha reveals the vehicle for that state. To those who seek the Mahayana teachings, the Buddha expounds them."[8] This statement refers to those teachings which are easy to believe and easy to understand, such as the *Kegon*, *Dainichi*, *Hannya*, Nirvana, and other sutras.

[In contrast, the Lotus Sutra says,] "At that time, through Bodhisattva Yakuō, the World-Honored One addressed the eighty thousand great seekers of the Law: 'Yakuō, do you see—within this great multitude of uncountable gods, dragon kings, *yakṣas*, *gandharvas*, *asuras*, *garuḍas*, *kiṃnaras*, *mahoragas*,[9] humans and nonhumans, as well as monks, nuns, laymen and laywomen—those who seek the rank of *śrāvaka* (*shōmon*), those who seek the rank of *pratyekabuddha* (*engaku*), and those who seek the path to Buddhahood? If any of them in the presence of the Buddha hears a single verse or phrase of the Lotus Sutra and experiences a single moment of rejoicing, then I hereby confer on him a prophecy that he shall attain supreme enlightenment."[10]

In the provisional sutras, Shakyamuni taught five precepts[11] for the beings of Humanity; ten good precepts[12] for those of Heaven; the four infinite virtues[13] for the god Bonten; a practice of impartial almsgiving for the Devil King; two hundred and fifty precepts for monks; five hundred precepts for nuns; the four noble truths[14] for *shōmon*; the twelve-linked chain of causation[15] for *engaku*; and the six *pāramitas* for bodhisattvas. This method of teaching is comparable to water that assumes the round or square shape of its container, or to an elephant that exerts just enough strength to subdue its enemy.

The Lotus Sutra is entirely different. It was preached equally for all, including the eight kinds of nonhuman beings and the four kinds of believers.[16] This method of teaching is comparable to a measuring rod that is used to eliminate uneven places, or to the lion, king of beasts, which always exerts its full power in attack, regardless of the strength of its opponent.

When one examines all the various sutras in the clear mirror of the Lotus Sutra, it is evident that the three sutras[17] of Dainichi Buddha and the three Jōdo or Pure Land sutras[18] are teachings expounded in accordance with the people's capacity. Yet because the teachings of Kōbō, Jikaku, and Chishō have for some reason been widely accepted, this truth was obscured in Japan more than four hundred years ago. [To uphold these men's teachings instead of the Lotus Sutra] is like exchanging a gem for a pebble or trading sandalwood for common lumber. Because Buddhism has by now become thoroughly confused, the secular world has also been plunged into corruption and chaos. Buddhism is like the body and society like the shadow. When the body is crooked, so is the shadow. How fortunate that all my disciples who follow the Buddha's true intention will flow naturally into the ocean of all-encompassing wisdom! But the Buddhist scholars of our time put their faith in teachings expounded according to the people's capacity and are therefore doomed to sink into the sea of suffering. I will explain in more detail on another occasion.

With my deep respect,
Nichiren

The twenty-sixth day of the fifth month

Notes

1. T9, 31b.
2. T25, 754b.
3. Chih-che is a title given to T'ien-t'ai.
4. T34, 110a.
5. *See* Five Periods in Glossary.
6. *Hokke Shūku*, DDZ3, 251.
7. The head temple of the Tō-ji (Eastern Temple) branch of the Shingon sect, located in Kyoto. It was originally built by Emperor Kammu in 796 as a temple for

the protection of the nation and later granted to Kōbō by Emperor Saga, becoming a center for the study of esoteric practices.

8. T12, 218b.

9. *See* Eight Kinds of Nonhuman Beings in Glossary.

10. T9, 30b–c.

11. The basic precepts to be observed by all people. They are: not to kill, not to steal, not to commit unlawful sexual acts, not to lie, and not to drink intoxicants.

12. Precepts for lay believers of Mahayana. They are prohibitions against the ten evils of killing, stealing, unlawful sexual intercourse, lying, flattery or irresponsible speech, defaming, duplicity, greed, anger, and the holding of mistaken views.

13. Reference is to the four kinds of measureless compassion (Jap: *Muryōshin*): (1) giving others happiness (*ji*), (2) removing them from suffering (*hi*), 93) rejoicing at seeing them become free from suffering and gain happiness (*ki*), and (4) abandoning attachments to love and hatred and being impartial toward everyone (*sha*). By the practice of these virtues, one is said to be able to attain rebirth in the Brahma Heaven. They are described in *Daichido Ron* (T25, 208c).

14. A fundamental doctrine of Buddhism, clarifying the cause of suffering and the way of emancipation. They are: (1) all existence is suffering, (2) suffering is caused by selfish craving, (3) the eradication of selfish craving brings about the cessation of suffering and enables one to attain nirvana, and (4) this eradication can be achieved by following the eightfold path.

15. An early doctrine of Buddhism showing the causal relationship between ignorance and suffering. The first link in the chain is ignorance. Then ignorance causes action; action causes consciousness; consciousness causes name and form; name and form cause the six sense organs; the six sense organs cause contact; contact causes sensation; sensation causes desire; desire causes attachment; attachment causes existence; existence causes birth; and birth causes old age and death.

16. Monks, nuns, laymen, and laywomen.

17. The *Dainichi*, *Kongōchō*, and *Soshitsuji* sutras.

18. The *Muryōju*, *Kammuryōju*, and *Amida* sutras.

25 THE TREATMENT OF ILLNESS

Nichiren wrote this letter to Toki Jōnin from Minobu on the twenty-sixth day of the sixth month, 1278 (some sources date the letter to 1282). When Toki heard that Shijō Kingo was going to Minobu he entrusted him with a summer robe and other offerings for Nichiren. He also informed Nichiren of the epidemic then raging in Kamakura, and sought his advice. This letter is Nichiren's reply. Its full title is "The Treatment of Illness and the Points of Difference Between Hinayana and Mahayana and Provisional and True Teachings" (*Jibyō Daishō Gonjitsu Imoku*). Its alternative title, used here, is *Jibyō Shō*.

***

I have received the summer robe you sent me through the offices of Shijō Kingo. Please inform all those who sent me various offerings that I have received everything he listed. I also wish to acknowledge receipt of the various offerings from Ōta Nyūdō[1] shown on the list you made. The teachings I will be discussing in this letter have already been explained in part in one of my letters to Shijō Kingo.[2] I hope you will ask him to show it to you.

Your letter says that the epidemics are raging all the more fiercely. The illnesses of human beings may be divided into two general categories, the first of which is illness of the body. Physical diseases comprise one hundred and one disorders of the earth element, one hundred and one imbalances of the water element, one hundred and one disturbances of the fire element, and one hundred and one disharmonies of the wind element,[3] a total of four hundred and four maladies. These illnesses do not require a Buddha to cure them. Skilled physicians such as Jisui, Rusui,[4] Jīvaka,[5] and Pien Ch'üeh[6] prescribed medicines that never failed to heal physical sickness.

The second category is illness of the mind. These illnesses arise from the three poisons of greed, anger, and stupidity and are of eighty-four thousand kinds.[7] They are beyond the healing powers of the two Brahman deities,[8] the three ascetics,[9] or the six non-Buddhist teachers.[10] Medicines prescribed by Shen Nung and Huang Ti[11] are even less effective.

Illnesses of the mind differ greatly in severity. The three poisons and their eighty-four thousand variations that afflict common mortals of the six paths can be treated by the Buddha of Hinayana and his teachings in the *Agon* sutras, or by the scholars and teachers of the Kusha, Jōjitsu,[12] and Ritsu sects. However, if these Hinayana believers, in following their teachings, should turn against the Mahayana, [the people will suffer from various diseases.] Or, even though they may not oppose Mahayana Buddhism, if the Hinayana countries think themselves equal to the Mahayana countries, their people will be plagued by sickness. If one attempts to cure such illnesses with Hinayana Buddhism, they will only become worse. They can be treated only by the votaries of the Mahayana sutras. [Even within the Mahayana,] if many followers of the *Kegon, Jimmitsu,*[13] *Hannya, Dainichi*, and other provisional Mahayana sutras, confusing the inferior with the superior, insist that the teachings of their sects are equal to or even surpass the Lotus Sutra, and if the ruler and others in high positions come to accept their assertion, then the three poisons and eighty-four thousand illnesses will all arise. Then, if those followers should try to cure these illnesses with the provisional Mahayana sutras on which they rely, the sicknesses will become all the more serious. Even if they try to use the Lotus Sutra, their efforts will fail because, although the sutra itself is supreme, the practitioners are persons who hold distorted views.

Further, the Lotus Sutra itself is divided into two categories, the theoretical teaching and the essential teaching. One is as different from the other as fire is from water or heaven from earth. The difference is even greater than that between the Lotus Sutra and the sutras that preceded it. These sutras and the theoretical teaching of the Lotus Sutra are certainly different, but still they have some points of similarity. Among the eight teachings[14] expounded by the Buddha, the *engyō* or perfect teaching of the earlier sutras and that of the theoretical teaching are similar to each other.[15] When the Buddha expounded the pre-Lotus Sutra and the theoretical teachings, he assumed different guises such as the inferior manifested body, the superior manifested body,[16] the bliss body, and the Dharma body,[17] yet he invariably depicted himself as having attained enlightenment for the first time in this world.

The difference between the theoretical and the essential teachings, however, is exceedingly great. Whereas in the former the Buddha is described as having first attained enlightenment during his lifetime, in the latter he is the Buddha who attained enlightenment in the remote past. The difference is like that between a one-hundred-year-old man and a one-year-old baby. The disciples of these two teachings are also as different as fire is from water, to say nothing of the difference between their lands.[18] One who confuses the essential teaching with the theoretical teaching would not have the sense to distinguish fire from water. The Buddha drew a distinct line between the two in his preaching, but during the more than two thousand years since his death, no one in the three countries of India, China, and Japan—or for that matter, in the entire world—has clearly understood the difference. Only T'ien-t'ai in China and Dengyō in Japan generally differentiated between the two. And the precept of the perfect and immediate enlightenment, in which the essential teaching is distinguished from the theoretical, still remained to be clarified.[19] In the final analysis, T'ien-t'ai and Dengyō perceived it in their hearts but did not reveal it for three reasons: first, the proper time had not yet come; second, the people had no capacity to accept it; and third, neither had been entrusted with the mission of expounding it. It is today, in the Latter Day of the Law, that the Bodhisattvas of the Earth will appear and propagate it.

The Latter Day of the Law is the proper time for the spread of the essential teaching, so the followers of the Hinayana, provisional Mahayana, and theoretical teachings will receive no benefit from their teachings, even though they are not guilty of any fault. These teachings can be likened to medicines compounded for use in springtime, which are ineffective if taken in the fall, or at least not as effective as they are in spring or summer. What is worse, these people are deluded as to the relative superiority of Hinayana and Mahayana or of the provisional and the true teachings. But the rulers of Japan in ancient times believed in the sutras they espoused, and erected temples and donated fields and farmland to their sects. Were these people to admit the truth of my assertion that their teachings are inferior, they would have no way to justify themselves and would in consequence lose the support of the ruler. For this reason, they become enraged, slandering the sutra of the true teaching and doing harm to its votary. The ruler, too, accepting the groundless accusations of these followers, persecutes the votary, because he wishes to side with the majority, because he cannot bear to abandon the teachings honored by the rulers of ancient times, because he is simply stupid and ignorant, or because he despises the votary of the true teaching. As a result, the gods who guard the true teaching, such as Bonten, Taishaku, the gods of the sun and moon, or the Four Heavenly Kings, punish the country, and the three calamities and seven disasters occur on an unprecedented scale. Hence the epidemics which have broken out this year as well as last year and in the Shōka era.[20]

Question: If, as you have stated, the gods inflict punishment on this country because it does harm to the votary of the Lotus Sutra, then epidemics should attack only the slanderers. Why is it that your own disciples also fall ill and die?

Answer: Your question sounds reasonable. But you are aware of only one side of the situation and not the other. Good and evil have been inherent in life since time without beginning. According to the provisional teachings and the sects based on them, both good and evil remain in one's life through all the stages of the bodhisattva practice up to the stage of *tōgaku*.[21] Hence the people at the stage of *tōgaku* or below have faults of some kind, [but not those at the highest stage]. In contrast, the heart of the Hokke sect[22] is the principle of *ichinen sanzen*, which reveals that both good and evil are inherent even in those at the highest stage, that of *myōgaku* or enlightenment. The fundamental nature of enlightenment manifests itself as Bonten and Taishaku, whereas the fundamental darkness manifests itself as the Devil of the Sixth Heaven. The gods hate evildoers, and demons hate good people. Because we have entered the Latter Day of the Law, it is natural that demons should be everywhere in the country, just like tiles, stones, trees, and grasses. Benevolent spirits are few because sages and worthies are rare in this world. One would therefore expect to find more victims of the epidemic among Nichiren's followers than among the believers of Nembutsu, teachers of Shingon, or priests of the Zen and Ritsu sects. For some reason, however, there is less affliction and death among Nichiren's followers. It is indeed mysterious. Is this because we are few in number, or because our faith is strong?

Question: Has there ever in the past been such a terrible outbreak of epidemics in Japan?

Answer: During the reign of Emperor Sujin, the tenth ruler after Emperor Jimmu, epidemics swept throughout Japan, claiming the lives of more than half the populace. But when Emperor Sujin had the people in each province worship the Sun Goddess and other deities, the epidemics ceased completely. Hence the name Sujin, which literally means "worshiping the gods." That was before Buddhism had been introduced to the country. The thirtieth, thirty-first and thirty-second rulers in the imperial line, along with many of their ministers, died of smallpox and other epidemic diseases. Prayers were once more offered to the same deities, but this time it was to no avail.

During the reign of the thirtieth ruler, Emperor Kimmei, Buddhist sutras, treatises, and priests were sent from the state of Paekche on the Korean peninsula to Japan, as well as a gilded bronze statue of Shakyamuni Buddha. Soga no Sukune[23] urged that the statue be worshiped. But Mononobe no Ōmuraji[24] and other ministers, along with the common people, joined in opposing the worship of the Buddha, saying that if honor were paid to him, it would enrage the native deities who then would bring ruin upon Japan. The emperor was still trying to decide which opinion to follow when the three calamities and seven disasters struck the nation on a scale never known before, and great numbers of the populace died of disease.

Mononobe no Ōmuraji seized this opportunity to appeal to the emperor, and as a result, not only were the Buddhist priests and nuns subjected to shame, but the gilded bronze statue of the Buddha was placed over charcoal and destroyed, and the Buddhist temple was likewise burned. At that time, Mononobe no Ōmuraji contracted a disease and died, and the emperor also passed away. Soga no Sukune, who worshiped the Buddha's statue, also fell ill.

Ōmuraji's son, the minister Mononobe no Moriya, declared that three successive emperors as well as his own father had died in the epidemic solely because homage had been paid to the Buddha. "Let it be known," he declared, "that Prince Shōtoku,[25] Soga no Umako,[26] and the others who revere the Buddha are all enemies of my father and of deceased emperors!" Hearing this, the Imperial Princes Anabe and Yakabe,[27] along with their ministers and thousands of retainers, all joined forces with Moriya. Not only did they burn images of the Buddha and their temples, but a battle broke out, and Moriya was killed in the fighting. For a period of thirty-five years after Buddhism had first been brought to this country, not a year passed without seeing the three calamities and seven disasters,[28] including epidemics. But after Mononobe no Moriya was killed by Soga no Umako and the gods were overpowered by the Buddha, the disasters abruptly ceased.

Outbreaks of the three calamities and seven disasters that occurred thereafter were for the most part due to confusion within Buddhism itself. But these would affect only one or two persons or one or two provinces, one or two clans or one or two areas. Such disasters occurred because of the anger of the gods, because Buddhism was slandered, or because of the people's distress.

The three calamities and seven disasters of these past thirty years or more, however, are due solely to the fact that the entire country of Japan hates me, Nichiren. In province after province, district after district, and village after village, everyone from the ruler on down to the common people seethes in such anger against me as the world has never seen. This is the first time that the fundamental darkness has erupted in the lives of common mortals caught in the illusions of thought and desire.[29] Even if they pray to the gods, the Buddha, or the Lotus Sutra, these calamities will only be aggravated. But it is different when the votary of the Lotus Sutra offers prayers to the essential teaching of the Lotus Sutra. In the final analysis, unless we demonstrate that this teaching is supreme, these disasters will continue unabated.

The Great Teacher T'ien-t'ai in his *Maka Shikan* described the ten objects of meditation[30] and the ten meditations,[31] but no one after him practiced them. In the days of Miao-lo and Dengyō some people practiced them to a certain extent but encountered few difficulties because there were no powerful opponents. The three obstacles and four devils described in the *Maka Shikan* will not arise to obstruct those who practice the provisional sutras. But now each and every one has risen to confront me. They are even more powerful than the three obstacles and four devils that T'ien-t'ai, Dengyō, and others had to face.

There are two ways of perceiving *ichinen sanzen*. One is theoretical and the other, actual. The *ichinen sanzen* of T'ien-t'ai and Dengyō was theoretical, but that which I practice now is actual. Because the way that I practice is superior, the difficulties attending it are that much greater. The practice of T'ien-t'ai and Dengyō was the *ichinen sanzen* of the theoretical teaching while mine is that of the essential teaching. These two are as different as heaven is from earth. You should bear this in mind when the time comes to face death.

With my deep respect,
Nichiren

The twenty-sixth day of the sixth month

Notes

1. Ōta Nyūdō is Ōta Jōmyō (1222–1283), a follower of Nichiren and an official employed by the Office of Legal Affairs of the Kamakura government. He lived in Shimōsa and was converted to Nichiren's teachings by Toki Jōnin around 1260.

2. This letter, known by its alternative title "The Two Kinds of Illness" (*Nibyō Shō*), carries the same date as the present letter. The full title of the letter is, "Reply to Lord Nakatsukasa Saemon-no-jō" (*Nakatsukasa Saemon-no-jō Dono Gohenji*).

3. Earth, water, fire, and wind were regarded as the constituent elements of all things. In the case of the human body, earth corrsponds to flesh, bone, skin, and hair; water to blood and sweat; fire to body temperature; and wind to the function of breathing. "One hundred and one" here does not necessarily indicate an exact number but simply a great many.

4. Jisui and Rusui (Sanskrit unknown) are a father and son, both excellent physicians, mentioned in the *Konkōmyō* Sutra (T26, 351c). According to this sutra, they lived countless kalpas ago. At one time an epidemic broke out and spread throughout the country. Jisui was too old to perform medical treatment, but Rusui mastered the medical arts and, in his father's place, saved the people.

5. Jīvaka was an Indian physician and a devout Buddhist. He treated King Bimbisāra, served as a minister to King Ajātaśatru, and when the king broke out in virulent sores, he succeeded in persuading him to reflect on his evil conduct and to seek the Buddha's teaching. His story is in the Nirvana Sutra (T12, 477a-b) and elsewhere.

6. Pien Ch'üeh was a physician in the Spring and Autumn period (722–481 B.C.) in China. In his boyhood he learned the medical arts and it is said to have been skilled in treating almost all kinds of diseases.

7. Here, not an exact number but a great many.

8. Śiva and Viṣṇu.

9. Kapila, Ulūka (Kanada), and Ṛṣabha. Kapila was a legendary figure, said to be the founder of the Samkhya school, one of the six major schools of Brahmanism in ancient India. Ulūka was the founder of the Vaiśesika school, another of the six schools. Ṛṣabha's teachings are said to have prepared the way for Jainism.

10. Influential thinkers in India during Shakyamuni's time who openly broke with the old Vedic tradition and challenged Brahman authority in the Indian social order. They are Pūraṇa-Kāśyapa, Maskari-gośālīputra, Ajita-keśakambala, Sañjayi-Vairāṭiputra, Kakuda Kātyāyāna, and Nirgrantha-jñātiputra.

11. Two of the Three Rulers, legendary ideal rulers of ancient China. They were also said to have been skilled in medical matters and were revered as patron deities and the inventors of certain medicines.

12. Two of the six sects of Nara. The Kusha sect is based on Vasubandhu's *Kusha Ron*, and the Jōjitsu sect is based on Harivarman's treatise, *Jōjitsu Ron*, said to be the pinnacle of Hinayana philosophical achievement.

13. Also called *Gejimmitsu* Sutra or *Gejimmikkyō* (T16, no.676). The basic text of the Hossō sect, which deals with such topics as the characteristics of the dharmas, ālaya-consciousness, and so forth.

14. A system by which T'ien-t'ai classified the sutras. *See* Eight Teachings in Glossary.

15. The perfect teaching of the pre-Lotus Sutra teachings and the perfect teaching

of the theoretical teaching both explain the concept of attaining Buddhahood in one's present form as a common mortal. However, the former amounts to a mere statement with no example of it ever having occurred, or else draws various distinctions and exceptions. The latter teaches that all people can without exception attain enlightenment, using examples.

16. The manifested body (Jap: *ōjin*; Skt: *nirmānakāya*) is one of the three bodies of the Buddha (sanshin; *see also* Three Bodies in Glossary), being the physical form in which the Buddha appears in this world in order to save people. T'ien-t'ai in his *Kannon Gishō* (T34, 933b) describes two different aspects manifested by the Buddha who displays his manifested body. The Buddha in the superior aspect (*shō ōjin*) manifests himself for the sake of bodhisattvas at or above the first stage of development, the forty-first of the fifty-two stages of bodhisattva practice. The Buddha in the inferior aspect (*retsu ōjin*) manifests himself for the sake of common mortals, men of the two vehicles, and bodhisattvas below the first stage of development.

17. Two of the three bodies of the Buddha. The bliss or reward body (Jap: *hōjin* or *hōshin*; Skt: *sambhogakāya*), the Buddha body received for meritorious actions, and the Dharma or Law body (Jap: *hosshin*; Skt: *dharmakāya*), the body of ultimate reality.

18. In the theoretical teaching that the Buddha expounded in his transient capacity, the Buddhaland is held to be a realm apart from this *sahā* world and the Buddha is said to have appeared in the *sahā* world only temporarily in order to expound the Law and save the people. In contrast, the *Juryō* (16th) chapter of the essential teaching indicates that the *sahā* world is itself the land in which the Buddha has always dwelt since his original enlightenment.

19. The term "essential teaching" has two meanings: the essential teaching of Shakyamuni's lifetime, or the latter fourteen chapters of the Lotus Sutra as contrasted with the theoretical teaching, or first fourteen chapters; and the essential teaching of the Latter Day of the Law. When the "essential teaching" is defined in this latter sense, the entire twenty-eight-chapter Lotus Sutra is regarded as the theoretical teaching.

20. That is, in 1259.

21. The fifty-first of the fifty-two stages of bodhisattva practice.

22. Here reference is to the Tendai sect.

23. Soga no Sukune refers to Soga no Iname or Iname no Sukune (d.570), an official of the Yamato period, who engaged in a struggle for power with Mononobe no Okoshi, leader of the conservative faction at court. Soga no Iname converted his home into a temple and paid homage to the Buddha image and other sacred articles. His daughters became consorts of Emperor Kimmei and one of them gave birth to Emperor Yōmei, father of Prince Shōtoku. Sukune was an honorary title given to high ministers or officials.

24. Mononobe no Ōmuraji is Mononobe Okoshi (n.d.), an official of the Yamato court. He criticized his rival at court, Ōtomo no Kanamura, also a member of a prominent family, for his handling of Korean affairs and overthrew the entire Ōtomo family. Later he opposed Soga no Iname, another important minister of the court.

25. Prince Shōtoku (574–622) was the second son of the thirty-first emperor, Yōmei. He was famous for his application of the spirit of Buddhism to government. As the regent for Empress Suiko, he carried out various reforms. He promulgated the Seventeen-Article Constitution in 604 and entered into diplomatic relations with the Sui dynasty, dispatching Ono no Imoko to China. Commentaries on the Lotus Sutra, Śrīmālā Sutra, and Vimalakīrti Sutra are attributed to him.

26. Soga no Umako (d.626) was a court official of the Yamato period and patron of Buddhism. In 587, when Emperor Yōmei died, a quarrel over the succession occurred between the prince backed by Mononobe no Moriya and the one backed by Soga no Umako. Umako attacked and killed Moriya, and proceeded to establish the position of the prince he supported, who became Emperor Sushun. Being told later that Emperor Sushun hated him, however, he had the emperor assassinated, and in his place set up his own niece, the consort of the deceased Emperor Bidatsu, who became Empress Suiko. He appointed Prince Shōtoku as regent to handle the affairs of government.

27. Anabe, also called Anahobe (d.587), was a son of Emperor Kimmei, and his mother was the daughter of Soga no Iname. According to the *Nihon Shoki* (Chronicles of Japan) and other sources, he could not ascend the throne upon the death of Emperor Bidatsu, and made another attempt to seize power at the death of Emperor Yōmei, conspiring with Mononobe no Moriya. However, he is said to have been killed by Soga no Umako, who supported another crown prince, Hatsusebe (Emperor Sushun). Yakabe (d.587), one of Prince Anahobe's closest friends, was also killed along with Anahobe.

28. *See* Three Calamities and Seven disasters in Glossary.

29. Not as yet having cut off the first of the three categories of illusion (Jap:*sanwaku*) formulated by T'ien-t'ai in the *Maka Shikan* (T46, 37, 62). They are: (1) illusions of thought and desire (*kenshi waku*), (2) illusions as numerous as particles of dust and sand (*jinja waku*), and (3) illusions of basic ignorance (*mumyō waku*).

30. Three obstacles and four devils devils (Jap: *sanshō shima*) are various obstacles to the practice of Buddhism. *See* Three obstacles and four devils in Glossary.

31. The ten objects of meditation (Jap: *jikkyō*) are a part of T'ien-t'ai's meditational system for perceiving *ichinen sanzen*. They are: (1) the phenomenal world, which exists by virtue of the five components, the relationship between the six sense organs and their six objects, and the six consciousnesses arising from this relationship; (2) earthly desires; (3) sickness; (4) karmic effect; (5) diabolical functions; (6) [attachment to a certain level of] meditation; (7) distorted views; (8) arrogance;, (9) [attachment to] the two vehicles; and (10) [attachment to] the state of bodhisattva. Through meditation on these ten objects, one realizes the limitations of the ten worlds. They are described in *Maka Shikan* (T46, 49a-b).

32. The ten meditations (Jap: *Jūjō kampō*) are ways to observe the truth of life, or *ichinen sanzen*. They are: (1) meditation on the region of the unfathomable, which means the truth of *ichinen sanzen*. This meditation is interpreted as the threefold contemplation in a single mind, and underlies the other nine. The other nine are meditations 2) to arouse compassion; (3) to enjoy security in the realm of truth; (4) to eliminate attachments; (5) to discern what leads to the realization of the true entity of life and what prevents it; (6) to make proper use of the thirty-seven conditions leading to enlightenment; (7) to remove obstacles to enlightenment while practicing the six *pāramitās*; (8) to recognize the stage of one's progress; (9) to stabilize one's mind; and (10) to remove the last barrier to enlightenment. They appear in *Maka Shikan* (T46, 52b.)

26 LETTER TO THE BROTHERS

The two brothers to whom this letter is addressed were the sons of Ikegami Saemon-no-tayū Yasumitsu, who held an important post in the government's Office of Construction and Repairs in Kamakura. The older brother, Munenaka (full name and title: Ikegami Emon-no-tayū Munenaka; d.1293) was converted to Nichiren's Buddhism probably in 1256, and the younger brother, Munenaga (full name and title: Ikegami Hyōe-no-sakan Munenaga; d.1283), shortly thereafter. The family estate was at Senzoku, Ikegami, in Musashi Province.

The father, Yasumitsu, was a loyal follower of the priest Ryōkan of the Gokuraku-ji, and vehemently opposed the beliefs of his two sons for over twenty years. In fact he went so far as to disown his elder son on two occasions, in 1275 and 1277. Nichiren sent letters of encouragement to the two brothers and their wives, urging them to maintain their faith. In 1278 the brothers finally succeeded in converting their father to Nichiren's teachings.

When Nichiren's health began to fail in the fall of 1282, at the urging of his disciples, he set out for the hot springs of Hitachi. While on his way he stayed at Munenaka's residence in Ikegami, and it was there that he passed away on the thirteenth day of the tenth month, 1282.

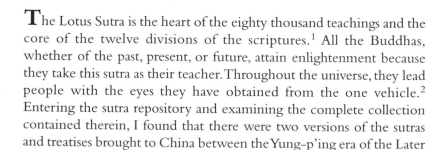

The Lotus Sutra is the heart of the eighty thousand teachings and the core of the twelve divisions of the scriptures.[1] All the Buddhas, whether of the past, present, or future, attain enlightenment because they take this sutra as their teacher. Throughout the universe, they lead people with the eyes they have obtained from the one vehicle.[2] Entering the sutra repository and examining the complete collection contained therein, I found that there were two versions of the sutras and treatises brought to China between the Yung-p'ing era of the Later

Han and the end of the T'ang dynasty.[3] There were 5,048 volumes of the older translations and 7,399 volumes of the newer translations.[4] Each sutra, by virtue of its contents, claims to be the highest teaching of all. However, comparison reveals that the Lotus Sutra is as superior to all the other sutras as heaven is to the earth. It rises above them like a cloud above the mud on the ground. If other sutras are compared to stars, the Lotus Sutra is like the moon; if they are as torches, stars or the moon, the Lotus Sutra is then as bright as the sun.

More specifically, the Lotus Sutra contains twenty important principles. The first two are the teachings of *sanzen-jintengō* and *gohyaku-jintengō*.[5] *Sanzen-jintengō* is explained in the seventh chapter entitled *Kejōyu-hon*. Suppose someone grinds a galaxy into dust. He then takes this dust with him and goes one thousand galaxies toward the east, where he drops one particle. He then proceeds another thousand galaxies eastward and drops the second particle. He continues on in this manner, dropping another particle and another until he has exhausted the entire galaxy[6] of dust particles. Then he gathers up all the galaxies along his journey, whether they received a particle or not, and reduces them all to dust. He places these dust particles in a row, allowing one entire kalpa to pass for the placement of each particle. When the first kalpa has passed, he places the second particle, and then the third, until as many kalpas have passed as there are particles of dust. The total length of time represented by the passage of all of these kalpas is called *sanzen-jintengō*.

It was this long ago—in the remote past indicated by *sanzen-jintengō*—that the three groups of *shōmon* disciples,[7] including Śāriputra, Mahākāśyapa, Ānanda, and Rāhula, learned the Lotus Sutra from a bodhisattva who was the sixteenth son of Daitsū Buddha.[8] However, deluded by evil people, they eventually abandoned the Lotus Sutra. They fell back into the *Kegon, Hannya, Daijuku,* or Nirvana Sutra, or further down into the *Dainichi, Jimmitsu,* or *Kammuryōju* Sutra, or even backslid to the Hinayana teachings of the *Agon* sutras. Continuing this descent, they fell down through relatively happy lives of the human and heavenly realms and finally into the paths of evil. During this period of *sanzen-jintengō* they were most often born into the hell of incessant suffering. Sometimes they were born in the seven major hells, or less frequently, in the hundred and some other hells.[9] On very rare occasions they were born into realms of hungry ghosts, animals, or Asura, and only after myriads of kalpas were they able to be born again as humans or heavenly beings.

The second volume of the Lotus Sutra states, "They dwell in hell so long that they come to think it as natural as playing in a garden, and the other evil paths seem like their own home."[10] Those who commit the ten evil acts[11] fall into the hell of Tōkatsu or Kokujō[12] and there must spend five hundred lifetimes or one thousand hell-years. Those who commit the five cardinal sins[13] fall into the hell of incessant suffering and, after staying there for one medium kalpa, are born again in this world.

Why is it, then, that those who abandon the Lotus Sutra fall into the hell of incessant suffering and have to stay there for such an unimaginably great number of kalpas? The sin of discarding one's faith in the sutra must at the time seem nowhere nearly as terrible as killing one's parents. However, even if one killed his parents in one, two, ten, one hundred, one thousand, ten thousand, one hundred thousand, one million, or even one billion lifetimes, he would not have to remain in hell for a period as long as *sanzen-jintengō*. Even if one were to kill one, two, ten, one hundred, one thousand, ten thousand, or as many as one billion Buddhas, would he have to dwell in hell for as long as *gohyaku-jintengō*? The three groups of *shōmon*, however, had to suffer through the period of *sanzen-jintengō*, and the great bodhisattvas, through that of *gohyaku-jintengō*, because of the sin they committed by discarding the Lotus Sutra. This shows what an unimaginably terrible sin it is.

To put this simply, if you strike at the air, your fist will not hurt, but when you hit a rock, you feel pain. The sin of killing an evil person is minor, compared to the sin of killing a good person, which is grave. If you kill someone who is not your kin, it is like striking mud with the fist, but if you kill your own parents, it is like hitting a rock. A dog may bark at a deer and not have its skull broken, but if it barks at a lion, its intestines will rot. An Asura tried to swallow the sun and the moon and had his head split into seven pieces.[14] Because Devadatta harmed the Buddha, the earth split open and swallowed him alive.[15] The seriousness of a sin depends on the person one harms.

The Lotus Sutra is the eye of all the Buddhas. It is the eternal master of Shakyamuni himself. If one discards one word or even one dot of the sutra, the sin is graver than that of one who kills his parents ten million times over, or even of one who sheds the blood of Buddhas everywhere in the universe. This is why those who forsook the Lotus Sutra had to suffer for as long as *sanzen-jintengō* or *gohyaku-jintengō*. Moreover, it is extremely difficult to meet a person who expounds this sutra exactly as the sutra directs. It is even more difficult than for a one-eyed turtle to find a piece of floating sandalwood or for someone to hang Mount Sumeru from the sky with the tiny fiber from a lotus stem.[16]

The Great Teacher Tz'u-en[17] was the disciple of Priest Hsüan-tsang and the teacher of Emperor T'ai-tsung. He was a saint who was not only well versed in the Sanskrit and Chinese scriptures but had memorized all of the Buddha's sutras. It is said of him that the Buddha's ashes fell from the tip of his writing brush and that light shone forth from his teeth. His contemporaries respected him as though he were the sun and the moon, and men in later ages earnestly sought out his teachings as guides for living. Even so, the Great Teacher Dengyō denounced him, writing, "Even though he praises the Lotus Sutra, he destroys its heart."[18] The quotation means that even though he intended to praise the Lotus Sutra, in the end, he destroyed it.

The Tripitaka Master Shan-wu-wei[19] was once the king of Udyana in India. He abdicated the throne, became a monk, and in the course of his Buddhist practice journeyed through more than fifty countries in India, finally mastering all the esoteric and exoteric teachings of Buddhism. Later he went to China and became the teacher of Emperor Hsüan-tsung. Every Shingon priest in both China and Japan has since become his follower. Though he was such a noble person, he died suddenly, tormented by Emma, the king of hell, although no one knows why. I, Nichiren consider that this happened because Shan-wu-wei was at first a votary of the Lotus Sutra, but when he read the *Dainichi* Sutra, he declared it superior to the Lotus Sutra.

Similarly, Śāriputra, Maudgalyāyana, and others were not doomed to wander through the evil paths for the period of *sanzen-jintengō* or *gohyaku-jintengō* because they had committed the ten evils or five cardinal sins. Nor was it because they had committed any of the eight rebellious acts.[20] It was because they met someone who was an evil influence, and discarded the Lotus Sutra to take faith in the provisional teachings.

According to the Great Teacher T'ien-t'ai, "If one befriends an evil person, he will lose his original mind."[21] "Original mind" means the heart which believes in the Lotus Sutra, while "lose" means to betray one's faith in the Lotus Sutra and follow other sutras. The Lotus Sutra reads, "but when they are given the medicine, they refuse to take it."[22] The Great Teacher T'ien-t'ai stated, "Those who had lost their minds would not take the excellent medicine, even though it was given them. Lost in suffering, they fled to other countries."[23]

Since this is so, the believers of the Lotus Sutra should fear those who interfere with their practice more than they fear bandits, burglars, midnight killers, tigers, wolves, or lions—even more than invasion by the Mongols. This world is the province of the Devil of the Sixth Heaven.[24] All of its people have been related to him since time without beginning. He has not only built the prison of twenty-five realms of existence[25] within the six paths and confined all humankind within it, but also made wives and children into shackles and parents and sovereigns into nets that block off the skies. To confound the Buddha nature that is the people's true mind, he causes them to drink the wine of greed, anger, and stupidity, and feeds them nothing but poisoned dishes that leave them prostrate on the ground of the three evil paths. When he happens on one with a seeking mind, he acts to obstruct him. If he sees that he is powerless to make a believer in the Lotus Sutra fall into evil, he tries to deceive him gradually by luring him toward the *Kegon* Sutra, which resembles the Lotus Sutra. This was done by the priests Tu-shun, Chih-yen, Fa-tsang, and Ch'eng-kuan.[26] Then, the priests Chia-hsiang and Seng-ch'üan[27] craftily deceived the believers in the Lotus Sutra into falling back upon the *Hannya* sutras. Hsüan-tsang and Tz'u-en led them toward the *Jimmitsu* Sutra, while Shan-wu-wei, Chin-kang-chih, Pu-k'ung, Kōbō, Jikaku, and Chishō[28] deluded them into following the *Dainichi* Sutra. Bodhidharma and Hui-k'o[29] caused them to stray into the Zen sect, while Shan-tao and Hōnen[30] tricked them into believing the *Kammuryōju* Sutra. In each case, the Devil of the Sixth Heaven possessed these Buddhist scholars in order to deceive the believers, just as foretold in the *Kanji* chapter of the Lotus Sutra: "Devils enter the body."[31]

The devil of fundamental ignorance can even enter the life of a bodhisattva who has reached the highest stage of practice and prevent him from attaining the Lotus Sutra's ultimate blessing—Buddhahood itself. How easily then can he obstruct those in any lower stage of practice. The Devil of the Sixth Heaven takes possession of the lives of wives and children and causes them to lead their husbands or parents astray. He also possesses the sovereign in order to threaten the votary of the Lotus Sutra, or causes parents to hinder the faith of devoted children. Prince Siddhartha wanted to renounce his title, but his son, Rāhula, had already been conceived. His father, King Śuddhodana, therefore, admonished him to wait until after the child was born before he left to become a monk. However, a devil delayed the childbirth for six years.[32]

In the distant past, Śāriputra began his practice of bodhisattva austerities during the Latter Day of Sendara Buddha. He had already practiced for sixty kalpas when the Devil of the Sixth Heaven became worried that in another forty kalpas, Śāriputra would complete his bodhisattva practice. The devil disguised himself as a Brahman, and begged Śāriputra for his eye. Śāriputra gave him an eye, but from that moment, he lost his will to practice and then gave up, thereby falling into the hell of incessant suffering for countless kalpas.[33] Sixty-eight million believers in the Latter Day of Daishōgon Buddha were deceived by Priest Kugan and three other priests so that they denounced Priest Fuji and as a result fell into the same hell for as many kalpas as there are particles of dust on earth.[34] The men and women in the Latter Day of Shishionnō Buddha followed Priest Shōi who observed the precepts, but mocked Kikon and also remained in hell for countless kalpas.[35]

It is the same with Nichiren's disciples. The Lotus Sutra reads, "Since hatred and jealousy abound even during the lifetime of the Buddha, how much worse will it be in the world after his passing?"[36] It also reads, "The people will be full of hostility, and it will be extremely difficult to believe."[37] The Nirvana Sutra reads, "By suffering sudden death, torture, slander, or humiliation, beatings with a whip or rod, imprisonment, starvation, adversity, or other relatively minor hardships in this lifetime, he will not have to fall into hell."[38] The *Hatsunaion* Sutra reads, "You may be poorly clad and poorly fed, seek wealth in vain, be born to an impoverished or heretical family, or be persecuted by your sovereign. It is due to the blessings obtained by protecting the Law that you can diminish in this lifetime your suffering and retribution."[39]

This means that we, who now believe in the True Law, once committed the sin of persecuting its votary in the past, and should therefore be destined to fall into a terrible hell in the future. However, the blessings gained by practicing the True Law are so great that we can change the karma that destines us to suffer terribly in the future by meeting relatively minor sufferings in this life. As the sutra describes, one's past slander may cause one to be born into a poor or heretical family or be persecuted by one's sovereign. A "heretical family" is one which slanders the True Law and "persecution by one's sovereign" means to live under the rule of an evil king. These are the two sufferings confronting you now. In order to expiate your past slanders, you are opposed by your parents who hold heretical views, and must live in the age of a sovereign who persecutes the votary of the Lotus Sutra. The sutra makes this absolutely clear. Cast off any thoughts you may have to the contrary. If you doubt that you committed slander in the past, you will not be able to withstand the minor sufferings of this life. Then, you might give in to your father's opposition and desert the Lotus Sutra against your will. Remember that should this happen, you are certain to fall into the hell of incessant suffering and drag your parents into it as well, causing all of you indescribable grief. To grasp this requires a great seeking spirit.

Each of you has continued your faith in the Lotus Sutra and can therefore rid yourselves of your heavy sins from the past. For example, the flaws in iron come to the surface when it is forged. Put into flames, a rock just turns to ashes, but gold is rendered into pure gold. This persecution more than anything else will prove your faith genuine, and the Jūrasetsu (Ten Goddesses)[40] of the Lotus Sutra will surely protect you. The demon who appeared to test Sessen Dōji was actually Taishaku.[41] The dove saved by King Shibi was Bishamon.[42] It is even possible that the Jūrasetsu have possessed your parents in order to test your faith. Any weakness will be cause for regret. The cart that overturns on the road ahead is a warning to the one behind.

In an age like this no one can help but thirst for the true way. You may hate this world, but you cannot escape. All Japanese are certain to meet with terrible misfortune in the immediate future. The revolt[43] that broke out on the eleventh day of the second month in the ninth year of Bun'ei (1272) was like blossoms being lashed by a gale or like bolts of silk burning in an inferno. Who can help but abhor a world like ours?

In the tenth month in the eleventh year of Bun'ei (1274), the people on Iki and Tsushima islands[44] were slaughtered at one stroke. How can we say that this is no concern of ours? The soldiers who went off to confront the invaders—how forlorn they must have been! They had to leave behind their aged parents, little children, young wives, and cherished homes to go out and defend a strange and foreboding sea. If they saw clouds on the horizon, they imagined them to be the enemy's banners. If they saw ordinary fishing boats, they thought them Mongol warships and were paralyzed with fear. Once or twice a day they climbed the hills to look out over the sea. Three or four times in the middle of the night they saddled and unsaddled their horses. They felt the stark reality of the Asura existence in their own lives. All this and the persecutions you have suffered as well can ultimately be blamed on the fact that this country's sovereign has become an enemy of the Lotus Sutra. His opposition was instigated by the slanderous priests who follow the Hinayana precepts[45] or the Nembutsu and Shingon doctrines. You must endure this trial and see for yourselves the blessings of the Lotus Sutra. Nichiren will also loudly call upon the heavenly gods. Now more than ever, you must neither show nor feel any fear.

Women are faint-hearted, and your wives have probably given up their belief. Yet you must grit your teeth and never slacken in your faith. Be as fearless as Nichiren when he faced Hei no Saemon.[46] Although theirs was not the road to enlightenment, the sons of Lord Wada and Lord Wakasa,[47] as well as the warriors under Masakado and Sadatō, fought to the death to preserve their honor. Death comes to all, even should nothing untoward ever happen. Therefore you must never be cowardly or make yourselves the subject of ridicule.

I am deeply worried about you both. Therefore I will relate a story that is important for you. There were two princes named Po-i and Shu-ch'i who were sons of the king of Hu-chu in China. Their father had willed his title to the younger brother, Shu-ch'i, yet after he passed away Shu-ch'i refused to ascend to the throne. Po-i urged Shu-ch'i to assume the title, but Shu-ch'i insisted that Po-i, the elder brother, do so instead. Po-i persisted, asking how the younger brother could contradict their father's will. Shu-ch'i agreed that their father's will clearly named him, yet he still refused the throne, claiming that he could not bear to push his elder brother aside.

Both brothers then abandoned their parents' country and traveled to another where they entered the service of King Wen of the Chou dynasty. Shortly thereafter, the country was attacked and King Wen was killed by King Chou of the Yin dynasty. Less than a hundred days after King Wen's death, his son, King Wu, prepared to do battle with King Chou, but Po-i and Shu-ch'i, holding fast to the reins of his horse, strove to dissuade him, saying, "You should be in mourning for three years after your father's death. If you now start a war, you will only dishonor his name." King Wu grew furious at this and was about to kill them both, but T'ai-kung Wang, his father's minister, restrained him.

The two were so loath to have anything more to do with this king that they went off to seclude themselves in Mount Shou-yang, where they lived solely on ferns. One day a person named Ma-tzu passed by and asked, "Why have you hidden yourselves in a place like this?" They told the whole story to Ma-tzu, who replied, "If that is so, don't these ferns also belong to the king?" Thus reproached, they immediately stopped eating the plants.

It is not the way of heaven to forsake sages. Thus a god appeared to them as a white deer and provided them with milk. After the deer had gone away, Shu-ch'i said, "Since the white deer's milk is so sweet to drink, its meat must taste even better!" Po-i tried to silence him, but heaven had already heard his words, and the brothers were abandoned at once. Thus, they eventually starved to death.[48] Even though a person acts wisely throughout his life, one careless word can ruin him. Not knowing what thoughts you may have in your hearts, I worry about you a great deal.

When Shakyamuni Buddha was a prince, his father, King Śuddhodana, could not bear losing his only heir and therefore would not allow him to renounce his royal station. The king kept two thousand soldiers posted at the city's four gates to prevent him from leaving. Nevertheless, the prince eventually left the palace against his father's will. In general, it is the son's duty to obey his parents, yet on the path to Buddhahood, not following one's parents may ultimately bring them good fortune. The *Shinjikan* Sutra explains the essence of filial piety as follows: "By renouncing one's obligations and entering nirvana one can truly repay those obligations in full."[49] That is, in order to enter the true way, one leaves his home against his parents' wishes and attains Buddhahood. Then he can truly repay his debt of gratitude to them.

In worldly affairs as well, if one's parents foment a rebellion, it is one's filial duty not to follow them. This is mentioned in the *Classic of Filial Piety*. When the Great Teacher T'ien-t'ai had commenced meditating on the Lotus Sutra, the apparitions of his deceased parents sat on his knees and tried to obstruct his practice of Buddhism. This was the work of the Devil of the Sixth Heaven, who took the form of his father and mother in order to oppose him.[50]

I have just cited the story of Po-i and Shu-ch'i. There is one more lesson you should learn from history. Emperor Ōjin, who now is Bodhisattva Hachiman, was the sixteenth ruler of Japan. Emperor Ōjin had two sons: the first was Prince Nintoku and the second, Prince Uji. The emperor transferred his throne to the younger brother, Uji. After their father passed away, Uji asked his elder brother to take the throne, but the elder brother reproached him, saying, "How can you refuse to comply with our father's will?"

They argued back and forth, and for three full years no one claimed the throne. As a result, the people suffered indescribable grief. It was like a curse upon the nation, and Prince Uji finally thought, "As long as I am alive, my brother will not assume the throne." So he committed suicide. At this Prince Nintoku was wracked with sorrow and fell into despair. Seeing this, Prince Uji came back to life in order to give words of encouragement to his brother; then he passed away again. It is recorded that when Nintoku at last ascended the throne, the nation became peaceful and received eighty boatloads of tribute each year from the three Korean kingdoms of Silla, Paekche, and Koguryo.[51]

There are other cases where the relationship between the sons of wise kings was not harmonious. What bonds have enabled you two brothers to continue on such good terms? Could you be princes Jōzō and Jōgen reborn, or the embodiments of Bodhisattvas Yakuō and Yakujō?[52] When your father disowned Munenaka, I expected that Munenaga would refuse to side with his brother, thereby making it even more difficult to reconcile your father and Munenaka. Yet if what Tsuruō told me is true, you two are determined to resolve this together. I am overjoyed to hear this surprising news, as I told you in my other letter. Could there ever be a more wonderful story than your own?[53]

The *Daitō Saiiki Ki* tells about a hermit who lived in the Deer Park at Benares, India, hoping to master occult powers. He learned to turn tiles and pebbles into jewels and change the forms of men and animals, but he could not yet ride on clouds or travel to the Palace of the Immortals. In order to accomplish these goals, he took as his disciple a man of integrity. Giving him a long sword, the hermit instructed him to stand in one corner of a meditation platform, telling him to hold his breath and utter not a word. If the disciple could remain silent through that whole night until dawn, the hermit was certain to master the occult. Determined, the hermit sat in the center of the platform with another long sword in hand and chanted incantations. Making his apprentice take a vow, he said, "Even at the cost of your life, say nothing!" The man answered, "Though I die, not a word will leave these lips."

In this manner they passed the night until, as dawn was just about to break, the apprentice cried out suddenly, and the hermit immediately failed in his attempt. He reproached the disciple, shouting, "How could you have broken your vow? This is deplorable!" Repenting deeply, the disciple said, "I dozed off for a little while, and in a dream, my previous master appeared and rebuked me. Yet I endured this, not uttering a word, for my debt of gratitude to you is much greater. My former master grew furious and threatened to behead me, but I still said nothing. Finally I was beheaded, and when I saw my own corpse proceding on its journey from death to the next life my sorrow was indescribable. Still, I did not speak. Eventually I was reborn in a Brahman family in southern India. The pain I felt on entering and leaving the womb was unbearable, yet I held my breath without crying. I grew up to be a young man and took a wife. My parents died; my child was born; I felt sorrow and joy but said not a word. Living on like this, I reached my sixty-fifth year. Then my wife said to me, 'If you still refuse to say anything, I will kill your beloved child.' The thought flashed through my mind that I was already in the last years of my life, and if my child were killed, I could not beget another. Feeling that I must shout . . . I suddenly awoke."

The hermit said, "We were not strong enough. You and I have been deceived by a devil. Our task has ended in failure." Lamenting, his disciple said, "Because I was so weak-willed, my teacher failed to master the occult." The hermit regretfully replied, "It is my fault for not having admonished you enough beforehand." Nonetheless, as the record states, his disciple was so grieved that he could not fulfill his obligation to his teacher that he brooded over it and died miserably.[54]

In China the occult evolved from Confucianism,[55] and in India it is found among the Brahman teachings. Yet it does not even approach the primitive *Agon* teachings of Hinayana Buddhism, much less the teachings of *tsūgyō*, *bekkyō*, or *engyō*.[56] Therefore, how could it measure up to the Lotus Sutra? The four devils[57] fiercely oppose the attainment of even such a shallow art as the occult. Therefore, how much greater are the tribulations that will confront the disciples of the votary of the Lotus Sutra, for he is the first to embrace and the first to propagate Nam-myoho-renge-kyo, the ultimate principle of the Lotus Sutra, in Japan. It is impossible to imagine, let alone describe in words.

The *Maka Shikan* is the Great Teacher T'ien-t'ai's masterwork and contains the essence of all the Buddhist sutras. During the five hundred years after Buddhism was introduced to China, there appeared seven great teachers to the north of the Yangtze River and three to the south.[58] Their wisdom was as brilliant as the sun and the moon, and their virtue was extolled far and wide, yet they were confused as to which sutras were shallow or deep, inferior or superior, and to the order in which they had been taught. It was the Great Teacher T'ien-t'ai[59] who not only clarified the teachings of Buddhism but also brought forth the wish-granting jewel of *ichinen sanzen* from the repository of the five characters of *Myōhō-renge-kyō* and bestowed it upon all people in the three countries.[60] This teaching originated in China. Not even the great scholars of India could formulate such a concept. So the Great Teacher Chang-an wrote, "We have never before heard of any teachings as lucid as the *Maka Shikan*,"[61] and "Even the great masters of India were not in a class with him."[62] The doctrine of *ichinen sanzen* revealed in the fifth volume of the *Maka Shikan* is especially profound. If you propagate it, devils will arise without fail. If they did not, there would be no way of knowing that this is the true teaching. One passage from the same volume reads, "As practice progresses and understanding grows, the three obstacles and four devils emerge, vying with one another to interfere . . . You should be neither influenced nor frightened by them. If you fall under their influence, you will be led into the paths of evil. If you are frightened by them, you will be prevented from practicing true Buddhism."[63] This quotation not only applies to me but also is a guide for my disciples. Reverently make this teaching your own and transmit it as an axiom of faith for future generations.

The three obstacles in this quotation are *bonnō-shō*, *gō-shō*, and *hō-shō*. *Bonnō-shō* are the obstacles to one's practice that arise from greed, anger, stupidity, and the like; *gō-shō* are the obstacles posed by one's wife or children, and *hō-shō* are the hindrances caused by one's sovereign or parents.[64] Of the four devils, the functions of the Devil of the Sixth Heaven are of this last kind. Of those people in Japan today who say, "I have attained concentration and insight, I have attained concentration and insight," who among them is facing the three obstacles and four devils? Yet many people claim they have mastered the *Maka Shikan*. The statement, "If you fall under their influence, you will be led into the paths of evil," does not indicate merely the three evil paths but also the worlds of Humanity and Heaven and, in general, all of the nine worlds. Therefore, all of the sutras except the Lotus Sutra—including those of the Kegon, Agon, Hōdō, and Hannya periods, as well as the Nirvana and *Dainichi* sutras—will lead people toward paths of evil. Also, with the exception of the Tendai sect, the adherents of the seven other major Buddhist sects[65] are in reality agents of hell who drive others toward evil paths. Even in the Tendai sect, there are those who profess faith in the Lotus Sutra yet actually lead others toward the pre-Lotus Sutra teachings. They, too, are agents of hell who cause people to fall into the evil paths.

Now you two brothers are like the hermit and his disciple. If either of you gives up halfway, you will both fail to attain Buddhahood. You are like the two wings of a bird or the two eyes of a man. And your wives are your support. Women support others and thereby cause others to support them. When a husband is happy, his wife will be fulfilled. If a husband is a thief, his wife will become one, too. This is not a matter of this life alone. A man and wife are as close as form and shadow, flowers and fruit, or roots and leaves, in every existence of life. Insects eat the trees they live in, and fish drink the water in which they swim. If grass withers, orchids grieve; if pine trees flourish, oaks rejoice.[66] Even trees and grass are so closely related. The *hiyoku* is a bird with one body and two heads. Both of its mouths nourish the same body. *Hiboku* are fish with only one eye each, so the male and female remain together for life. A husband and wife should be like them.

You two wives should have no regrets even if your husbands do you harm because of your faith in this teaching. If both of you unite in encouraging your husband's faith, you will follow the path of the Dragon King's daughter[67] and become the model for women attaining enlightenment in the evil Latter Day of the Law. Insofar as you can act this way, no matter what may happen, I, Nichiren, will tell the two saints, the two heavenly gods,[68] and the Ten Goddesses as well as Shakyamuni and Tahō Buddhas to make you Buddhas in every future existence. The *Rokuharamitsu* Sutra states that one should become the master of the mind rather than let the mind master one.[69]

Whatever trouble may occur, regard it as no more than a dream and think only of the Lotus Sutra. Nichiren's teaching was especially difficult to believe at first, but now that my prophecies have been fulfilled, those who slandered without reason have come to repent. Even if other men and women become my believers in the future, they will not replace you in my heart. Among those who believed at first, many later discarded their faith, fearing that society would reject them. Among these are some who oppose me more furiously than those who slandered from the beginning. In Shakyamuni's lifetime, Priest Sunakṣatra at first believed the Buddha, then later not only backslid but slandered so viciously that even the Buddha could not save him from falling into the hell of incessant suffering.[70] This letter was especially written for Munenaga. It should also be read to his wife and Munenaka's. Nam-myoho-renge-kyo, Nam-myoho-renge-kyo.

Nichiren

The sixteenth day of the fourth month in the twelfth year of Bun'ei (1275)

Notes

1. All the Buddha's teachings and the twelve divisions of the scriptures.

2. The Lotus Sutra.

3. A.D. 58–90.

4. The new translations refer to those made by Hsüan-tsang (602–664) and later; the old translations refer to works translated before this time, chiefly those rendered by Kumārajīva (344–409) and Paramārtha (499–569).

5. *Sanzen-jintengō* is explained later in the text; *gohyaku-jintengō* is described in the *Juryō* (16th) chapter of the Lotus Sutra. These terms do not appear as such in the sutra. *See also: sanzen-jintengō* and *gohyaku-jintengō* in Glossary.

6. The term "galaxy" is used here to translate *sanzen daisen sekai*, one thousand times three thousand great worlds, an immeasurable distance of space.

7. The three groups of disciples (Jap: *sanshū no shōmon*) who attained Buddhahood on the basis of their innate capacity to understand the teachings: the one of superior capacity who was enlightened directly on hearing the preaching, Śāriputra; those of medium capacity who awakened to the teaching on the basis of the parables, Mahākāśyapa and others; those of inferior capacity who gained understanding on the basis of the exposition of their relationship with Shakyamuni from the remote past, Pūrṇa and others.

8. Daitsū Buddha is a Buddha who appeared in the remote past. He is described in the *Kejōyu* (7th) chapter of the Lotus Sutra. He had sixteen sons, all of whom preached the Lotus Sutra. The youngest son was born in this *sahā* world as Shakyamuni.

9. The *Shōbō Nenjo* Sutra (T17, no.721) describes the eight hot hells, situated one above the other beneath Jambudvīpa, each of which has sixteen subsidiary hells associated with it, making a total of 136 hells. The hell of incessant suffering (also known as the Avīci Hell) is the eighth and most fearsome of the hells. There are also eight cold hells. They are also explained by T'ien-t'ai in his *Hokke Gengi* (T33, 758c).

10. T9, 15c-16a.

11. The three physical evils of killing, theft, and adultery; the four verbal evils of lying, flattery, slander, and duplicity; the three mental evils of greed, anger, and stupidity. They are described in the *Kusha Ron* (T29, 85ff.).

12. Tōkatsu and Kokujō are the first and the second of the hot hells.

13. To kill a father, a mother, an arhat, shed the blood of a Buddha, and to destroy the harmony of the Sangha.

14. This refers probably to the *asura* Asurin, associated with eclipses, who increased greatly the size of his body and mouth and tried to swallow the sun and moon. The story is found in the *Zōichi Agon* Sutra (T2, 560a).

15. The story of Devadatta's fall into hell is found in the *Daichido Ron* (T25, 165a) and elsewhere.

16. The turtle and the log simile is from the Lotus Sutra (T9, 60b). It is frequently used by Nichiren; usually the blind turtle must find a hole in the floating log just the right size to accommodate itself. The account of Mount Sumeru suspended from a lotus-root fiber is from the Nirvana Sutra (T12, 471b).

17. Tz'u-en (632–682), better known as K'uei-chi, was the foremost disciple of Hsüan-tsang (602–660). He was the organizer of the Fa-hsiang (Hossō) teachings. Tz'u-en is the name of the temple at which he lived.

18. *Hokke Shūku* (DDZ3, 252).

19. Shan-wu-wei (Skt: Śubhakarasimha; Jap; Zemmui; 637–735) introduced esoteric teachings to China in 716. He was closely associated with the court and translated several scriptures into Chinese.

20. These refer to civilian rather than specifically Buddhist offenses set forth in the Ritsuryō Code. They are: (1) attempts on the emperor's life; (2) plots to destroy imperial graves or palaces; (3) treason; (4) murder of an older relative, such as a grandparent, parent, sister, or brother; (5) murder of other senior relatives or of one's wife; (6) disrespectful acts against the emperor or imperial shrines; (7) unfilial acts against a grandparent; and (8) killing one's master, teacher, or superior.

21. *Hokke Gengi* (T33, 761b).

22. T9, 43a.

23. *Hokke Gengi* (T33, 755c).

24. The Devil of the Sixth Heaven is Takejizaiten, who resides in the sixth heaven of the world of desire. He is described in the *Daichido Ron* (T25, 123a) and elsewhere.

25. The twenty-five realms of existence in the world of desire are: the four lower realms: hell, hungry ghosts, animals, and asura; the four continents of the realm of humanity; the six heavens of the desire world. In the realm of form, Brahma heaven, the four dhyana heavens, the heaven free from intellectual activity, and the five pure dwelling heavens (counted as one heaven) all in the realm of pure form; and the four heavens of the realm without form.

26. Tu-shun (557–640), Chih-yen (602–668), Fa-tsang (643–712), and Ch'eng-kuan (738–839). The founder and successive patriarchs of the Hua-yen (Kegon) school.

27. Chia-hsiang (better known as Chi-tsang, 547–623) is sometimes regarded as the founder of the San-lun (Sanron) school. Seng-ch'üan was an early San-lun practitioner.

28. Shan-wu-wei (Śubhakarasimha, 537–735), Chin-kang-chih (Vajrabodhi, 671–741), and Pu-k'ung (Amoghavajra, 705–774) were Indian masters who brought esoteric Buddhism to China. Kōbō is Kūkai (774–835), the founder of the Shingon sect in Japan; Jikaku (Ennin, 794–866) and Chishō (Enchin, 814–891) were Tendai masters who incorporated esoteric doctrines in their teachings.

29. Bodhidharma and Hui-k'o are the putative founders of Ch'an (Zen) in China.

30. Shan-tao (613–681) was an important Pure Land leader in China. Hōnen (1133–1212) was the founder of the Jōdo (Pure Land) sect in Japan.

31. T9, 36c.

32. This story is found in *Daichido Ron* (T25, 182a).

33. This story is also found in *Daichido Ron* (T25, 145a) and elsewhere. It tells how, while Śāriputra was practicing the bodhisattva way, a Brahman begged him for his eye. Śāriputra gave it to him, but the Brahman was so revolted by its smell that he dropped and crushed it. Seeing this, Śāriputra withdrew from his practice and as a result fell into Avīci Hell for countless kalpas.

34. Based on a story in the *Butsuzō* Sutra (T15, 794c–795a). Daishōgon Buddha lived 68 million years and had 68 million disciples. However, three months after he entered nirvana all his disciples did likewise, so that there was no one left to pass on the teaching. Those who came later, influenced by his reputation, became monks; however, not knowing the depth of the Buddhadharma, a hundred years later these monks split into five groups. Kugan and three other priests denounced the priest Fuji,

who was the only one to understand Buddhism. Because of their heretical views they all fell into the Avīci Hell.

35. This story is from the *Shohō Mugyō* Sutra (T15, 759a-b).

36. T9, 31b.

37. T9, 39a.

38. Nirvana Sutra (Southern version, T12, 705a).

39. T12, 877c.

40. The Ten Goddesses (Skt: Rakṣīsī) are the daughters of Kishimojin (Hārītī), described in the *Darani* (26th) chapter of the Lotus Sutra. The mother and daughters vow to protect the votaries of the Lotus Sutra. In other texts they appear as evil demons; the Lotus Sutra, however, describes them as protectors of the followers of the Lotus Sutra.

41. Reference is to a story in the Nirvana Sutra (T12, 45a), frequently cited by Nichiren, in which a demon tests Sessen Dōji, who is Shakyamuni in a previous existence. In the end the demon proves to be Taishaku (Indra).

42. King Shibi was the name under which Shakyamuni, in a previous existence, engaged in bodhisattva practice. To test his progress as a bodhisattva, Indra and Bishamon turned themselves into a hawk and a pigeon respectively. King Shibi protected the pigeon in his clothing, but in order to rescue the hawk, which was starving, cut off a piece of his own thigh and fed it to the hawk. *Bosatsu Honjō Manron* (T3, 333b-c).

43. Hōjō Tokimune (1251–1284), suspecting his half-brother, Tokisuke (? –1272), of plotting against the regency, had him killed.

44. Reference is to the invasion of these islands by Mongol troops.

45. The term used here is *jisai*, to refrain from eating after noon, one of the Hinayana precepts. Reference is presumably to the Ritsu sect, whose leader, Ryōkan, Nichiren considered his archenemy.

46. Hei no Saemon (? –1291) is the shogunal official who opposed Nichiren and attempted to have him executed at Tatsunokuchi.

47. Lord Wada is Wada Yoshimori (1147–1212), a Kamakura military figure, who fought against the Hōjō and whose entire family was wiped out. Lord Wakasa is Miura Yasumura (? –1247), who was related to the Hōjō by marriage but was accused of treason; he and his entire family were destroyed in battle. Taira no Masakado (d.940) led the first major rebellion against the central government. In 939 he rebelled against the imperial court and proclaimed himself the new emperor. His cousin, Taira no Sadamori (n.d.), crushed his forces and killed him. Abe no Sadatō (1019–1062) was head of a powerful family in northern Japan. He revolted against the imperial rule but was defeated and his forces destroyed.

48. Po-i and Shu-ch'i are exemplars, praised for their virtue by Confucius and Mencius. Their stories appear in the *Shih Chi* (Records of the Historian).

49. The precise quotation is not found in the sutra. The passage is a famous one and is frequently recited at ordination ceremonies.

50. This encounter is described in the biography of Chih-i (T'ien-tai) in the *Zoku Kōsō Den* (T50, 565a).

51. This story appears in the *Nihon Shoki* under Nintoku Tennō.

52. The *Myōshōgonnō* (27th) chapter of the Lotus Sutra states that Yakuō and Yakujō, bodhisattvas who cure physical and mental diseases, are the embodiments of

Jōzō and Jōgen, princes possessed of supernatural powers in a kingdom that existed incalculable kalpas in the past.

53. Munenaka, the elder brother is given here as Tayū-no-sakan; Munenaga, the younger brother as Hyōe-no-sakan. Tsuruō is not identified.

54. *Daitō Saiiki Ki* (T51, 906c–907a).

55. Nichiren is obviously referring to Taoism here.

56. Reference is to the Four Teachings of Doctrine (*kehō no shikyō*) by which Chegwan, on the basis of T'ien-t'ai's writings, classified Buddhist scriptures. They are: (1) the tripitaka teaching (*zōkyō*), consisting of sutras, *vinaya*, and *abhidharma*, corresponding to Hinayana teachings; (2) the connecting or shared teaching (*tsugyō*), which includes the *Hōdō* or *Vaipulya*, early Mahayana teachings; (3) the specific or distinctive teaching (*bekkyō*), which includes *Hannya* or Wisdom sutras, and (4) the complete or perfect teaching (*engyō*), which includes the Lotus and Nirvana sutras. These are discussed in *Tendai Shikyō Gi* (T46, 774c ff.).

57. The four devils are associated with the three obstacles (mentioned below). The four devils are: (1) *bonnō-ma*, obstructions arising from the three poisons (*sandoku*): greed, anger, and stupidity; (2) *on-ma*, obstacles occasioned by the coming together of the five *skandhas*, or components: form, perception, conception, volition, and consciousness; (3) *shi-ma*, the obstacle of death that brings to an end one's practice of Buddhism; and (4) *tenji-ma*, obstruction of the devil of the Sixth Heaven, which takes the form of oppression by men of power, and is the most difficult to do away with.

58. Nichiren writes in the text: "Ten teachers of North and South (*Namboku no jūshi*)." In most other instances he refers to these teachers as translated above in the text.

59. Nichiren refers to T'ien-t'ai here by his other title, Chih-she ta-shih (Chisha Daishi).

60. India, China, and Japan.

61. The initial passage in the *Maka Shikan*, T'ien-t'ai's major work, recorded by Chang-an (T46, 1a).

62. *Hokke Gengi* (T33, 704c).

63. T46, 49a.

64. The three obstacles are associated with the four devils, above. They are mentioned in the Nirvana Sutra (T12, 428c) and elsewhere.

65. Here reference is to the three Hinayana sects: Kusha, Jōjitsu, and Ritsu, and the four Mahayana sects: Sanron, Hossō, Kegon, and Shingon.

66. This passage alludes to the *T'an-shih fu* ("Lamentation on Passing Away") by Lu Chi (261–303), contained in *Wen-hsüan* 16.

67. The *Daibadatta* (12th) chapter of the Lotus Sutra describes the attainment of Buddhahood by the daughter of the Dragon King.

68. The two saints are Yakuō and Yūze, bodhisattvas who protect the Lotus Sutra and appear in the *Darani* (26th) chapter of the Lotus Sutra. The two gods are Bishamonten and Jikokuten, two of the Four Heavenly Kings.

69. T8, 898b. The full title of the sutra is *Daijō Rishu Rokuharamitsu* Sutra.

70. The story of Zenshō biku (Sunakṣatra) appears in the Nirvana Sutra (T12, 560b).

27 THE THREE OBSTACLES AND FOUR DEVILS

This letter was written to Hyōe-no-sakan Munenaga, the younger of the two Ikegami brothers, to whom the preceding "Letter to the Brothers" is addressed. The letter is dated the twentieth of the eleventh month, 1277, and is designed to bolster the resolve of the younger brother. The elder brother, Munenaka, had twice been disowned, in 1275 and again in 1277, by the father, Yasumitsu, who was a loyal follower of Ryōkan, the prominent Kamakura priest who was Nichiren's archenemy.

"The Three Obstacles and Four Devils" (*Sanshō Shima no Koto*) is an alternative title for this letter. It is otherwise referred to as *Hyōe Sakan Dono no Gohenji* (Reply to Lord Hyōe Sakan).

The two men you sent have arrived here, bringing your various offerings. I also received a message from the Priest Nisshō[1] regarding your faith.

In this letter I want to advise you about what is most important for you. In the Former and Middle Days of the Law, the world did not fall into decline because saints and sages appeared frequently and the gods protected the people. In the Latter Day of the Law, however, people have become so greedy that strife rages incessantly between sovereign and subject, parent and child, elder and younger brother, and all the more so among people who are unrelated. When such conflict occurs, the gods abandon the country and then the three calamities and seven disasters[2] begin, until one, two, three, four, five, six, or seven suns appear in the sky.[3] Plants wither and die, large and small rivers dry up, the earth smolders like charcoal, and the sea becomes like boiling oil. Eventually flames fill the atmosphere, arising from the hell of incessant suffering and reaching the Brahma-heaven. Such is the devastation that will occur when the world reaches its final dissolution.

Everyone, whether wise or foolish, considers it natural for children to obey their parents, for subjects to be loyal to their sovereign, and for disciples to follow their master. Recently, however, it appears that the people of our day, drunk with the wine of greed, anger, and stupidity,[4] make it a rule to betray their sovereign, despise their parents, and scoff at their teachers. You should read again and again the previous letter[5] in which I explained that one should of course obey his parents as well as his sovereign and teacher, but should they commit evil, admonishing them is in fact being loyal to them.

Recently your elder brother, Uemon no Sakan, was again disowned by your father. I told your wife when she came to visit me here that he was certain to be disowned again, and since your faith was quite unstable, she should be prepared for the worst. This time I am sure that you will give up your faith. If you do, I have not the slightest intention of reproaching you for it. Likewise, neither should you blame me, Nichiren, when you have fallen into hell. It is in no way my responsibility. It is an undeniable fact that fire can at once reduce even a thousand-year-old field of pampas grass to ashes, and that the merit one has formed over a hundred years can be destroyed with a single careless word.

Your father now seems to have become the enemy of the Lotus Sutra, yet your brother will now become one of its votaries.[6] You, who think only of immediate affairs, will obey your father, and deluded people will therefore praise you for your filial devotion. Munemori obeyed his father's tyrannous commands and was finally beheaded at Shinohara. Shigemori disobeyed his father and preceded him in death.[7] Who was truly the better son? If you obey your father who is an enemy of the Lotus Sutra and abandon your brother who is a votary of the supreme teaching, are you then being filial? In the final analysis, what you should do is resolve to pursue the way of Buddhism single-mindedly just as your brother is doing. Your father is like King Myōshōgon and you brothers are like the princes Jōzō and Jōgen.[8] The age is different but the principle of the Lotus Sutra remains the same. Recently Hōjō Yoshimasa,[9] the lord of Musashi Province, abandoned his vast territory and his many subjects in order to retire from all worldly affairs. If you ingratiate yourself with your father for the sake of a small private estate, neglect your faith and fall into the evil states of existence, you should not blame me, Nichiren. Yet despite this warning, I feel that this time you will discard your belief.

I state this out of pity because you have been faithful until now, but you may fall into the evil states of existence in spite of your past faith. If, by one chance out of a hundred or a thousand, you should decide to follow my advice, then confront your father and say: "Since you are my father, I should by rights obey you, but since you have become an enemy of the Lotus Sutra, I would be unfilial if I were to do so in this matter. Therefore, I have resolved to break with you and follow my brother. If you should disown him, be aware that you are disowning me too." You should not have the slightest fear in your heart. It is lack of courage that prevents one from attaining Buddhahood, although he may have professed faith in the Lotus Sutra many times since the remotest past.

There is definitely something extraordinary in the ebb and flow of the tide, the rising and setting of the moon, and the way in which summer, autumn, winter and spring give way to each other. Something uncommon also occurs when an ordinary person attains Buddhahood. At such a time, the three obstacles and four devils will invariably appear, and the wise will rejoice while the foolish will retreat. I have long been waiting to tell you this, either through my own messenger or by some other means. So I greatly appreciate your sending these messengers to me. I am sure that if you were about to abandon your faith, you would not have sent them. Thinking it may still not be too late, I am writing this letter.

To attain Buddhahood is difficult indeed, more difficult than the feat of placing a needle atop the Mount Sumeru of this world and then casting a thread from atop the Mount Sumeru of another world directly through the eye of this needle. And the feat is even more difficult if it must be done in the face of a contrary wind. The Lotus Sutra states, "During countless millions and millions of kalpas of inconceivable duration, rare are the times when this Lotus Sutra has been heard. During countless millions and millions of kalpas of inconceivable duration, rare are the times when the Buddhas, the World-Honored Ones, preach this sutra. Therefore, the practitioners after the Buddha's death, on hearing such a sutra as this, should not have any doubts."[10] This passage is extremely unusual even among the twenty-eight chapters of the Lotus Sutra. From the *Jo* to the *Hosshi* chapters, humans, heavenly beings, the four kinds of believers, and the eight kinds of nonhuman beings below the stage of *tōgaku*[11] were many in number, but there was only one Buddha, Shakyamuni. Thus, these chapters are more important [than the pre-Lotus Sutra teachings] but less important [than those chapters of the Lotus Sutra which describe the ceremony in the air]. The twelve chapters from *Hōtō* to *Zokurui* are the most important of all. This is because in the presence of Shakyamuni Buddha there appeared a tower decorated with many treasures.[12] It was as if the sun had risen in front of the moon. All the Buddhas in the universe were seated under the trees, and it seemed as though the light of a fire shone over all the grass and trees in the universe. It was in this setting that the above passage was expounded.

The Nirvana Sutra states, "People have been suffering since uncountable kalpas ago. The bones each individual leaves behind in a kalpa pile up as high as Mount Vipula in Rājagṛha, and the milk he sucks is equal to the water of the four oceans.[13] The blood one sheds surpasses the quantity of water in the four oceans, and so do the tears he sheds in grief over the death of parents, brothers and sisters, wives, children, and relatives. And though one used all the plants and trees growing in the earth to make four-inch tallies to count them, one could not count all the parents one has had in the past existences of life."[14] These are the words the Buddha uttered lying in the grove of sāla trees on the final day of his earthly life. You should pay the strictest attention to them. They mean that the number of parents who gave birth to you since innumerable kalpas ago could not be counted even with tallies made by cutting all the plants and trees growing on all the worlds of the universe into four-inch pieces.

Thus you have had a countless number of parents in your past existences, yet during that time you have never encountered the Lotus Sutra. From this we see that it is easy to have parents, but very difficult to encounter the Lotus Sutra. Now if you disobey the words of a parent, one who is easy to come by, and follow a friend of the Lotus Sutra, one who can rarely be encountered, you will not only be able to attain Buddhahood, but will also be able to lead to enlightenment the parent whom you disobeyed. For example, Prince Siddhārtha[15] was the eldest son of King Śuddhodana. His father wanted him to succeed to the throne and rule the nation, and actually ceded the throne to him, but the prince went against his father's wishes and escaped from the city at night. The king was angry at him for being unfilial, but after Siddhārtha had attained Buddhahood, he set about first of all to save his parents, King Śuddhodana and Lady Māyā.

No parent would ever urge his son to renounce the world in order to attain enlightenment. But however that may be, in your case, the priests and followers of the Ritsu and Nembutsu sects have egged on your father to join with them so that they may make both you and your brother abandon your faith. I am told that Ryōka-bō[16] is persuading others to chant one million Nembutsu in an attempt to cause discord among people and destroy the seeds of the Lotus Sutra. Hōjō Shigetoki[17] seemed to be an admirable person. But deluded by the Nembutsu believers, he treated me with enmity, and as a result, he and his entire clan have been all but ruined. Only Hōjō Naritoki,[18] lord of Echigo Province, has survived. You may think that those who believe in Ryōka-bō are prospering, but you should see what has become of the Nagoe clan,[19] who paid for the building of Zenkō-ji, Chōraku-ji, and a temple to house a huge Buddha image.[20] Again, Hōjō Tokimune[21] is the ruler of Japan, but by his conduct he has called down on himself an enemy almost as great as the entire world.[22]

Even if you abandon your brother and take his place in your father's favor, you will never prosper in ten million years. There is no knowing what will become of you even in the near future—you may face ruin in this very lifetime. Therefore, you should resolve to give all your thought to your next existence. Having written all this, it occurs to me that this letter may be futile and I tire of going on. But it may serve as a reminder to you in the future.

With my deep respect,
Nichiren

The twentieth day of the eleventh month

Notes

1. Nisshō (1221–1323) was one of Nichiren's six senior priest-disciples. He devoted himself to propagation mainly in Kamakura, but after Nichiren's death, he was influenced by his former ties with the Tendai sect and turned against Nichiren's teachings.

2. *See* Three Calamities and Seven Disasters in Glossary.

3. Reference is to an unusual phenomenon when the sun is seen as a multiple image. Such illusions involving the sun have appeared in the form of many bright disks arcing outward from the sun. Scientists say that they are caused by reflection or refraction of light by ice crystals floating in the stratosphere.

4. Generally known as the three poisons (*sandoku*), the fundamental evils inherent in life that give rise to human suffering.

5. The "Letter to the Brothers," dated the sixteenth day of the fourth month, 1275.

6. The elder brother, Munenaka, was already a votary of the Lotus Sutra in that he had been practicing the sutra according to Nichiren's instruction. This statement implies that because Munenaka will willingly accept disinheritance and the accompanying social sanctions rather than renouce his faith, he was in effect giving his life for the Lotus Sutra.

7. Munemori (1147–1185) and Shigemori (1138–1179) were brothers and warriors belonging to the Taira clan, which took control of the Japanese court in the mid-twelfth century and held supreme power until defeated by the Minamoto clan in 1185. The head of the ruling clan, Taira no Kiyomori (1118–1181), installed himself in the highest government position and abused his authority. His first son, Shigemori, remonstrated with his father when he tried to confine the retired emperor Goshirakawa, while the third son, Munemori, followed his father's instructions. Shigemori died of illness and Munemori, after the Taira forces were destoryed at Dannoura, attempted to drown himself, but was rescued and eventually was beheaded at Shinohara in Ōmi Province.

8. Jōzō and Jōgen were the sons of King Myōshōgon who are described in the *Myōshōgonnō* (27th) chapter of the Lotus Sutra. At their mother's urging, the two sons displayed mystic powers before their father, a follower of Brahmanism, causing him to turn to Buddhism.

9. Hōjō Yoshimasa (1243–1281) was a top official of the Kamakura government who held important posts such as adviser to the regent and provincial governor. He resigned from his position to enter the priesthood in 1277.

10. T9, 51c.

11. *Tōgaku* is the fifty-first of the fifty-two stages of bodhisattva practice, the last being *myōgaku*, or full enlightenment. *Tōgaku* is thus the highest stage of a bodhisattva.

12. The Treasure Tower of Tahō Buddha, which appeared in the *Hōtō* (11th) chapter of the Lotus Sutra.

13. The four oceans that surround all four sides of Mount Sumeru.

14. T12, 496b.

15. The given name of Shakyamuni Buddha before his renunciation of the world.

16. Ryōka-bō refers to Ryōkan (1217–1303), a priest of the Gokuraku-ji, a temple of the Ritsu sect. Ryōka of Ryōka-bō is a phonetic change of Ryōkan and means "two fires." In the third month of 1275, a fire broke out in the Gokuraku-ji where Ryōkan was then living, and the flames spread to the palace of the shogunate. The temple and part of the palace were burned to the ground. Sarcastically, therefore, Nichiren refers to Ryōkan as "Ryōka"-bō (priest double-fire).

17. Hōjō Shigetoki (1198–1261) was the third son of Hōjō Yoshitoki (1163–1224), the second regent. He built the Gokuraku-ji for Ryōkan and Nichiren refers to him here as Gokurakuji-dono, the name by which he was known after he joined the priesthood and retired to this temple.

18. Hōjō Naritoki (n.d.) was the fifth son of Hōjō Shigetoki. He became Echigo no kami (by which title Nichiren refers to him here) in 1275.

19. Nagoe was formerly a place name within Kamakura where the clan of Hōjō Tomotoki (1193–1245), the younger brother of Hōjō Yasutoki (1183–1242), the third regent of the Kamakura government, had its residence.

20. A temple by the name of Zenkō-ji no longer exists in Kamakura. The Chōraku-ji was a large temple of the Pure Land sect. The temple to house a huge Buddha image is known as Kōtoku-in. A large wooden statue of Amida and the building to house it was begun in 1238 and completed in 1243. In 1248 both building and statue were destroyed by a typhoon. The present bronze statue was constructed in 1252 and installed in a great Buddha Hall. The Buddha Hall was subsequently destroyed several times by fire and the statue, known as the Kamakura Daibutsu, stands in the open today.

21. Hōjō Tokimune (1251–1284) was the eighth regent of the Kamakura government. Nichiren refers to him as Kōdono.

22. This enemy is, of course, the Mongols, who invaded in 1274.

28 Recitation of the Hōben and Juryō Chapters

Nichiren wrote this letter in 1264, while living in Kamakura, to the wife of Hiki Daigaku Saburō Yoshimoto (1202–1286). Yoshimoto had studied Confucianism in Kyoto and had served the Retired Emperor Juntoku. He later went to Kamakura where he was employed by the military government as a Confucian scholar. He is said to have become a follower of Nichiren around 1260. Both Yoshimoto and his wife were strong believers. The present letter is in reply to an inquiry by Yoshimoto's wife in which she asked about the formalities to be observed in the worship of the Lotus Sutra.

This letter is most commonly referred to by the title *Gessui Gosho* (Letter on Menstruation). Here it is given its alternative title, "Recitation of the *Hōben* and *Juryō* Chapters" (*Hōben Juryō Dokuju no Koto*).

In the letter that you sent by messenger, you say that you used to recite one chapter of the Lotus Sutra each day, completing the entire sutra in the space of twenty-eight days, but that now you simply read the *Yakuō* chapter[1] once each day. You ask [if this is satisfactory, or] if it would be better to return to your original practice of reading each chapter in turn.

In the case of the Lotus Sutra, one may recite the entire sutra of twenty-eight chapters in eight volumes every day; or one may recite only one volume, or one chapter, or one verse, or one phrase, or one word; or one may simply chant the daimoku, Nam-myoho-renge-kyo, only once a day, or chant it only once in the course of a lifetime; or hear someone else chant it only once in a lifetime and rejoice in the hearing; or rejoice in hearing the voice of someone else rejoice in the hearing, and so on to fifty removes from the original individual who first chanted the daimoku.[2]

In such a case, of course, the spirit of faith would become weak and the feeling of rejoicing much diluted, like the vague notions that might occur to the mind of a child of two or three, or like the mentality of a cow or a horse, unable to distinguish before from after. And yet the blessings gained by such a person are a hundred, a thousand, ten thousand, a hundred thousand times greater than those gained by persons of excellent innate ability and superior wisdom who study other sutras: persons such as Śāriputra, Maudgalyāyana, Monju, and Miroku, who had committed to memory the entire texts of the various sutras.

The Lotus Sutra itself tells us this, and the same opinion is expressed in the sixty volumes of commentary[3] by T'ien-t'ai and Miao-lo. Thus, the sutra states [concerning these blessing], "Even if their quantity were to be measured with the Buddha wisdom, their limit could not be found."[4] Not even the wisdom of the Buddha can fathom the blessings such a person will obtain. The Buddha wisdom is so marvelous that it can know even the number of raindrops that fall in this major world system of ours during a period of seven days or twice seven days. And yet we read that the blessings acquired by one who recites no more than a single word of the Lotus Sutra are the one thing alone it cannot fathom. How, then, could ordinary persons like ourselves, who have committed so many grave offenses, be capable of understanding such blessings?

Great as such blessings may be, however, it is now some twenty-two hundred years and more since the Buddha's passing. For many years, the five impurities[5] have flourished, and good deeds in any connection are rare indeed. Now, even though a person may do good, in the course of doing a single good deed he accumulates ten evil ones, so that in the end, for the sake of a small good, he commits great evil. And yet, in his heart, he prides himself on having practiced "great good"—such are the times we live in.

Moreover, you have been born in the remote land of Japan, a tiny island country in the east separated by two hundred thousand ri[6] of mountains and seas from the country of the Buddha's birth. What is more, you are a woman, burdened by the five obstacles and bound by the three obediences.[7] How indescribably wonderful, therefore, that in spite of these hindrances, you have been able to take faith in the Lotus Sutra!

Even the wise or the learned, such as those who have pored over all the sacred teachings propounded by the Buddha in the course of his lifetime, and who have mastered both the exoteric and esoteric doctrines, are these days abandoning the Lotus Sutra and instead reciting the Nembutsu. What good karma must you have formed in the past, then, to have been born a person able to recite even so much as a verse or a phrase of the Lotus Sutra!

When I read over your letter, I felt as though my eyes were beholding something rarer than the *udumbara* flower, something even less frequent than the one-eyed turtle encountering a floating log with a hollow in it that fits him exactly.[8] Moved to heartfelt admiration, I thought I would like to add just one word or one expression of my own rejoicing, endeavoring in this way to enhance your merit. I fear, however, that as clouds darken the moon or as dust defiles a mirror, my brief and clumsy attempts at description will only serve to cloak and obscure the incomparably wonderful blessings you will receive, and the thought pains me. Yet, in response to your question, I could scarcely remain silent. Please understand that I am merely joining my one drop to the rivers and the oceans or adding my candle to the sun and the moon, hoping in this way to increase even slightly the volume of the water or the brilliance of the light.

First of all, when it comes to the Lotus Sutra, whether one recites all eight volumes, or only one volume, one chapter, one verse, one phrase, or simply the daimoku or title, you should understand that the blessings that result are in all cases the same. It is like the water of the great ocean, a single drop of which contains water from all the countless streams and rivers, or like the wish-granting jewel, which, though only a single jewel, can shower all kinds of treasures upon the wisher. And the same is true of a hundred, a thousand, ten thousand, or a hundred thousand such drops of water or such jewels. A single character of the Lotus Sutra is like such a drop of water or such a jewel, and all the hundred million characters[9] of the Lotus Sutra are like a hundred million such drops or jewels.

On the other hand, a single character of the other sutras, or the name of any of the various Buddhas, is like one drop of the water of some particular stream or river, or like only one stone from a particular mountain or a particular sea. One such drop does not contain the water of countless other streams and rivers, and one such stone does not possess the virtues that inhere in innumerable other kinds of stones.

Therefore, when it comes to the Lotus Sutra, it is praiseworthy to recite any chapter you have placed your trust in, whichever chapter it might be.

Generally speaking, among all the sacred teachings of the Tathagata, none has ever been known to contain false words. Yet when we consider the Buddhist teachings more deeply, we find that even among the Tathagata's golden words there exist various categories, such as Mahayana and Hinayana, provisional and true teachings, and exoteric and esoteric doctrines. These distinctions arise from the sutras themselves, and accordingly we find that they are roughly outlined in the commentaries of the various scholars and teachers.

To state the essence of the matter, among the doctrines propounded by Shakyamuni Buddha in the fifty or more years of his teaching life, those put forward in the first forty or so years are of questionable nature. We can say so because the Buddha himself clearly stated in the *Muryōgi* Sutra, "In these more than forty years, I have not yet revealed the truth."[10] And in the Lotus Sutra, the Buddha himself proclaims concerning its every word and phrase: "Honestly discarding the provisional teachings, I will expound only the supreme Way."[11]

Moreover, Tahō Buddha appeared from the depths of the earth to add his testimony, declaring, "The Lotus Sutra. . . . All that you [Shakyamuni Buddha] have expounded is the truth."[12] And the Buddhas of the ten directions all gathered at the assembly where the Lotus Sutra was being preached and extended their tongues to give further support to the assertion that within the Lotus Sutra there is not a single word that is false. It was as though a great king, his consort and his most venerable subjects had all with one accord given their promise.

Suppose that a man or a woman who recites even a single word of the Lotus Sutra should be destined to fall into the evil paths because of having committed the ten evil acts,[13] the five cardinal sins, the four major offenses,[14] or countless other grave misdeeds. Even though the sun and moon should never again emerge from the east, though the great earth itself should turn over, though the tides of the great ocean should cease to ebb and flow, though a broken stone should be made whole or the waters of the streams and rivers cease to flow into the ocean, no woman who has put her faith in the Lotus Sutra would ever be dragged down into the evil paths as a result of worldly offenses.

If a woman who has put her faith in the Lotus Sutra should ever fall into the evil paths as a result of jealousy or ill temper or because of excessive greed, then Shakyamuni Buddha, Tahō Buddha and the Buddhas of the ten directions would immediately be guilty of breaking the vow they have upheld over the span of countless major kalpas never to tell a lie. Their offense would be even greater than the wild falsehoods and deceptions of Devadatta or the outrageous lies told by Kokālika.[15] But how could such a thing ever happen? Thus a person who embraces the Lotus Sutra is absolutely assured of its blessings.

On the other hand, though one may not commit a single evil deed in his entire lifetime, but instead observe the five precepts,[16] the eight precepts,[17] the ten precepts,[18] the ten good precepts,[19] the two hundred and fifty precepts,[20] the five hundred precepts,[21] or countless numbers of precepts; though he may learn all the other sutras by heart, make offerings to all the other Buddhas and bodhisattvas and accumulate immeasurable merit; if he but fails to put his faith in the Lotus Sutra; or if he has faith in it but considers that it ranks on the same level as the other sutras and the teachings of the other Buddhas; or if he recognizes its superiority but constantly engages in other religious disciplines, practicing the Lotus Sutra only from time to time; or if he associates on friendly terms with priests of the Nembutsu, who do not believe in the Lotus Sutra but slander the Law; or if he thinks that those who insist the Lotus Sutra does not suit the people's capacity in the latter age are guilty of no fault, then all the merit of the countless good acts he has performed throughout the course of his life will suddenly vanish. Moreover, the blessings resulting from his practice of the Lotus Sutra will for some time be obscured, and he will fall into the great citadel of the Avīci Hell as surely as rain falls from the sky or rocks tumble down from the peaks into the valleys.

Yet even though one may have committed the ten evil acts or the five cardinal sins, so long as he does not turn his back on the Lotus Sutra, he will without doubt be reborn in the Pure Land and attain Buddhahood in his next existence. On the other hand, we read in the sutra that even a person who observes the precepts, embraces all other sutras, and believes in the various Buddhas and bodhisattvas, if he fails to take faith in the Lotus Sutra, is certain to fall into the evil paths.

Limited though my ability may be, when I observe the situation in the world these days, it seems to me that the great majority of both lay believers and members of the clergy are guilty of slandering the Law.

But to return to your question: As I said before, though no chapter of the Lotus Sutra is negligible, among the entire twenty-eight chapters, the *Hōben* chapter and the *Juryō* chapter are particularly outstanding. The remaining chapters are all in a sense the branches and leaves of these two chapters. Therefore, for your regular recitation, I recommend that you practice reading the prose sections of the *Hōben* and *Juryō* chapters. In addition, it might be well if you wrote out separate copies of these sections. The remaining twenty-six chapters are like the shadows that accompany a form or the value inherent in a jewel. If you recite the *Juryō* and *Hōben* chapters, then the remaining chapters will naturally be included even though you do not recite them. It is true that the *Yakuō* and *Devadatta* chapters[22] deal specifically with women's attainment of Buddhahood or rebirth in the Pure Land. But the *Devadatta* chapter is a branch and leaf of the *Hōben* chapter, and the *Yakuō* chapter is a branch and leaf of the *Hōben* and *Juryō* chapters.[23] Therefore, you should regularly recite these two chapters, the *Hōben* and *Juryō*. As for the remaining chapters, you may turn to them from time to time when you have a moment of leisure.

Also, in your letter you say that three times each day you bow in reverence to the seven characters of the daimoku, and that each day you repeat the words *Namu-ichijō-myōten*[24] ten thousand times. However, at times of menstruation you refrain from reading the sutra. You ask if it is acceptable to recite the daimoku and the *Namu-ichijō-myōten* [without facing the object of worship] at such times. You also ask whether you should refrain from reading the sutra merely during your menstrual period, or, if not, how many days following the end of your period you should wait before resuming recitation of the sutra.

This is a matter that concerns all women and about which they always inquire. In past times, too, we find many persons addressing themselves to this question concerning women. But because the sacred teachings put forward by the Buddha in the course of his lifetime do not touch upon this point, no one has been able to offer any clear scriptural proof upon which to base an answer. In my own study of the sacred teachings, though I find clear prohibitions against the impurity of certain sexual acts or the consumption of meat or wine or the five spicy foods[25] on specific days of the month, I have never come across any passage in the sutras or treatises that speaks of avoidances connected with menstruation.

While the Buddha was in the world, many women in the prime of life became nuns and devoted themselves to the Buddhist Law, but they were never shunned on account of their menstrual period. Judging from this, I would say that menstruation does not represent any kind of pollution coming from an external source. It is simply a characteristic of the female sex, a phenomenon related to the perpetuation of the seed of birth and death. Or in another sense, it might be regarded as a kind of chronically recurring illness. In the case of feces and urine, though these are substances produced by the body, so long as one observes cleanly habits, there are no special prohibitions to be observed concerning them. Surely the same must be true of menstruation. That is why, I think, we hear of no particular rules for avoidance pertaining to the subject in India or China.

Japan, however, is a land of the gods. And it is the way of this country that, although the Buddhas and bodhisattvas have manifested themselves here in the form of gods,[26] strangely enough, these gods, in many cases, do not conform to the sutras and treatises. Nevertheless, if one goes against them, one is likely to incur actual punishment.

When we scrutinize the sutras and treatises with care, we find that there is a doctrine called the *zuihō bini* precept[27] that corresponds to such cases. The gist of this precept is that, so long as no seriously offensive act is involved, then, even though one should depart to some slight degree from the teachings of Buddhism, one should avoid going against the manners and customs of the country. This is a precept expounded by the Buddha. But it appears that some wise men, unaware of this fact, claim that because the gods are demonlike beings, they are unworthy of reverence. And by insisting upon the rightness of their views, it appears that they do injury to the faith of many believers.

If we go by this *zuihō bini* precept, then since the gods of Japan have in most cases desired that prohibitions be observed regarding the period of menstruation, people born in this country would probably do well to be aware of and honor such prohibitions.

However, I do not think that such prohibitions should interfere with a woman's daily religious devotions. I would guess that it is persons who never had any faith in the Lotus Sutra to begin with who tell you otherwise. They are trying to think of some way to make you stop reciting the sutra, but they do not feel they can come right out and advise you to cast the sutra aside. So they use the pretext of bodily impurity to try to distance you from it. They intimidate you by telling you that if you continue your regular devotions during a period of pollution, you will be treating the sutra with disrespect. In this way they mean to trick you into committing a fault.

I hope you will keep in mind all that I have said regarding this matter. On this basis, even if your menstrual period should last as long as seven days, if you feel so inclined, then dispense with the reading of the sutra and simply recite Nam-myoho-renge-kyo. Also, when making your devotions, you need not bow facing the sutra.

If unexpectedly you should feel yourself approaching death, then even if you are eating fish or fowl,[28] if you are able to read the sutra, you should do so, and likewise chant Nam-myoho-renge-kyo. Needless to say, the same principle applies during your period of menstruation.

Reciting the words *Namu-ichijō-myōten*[29] amounts to the same thing. But it is better if you just chant Nam-myoho-renge-kyo, as Bodhisattva Vasubandhu and the Great Teacher T'ien-t'ai did. There are specific reasons why I say this.

Respectfully,
Nichiren

The seventeenth day of the fourth month in the first year of Bun'ei (1264), cyclical sign kinoe-ne.

Notes

1. The twenty-third chapter of the Lotus Sutra. It contains a passage (T9, 54c) stating that a woman who practices the Lotus Sutra will at life's end go directly to the Pure Land, and was therefore considered to have particular relevance to women's attainment of enlightenment.

2. Nichiren refers here to the principle of "continual propagation to the fiftieth person," described in the *Zuiki Kudoku* (18th) chapter of the Lotus Sutra. Suppose, the text says, a person were to hear the Lotus Sutra and rejoice, then preach it to a second person, who also rejoices and in turn preaches it to a third, and so on, until a fiftieth person hears the sutra. The benefit received by this person on hearing the sutra, even at fifty removes, would be countless millions of times greater than that of someone who for eighty years makes offerings to the beings of four billion *asōgi* worlds and enables them all to attain the state of arhat (T9, 46c).

3. T'ien-t'ai's three major works (the *Hokke Gengi*, *Hokke Mongu*, and *Maka Shikan*), each consisting of ten volumes, and Miao-lo's commentaries on these three works (the *Hokke Gengi Shakusen*, *Hokke Mongu Ki*, and *Maka Shikan Bugyōden Guketsu*), each also consisting of ten volumes.

4. T9, 54b.

5. The five impurities, also called the five defilements (Jap: *gojoku*), are impurities of the kalpa or age, of desire or agony, of the people, of thought (or views) and of the life span itself. They are mentioned in the *Hōben* (2d) chapter of the Lotus Sutra (T9, 7b).

6. A unit of linear measurement, originally defined as 6 *chō* (0.65 km), but from the Heian period (794–1185) on, commonly understood as 36 *chō* (3.93 km).

7. The five obstacles (Jap: *goshō*) are limitations that traditionally are said to bind

women in Buddhist and secular thought. They are: a woman cannot become a Bonten, a Taishaku, a devil king, a wheel-turning king, or a Buddha. The three obediences (*sanjū*) derive from Confucianism and require that a woman obey her parents in childhood, her husband after marriage, and her sons in old age. Virtually identical pronouncements are found also in Buddhist works (*Kegon* Sutra, T10, 790b and *Daichido Ron*, T25, 748b).

8. These are both Buddhist metaphors for something of very rare occurrence; they are mentioned frequently by Nichiren. The *udumbara* is a legendary plant said to bloom once every three thousand years to herald the advent of a wheel-turning king or a Buddha. The one-eyed turtle is mentioned in the *Myōshōgonnō* (27th) chapter of the Lotus Sutra (T9, 60c).

9. This is a figurative expression; the Lotus Sutra actually consists of 69,384 characters.

10. T9, 386b.

11. T9, 10a.

12. T9, 32c.

13. Evils condemned in the *Kusha Ron* (T29, 85a-b). They are killing, stealing, unlawful sexual intercourse, lying, flattery (or random and irresponsible speech), defaming, duplicity, greed, anger, and stupidity, or the holding of mistaken views.

14. The four major offenses are the first four of the ten evil acts: killing, stealing, sexual intercourse, and lying (in particular, claiming to have attained some insight or understanding that one does not in fact possess). These are especially grave transgressions that for monks carried the penalty of automatic expulsion from the Buddhist order. They are described in *Shibun Ritsu Biku Kaihon* (T22, 1015c).

15. Kokālika was a member of the Śākya tribe and an enemy of Shakyamuni Buddha. He fell under the influence of Devadatta and slandered the disciples Śāriputra and Maudgalyāyana and is said to have fallen into hell alive. His story appears in the Nirvana Sutra (T12, 560b).

16. Basic precepts to be observed by lay Buddhists: not to kill, not to steal, not to commit unlawful sexual intercourse, not to lie, and not to drink intoxicants. They are found in *Kusha Ron* (T29, 72b-c).

17. The eight precepts (Jap: *hachikai* or *hassaikai*) that are to be observed by lay Buddhists on specific days of the month. They correspond to the precepts for novice monks and nuns and are: (1) not to take life, (2) not to steal, (3) not to engage in sexual activity, (4) not to lie, (5) not to drink intoxicants, (6) not to wear ornaments or perfume, nor go to listen to singing or to watch dancing, (7) not to sleep on an elevated or broad bed, and (8) not to eat at irregular hours, that is, after the noon hour. *Kusha Ron* (T29, 72c-73a).

18. Ten precepts for both male and female novices of the Buddhist Order. They consist of the five precepts listed in note 16, as well as (6) not to wear ornaments or perfume, (7) not to go to listen to singing or to watch dancing, (8) not to sleep on an elevated or broad bed, (9) not to eat at irregular hours (after noon), and (10) not to own valuables such as gold and silver. They are described in the *Bommō* Sutra (T24, 1004 ff.).

19. The ten good precepts are precepts for lay believers of Mahayana; they are prohibitions against the ten evil acts listed in note 13. They are listed in the *Shōbō Nenjo* Sutra (T17, 6–7).

20. The two hundred and fifty precepts are the rules of dicipline to be observed by

fully ordained Hinayana monks. They are discussed in the *Shibun Ritsu Gyōji Shō* (T40, 50 ff.) and elsewhere.

21. The five hundred precepts are the rules for duly ordained Hinayana nuns. The 500 is not a literal figure; the number varies with the source. The *Shibun Ritsu* (T22, 714 ff.) lists 348.

22. The *Devadatta* (12th) chapter of the Lotus Sutra tells the story of the dragon king's daughter, who in a single moment attained supreme enlightenment through the power of the Lotus Sutra. She was considered to represent women's potential for Buddhahood.

23. "Branch and leaf" indicates a less essential or less important element.

24. *Namu ichijō myōten*, "Devotion to the mystic sutra of the one vehicle," is an expression of devotion to the Lotus Sutra, evidently chanted as a mantra.

25. The five spicy foods are the five kinds of pungent roots: leeks, scallions, onions, garlic, and ginger. Consumption of these foods was thought to produce irritability, anger, and sexual desire, and was accordingly forbidden by the monastic precepts.

26. Nichiren is referring to the widespread belief that Japanese deities were incarnations or manifestations (Jap: *suijaku*) of Buddhas and bodhisattvas. This concept, which took firm hold around the tenth century, reflected a tendency toward a synthesis of Buddhist and Shinto elements.

27. The precept of adapting to locality. The concept is mentioned in passages in the *Gobun Ritsu* (T22, 153a) and the preface to the *Shibun Ritsu Gyōji Shō* (T40, 2a), although the term *zuihō bini* does not appear. The precept states that in matters that the Buddha himself did not expressly permit or forbid, one may act in accordance with local custom, provided that the fundamental principles of Buddhism are not violated.

28. Eating flesh was also considered a source of pollution.

29. In the expression *ichijō myōten*, *ichijō* refers to the Lotus Sutra and *myōten* means mystic text.

29 THE ESSENCE OF THE JURYŌ CHAPTER

This letter is dated the seventeenth day of the fourth month, but the year of its composition is not indicated, nor is the recipient of the letter named. Some date the letter to 1271; however, a later date may well be possible. The content of the letter parallels in many ways passages in the lengthy treatise, *Kaimoku Shō*, "The Opening of the Eyes," which was written in 1272. Some authorities hold that it antedates this work, although a positive determination of the date of composition of this letter cannot be arrived at.

When the Lord Shakyamuni expounded the *Juryō* chapter, he said, making reference to what all living beings had heard in the pre-Lotus Sutra teachings and in the theoretical teaching of the Lotus Sutra: "All gods, men, and *asuras* of this world believe that after leaving the palace of the Shakyas, Shakyamuni Buddha seated himself at the place of meditation not far from the city of Gayā[1] and attained the supreme enlightenment."[2] This statement shows the idea held by all the Buddha's disciples and the great bodhisattvas from the time they heard Shakyamuni preach his first sermon in the *Kegon* Sutra, up through the time he expounded the *Anrakugyō* chapter[3] of the Lotus Sutra.

We find two flaws in the pre-Lotus Sutra teachings. First, [as Miao-lo says,] "Because they teach that the Ten Worlds are separate from one another, they fail to move beyond the provisional doctrines."[4] That is, they do not reveal the theory of *ichinen sanzen*, the principle of discarding the provisional and revealing the true,[5] or the capacity of those in the two vehicles to attain Buddhahood, all of which are implicit in the doctrine of the ten factors[6] stated in the *Hōben* chapter of the theoretical teaching.

Second, "Because they teach that Shakyamuni first attained enlightenment in this world, they fail to discard the Buddha's provisional status."[7] Thus they do not reveal the Buddha's original enlightenment expounded in the *Juryō* chapter. These two great doctrines [the attainment of Buddhahood by those of the two vehicles and the Buddha's original enlightenment] are the core of the Buddha's lifetime teachings, the very heart and marrow of all the sutras.

The theoretical teaching states that persons in the two realms of *shōmon* and *engaku* can attain Buddhahood, thus avoiding one of the shortcomings found in the sutras expounded during the first forty years and more of the Buddha's preaching. However, since the *Juryō* chapter had not yet been expounded, the true doctrine of *ichinen sanzen* remained obscure and the enlightenment of those in the two vehicles was not assured. In these respects the theoretical teaching does not differ from the moon's reflection on the water or rootless plants drifting on the waves.

The Buddha also stated: "However, men of devout faith, the time is limitless and boundless—a hundred, thousand, ten thousand, hundred thousand, nayuta[8] kalpas—since I in fact attained Buddhahood."[9] With this single proclamation, he refuted as great falsehoods the words of the *Kegon* Sutra, which states that Shakyamuni attained Buddhahood for the first time in this world;[10] the *Agon* sutras, which speak of his "first attainment of the path";[11] the Vimalakīrti Sutra, which reads, "For the first time the Buddha sat beneath the tree";[12] the *Daijuku* Sutra, which states, "It is sixteen years since the Buddha first attained enlightenment";[13] the *Dainichi* Sutra, which describes the Buddha's enlightenment as having taken place "some years ago when I sat in the place of meditation";[14] the *Ninnō* Sutra, which refers to the Buddha's enlightenment as an event of "twenty-nine years ago";[15] the *Muryōgi* Sutra, which states, "Previously I went to the place of meditation";[16] and the *Hōben* chapter of the Lotus Sutra, which says, "When I first sat in the place of meditation."[17]

When we come to the *Juryō* chapter of the essential teaching, the belief that Shakyamuni attained Buddhahood for the first time in India is demolished, and the effects [enlightenment] of the four teachings[18] are likewise demolished. When the effects of the four teachings are demolished, their causes are likewise demolished. "Causes" here refers to Buddhist practice [to attain enlightenment] or to the stage of disciples engaged in practice. Thus the causes and effects as expounded in both the pre–Lotus Sutra teachings and the theoretical teaching of the Lotus Sutra are wiped out, and the cause and effect of the Ten Worlds[19] in the essential teaching are revealed. This is the doctrine of original cause and original effect. It teaches that the nine worlds are all present in the beginningless Buddhahood, and that Buddhahood exists in the beginningless nine worlds. It is the true mutual possession of the Ten Worlds, the true hundred worlds, and thousand factors,[20] the true *ichinen sanzen*.

Considered in this light, it is evident that Vairocana Buddha seated on a lotus pedestal as depicted in the *Kegon* Sutra, the sixteen-foot Shakyamuni described in the *Agon* sutras,[21] and the other provisional Buddhas mentioned in the *Hōdō*, *Hannya*, *Konkōmyō*, *Amida*, and *Dainichi* sutras are no more than reflections of the Buddha of the *Juryō* chapter. They are like fleeting images of the moon in the sky mirrored on the surface of the water held in vessels of varying sizes. The learned priests and scholars of the many sects are first of all confused as to the meaning of the sutras upon which their own doctrines are based, and more fundamentally, they are ignorant of the teaching expounded in the *Juryō* chapter of the Lotus Sutra. As a result, they mistake the reflection of the moon on the water for the real moon shining in the sky. Some of them enter the water and try to grasp it with their hands, while others try to snare it with a rope. As the Great Teacher T'ien-t'ai says, "They know nothing of the moon in the sky, but gaze only at the moon in the pond."[22] He means that those attached to the pre–Lotus Sutra teachings or the theoretical teaching of the Lotus Sutra are not aware of the moon shining in the sky but see only its reflection in the pond.

The *Sōgi Ritsu*[23] also tells of five hundred monkeys who, emerging from the mountains, saw the moon reflected in the water and tried to seize it. However, as it was only a reflection, they fell into the water and drowned. This writing equates the monkeys with Devadatta and the group of six monks[24] [who lived in the Buddha's lifetime].

Were it not for the presence of the *Juryō* chapter among all the teachings of Shakyamuni, they would be like the heavens without the sun and moon, a kingdom without a king, the mountains and seas without treasures or a person without a soul. This being so, without the *Juryō* chapter, all the sutras are meaningless. Grass without roots will die in no time, and a river without a source will not flow far. A child without parents is looked down upon. Nam-myoho-renge-kyo, the heart of the *Juryō* chapter, is the mother of all Buddhas throughout the ten directions and the three existences of past, present, and future.

With my deep respect,
Nichiren

The seventeenth day of the fourth month

Notes

1. A city in Magadha, about ninety-six km southwest of Pāṭaliputra, India. Buddhagayā, where Shakyamuni gained enlightenment, is near Gayā.

2. T9, 42c.

3. The fourteenth chapter of the twenty-eight chapter Lotus Sutra and the last chapter of the "theoretical" teaching.

4. *Hokke Gengi Shakusen* (T33, 950b).

5. A principle set forth by T'ien-t'ai in the *Maka Shikan* (T46, 54a) on the basis of the Lotus Sutra. By "the provisional" here Nichiren refers to all the sutras expounded during the first forty-two years of Shakyamuni's teaching, and "the true" to the Lotus Sutra. *See also* in Glossary: *ichinen sanzen.*

6. *See* Ten Factors in Glossary.

7. A continuation of the passage from *Hokke Gengi Shakusen* (T33, 950b).

8. An Indian numerical unit. The *Kusha Ron* (T29, 63b) defines it as one hundred billion (10^{11}). Other sources define it as 10^7.

9. T9, 42b.

10. T10, 1b.

11. *Zō Agon Sutra* (T2, 122b); *Zōichi Agon Sutra* (T2, 593a).

12. T14, 537c.

13. T13, 1b.

14. T18, 9b.

15. T8, 825b.

16. T9, 386a.

17. T9, 9c.

18. T'ien-t'ai classified Buddhist sutras into eight teachings, four teachings of doctrine (Jap: *kehō no shikyō*) and four teachings of method (*kegi no shikyō*). Indicated here are the four teachings of doctrine: (1) the Tripitaka teaching (*zōkyō*), which corresponds to the Hinayana; (2) the connecting teaching (*tsūgyō*), or introductory Mahayana; (3) the specific teaching (*bekkyō*), a higher level of provisional Mahayana; and (4) the perfect teaching (*engyō*), or true Mahayana. Strictly speaking, the perfect teaching refers to the Lotus Sutra; however, from a broad perspective some of the teachings of other sutras are similar to those of the Lotus Sutra, and it is in this sense

that the expression "four teachings" is used here, indicating all of the pre-Lotus teachings. The "effects of the four teachings" indicates the enlightenment one is said to attain by practicing the four teachings. *See also* Eight Teachings in Glossary.

19. Here "cause" or the stage of practice is equated with the nine worlds of delusion in which the Buddha nature still remains dormant, and "effect" to Buddhahood, or enlightenment, the tenth world. By indicating that the Buddha still retains all the nine worlds even after attaining enlightenment, the *Juryō* (16th) chapter demonstrates that cause (nine worlds) and effect (Buddhahood) exist simultaneously, thus substantiating the mutual possession of the Ten Worlds. *See also* Ten Worlds in Glossary.

20. An expansion of the doctrine of mutual possession. At each moment life experiences one of ten conditions, that is the Ten Worlds. Each of these worlds possesses the potential for all ten within itself, thus making one hundred possible worlds. Each of these hundred worlds possesses the ten factors (*jūnyoze*), thus becoming one thousand factors. *See* Ten Factors in Glossary.

21. The term translated as sixteen-foot Shaka (*jōroku no shō Shaka*), literally one *jō* six *sun* (approx. 4,85 meters) is the Buddha as seen by ordinary people, *shōmon. engaku*, and beginning bodhisattvas. In the *Agon* sutras Shakyamuni preaches Hinayana teachings; therefore the Shakyamuni of the *Agon* sutras is inferior to the Shakyamuni who preaches the Mahayana teachings.

22. *Hokke Gengi* (T33, 766b).

23. *Maka Sōgi Ritsu* (T22, 284a).

24. Monks whose misconduct is said to have caused the necessity to formulate the precepts. They are: Nanda, Upananda, Kālodayin, Chanda, Aśvaka, and Punarvasu.

30 THE PERSECUTION AT TATSUNOKUCHI

Nichiren wrote this letter on the twenty-first day of the ninth month, 1271, to his loyal follower, Shijō Kingo. This was only nine days after Nichiren had barely escaped execution at Tatsunokuchi. Nichiren had been sentenced to exile on Sado Island under the supervision of Hōjō Nobutoki, the constable of Sado. The plan was for Nichiren to be escorted to the residence in Echi of Homma Rokurōzaemon Shigetsura, Nobutoki's deputy, from where he was to be taken to Sado. Hei no Saemon, a high government official and archenemy of Nichiren, decided on his own to have Nichiren executed while on the way to Homma's residence. An attempt to behead Nichiren was made at Tatsunokuchi, but the attempt failed and Nichiren's scheduled exile was later enforced.

This letter is most frequently referred to as *Shijō Kingo Goshōsoku* (Letter to Lord Shijō Kingo). Its alternative title is *Tatsunokuchi Gosho* (Tatsunokuchi Letter) or, as rendered here, "Persecution at Tatsunokuchi."

I cannot adequately express my gratitude for your frequent letters. At the time of my persecution on the twelfth of last month,[1] you not only accompanied me to Tatsunokuchi but declared that you would die by my side. I was deeply moved!

How many are the places where I died in past existences for the sake of my family, lands, and kin! I have given up my life on mountains, seas, and rivers, on the seashore and by the roadside, but never once did I die for the Lotus Sutra or suffer persecution for the daimoku. Hence none of the ends I met enabled me to reach enlightenment. Because I did not attain Buddhahood, the seas and rivers where I died are not the Buddha land.

In this life, however, as the votary of the Lotus Sutra, I was exiled and almost put to death—exiled to Itō and nearly beheaded at Tatsunokuchi. Tatsunokuchi in Sagami Province is the place where Nichiren gave his life. Because he died there for the Lotus Sutra, how could it be anything less than the Buddha land? A passage from the sutra reads, "In the Buddha lands of the ten directions there is only the Law of the one vehicle."[2] Doesn't this bear out my assertion? The "one supreme vehicle" is the Lotus Sutra. There is no true teaching other than the Lotus Sutra in any of the Buddha lands throughout the universe. The Buddha's expedient teachings are excluded, as the sutra explains elsewhere.[3] This being so, then every place where Nichiren meets persecution is the Buddha land.

Of all the places in this world, it is at Tatsunokuchi in Katase of Sagami Province where Nichiren's life dwells.[4] Because he gave his life there for the sake of the Lotus Sutra, Tatsunokuchi may well be called the Buddha land. This principle is found in the *Jinriki* chapter, where it states, "Whether in a forest, in a garden, on in mountain valleys, or the wild wilderness, . . .the Buddhas enter parinirvana."[5]

You accompanied Nichiren, vowing to give your life as a votary of the Lotus Sutra. Your deed is infinitely greater than that of Hung Yen,[6] who tore open his stomach and inserted the liver of his dead lord, Duke Yi, to save him from shame and dishonor. When I reach Eagle Peak, I will first tell how Shijō Kingo, like Nichiren, resolved to die for the Lotus Sutra.

Secretly I learned that I am to be exiled to Sado by order of Regent Hōjō. Of the three heavenly gods, the god of the moon saved my life at Tatsunokuchi by appearing as a shining object, and the god of the stars descended four or five days ago to greet me.[7] Now only the god of the sun remains, and he is certain to protect me. How reassuring! The *Hosshi* chapter states, "[The Buddha] will send gods in various guises to protect the votary of the Lotus Sutra."[8] This passage leaves no room for doubt. The *Anrakugyō* chapter reads, "Neither swords nor staves will harm him."[9] The *Fumon* chapter states, "The sword will instantly be broken into pieces."[10] There is nothing false in these quotations. Strong and steadfast faith is the vital thing.

With my deep respect,
Nichiren

The twenty-first day of the ninth month in the eighth year of Bun'ei (1271)

Notes

1. Twelfth day of the ninth month, 1271.
2. T9, 8a.
3. Continuation of the above passage.
4. The translation is simplified here to eliminate repetitive use of geographic names.
5. T9, 52a.
6. Duke Yi of the state of Wei loved cranes and lived extravagantly, losing the support of the public. While his minister Hung Yen was away on a journey, enemies attacked Wei and killed Duke Yi. They ate the duke's flesh except for his liver, and then left the land. Returning, Hung Yen saw the disastrous scene and wept. He cut open his own stomach and inserted the duke's liver in it to save him from shame and dishonor.
7. On the night of the thirteeth day of the ninth month, while Nichiren was con fined at Homma Rokurōzaemon Shigetsura's residence in Echi, a luminous object fell from the sky and hung suspended before him in the branches of a plum tree. In scientific terms, this seems to have been a phenomenon caused by atmospheric discharge.
8. T9, 32b.
9. T9, 39b.
10. T9, 57c.

31 *THE CAUSAL LAW OF LIFE*

When Shijō Kingo visited Nichiren on Sado Island in the fourth month of 1272, Nichiren entrusted him with this letter for his wife, Nichigennyo. Nichigennyo was the name Nichiren had given to Kingo's wife who, along with her husband, was a devoted supporter of Nichiren's teachings. At the start of the letter, Nichiren urges her to share the letter with Tōshirō's wife. Little is known of Tōshirō; it is believed that he was a government official whose wife was close to Nichigennyo.

This letter, rendered here as The Causal Law of Life, is entitled *Dōshō Dōmyō Gosho* and refers to two heavenly messengers that dwell on a person's shoulders from the time of birth and observe all actions. They thus symbolize the workings of the law of cause and effect in life.

❧

I hope you will read this letter over and over again together with Tōshirō's wife. The sun dispels darkness, no matter how deep. A woman's heart may be likened to darkness, and the Lotus Sutra to the sun. A baby may not always recognize its mother, but a mother never forgets her own baby. Shakyamuni Buddha may be likened to the mother and a woman to the baby. If two people long for one another, then they will never be parted. But though one person yearns for the other, if the other does not feel the same way, then they will be united at times but separated at others. The Buddha may be likened to the one who always longs for the other, and a woman to the one who does not. But if we truly yearn for Shakyamuni Buddha, how could he ever fail to reveal himself to us?

You may call a rock a jewel, but that does not make it one. You may call a jewel a rock, but it remains a jewel. In our age, the doctrines of the Nembutsu and other sects that are based upon the Buddha's provisional teachings are all like rocks. People may say that the Nembutsu is equal to the Lotus Sutra, but that does not in fact make it so. And people may slander the Lotus Sutra, but that does not affect it any more than calling a jewel a rock affects the jewel.

In the past there was an evil ruler in China named Emperor Hui-tsung.[1] Led astray by Taoist priests, he destroyed Buddhist statues and sutras and forced all the priests and nuns to return to secular life until not one remained in the religious calling. Among the priests was one named the Tripitaka Master Fa-tao who refused to be cowed by the Imperial command. As a result, he was branded on the face and exiled to the region south of the Yangtze River.[2] I was born in an age when the rulers put their faith in the Zen sect, which is fully as heretical as the Taoist priests, and I too, like Fa-tao, have met with great difficulties.

You two women were born as commoners and now live in Kamakura, [the seat of the military government] yet you believe in the Lotus Sutra without concern for the prying eyes of others or the danger it may pose for your lives. This is nothing short of extraordinary. I can only imagine your faith to be like the magic jewel that, when placed in muddy water, miraculously cleanses it. You are like someone who, when taught something new by a wise man, believes his every word and thus grasps the truth. Is this because Shakyamuni Buddha and the Bodhisattvas Fugen, Yakuō, and Shukuōke[3] are dwelling in your hearts? The Lotus Sutra declares that people throughout the world are able to believe in the sutra because of the aid extended by Bodhisattva Fugen.[4]

A woman is like a wisteria, a man like a pine. The wisteria cannot stand for a moment if it is separated from the pine tree that supports it. And yet, in this turbulent age, when you do not even have servants you can rely on, you have sent your husband here to Sado Island. This shows that your faith is more solid than the earth, and the earthly gods must certainly realize this. Your faith is loftier than the sky, and the heavenly gods Bonten and Taishaku must also be aware of it. The Buddha taught that people from the very moment of their birth are attended by two messengers called Dōshō and Dōmyō,[5] who follow them as closely as their own shadows, never leaving them for an instant. These two take turns reporting to heaven the person's good and evil acts, both major and minor, without overlooking the slightest detail. Therefore, heaven must already know about your great faith. How encouraging!

Nichiren

The fourth month

Notes

1. Hui-tsung (1082–1135) was the eighth emperor of the Northern Sung dynasty. He ascended the throne in 1100, but took little interest in ruling, devoting his time to calligraphy and painting. He was a follower of Taoism and made efforts to suppress Buddhism.

2. Fa-tao (1086–1147) remonstrated with Emperor Hui-tsung when the latter took steps to suppress Buddhism. For his actions he was branded on the face and exiled to Tao-chou. He was later pardoned; the emperor, however, was captured by the invading Chin forces and taken to Manchuria where he lived until his death in 1135. *Busso Tōki* (T49, 421a).

3. A bodhisattva who appears in the *Yakuō* (23d) chapter of the Lotus Sutra to play the role of questioning the Buddha. In this chapter Shakyamuni Buddha orders Bodhisattva Shukuōke to protect the Lotus Sutra with his occult power.

4. As described in chapter twenty-eight of the Lotus Sutra.

5. These two heavenly messengers appear in the *Kegon* Sutra (T9, 680c). In the *Muryōōju Kyō Gisho* (T37, 124b), Dōshō is female, dwells on the right shoulder, and reports the evil a person has committed; Dōmyō is male, dwells on the left shoulder, and reports the good. In the *Shikan Bugyōden Guketsu* (T46, 401a), both messengers are born at the same time a person is born and have the same name as that person.

32 LETTER TO NICHIMYŌ SHONIN

Nichiren wrote this letter from Ichinosawa on Sado Island on the twenty-fifth day of the fifth month, 1272. The letter was addressed to a young widow who lived in Kamakura, of whom virtually nothing is known. She undertook, however, the long and perilous journey from Kamakura to Sado to visit Nichiren, accompanied by her infant daughter Oto Gozen. Nichiren was so impressed with this demonstration of faith that he gave her the Buddhist name Nichimyō Shonin, or Saint Nichimyō, in recognition of her courage and loyalty. After Nichiren went to live on Mount Minobu she visited him there, and later, in the eighth month of 1275 Nichiren sent her a letter addressed to her daughter, entitled "The Supremacy of the Law," suggesting that she was welcome to stay at Mount Minobu should there be the need. (See Letter 38.)

Once there was a person named Gyōbō Bonji.[1] He traveled from country to country for twelve years in search of the teachings of a Buddha. In those days none of the Three Treasures—the Buddha, the Law, and the Priesthood—had yet appeared. Nevertheless, Bonji continued his quest for Buddhism as desperately as a thirsty man seeks water or as a starving person looks for food. One day a Brahman came to him and said, "I possess a verse of the sacred teaching. If you are a true seeker of Buddhism, I will impart it to you." Bonji beseeched him to do so. The Brahman said, "To prove your sincerity, first peel off your skin for parchment, break off one of your bones for a writing brush, grind up its marrow for pigment, and draw your blood to mix the ink. If you are willing to do all this, I will teach you the Buddha's verse."

Bonji was overjoyed. He peeled off his skin, dried it, and made parchment of it. When he had done all the things demanded of him just as he had been told, the Brahman suddenly vanished. Bonji bewailed his fate, now gazing up to heaven, now flinging himself to the ground. The Buddha, feeling his sincerity, emerged from beneath the earth and taught him: "Practice that which accords with the Law; do not practice that which contradicts it. One who practices the Law will dwell in peace and security both in this life and the next." The moment Bonji heard this, he became a Buddha. This teaching consists of twenty Chinese characters.[2]

Once [in one of his previous existences] when Shakyamuni was a wheel-turning king engaged in bodhisattva practice, he revered an eight-character phrase which stated: "He who is born is destined to die. To extinguish this cycle is to enter the joy of nirvana." As an offering to the eight characters, he transformed his own body into a thousand burning candles. Moreover, he inscribed those characters on stone walls and main roads so that those who read them would arouse the aspiration for enlightenment. The light of those candles reached as high as the Trayastriṃśa Heaven, where it served as illumination for Taishaku and the other deities.[3]

In another past existence Shakyamuni was carrying out bodhisattva austerities in search of Buddhism. One day a leper said to him, "I possess the true teaching which consists of twenty characters. If you will massage my leprous body, embrace and lick it, feeding me two or three pounds of your own flesh every day, I will impart the teaching to you." Shakyamuni did exactly as the leper said. As a result, he obtained the twenty-character teaching and attained Buddhahood. The teaching went, "The Tathagata is enlightened to the truth of nirvana, and has forever freed himself from the sufferings of birth and death. Anyone who wholeheartedly listens to him will surely obtain immeasurable happiness."[4]

There was once a person called Sessen Dōji who lived in the Snow Mountains. Although he had mastered all non-Buddhist teachings, he had not yet encountered Buddhism. Then, one day, he happened to hear a terrifying demon recite a verse which began: "All is changeable, nothing is constant. This is the law of birth and death." The demon, however, spoke only the first eight characters of the verse, leaving the rest unsaid. Although Sessen Dōji was exceedingly glad to have heard the first eight characters, he felt as though he had been given only half the wish-granting jewel. It was like a plant that flowers but bears no fruit. When he asked for the remaining eight characters, the demon replied, "I have had nothing to eat for several days. I am too dazed with hunger to preach the remaining eight characters. First give me some food!" Dōji asked, "What do you eat?" The demon answered, "I feed on the warm flesh and blood of human beings. Though I can fly anywhere throughout the four continents in the space of a moment, I can obtain no warm flesh and blood. Human beings are protected by heaven, so I cannot kill them unless they commit evil."

Sessen Dōji said, "I will make you an offering of my own body, so teach me the remaining eight characters." The demon said, "You are a cunning fellow, aren't you? Surely you are trying to deceive me." Dōji replied, "If one is offered gold and silver in exchange for tiles and stones, should he not accept it? If I die to no purpose on this mountain, then my body will be devoured by kites, owls, wolves, and tigers, and will bring me no benefit whatsoever. On the other hand, if I give my life for the remaining eight characters, it will be like exchanging filth for food."

The demon was still suspicious. Dōji assured him, saying, "I have guarantors to vouch for my honesty. Like the Buddhas of ages past, I call upon Bonten, Taishaku, the gods of the sun and the moon, and the Four Heavenly Kings to be my witnesses." Finally the demon consented to impart the second half of the verse. Dōji removed his deerskin garment and spread it out for the demon to sit upon. Then he knelt down and joined his palms together in supplication, begging the demon to be seated. The fierce demon complied and began to recite, "Extinguishing the cycle of birth and death, one enters the joy of nirvana." When Dōji had learned the entire verse, he inscribed it on trees and stones. This completed, he cast himself into the demon's mouth. Dōji was actually Shakyamuni in one of his past existences, while the demon was Taishaku in disguise.[5]

Bodhisattva Yakuō burnt his elbows for seventy-two thousand years as an offering to the Lotus Sutra.[6] Bodhisattva Fukyō was for many years abused, humiliated, beaten, and stoned by countless monks, nuns, laymen, and laywomen because he venerated them by uttering the twenty-four characters which read: "I deeply respect you. I would not dare despise you or be arrogant, for you will all practice the bodhisattva way and surely attain Buddhahood."[7] Bodhisattva Fukyō was the Lord Shakyamuni in one of his past lifetimes. King Suzudan performed menial labor in the service of the hermit Ashi[8] for a thousand years in order to receive the five characters of Myōhō-renge-kyō. He even went so far as to make a bed of his own body for his master. As a result, he was reborn as Shakyamuni Buddha.

Myōhō-renge-kyō consists of eight volumes. Reading these eight volumes is in effect equal to reading sixteen, for the sutra was expounded by Shakyamuni Buddha and verified by Tahō Buddha. The sixteen volumes, in turn, represent innumerable volumes, for their truth was verified by all the Buddhas of the ten directions. In the same way, each character in the sutra equals two, for it was uttered by Shakyamuni and confirmed by Tahō. Again, a single character equals innumerable others, for the validity of the sutra was attested to by all the Buddhas of the ten directions. A single wish-granting jewel can cause as many treasures to rain down as would two such jewels or, even more, as would innumerable jewels. Likewise, each character in the Lotus Sutra is like a jewel, and since it stands for innumerable others, it is like an uncountable number of jewels. The character *myō* [of Myōhō-renge-kyō] was uttered by two tongues, the tongues of Shakyamuni and Tahō. The tongues of these two Buddhas are like an eight-petaled lotus flower, one petal overlapping another, on which rests a jewel, the character of *myō*.

The jewel of the character *myō* contains all the benefits which Shakyamuni Buddha received by practicing the six *pāramitās* in his past existences: the benefits he obtained through the practice of almsgiving by offering his body to a starving tigress[9] and by giving his life in exchange for that of a dove;[10] the benefits he obtained when he was King Shudama, who, in order to observe the precepts, kept his word though it meant his death;[11] the benefits he obtained as a hermit called Ninniku by enduring the tortures inflicted upon him by King Kari;[12] the benefits he obtained as Prince Nōse[13] and as the hermit Shōjari,[14] and all his other benefits. We, people in the evil age of the Latter Day of the Law, have not formed even a single good cause, but Shakyamuni [by bestowing upon us the character *myō*] has granted us as many benefits as if we ourselves had fulfilled all the practices of the six *pāramitās*. This precisely accords with his statement, "Now this threefold world is all my domain. The living beings in it are all my children."[15] Bound as we common mortals are by earthly desires, we can instantly attain the same virtues as the Lord Buddha Shakyamuni, for we receive all the virtues which he accumulated. The sutra states, "At the start I pledged to make all people perfectly equal to me, without any distinction between us."[16] This means that those who believe in and practice the Lotus Sutra are equal to Shakyamuni Buddha.

To illustrate, a father and mother unite in conjugal harmony to give birth to a child. No one can dispute that the child is the flesh and blood of its parents. A calf begotten by an ox king will become an ox king; it will never become a lion king. A cub sired by a lion king will become a lion king; it will never become a human king or heavenly king. Now the votaries of the Lotus Sutra are the children of Shakyamuni Buddha, as the sutra states, "The living beings in it are all my children." It is not difficult for them to become kings of the Law just as Shakyamuni Buddha did.

Unfilial children, however, are not allowed to succeed their parents. King Yao[17] had an heir named Tan Chu, and King Shun had a prince named Shang Chün. As both sons were lacking in filial piety, they were disowned by their respective fathers and demoted to the rank of commoners. Ch'ung Hua and Yü were the children of commoners, but both were extremely filial. Hearing of this, King Yao and King Shun summoned Ch'ung Hua and Yü, respectively, and abdicated their thrones to them. Commoners became royalty in a day. Just as a commoner can become a king, so can an ordinary person become a Buddha instantly. This is the heart of the doctrine of *ichinen sanzen*.

How, then, can we obtain this benefit? Should we peel off our skins as Gyōbō Bonji did, follow Sessen Dōji's example and offer our bodies to a demon, or emulate Bodhisattva Yakuō in burning our elbows? As the Great Teacher Chang-an stated, "You should distinguish between the *shōju* and *shakubuku* methods and never adhere solely to one or the other."[18] What practice one should perform in order to master the True Law and attain Buddhahood depends upon the times. Were there no paper in Japan, then you should peel off your skin. Had the Lotus Sutra not yet been introduced to our country and the only individual to appear who knew it was a demon, then you should offer your body to him. Were there no oil available in our land, then you should burn your elbows. But of what use is it to peel off one's skin when the country is abundantly supplied with excellent paper?

Hsüan-tsang journeyed throughout India in search of the Law for seventeen years, covering a distance of a hundred thousand *ri*. Dengyō remained in China for only two years, but he traveled three thousand *ri* across the billowing sea to arrive there. They were both men, sages and worthies at that, and theirs was a more virtuous age. Never have I heard of a woman who journeyed a thousand *ri* in search of Buddhism as you did. True, the dragon king's daughter attained enlightenment without changing her dragon form, and the nun Mahāprajāpati[19] received a prediction that she would become a Buddha in the future. I am not certain, but they may have been female forms assumed by

Buddhas or bodhisattvas. After all, those events occurred in the Buddha's lifetime.

A woman's nature differs from a man's just as fire differs from water, fire being hot and water cold. Fishermen are skilled in catching fish, and hunters are proficient in trapping deer. A sutra states that it is a woman's nature to be jealous, but no sutra says that women are good at seeking Buddhism. A woman's mind is compared to a breeze; even if it were possible to bind the wind, one could never grasp a woman's mind. A woman's mind is likened to characters written on the surface of water; they do not remain a moment. A woman is compared to a liar; one cannot tell whether a liar's words are true or false. A woman's mind is compared to a river, for all rivers meander.

The Lotus Sutra, however, is the teaching which contains Shakyamuni's declaration that he would now "honestly discard the provisional teachings."[20] It is the sutra of which Tahō Buddha said, "All that you [Shakyamuni Buddha] have expounded is the truth."[21] It demands that its believers be "honest and upright, gentle in mind,"[22] "gentle, peaceful and upright,"[23] and so on. Those who believe in this sutra, therefore, must have minds that are as straight as a tight-stretched bowstring or a carpenter's inking line. One may call dung sandalwood, but it will not have the sandalwood's fragrance. A liar never becomes a truthful person simply because one calls him honest. All the sutras are the Buddha's golden teachings, his true words. When compared with the Lotus Sutra, however, they are false, flattering, abusive, or forked-tongued.[24] The Lotus Sutra alone is the truth of truths. Only honest people are able to take faith in this sutra, a teaching free from all false-hood. Certainly you are a woman of true words.

Think of it! Even were one to meet a person who could cross the ocean carrying Mount Sumeru on his head, one could never find a woman like you. Even though one might find a person who could steam sand and make boiled rice of it, one could never meet a lady of your virtue. Let it be known that Shakyamuni Buddha, Tahō Buddha, all the Buddhas of the ten directions, great bodhisattvas such as Jōgyō and Muhengyō, Bonten, Taishaku, the Four Heavenly Kings, and other deities will protect you and be with you always, just as a shadow accompanies the body. You are undoubtedly the foremost votary of the Lotus Sutra among the women of Japan. Therefore, following the example of Bodhisattva Fukyō, I bestow on you the Buddhist name, Nichimyō Shonin.[25]

From Kamakura in Sagami Province to the northern province of

Sado is a journey of more than a thousand *ri* over treacherous mountains and the raging sea. The wind and rain make untimely onslaughts; bandits lurk in the mountains and pirates lie in wait on the sea. The people at every stage and every post town are as bestial as dogs or tigers, and you must have felt as though you were undergoing the sufferings of the three evil paths. Moreover, we live in troubled times. Since last year our country has been filled with rebels, and finally, on the eleventh day of the second month of this year, a battle broke out.[26] It is now almost the end of the fifth month, but society has not yet been restored to tranquillity. Nevertheless, despite all the risks involved, you traveled to Sado carrying your infant daughter, since her father, from whom you have long been separated, was not to be depended upon for her care.

I cannot even imagine the hardships you must have suffered during your journey, much less describe them in words, so I will lay down my writing brush.

Nichiren

The twenty-fifth day of the fifth month in the ninth year of Bun'ei (1272)

Notes

1. Gyōbō Bonji is the name of Shakyamuni when he practiced austerities in a past existence. The story appears in *Daichido Ron* (T25, 412a).

2. Nichiren has combined the stories of two different Bonji here. Aihō Bonji, who hears the twenty-character verse, is described in a different story in *Daichido Ron* (T25, 178c).

3. This story appears in the *Hōon* Sutra (T3, 134c). The wheel-turning king was an ideal ruler in Indian mythology. In Buddhism wheel-turning kings are regarded as kings who rule the world by justice rather than force. They possess the thirty-two distinguishing marks and rule the four continents surrounding Mount Sumeru by turning the wheels that are given them at the time of their coronation. These wheels are of four kinds, gold, silver, copper, and iron. The Trayastriṁśa Heaven is also called the Heaven of the Thirty-three Gods, and is the second heaven of the world of desire. Located on a plateau at the top of Mount Sumeru, thirty-three gods, including Taishaku, live here. Taishaku rules from his palace in the center and the other thirty-two gods live on four peaks, eight gods to a peak, in each of the plateau's four corners.

4. This story appears in the Nirvana Sutra (T12, 497b).

5. This lengthy story is found in the Nirvana Sutra (T12, 450a-451a). Sessen Dōji

is the name of Shakyamuni in a previous lifetime. The wish-granting jewel is said to be a jewel that possesses the power of providing whatever one desires.

6. The story of Bodhisattva Yakuō appears in the twenty-third chapter of the Lotus Sutra.

7. The story of Bodhisattva Fukyō appears in the twentieth chapter of the Lotus Sutra. The quotation is at T9, 50c.

8. This story is recounted in the *Devadatta* (12th) chapter of the Lotus Sutra (T9, 34c), although the name of Suzudan is not specifically mentioned. Ashi is referred to as a former incarnation of Devadatta.

9. This story appears in the *Konkōmyō Saishōō* Sutra (T16, 354b). In a past existence, as Prince Satta, son of King Makarada, Shakyamuni found an injured tigress that had given birth, but was too weak with hunger to feed her cubs. At that time he gave his body as an offering to feed her.

10. According to the *Bosatsu Honjō Manron* (T3, 333b-c), one day the god Bishukatsuma disguised himself as a dove and Taishaku changed into a hawk in order to test King Shibi. The hawk pursued the dove, which flew into King Shibi's robes for protection. In order to save the dove, King Shibi offered his own flesh to the hungry hawk. King Shibi was Shakyamuni in one of his past existences when he was carrying out the *pāramitā* of almsgiving.

11. Shudama, also called Fumyō, was the name of Shakyamuni when he was a king in a past existence engaged in the *pāramitā* of observing precepts. According to the *Daichido Ron* (T25, 89a), King Fumyō and 99 other kings (the *Ninnō* Sutra, T8, 840b, says 999) had been captured by King Rokusoku and were about to be killed. King Fumyō asked King Rokusoku to let him keep a promise he had made to give offerings to a certain monk. King Rokusoku granted him seven days' grace to fulfill his promise and King Fumyō returned to his country, where he gave the monk offerings and transferred the throne to his son. After proclaiming to the people that keeping one's promise is the most important precept, he returned to King Rokusoku; the latter was so impressed by Fumyō's sincerity that he released him and the other kings, and also converted to Buddhism.

12. This story appears in the *Kengu* Sutra (T4, 359c-360a) and the *Daichido Ron* (T25, 166c). The hermit Ninniku was Shakyamuni when he was carrying out the *pāramitā* of forbearance in a past existence. Ninniku once preached the practice of forbearance to the female attendants of King Kari of Vārānāsī. The king assumed that the hermit had been trying to seduce them and flew into a rage. Being informed that the hermit was engaged in the practice of forbearance, the king cut off his hands, legs, ears, and nose. But the hermit did not flinch. His blood turned into milk, and his body restored itself. Seeing this, the king repented his conduct and thereafter protected the hermit.

13. This story appears in the *Kengu* Sutra (T4, 405a ff) and the *Daichido Ron* (T25, 151a ff). Born to a royal family, Prince Nōse felt pity for the poor and suffering people of his country and implored his father to give all his treasures to them. When his father had exhausted his treasures, the prince went into the sea to look for a fabulous wish-granting jewel owned by the dragon king. He faced many obstacles but finally found the jewel, and, bringing it back with him, caused treasures to rain down upon the people. The prince was Shakyamuni in a past existence.

14. The name of Shakyamuni when he was a hermit practicing the *pāramitā* of meditation in a past existence. According to the *Daichido Ron* (T25, 188a-b), while

Shōjari was engaged in meditation, a bird happened to build a nest in his hair and laid several eggs. One day he gained a great insight, but, being aware of the eggs on his head, he did not move until they hatched and the baby birds were able to fly away.

15. T9, 14c.

16. T9, 8c.

17. Yao and Shun were legendary kings in ancient China, who were highly respected by the people for their excellent rule.

18. *Nehangyō Sho* (T38, 84c). *Shōju* here does not indicate a method of Buddhist propagation, but rather, seeking the Law for one's own enlightenment as opposed to propagating it to others (*shakubuku*).

19. Mahāprajāpatī was a younger sister of Māyā, Shakyamuni's mother. After Māyā's death, she married Śuddhodana, his father, and raised Shakyamuni. After Śuddhodana's death, she renounced secular life and followed Shakyamuni's teachings. The *Kanji* (13th) chapter of the Lotus Sutra predicts that she will become the Buddha Beheld with Joy by All Sentient Beings (T9, 36a).

20. T9, 10a.

21. T9, 32c.

22. T9, 43b.

23. T9, 43c.

24. These correspond to the four verbal evils of lying, flattery (or random and irresponsible speech), defamation, and duplicity.

25. Acccording to the *Fukyō* (20th) chapter of the Lotus Sutra, Bodhisattva Fukyō propagated a teaching consisting of twenty-four characters and showed respect toward all people for their innate Buddha nature. He predicted that all would become Buddhas in the future. In the same spirit, Nichiren gave the recipient of this letter the Buddhist name Nichimyō Shonin. *Nichi* of *Nichimyō* comes from Nichiren, indicating the sun, and *myō* is that of Myōhō-renge-kyō. *Shonin* here means a sage.

26. Hōjō Tokisuke (1247–1272), an elder half brother of the regent Hōjō Tokimune (1251–1284), had been plotting to seize power, but Tokimune heard of the plot and quickly suppressed it by having his brother killed.

33 REPLY TO KYŌ'Ō

This brief letter was written on the fifteenth day of the eighth month, 1273, and was addressed to Kyō'ō, Shijō Kingo's infant daughter. However, since Kyō'ō was then only one year old, the letter was meant, most likely, for Shijō Kingo and his wife Nichigen-nyo. They had two children, Kyō'ō and Tsukimaro, both apparently named by Nichiren. Nichiren was living in exile at Ichinosawa on Sado Island at the time that he sent this letter.

Just when I was longing to hear from you once again the messenger, whom you troubled to send, arrived. In my present circumstances, your gift of money is far more valuable than any treasure to be found on land or sea.

Since I heard from you about Kyō'ō Gozen, I have been praying to the gods of the sun and moon for her every moment of the day. Always cherish the Gohonzon which I sent some time ago for her protection. This Gohonzon was never known, let alone inscribed, by anyone in the Former or Middle Day of the Law. The lion, king of beasts, is said to advance three steps, then gather himself to spring, unleashing the same power whether he traps a tiny ant or attacks a fierce animal. In inscribing this Gohonzon for her protection, Nichiren is equal to the lion king. This is what the sutra means by "the power of an attacking lion."[1] Believe in this mandala with all your heart. Nam-myoho-renge-kyo is like the roar of a lion. What sickness can therefore be an obstacle?

It is written that those who embrace the daimoku of the Lotus Sutra will be protected by Kishimojin and her ten daughters.[2] Such persons will enjoy the happiness of Aizen and the good fortune of Bishamon.[3] Wherever your daughter may frolic or play, no harm will come to her; she will be free from fear like the lion king. Among Kishimojin's ten daughters, the protection of Kōdainyo[4] is the most profound. But your faith alone will determine all these things. A sword will be useless in the hands of a coward. The mighty sword of the Lotus Sutra must be wielded by one courageous in faith. Then he will be as strong as a demon armed with an iron staff. I, Nichiren, have inscribed my life in *sumi*,[5] so believe in the Gohonzon with your whole heart. The Buddha's will is the Lotus Sutra, but the soul of Nichiren is nothing other than Nam-myoho-renge-kyo. Miao-lo states in his interpretations, "The revelation of the Buddha's original enlightenment is the heart of the sutra."[6]

Kyō'ō Gozen's misfortunes will change into fortune. Muster your faith and pray to this Gohonzon. Then what is there that cannot be achieved? You should believe the Lotus Sutra when it says, "This sutra fulfills one's desires. It is the pond's cool, clear water that quenches thirst,"[7] and "They will have peace and security in this life and good circumstances in the next."[8] When I am pardoned from exile to this province, I will hasten to Kamakura where we will meet. If one considers the power of the Lotus Sutra, he will find perpetual youth and eternal life before his eyes. My only worry is that she may die young; therefore, I am praying with all my might for the gods to protect her. Raise her to be like Lady Jōtoku[9] or the Dragon King's daughter. Nam-myoho-renge-kyo, Nam-myoho-renge-kyo.

Respectfully,
Nichiren

Notes

1. T9, 41a.

2. Kishimojin (Skt: Hāritī) was originally a female demon, the mother of countless children. She is described in the *Darani* (26th) chapter of the Lotus Sutra, where she has ten daughters. The mother and daughters vow to protect the votaries of the Lotus Sutra. The ten daughters (Skt: *rākṣasī*; Jap: *jūrasetsu*) are also referred to as the ten demon daughters and Ten Goddesses.

3. Aizen (Skt: Vidyaraja) is a Buddhist deity who is said to purify peoples' earthly desires and free them from illusions and the sufferings desires cause. Bishamon (Skt: Vaiśravaṇa) is one of the Four Heavenly Kings.

4. Kōdainyo (Skt: Kunti) is one of the ten daughters of Kishimojin.

5. Black Chinese ink.

6. *Hokke Mongu Ki* (T34, 352b).

7. T9, 54b.

8. T9, 19b.

9. A faithful believer, mentioned in the *Fumbetsu Kudoku* (27th) chapter of the Lotus Sutra. She is the mother of Jōzō and Jōgen, whose display of occult powers enabled them to convert their father to Buddhism.

34 REBUKING SLANDER OF THE LAW AND ERADICATING SINS

This lengthy letter was sent by Nichiren to his loyal follower in Kamakura, Shijō Kingo. Written while in exile at Ichinosawa on Sado Island, the letter includes no specific date, although the year of composition was 1273, and Nichiren had already been living on this island for well over a year, under the most difficult of conditions.

※

I have read your letter carefully. In the past as well, when I was exiled to the province of Izu[1] on account of the Lotus Sutra, I rejoiced at heart, though when I say so I suppose people will think that I am speaking immodestly.

If, since the beginningless past, I had ever incurred blame for the sake of the Lotus Sutra, whether I was sincerely devoted to it or not, would I then have been born in this lifetime as a mere common mortal? [Therefore, when I was condemned to exile,] though I felt downcast for a while, seeing that it was for the sake of the Lotus Sutra, I was also delighted for I thought that I might thereby eradicate to some small extent the sins of my previous existences. However, the various grave offenses represented by the ten evil acts,[2] the four major offenses,[3] the six major offenses,[4] the eight major offenses,[5] the ten major offenses,[6] the five sins that condemn one to the hell of incessant suffering,[7] the slander of the True Law, and the sin of incorrigible disbelief, accumulated since the beginningless past, must be huger than huge mountains, deeper than the great sea.

When it comes to the five cardinal sins, the commission of even one of them will condemn one to the hell of incessant suffering for the space of an entire kalpa. A kalpa is the length of time it takes for the life span of human beings to decrease from eighty thousand years to ten years, decreasing at the rate of one year every hundred years, and then to increase again to eighty thousand years at the same rate.[8] One who murders one's parent will fall into the hell of incessant suffering and undergo its terrible pain without a moment's respite for such a period of time.

As for the person who slanders the Lotus Sutra, though he may not be serious at heart, if he so much as manifests the outward appearance of animosity, or if he disparages the sutra even in jest, or if he makes light, not of the sutra itself, but of those who act in its name, then, the sutra says, he will fall into the hell of incessant suffering for countless kalpas of the kind described above.

The people who cursed and struck Bodhisattva Fukyō at first behaved with such animosity, though later they took faith and became followers of the Lotus Sutra, looking up to Fukyō and treating him with great respect, honoring him as the heavenly deities would Taishaku, and standing in awe of him as we do the sun and moon. However, they were unable to wipe out the great offense of their initial slander, so that for a thousand kalpas they were condemned to the Avīci Hell, and for twenty billion kalpas they were abandoned by the Three Treasures.

If one were to liken the [retribution for the] five cardinal sins and slander of the Law to illness, then the five cardinal sins would be comparable to sunstroke, which affects one suddenly. Slander of the Law, on the other hand, is like white leprosy, which does not appear to be so serious at first, but bit by bit becomes very serious indeed. Those persons who commit slander of the Law are in most cases reborn in the hell of incessant suffering, or, in some few cases, in one of the six lower paths. If they are reborn in the realm of human beings, then, the sutra tells us, they will suffer on account of poverty, low status, white leprosy, and so forth.

When I, Nichiren, hold up the bright mirror of the Lotus Sutra before my own person, all is spotlessly revealed, and there can be no doubt that, in my previous existences, I was guilty of slandering the Law. If in my present existence I do not wipe out that offense, then in the future how can I escape the pains of hell?

How could I gather together all the grave offenses that I have accumulated in age after age since the far distant past and eradicate them all in my present lifetime, so that I may be spared great pain in the future? When I pondered this question, it occurred to me that now, in the present age [of the Latter Day of the Law], slanderers of the Law fill every province of the nation. What is more, the ruler of the nation is himself the foremost perpetrator of such slander. If in such a time I do not expunge these heavy sins, then at what time can I expect to do so?

Now if I, Nichiren, insignificant person that I am, were to go here and there throughout the country of Japan denouncing these slanders, then innumerable persons among the four categories of Buddhists[9] who follow erroneous doctrines would in one instant join their innumerable voices in reviling me. At that time the ruler of the nation, allying himself with those monks who slander the Law, would come to hate me and try to have me beheaded or order me into exile. And if this sort of thing were to occur again and again, then the grave offenses that I have accumulated over countless kalpas could be wiped out within the space of a single lifetime. Such, then, was the great plan that I conceived; and it is now proceeding without the slightest deviation. So when I find myself thus sentenced to exile, I can only feel that my wishes are being fulfilled.

Nevertheless, being no more than a common mortal, I have at times been apt to regret having embarked upon such a course. And if even I am beset by such feelings, then how much more so in the case of a woman such as your wife, who is ignorant of all the circumstances surrounding the matter! Persons like you and her do not fully comprehend the Buddhist teachings, and it pains me to think how greatly you must regret that you ever elected to follow Nichiren. And yet, contrary to what one might expect, I hear that you two are even firmer and more dedicated in your faith than I myself, which is indeed no ordinary matter! I wonder if Shakyamuni, the lord of teachings, himself may have entered and taken possession of your hearts, and it moves me so that I can barely restrain my tears.

The Great Teacher Miao-lo says in his commentary (*Hokke Mongu Ki*, seven): "Therefore we know that if, in the latter age, one is able to hear the Law even briefly, and if, having heard it, one then arouses faith in it, this comes about because of the seeds planted in a previous existence."[10] And he also says (*Maka Shikan Bugyōden Guketsu*, two): "Being born at the end of the Middle Day of the Law, I have been able to behold these true words of the sutra. Unless in a previous existence one has planted the seeds of auspicious causation, then it is truly difficult to encounter such an opportunity."[11]

During the first forty or more years of his teaching life, Shakyamuni kept secret the five characters of Myōhō-renge-kyō. Not only that, he still remained silent concerning them when he preached the first fourteen chapters of the Lotus Sutra, which comprise the theoretical teaching. It was only with the *Juryō* chapter that he spoke openly regarding the two characters *renge*, which [represent the five characters Myōhō-renge-kyō and] indicate the True Effect and the True Cause.[12] The Buddha did not entrust these five characters to Monju, Fugen, Miroku, Yakuō, or the others of their group. Instead he summoned forth the bodhisattvas Jōgyō, Muhengyō, Jyōgyō, Anryugyō, and their followers from the great earth of Tranquil Light[13] and transferred the five characters to them.

What took place then was no ordinary ceremony. The Tathagata Tahō, who lives in the world of Treasure Purity, made his appearance, seated in a tower that emerged from the earth and was adorned with seven kinds of gems.[14] Shakyamuni Buddha purified four hundred billion nayuta worlds in addition to this major world system, planted them with rows of jewel trees measuring five hundred *yojana*[15] high at intervals of an arrow's flight, placed a lion throne five *yojana* in height beneath each jewel tree, and seated on these thrones all the Buddhas from the ten directions, who were his emanations.

Thereupon Shakyamuni Buddha removed his dusty robe, opened the Treasure Tower, and took a seat beside the Tathagata Tahō. It was as though the sun and moon were to appear side by side in the blue sky, or as though Taishaku and the King Born from the Crown of the Head[16] were to sit together in the Hall of the Good Law. Monju and the other bodhisattvas of this world, as well as Kannon and the other bodhisattvas of the other words, were gathered together in open space throughout the ten directions like so many stars filling the sky.

At this time there were gathered together in this place the great bodhisattvas such as Dharma Wisdom, Forest of Merits, Diamond Banner, Diamond Repository, and others, equal in number to the dust particles of the worlds of the ten directions, who had gathered at the seven places and eight assemblies of the *Kegon* Sutra[17] and were disciples of Vairocana Buddha who sits on the lotus pedestal of the worlds of the ten directions;[18] the Buddhas and bodhisattvas who had gathered like clouds at the Great Treasure Chamber[19] when the *Hōdō* sutras were preached; Subhūti, Taishaku, and the thousand Buddhas who had gathered to hear the *Hannya* sutras;[20] the four Buddhas and four bodhisattvas,[21] belonging to the nine honored ones on the eight-petaled lotus, who appear in the *Dainichi* Sutra; the thirty-seven honored ones[22] of the *Kongōchō* Sutra; and the Buddhas and bodhisattvas of the worlds of the ten directions who gathered at the city of Kuśinagara to listen to the Nirvana Sutra.[23] All these figures were recognized by Monju, Miroku, and the others of their group, who talked together with them, so it appeared that the great bodhisattvas Monju and Miroku were quite accustomed to their being in attendance.

But after those four bodhisattvas who emerged from the earth had made their appearance, then Bodhisattva Monjushiri, whose teaching Shakyamuni Buddha was the ninth to inherit,[24] and who is the mother of the Buddhas of the three existences,[25] as well as Bodhisattva Miroku, who will succeed Shakyamuni Buddha after his next rebirth—when these two, Monju and Miroku, stood beside these four bodhisattvas, they seemed to be of no significance whatsoever. They were like humble woodsmen mingling in the company of exalted lords, or like apes and monkeys seating themselves by the side of lions.

Shakyamuni summoned the four bodhisattvas and entrusted them with the five characters of Myōhō-renge-kyō. And this entrustment, too, was no ordinary affair, for the Buddha first manifested ten mystic powers.[26] When Shakyamuni extended his long broad tongue[27] upward as far as the limit of the world of form, all the other Buddhas did likewise, so that the tongues of the Buddhas extended up into the air above the four hundred billion nayuta worlds like a hundred, thousand, ten thousand, hundred thousand red rainbows filling the sky. Marvelous indeed was the sight!

In this manner the Buddha displayed the wonders of his ten mystic powers, and, in what is termed the transfer of the essence, he extracted the heart and core of the Lotus Sutra and transferred it to the four bodhisattvas. He fervently enjoined them to bestow it after his passing upon all beings of the ten directions. After that, he again manifested yet another mystic power[28] and entrusted this sutra, the Lotus, and the other sacred teachings preached during his lifetime, to Monju and the other bodhisattvas of this and other worlds, to the persons of the two vehicles, and to the heavenly and human beings, dragon deities, and others.

These five characters Myōhō-renge-kyō were not entrusted even to Mahākāśyapa, Śāriputra, or the other disciples, though these men had from the outset attended the Buddha as closely as a shadow follows the form. But even setting that aside, why did the Buddha refuse to entrust them to the bodhisattvas such as Monju and Miroku? Even though they may have been lacking in capability, it would seem unlikely that he should reject them. There are in truth many puzzling aspects about the matter. But the fact was that the bodhisattvas from other worlds were rejected because their connection with this world was slight; or in other cases, although the bodhisattvas were of this *sahā* world, they had only recently established connections with this world; or in still other cases, some were rejected because, although they were disciples of the Buddha, they had not been among his disciples when he first aroused the aspiration for enlightenment [in the remote past]. Thus among those who had been his disciples during the forty or more years preceding the preaching of the Lotus Sutra, or during the preaching of the theoretical teaching, the first fourteen chapters of the Lotus Sutra, there was not one who could be called an original disciple. We see from the sutra that only these four bodhisattvas had been the disciples of Shakyamuni, the lord of teachings, since the remote past of *gohyaku-jin-tengō*; from the time he had first aroused the aspiration for enlightenment, they had never followed any other Buddha, nor had they required the instruction of the theoretical and essential teachings.[29]

Thus T'ien-t'ai says: "[The great assembly] witnessed the Bodhisattvas of the Earth alone making this pledge."[30] And he also states: "These are my [Shakyamuni's] disciples, destined to propagate my Law."[31] Miao-lo says: "The sons will disseminate the Law of the father."[32] And Tao-hsien states: "Because the Law is that realized by the Buddha in the remote past, it was transferred to those who were his disciples in that distant time."[33] Thus these five characters Myōhō-renge-kyō were entrusted to these four bodhisattvas.

Nevertheless, after the Buddha's passing, during the thousand years of the Former Day of the Law, the thousand years of the Middle Day of the Law, and the two hundred twenty or more years that have elapsed since the beginning of the Latter Day of the Law, nowhere in India, China, Japan or any other place in the entire world have these four bodhisattvas so much as once made their appearance. Why is that?

Bodhisattva Monjushiri, though he was not specifically entrusted with the teachings of Myōhō-renge-kyō, remained in this world for four hundred fifty years following the passing of the Buddha to spread the Mahayana sutras, and even in the ages thereafter he from time to time descended from the Fragrant Mountain or Mount Clear and Cool, assuming the form of an eminent monk in order to propagate the Buddhist teachings.[34] Bodhisattva Yakuō took on the form of the Great Teacher T'ien-t'ai, [Bodhisattva] Kanzeon became the Great Teacher Nan-yüeh,[35] and Bodhisattva Miroku became Fu Ta-shih.[36]

Moreover, the disciples Mahākāśyapa and Ānanda worked to spread the teachings of the Buddha after his passing for twenty and forty years, respectively. And yet in all this time, the Buddha's legitimate heirs, to whom the teachings of Myōhō-renge-kyō had been entrusted, failed to make their appearance.

During this period of twenty-two hundred years and more, worthy rulers and sage rulers have honored painted images or wooden images of Shakyamuni, the lord of teachings, as their principal object of worship. But although they have made depictions of the Buddhas of the Hinayana and the Mahayana teachings; of the *Kegon*, Nirvana, and *Kammuryōju* sutras; of the theoretical teaching of the Lotus Sutra and of the *Fugen* Sutra; of the Buddha of the *Dainichi* and the other Shingon sutras; and of the Buddhas Shakyamuni and Tahō of the *Hōtō* chapter,[37] the Shakyamuni of the *Juryō* chapter[38] has never been depicted in any mountain temple or monastery anywhere. It is very difficult to fathom why this should be.

Shakyamuni Buddha made specific reference to the fifth five hundred years[39] and never designated the two thousand years of the Former and Middle Days of the Law as the time for the propagation of the Lotus Sutra. The Great Teacher T'ien-t'ai said: "In the fifth five hundred years, the Mystic Way shall spread and benefit mankind far into the future,"[40] indicating that its propagation should be left to the future. The Great Teacher Dengyō wrote: "The Former and Middle Days are almost over, and the Latter Day is near at hand."[41] In this way, he himself judged that the close of the Middle Day of the Law was not yet the time for the propagation of the Lotus Sutra.

Are we to assume, then, that the countless great bodhisattvas who sprang up from the earth intend to remain silent and unmoving and to go back upon the promise that they made when the teachings were entrusted to them by Shakyamuni, Tahō, and the other Buddhas of the ten directions?

Yet even the worthy men described in the non-Buddhist scriptures know that one must await the time. The cuckoo always waits until the fourth or fifth month to sing his song. Similarly, we read in the sutra that these great bodhisattvas must likewise wait until the Latter Day of the Law to appear.

Why do I say this? Both Buddhist and non-Buddhist writings make clear that, before a certain destined event actually occurs, omens will always appear. Thus when the spider spins its web, it means that some happy event will take place, and when the magpie calls, it means that a visitor will arrive.[42] Even such minor events have their portents. How much more so do major occurrences! Thus the six auspicious happenings[43] described in the *Jo* chapter of the Lotus Sutra are great omens exceeding in magnitude any other major signs appearing in the entire life of Shakyamuni Buddha. And the great omens described in the *Yujutsu* chapter are immeasurably greater in magnitude than these.[44]

Therefore, T'ien-t'ai says: "By observing the fury of the rain, we can tell the greatness of the dragon that caused it, and by observing the flourishing of the lotus flowers, we can tell the depth of the pond in which they grow."[45] And Miao-lo states: "Wise men can see omens and what they foretell, as snakes know the way of snakes."[46]

Now I, too, in discerning the significance of omens, must share some portion of the wise man's power. The great earthquake that struck in the first year of the Shōka era (1257), (when the reverse marker of Jupiter was in the sector of the sky with the cyclical sign *hinoto-mi*), on the twenty-third day of the eighth month, at the time when the Hour of the Dog gives way to the Hour of the Boar (9:00 P.M.), and also the great comet that appeared in the first year of the Bun'ei era (1264), (when the reverse marker was in the sector of the sky with the cyclical sign *kinoe-ne*), on the fourth day of the seventh month[47]—these are major portents such as have never before occurred during the twenty-two hundred or more years since the Buddha's passing. I wonder if they are not great signs indicating that those great bodhisattvas are now about to make their appearance in this world bearing the great Law.

Ten-feet-high waves do not rise up in a foot-wide pond, and the braying of a donkey cannot cause the winds to blow. Though the government of Japan today is in chaos and the common people cry out in distress, such conditions alone could scarcely cause the appearance of such major omens. Who knows but what these are great signs foretelling that though the Lotus Sutra has perished, it is in fact eternal!

During the two thousand and more years [since the Buddha's passing], there have been evil rulers who were cursed by their subjects and traitorous persons who were hated by all. But Nichiren, though guilty of no fault, has without respite for the past twenty years and more been cursed and abused, assaulted with swords and staves, and stoned with rocks and tiles, by people both high and low. This is no common affair!

Mine is like the case of Bodhisattva Fukyō, who, toward the end of the Law of the Buddha Ionnō, was cursed and reviled over a period of many years. Moreover, Shakyamuni Buddha cited the example of this bodhisattva and predicted that, in the Latter Day of the Law, after his own passing, events would unfold in the same manner as in Fukyō's time. And yet whether here close at hand in Japan or whether in the far distant land of China, such a thing has never yet been known to happen for the sake of the Lotus Sutra.

Because people hate me, they do not mention the significance of my suffering. If I mention it myself, it may seem to be self-adulation. If I fail to mention it, however, I will commit the offense of negating the Buddha's words. I speak of it because to hold one's own life lightly but to value the Law is the way of a worthy man.

I, Nichiren, resemble Bodhisattva Fukyō. Whether the ruler of a nation murders his parents or a lowly subject does away with his father and mother, though the murderers differ greatly in social position, because the crime is identical, both will fall into the hell of incessant suffering. Similarly, though Bodhisattva Fukyō and I stand on different levels, we perform the same action. Therefore, if Bodhisattva Fukyō is destined to attain Buddhahood, can there be any doubt that I will gain the fruit of Buddhahood as well?

Bodhisattva Fukyō was cursed by arrogant monks who observed all the two hundred and fifty precepts.[48] I, Nichiren, am slandered and reviled by Ryōkan,[49] who is known as the foremost observer of the precepts. The monks who cursed Fukyō, though they followed him in the end, still had to suffer in the Avīci Hell for one thousand kalpas. But Ryōkan has yet to seek my teachings. Hence I do not know [the full gravity of his offense]. He may be destined to suffer in hell for countless kalpas. Pitiful! Pitiful!

Question: With regard to the great earthquake that occurred in the Shōka era, in your admonitory essay, the *Risshō Ankoku Ron*,[50] which you entrusted to Yadoya Nyūdō[51] for submission to His Lordship, the late lay priest of Saimyō-ji,[52] on the sixteenth day of the seventh month in the first year of the Bunnō era (1260), (when the reverse marker of Jupiter was in the sector of the sky with the cyclical sign *kanoe-saru*), you stated your opinion that heaven and earth had become angered because people in Japan were destroying Buddhism by their reliance on Hōnen's *Senchaku Shū*,[53] and that this error would bring about rebellion within the country and invasion from countries abroad. But now you say that the earthquake was an auspicious omen of the propagation of the Lotus Sutra. How do you explain the discrepancy between these two views?

Answer: That is a very good question. The fourth volume of the Lotus

Sutra says: "Since hatred and jealousy toward this sutra abound even during the lifetime of the Buddha, how much worse will it be in the world after his passing!"[54] And in the seventh volume, referring again to the time "after his passing" when things will be "much worse," the Buddha says: "In the fifth five hundred years after my death, widely declare and spread [the Lotus Sutra]."[55] So we see that the hatred that abounds after the passing of the Buddha will come about in the fifth five hundred years when Myōhō-renge-kyō will spread. And immediately following the above passage, the Buddha warns of dangers from "the devil, the devil's people, or the deities, dragons, yakṣas, and kumbhāṇḍas."[56]

When the chief priest Hsing-man[57] laid eyes on the Great Teacher Dengyō, he exclaimed, "The sacred words will not become extinct. Now I have encountered this man! All the doctrines that I have learned I will transfer to this ācārya[58] from the country of Japan." And the situation today is just the same. Now, in the beginning of the Latter Day of the Law, the time has come for the five characters of Myōhō-renge-kyō to be propagated so that all persons throughout the country of Japan may receive the seed of the Buddha's teachings.

When a woman of low station becomes pregnant with the ruler's child, the other women grow jealous and angered. And when a person of humble background is presented with a jewel from the king's crown, then great troubles are bound to arise. Thus the sutra says, "In the world at that time the people will resent [the Lotus Sutra] and find it extremely difficult to believe."[59]

The Nirvana Sutra declares: "If troubles are inflicted upon a sage, then the country where he dwells will be attacked by other countries."[60] And the Ninnō Sutra states essentially the same thing. If I, Nichiren, am attacked, then from heaven and earth and the four directions, great calamities will pour down like rain, jet up like fountains, or come surging forward like waves. If the crowd of monks, those hordes of locusts who afflict the nation, and the ministers in power in the government persist in their ever-increasing slanders and accusations against me, then great disasters will occur in growing magnitude.

When an asura demon tried to shoot at the god Taishaku, his arrow rebounded and pierced him in the eye.[61] And when the garuda[62] birds attempt to attack the dragon king Anavatapta,[63] flames erupt from their own bodies and consume them. Is the votary of the Lotus Sutra inferior to Taishaku or the dragon king Anavatapta?

The Great Teacher Chang-an wrote: "He who destroys or brings confusion to the Buddhist Law is an enemy of the Law. If one befriends another person but lacks the mercy to correct him, he is in fact his enemy."[64] And he also says: "He who makes it possible for the offender to rid himself of evil thus acts like a parent to the offender."

All the people throughout Japan have been led astray by the wild assertions of Hōnen, who tells them to "discard, close, ignore and abandon" [all sutras other than the sutras of his sect], or of the men of the Zen sect, who speak of a "special transmission outside the sutras,"[65] so that there is not a single one who is not destined to fall into the great citadel of the hell of incessant suffering. So believing, over the past twenty years and more I have never ceased to cry out in a loud voice against these errors, fearing neither the ruler of the nation nor the common people. I am in no way inferior to the outspoken ministers Lung-p'eng[66] and Pi Kan[67] of old. I am like the thousand-armed Kannon,[68] the bodhisattva of great compassion, who strives to rescue at once all the beings confined to the hell of incessant suffering.

When several children are caught in a fire, though the parents wish to save them all at the same time, having only two arms, they must decide which child to save first and which to leave until after. [The true teaching of the Buddha] is a parent with a thousand arms, ten thousand arms, or a hundred thousand arms. The sutras preached before the Lotus Sutra have only one or two arms, as it were. But the Lotus Sutra, which "instructs all living beings, causing them all to enter the Buddha Way,"[69] is a veritable bodhisattva of innumerable arms.

If we go by the Lotus Sutra and the commentary of Chang-an, then Nichiren is a compassionate father and mother to all the people of Japan. Heaven may be lofty, but it has sharp ears and can hear what is happening. Earth may be deep, but it has keen eyes with which to observe. Heaven and earth by now know [how the situation stands]. And yet I, who am father and mother to all people, am cursed and reviled and sent into exile. The abuses of government that have taken place in this country in the past two or three years are such as have never been heard of in former ages, and exceed all bounds of reason.

In your letter you mentioned your filial devotion to your deceased mother. Reading it, I was so moved that I could barely hold back my tears.

Long ago in China there were five young men, including Yüan-chung.[70] They had originally been strangers from different districts and had different surnames, but they took a vow to be brothers and never turned against one another, and in time they amassed three thousand in treasure.

All the young men were orphans and, grieved at this fact, when they met an old woman along the road, they decided to honor her as their mother. They did so for twenty-four years, never going against her wishes in the slightest.

Then the mother suddenly fell ill and was unable to speak. The five sons gazed up at the sky and said, "Our efforts to care for our mother have not been appreciated, and she has been seized by an illness that prevents her from speaking. If Heaven will grant our filial feelings any recognition, we pray that it will restore the power of speech to her."

At that time the mother said to her five sons, "In past times I was the daughter of a man named Yang Meng of the district of T'ai-yüan.[71] I was married to one Chang Wen-chien of the same district, but he died. At that time, I had a son named Wu-i. When he was seven, rebellion broke out in the area, and I do not know what became of him. You, my five sons, have taken care of me for twenty-four years, but I have never told you of this. My son Wu-i had markings like the seven stars of the Big Dipper on his chest, and on the sole of his right foot he had a black mole." When she had finished saying this, she died.

As the five sons were accompanying her body to the burial ground, they encountered the magistrate of the district along the road. The magistrate happened to drop a bag containing important documents, and the five young men, being accused of stealing it, were arrested and bound. When the magistrate confronted them, he demanded, "Who are you?" whereupon the five young men told him all they had learned from their mother.

When he heard this, the magistrate almost toppled from his seat, gazing up at the heavens, then bowing to the earth in tears. He freed the five men from their bonds, led them to his seat, and said, "I am Wu-i, and it was my mother you took care of! For these past twenty-four years I have known many pleasures, but because I could never cease thinking about my beloved mother, they were never real pleasures to me!" In time he presented the five men to the ruler of the country, and each was appointed to be the head of a prefecture.

In this way, even strangers were rewarded when they came together and treated someone as a parent. How much more so will be the case with actual brothers and sisters when they treat each other kindly and take care of their own father and mother! How could Heaven possibly fail to approve?

Jōzō and Jōgen[72] used the Lotus Sutra to lead their father, who held erroneous views, to salvation. Devadatta was an enemy of the Buddha, and was condemned by the sutras preached during the first forty or more years of the Buddha's teaching life. The moment of his death was terrifying; the earth split open and he fell into the hell of incessant suffering. But in the Lotus Sutra he was summoned back and received the prediction that he would become the Tathagata Heavenly King. King Ajātaśatru killed his father, but just before the Buddha entered nirvana, he heard the teachings of the Lotus Sutra and was able to escape the great sufferings of the Avīci Hell.

This province of Sado is like the realm of beasts. Moreover, it is full of disciples of Hōnen, who hate me a hundred, a thousand, ten thousand, or a hundred thousand times more than did the people of Kamakura. I am never certain whether I am going to survive the day. But thanks to the warm support of both of you, I have managed to sustain my life thus far. When I consider this, I suppose that since Shakyamuni, Tahō, and the other Buddhas of the ten directions and great bodhisattvas as well all make offerings and pay reverence to the Lotus Sutra, these Buddhas and bodhisattvas must be informing your parents each hour of the night and day [that you are assisting me]. And the fact that you now enjoy your lord's favor must also be due to the protection you receive from your parents.

Do not think of your siblings as siblings. Just think of them as your own children. It is true that, among children, there are those like the young of the owl, which are said to eat their own mother, or like those of the *hakei*[73] beast, which watch for the chance to devour their own father. Though your own son, Shirō,[74] takes care of his parents, if he is a bad person, perhaps there is nothing to be done. However, even a stranger, if you open up your heart to him, may be willing to lay down his life for you. So if you treat your younger brothers as though they were your own sons, they may become your allies for life, and of course it will make a favorable impression on others as well. And if you likewise think of your younger sisters as daughters, then why would they not respond with filial devotion?

When I was exiled to this place, I assumed that no one would come to visit me. But I have no fewer than seven or eight persons with me here, and if it were not for your consideration, I do not know how we could manage to keep the whole group in provisions. I am certain that this is all because the words of the Lotus Sutra have entered into your bodies in order to give us aid. I am praying that, no matter how troubled the times may become, the Lotus Sutra and the ten demon daughters will protect all of you, praying as earnestly as though to pro-

duce fire from damp wood or to obtain water from parched ground.
There are many other matters to be discussed, but I will close here.

Nichiren

Notes

1. Nichiren was exiled to Izu from the fifth month of 1261 through the second month of 1263.

2. The ten evil acts are: killing, stealing, unlawful sexual intercourse, lying, flattery (or random and irresponsible speech), defaming, duplicity, greed, anger, stupidity, or the holding of mistaken views.

3. Also referred to as the four unpardonable offenses. They are especially grave offenses that for monks carry the penalty of automatic expulsion from the Buddhist Order. They are killing, stealing, sexual intercourse, and lying (in particular, claiming to have gained some insight or understanding that one does not in fact possess).

4. The six major offenses are the violation of the six precepts to be observed by nuns of Mahayana Buddhism. They are the four major offenses plus the offense of speaking ill of the misdeeds of other Buddhists and the offense of selling liquor. They are detailed in the *Ubasokukai* Sutra (T24, 1047c).

5. The eight major offenses are violations of prohibitions for bodhisattvas. They consist of the four major offenses, plus those of praising oneself and disparaging others, begrudging offerings or sparing one's efforts to teach the Law, giving way to anger and refusing to accept apology, and speaking ill of the True Law. They are described in the *Bosatsu Zenkai* Sutra (T30, 1015a).

6. The ten major offenses are violations of the ten major precepts. They are the offenses of killing, stealing, sexual misconduct, lying, selling liquor, speaking ill of the misdeeds of other Buddhists, praising oneself and disparaging others, begrudging offerings and sparing one's efforts to teach the Law, giving way to anger and refusing to accept apology, and speaking ill of the Three Treasures. They are described in the *Bosatsu Yōraku Hongō* Sutra (T24, 1012b) and elsewhere.

7. The five cardinal sins (Jap: *go gyakuzai*) are the most serious offenses in Buddhism. Explanations vary according to different sutras and treatises. The most common version is: (1) killing one's father, (2) killing one's mother, (3) killing an arhat, (4) injuring a Buddha, and (5) causing disunity within the Buddhist Order. Nichiren refers to them here as the *go mugen*, the five crimes leading to the hell of incessant suffering (*mugen jigoku*).

8. According to ancient Indian cosmology, the human life span undergoes repeated cyclic periods of increase and decrease. *See also* Kalpa in Glossary.

9. Monks, nuns, laymen, and laywomen.

10. This passage actually appears in volume 8 of the *Hokke Mongu Ki* T34, 301b).

11. T46, 216b.

12. Respectively, the enlightenment attained by the Buddha in the remote past and the cause of that enlightenment. "True Effect" and "True Cause" also indicate, respec-

tively, the world of Buddhahood (effect) and the nine worlds (cause), which are both eternally inherent in life.

13. The great earth of Tranquil Light (Jap: *Jakkō no daichi*) is the land from which the Bodhisattvas of the Earth welled forth, as described in the *Yujutsu* (15th) chapter of the Lotus Sutra. *See also* Bodhisattvas of the Earth in Glossary.

14. Gold, silver, lapis lazuli, giant clam shell, coral, pearl, and carnelian.

15. A unit of measurement in ancient India, equal to the distance that the royal army could march in a day. Approximations vary as widely as 9.6, 18, and 24 kilometers.

16. The King Born from the Crown of the Head, Mūrdhagata or Māndhāta in Sanskrit, appears in the *Chōshōō Koji* Sutra (T1, 822b ff.) and elsewhere. He is said to have been born from the top of King Uposatha's head, and grew up to become a gold-wheel-turning king. He ruled the four continents surrounding Mount Sumeru and finally ascended to the Trāyastriṃśa Heaven on the summit of Mount Sumeru. According to the Nirvana Sutra (T12, 439a), he was welcomed there by the god Taishaku, who seated him by his side in the Hall of the Good Law. Later, however, he attempted to displace Taishaku, lost his powers, and fell to earth, where he took sick and died.

17. The preaching of the *Kegon* Sutra (the sixty-volume old translation) is described as occurring in eight successive assemblies in seven different locations, beginning at the place of Shakyamuni Buddha's enlightenment and then shifting to various heavens. The new (eighty volume) translation lists nine assemblies in seven locations.

18. In the *Kegon* Sutra Vairocana is depicted as seated in the center of a vast lotus blossom, which constitutes all the worlds of the universe.

19. The name of the great court, located between the worlds of desire and form, where the *Daijuku* Sutra, one of the *Hōdō* sutras, was preached. It is described at the beginning of the sutra (T13, 1b).

20. Subhūti was one of Shakyamuni's ten major disciples. The *Hannya* sutras, several of which are addressed to him, depict him as the foremost in understanding the doctrine of Emptiness. It is said that when the Buddha preached on the perfection of wisdom, the theme of the *Hannya* sutras, one thousand Buddhas appeared in each of the ten directions to listen to him, and Taishaku was also present as the ruler of the Trāyastriṃśa Heaven.

21. Buddhas and bodhisattvas described in the *Dainichi* Sutra, who are pictured in the court of the eight-petaled lotus appearing in the center of the Womb Realm mandala, one of the objects of worship in the esoteric teaching. In this mandala Dainichi sits in the center of the lotus, with four Buddhas and four bodhisattvas seated respectively on the eight petals. Together, they are known as the nine honored ones on the eight-petaled lotus.

22. Five Buddhas, centering around Dainichi, and thirty-two bodhisattvas described in the *Kongōchō* Sutra, one of the scriptures of esoteric Buddhism. They are depicted in the Diamond Realm mandala.

23. The Nirvana Sutra is said to have been preached in a grove of sāla trees north of the city of Kuśingara.

24. According to the first chapter of the Lotus Sutra, in the distant past, Monjushiri (or Monju) was a bodhisattva called Myōkō, a disciple of a Buddha called Nichigatsu Tōmyō. After that Buddha's death, Myōkō continued to embrace the Lotus Sutra, which his teacher had expounded. Nichigatsu Tōmyō's eight sons, fathered before he

entered religious life, practiced under Myōkō's guidance until they attained Buddhahood. The last of them to attain Buddhahood was called Nentō Buddha. Nentō figures in other sources as the Buddha under whom Shakyamuni first aroused the aspiration for enlightenment; in this sense, Shakyamuni was "ninth to inherit Monjushiri's teachings.

25. The *Shinjikan* Sutra (T3, 305a) and other sutras refer to Monjushiri as the mother of all Buddhas. He is so called because he represents the supreme wisdom essential to attaining enlightenment.

26. The ten mystic powers are the ten supernatural signs that the Buddha displays in the *Jinriki* (21st) chapter of the Lotus Sutra. They are described and interpreted by T'ien-t'ai in his *Hokke Mongu* (T34, 141c ff.).

27. One of the thirty-two marks of a Buddha.

28. At the beginning of the *Zokurui* (22d) chapter of the Lotus Sutra, Shakyamuni Buddha strokes with his right hand the heads of all the assembled bodhisattvas, and then makes a general transfer of the Law to all of them.

29. In the theoretical teaching, the *shōmon* disciples first heard the teaching of the one vehicle, grasped its significance, and then received Shakyamuni's prediction that they would attain Buddhahood in the future. Next, in the essential teaching, the assembly learned that Shakyamuni had not attained enlightenment for the first time during his current lifetime in India, as they had previously assumed, but has in fact been the Buddha since the remote past. The Bodhisattvas of the Earth, however, having been the Buddha's disciples since the time of his original enlightenment, did not need to go through the process of instruction.

30. *Hokke Mongu* (T34, 141c).

31. *Hokke Mongu* (T34, 124c).

32. *Hokke Mongu Ki* (T34, 324a).

33. *Hokke Mongu Fushō Ki* (ZZ1, 45, 2, 105). Tao-hsien was a priest of the Tendai school in T'ang China, said to have been a disciple of Miao-lo. This work is a ten-volume commentary on Miao-lo's *Hokke Mongu Ki*.

34. According to the *Monjushiri Hatsunehan* Sutra (T14, 480c–481b), 450 years following the Buddha's death, Bodhisattva Monjushiri (or Monju) went to the Snow Mountains, where he expounded the Buddhist teachings for five hundred hermits. Later he assumed the form of a monk and, descending from the mountains, led many people to salvation. He later lived in a stupa on a mountain to the north of the Snow Mountains. According to the *Kegon* Sutra (T10, 241b), Monju lives on Mount Ch'ing-liang in the east, which later came to be identified with Mount Wu-t'ai in China.

35. The reappearance of Yakuō and Kanzeon (or Kannon) as T'ien-t'ai and Nan-yüeh, respectively, is mentioned in a note to the text of the *Hokke Denki* (T51, 56b).

36. Fu Ta-shih (497–569), also known as Fu Hsi, was a celebrated priest of the Northern and Southern Dynasties period. His biography in the *Shakushi Keiko Ryaku* (T49, 596c) states that he descended from the Fourth Heaven of the Desire Realm, known as the Tuṣita Heaven. This heaven is the abode of Bodhisattva Miroku (Maitreya), who is awaiting his rebirth to succeed Shakyamuni as the future Buddha. The term "ta-shih" can be construed to mean bodhisattva; thus Nichiren states that Miroku became Fu Ta-shih.

37. The *Hōtō* is the eleventh chapter of the Lotus Sutra, which describes how the Buddhas Shakyamuni and Tahō sat side by side in the Treasure Tower. It belongs to the theoretical teaching, or the first fourteen chapters of the sutra.

38. Shakyamuni of the *Juryō* (16th) chapter, the eternal Buddha.

39. According to the Lotus Sutra, the time when the Mystic Law will spread. *See* Fifth five-hundred-year period in Glossary.

40. *Hokke Mongu* (T34, 2c).

41. *Shugo Kokkai Sho* (DDZ2, 349).

42. Both examples appear in T'ien-t'ai's *Hokke Gengi* (T33, 750a).

43. The six auspicious happenings, also called the six portents (Jap: *rokuzui*), which herald the preaching of the Lotus Sutra in this world. They are: (1) the Buddha preaches the *Muryōgi* Sutra, an introductory teaching to the Lotus Sutra; (2) he enters into profound meditation; (3) four kinds of exquisite flowers rain down from the heavens; (4) the earth trembles in six different ways; (5) seeing these portents, the people rejoice and, placing their palms together, single-mindedly behold the Buddha; (6) the Buddha emits a beam of light from the tuft of white hair between his brows, illuminating eighteen thousand worlds to the east. The *Jo* (1st) chapter goes on to describe the six signs occurring in other worlds: (1) all beings in the six worlds (from the lowest hell to the highest heaven) are seen; (2) all Buddhas in other lands are seen; (3) all sutras that these Buddhas are preaching can be heard; (4) all monks, nuns, laymen, and laywomen can be seen; 5) all bodhisattvas can be seen; and (6) the nirvana of all Buddhas can be seen.

44. This refers to the ground splitting open and the countless bodhisattvas emerging from the earth.

45. *Hokke Mongu* (T34, 125b).

46. *Hokke Mongu Ki* (T34, 362b).

47. The comet first appeared on the twenty-sixth day of the sixth month, began to shine with renewed brilliance on the fourth day of the seventh month, and continued to shine into the eighth month.

48. The rules of discipline to be observed by ordained monks of Hinayana.

49. Ryōkan (1217–1303) was a prominent priest of the Shingon-Ritsu sect who entered the priesthood at seventeen and received the precepts from Eizon (1202–1290), considered the restorer of the Ritsu sect. In 1261 he went to Kamakura where he was named the chief priest of the Kōsen-ji, founded by a Hōjō regent. Later he was named chief priest of the Gokuraku-ji, founded by Hōjō Shigetoki. Nichiren considered him an archenemy and writes disparagingly of his talents.

50. The *Rissho Ankoku Ron* is one of Nichiren's major works. See translation in *The Selected Writings of Nichiren* (New York, Columbia University Press, 1990).

51. Yadoya Mitsunori (n.d.), an official of the Kamakura government.

52. The lay priest of Saimyō-ji refers to Hōjō Tokiyori (1227–1263), the fifth regent of the Kamakura shogunate.

53. The full title of this work by Hōnen (1133–1212) is *Senchaku Hongan Nembutsu Shū*, composed in 1198. It advocates the chanting of the Nembutsu alone as the sole way to rebirth in the Pure Land and urges the rejection of all other Buddhist teachings.

54. T9, 31b.

55. T9, 54c.

56. *Yakṣas* were originally beings who serve Kumbera, the god of wealth in Indian mythology. Later they were incorporated into Buddhism as one of the eight kinds of nonhuman beings who protect Buddhism. They are regarded as followers of the god Bishamon, though some sutras depict them as fierce and ugly beings that feed on

human flesh. *Kumbhāṇḍas* are a kind of evil spirit, said to possess testicles the size of water jars.

57. Hsing-man (n.d.) was a T'ien-t'ai priest who first studied the *Vinaya* and then became a disciple of Miao-lo. When Dengyō arrived at Mount T'ien-t'ai from Japan in 804, Hsing-man taught him the T'ien-t'ai doctrine and entrusted him with the major works of the school.

58. *Ācārya* (Jap: *ajari*) is an honorific title meaning teacher, conferred upon a priest who guides the conduct of disciples and serves as an example to them. This quotation is found in *Eizan Daishi Den* (DDZ5, *furoku* 18).

59. T9, 39a.

60. This quotation has not been identified.

61. The source of this story has not been traced.

62. A huge bird in Indian mythology that is said to feed on dragons.

63. A dragon said to live in the Icy Lake lying north of the Snow Mountains. A description of this dragon is found in the *Jōagon* Sutra (T1, 117a).

64. This and the following quotation are from *Nehangyō Sho* (T38, 80b).

65. Hōnen makes this statement in the *Senchaku Shū* (T83, 2, 17–19). Zen is said to advocate the transmission of the teaching from mind to mind and not to base itself on the sutras.

66. Lung-p'eng is Kuan Lung-p'eng, a minister to King Chieh, the last king of the Hsia dynasty (c.2205–c.1766 B.C.). According to the *Shih Chi*, King Chieh led a dissolute life and caused his people great distress. Kuan Lung-p'eng remonstrated with him, but Chieh gave no ear to his admonitions and had him beheaded. After that the Hsia dynasty rapidly declined and was destroyed by King T'ang of the Yin dynasty.

67. Pi Kan is said to have been either a son of King Chou of the Yin dynasty or his minister. According to the *Shih Chi*, King Chou was so absorbed in his affection for his concubine Ta Chi that he totally neglected government affairs. When Pi Kan remonstrated with him, King Chou flew into a rage. Prompted by Ta Chi, he announced his intention to test the ancient saying that a sage has seven holes in his heart, and so had Pi Kan killed and his chest torn open. Thereafter the kingdom quickly fell into disorder and was destroyed by King Wu of the Chou dynasty.

68. The thousand-armed Kannon is one of the many iconographic forms of Kannon or Kanzeon, representing the bodhisattva's compassion.

69. T9, 8a.

70. Yüan-chung was an orphan from the state of Wei during the Chou dynasty. The story of these five persons appears in Miao-lo's *Maka Shikan Bugyōden Guketsu* (T46, 265a-b).

71. Located in present-day Shansi Province.

72. Jōzō and Jōgen were sons of King Myōshōgon who appear in the *Myōshōgonnō* (27th) chapter of the Lotus Sutra. They were instrumental in causing their father to convert to Buddhism. Nichiren frequently cites their story.

73. A beast, resembling a tiger, that is said to eat its father.

74. Details of Shirō are not known. No other of Nichiren's letters indicates that Shijō Kingo had a son. One of his younger brothers was named Shirō but it is not certain if this is to whom Nichiren was referring.

35 ON RECOMMENDING THIS TEACHING TO YOUR LORD

Nichiren sent this letter to Shijō Kingo on the twenty-sixth day of the ninth month, 1274, from his place of retirement on Mount Minobu. Shijō was among Nichiren's strongest supporters and, as a samurai in service to the Ema family, a branch of the ruling Hōjō, had access to the higher echelons of government. Lord Ema had ties to both Ryōkan of the Gokuraku-ji and to the Jōdo sect temple, Chōraku-ji, and was not receptive to Shijō's attempts to convert him to Nichiren's teachings. At one point he threatened to transfer Kingo to the remote province of Echigo if he would not renounce his faith in the Lotus.

The full title of this letter is "On Recommending This Teaching to Your Lord and Thereby Avoiding the Offense of Complicity in Slander" (*Shukun Ni'nyū Shihōmon Men Yodōzai Ji*). The alternative title is *Yodōzai no Koto* (The Offense of Complicity in Slander). The "offense of complicity in slander" refers to the slander that occurs when one, although not committing slander oneself, makes offerings to enemies of the Lotus Sutra, or fails to admonish them.

I have received two kan[1] of coins.

The foremost treasure of sentient beings is nothing other than life itself. Those who take life are doomed to fall into the three evil paths. Wheel-turning kings observed the precept of "not to kill" as the first of the ten good precepts.[2] The Buddha preached the five precepts[3] at the starting point of the Hinayana sutras and made "not to kill" the first of them. The Buddha also taught "not to kill" as the first of the ten major precepts[4] in the *Bommō* Sutra of Mahayana. The *Juryō* chapter of the Lotus Sutra contains the blessings of Shakyamuni Buddha's precept "not to kill."[5] Consequently, those who take life will be forsaken by all the Buddhas of the three existences, and the gods of the six heavens of the world of desire[6] will not protect them. The scholars of our time are aware of this, and I, Nichiren, also have a general understanding of it.

However, the circumstances of killing vary, and the offense of the person killed may be heavy or light. If one kills the murderer of his parents, sovereign, or teacher, then although he commits the same offense of killing, his grave sin will in effect become a lighter one. This, too, is something our contemporary scholars know. But even bodhisattvas with their great compassion, if they make offerings to the enemies of the Lotus Sutra, are certain to fall into the hell of incessant suffering. On the other hand, even those who commit the five cardinal sins, if they hate those enemies, will definitely be reborn in the human or heavenly realms. King Sen'yo[7] and King Utoku,[8] who had respectively destroyed five hundred and innumerable enemies of the Lotus Sutra, became the Shakyamuni Buddha of this world. Shakyamuni's disciples, such as Mahākāśyapa, Ānanda, Śāriputra, Maudgalyāyana, and other countless followers, were those who, at that time, had been in the vanguard of the battle and had scattered the enemy, killing them, injuring them, or rejoicing in the fight. The monk Kakutoku became Kashō Buddha. He was a most compassionate votary of the Lotus Sutra who, at that time, urged King Utoku to attack the enemies of the sutra as he would one who has been betraying his father and mother since a previous lifetime.

Our present day corresponds to that time. If the ruler would accept Nichiren's words, he would become like the two kings. Yet he not only rejected them but actually sided with the enemies of the Lotus Sutra, so that the entire nation attacks me, Nichiren. From the ruler down to the common people, all have become slanderers whose offense exceeds even the five cardinal sins. All of you belong to the side of the ruler. Although in your heart you are of the same mind as Nichiren, your person is in service to your lord; thus it would seem extremely difficult for you to avoid the offense of complicity in slander. Nevertheless, you have communicated this teaching to your lord and urged him to take faith in it. How admirable! Even though he may not accept it now, you have been able to avoid the offense of complicity. From now on, you should be careful in what you say. The heavenly gods will protect you without fail, and I myself will tell them to do so.

Please take every possible precaution. Those who hate you will be all the more vigilant in watching for a chance to do you harm. Don't attend any further drinking parties at night. What dissatisfaction can there be in drinking in your wife's company alone? Even if you attend banquets with others in the daytime, never relax your guard. Your enemies will have no opportunity to attack you, unless they take advantage of a time when you are drinking. You cannot be too careful.

With my deep respect,
Nichiren

The twenty-sixth day of the ninth month

Notes

1. An old monetary unit consisting of one thousand coins strung together with a cord.

2. The ten good precepts are admonitions against the ten evil acts: killing, stealing, unlawful sexual intercourse, lying, flattery (or random and irresponsible speech), defaming, duplicity, greed, anger, and stupidity, or the holding of mistaken views. They are listed in the *Shōbō Nenjo* Sutra (T17, 6c ff.).

3. The five basic precepts to be followed by lay Buddhists: not to kill, not to steal, not to commit unlawful sexual intercourse, not to lie, and not to drink intoxicants.

4. The ten major precepts for Mahayana bodhisattvas, set forth in the *Bommō* Sutra (T24, 1004b-c): not to kill, not to steal, not to commit sexual misconduct, not to lie, not to sell liquor, not to discuss others' faults, not to praise oneself or disparage others, not to begrudge offerings or spare one's efforts for the sake of Buddhism, not to give way to anger, and not to speak ill of the Three Treasures.

5. Because this chapter teaches that the Buddha nature, transcending birth and death, is eternally inherent in the lives of all people, Nichiren says that it contains the benefit of the precept "not to kill."

6. The six heavens that lie between the earth and the Brahma heaven. They are: (1) the Heaven of the Four Heavenly Kings (Shitennō Ten); (2) the Trāyastriṃṡa Heaven (Heaven of the Thirty-three Gods or Tōri-ten); (3) the Yāma Heaven, where the seasons are always fine; (4) the Tuṣita or Tosotsu-ten, the heaven in which bodhisattvas are born before they become Buddhas on earth; it is the home of Maitreya, the future Buddha; (5) the Joy-born Heaven (Skt: Nirmānarati; Jap: Keraku-ten), where mutual smiling causes impregnation, and children are born by metamorphosis; and (6) the Parinirmaita-vaśavartin (Jap: Takejizai-ten), whose inhabitants enjoy pleasures provided by others. Māra, the devil king, dwells here; he is frequently referred to as the Devil of the Sixth Heaven. The Heaven of the Four Heavenly Kings is located halfway up Mount Sumeru and the Heaven of the Thirty-three Gods is on a plateau at the top of Mount Sumeru. The other four heavens are suspended above Mount Sumeru.

7. Sen'yo is the name of Shakyamuni in a previous existence. According to the

Nirvana Sutra (T12, 434c), King Sen'yo was the ruler of a great kingdom who had faith in the Mahayana sutras. When five hundred Brahmans slandered the Mahayana teachings, he had them put to death. Because of this act, the sutra says, he was never in danger of falling into hell.

8. Utoku was the name of Shakyamuni in another previous lifetime. At that time, long after the death of the Buddha Kangi Zōyaku, when that Buddha's teachings were about to perish, Utoku was a king in Kuśinagara. According to the Nirvana Sutra (T12, 383c-384b), when many evil monks who violated the precepts armed themselves to attack the monk Kakutoku, who alone correctly upheld the Buddha's Law, King Utoku himself was fatally wounded. As a result of his willingness to give up his life for the Law, he was eventually reborn as Shakyamuni Buddha, and Kakutoku was reborn as Kashō Buddha, the Buddha who preceded Shakyamuni.

36 *THE DIFFICULTY OF SUSTAINING FAITH*

This brief letter is one of thirty-seven still extant addressed by Nichiren to his faithful disciple, Shijō Kingo. The letter is dated the third day of the twelfth month, 1275, and was sent from Mount Minobu. At this time Kingo was under great pressure from Lord Ema and other warriors to renounce his support for Nichiren. This letter was written to encourage Kingo and strengthen his resolve.

"The Difficulty of Sustaining Faith" (*Shikyō Nanji Gosho*) is an alternative title for this letter, descriptive of its contents. It is also known as *Shijō Kingo Dono Gohenji* (Reply to Lord Shijō Kingo), identified by the year 1275.

$$\sim$$

About the difficulty of sustaining faith in this sutra: According to Nisshō,[1] you said to him, "I have been practicing this sutra correctly since last year, when you told me that those who embrace this sutra will enjoy peace and security in this life and good circumstances in the next. But instead I have been deluged by hardships." Is this true, or did he give me a false report? In either case, I will take advantage of this opportunity to resolve any doubts you may have.

A passage from the Lotus Sutra reads, ". . . difficult to believe and difficult to understand."[2] Many hear about and accept this sutra, but few continue their faith in the face of great obstacles. To accept is easy; to continue is difficult. But Buddhahood lies in continuing faith. Those who embrace this sutra should be prepared to meet difficulties. It is certain, however, that they will "quickly obtain the supreme enlightenment."[3] To "sustain faith" means to cherish Nam-myoho-renge-kyo, the teaching by which all Buddhas throughout past, present and future attain enlightenment. The sutra reads, "We will uphold what the Buddha has entrusted to us."[4] The Great Teacher T'ien-t'ai stated, "One accepts out of the power of faith and continues because of the power of prayer."[5] Another part of the sutra reads, "It is difficult to sustain faith in this sutra. One who embraces it even for a short time will delight me and all other Buddhas."[6]

A fire burns higher when logs are added, and a strong wind makes the *gura*[7] swell. The pine tree lives for a thousand years, and therefore its boughs become bent and twisted. The votary of the Lotus Sutra is like the fire and the *gura*, while his persecutions are like the logs and wind. The votary of the Lotus Sutra is the Buddha of eternal life; no wonder his practice is hindered, just as the pine tree's branches are bent and twisted. From now on, you should always remember the words, "It is difficult to sustain faith in this sutra."

With my deep respect,
Nichiren

The sixth day of the third month in the twelfth year of Bun'ei (1275)

Notes

1. Nisshō (1221–1323) was one of the six senior disciples of Nichiren. Nichiren refers to him by the name Ben Ajari. He was Nichiren's first disciple among the priesthood, but after Nichiren's death he returned to Kamakura and established his own temple, which was associated with the Tendai sect.
2. T9, 31b.
3. T9, 34b.
4. T9, 36c.
5. *Hokke Mongu* (T34, 107c).
6. Lotus Sutra (T8, 334b).
7. *Gura* (Skt: *kalākula*) are imaginary insects that swell rapidly in strong winds.

37 THE EIGHT WINDS

This letter is another of the many letters Nichiren wrote to Shijō Kingo, his loyal disciple in Kamakura. Kingo had been ordered in 1276 to move from his estate near Kamakura to the distant province of Echigo because of unpleasantness that arose as a result of Kingo's adherence to Nichiren's teachings. Nichiren cautioned Kingo to remain in the good graces of his lord, reminding him that Lord Ema had protected him at the time of Nichiren's exile to Sado. The letter is not dated, but it is known to have been written in 1277 while Kingo was still in Kamakura.

"The Eight Winds" (*Happū Shō*) is the alternative title of this letter. It is also known by the title common to several letters to this disciple, *Shijō Kingo Dono Gohenji* (Reply to Lord Shijō Kingo) for 1277.

I had been anxious about you because I had not heard from you in so long. I was overjoyed to receive your messenger, who arrived with your many gifts. I am going to bestow the Gohonzon upon you.

About the problem of your transfer to another estate: I have studied Lord Ema's letter to you and your letter to me, and compared them. I anticipated this problem even before your letter arrived. Since your lord regards this as a matter of utmost importance, I would surmise that other retainers have spoken ill of you to him, saying, "Yorimoto[1] shows a lack of respect for you in his unwillingness to move to a new estate. There are many selfish people, but he is more selfish than most. We would advise you to show him no further kindness for the time being." You must be aware of where the real problem lies, and act cautiously.

As vassals, you, your family, and your kinsmen are deeply indebted to your lord. Moreover, he showed you great clemency by taking no action against your clan when I was exiled to Sado and the entire nation hated me. Many of my disciples had their land seized by the government, and were then disowned or driven from their lords' estates. Even if he never shows you the slightest further consideration, you should not hold a grudge against your lord. It is too much to expect another favor from him, just because you are reluctant to move to a new estate.

A truly wise man will not be carried away by any of the eight winds: prosperity, decline, disgrace, honor, praise, censure, suffering, and pleasure.[2] He is neither elated by prosperity nor grieved by decline. The heavenly gods will surely protect one who does not bend before the eight winds. But if you nurse an unreasonable grudge against your lord, they will not protect you, not for all your prayers.

When a person goes to court he may win his case, but then again he may lose, when he could have obtained satisfaction outside of court. I considered how the night guards might win their case. I felt great pity for them; they were deeply troubled and their houses and lands had been confiscated just because they were Nichiren's disciples. I said, however, that I would pray for them, provided they did not go to court. They agreed, and promised not to go. When they did sue, I feared no action would be taken, because so many people are petitioning the courts and embroiled in bitter lawsuits. So far their case is still pending.

Hiki Yoshimoto[3] and Ikegami Munenaka[4] had their prayers answered because they followed my advice. Hakiri Sanenaga[5] seems to believe my teachings, but he ignored my suggestions about his lawsuit, and so I was concerned about its progress. Some good seems to have come of it, perhaps because I warned him that he would lose unless he followed my advice. But he chose not to, and the outcome has been less fruitful than he expected.

If master and disciple pray with differing minds, their prayers will be as futile as trying to kindle a fire on water. Even if they pray with one mind, their prayers will go unanswered if they have long slandered true Buddhism by adhering to inferior teachings. Eventually both will be ruined.

Myōun[6] was the fiftieth successor to the high priesthood of the Tendai sect. He was punished by the retired emperor in the fifth month of the second year of Angen (1176) and ordered into exile on Izu. En route, however, he was rescued at Ōtsu by his monks from the Enryaku-ji on Mount Hiei. He reassumed his position as high priest, but in the eleventh month of the second year of Juei (1183), he was captured by Minamoto no Yoshinaka[7] and beheaded. In saying that he was banished and executed, I do not mean to imply any fault. Even saints and sages undergo such things.

When civil war broke out between Yoritomo of the Minamoto clan and Kiyomori of the Taira clan, more than twenty of Kiyomori's clansmen signed a pledge and affixed their seals. They vowed: "We will look to Enryaku-ji as our clan's temple. We will revere the three thousand monks as own parents. The joys and sorrows of the temple will be our joys and sorrows." They donated the twenty-four districts of Ōmi Province to the temple. Then Myōun and his disciples employed all the esoteric rites of the Shingon sect in their prayers to vanquish the enemy, and even ordered their armed monks to shoot arrows at the Minamoto soldiers. However, Minamoto no Yoshinaka and one of his retainers, Higuchi,[8] accompanied by a mere five or six men, climbed Mount Hiei and burst into the main hall.[9] They dragged Myōun from the altar where he was praying for victory, bound him with a rope, rolled him down the west slope of the mountain like a big stone, and then beheaded him. But still the Japanese do not shun the Shingon sect, nor have they ever questioned why their prayers go unanswered.

During the fifth, sixth, and seventh months of the third year of Jōkyū (1221), the Kyoto Imperial Court waged war against the Kamakura regime.[10] At that time the temples of Enryaku-ji, Tō-ji, Onjō-ji, and the seven great temples of Nara[11] each performed all the most esoteric rites of Shingon in their prayers to the gods Tenshō Daijin, Hachiman, and Sannō.[12] Forty-one of the most renowned priests, including the late Archbishop Jien[13] of the Tendai sect, the bishops of Tō-ji and Ninna-ji, and Jōjūin of Onjō-ji temple, prayed repeatedly for Hōjō Yoshitoki's[14] defeat. The second son of Emperor Gotoba also began praying in the Hall for State Ceremonies on the eighth of the sixth month. The Imperial Court proclaimed that it would be victorious within seven days. But on the seventh day, the fourteenth day of the sixth month, the battle ended in defeat, and the second son died of extreme grief because his beloved page, Setaka,[15] had been beheaded. Yet despite all this, no one ever wondered what was wrong with the Shingon doctrines. The two religious ceremonies which incorporated all the esoteric rituals of Shingon—the first conducted by Myōun and the second by Jien—resulted in the complete collapse of the Japanese Imperial Court. Now for the third time, a special religious ceremony is being held to ward off the Mongol invasion.

The present regime will surely suffer the same fate, but you should keep this strictly to yourself.

As for your own problem, I advise you not to go to court. Do not harbor a grudge against your lord, nor leave your present estate. Stay on in Kamakura. Attend your lord less frequently than before; serve him only from time to time. Then your wish can be fulfilled. Never lose your composure. Do not be swayed by your desires, nor by your concern for status, nor by your temper.

Notes

1. Yorimoto is Shijō Kingo's given name.

2. The eight winds are mentioned in the *Butsujikyō Ron* (T26, 315b) and elsewhere.

3. Hiki Yoshimoto (1202–1286) was an official teacher of Confucianism who is said to have converted to Nichiren's teaching on reading a draft of the *Risshō Ankoku Ron*. Nichiren refers to him here as Daigaku Dono; his full name was Hiki Daigaku Saburō Yoshimoto.

4. Ikegami Munenaka (d.1293) was the elder son of an important official in the Kamakura government. Nichiren refers to him here as Emon-no-tayū. *See* Letter 26: Letter to the Brothers.

5. Hakiri Sanenaga (1222–1297) was the steward of the Minobu area of the southern part of Kai Province. He had been converted to Nichiren's teachings by Nichiren's disciple Nikkō (1246–1333) and welcomed Nichiren to Minobu when Nichiren moved to Mount Minobu. After Nichiren's death he abandoned his faith.

6. Myōun (1115–1183) became the fifty-fifth (and later the fifty-seventh) chief priest of the Enryaku-ji, the Tendai temple on Mount Hiei. He was involved in an attack by Mount Hiei monks on the Imperial court and was sentenced to exile by the retired emperor Goshirakawa. Nichiren relates his history below in the text.

7. Minamoto no Yoshinaka (1154–1184) was a cousin of Yoritomo, the head of the Minamoto clan, who assisted the latter in his revolt against the Taira.

8. Higuchi Kanemitsu (?–1194) was a retainer of Yoshinaka, who later fell into disfavor and was executed.

9. The Kompon Chūdō, the main building of the temple complex at Enryaku-ji. It was constructed by Dengyō in 788.

10. The incident, known as the Jōkyū disturbance, clearly established the power of the Hōjō Regency.

11. Tō-ji was a major Shingon temple in Kyoto. Onjō-ji, also known as Mii-dera, is located in Ōtsu and was the head temple of the Jimon branch of Tendai. The seven Nara temples at this time were: Tōdai-ji, Kōfuku-ji, Gangō-ji, Daian-ji, Yakushi-ji, Saidai-ji, and Hōryū-ji. None of them was directly connected to the Shingon sect.

12. Sannō refers to the Hie (also called Hiyoshi) Shrine in Sakamoto. It was the guardian shrine of Mt. Hiei.

13. Jien (1155–1225) served four times as the head priest of the Tendai sect. He is celebrated also as a poet and the author of the important historical work *Gukan Shō*.

14. Hōjō Yoshitoki (1164–1224) was the second regent of the Kamakura government.

15. Setaka was the sixth son of Sasaki Hirotsuna (?–1221), a warrior who supported Emperor Gotoba.

38 *THE SUPREMACY OF THE LAW*

This letter, dated the fourth day of the eighth month, 1275, was sent from Minobu, and is addressed to Oto, the infant daughter of Nichimyō Shonin. Virtually nothing is known of Nichimyō other than that she visited Nichiren, accompanied by her daughter, while he was in exile on Sado Island. This was a dangerous journey and Nichiren was greatly impressed by the loyalty she exhibited. The letter, although addressed to Oto, was obviously meant for the mother.

The alternative title for this letter, translated here as "The Supremacy of the Law," is more literally rendered as *Shinkyō Hōjū Shō* (The Body Is Insignificant While the Law Is Supreme). The phrase is derived from a passage in the *Nehangyō Shō* by Chang-an (Miao-lo). The standard title for this letter is *Oto Gozen Goshōsoku* (Letter to Oto Gozen). *See also* Letter 31.

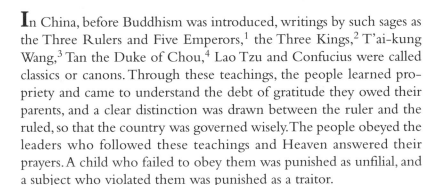

In China, before Buddhism was introduced, writings by such sages as the Three Rulers and Five Emperors,[1] the Three Kings,[2] T'ai-kung Wang,[3] Tan the Duke of Chou,[4] Lao Tzu and Confucius were called classics or canons. Through these teachings, the people learned propriety and came to understand the debt of gratitude they owed their parents, and a clear distinction was drawn between the ruler and the ruled, so that the country was governed wisely. The people obeyed the leaders who followed these teachings and Heaven answered their prayers. A child who failed to obey them was punished as unfilial, and a subject who violated them was punished as a traitor.

When the Buddhist scriptures were first brought to China from India, some people said that they should be accepted, while others said they should be rejected. A conflict arose, and the ruler summoned the two groups to meet and debate the issue. The adherents of non-

Buddhist teachings were defeated by the supporters of Buddhism. After that, whenever the two groups engaged in polemics, the devotees of non-Buddhist scriptures were defeated by the Buddhists as easily as ice melts in the sun or as fire is extinguished by water. Eventually they ceased to offer any effective opposition to Buddhism.

As more Buddhist sutras were brought to China, it became apparent that some were superior in content or more profound than others. They belonged to different categories such as Hinayana and Mahayana, exoteric and esoteric, provisional and true. To illustrate, all stones are invariably inferior to gold, but gold itself is divided into several grades. No gold found in the human world can match the gold mined from the Jambu River.[5] But the gold from the Jambu River is in turn far less valuable than the gold stored in the Brahma Heaven. In the same way, all the Buddhist sutras are like gold, but some are finer and more profound than others.

Those sutras that are called Hinayana are like small boats. They can carry two or three passengers, but not a hundred or a thousand. Even with only two or three persons aboard, they must remain close to this shore and cannot cross over to the other shore. They can be loaded with a small amount of cargo, but not with a large amount. In contrast, the Mahayana sutras are like those huge vessels which, carrying ten or twenty people and loaded with large quantities of cargo, can sail from Kamakura as far as Tsukushi Province in the south or Mutsu Province in the north.

But the ship of the true Mahayana sutra is incomparably greater than those ships that are the other Mahayana sutras. Loaded with a hoard of rare treasures and carrying a hundred or a thousand passengers, it can sail all the way to the land of Korea. The Lotus Sutra, the teaching of the one vehicle, is precisely this kind of sutra. Devadatta was the most evil man in the entire world, but the Lotus Sutra predicted that he would become a Buddha called the Tathagata Heavenly King. Although Ajātaśatru was a wicked king who killed his own father, he was among those present when the Lotus Sutra was preached and, after hearing only a verse or a phrase, took faith in it and thereby formed a relationship with the sutra. The dragon king's daughter, a woman with a reptile's body, attained Buddhahood by listening to Bodhisattva Monjushiri preach the Lotus Sutra. Furthermore, the Buddha designated the evil era of the Latter Day of the Law as the very time for the Lotus Sutra to be propagated, and bequeathed it to the men and women of that impure age. The Lotus Sutra, the teaching of the one vehicle, is then a sutra as great and powerful as the ships of the China trade.

Thus, all the Buddhist sutras are to the non-Buddhist scriptures as gold is to stones. And all the various Mahayana sutras, such as the *Kegon, Dainichi, Kammuryōju, Amida,* and *Hannya* sutras, are to the Lotus Sutra as fireflies are to the sun or the moon, or anthills to Mount Hua.[6] Moreover, there is superiority and inferiority not only among the sutras, but also among their adherents. The various teachers of Shingon, who believe in the *Dainichi* Sutra, are like fire being put out by water or dew being blown away by the wind when confronted in debate by the votary of the Lotus Sutra. People say that if a dog barks at a lion, its intestines will rot. The *asura* demon who shot an arrow at the sun had his head split into seven pieces. The Shingon teachers are like the dog or the *asura*, while the votary of the Lotus Sutra is like the sun or the lion.

Before the sun rises, ice is as hard as metal. Fire, when untouched by water, is as hot as molten iron. But even the hardest ice easily melts away in the sun of summer, and even the hottest fire is easily extinguished by water. The various Shingon teachers appear to be most dignified and wise, but they are like one who, forgetful of the sun, expects ice to remain hard forever or who, not taking water into account, thinks that fire will burn indefinitely.

As you know, before the Mongol attack, the arrogance of the people of our day knew no bounds. Since the tenth month of last year, however, none of them has dared to assume a haughty attitude, for, as you have heard, I, Nichiren, alone predicted this foreign invasion. If the Mongols attack our country again, none of the people will have the courage to face them. They will be like a monkey terrified by a dog or a frog cowering before a snake. This is all because the nation has allowed the priests of the Shingon, Nembutsu, Ritsu, and other sects to hate Nichiren, who is the votary of the Lotus Sutra and an emissary of Shakyamuni Buddha, and thereby brought harm upon itself. Thus it incurred the wrath of Heaven, with the consequence that all its people have become cowards. In their terror of another Mongol invasion, they are like fire fearful of water, a tree dreading the ax, a pheasant frightened out of its wits at the sight of a hawk, or a mouse threatened by a cat. Not one of them will escape. What will they do then? Soldiers look upon the general as their soul. If the general loses heart, his soldiers will become cowards.

A woman's soul is her husband. Without him, she has no soul.

Nowadays, even married women find it difficult to get along in the world. Though you have no husband, you lead your life more courageously than those who are married. Furthermore, you maintain your faith in the Buddhist gods and continue to worship the Buddha. You are indeed a remarkable woman.

While I was in Kamakura, aside from the evident heresy of the adherents of the Nembutsu and other sects, I had no way of determining whether the faith of individual believers in the Lotus Sutra was deep or shallow. This I came to know only after I had incurred the displeasure of the authorities and had been exiled to Sado. Though no one else came to visit me, you, a woman, not only sent me various offerings but personally made the journey to see me. It was almost too amazing to be true. And in addition, you have now called on me here in Minobu. I know of no words with which to thank you. Certainly the Buddhist gods will protect you and the Ten Goddesses will have compassion for you. The Buddha promised in the Lotus Sutra that, for a woman, the sutra will serve as a lantern in the darkness, as a ship when she crosses the sea, and as a protector when she travels through dangerous places.[7]

When the Tripitaka Master Kumārajīva was carrying the Lotus Sutra to China, the Heavenly King Bishamon[8] dispatched a vast number of troops to escort him safely over the Pamirs. When Priest Dōshō[9] read the Lotus Sutra in the field, innumerable tigers gathered to protect him. There is no reason why you should not be protected in the same way. The thirty-six deities on earth[10] and the twenty-eight gods of the constellations in the heavens[11] will lend you protection. Furthermore, each person has two heavenly gods who always accompany him, just as the shadow follows the body. One is named Dōshō and the other Dōmyō.[12] Perched respectively on one's left and right shoulders, they report all of his deeds to Heaven. Therefore Heaven never punishes those who have not committed any error, let alone a person of your virtue.

That is why the Great Teacher Miao-lo stated, "The stronger one's faith, the greater the gods' protection."[13] So long as one maintains firm faith, he is certain to receive the great protection of the gods. I say this for your sake. I know your faith has always been admirable, but now you must strengthen it more than ever. Only then will the Ten Goddesses lend you greater protection. You need not seek far for an example. Everyone in Japan, from the sovereign on down to the common people, all without exception tried to do me harm, but I have survived until this day. This is because, although I am alone, I have firm faith [in the Lotus Sutra].

If a boat is handled by an unskilled steersman, it may capsize and drown everyone aboard. Likewise, even if someone has great physical strength, if he lacks a resolute spirit, he cannot give full play to his abilities. In this country, there are many wise persons, but they cannot utilize their wisdom because they are governed by foolish leaders.

In the last Mongol invasion, tens of thousands of soldiers as well as civilians, both male and female, in Iki, Tsushima, and the nine provinces [Kyushu] were killed, captured, drowned in the sea, or fell from cliffs to their death. If the Mongols attack again, this time they will wreak incomparably greater havoc. Kyoto and Kamakura will meet the same fate as Iki and Tsushima in the past. Prepare in advance and flee to some other place. At that time, those who declared they would not see or listen to me will join their palms together and take faith in the Lotus Sutra. Even the adherents of the Nembutsu and Zen sects will chant Nam-myoho-renge-kyo.

The Lotus Sutra states that if there are men and women who have firm faith in this sutra, the Buddha will support them on his shoulders and carry them on his back.[14] When the Tripitaka Master Kumārāyana[15] traveled [to Kucha], a wooden statue of Shakyamuni carried him on its back by night. When I was about to be beheaded, the Lord Buddha Shakyamuni took my place. It is the same in the present as it was in the past. All of you are my followers, so how could you fail to attain Buddhahood?

No matter whom you may marry, you must not follow him if he is an enemy of the Lotus Sutra. Strengthen your faith more than ever. Ice is made of water, but it is colder than water. Blue dye is produced from indigo, but if something is dyed in it repeatedly, it becomes bluer than the indigo plant itself.[16] The Lotus Sutra itself does not change, but as you continue to strengthen your faith in it, you will be filled with more vitality and receive more blessings than other people do.

Wood is vulnerable to fire, but sandalwood cannot be burned. Fire is extinguished by water, but the fire that cremated the Buddha's remains could not be quenched. Although flowers are scattered by the wind, those that bloom in the [five] heavens of purity[17] do not wither. Water evaporates in a time of great drought, but not if it enters the Yellow River. The wicked king named Dammira did not incur punishment even when he cut off the head of an Indian monk. But when he beheaded the Venerable Āryasimha,[18] his sword fell to the ground, and his arm with it. When King Puṣyamitra[19] burned the Kukkuṭārāma Monastery to ashes, his head was split by the staves of the twelve gods.[20]

Likewise the people of Japan, by becoming enemies of the Lotus Sutra, bring ruin on themselves and their country. And because I proclaim this, I am called arrogant by those of little understanding. But I do not speak out of arrogance. It is simply that if I did not speak out, I would not be the votary of the Lotus Sutra. Moreover, when my words prove later to be true, people will be able to believe all the more readily. And because I write this down now, the people of the future will recognize my wisdom.

[A commentary[21] on the Nirvana Sutra states that] the body is insignificant while the Law is supreme, and [that] one should give his life in order to propagate the Law. Because my body is insignificant, I am struck and hated, but because the Law is supreme, it will spread without fail. If the Lotus Sutra spreads, my mortal remains will be respected, and if my remains are respected, they will benefit the people. Then I will come to be revered as highly as the Great Bodhisattva Hachiman is now. You should understand that at that time, the men and women who aided me will be honored as greatly as Takeshiuchi[22] and Wakamiya.[23]

The benefits which come from opening the eyes of even one blind person are beyond description. How then is it possible to describe the benefits that derive from opening the blind eyes of all the Japanese people, and from giving the gift of sight to all human beings throughout Jambudvīpa and the other three continents of the earth? In the fourth volume of the Lotus Sutra we read, "After the Buddha's death, those who can comprehend its [the sutra's] meaning serve as the eyes of all heavenly beings and of the people of the world."[24] Those who maintain their faith in the sutra act as the eyes of all gods and people. Therefore, those Japanese who are hostile to me are in effect gouging out the eyes of all heavenly and human beings. As a result, heaven is enraged and day after day rains down disasters, while earth is infuriated and month after month one calamity after another occurs.

Taishaku was a heavenly lord, yet he greatly respected the fox who taught him the Law.[25] As a result, he was reborn as the Lord Shakyamuni Buddha. Sessen Dōji[26] honored a demon as his teacher and became the lord of the threefold world. Saints and sages of old did not reject the Law, no matter what the appearance of its teachers. I, Nichiren, may be a stupid man, but I am surely not inferior to a fox or a demon. The noblest people in the present age are in no way superior to Taishaku or Sessen Dōji, yet because of my low social position, they have rejected my wise words. That is why the country is now on the brink of ruin. How lamentable! And what I find even sadder is that I will be unable to save my disciples who have pitied my sufferings.

Should any calamity befall us, you should immediately come to visit me here, where you will be welcomed wholeheartedly. Should the worst happen, then let us starve together among these mountains. I would imagine your daughter, Oto, has become a fine and intelligent young girl. I will write you again.

Nichiren

The fourth day of the eighth month

Notes

1. Legendary rulers of ancient China said to have realized model governments. The Three Rulers are Fu Hsi, Shen Nung, and Huang Ti. The Five Emperors are Shao Hao, Chaun Hsü, Ti Kao, T'ang Yao, and Yü Shun, who reigned after the Three Rulers.

2. King (or Emperor) Yü of the Hsia dynasty, King T'ang of the Yin dynasty, and King Wen of the Chou dynasty. They are said to have reigned after the Five Emperors.

3. T'ai-kung Wang was a general who served King Wen and, after the king's death, served King Wu, Wen's son. He fought valiantly in the battle with Emperor Chou of the Yin dynasty and contributed to the prosperity of the Chou dynasty.

4. Tan the Duke of Chou was a younger brother of King Wu. After Wu's death, Ch'eng, King Wu's son, was still a child, so Tan administered the affairs of state for him as regent.

5. Imaginary reddish-yellow gold of the highest quality said to have been mined from the mythological Jambu River that flows beneath a forest of *jambu* trees.

6. One of the five sacred mountains in China.

7. T9, 54c.

8. Bishamon is one of the Four Heavenly Kings, who lives halfway down the slopes of Mount Sumeru and protects the north. This god is said always to protect the place where the Buddha preaches and to listen to the Buddha's teachings. The story of Bishamon dispatching troops to escort Kumārajīva appears in *Hokke Denki* (T51, 52c).

9. Dōshō (629–700) was the founder of the Hossō sect in Japan. In 653 he went to China where he studied the Hossō doctrine under Hsüan-tsang. After staying in China for eight years he returned to Japan where he propagated the Hossō teaching. The story of the tigers gathering to protect him appears in the *Nihon Ryōiki* (Account of Miraculous Stories in Japan).

10. Benevolent deities appearing in the *Kanjō* Sutra (T21, 501c–502b), whose role is to protect those who embrace the Three Treasures: the Buddha, the Law, and the Priesthood.

11. Gods of the twenty-eight celestial houses or lunar mansions. According to tradition, the heavens are divided into four houses of seven major heavenly bodies each, corresponding respectively to the four directions and four seasons: east, or spring; south, summer; west, autumn; and north, winter. They are described in the *Shukuyō* Sutra (T21, 387a ff.) and elsewhere.

12. Dōshō and Dōmyō are two gods said to dwell on a person's shoulders from birth and to report good and evil actions. *See* Letter 31: The Causal Law of Life.

13. *Maka Shikan Bugyōden Guketsu* (T46, 401a).

14. T9, 31a.

15. Kumārāyana was the father of Kumārajīva, and the son of a chief minister of one of the ancient Indian kingdoms. He was a devout Buddhist, yet his king harbored so much hostility against Buddhism that he had to leave the country. He crossed the Pamir range to the north, traveling toward China. When the king of Kucha heard that Kumārāyana had forsaken a high position because of his faith in Buddhism, he gave him an official welcome and offered him another high post and the hand of his sister, Jīvaka, who also had a deep interest in Buddhism. They were married and named their first son Kumārajīva, combining their names. According to legend, when Kumārāyana left India he brought with him a statue of Shakyamuni Buddha. It is said that by day he carried the statue, and by night the statue carried him. This story appears in the *Hōbutsu Shū* (DBZ 147, 310).

16. This expression is found in chapter 1 of the *Hsün Tzu*.

17. A reference to the five highest of the eighteen heavens in the world of form, where one who reaches the third stage of enlightenment in Hinayana Buddhism ("non-returner") is reborn. It is said that no wind blows in these heavens. *Abidatsuma Jūimonsaku Ron* (T26, 427a).

18. Āryasiṃha was the last of Shakyamuni's twenty-four successors. He lived in central India during the sixth century. According to the *Fu Hōzō Innen Den* (T50, 321c), when he was propagating Buddhism in Kashmir, King Dammira (Sanskrit unknown), an enemy of Buddhism, destroyed many Buddhist temples and stupas and murdered a number of priests. He finally beheaded Āryasiṃha. It is said that instead of blood, pure white milk gushed from his neck.

19. Puṣyamitra was a king in India around the second century B.C. Though a descendant of Aśoka, he became an enemy of Buddhism. He originally served as commander in chief to Bṛhadratha, the last king of the Maurya dynasty, but he murdered Bṛhadratha and founded the Śunga dynasty, ruling northern India from his capital in Pāṭaliputra. He slandered Buddhism, killed many monks, and destroyed the Kukkuṭārāma Monastery, a major center of Buddhism built by Aśoka. *Zōagon* Sutra (T2, 181b–c).

20. Usually the twelve heavenly gods that protect the world, but here the reference appears to be to the two guardian deities of the Kukkuṭārāma Monastery. According to the *Aikuō Den* (T50, 111b) these two deities killed Puṣyamitra and his troops when they came to destroy the monastery by dropping a huge rock on them. The *Aikuō* Sutra (T50, 149b) credits two *yakṣas* with dropping the rock.

21. Miao-lo (Chang-an), *Nehangyō Sho* (T38, 114b).

22. Takeshiuchi was a general and statesman of the Yamato era (300–710) who appears in the *Nihon Shoki* (Chronicles of Japan). He served Emperor Ōjin, who was said to have been reborn as Bodhisattva Hachiman.

23. Reference is to the shrine built in 1063 by Minamoto no Yoriyoshi (988–1075) at Tsurugaoka for the emanation of the spirit of the Iwashimizu Hachiman Shrine. Even after Minamoto no Yoshitomo relocated the shrine in 1180 to Kitayama in Kamakura, it still retained the name of Tsurugaoka.

24. T9, 34c.

25. This story is found in the *Maka Shikan Bugyōden Guketsu* (T46, 272a–b). Once there was a fox on Mount Shita, India. Chased by a lion, it accidentally fell into a dry well and remained there for three days. On the brink of starvation, it resolved to dedicate itself to the Buddhist Law and recited a verse expressing its desire to expiate its past offenses. When the fox's voice reached the god Taishaku on the summit of Mount Sumeru, Taishaku rescued it and asked it to preach the Law to him and to the other heavenly deities.

26. The story of Sessen Dōji is frequently mentioned by Nichiren. It appears in the Nirvana Sutra (T12, 450a).

39 A WARNING AGAINST BEGRUDGING ONE'S FIEF

Nichiren sent this letter to Shijō Kingo in the latter part of 1277 in order to give him support in the strained relationship that had developed between Kingo and his lord, Ema Chikatoki. In the sixth month there had been a debate between Nichiren's disciple, Sammi-bō, and a certain Ryūzō-bō, a Tendai priest who had been expelled from the Enryaku ji on Mount Hiei and had later come to Kamakura where he won the patronage of Ryōkan. Shijō Kingo had been present at this debate, held at Kuwagayatsu in Kamakura, in which Sammi-bō decisively defeated his opponent. Enemies of Kingo, however, accused him of having forcibly disrupted the debate with his own followers. Lord Ema was outraged and demanded that Kingo sign a pledge disavowing his faith in the Lotus Sutra. This Kingo refused to do and informed Nichiren of his decision. Nichiren wrote this letter to encourage Kingo and sent a petition addressed to Lord Ema in which he defended Kingo and praised the faithful service that Kingo had extended toward his lord. This petition, however, was apparently never submitted.

The title of this letter, "A Warning Against Begrudging One's Fief" (*Fukashaku Shoryō no Koto*) is the alternative title of this letter. It is usually referred to by the same title as that of many of Nichiren's letters to Shijō Kingo: *Shijō Kingo-dono Gohenji* (Reply to Lord Shijō Kingo).

Your letter dated the twenty-fifth of last month arrived at the Hour of the Cock (5:00–7:00 P.M.) on the twenty-seventh of the same month. On reading your lord's official letter [ordering you to submit a written oath renouncing your faith in the Lotus Sutra] and your own pledge not to write such an oath, I feel that your resolve is as rare as seeing the *udumbara*[1] plant in blossom and as admirable as the fragrance of budding red sandalwood.

Śāriputra, Maudgalyāyana, and Mahākāśyapa were great arhats who had acquired the three insights and the six supernatural powers.[2] Moreover, they were bodhisattvas who, by hearing the Lotus Sutra, had attained the first stage of development[3] and the first stage of security,[4] achieving the perception of nonbirth and nonextinction.[5] Yet even these people deemed themselves unable to endure the great persecutions that attend the propagation of the Lotus Sutra in the *sahā* world during the Latter Day of the Law, and declined to accept the task. How then could a common mortal in the Latter Day, who has not yet eradicated the three categories of illusion,[6] become a votary of this sutra?

Even though I, Nichiren, may have been able to withstand attacks by sticks and staves and tiles and stones, vilification and persecution by the sovereign, how could lay believers, who have wives and children and are ignorant of Buddhism, possibly do the same? They might have done better never to have taken faith in the Lotus Sutra in the first place. Should they prove unable to carry their faith through to the end, upholding it only for a short time, they will be mocked by others. So thinking, I had felt pity for you. Yet, during the repeated persecutions I suffered as well as throughout my two sentences of exile,[7] you demonstrated unshakable resolve. That alone was wondrous enough, but now, despite your lord's threats, you have written a pledge to carry through your faith in the Lotus Sutra even at the cost of your two fiefs. I can find no words sufficient to praise you.

The Buddha doubted whether even Bodhisattvas Fugen and Monju could undertake the propagation of the Lotus Sutra in the latter age, and he therefore entrusted the five characters of Myōhō-renge-kyō to Jōgyō and the other three leaders of the countless Bodhisattvas of the Earth. Now, pondering the meaning of this affair, I wonder if Bodhisattva Jōgyō could have lodged himself in your body in order to assist me, Nichiren. Or perhaps it may be the merciful design of the Lord Buddha Shakyamuni.

The fact that those of your lord's retainers [who resent you] are growing more presumptuous must surely be the work of Ryōkan and Ryūzō.[8] Should you write an oath discarding your faith, that crowd will only become more arrogant than before, and they will certainly mention it to everyone they meet. Then all my disciples in Kamakura will be hounded until not a one remains.

It is the nature of common mortals not to know what awaits them in the future. Those who know it well are called worthies or sages. Passing over examples from the past, I will cite one from the present. Lord Hōjō Yoshimasa[9] relinquished both his domains and became a lay priest. I hear that, in the end, he abandoned all his many estates, forsook his sons and daughters as well as his wife, and secluded himself from the world. You have neither sons nor brothers on whom you can rely. All that you have is your two fiefs. This life is like a dream. One cannot know if he will live until tomorrow. Even if you should become the most wretched of beggars, never disgrace the Lotus Sutra. Since life is so short in any event, you should not weep over your fate. As you yourself wrote in your letter, you must act and speak without the least servility. Fawning or flattery will only do you more harm. Even if your fiefs should be confiscated or you yourself driven out, think that it is due to the workings of the Ten Goddesses,[10] and wholeheartedly entrust yourself to them.

Had I, Nichiren, not been exiled but remained in Kamakura, I would certainly have been killed in the battle.[11] In like manner, because remaining in your lord's service might prove to be to your detriment, Shakyamuni may well have contrived matters [so that you are forced to leave].

I have written a petition[12] on your behalf. There are several priests [who are my disciples in Kamakura], but they are too unreliable. I was thinking of sending Sammi-bō.[13] However, since he has still not recovered from his illness, I am sending this other priest[14] in his stead. Have either Daigaku Saburō, Taki no Tarō, or Lord Toki[15] make a clean copy of the petition when he has time, and present it to your lord. If you can do so, this matter of yours will be resolved. You need not be in great haste; rather, you should band solidly together with your fellow believers. As for the others, let them clamor against you as they will. Then, if you can submit the petition, news of it may spread throughout Kamakura, and perhaps even reach the regent himself. This will mean misfortune changing into fortune.

I explained to you the teachings of the Lotus Sutra some time ago. Matters of minor consequence arise from good, but a matter of great import assuredly means that disaster will change into great fortune. If people read this petition, the enemies of Buddhism will be exposed. You have only to state briefly, "I do not intend to leave my lord's clan and return my fief of my own will. Yet, if my lord should confiscate it, I will regard it as an offering to the Lotus Sutra and an occasion for rejoicing." Say this in a scathing tone.

You must in no way behave in a servile fashion toward the magistrate.[16] Tell him, "This fief of mine is not one which my lord bestowed upon me for any ordinary reason. He awarded it to me because I saved his life with the medicine of the Lotus Sutra when he fell seriously ill. If he takes it from me, his illness will surely return. At that time, even if he should apologize to me, Yorimoto, I will not accept it." Having had your say, take your leave in an abrupt manner.

Under no circumstances should you attend any gatherings. Maintain a strict guard at night. Be on close terms with the night watchmen,[17] and request their assistance. You should always be in company with them. If you are not ousted this time, the chances are nine to one that your fellow samurai will make an attempt on your life. No matter what, do not die shamefully.

Nichiren

The seventh month in the third year of Kenji (1277), cyclical sign hinoto-ushi.

Notes

1. An imaginary flower said to bloom once every three thousand years to herald the advent of either a Buddha or a gold-wheel-turning king, who was said to rule the four continents surrounding Mount Sumeru.

2. Powers that Buddhas, bodhisattvas, and arhats possess. The three insights (Jap: *sammyō*) are the ability to know the past, know the future, and to eradicate illusions. The six supernatural powers (Jap: *rokutsū*) are the power of being anywhere at will, the power of seeing anything anywhere, the power of hearing any sound anywhere, the power of knowing the thoughts of all other minds, the power of knowing past lives, and the power of eradicating illusions.

3. The forty-first of the fifty-two stages of bodhisattva practice. It is the stage of joy at which one rejoices at realizing a partial aspect of the truth. *See* Fifty-two stages of bodhisattva practice in Glossary.

4. The eleventh of the fifty-two stages of bodhisattva practice. At this stage one arouses the aspiration for Buddhahood. *See* Fifty-two stages of bodhisattva practice in Glossary.

5. The stage at which one perceives that the true aspect of all phenomena is neither born nor dies, and thereby dwells in security.

6. The three categories of illusion (Jap: *sanwaku*) are (1) illusions of thought and desire possessed by persons in the six paths; (2) illusions preventing bodhisattvas from saving others; and (3) the forty-two basic illusions that prevent a bodhisattva from attaining enlightenment. They are described in the *Maka Shikan* (T46, 37c).

7. The "repeated persecutions" refers to incidents such as the attack on Nichiren's home at Matsubagayatsu in Kamakura in 1260 and the attack on Nichiren by Tōjō Kagenobu and his men at Komatsubara in Awa in 1264. The two exiles are the Izu exile from the fifth month, 1261 to the second month 1263 and the exile to Sado Island, from the tenth month, 1271 to the third month, 1274.

8. Ryōkan (1217–1303) was a prominent priest of the Shingon-Ritsu sect who entered the priesthood at seventeen and received the precepts from Eizon (1202–1290), considered the restorer of the Ritsu sect. He became chief priest of the Gokuraku-ji in Kamakura. Nichiren considered him an archenemy. Ryūzō (dates unknown) was a Tendai priest who, according to an entry in the *Tendai zasu ki* for the twenty-seventh day of the fourth month, 1275, was expelled from the Enryaku-ji on Mount Hiei for allegedly eating human flesh. He fled to Kamakura where he won the patronage of Ryōkan. Ryūzō was defeated in debate with Nichiren's disciple Sammi-bō at Kuwagayatsu in Kamakura in 1277.

9. Hōjō Yoshimasa (1242–1281) was the lord of Musashi Province. He held various positions in the Kamakura government and in 1276 became *rensho* (cosigner) as deputy to the regent Hōjō Tokimune. "Both his domains" here refers to Suruga and Musashi provinces. Nichiren refers to him as Musashi no Kō-dono.

10. The Ten Goddesses (Jap: Jūrasetsu; Skt: Rākṣasī), also known as the Ten Demon Daughters, are the daughters of Kishimojin (Skt: Hāritī) described in the *Darani* (26th) chapter of the Lotus Sutra. The mother and daughters vow to protect the votaries of the Lotus Sutra.

11. Reference is probably to the conflict that broke out between Regent Hōjō Tokimune and his elder half brother Hōjō Tokisuke in the second month of 1272.

12. The petition, known as the "Yorimoto chinjō" or "Letter of Petition from Yorimoto," that Nichiren wrote to Lord Ema on Shijō Kingo's behalf. Yorimoto is part of Shijō's full name and title: Shijō Nakatsukasa Saburō Zaemon-no-jō Yorimoto. Kingo is an equivalent of the title Saemon-no-jō. The petition was apparently never submitted to Lord Ema.

13. Sammi-bō (dates unknown) was one of Nichiren's early disciples. A native of Shimōsa, he studied extensively on Mount Hiei; skilled in debate, he was highly esteemed for his great learning. He readily defeated Ryūzō in the debate at Kuwagayatsu. Later he abandoned Nichiren's teachings and met with a violent death.

14. Not identified.

15. Daigaku Saburō (1202–1286), also called Hiki Yoshimoto, was an official teacher of Confucianism for the Kamakura shogunate. It is said that he converted to Nichiren's teachings upon reading a draft of the *Risshō Ankoku Ron*. Taki no Tarō is also said to have been a teacher of Confucianism, but no detailed information about him is known. Lord Toki, or Toki Jōnin, served as a retainer to a certain Lord Chiba and was one of Nichiren's leading disciples in Shimōsa Province. He was a man of considerable erudition, and Nichiren entrusted him with many of his important works.

16. The magistrate (Jap: *bugyō*) is an administrative official who carries out the orders received from a superior. In this case, the official who would be assigned to execute Lord Ema's orders ousting Shijō Kingo.

17. Men thought to have been Shijō Kingo's escorts, who lived in his residence. Their estates had been confiscated because of their belief in Nichiren's teachings. One theory has it that they were Shijō Kingo's younger brothers, but this is by no means certain.

40 THE REAL ASPECT OF THE GOHONZON

This letter is a reply addressed to Lady Nichinyo sent by Nichiren from Minobu on the twenty-third day of the eighth month, 1277. Uncertainty surrounds the identity of Lady Nichinyo; she was thought to be either the wife of Ikegami Munenaka, the older of the Ikegami brothers, or the daughter of Lady Matsuno. She was apparently a middle-aged lady of good education and considerable affluence. As a recipient of a Gohonzon, or object of worship, she was evidently a sincere believer. This letter contains a clear description of the Gohonzon, outlining the figures represented and their significance.

The title "The Real Aspect of the Gohonzon" (*Gohonzon Sōmyō Shō*) is an alternative title. The letter is known also as *Nichinyo Gozen Gohenji* (Reply to Lady Nichinyo).

﹌﹌﹋

I have received your offerings to the Gohonzon of five *kan*[1] of coins, one horse-load of rice, and fruit. Of the fifty years of teachings in the Buddha's lifetime, only during his last eight was this teaching revealed. The Lotus Sutra, which was expounded during that period, explains the Gohonzon in the eight chapters from the *Yujutsu* through the *Zokurui* chapter. After the Buddha's death, in the two thousand years of the Former and Middle Days of the Law, not even the term "object of worship of the essential teaching" was mentioned, let alone the object itself being inscribed. Nor was there anyone capable of inscribing it. T'ien-t'ai, Miao-lo, and Dengyō perceived it in their hearts but for some reason never expounded it, just as Yen Hui[2] realized the true meaning of Confucius' teaching but kept it secret. Yet the sutra itself as well as T'ien-t'ai and Miao-lo's annotations explicitly state that the Gohonzon will appear in the first five hundred years of the Latter Day of the Law, a little more than two thousand years after the Buddha's death.

Now, over two hundred years have passed since the beginning of the Latter Day of the Law. How awesome that Nichiren was the first to inscribe this great mandala as the banner of propagation of the Lotus Sutra, when even such great masters as Nāgārjuna, Vasubandhu, T'ien-t'ai, and Miao-lo were unable to do so! This mandala is in no way Nichiren's invention. It is the object of worship which perfectly depicts Lord Shakyamuni in the Treasure Tower and all the other Buddhas who were present, as accurately as the print matches the woodblock. The five characters of the Lotus Sutra's title are inscribed in the center of the Treasure Tower, while the Four Heavenly Kings are seated at the four corners. Shakyamuni and Tahō Buddhas, as well as the four leaders of the Bodhisattvas of the Earth, are lined across the top. Seated below them are the Bodhisattvas Fugen and Monju, as well as Śāriputra, Maudgalyāyana, and others. Beside them are posted the gods of the sun and the moon, the Devil of the Sixth Heaven, the Dragon King and *asura*; Fudō and Aizen take up their stations to the south and north, respectively. The evil and treacherous Devadatta and the Dragon King's ignorant daughter attend, too. The demon Kishimojin appears with her ten daughters, who sap the lives of people throughout the universe. Also present are the guardian deities of Japan: Tenshō Daijin and Bodhisattva Hachiman, representing the seven ranks of heavenly gods, the five ranks of earthly gods,[3] and all other major and minor gods in general. As all the gods appear in their essence, so must they appear in their manifestations. The *Hōtō* chapter states, "All the assembly were lifted and present in the air."[4] Dwelling in the Gohonzon are all the Buddhas, bodhisattvas, and great saints, as well as the eight groups of sentient beings of the two realms[5] who appear in the first chapter of the Lotus Sutra. Illuminated by the five characters of the Mystic Law, they display the enlightened nature they inherently possess. This is the true object of worship.

This manifestation is what the sutra means by "all phenomena reveal the true entity."[6] Miao-lo states, "The true entity is invariably revealed in all phenomena, and all phenomena invariably possess the Ten Factors. The Ten Factors invariably function within the Ten Worlds, and the Ten Worlds invariably entail both life and its environment."[7] T'ien-t'ai states, "The profound principle of 'true entity' is the original Law of Myōhō-renge-kyō."[8] The Great Teacher Dengyō wrote, "The entity of *ichinen sanzen* is the Buddha who obtained enlightenment for himself, and that Buddha assumes no august attributes."[9] Therefore this Gohonzon is the supreme mandala never before known, for it has not appeared until more than twenty-two hundred and twenty years after the Buddha's death.

A woman who devotes herself to the Gohonzon invites happiness in this life; and in the next, the Gohonzon will be with her and protect her always. Like a lantern in the dark, like a strong supporting arm on a treacherous path, the Gohonzon will protect you, Lady Nichinyo, wherever you go. Therefore you should ward off slanderers as you would prevent a courtesan from entering your house. That is the meaning of "Part with bad friends and seek out good ones."[10]

Never seek this Gohonzon outside yourself. The Gohonzon exists only within the mortal flesh of us ordinary people who embrace the Lotus Sutra and chant Nam-myoho-renge-kyo. The body is the palace of the ninth consciousness,[11] the unchanging reality which reigns over all life's functions. To be "endowed with the Ten Worlds" means that all the Ten Worlds without exception are contained in the one world of Buddhahood. That is why the Gohonzon is called a mandala. Mandala is a Sanskrit word meaning "perfectly endowed" or "cluster of blessings." The Gohonzon is found in faith alone. As the sutra states, "Only with faith can one enter Buddhahood."[12]

Since Nichiren's disciples, both priests and laymen, believe in the supremacy of the Lotus Sutra, which states, ". . . honestly discarding the provisional teachings"[13] and "Never accept even a single phrase from other sutras,"[14] they can enter the Treasure Tower of the Gohonzon. How reassuring! Make every possible effort for the sake of your next life. The most important thing is to chant only Nam-myoho-renge-kyo and attain enlightenment. All depends on the strength of your faith. To have faith is the basis of Buddhism. That is why the fourth volume of the *Maka Shikan* states, "Buddhism is a vast ocean, but only those with faith can enter."[15] In interpreting this passage, Miao-lo writes in the fourth volume of his *Guketsu*, "Even Confucius teaches that faith is first and foremost. This is all the more true with the profound doctrines of Buddhism! Without faith, how can one possibly approach them? That is why the *Kegon* Sutra defines faith as the basis of practice and the mother of blessings."[16] The first volume of the *Maka Shikan* further states, "How does one hear, believe in, and practice the perfect teaching to attain perfect enlightenment?"[17] Volume one of the *Guketsu* interprets this: "To 'believe in the perfect teaching' means to awaken faith through doctrine and make faith the basis of practice."[18] A non-Buddhist text tells of the Emperor of Han, who so implicitly believed his aide's report that he found the river actually frozen.[19] Another relates how Li Kuang, eager to revenge his father, pierced with his arrow a boulder hidden in the grass.[20] T'ien-t'ai and Miao-lo's annotations make it absolutely clear that faith is the cornerstone. Because the Han emperor believed without doubt in his retainer's words, the river froze over. And Li Kuang was able to pierce a rock with his arrow because he fully believed it to be the tiger that had killed his father. Faith is still more powerful in the world of Buddhism.

Embracing the Lotus Sutra and chanting Nam-myoho-renge-kyo encompass all five practices that the Great Teacher Dengyō personally inherited from Priest Tao-sui[21] when he journeyed to China. This is the primary teaching for Nichiren's disciples and believers. It is the practice that appears in the *Jinriki* chapter. I will give you more details later.

Respectfully,
Nichiren

The twenty-third day of the eighth month in the third year of Kenji (1277)

Notes

1. An old monetary unit consisting of one thousand coins strung together with a cord.
2. Yen Hui (514–483 B.C.) was one of Confucius' favored disciples. Nichiren refers to him here by his other name, Yen Yüan.
3. The seven heavenly gods who ruled Japan and the five earthly gods who are said to have existed before the time of Emperor Jimmu.
4. T9, 33c.
5. The two realms are those of desire and form, two divisions of the threefold world. The eight groups of sentient beings are enumerated in the *Jo* (1st) chapter of the Lotus Sutra. They are: (1) beings in the realm of desire, (2) beings in the realm of form, (3) dragon kings, (4) *kimnara* kings (gods with beautiful voices), (5) *gandharva* kings (gods of music), (6) *asura* kings, (7) *garuda* kings (birds that prey on dragons), and (8) human kings.
6. T9, 5c.
7. *Kongōbei Ron* (T46, 785c).
8. Source not identified.

9. This quotation is said to derive from the *Himitsu Shōgon Ron*, a work by Dengyō that is no longer extant.

10. T9, 16b.

11. The *amala*, the pure, unstained consciousness, the last of the nine consciousnesses. Here Nichiren relates it to Nam-myoho-renge-kyo.

12. T9, 15b.

13. T9, 10a.

14. T9, 16a.

15. T46, 45c.

16. T46, 272c.

17. T46, 2a.

18. T46, 152b.

19. Emperor Kuang-wu (6 B.C.–A.D. 57), the founder of the Later Han dynasty, before he became emperor, was defeated in battle. While retreating, his trusted aide, Wang Pa, pretended that the river ahead of them that they needed to cross was frozen. The emperor-to-be put so much faith in Wang Pa that when the troops reached the river it actually was frozen and his army was able to cross.

20. Li Kuang (d.119 B.C.) was a general of the Former Han dynasty. According to the *Shih Chi* (Records of the Historian), chapter 109, he served the Emperor Wu and excelled in archery. The *Konjaku Monogatari* (Tales of Times Now Past), volume ten, relates the story of his vendetta against a tiger that is said to have killed his mother. Another source says, as does Nichiren, that it was the father who was killed. *See also* Letter 42: General Stone Tiger.

21. Tao-sui (n.d.) was the tenth successor of the T'ien-t'ai school in China. He studied under Miao-lo and devoted himself to transmitting the doctrines to his followers, including Dengyō from Japan.

41 THE THREE KINDS OF TREASURE

Nichiren sent this letter from Mount Minobu to Shijō Kingo in Kamakura on the eleventh day of the ninth month, 1277. Around 1274 Kingo began making efforts to convert his lord to Nichiren's teachings, but Lord Ema did not take kindly to his efforts. He reduced the size of Kingo's holdings and threatened to send him to the remote area of Echigo. Kingo's colleagues broadcast scurrilous reports about him and Kingo was accused of fomenting trouble at a debate in which the Tendai priest Ryūzō-bō was bested by Nichiren's disciple, Sammi-bō. Nichiren cautions Kingo and instructs him on the best course of behavior under his trying circumstances. Later that year Lord Ema fell ill and Kingo helped cure him with his medical skills. Ema was most grateful and restored and later even increased Kingo's land holdings.

The "Three Kinds of Treasure" (*Sanshu no Zaihō Gosho*) is the alternative title of this letter. It is more frequently referred to as *Sushun Tennō Gosho* (The Story of Emperor Sushun).

I have received the various articles from your messenger, including a white winter robe and a string of coins, as well as the goods mentioned in Lord Toki's[1] letter. The persimmons, pears, and fresh and dried seaweed are particularly welcome.

I am most grieved over your lord's illness. Although he has not professed faith in the Lotus Sutra, you are a member of his clan, and it is thanks to his consideration that you are able to make offerings to the sutra. Therefore all of your gifts are in effect prayers for your lord's recovery. Think of a small tree under a large one, or grass by a great river. Though they do not receive rain or water directly, they nonetheless thrive, partaking of dew from the large tree or drawing moisture from the river. The same holds true with the relationship between you and your lord. To give another example, King Ajātaśatru was an enemy of the Buddha. But because Jīvaka,[2] a minister in the king's court, believed in the Buddha and continually made offerings to him, the blessings accruing from his actions are said to have returned to Ajātaśatru.

Buddhism teaches that when the Buddha nature manifests itself from within, it will obtain protection from without. This is one of its fundamental principles. The Lotus Sutra says, "I deeply respect you."[3] The Nirvana Sutra states, "All living things possess the Buddha nature."[4] Aśvaghoṣa's *Daijō Kishin Ron* says, "When the Buddha nature continuously manifests itself, it will quickly extinguish illusions and reveal the Law body."[5] Bodhisattva Maitreya's *Yuga Ron*[6] contains a similar statement. An inconspicuous deed will produce a conspicuous benefit.

The Devil of the Sixth Heaven probably knew the aforementioned principle, and he therefore possessed your colleagues, causing them to invent that preposterous lie[7] in order to prevent you from making offerings to the Lotus Sutra. However, since your faith is profound, the Ten Goddesses must have come to your aid and thus caused your lord's illness. He does not regard you as his enemy, but since he once acted against you in giving credit to the false accusations of your colleagues, he has become seriously ill and the malady persists.

Ryūzō-bō,[8] whom these people count on as their pillar of strength, has already been toppled, and those who spoke falsely of you have contracted the same disease as your lord. Ryōkan[9] is even more slanderous than they. He will probably encounter some bad accident, or stir up major trouble and find himself in serious distress. Surely he will not escape unharmed.

As things stand now, I have a feeling you are in danger. Your enemies are sure to make an attempt on your life. In backgammon, if two stones of the same color are placed side by side, they cannot be hit by an opposing stone. A cart, as long as it has two wheels, does not lurch all over the road. Likewise, if two men go together, an enemy will hesitate to attack. Therefore, no matter what faults you may find with your younger brothers, do not let them leave you alone even for a moment.

Your face bears definite signs of a hot temper. But you should know that the gods will not protect a short-tempered person, no matter how important they may think he is. If you should be killed, even though you might attain Buddhahood after your death, your enemies would be delighted, but we would feel only grief. This would indeed be regrettable. While your foes busy themselves plotting against you, your lord places greater confidence in you than before. Therefore, although they appear to have quieted down, inwardly they are no doubt seething with hate. So you should at all times behave unobtrusively in their presence. Pay greater respect to the other retainers of the clan than you have in the past. For the time being, when members of the Hōjō clan are visiting your lord, refrain from calling on him, even if he should summon you.

If the worst should happen and your lord should die, your enemies would become masterless and would have nowhere to turn, though they do not seem to consider that fact. Unreasoning as they are, when they see you report to work more and more frequently, their hearts are bound to be fired with jealousy and their breath come in pants.

If the young nobles of the Hōjō clan or the wives of those in power should inquire about your lord's illness, no matter who the person may be, get down on your knees, place your hands properly, and reply thus: "His malady is entirely beyond my poor skill to cure. But no matter how often I decline, he insists that I treat him. Since I am in his service, I cannot help but do as he says." Leave your hair untended, and refrain from wearing well-starched court dress, bright robes, or other colorful clothing. Be patient and continue in this way for the time being.

Perhaps you are well aware of it, but let me cite the Buddha's prediction about what the Latter Day of the Law will be like. In essence he states, "It will be a chaotic age in which even a sage will find it difficult to live. He will be like a stone in a great fire, which for a while seems to endure the heat but finally chars and crumbles to ashes. Worthy men will advocate the five great principles of humanity,[10] but they themselves will find it hard to practice them." Thus the saying goes, "Do not remain in the seat of honor too long."

Many people have plotted to undo you, but you have avoided their intrigues and emerged victorious. Should you lose your composure now and fall into their trap, you will be, as people say, like a boatman who rows his boat with all his might only to have it capsize just before he reaches the shore, or like a person who is served no tea at the end of his meal.

While you are in your lord's mansion, if you stay in the room assigned to you, nothing will happen to you. But on your way to work at dawn or returning from it at dusk, your enemies are bound to be lying in wait for you. Also, be very careful in and around your house in case someone should be hiding beside the double doors, inside the family sanctuary, under the floor, or in the space above the ceiling. This time your foes will use even more cunning in their plots than before. In the end, no one will be more dependable in an emergency than the night watchmen of Egara[11] in Kamakura. However disagreeable it may be to you, you should associate with them amicably.

Minamoto no Yoshitsune[12] found it utterly impossible to defeat the Heike until he won Shigeyoshi[13] over to his side and in that way vanquished the rival clan. Shogun Minamoto no Yoritomo[14] sought to take revenge on Osada[15] for his father's death, but he would not behead the murderer until after he had conquered the Heike. It is even more vital for you to master your emotions and ally yourself with your four brothers. They had risked their lives to acquire their mansions, and these were confiscated by their lord because of their faith in the Lotus Sutra and because of their belief in Nichiren. Be considerate of those who believe in Nichiren and the Lotus Sutra, no matter what they may have done in the past. Moreover, if they frequent your house, your enemies will be afraid to attack you at night. It is not as if they were trying to avenge their fathers' deaths; certainly they do not want their plot to come out into the open. To one such as you who must avoid being seen, these four are the most dependable warriors. Always maintain friendly relations with them. But since you are hot-tempered by nature, you might not take my advice. In that case, it will be beyond the power of my prayers to save you.

Ryūzō-bō and your elder brother plotted evil against you. Therefore, Heaven so contrived that the situation would develop exactly as you wished. Then how can you now dare to go against the wish of Heaven? Even if you had accumulated a thousand or ten thousand treasures, of what use would they be if your lord should forsake you? He already looks to you as if you were his own parent, following you as water follows the shape of its container, longing for you as a calf longs for its mother, relying on you as an elderly person relies on his staff. Is his regard for you not due to the aid of the Lotus Sutra? How envious your fellow retainers must be! You must hurry and bring your four brothers over to your side and report to me how the matter goes. Then I will fervently pray to the gods for your protection. I have already informed them of how deeply you grieve over the death of your father and mother. Shakyamuni Buddha will surely extend them his especial consideration.

Over and over I recall the moment,[16] unforgettable even now, when I was about to be beheaded and you accompanied me, holding the reins of my horse and weeping tears of grief. Nor could I ever forget it in any lifetime to come. If you should fall into hell for some grave offense, no matter how Shakyamuni might urge me to become a Buddha, I would refuse; I would rather go to hell with you. For if you and I should fall into hell together, we would find Shakyamuni Buddha and the Lotus Sutra there. It would be like the moon illuminating the darkness, like cold water pouring into hot, like fire melting ice, or like the sun dispelling the darkness. But if you depart from my advice even slightly, then do not blame me for what may happen.

The plague which is raging at present will, as you predict, strike those in the higher ranks of society at the turn of the year. This is perhaps the design of the Ten Goddesses. For the time being stay calm and observe how things develop. And do not go around lamenting to others how hard it is for you to live in this world. To do so is an act utterly unbecoming to a worthy man. If one behaves in this way, then after he dies, his wife, overcome with sorrow at losing her husband, will tell other people about the shameful things he did, though she has no real intention of doing so. And that will in no way be her fault but solely the result of his own reprehensible behavior.

It is rare to be born a human being. The number of those endowed with human life is as small as the amount of earth one can place on a fingernail. Life as a human being is hard to sustain—as hard as it is for the dew to remain on the grass. But it is better to live a single day with honor than to live to one hundred and twenty and die in disgrace. Live so that all the people of Kamakura will say in your praise that Shijō Kingo is diligent in the service of his lord, in the service of Buddhism, and in his concern for other people. More valuable than treasures in a storehouse are the treasures of the body, and the treasures of the heart are the most valuable of all. From the time you read this letter on, strive to accumulate the treasures of the heart!

I would like to relate an incident that is customarily kept secret. In the history of Japan, there have been two emperors who were assassinated. One of them was the thirty-third emperor Sushun. He was the son of Emperor Kimmei and an uncle of Prince Shōtoku.[17] One day he summoned Prince Shōtoku and said, "We hear that you are a man of unsurpassed wisdom. Examine Our physiognomy and tell Us what you see there!" The prince declined three times, but the emperor insisted that he obey the Imperial command. Finally, no longer able to refuse, the prince reverently examined Sushun's physiognomy and then reported, "Your Majesty's countenance indicates that you will be assassinated by someone."

The emperor's complexion changed color. "What evidence do you have to support such a contention?" he asked. The prince replied, "I see red veins running over your eyes. This is a sign that you will incur the enmity of others." Thereupon the emperor asked, "How can We escape this fate?" The prince said, "It is difficult to evade. But there are soldiers known as the five great principles of humanity. As long as you keep these warriors on your side, you will be safe from danger. In the Buddhist scriptures these soldiers are referred to as 'forbearance,' one of the six *pāramitās*."[18]

For some time after that, Emperor Sushun faithfully observed the practice of forbearance. But, being irascible by nature, he violated the precept one day when one of his subjects presented him with a young wild boar. He withdrew the metal rod that was attached to his sword scabbard and stabbed the boar in the eyes with it, saying, "One of these days this is what We will do to that fellow We hate!" Prince Shōtoku, who happened to be present, exclaimed, "Ah, what a fearful thing to do! Your Majesty will surely arouse the enmity of others. These very words you have spoken will be the sword that wounds you." The prince then ordered articles of value to be brought out and divided among those who had heard the emperor's remark, [hoping to buy their silence]. One of them, however, told the high minister Soga no Umako[19] about the episode. Umako, believing that he was the one the emperor hated, won over Atai Goma, son of Azumanoaya no Atai Iwai,[20] and had him kill the emperor.

Thus even a ruler on a throne must take care not to give unreserved expression to his thoughts. Confucius held to the proverb "Nine thoughts to one word,"[21] which means that he reconsidered nine times before he spoke. Tan, the Duke of Chou,[22] was so earnest in receiving callers that he would bind up his hair three times in the course of washing it, or spit out his food three times in the course of a meal, in order not to keep them waiting. Think carefully about what I mean by this so you will have no cause to reproach me later. Such thoughtfulness is surely a part of Buddhism.

The key to all of Shakyamuni's teachings is the Lotus Sutra, and the key to the practice of the Lotus Sutra is expounded in the *Fukyō* chapter. What does Bodhisattva Fukyō's profound respect for people signify? The real meaning of the Lord Shakyamuni Buddha's appearance in this world lay in his behavior as a human being. How profound! The wise may be called human, but the thoughtless are no more than animals.

Nichiren

The eleventh day of the ninth month in the third year of Kenji (1277)

Notes

1. Toki Jōnin (Toki Gorō Tanetsugu, 1216?–1299?) was an official serving the Kamakura government on the military tribunal. He was a staunch follower of Nichiren.

2. Jīvaka was an Indian physician in Shakyamuni's time. He was a devout Buddhist and served as a minister to King Ajātaśatru.

3. T9, 50c.

4. T12, 522c.

5. T32, 579a. For Law Body, *see* Three Bodies in Glossary.

6. The *Yuga Ron* (T30, no. 1579) by Maitreya, Buddhist scholar of the third or fourth century in India, was translated into Chinese by Hsüan-tsang during the T'ang dynasty.

7. The report that Shijō Kingo's associates are said to have made to Lord Ema that Shijō had forcibly attempted to disrupt the debate between Nichiren's disciple Sammi-bō and Ryūzō-bō, held at Kuwagayatsu in the sixth month of 1277.

8. Ryūzō-bō was a Tendai priest from the Enryaku-ji on Mount Hiei. A story has it that he was banished from Mount Hiei for eating human flesh. *Tendai Zasu Ki* (entry for the twenty-seventh day of the 4th month, 1275. *Gunsho Ruiju* 4, part 2, p. 685). Later he appeared in Kamakura where he continued preaching from a cottage in Kuwagayatsu. He is said to have gained considerable popularity until he was defeated in debate by Sammi-bō.

9. Ryōkan Ninshō (1217–1303), was a famous priest of the Shingon-Ritsu sect who enjoyed the favor of the Kamakura government. Nichiren considered him his archenemy and wrote disparagingly of his talents.

10. These are the five constant virtues of Confucianism: benevolence, righteousness, propriety, wisdom, and good faith.

11. Egara is a place name in Kamakura where government buildings were located. The night watchmen are said to have been the four younger brothers of Shijō Kingo whose lands were confiscated because of their belief in Nichiren's teachings, and who were thus obliged to take menial positions.

12. Minamoto no Yoshitsune (1159–1189) was a younger half brother of Minamoto no Yoritomo (1147–1199), founder of the Kamakura government. In 1180, when Yoritomo raised an army against the rival Taira or Heike clan, Yoshitsune joined forces with him and later defeated the Taira army. After the battle Yoshitsune

incurred Yoritomo's displeasure and escaped to Hiraizumi in the northern part of Japan, where he placed himself under the protection of the Fujiwara family but, under pressure from Yoritomo, he was obliged to commit suicide.

13. Taguchi Shigeyoshi (n.d.) was the head of a powerful family in Awa, a province on the island of Shikoku. Although a member of the Taira family, he informed Yoshitsune of the internal conditions of the Taira army as well as the weak points of their position. This helped bring about the downfall of the Taira clan.

14. Minamoto no Yoritomo (1147–1199) was the founder of the Kamakura shogunate. He defeated the rival Taira clan at the battle of Dannoura in 1185, and established a military government in Kamakura. However, he made no attempt to dismantle the government machinery already in existence in Kyoto and deliberately sought recognition for his actions from the emperor and the court. In 1192 he succeeded in obtaining the prestigious military title of shogun.

15. Osada Tadamune (n.d.) was a samurai in Owari province in central Japan. In 1159 Minamoto no Yoshitomo (1123–1160), the father of Yoritomo, battled with the Taira army and was defeated. Fleeing, he hid in the house of Osada Tadamune. On the Taira's order, Osada led Yoshitomo into the bath and there killed him. Later, when Yoritomo raised an army, Tadamune and his son, Kagemune, sided with Yoritomo, but were killed, the story has it, at Yoritomo's command after the fall of the Taira.

16. Reference is to the Tatsunokuchi Persecution of 1271, when Nichiren was almost beheaded.

17. *See* Letter 25, note 25.

18. The six *pāramitā* (Jap: *ropparamitsu*) are the six practices for Mahayana bodhisattvas in their progress toward Buddhahood: charity, or giving, observing the precepts, forbearance, assiduousness, meditation, and wisdom.

19. Soga no Umako (d.626) was the chief minister, who succeeded to the position in 570 on the death of his father, Soga no Iname. In 587, he defeated the Mononobe family, the strongest opponents of Buddhism. In the following year the prince chosen by Umako ascended the throne to become Emperor Sushun. Under the protection of the Soga clan, Buddhism soon began to flourish, and by the end of the sixth century, it was well established in the Yamato area. Unfortunately, Soga no Umako's political record did not match his pious efforts to promote Buddhism, for he proceeded to consolidate his power by having Emperor Sushun assassinated in 592, and placing on the throne his own niece, Empress Suiko.

20. Atai Goma is Azumanoaya Goma (n.d.), also known as Yamatonoaya Koma. His family had come to Japan from the mainland during the time of Emperor Ōjin and were responsible for supervising foreign artisans. The family had great economic and political power and were allied with the Soga clan. Atai Goma is said to have been killed after having been discovered in an illicit affair with an imperial concubine.

21. *Analects*, chapter 16.

22. Tan, the Duke of Chou, was the younger brother of Emperor Wu. After Wu's death, Ch'eng, Emperor Wu's son, was still a child, so Tan administered affairs of state for him as regent.

42 GENERAL STONE TIGER

This letter, written on the twenty-second day of the intercalary tenth month, 1278, was sent to Shijō Kingo by Nichiren from Mount Minobu. Evidently Kingo had sent Nichiren various medicines that helped to alleviate his illness. At this time a virulent epidemic was sweeping throughout Japan, and Kingo's lord became violently ill. Despite the lord's antagonism toward Nichiren's teachings, he felt the need to turn to Kingo for help. Lord Ema was most grateful for Kingo's ministrations and awarded him additional lands and returned those that had previously been confiscated. Yet Nichiren warns Kingo to be constantly on guard and to always travel with soldiers in escort.

"General Stone Tiger" (*Sekko Shōgun Gosho*) is the alternative title for this letter. It is more frequently referred to by the title *Shijō Kingo-dono Gohenji* (Reply to Lord Shijō Kingo), 1278.

On the twenty-second of this month I received all that you sent me from Shinano—three *kan*[1] of coins, a sack of polished rice, fifty rice cakes, one large and one small bamboo container of sake, five bundles of dried persimmons, and ten pomegranates, as well as the list you enclosed with these gifts.

A sovereign is supported by the people, and they in turn live under his protection. Clothes protect us from cold and food sustains us, just as oil keeps a fire burning and water enables fish to live. Birds nest high in the trees in fear that men will harm them, but they come down to feed and are caught in snares. Fish living at the bottom of a pond fear that it is too shallow and dig holes to hide in, yet lured by bait, they take the hook. No treasure possessed by man is more precious than food and drink, clothing and medicine.

I, Nichiren, am not as healthy as others, and in addition, I dwell in this remote mountain forest. This year was especially difficult, with widespread epidemics and famine in spring and summer, which worsened in autumn and winter. My sickness grew worse again, too, but you prescribed various medicines and sent them to me along with quilted silk clothes. Thanks to your remedies, I improved steadily; I have now recovered and feel much better than before. The *Yuga Ron* of Bodhisattva Maitreya[2] and the *Dai Ron*[3] of Bodhisattva Nāgārjuna both state that if one's illness is caused by immutable karma, even the most excellent medicine will turn to poison, but if he believes in the Lotus Sutra, poison will change into medicine. Although unworthy, Nichiren propagates the Lotus Sutra; hence devils have competed to deprive him of food. Understanding this, I have no complaint, but I believe that I survived this time only because Shakyamuni Buddha sent you to assist me.

So much for that. I was extremely concerned about your journey home last time, and I am overjoyed to hear that you arrived safely in Kamakura. Such was my anxiety that I asked everyone who came here from Kamakura about you. One said that he had met you at Yumoto, another that he had encountered you further on at Kōzu, and when a third told me that he had seen you in Kamakura, I felt greatly relieved. From now on, you must not come to visit me in person unless absolutely necessary. When you have something urgent to tell me, send a messenger. Indeed, I was deeply worried about your last trip. An enemy will try to make you forget the danger so that he can attack. If you should have to travel, do not spare the cost of a good horse. Bring along your best soldiers to defend you against a surprise attack, and ride a horse which can easily carry you in your armor.

In the eighth volume of the *Maka Shikan* and in the eighth volume of Miao-lo's *Guketsu* it is said, "The stronger one's faith, the greater the gods' protection."[4] This means that the protection of the gods depends on the strength of one's faith. The Lotus Sutra is a keen sword, but its might depends upon the one who wields it.

Among those who propagate this sutra in the Latter Day of the Law, who could compare with Śāriputra, Mahākāśyapa, Kannon, Myōon, Monju, and Yakuō? Śāriputra and Mahākāśyapa, who were of the two vehicles, had destroyed all illusions of thought and desire, thus freeing themselves from the six paths. The others, all bodhisattvas, had eradicated the forty-one illusions[5] and were approaching perfection, like the harvest moon on the night before it reaches fullness. Nevertheless Shakyamuni Buddha refused to entrust the mission of propagation to any of these people and gave it instead to the Bodhisattvas of the Earth. Thus these Bodhisattvas of the Earth are the ones who had thoroughly forged their faith.

The mother of the mighty warrior General Li Kuang[6] was devoured by a ferocious tiger. The General spied the beast and shot it with an arrow, but then discovered that what he had seen was only a rock. The arrow lodged itself deep in the rock. He was surprised and tried to duplicate his feat but could not penetrate the stone a second time. Later he came to be known as General Stone Tiger. Your strength of purpose is comparable to his. Though enemies lurk in wait for you, your resolute faith in the Lotus Sutra has forestalled persecutions before they could begin. Realizing this, you must strengthen your faith more than ever. It is impossible to say all I want to in one letter.

With my deep respect,
Nichiren

The twenty-second day of the tenth intercalary month in the first year of Kōan (1278)

Notes

1. An old monetary unit consisting of a thousand coins strung together on a cord.

2. Reference is to the *Yuga Shiji Ron* (T30, no. 1579) by Maitreya, an Indian scholar of the third to fourth century.

3. The *Daichido Ron* (T25, no. 1509).

4. Nichiren quotes a passage from Miao-lo's *Maka Shikan Bugyōden Guketsu* (T46, 401a) that is a rephrasing of a passage of similar import in T'ien-t'ai's *Maka Shikan* (T46, 110a).

5. There are fifty-one stages of ignorance or illusions that the bodhisattva must pass through in his progress toward the fifty-second stage, *myōgaku*, enlightenment or Buddhahood. The first ten stages, those of faith, are not included here. Thus the forty-one are ten stages of security, ten stages of practice, ten stages of devotion, ten stages of development, and *tōgaku*, a stage almost equal to enlightenment.

6. *See* Letter 40, note 20.

43 THE STRATEGY OF THE LOTUS SUTRA

This letter, dated the twenty-third day of the tenth month, 1279, is in reply to a letter to Nichiren from Shijō Kingo, informing him that he had been ambushed by enemies among his fellow samurai, but had managed to escape unharmed.

The title "The Strategy of the Lotus Sutra" (*Hoke Kyō Heihō no Koto*) is an alternative title. It is better known as *Shijō Kingo-dono Gohenji* (Reply to Lord Shijō Kingo). The letter also is called by the alternative title "Letter on Swordmanship" (*Kengyō Sho*).

I have carefully read your letter in which you described the recent skirmish with powerful enemies. So they have finally attacked you. It is a matter of rejoicing that your usual prudence and courage, as well as your firm faith in the Lotus Sutra, enabled you to survive unharmed.

When one comes to the end of his good fortune, no strategy whatsoever will avail. When one's blessings are exhausted, even his retainers will no longer follow him. You survived because you still possess good fortune. Moreover, in the *Zokurui* chapter, the heavenly gods pledged to protect the votary of the Lotus Sutra. Of all the guardian deities in heaven, it is the gods of the sun and moon who visibly protect us. How can we doubt their protection? Marishiten[1] in particular serves the god of the sun. Could the vassal Marishiten abandon the votary of the Lotus Sutra when her lord, the god of the sun, protects him? In the first chapter, Taishaku appears with his twenty thousand retainer gods. The god of the moon, the god of the stars, the god of the sun, and the Four Heavenly Kings were seated together with their ten thousand retainer gods. Marishiten must be among the thirty thousand heavenly gods who were present at the ceremony. Otherwise, she could only abide in hell.

You must have escaped death because of this deity's protection. She gave you skill in swordsmanship, while Nichiren has bestowed upon you the five characters of Myōhō-renge-kyō. Never doubt that all gods protect those who embrace the Lotus Sutra. Marishiten also embraces the Lotus Sutra and thus helps all people. Even the incantation, "Those who join the battle are all on the front line,"[2] is related to the Lotus Sutra, where it says, "learning, government, language, and daily living will accord with the True Law."[3] Therefore you must summon up the power of faith more than ever. Do not blame the heavenly gods if you exhaust your good fortune and lose their protection.

Masakado[4] was renowned as a brave general who had mastered the art of war, yet he was defeated by the emperor's armies. Even Fan K'uai and Chang Liang[5] had their failures. Faith alone is what really matters. No matter how earnestly Nichiren prays for you, if you lack faith, it will be like trying to set fire to wet tinder. Spur yourself to muster the power of faith. Regard your survival as wondrous. Employ the strategy of the Lotus Sutra before any other. Then, just as the sutra says, "All enemies are crushed."[6] These golden words will never prove false. Believe them wholeheartedly. The heart of strategy and swordsmanship derives from the Mystic Law. A coward cannot have any of his prayers answered.

With my deep respect,
Nichiren

The twenty-third day of the tenth month

Notes

1. Marishiten (Skt: Marīci) is originally the personification of the sun's rays. She is characterized as an invisible god whose occult powers enable her to defeat an enemy without being wounded or captured. She is pictured as holding a fan in her left hand. The belief was that if you prayed to her you would avert disaster and be able to gain the techniques for hiding the body. She is venerated as a protective deity of the warrior.

2. A quote from a fourth century Taoist work, the *Pao-p'u-tzu* that was used as a

spell by Chinese soldiers who believed that reciting this phrase while drawing four vertical lines and five horizontal lines in the air would protect them from harm. This ritualistic practice later spread to Japan and was widely adopted among the samurai of the Kamakura period. Here Nichiren indicates that the votary of the Lotus Sutra will be protected in all his activities.

3. T9, 50a.

4. Taira no Masakado (d.940), a warrior who gained control of the Kanto area and in 939 rebelled against the Imperial court and declared himself the "New Emperor." He was killed by troops under the leadership of Fujiwara no Hidesato.

35. Fan K'uai (d.189 B.C.) and Chang Liang (d.168 B.C.) were military leaders and strategists who assisted Emperor Kao-tsu in unifying China and founding the Former Han dynasty. They are known for their courage and loyalty in the face of numerous difficulties.

6. T9, 54c.

44 *THE MEANING OF FAITH*

Nichiren wrote this brief letter to Myōichi-ama on the eighteeenth day of the fifth month, 1280. Myōichi-ama was a relative of Nisshō, one of the six senior priests, and lived in Kamakura. She was a steadfast believer, of good education, but suffered from poor health. Her husband was also a believer and their fief was confiscated because of their faith. After her husband died Myōichi-ama was left with two small children, but despite her many difficulties, always remained loyal to Nichiren.

"The Meaning of Faith" (*Shinjin Hongi no Koto*) is an alternative title for this letter. It is known also as *Myōichi-ama Gozen Gohenji* (Reply to Lady Myōichi-ama).

What we call faith is nothing extraordinary. As a woman cherishes her husband, as a man will give his life for his wife, as parents will not abandon their children, or as a child refuses to leave his mother, so should we put our trust in the Lotus Sutra, Shakyamuni, Tahō, and all the Buddhas and bodhisattvas of the ten directions, as well as the heavenly gods and benevolent deities, and chant Nam-myoho-renge-kyo. This is what is meant by faith. Moreover, you should ponder the sutra passages "Honestly discarding the provisional teachings,"[1] and "Not accepting even a single verse from any of the other sutras,"[2] and never be of a mind to abandon them, just as a woman will not throw away her mirror or as a man always wears his sword.

Respectfully,
Nichiren

The eighteenth day of the fifth month

Notes

1. Lotus Sutra (T9, 10a).
2. Lotus Sutra (T9, 16a).

45 THE SWORDS OF GOOD AND EVIL

This letter was written to Hōjō Yagenta, a lay believer in Kamakura; it is dated the twenty-first day of the second month, with no year indicated, but it is believed to be 1274. The letter was sent by Nichiren from Ichinosawa on Sado Island, seven days after a pardon had been issued (fourteenth day of the second month), but that did not reach Nichiren until the eighth day of the third month. Little is known of Yagenta, although he is believed to have been an early follower of Nichiren's teachings. He was a recipient in 1268 of one of the eleven letters that Nichiren wrote remonstrating with the government when a delegate from Kublai Kahn arrived bearing a manifesto demanding Japan's surrender.

"The Swords of Good and Evil" (*Zennaku Nitō Gosho*) is again an alternative title to this letter. It is also known as *Yagenta-dono Gohenji* (Reply to Lord Yagenta).

Nichiren is the most perverse person in Japan. The reason is this: Nichiren proclaims that because the people revere Amida, Dainichi, Yakushi and other Buddhas even more than their own parents and lords, the three calamities and seven disasters[1] are occurring in greater magnitude than in any previous age, and natural disasters are now more terrible than ever. I am forever reminding them that they will not only ruin themselves and destroy the country in this lifetime, but will fall into the hell of incessant suffering in the next. Hence I have suffered this persecution. I might be compared to a summer insect that flies into a flame or a mouse that dashes in front of a cat. I am like an animal that knows it is in danger and yet pays no heed. But I risk my life as a matter of conscious choice; therefore I, Nichiren, am a perverse person.

It is also true that stones are split open for their hidden gems, deer

347

are slain for their hides and meat, fish are caught for their flavor, the kingfisher is killed for its gorgeous feathers, and a beautiful woman is envied for her beauty. This is the case with Nichiren. Because he is the votary of the Lotus Sutra, he has suffered all manner of persecution at the hands of the three powerful enemies.[2] How wondrous that you have, nonetheless, become a disciple of such a person! There must be some profound reason for our relationship. Make every possible effort to deepen your faith and reach the pure land of Eagle Peak.

I have received the two swords[3]—a long and a short one—to be offered in prayer. The long sword must have been made by a renowned swordsmith. It is fully equal to the celebrated swords Amakuni, Onikiri and Yatsurugi,[4] or to those famous Chinese swords Kan-chiang and Mo-yeh.[5] You have offered this sword to the Lotus Sutra. While you wore it at your side, it was an evil sword, but now that it has been offered to the Buddha, it has become a sword for good, just like a demon who professes Buddhism. How strange, how wonderful!

In the next life you should use this sword as your walking stick. The Lotus Sutra is the staff which helps all Buddhas of the three existences as they enter upon the path to enlightenment. However, you should rely upon Nichiren as your staff. When one uses a staff, he will not fall on treacherous mountain paths or rough roads, and when led by the hand, he will never stumble. Nam-myoho-renge-kyo will be your unbreakable staff to take you safely over the mountains of death. Shakyamuni and Tahō Buddhas as well as the Four Bodhisattvas headed by Jōgyō will lead you by the hand on your journey. Should Nichiren die before you, I will come to meet you at the moment of your death. If you should die before I do, I will be sure to tell King Emma everything about you. All that I tell you is true. According to the Lotus Sutra, Nichiren is the guide on the difficult road to enlightenment. Devote yourself single-mindedly to faith with the aim of reaching Eagle Peak.

Money serves various purposes according to our needs. The same is true of the Lotus Sutra. It will be a lantern in the dark or a boat at a crossing. At times it will be water, and at other times, fire. This being so, the Lotus Sutra assures us of "peace and security in this life and good circumstances in the next."[6]

Of all the many places in Japan, Nichiren was born in the province of Awa. It is said that when the Sun Goddess discovered the land of Japan, she first dwelt in Awa Province. A shrine of the Sun Goddess stands in Awa. This goddess is the merciful parent of the entire nation, so this province must be of great significance. What destiny caused Nichiren to be born in this same province? No reward could be greater. That is not the main point of this letter, so I will not go into further detail. But you should think about what I mean.

I will pray to the gods with all my heart. Hold fast to your faith so that your wish will be fulfilled. Tell your wife all that I have said.

With my deep respect,
Nichiren

The twenty-first day of the second month.

Notes

1. The three calamities and seven disasters (Jap: *sansai shichinan*) are described in various sutras. The three calamities are of two kinds: the three greater calamities of fire, water and wind that destroy a world at the end of the Kalpa of Decline, and the three lesser calamities of high grain prices (especially those caused by famine), warfare and pestilence (*Kusha Ron*, T29, 65c-66a). The *Yakushi* Sutra (T14, 407c) gives the seven disasters as pestilence, foreign invasion, internal strife, unnatural changes in the heavens, solar and lunar eclipses, unseasonable typhoons and storms, and drought. The *Ninnō* Sutra (T8, 832b-c) gives extraordinary heavenly phenomena, such as eclipses, changes among planets and stars, fires, floods, typhoons, drought, and foreign invasion or internal strife.

2. The three powerful enemies (Jap: *sanrui no gōteki*) are three types of people described in the *Kanji* (13th) chapter of the Lotus Sutra. They are: (1) lay people ignorant of Buddhism who denounce the votaries of the Lotus Sutra and attack them with swords and staves; (2) arrogant and cunning priests who slander the votaries; and (3) those who enjoy the respect of the general public and who, in fear of losing fame or profit, induce the authorities to persecute the votaries of the Lotus Sutra.

3. A sword made by the renowned swordsmith Munechika, housed at the Taiseki-ji, is said to be one of these two swords.

4. The Amakuni sword was made by a swordsmith of the same name during the Nara period. The Onikiri sword was a cherished possession of the Minamoto clan. The Yatsurugi sword is thought to be the sacred sword of the Yatsurugi Shrine, associated with the Atsuta shrine in present-day Nagoya.

5. Kan-chiang and his wife Mo-yeh forged two superb swords for the king of Wu; the swords were named after them.

6. T9, 19b.

46 HERITAGE OF THE ULTIMATE LAW OF LIFE

This letter, dated the eleventh day of the second month, 1272, was sent by Nichiren to Sairen-bō Nichijō, a Tendai priest who, for unexplained reasons, was also living in exile on Sado Island. Little is known of Sairen-bō; originally from Kyoto, he had studied at Mount Hiei before his exile. He was present at the Tsukahara debate, held at the Sammai-dō, Nichiren's residence at Tsukahara, on the sixteenth and seventeenth of the first month, 1272. In this debate Nichiren bested Pure Land, Shingon, and other priests from Sado and also from various provinces of northern Japan. He made several converts, among them Sairen-bō. Nichiren discusses this debate in detail in "On Various Actions of the Priest Nichiren" (*Shuju Ofurumai Gosho*): *Selected Writings of Nichiren* (New York, Columbia University Press, 1990). Sairen-bō was a highly educated priest to whom Nichiren sent several important letters. After leaving Sado, Sairen-bō is said to have founded a temple, the Honkoku-ji, in Shimoyama in the province of Kai. One source gives his death date as 1308.

I have just carefully read your letter. To reply, the ultimate law of life and death as transmitted from the Buddha to all living beings is Myōhō-renge-kyō. The five characters of Myōhō-renge-kyō were transferred from the two Buddhas inside the Treasure Tower, Shakyamuni and Tahō, to Bodhisattva Jōgyō, carrying on a heritage unbroken since the infinite past. *Myō* represents death, and *hō* represents life. Life and death are the two phases passed through by the entities of the Ten Worlds, the entities of all sentient beings which embody the law of cause and effect (*renge*).

T'ien-t'ai said, "You must realize that the interrelated actions and reactions of sentient beings and their environments all manifest the law of the simultaneity of cause and effect."[1] "Sentient beings and their environments" here means the reality of life and death. The law of simultaneity of cause and effect is clearly at work in everything that lives and dies.

The Great Teacher Dengyō said, "Birth and death are the mysterious workings of the life essence. The ultimate reality of life lies in existence and nonexistence."[2] No phenomena—heaven or earth, Yin or Yang, the sun or the moon, the five planets, or any life-condition from Hell to Buddhahood—are free from birth and death. Thus the life and death of all phenomena are simply the two phases of Myōhō-renge-kyō. In his *Maka Shikan*, T'ien-t'ai says, "The emergence of all things is the manifestation of their intrinsic nature, and their extinction, the withdrawal of that nature into the state of latency."[3] Shakyamuni and Tahō Buddhas, too, are the two phases of life and death.

Shakyamuni who attained enlightenment countless kalpas ago, the Lotus Sutra which leads all people to Buddhahood, and we ordinary human beings are in no way different or separate from each other. Therefore, to chant Myōhō-renge-kyō with this realization is to inherit the ultimate law of life and death. To carry on this heritage is the most important task for Nichiren's disciples, and that is precisely what it means to embrace the Lotus Sutra.

For one who summons up his faith and chants Nam-myoho-renge-kyo with the profound insight that now is the last moment of his life, the sutra proclaims: "After his death, a thousand Buddhas will extend their hands to free him from all fear and keep him from falling into the evil paths."[4] How can we possibly hold back our tears at the inexpressible joy of knowing that not just one or two, nor only one or two hundred, but as many as a thousand Buddhas will come to greet us with open arms!

One who does not have faith in the Lotus Sutra will instead surely find the wardens of hell confronting him and seizing him by the hands, just as the sutra warns, "After he dies, he will fall into the hell of incessant suffering."[5] How pitiful! The ten kings of hell[6] will then pass judgment on him, and the heavenly messengers[7] who have been with him since his birth will berate him for his evil deeds.

Just imagine that those thousand Buddhas extending their hands to all Nichiren's disciples who chant Nam-myoho-renge-kyo are like so many melons or moonflowers extending their slender vines. My disciples have been able to receive and embrace the Lotus Sutra by virtue of the strong ties they formed with this teaching in their past existences. They are certain to attain Buddhahood in the future. The heritage of the Lotus Sutra flows within the lives of those who never forsake it in any lifetime whatsoever—whether in the past, the present or the future. But those who disbelieve and slander the Lotus Sutra will "destroy the seeds for becoming a Buddha in this world."[8] Because they cut themselves off from the potential to attain enlightenment, they do not share the ultimate heritage of faith.

All disciples and believers of Nichiren should chant Nam-myoho-renge-kyo with one mind (*itai dōshin*), transcending all differences among themselves[9] to become as inseparable as fish and the water in which they swim. This spiritual bond is the basis for the universal transmission of the ultimate law of life and death. Herein lies the true goal of Nichiren's propagation. When you are so united, even the great hope for *kōsen-rufu* can be fulfilled without fail. But if any of Nichiren's disciples should disrupt the unity of *itai dōshin*, he will be like a castle-holder who destroys his own castle.

Nichiren has been trying to awaken all the people of Japan to faith in the Lotus Sutra so that they too can share the heritage and attain Buddhahood. But instead they attacked me time and again, and finally had me banished to this island. You have followed Nichiren, however, and met with sufferings as a result. It pains me deeply to think of your anguish. Gold can neither be burned by fire nor corroded or swept away by water, but iron is vulnerable to both. A wise person is like gold and a fool like iron. You are like pure gold because you embrace the "gold" of the Lotus Sutra. The Lotus Sutra reads in part, "Sumeru is the loftiest of all mountains. The Lotus Sutra is likewise the loftiest of all the sutras."[10] It also states, "[The good fortune of the believer] cannot be burned by fire or washed away by water."[11]

It must be ties of karma from the distant past that have destined you to become my disciple at a time like this. Shakyamuni and Tahō Buddhas certainly realize this truth. The sutra's statement, "In lifetime after lifetime they were always born together with their masters in the Buddha lands throughout the universe,"[12] cannot be false in any way.

How admirable that you have asked about the transmission of the ultimate law of life and death! No one has ever asked me such a question before. I have answered in complete detail in this letter, so I want you to take it deeply to heart. The important point is to carry out your practice, confident that Nam-myoho-renge-kyo is the very lifeblood which was transferred from Shakyamuni and Tahō to Bodhisattva Jōgyō.

The function of fire is to burn and give light. The function of water is to wash away filth. The winds blow away dust and breathe life into plants, animals, and human beings. The earth nourishes the grasses and trees, and heaven provides nourishing moisture. Myōhō–renge–kyō too works in all these ways. It is the cluster of blessings brought by the Bodhisattvas of the Earth. The Lotus Sutra says that Bodhisattva Jōgyō should now appear to propagate this teaching in the Latter Day of the Law, but has this actually happened? Whether or not Bodhisattva Jōgyō has already appeared in this world, Nichiren has at least made a start in propagating this teaching.

Be resolved to summon forth the great power of your faith, and chant Nam-myoho-renge-kyo with the prayer that your faith will be steadfast and correct at the moment of your death. Never seek any other way to inherit the ultimate law of birth and death and manifest it in your life. Only then will you realize that earthly desires are enlightenment and the sufferings of life and death are nirvana. Without the lifeblood of faith, it would be useless to embrace the Lotus Sutra.

I am always ready to clear up any further questions you may have.

With my deep respect,
Nichiren, the Śramaṇa of Japan

The eleventh day of the second month in the ninth year of Bun'ei (1272)

Notes

1. *Hokke Gengi* (T33, 772c).
2. *Tendai Hokkeshū Gozu Hōmon Yōsan* (DDZ5, 59).
3. *Maka Shikan* (T46, 56c).
4. Lotus Sutra (T9, 61c).
5. Lotus Sutra (T9, 15b).
6. The ten kings of hell are symbolic figures from popular religious tradition. They are described in the *Jizō Juō* Sutra (ZZ2b, 23, 4).
7. These messengers (Jap: *gushōjin*) are mentioned in the *Yaskushi Hongan* Sutra (T14, 407b). They are equated with the heavenly messengers Dōshō and Dōmyō, said to dwell on one's shoulders and to report every good and bad deed to the king of hell. Dōshō is female, dwells on the right shoulder, and reports evil deeds; Dōmyō is male, resides on the left shoulder, and reports good actions. They are mentioned in the *Kegon*

Sutra (T9, 680b) and elsewhere and are frequently referred to by Nichiren. *See* Letter 31. The Causal Law of Life.

    8. T9, 15b.

    9. Literally, "without any thought of self and others, this or that."

    10. T9, 54a.

    11. T9, 54c.

    12. T9, 26c.

47 ON THE TREASURE TOWER

Nichiren sent this letter, dated the thirteenth day of the third month, 1272, to his disciple Abutsu-bō Nittoku, more commonly known by his temple name Abutsu-bō; his original name was Endō Tamemori. One story has it that he was a samurai serving retired Emperor Juntoku and had accompanied him to Sado after he was exiled there after the Jōkyū Disturbance of 1221. It is more likely, however, that he was either a native of Sado Island, or had lived there for a long time. He went to Tsukahara to debate with Nichiren and was converted to Nichiren's teaching. He and his wife Sennichi-ama became loyal supporters of Nichiren and brought him food and other necessities for much of the time he was on the island. After Nichiren had retired to Mount Minobu, Abutsu-bō made three visits there despite his great age. He died in 1279 at the age of ninety-one.

"On the Treasure Tower" (*Hōtō Gosho*) is the alternative title of this letter. It is also known as *Abutsu-bō Gosho* (Letter to Abutsu-bō).

I have read your letter with great care. I have also received your offering to the Treasure Tower of one *kan*[1] of coins, polished rice, and other articles. This I have respectfully reported to the Gohonzon and to the Lotus Sutra. Please rest assured.

In your letter you ask: "What is signified by the Treasure Tower, with Tahō Buddha seated in it, appearing from within the earth?" The appearance of this bejeweled stupa [in the eleventh chapter of the Lotus Sutra] is of great importance. In the eighth volume of his *Hokke Mongu*, the Great Teacher T'ien-t'ai explained the appearance of the Treasure Tower. He stated that it had two distinct functions: to lend credence to the preceding chapters and to pave the way for the revelation to come.[2] Thus, the Treasure Tower appeared in order to verify the theoretical teaching and to introduce the essential teaching. To put

355

it another way, the closed Tower symbolizes the theoretical teaching and the open Tower, the essential teaching. This represents the two principles of object (*kyō*) and subject (*chi*), or reality and wisdom. However, this is extremely complex, so I will not go into further detail now. In essence, the appearance of the Treasure Tower indicates that the three groups of Shakyamuni's disciples[3] attained enlightenment only when they heard the Lotus Sutra and perceived the Treasure Tower within their own lives. Now Nichiren's disciples are doing the same. In the Latter Day of the Law, there is no Treasure Tower other than the figures of the men and women who embrace the Lotus Sutra. It follows, therefore, that those who chant Nam-myoho-renge-kyo, irrespective of social status, are themselves the Treasure Tower and likewise they themselves are Tahō Buddha. There is no Treasure Tower other than Myōhō-renge-kyō. The daimoku of the Lotus Sutra is the Treasure Tower, that is to say, the Treasure Tower is Nam-myoho-renge-kyo.

Now the entire body of Abutsu Shonin is composed of the five universal elements[4] of earth, water, fire, wind, and *kū* (space) These five elements are also the five characters of the daimoku. Therefore, Abutsu-bō is the Treasure Tower itself, and the Treasure Tower is Abutsu-bō himself. No other knowledge is purposeful. It is the Treasure Tower adorned with seven kinds of gems—listening to the true teaching, believing it, keeping the precepts, attaining peace of mind, practicing assiduously, unselfishly devoting oneself, and forever seeking self-improvement. You may think you offered gifts to the Treasure Tower of Tahō Buddha, but that is not so. You, yourself, are a true Buddha who possesses the three enlightened bodies.[5] You should chant Nam-myoho-renge-kyo with this conviction. Then, the place wherein you dwell and chant daimoku is the place of the Treasure Tower. The sutra reads: "Wherever one teaches the Lotus Sutra, this Treasure Tower of mine will rise and appear before him."[6] Faith like yours is so extremely rare that I will inscribe the Treasure Tower especially for you. You should never transfer it to anyone but your son. You should never show it to others unless they have steadfast faith. This is the reason for my advent in this world.

Abutsu-bō, you deserve to be called a leader of this northern province. Could it be that Bodhisattva Jyōgyō was reborn into this world as Abutsu-bō and visited me? How marvelous! It is beyond my power to understand why you have such pure faith. I will leave it to Bodhisattva Jōgyō when he appears, as he has the power to know these things. I am not saying all this without good reason. You and your wife should worship this Treasure Tower privately. I will explain more later.

With my deep respect,

Nichiren

The thirteenth day of the third month in the ninth year of Bun'ei (1272)

Notes

1. An old monetary unit consisting of 1,000 coins strung together on a cord.
2. T34, 113a.
3. Disciples of superior, intermediate, and inferior capacity.
4. The five basic elements that comprise the universe. By saying that Abutsu-bō has these components Nichiren defines the human being as a microcosm of the universe.
5. The Law or Dharma body, the bliss or reward body, and the manifested body. *See* Three Bodies in Glossary.
6. Lotus Sutra (T9, 36b).

Nichiren sent this letter to Sairen-bō from Ichinosawa on Sado Island on the seventeenth day of the fifth month, 1273. Sairen-bō was a highly educated priest who had been converted by Nichiren and in whom Nichiren placed considerable trust. See introduction to Letter 46.

Question: In the *Hōben* chapter of volume one of the Lotus Sutra is the passage:"The true entity of all phenomena can only be understood and shared between Buddhas. This reality consists of the appearance, nature . . . and their consistency from beginning to end."[1] What does this passage mean?

Answer: It means that all beings and their environments in any of the Ten Worlds, from Hell at the lowest to Buddhahood at the highest, are, without exception, the manifestations of Myōhō-renge-kyō. Where there is an environment, there is life within it. Miao-lo states, "Both life (*shōhō*) and its environment (*ehō*) always manifest Myōhō-renge-kyō."[2] He also states, "The true entity is invariably revealed in all phenomena, and all phenomena invariably possess the Ten Factors. The Ten Factors invariably function within the Ten Worlds, and the Ten Worlds invariably entail both life and its environment."[3] And, "Both the life and environment of Hell exist within the life of Buddha. On the other hand, the life and environment of Buddha do not transcend the lives of common mortals."[4] Such precise explanations leave no room for doubt. Thus, all life in the universe is clearly Myōhō-renge-kyō. Even the two Buddhas, Shakyamuni and Tahō, are the functions of Myōhō-renge-kyō who appeared to bestow its blessings upon humankind. They manifested themselves as the two

Buddhas and, seated together in the Treasure Tower, nodded in mutual agreement.

No one but Nichiren has ever revealed these teachings. T'ien-t'ai, Miao-lo, and Dengyō knew in their hearts but did not declare them aloud. There was reason for their silence: the Buddha had not entrusted them with this mission, the time had not yet come, and they had not been the Buddha's disciples from ages past. No one but Jōgyō, Muhengyō, and the other leaders of the Bodhisattvas of the Earth can appear during the first five hundred years of the Latter Day to spread the Law of Myōhō-renge-kyō. Only they are qualified to inscribe the object of worship which physically manifests the ceremony of the two Buddhas seated together in the Treasure Tower. This is because both the Law and the object of worship are the reality of *ichinen sanzen* revealed in the *Juryō* chapter of the essential teaching.

The two Buddhas, Shakyamuni and Tahō, are merely functions of the true Buddha, while Myōhō-renge-kyō actually is the true Buddha. The sutra explains this as "the Tathagata's secret and his mystic power."[5] The "secret" refers to the entity of the Buddha's three bodies and the "mystic power" to their functions. The entity is the true Buddha and the function, a provisional Buddha. The common mortal is the entity of the three bodies, or the true Buddha. The Buddha is the function of the three bodies, or a provisional Buddha. Shakyamuni is thought to have possessed the three virtues of sovereign, teacher, and parent for the sake of us common mortals, but on the contrary, it is the common mortal who endowed him with the three virtues.

T'ien-t'ai explains the Tathagata as follows: "*Nyorai* is the title of the Buddhas of the ten directions and three existences, of the two Buddhas[6] and the three Buddhas,[7] and of all the Buddhas, true and provisional."[8] Here the "true Buddha" is the common mortal, whereas "provisional Buddhas" means the Buddha. Nevertheless, there is a clear distinction between a Buddha and a common mortal, in that a common mortal is deluded while a Buddha is enlightened. The common mortal fails to realize that he himself possesses both the entity and the function of the Buddha's three bodies.

"All phenomena" in the sutra refers to the Ten Worlds, and the "true entity"[9] is what permeates the Ten Worlds. Reality[9] is another expression for Myōhō-renge-kyō; hence Myōhō-renge-kyō is manifest in all phenomena. Hell appears hellish; that is the reality of Hell. When Hungry Ghosts emerge, the reality of Hell is no longer present. A Buddha exhibits the reality of a Buddha, and a common mortal, that of a common mortal. All phenomena are themselves manifestations of Myōhō-renge-kyō. This is the meaning of "all phenomena reveal the true entity." T'ien-t'ai states, "The profound principle of 'true entity' is the original law of Myōhō-renge-kyō,"[10] thus identifying the phrase "true entity" with the theoretical teaching and "the original law of Myōhō-renge-kyō" with the essential teaching. You should ponder this passage deep in your heart.

Although not worthy of the honor, Nichiren was nevertheless the first to spread the Mystic Law entrusted to Bodhisattva Jōgyō for propagation in the Latter Day of the Law. Nichiren was also the first to inscribe the Gohonzon, which is the embodiment of the Buddha from the remote past as revealed in the *Juryō* chapter of the essential teaching, of Tahō Buddha who appeared when the *Hōtō* chapter of the theoretical teaching was preached, and the Bodhisattvas of the Earth who emerged with the *Yujutsu* chapter. No matter how people may hate Nichiren, they cannot possibly alter the fact of his enlightenment.

To have exiled Nichiren to this remote island is therefore a sin that can never be expiated, even with the passing of countless kalpas. A passage from the *Hiyu* chapter reads, "Not even a kalpa would be time enough to explain the full gravity of this sin."[11] On the other hand, not even the wisdom of the Buddha can fathom the blessings one will obtain by giving alms to Nichiren and by becoming his disciple. The *Yakuō* chapter reads, "Not even with the Buddha's wisdom can one measure these benefits."[12]

Nichiren alone began to carry out the task of the Bodhisattvas of the Earth. He may even be one of them. If Nichiren should be a Bodhisattva of the Earth, then so must his disciples. The *Hosshi* chapter states, "If there is someone, whether man or woman, who secretly teaches to one person even a single phrase of the Lotus Sutra, let it be known that he is the envoy of the Buddha, sent to carry out the Buddha's work."[13] Who else but us can this possibly refer to?

When one is praised highly by others, he feels there is no hardship he cannot bear. Such is the courage which springs from words of praise. The votary born in the Latter Day of the Law who propagates the Lotus Sutra will encounter the three powerful enemies, who will cause him to be exiled and even sentence him to death. Yet Shakyamuni Buddha will enfold in his robe of mercy those who nonetheless persevere in propagating. All gods will make them offerings, support them with their shoulders, and carry them on their backs. They possess supreme good fortune and qualify as leaders of all mankind. Thus extolled by Shakyamuni Buddha, Tahō Buddha and all of the other Buddhas and bodhisattvas, the seven ranks of heavenly gods and five ranks of earthly gods,[14] Kishimojin and her ten daughters, the Four Heavenly Kings, Bonten, Taishaku, King Emma, the gods of the waters and winds, the gods of the seas and mountains, Dainichi Buddha, Bodhisattvas Fugen and Monju and the gods of the sun and the moon, Nichiren has been able to endure countless harsh trials. When praised, one does not consider his personal risk, and when criticized, he can recklessly cause his own ruin. Such is the way of common mortals.

No matter what, maintain your faith as a votary of the Lotus Sutra, and forever exert yourself as Nichiren's disciple. If you are of the same mind as Nichiren, you must be a Bodhisattva of the Earth. And since you are a Bodhisattva of the Earth, there is not the slightest doubt that you have been a disciple of the Buddha from the remotest past. The *Yujutsu* chapter states, "I have taught these people since the remotest past."[15] There should be no discrimination among those who propagate the five characters of Myōhō-renge-kyō in the Latter Day of the Law, be they men or women. Were they not Bodhisattvas of the Earth, they could not chant the daimoku. Only I, Nichiren, at first chanted Nam-myoho-renge-kyo, but then two, three and a hundred followed, chanting and teaching others. Likewise, propagation will unfold this way in the future. Doesn't this signify "emerging from the earth"? At the time of *kōsen-rufu*, the entire Japanese nation will chant Nam-myoho-renge-kyo, as surely as an arrow aimed at the earth cannot miss the target.

But now you must build your reputation as a votary of the Lotus Sutra and devote yourself to it. Shakyamuni Buddha and Tahō Buddha, seated in the Treasure Tower in the air, surrounded by all other Buddhas and bodhisattvas, nodded in agreement. What they decided upon was solely for the perpetuation of the True Law throughout the Latter Day. Tahō Buddha had offered Shakyamuni Buddha a place beside him, and when they unfurled the banner of Myōhō-renge-kyō, the two leaders of the entire multitude made their decision together. Could there have been anything false in their decision? Their ultimate purpose in meeting was to provide a way for all of us ordinary people to attain Buddhahood.

Although I was not at that ceremony, in looking at the sutra, this is crystal-clear. On the other hand, I may have been at the ceremony, but since I am a common mortal, it is beyond my power to know the past.

There is no doubt, however, that in the present life I am the votary of the Lotus Sutra, and that in the future I will therefore reach the seat of enlightenment. Judging the past from this point of view, I must have been at the ceremony in the air. There can be no discontinuity between past, present, and future.

Because I view things this way, I feel immeasurable delight even though I am now an exile. Joy as well as sorrow brings us to tears. Tears express our feeling for both blessings and misfortune. The one thousand arhats shed tears in memory of the Buddha, and in tears Bodhisattva Monju chanted Myōhō-renge-kyō. From among those one thousand arhats, the venerable Ānanda replied in tears, "Thus I heard."[16] Thereupon the tears of all the others fell, wetting their ink-stones, and they wrote "Myōhō-renge-kyō" followed by "Thus I heard." I, Nichiren, now feel exactly as they did. I am now in exile because I spread the teaching of Myōhō-renge-kyō. I spread this teaching because I, too, "heard thus": Shakyamuni Buddha and Tahō Buddha left Myōhō-renge-kyō for the Japanese and all people in the future.

I cannot hold back my tears when I think of the great persecution confronting me now, or when I think of the joy of attaining Buddhahood in the future. Birds cry, but never shed tears. I, Nichiren, do not cry, but my tears flow ceaselessly. I shed my tears not for worldly affairs but solely for the sake of the Lotus Sutra. So indeed, they must be tears of amṛta.[17] The Nirvana Sutra states that while the tears one sheds throughout his many existences on the death of his parents, brothers, sisters, wives, children, and followers may surpass the quantity of water in all the seas, he weeps not a drop for Buddhism.[18] One becomes a votary of the Lotus Sutra by virtue of his practice in past existences. It is karmic relationships that determine which among so many of the same kind of trees are made into images of Buddha. It is also because of karma that some Buddhas are born as provisional ones.

In this letter, I have written my most important teachings. Grasp their meaning and make them part of your life. Believe in the Gohonzon, the supreme object of worship in the world. Forge strong faith and receive the protection of Shakyamuni, Tahō and all the other Buddhas. Exert yourself in the two ways of practice and study. Without practice and study, there can be no Buddhism. You must not only persevere yourself; you must also teach others. Both practice and study arise from faith. Teach others to the best of your ability, even if only a single sentence or phrase. Nam-myoho-renge-kyo, Nam-myoho-renge-kyo.

With my deep respect,
Nichiren

The seventeenth day of the fifth month

POSTSCRIPT:

I have already passed on to you many of my important teachings. Those I have revealed to you in this letter are especially important. Is there not a mystic bond between us? Are you not the embodiment of one of the Four Bodhisattvas of the Earth headed by Jōgyō who led bodhisattvas equal in number to the sands of the sixty thousand Ganges rivers? There must be some profound reason for our relationship. I have given you some of the most important teachings relating to my own life and practice. Nichiren may be one of the countless Bodhisattvas of the Earth, for I have been chanting Nam-myoho-renge-kyo out of my desire to guide all the men and women in Japan. Hence the phrase of the sutra:"[Among the bodhisattvas are four who led the entire multitude:] The first is called Jōgyō; [the second, Muhengyō; the third, Jyōgyō; and the fourth, Anryūgyō.] They are the four highest leaders."[19] Our deep relationship in the past has made you one of my disciples. By all means keep these matters to yourself. Nichiren has herein committed to writing the teachings of his own enlightenment. I will end here.

Notes

1. T9, 5c.
2. *Hokke Mongu Ki* (T34, 360a).
3. *Kongōbei Ron* (T46, 785c).
4. *Kongōbei Ron* (T46, 781a). The renderings of the above two quotations are not precise translations, but convey the sense of the original.
5. Lotus Sutra (T9, 42b).
6. The two Buddhas indicate a Buddha in his true, original state (the Law or

Dharma body, *hosshin*) and the form in which he appears in the world to save people (the manifested body, *ōjin*).

7. This refers to the three bodies of the Buddha. *See* Three Bodies in Glossary.

8. *Hokke Mongu* (T34, 127c).

9. Reality is another translation for the "true entity" of all phenomena.

10. Source unknown.

11. T9, 16a.

12. T9, 54b.

13. T9, 30c.

14. According to Japanese mythology, these are the seven ranks of heavenly gods and five ranks of earthly gods that existed before the time of the first emperor, Jimmu.

15. T9, 41b.

16. A phrase that commonly opens many sutras. The "I" indicates the person who recites what the Buddha taught, so that it might be put into the sutra.

17. According to ancient Indian legend, *amṛta* was the sweet-tasting drink of immortality.

18. The exact passage to which Nichiren is referring has not been determined.

19. T9, 40a.

49 BESTOWAL OF THE MANDALA OF THE MYSTIC LAW

Neither the date of composition nor the name of the recipient of this letter is known; however, the text indicates that it was written to a woman, and the general assumption is that the recipient was Sennichi-ama, the wife of Abutsu-bō. Both Abutsu-bō and his wife were loyal supporters of Nichiren during his stay on Sado, and they supplied him with food and other necessities during his exile.

~~~~~~

I am bestowing upon you the Gohonzon of Myōhō-renge-kyō. Though [the daimoku of] this mandala is written in but five or seven characters,[1] it is the teacher of all Buddhas throughout the three existences and the seal that guarantees the enlightenment of all women. It will be a lamp in the darkness of the road to the next world and a fine horse to carry you over the mountains of death. It is like the sun and the moon in the heavens or Mount Sumeru on earth. It is a ship to ferry people over the sea of suffering. It is the teacher who leads all people to enlightenment. This mandala has never yet been revealed or propagated anywhere in the world in the more than 2,220 years since the Buddha's passing.

[The prescription of] medicine differs according to the illness. Ordinary medicine will help a slight ailment, but for grave illnesses, elixir should be used. During the 2,220 or more years since the Buddha's death, the people's illnesses, that is, their illusions and negative karma, were not serious, and a succession of learned priests appeared in order to act as physicians and dispense medicine appropriately as these illnesses required. These learned priests came from the

Kusha, Jōjitsu, Ritsu, Hossō, Sanron, Shingon, Kegon, Tendai, Jōdo, and Zen sects. Each of these sects prescribed its own medicine. For example, the Kegon sect set forth the principle of the six forms and the ten mysteries,[2] the Sanron sect advocated the middle path of the eight negations,[3] the Hossō sect stressed the perception that all phenomena derive from consciousness only,[4] the Ritsu sect upheld the two hundred and fifty precepts,[5] the Jōdo sect invoked the name of Amida Buddha, the Zen sect expounded the attainment of Buddhahood by perceiving one's true nature, the Shingon sect propounded the meditation on the five elements,[6] and the Tendai sect established the theory of *ichinen sanzen*.

Now, however, we have entered the Latter Day of the Law, and the medicines of these various sects no longer cure the people's illnesses. Moreover, all the Japanese have become *icchantika* and people of grave slander. Their offense is even worse than that of killing one's father or mother, fomenting a rebellion, or injuring a Buddha. Japan is filled with individuals whose offenses exceed even those of one who were to singlehandedly remove the eyes of all the human beings of a major world system, or raze all temples and stupas in the worlds of the ten directions. Consequently, the heavenly deities glare down furiously upon our nation day after day while the earthly deities tremble in continual rage. Nevertheless, all the people of our day believe themselves to be without fault, and none doubts that he will be reborn in the Pure Land and attain enlightenment.

The blind cannot see or comprehend the shining sun, and someone who is sound asleep will not even feel an earthquake reverberating like a great drum. So too it is with all the people of Japan [who do not realize their own offenses]. The offenses committed by the men are heavier than those committed by the women. In like manner, the nuns' offenses are heavier than the laymen's and the priests' more serious than the nuns.' Among the priests, the offenses of those who observe the precepts are worse than those of the priests who violate them, and those of the learned priests are graver still.[7] Such priests are like those with white leprosy among lepers, and among those with white leprosy, the most malignant.

Then, what great physician or what efficacious medicine can cure the illnesses of all people in the Latter Day of the Law? They cannot be cured by the mudras and mantras of Dainichi Buddha, the forty-eight vows of Amida Buddha,[8] or the twelve great vows of Yakushi Buddha,[9] not even his pledge to "heal all ills." Not only do such medicines fail to cure these illnesses; they aggravate them all the more.

The Lord Shakyamuni assembled Tahō Buddha as well as all the other Buddhas, who were his own emanations, from throughout the ten directions and left one great medicine—the five characters of Myōhō-renge-kyō—for the people of the Latter Day of the Law. He refused to entrust it to any of the bodhisattvas such as Hōe, Kudokurin,[10] Kongōsatta,[11] Fugen, Monju, Yakuō, and Kannon, let alone to Mahākāśyapa, Śāriputra [or any other man of the two vehicles]. Rather, there were four great bodhisattvas, including Jōgyō, who had been disciples of Shakyamuni Buddha since *gohyaku-jintengō*. Not even for a moment had they ever forgotten the Buddha. Shakyamuni summoned these bodhisattvas and transferred Myōhō-renge-kyō to them.

A woman who takes this efficacious medicine will be surrounded and protected by these four great bodhisattvas at all times. When she rises to her feet, so will the bodhisattvas, and when she walks along the road, they will also do the same. She and they will be as inseparable as a body and its shadow, as fish and water, as a voice and its echo, or as the moon and its light. Should these four great bodhisattvas desert the woman who chants Nam-myoho-renge-kyo, they would incur the wrath of Shakyamuni, Tahō, and all the other Buddhas of the ten directions. You may be certain that their offense would be greater than even that of Devadatta, their falsehood more terrible than Kokālika's.[12] How reassuring! Nam-myoho-renge-kyo, Nam-myoho-renge-kyo.

Nichiren

Notes

1. The five characters *myō, hō, ren, ge, kyō* are often used synonymously by Nichiren with the seven characters: Nam (namu)-myo-ho-renge-kyo.

2. The six forms and ten mysteries of the Kegon are an analysis of the world from the standpoints of both difference and identity. The six forms are the six integral aspects of all things: the whole containing the parts, the interdependency of the parts making the whole, the unity of the parts in the whole, the variety of the parts, the variety making the whole, and the identity of the parts. *Kegon Gokyō Shō* (T45, 507c). The ten mysteries are the ten characteristics of the interrelationship of all phenomena. They are described in the *Kegon Ichijō Jūgenmon* (T45, 515b).

3. Eight expressions of negation in Nāgārjuna's *Chū Ron* (T30, 1b): "Neither birth

nor extinction, neither cessation nor permanence, neither uniformity nor diversity, neither coming nor going." The doctrine of the eight negations indicates that the Middle Way or true nature of all phenomena cannot be defined as either existence or nonexistence; it is nonsubstantial (*kū*) and transcends all duality.

4. The perception that all phenomena arise from the *ālaya* consciousness.

5. Rules of conduct to be observed by fully ordained monks of Hinayana Buddhism.

6. An esoteric form of meditation intended to let one realize that self and environment are composed of the five elements earth, water, fire, wind, and space; that the five parts of the body, namely crown, face, chest, abdomen, and knees, are governed by the five syllables of the esoteric mantra, *Avarahakha*; and that one's own life is ultimately one with the five Buddhas who are embodiments of the five aspects of Dainichi Buddha's wisdom. They are described in *Dainichi Kyō Sho* (T39, 727c).

7. In this passage Nichiren is saying that the more highly respected the perpetrator, the heavier in effect the offense will be. Men had the greater influence in Japanese society, so their errors with respect to Buddhism made a heavier impact than the same errors committed by women. Similarly, the clergy carried more influence than the laity, and among the clergy, those priests who observed the precepts and were well learned commanded the highest respect; thus their slanders had a graver influence on society as a whole than anyone else's.

8. Vows made by Amida Buddha while still engaged in bodhisattva practice as Bodhisattva Hōzō, as described in the *Muryōju* Sutra (T12, 267c ff.). Among these vows, the eighteenth vow—that all who place their trust in Amida Buddha shall obtain rebirth in the Pure Land—is the one most emphasized by the Pure Land sect.

9. The twelve great vows are the vows that Yakushi Buddha made as a bodhisattva to cure all illnesses and lead all people to enlightenment. *Yakushi Rurikō Hongan Kudoku* Sutra (T14, 405a-b).

10. Hōe and Kudokurin are two of the four major bodhisattvas mentioned in the *Kegon* Sutra (T10, 81a; 99c).

11. Kongōsatta (Skt: Vajrasattva) is traditionally the second of the first eight patriarchs of the Shingon sect. He is said to have received the esoteric teaching directly from Dainichi Buddha.

12. Kokālika was a member of the Shakya tribe and an enemy of Shakyamuni. He fell under Devadatta's influence and slandered Śāriputra and Maudgalyāyana. He is said to have fallen into hell alive. His story appears in various sources; the exact source that Nichiren used cannot be traced.

50 LETTER TO ICHINOSAWA NYŪDŌ

Nichiren wrote this letter at Minobu on the eighth day of the fifth month, 1275. The letter was addressed to Ichinosawa Nyūdō's wife, Nichigaku, but since the letter contains cautionary remarks addressed to her husband, it has come to be known by the title it now bears, "Letter to Ichinosawa Nyūdō." In the first month of 1272 Nichiren had triumphed in a debate with representatives of various sects of Buddhism, which was held at the dilapidated building he lived in at Tsukahara. In the fourth month he was able to move to the home of Ichinosawa Nyūdō, where he lived the remaining two years of his stay on Sado. Nichiren was successful in converting Nichigaku, the wife, but he had more problems in converting Ichinosawa himself, who remained attached to Pure Land teachings.

※

In the first year of the Kōchō era (1261), when the reverse marker of Jupiter was in the sector of the sky with the cyclical sign *kanoto-tori*, on the twelfth day of the fifth month, I incurred the displeasure of the government authorities and was exiled to the village of Itō in the province of Izu. It is the place where the subcommander of the Imperial Guard Minamoto no Yoritomo[1] was banished. However, before long, in the third year of the Kōchō era (1263), the year with the cyclical sign *mizunoto-i*, on the twenty-second day of the second month, I was pardoned and allowed to return to Kamakura.

Then, in the eighth year of the Bun'ei era (1271), the year with the cyclical sign *kanoto-hitsuji*, on the twelfth day of the ninth month, I once more incurred the displeasure of the government and was summarily sentenced to have my head cut off. Because of certain circumstances, the execution was temporarily postponed. Instead, I was placed in the custody of the former governor of Musashi,[2] who held

369

the island province of Sado in the north as part of his feudal domain. In accordance with the designs of his retainers, I was sent to that island.

The inhabitants of the island are a wild and barbarous lot, with no understanding of the law of cause and effect. Needless to say, they treated me very roughly. Nevertheless, I did not harbor the slightest resentment against them. The reason is this: Even the ruler of the country of Japan, the lord of Sagami,[3] whom one would expect to have at least some understanding of principles, failed to investigate the circumstances of my case, though I was in fact attempting to aid the nation. Instead, contrary to all reason and justice, he had me condemned to death. Therefore, even the good men among his subjects were not to be counted upon, and so there was surely no point in hating the evil ones.

Since the time I began declaring this teaching, I have resolved to dedicate my life to the Lotus Sutra and to spread my name in the pure lands of the Buddhas of the worlds in the ten directions. Hung Yen took the liver of his dead lord, Duke Yi of Wei, cut open his own stomach and inserted the liver before he died.[4] Yü Jang, because his lord, Chih Po, had suffered disgrace, fell on his sword to avenge the wrong.[5] These men went to such lengths to repay what was no more than a worldly debt of gratitude. The reason why people continue to transmigrate through the six paths for countless kalpas without ever being able to attain Buddhahood is because they begrudge their bodies and do not lay down their lives for the sake of the Lotus Sutra.

The bodhisattva called Kiken[6] for a period of twelve hundred years burned his own body as an offering to the Buddha Pure Bright Excellence of Sun and Moon, and for seventy-two thousand years he burned his arms as an offering to the Lotus Sutra, after which he was reborn as Bodhisattva Yakuō. Bodhisattva Fukyō over a period of many kalpas suffered abuse and ridicule and was attacked with sticks and staves, tiles and rocks, all for the sake of the Lotus Sutra. But was he not reborn as Shakyamuni Buddha? Thus we can see that the path to Buddhahood requires different forms of practice depending upon the age.

In our present day, the Lotus Sutra is of course supreme as it was in the past. And yet, because the way of practicing it differs from age to age, even if one were to retire to the mountain forests and read and recite it, or live in the villages and expound its doctrines, or observe all the various precepts or even burn one's arms as an offering, he would nevertheless fail to attain Buddhahood.

It would seem as though the teachings of Buddhism are now flourishing in Japan. And yet there is something strange in regard to these teachings, though people are unaware of it. They are like insects that unwittingly fly into a flame, or birds that enter the mouth of a serpent.

The teachers of the Shingon sect and the adherents of the Kegon, Hossō, Sanron, Zen, Pure Land, and Ritsu sects all believe that they have grasped the Law and freed themselves from the sufferings of birth and death. But the founders who first established these sects failed to discern the true meaning of the sutras upon which they based their teachings. They proceeded only in a shallow manner, employing the sutras in a way that fitted with their own ideas. In doing so, they went against the Lotus Sutra, which means that their teachings were not in accord with the true intention of the Buddha. They were unaware of this, however, and as they proceeded to propagate their doctrines, both the rulers of the nation and the common people came to believe in them. In addition, these doctrines spread to other countries, and many years have gone by since they were first propagated. As a result, the scholars of this latter age, unaware that the founders of these sects were in error, look up to those who practice and propagate their teachings as men of wisdom.

If the source is muddy, the stream will not flow clear; if the body is bent, the shadow will not stand upright. Shan-wu-wei and the others who founded the Shingon sect were already destined for hell. Perhaps among them there were some who repented in time and hence managed to avoid falling into hell. Or perhaps there were some who merely propagated the teachings of their own sutras and neither praised nor attacked the Lotus Sutra, and thus, though they could not free themselves from the sufferings of birth and death, were nevertheless able to avoid falling into the evil paths. But the people of this latter age are not aware of these matters, and instead all alike put their faith in these teachings. They are like people who board a damaged vessel and set out upon the great sea, or like people who, drunk with wine, lie down to sleep in the midst of a fire.

When I, Nichiren, perceived this state of affairs, I immediately aroused the aspiration for enlightenment [in order to save them] and began to speak out regarding the matter. I was aware from the beginning that, no matter how I addressed them, the people of the time would probably not believe me, and that I would on the contrary most likely be sentenced to exile or execution.

The nation of Japan today has turned its back on the Lotus Sutra and cast aside Shakyamuni Buddha. For that reason, its people are not only bound to fall into the great citadel of the Avīci Hell in their next existence, but they will surely encounter great troubles in their present existence as well. That is to say, invaders will come from a foreign land, and everyone, from the ruler on down to the common people, will lament with a single voice.

To illustrate, if a thousand brothers join together to slay their parent, the burden of guilt will not be divided among them in a thousand portions. Rather each and every one of the brothers must [receive the full karmic retribution, and all alike will] fall into the great citadel of the hell of incessant suffering, to remain there for the space of a kalpa. And the same is true of [the people of] this country of Japan.

Since the far-off time of *gohyaku-jintengō*, this *sahā* world has been the domain of Shakyamuni Buddha, the lord of teachings. Of the vast earth, the skies, the mountains and seas, the plants and trees, there is not a single portion that belongs to any other Buddha. And all the living beings within it are likewise the children of Shakyamuni.

For example, it is said that at the beginning of a Kalpa of Formation,[7] the god Bonten descends from on high and gives birth to the various beings who inhabit the six paths.[8] Just as Bonten is then the parent of all those beings, in the same way Shakyamuni Buddha is the parent of all living beings in this world. Moreover, the Lord Buddha Shakyamuni is the enlightened teacher for all the living beings in this country of ours. It is thanks to our teacher that we can understand who our parents are. It is owing to Shakyamuni that we can distinguish black from white.

But because of the teachings of men like Shan-tao[9] and Hōnen, who have been possessed by the Devil of the Sixth Heaven, the practitioners of the Nembutsu proceed to build Amida halls throughout the country. They build Amida halls in each district, each village, and each hamlet, or the general populace build Amida halls in their own houses, or people make painted or wooden images of Amida Buddha to put up in their houses and dwellings. The name of Amida is on everyone's lips, some chanting it in a loud voice, some chanting it ten thousand times, some chanting it sixty thousand times [a day]. And persons with a degree of wisdom make haste to encourage them in these practices. This is like adding dried grass to a fire, or loosing winds to blow upon the waters and stir them up.

Of the inhabitants of this country, there is not one who is not a disciple and subject of the Lord Shakyamuni. If a person does not paint or carve a single image of Amida or of any Buddha other than

Shakyamuni, or does not chant Amida's name, then, although he may be an evil person, he still has not clearly shown that he has rejected Shakyamuni Buddha. But all those persons who worship Amida Buddha exclusively have already clearly shown that they have rejected Shakyamuni Buddha. Those who chant the vain and profitless formula of the Nembutsu—they are the truly evil ones!

This Buddha, who is neither father nor mother to them, nor sovereign nor teacher, they treat with the kind of tenderness one might show to a beloved wife. At the same time, they cast aside Shakyamuni, our real sovereign, parent, and enlightened teacher, and fail to open their mouths to recite the Lotus Sutra, which is like a wet nurse to us. How can they be called anything but unfilial?

And these unfilial persons number not just one or two, a hundred or a thousand; they include not just the inhabitants of one or two provinces. From the ruler on down to the common people, everyone in the entire land of Japan, without a single exception, is guilty of committing three of the cardinal sins![10]

As a result, the sun and moon change color and glare down on this, the earth shakes and heaves in anger, great comets fill the sky, and huge fires break out all over the land. Yet these persons fail to perceive their error and instead take pride in what they do, saying, "We unceasingly recite the Nembutsu, and in addition we build Amida halls and pay honor to Amida Buddha!"

Such ways may seem wise, but in fact they are worthless. Suppose there is a young couple. The husband is so in love with his wife, and the wife thinks so tenderly of her husband, that they completely forget about their parents. As a result, the parents go about in thin clothing, while the bedroom of the young couple is warm and snug. The parents have nothing to eat, while the young couple's stomachs are full. Such young people are committing the worst kind of unfilial conduct, and yet they fail to see that they are doing wrong. And a wife who would deliberately turn her back on her own mother, a husband who would go against his own father—are they not guilty of an even graver offense?

Amida Buddha dwells in a region ten billion Buddha lands away and has not the slightest connection with this *sahā* world. However one may claim [that such a conneciton exists], there is no basis for it. It is like trying to mate a horse with an ox, or a monkey with a dog!

I, Nichiren, am the only person who is aware of this. If, begrudging my life, I should refrain from speaking out, I would not only be failing to repay the debt of gratitude I owe to my country, but I would also be acting as the enemy of the Lord Buddha Shakyamuni. On the other hand, I knew from the outset that if I set aside my fears and declared matters exactly as they are, I would be sentenced to death. And even if I should escape the death penalty, I would surely be condemned to exile. So great is the debt of gratitude I owe the Buddha, however, that I have not let myself be intimidated by others but have spoken out on these matters.

Just as I anticipated, I was exiled no less than twice. During the second of these sentences, in the summer of the ninth year of the Bun'ei era (1272), I was sent to a place called Ichinosawa in Ishida village in the province of Sado. The headman and his men in the region to which I had been assigned, in both official and unofficial matters, treated me with greater malice than if I had been a lifelong enemy of their parents or a foe from some previous existence. But the nyūdō of the lodgings[11] where I was put up, as well as his wife and servants, though they seemed fearful at first, privately came to look on me with pity, perhaps because of some bond formed between us in a previous existence.

The rations of food that I received from the headman were very scanty. And since I had a number of disciples with me, we often had no more than two or three mouthfuls of rice to a person. Sometimes we portioned out the food on square trays made of bark, and sometimes we simply received it in the palms of our hands and ate it then and there. The master of the house in private treated us with compassion. Though outwardly he appeared to be fearful of the authorities, at heart he had great pity for us, something that I will never forget in any future lifetime. At that time, he meant more to me than the very parents who gave me birth. However great the obligations I incurred with respect to him, I must endeavor to somehow repay them. Even more, I must not fail to do what I had promised him.

The nyūdō was deeply concerned at heart about the life to come, and had for a long time devoted himself to chanting the Nembutsu. Moreover, he had constructed an Amida hall and dedicated his lands in offering to Amida Buddha. He was also afraid of how the steward of the area[12] might react, and so he did not come forward and take faith in the Lotus Sutra. From his point of view, this was probably the most reasonable course to take. But at the same time, he will without doubt fall into the great citadel of the hell of incessant suffering. I had thought, for example, that even if I were to send him a copy of the

Lotus Sutra, he would not be willing to abandon the practice of the Nembutsu out of his fear of worldly opinion, and so it would simply be like adding water to fire. There was no doubt but that the flood of his slander of the Law would extinguish the small flame of his faith in the Lotus Sutra. And if he were to fall into hell, I, Nichiren, would in turn be to blame. Thus, while asking myself anxiously again and again what ought to be done, I have so far not sent him a copy of the Lotus Sutra.

[In the midst of all this,] I received word that the copy of the Lotus Sutra that I had earlier intended to send him had been destroyed in a fire in Kamakura. More than ever it seemed as though the *nyūdō* had no connection with the Lotus Sutra, and I wondered at myself for ever having promised to send him a copy.

Moreover, when the nun of Kamakura[13] was leaving Sado to return home, she found herself in difficulty for money to cover her journey. Although reluctant to do so, I asked the *nyūdō* to provide for her expenses, though I regret having made such a request. I could of course simply return the sum of money to him along with interest. But my disciples point out that I would still be failing to keep my original promise. I am faced with difficulties any way I turn, and yet I am afraid that people may think I am given to irresponsible and deceitful behavior. Therefore I feel I have no choice but to send a copy of the entire Lotus Sutra in ten volumes.[14] Since the *nyūdō's* grandmother seems at heart to be more deeply drawn to the sutra than does the *nyūdō* himself, I entrust it to you for her sake.

The things I, Nichiren, say sound like the words of a fool, and so no one heeds them. Nevertheless, I must note that in the tenth month of the eleventh year of the Bun'ei era (1274), cyclical sign *kinoe-inu*, when the kingdom of the Mongols launched an attack on Tsukushi,[15] the defenders of the island of Tsushima held fast, but Sō,[16] the vice governor of Tsushima, fled. As a result, the Mongols were able to attack the peasants and other commoners, killing or taking prisoners among the men, and herding the women together and tying them by the hands to their ships or taking them prisoner. Not a single person escaped.

In the attack on the island of Iki the same thing happened. And when the Mongol ships pressed on [to Tsukushi], the magistrate[17] who was in charge of the area, the former governor of Buzen, fled in defeat. Several hundred of the Matsuratō men[18] were struck down or taken prisoner, and the population of one coastal village after another suffered the same fate as the people of Iki and Tsushima.

And when the Mongols attack the next time, what will it be like? When thousands and millions of fighting men from their country come swarming and pressing upon Japan, what will happen?

Their forces in the north will first of all attack the island of Sado. In no time at all, they will kill the stewards and constables of the area. And when the common people attempt to flee to the northern mountains, they will be killed or taken prisoner, or will perish in the mountains.

We must stop to consider why such terrible things should occur. The reason, as I stated earlier, is that every single person in this country has committed three of the cardinal sins. Therefore, Bonten, Taishaku, the gods of the sun and moon and the Four Heavenly Kings have entered into the body of the Mongol ruler and are causing him to chastise our nation.

I, Nichiren, may be a fool, but, having declared myself to be the messenger of Shakyamuni Buddha and the votary of the Lotus Sutra, it is nothing short of amazing that my words go unheeded. And because of this failure, the nation now faces ruin. Not only are my words not heeded, but I have been driven out of province after province, been dragged about, attacked and beaten, or sent into exile, and my disciples have been killed or had their lands taken away from them.

If someone were to mete out such treatment to an actual messenger of his parents, could that person's actions possibly be condoned? And I, Nichiren, am parent to all the people of Japan, I am their sovereign, I am their enlightened teacher! Should they turn against one like me?

It is absolutely certain that those who chant the Nembutsu are destined to fall into the hell of incessant suffering. You may depend on it!

When the Mongols come to make their assault, what will you do? Even if you should put this copy of the Lotus Sutra on your head or hang it around your neck and flee to the northern mountains, the fact remains that over a period of many years you have given support to the Nembutsu believers and have recited the Nembutsu yourself, and in doing so have made yourself the enemy of Shakyamuni Buddha and of the Lotus Sutra.

If at that time you should lose your life, you must bear no resentment toward the Lotus Sutra. And when you are brought before King Emma in his palace, what will you say? At that time, though you may feel foolish in saying so, you will probably declare that you are a follower of Nichiren.

But enough of that. As for this copy of the Lotus Sutra that I am sending, you should ask Gakujō-bō[19] to read it for you regularly. But whatever anyone may say, you must not allow any of the Nembutsu priests, Shingon teachers, or observers of the precepts[20] to look at it. And though people may claim to be disciples of Nichiren, if they do not possess some proof of that fact from my hand, you must not trust them.

With my deep respect,
Nichiren

The eighth day of the fifth month

Notes

1. Minamoto no Yoritomo (1147–1199) was the founder of the Kamakura shogunate, the first military government in Japan. In 1159 he joined his father, Yoshitomo (1123–1160) in an attempt to overthrow the powerful warrior Taira no Kiyomori (1118–1181), an event known as the Heiji War. Yoshitomo was killed and Yoritomo captured and, in 1160, banished to the province of Izu; he remained there until 1180 when he led a revolt against the Taira clan, which dominated the imperial court. In 1192, he was granted the title of shogun and established a military government in Kamakura.

2. The Former Governor of Musashi refers to Hōjō Nobutoki (1238–1323), who held the post of the governor of Musashi (now Tokyo, Saitama, and eastern Kanagawa prefectures) from 1267 to 1273. He was also the constable of Sado Province. While Nichiren was in exile there, he sent three private orders forbidding anyone to extend him assistance. (See also *Selected Writings of Nichiren*, pp. 334–335.)

3. The lord of Sagami is Hōjō Tokimune (1251–1284), the eighth regent of the Kamakura government. He concurrently held the post of governor of Sagami Province, where Kamakura, the seat of government, was located.

4. This story, often referred to by Nichiren, appears in the *Shih Chi*. Duke Yi of the state of Wei loved cranes and lived extravagantly, losing the support of the public. While his minister Hung Yen was away on a journey, enemies attacked Wei and killed Duke Yi. They ate the duke's flesh except for his liver, and then left the land. Returning, Hung Yen saw the disastrous scene and wept. He cut open his own stomach and inserted the duke's liver in it to save him from shame and dishonor, and so died.

5. According to the *Shih Chi*, Yü Jang of Chin first served the Fan and Chung-hang families but was not given an important position. Later Yü Jang served Chih Po, who treated him with great favor. Chih Po was in time killed by Hsiang-tzu, the lord of Chao. To revenge his lord, and in order to approach Hsiang-tzu, Yü disguised himself as a leper by lacquering his body, and made himself mute by drinking lye. But his assas-

sination attempt failed, and he was caught. Hsiang-tzu, understanding his feeling of loyalty, gave his robe to Yü Jang, who stabbed it three times to show his enmity for the man who had killed his lord, and then turned his sword upon himself.

6. Issai Shujō Kiken (Gladly Seen by All Living Beings) is a bodhisattva who appears in the *Yakuō* (23d) chapter of the Lotus Sutra as a previous incarnation of Bodhisattva Yakuō. He learned the Lotus Sutra from a Buddha called Nichigatsu Jōmyōtoku (Pure Bright Excellence of Sun and Moon) and, in gratitude, anointed himself with oil and burned his body as an offering for twelve hundred years. He was reborn in Nichigatsu Jōmyōtoku's realm and again served this Buddha. After Nichigatsu Jōmyōtoku's death, he burned his arms as another offering for seventy-two thousand years.

7. The period corresponding to the first stage in the cycle of formation, continuance, decline, and disintegration that a world is said to undergo. In this kalpa, a world takes shape and living beings appear. *See also* Kalpa in Glossary.

8. This tradition probably stems from the ancient Indian belief in Brahma (Jap: Bonten) as the creator deity. *See also* Bonten in Glossary.

9. Shan-tao (613–681) is regarded as the third patriarch of the Pure Land school in China.

10. Here, the three offenses of turning against one's sovereign, parent, and teacher, in other words, Shakyamuni Buddha.

11. A reference to Ichinosawa Nyūdō, to whose wife this letter was addressed. *Nyūdō* means a lay priest, or one who has been tonsured as a priest but continues to live as a layman.

12. Reference is to Homma Rokurō Zaemon (n.d.), a retainer of Hōjō Nobutoki. His fief was at Echi in Sagami Province, but he also served as steward of Niiho on Sado Island and as deputy constable of the island itself.

13. Identity uncertain. This may perhaps refer to the woman known as Nichimyō Shonin, who journeyed to Sado from Kamakura with her infant daughter to visit Nichiren during his exile on Sado Island.

14. The entire Lotus Sutra, consisting of eight volumes, along with the one-volume *Muryōgi* Sutra and the one-volume *Fugen* Sutra, which serve respectively as a prologue and an epilogue to the Lotus Sutra.

15. Tsukushi is an ancient name for the southern island of Kyushu. When Kyushu was divided into provinces during the Nara period, Tsukushi came to refer to the provinces of Chikuzen and Chikugo. This area formed the front line of defense against the Mongols, and many warriors were dispatched there from throughout the country. Tsushima and Iki, mentioned subsequently, are islands off the coast of Kyushu that bore the brunt of the Mongol attack.

16. Sō no Sukekuni (1207–1274) was a warrior descendant of the Taira clan. He was the deputy constable of the island province of Tsushima. Nichiren refers to him as Sō no Sōma no Jō.

17. This magistrate is Shōni Shigeyoshi (1198–1281), the constable of Iki, Tsushima, Chikuzen, Buzen, and Hizen provinces. He concurrently held the post of magistrate, and was therefore responsible for overseeing the judiciary, temples and shrines, civil engineering projects, and so forth in the Kyushu area. After the Mongol attack in 1274, he became a *nyūdō*, or lay priest, assuming the name Kakue. Nichiren refers to him in the text as Bugyō Nyūdō Buzen Zenji.

18. Matsuratō men were memebers of a league of warriors who controlled the Matsura region in Hizen Province (now Nagasaki and Saga prefectures) from the twelfth through the fifteenth centuries. In the battle of Dannoura in 1185, they fought on the losing, Taira, side, but submitted to Minamoto no Yoritomo and received appointments to become officials of local manors.

19. Gakujō-bō (d.1301) was a disciple of Nichiren's who is said to have lived at Ichinosawa on Sado Island. Originally a Shingon believer, he converted to Nichiren's teaching. He propagated the teachings widely, establishing a temple, the Jissō-ji on the island.

20. Reference is to monks of the Zen and Ritsu sects.

51 *THE SUTRA OF TRUE REQUITAL*

Nichiren wrote this letter in reply to a communication from Sennichi-ama on Sado Island, on the twenty-eighth day of the seventh month, 1278. Sennichi-ama was the wife of the lay disciple Abutsu-bō, who was paying his third visit to Nichiren at Mount Minobu, and had brought a letter from his wife with him. Little is known of Sennichi-ama; legend has it that she served as an attendant to a court lady who had accompanied the party of the Retired Emperor Juntoku, who was banished to Sado after the Jōkyū Disturbance of 1221, but it is more likely that she was a native of the island itself. At any rate, she and her husband were devoted followers of Nichiren and supplied him with food, writing materials, and other necessities for more than two years until his pardon in 1274.

"The Sutra of True Requital" (*Shinjitsu Hōon Kyō no Koto*) is an alternative title for this letter. It is more frequently referred to as *Sennichi-ama Gozen Gohenji* (Reply to Sennichi-ama).

In the first year of the Kōan era (1278), when the reverse marker of Jupiter was in the sector of the sky with the cyclical sign *tsuchinoe-tora*, on the sixth day of the seventh month, a letter from Sennichi-ama of the province of Sado was brought to me here deep in the mountains at a place called Mount Minobu in the village of Hakiri, the province of Kai in Japan, being delivered to me by Abutsu-bō, her husband.

In the letter, she says that she had been concerned about the faults and impediments that prevent women from gaining enlightenment,[1] but that since, according to my teaching, the Lotus Sutra places the highest importance on women attaining Buddhahood, she is therefore relying upon this sutra in all matters.

We may stop to ask ourselves: Who was the Buddha who preached this sutra known as the Lotus Sutra? To the west of this land of Japan, west again from China, far, far west beyond the deserts and mountain ranges, in the land called India, there was a great king named Śuddhodana. The son and heir of this great ruler, when he reached the age of nineteen, cast aside his position, withdrew to Mount Daṇḍaka,[2] and took up the religious life. At the age of thirty he became a Buddha. His body took on a golden color, and his spirit became capable of viewing everything in the three existences. This Buddha, whose mind reflected as though in a mirror all that had happened in the past and would happen in the future, spent more than fifty years expounding all the various sutras of his teaching life.

During the first thousand years after the Buddha's passing, these various sutras gradually spread throughout the land of India, but they were not yet transmitted to China or Japan. It was 1,015 years after the death of the Buddha when Buddhism was first introduced to China, but the Lotus Sutra was not among the texts transmitted at that time.

Some two hundred or more years after Buddhism was introduced to China, the Tripitaka Master Kumārāyana[3] lived in a country called Kucha, located between India and China. His son, Kumārajīva, journeyed from Kucha to India, where he received instruction in the Lotus Sutra from the Tripitaka Master Śūryasoma.[4] On entrusting him with the sutra, Śūryasoma said to him, "This Lotus Sutra has a deep connection with a country to the northeast."

With these words in mind, Kumārajīva set out to carry the sutra to the region east of India, to the land of China. Thus it was more than two hundred years after Buddhism had been introduced to China, during the reign of a ruler of the Later Ch'in dynasty,[5] that the Lotus Sutra was first brought to that country.

Buddhism was introduced to Japan during the reign of the thirtieth sovereign, Emperor Kimmei,[6] on the thirteenth day, a day with the cyclical sign *kanoto-tori*, of the tenth month of the thirteenth year of his reign, a year with the cyclical sign *mizunoe-saru* (552), by King Sŏng-myŏng of the kingdom of Paekche[7] to the west of Japan. This occurred four hundred years after the introduction of Buddhism to China and more than fourteen hundred years after the Buddha's passing.

The Lotus Sutra was among the texts brought to Japan at that time. Later, however, Prince Shōtoku,[8] the son of the thirty-second sovereign, Emperor Yōmei, sent an envoy to China to procure another copy of the Lotus Sutra, and propagated its teachings throughout Japan. Since then, more than seven hundred years have passed.

Already, over 2,230 years have gone by since the death of the Buddha. Moreover, the lands of India, China, and Japan are separated one from another by mountains upon mountains, rivers upon rivers, and sea after sea. Their inhabitants, their ways of thinking, and the character of their lands all differ from each other; they speak different languages and follow different customs. How, then, can ordinary human beings like ourselves possibly understand the true meaning of the Buddhist teachings?

The only way to do so is to examine and compare the words found in the various sutras. These various sutras all differ from one another, but the one known as the Lotus Sutra is in eight volumes. In addition, there are the *Fugen* Sutra, which urges the propagation of the Lotus Sutra, and the *Muryōgi* Sutra, which serves as an introduction to the Lotus Sutra, each consisting of one volume. When we open the Lotus Sutra and look into it, it is like seeing our own face reflected in a bright mirror, or like being able to discern the colors of all the plants and trees once the sun has risen.

In reading the *Muryōgi* Sutra, which serves as an introduction, we find a passage that says, "In these more than forty years, I [Shakyamuni Buddha] have not yet revealed the truth." In the first volume of the Lotus Sutra, at the beginning of the *Hōben* chapter, we read, "The World-Honored One has long expounded his doctrines and now must reveal the truth." In the fourth volume, in the *Hōtō* chapter, there is a passage that states clearly, "The Lotus Sutra of the Wonderful Law . . . all that you [Shakyamuni] have expounded is the truth." And the seventh volume contains the obvious passage of proof that mentions the tongue reaching to the Brahma Heaven.[9]

In addition to these passages, we should note that the other sutras that preceded or followed the Lotus Sutra have been compared to the stars, to streams and rivers, to minor rulers or to hills, while the Lotus Sutra has been compared to the moon, to the sun, to the great ocean, to a great mountain, or to a great king.[10]

These statements are not something I myself have said. They are in every case the golden words of the Tathagata, words that express the judgment of all Buddhas in the ten directions. And all bodhisattvas, persons of the two vehicles, Bonten, Taishaku, and the gods of the sun and moon, which shine now in the sky like bright mirrors, witnessed these statements being made. The words of these sun and moon deities, too, are recorded in the Lotus Sutra. All the ancient gods of India, China, and Japan were also present in the assembly, and none of the gods of Japan such as Tenshō Daijin, the Great Bodhisattva Hachiman, or the deities of Kumano[11] and Suzuka[12] dispute this view.

This sutra is superior to all other sutras. It is like the lion king, the monarch of all creatures that run on the ground, and like the eagle, the king of all creatures that fly in the sky. The *Namu Amida Butsu* Sutra[13] and the other sutras are mere pheasants or rabbits by comparison, to be seized by the eagle as their tears flow down or to be pursued by the lion while fear grips their bowels. And the same is true of the Nembutsu believers, the Ritsu priests, the Zen priests, and the Shingon teachers. Face to face with the votary of the Lotus Sutra, their color will drain away and their spirits will fail.

As for what sort of doctrines are taught in this wonderful Lotus Sutra: Beginning with the *Hōben* chapter in the first volume, it teaches that bodhisattvas, persons of the two vehicles, and ordinary common mortals are all capable of attaining Buddhahood. But at this point there are no examples to prove this assertion. It is like the case of a guest whom one meets for the first time. His appearance is attractive, his spirit is forthright, and on hearing him speak, we have no reason to doubt him. Yet because we have never seen him before and have no proof of the things he says, we find it difficult to believe him on the basis of his words alone. But if we repeatedly see evidence to support the major points he made at that time, we will be able to trust what he says from then on as well.

For all those who wished to believe the Lotus Sutra and yet could not do so with complete certainty, the fifth volume presents what is the very heart and core of the entire sutra, the doctrine of attaining Buddhahood in one's present form. It was as though a black object were to become white, black lacquer to become like snow, an unclean thing to become clean and pure, or a wish-granting jewel to be thrust into muddy water. Here it is told how a reptile-like woman, the dragon king's daughter, attained Buddhahood in her present form. And at that moment, no one any longer doubted that it is possible for women to attain Buddhahood as well. Thus the Lotus Sutra uses the enlightenment of women as a model [to reveal that Buddhahood is accessible to all].

For this reason, the Great Teacher Dengyō, the founder of the Enryaku-ji on Mount Hiei who first spread the true teachings of the Lotus Sutra in Japan, comments on this point where he states, "Neither teachers nor disciples need undergo countless kalpas of austere practice in order to attain Buddhahood. Through the power of the Lotus Sutra they can do so in their present form."[14] And the Great Teacher T'ien-t'ai Chih-che of China, who first expounded the true meaning of the Lotus Sutra in that country, remarks, "The other sutras predict Buddhahood for men only and not for women. . . . Only this [Lotus] sutra predicts Buddhahood for all."[15]

Do not these interpretations make clear that, among all the teachings of the Buddha's lifetime, the Lotus Sutra stands in first place, and that among the teachings of the Lotus Sutra, that of women attaining Buddhahood is foremost? For this reason, though the women of Japan may be condemned in all sutras other than the Lotus Sutra as incapable of attaining Buddhahood, as long as the Lotus Sutra guarantees their enlightenment, what reason have they to be downcast?

Now I, Nichiren, have been born as a human being, something difficult to achieve, and I have encountered the Buddhist teachings, which are but rarely to be met. Moreover, among all the teachings of Buddhism, I have been able to meet the Lotus Sutra. When I stop to consider my good fortune, I realize that I am indebted to my parents, indebted to the ruler, and indebted to all living beings.

With regard to the debt of gratitude owed to one's parents, one's father may be likened to heaven and one's mother to the earth, and it would be difficult to say to which parent one is the more indebted. But it is particularly difficult to repay the great kindness of one's mother.

If, in desiring to repay it, one seeks to do so by following the outer scriptures such as the *Three Records* and the *Five Canons* or the *Classic of Filial Piety*,[16] he will be able to provide for his mother in this life, but he cannot assist her in the life to come. Although he may provide for her physically, he will be unable to save her spiritually.

On turning to the inner scriptures, those of Buddhism, because the more than five thousand or seven thousand volumes of Hinayana and Mahayana sutras teach that women cannot attain Buddhahood, they offer no way to requite the debt owed to one's mother. The Hinayana teachings flatly deny that a woman can attain Buddhahood. The Mahayana sutras in some cases seem to say that a woman may attain Buddhahood or may be reborn in a pure land, but this is simply a possibility mentioned by the Buddha and no examples are given of such a thing actually having happened.

Only the Lotus Sutra reveals that a woman can attain Buddhahood, and therefore I have come to realize that this sutra is the very one that makes possible true requital for a mother's kindness. To repay that debt, I have vowed to enable all women to chant the daimoku of this sutra.

However, the women of Japan have all been led astray by priests like Shan-tao of China or Eshin, Eikan, and Hōnen[17] of Japan, so that throughout the entire country, not a one of them chants Nam-myoho-renge-kyo, which should be their foundation. All they do is chant Namu Amida Butsu once a day, ten times a day, a hundred thousand billion times, or thirty thousand or a hundred thousand times. All their lives, every hour of the day and night, they do nothing else. Both those women who are steadfast in their pursuit of enlightenment and those who are evil make the invocation of Amida's name their basis. And the few women who seem to be devoting themselves to the Lotus Sutra do so only as though whiling away time waiting for the moon to rise, or as though reluctantly spending time with a man who does not please them until they can meet their lover.

Thus among all the women of Japan, there is not one whose actions accord with the spirit of the Lotus Sutra. They do not chant the daimoku of the Lotus Sutra, which is the highest way to requite a mother's kindness, but instead devote their hearts to Amida. And because they do not base themselves on the Lotus Sutra, Amida extends no aid. Reciting the name of Amida Buddha is no way for a woman to gain salvation; rather it will invariably plunge her into hell.

In grieving over what is to be done, [I have realized that, in any event,] if one wishes to assist one's mother, the recitation of the name of Amida Buddha [is not the way to go about it, since it] creates the karma that destines a person to the hell of incessant suffering. Such recitation is not included among the five cardinal sins, and yet it is worse than the five sins. A person who murders his father and mother destroys their physical bodies, but he does not condemn them to fall into the hell of incessant suffering in their next existence.

Today the women of Japan, who could without fail attain Buddhahood through the Lotus Sutra, have been deceived into reciting the formula Namu Amida Butsu exclusively. Because this does not appear to be an evil act, they have been misled. Because the Nembutsu is not the seed of Buddhahood, one who chants it will never become a Buddha. By clinging to the minor good of reciting Amida Buddha's name, one deprives oneself of the major good of the Lotus Sutra. Thus this minor good of the Nembutsu is worse in its effect than the great evil of the five cardinal sins.

It is like the case of Masakado,[18] who during the Shōhei era seized control of eight provinces in the Kanto region, or like Sadatō,[19] who during the Tenki era took possession of the region of Ōshū. Because these men caused a division to arise between the people of their region and the sovereign, they were declared enemies of the court and in the end were destroyed. Their plots and rebellions were worse than the five cardinal sins.

Buddhism in Japan today reminds us of these men, marked as it is by strange plots and rebellions. The Lotus Sutra represents the supreme ruler, while the Shingon sect, Jōdo sect, Zen sect and Ritsu priests, by upholding various minor sutras such as the *Dainichi* Sutra and the *Kammuryōju* Sutra, have become the deadly enemies of the Lotus Sutra. And yet women throughout Japan, unaware of the foolishness of their own minds, think that Nichiren, who can save them, is their foe, and mistake the Nembutsu believers and the Zen, Ritsu, and Shingon priests, who are in fact deadly enemies, for good friends and teachers. And because they look upon Nichiren, who is trying to save them, as a deadly enemy, these women all join together to slander him to the government authorities, so that after having been exiled to the province of Izu in the past, he was once again exiled to the province of Sado.

I, Nichiren, having taken my vow, have this to say. There is absolutely no fault on my part. And even if I should be mistaken, the fact remains that I have made a vow to save all the women of this country of Japan, and that sincerity cannot be ignored—especially since what I am saying is in complete accord with the Lotus Sutra itself.

If the women of Japan do not choose to put faith in me, then they should let the matter rest there. On the contrary, however, they set about attacking me. But am I in error?

How do Shakyamuni, Tahō, the Buddhas of the ten directions, the bodhisattvas, the people of the two vehicles, Bonten, Taishaku, and the Four Heavenly Kings plan to deal with this matter? If I were in error, they would surely make that plain. We could certainly expect that much from the deities of the sun and moon, which are shining right before our eyes. Moreover, all these deities not only listened to the words of Shakyamuni Buddha, but vowed to punish one who persecutes the votary of the Lotus Sutra, saying, "May his head be split into seven pieces."[20] What then do they intend to do? Because I, Nichiren, strongly called them to task in this manner, Heaven has inflicted punishment upon this nation of ours, and these epidemics have appeared.

By rights Heaven should command another nation to punish our country, but too many people of both sides would perish. Therefore, Heaven's design is to avoid a general conflict but instead to first destroy the people [in this epidemic]—which is in effect cutting off the ruler's hands and feet—and thus compel the ruler and high ministers of this nation [to honor the Lotus Sutra]. In this way it intends to wipe out the enemies of the Lotus Sutra and make way for the propagation of the True Law.

Nevertheless, when I was exiled to the province of Sado, the constable of the province and the other officials, following the designs of the regent, treated me with animosity. And the ordinary people went along with their orders. In addition, the Nembutsu believers and the Zen, Ritsu, and Shingon priests in Kamakura sent word that by no means should I be allowed to return there from the island of Sado, and Ryōkan of Gokuraku-ji and others persuaded Hōjō Nobutoki, the former governor of the province of Musashi, to issue private letters of instruction, which were carried to Sado by Ryokan's disciples, ordering that I be persecuted. Thus it seemed that I could not possibly escape with my life. Whatever Heaven's design in the matter may have been, every single steward and Nembutsu believer worthy of the name kept strict watch on my hut day and night, determined to prevent anyone from communicating with me. Never in any lifetime will I forget how under those circumstances you, with Abutsu-bō, carrying a wooden container of food on his back, again and again came in the night to bring me aid. It was as though my deceased mother had suddenly been reborn in the province of Sado!

Once in China there was a man named Liu Pang,[21] the lord of P'ei. Because there were signs about him indicating that he would become a ruler, the First Emperor of the Ch'in dynasty decreed that unparalleled rewards would be bestowed upon anyone who would kill Liu Pang. Liu Pang thought it would be too dangerous to try to conceal himself in the country villages, and so he entered the mountains, where he remained hidden for seven days, and then for another seven. At that time, he believed that his life was as good as lost. But Liu Pang had a wife of the Lü family who went searching for him in the mountains and from time to time would bring him food to keep him alive.

Being Liu Pang's wife, she could not help but feel compassion for him. But in your case, were you not concerned about the life to come, how could you have shown me such devotion? And that is also the reason why you have remained steadfast throughout, even when you were driven from your place, fined, or had your house taken from you. In the Lotus Sutra, it is said that one who in the past has made offerings to tens of billions of Buddhas shall, when reborn in a later existence, be unshakable in faith.[22] You, then, must be a woman who has made offerings to tens of billions of Buddhas.

In addition, it is easy to sustain our concern for someone who is before our eyes, but quite a different thing when he or she is far away, even though in our hearts we may not forget that person. Nevertheless, in the five years from the eleventh year of the Bun'ei era (1274) until this year, the first year of the Kōan era (1278), that I have been living here in the mountains, you have three times sent your husband from the province of Sado to visit me. What profound sincerity! Your faith is weightier than the great earth, deeper than the great sea!

Shakyamuni Buddha, when he was Prince Satta[23] in a previous existence, gained merit by feeding his body to a starving tigress, and when he was King Shibi,[24] he gained merit by giving his flesh to a hawk in exchange for the life of a dove. And he declared in the presence of Tahō and the Buddhas of the ten directions that, in the Latter Day of the Law, he would transfer this merit to those who believe in the Lotus Sutra as you do.

You say in your letter that the eleventh day of the eighth month of this year will mark the thirteenth anniversary of your father's death. You also note that you are enclosing an offering of one *kan* of coins. It is extremely kind of you to do so. Fortunately, I happen to have a copy of the Lotus Sutra in ten volumes[25] that I am sending you. At times when you are thinking fondly of me, you may have Gakujō-bō[26] read it aloud for you so you can listen to the words. And in a future existence, you may use this copy of the sutra as a token of proof with which to search me out.

In view of the epidemics that have raged the year before last, last year and this year as well, I had been anxious about how all of you were faring and praying earnestly to the Lotus Sutra for your safety, but still I was feeling uneasy. Then, on the twenty-seventh day of the seventh month, at the Hour of the Monkey (3:00–5:00 P.M.), Abutsu-bō appeared. I asked him first of all how you were, and how Kō Nyūdō[27] was. He told me that neither of you had fallen ill, and that Kō Nyūdō had set out along with him but, because the early rice was nearly ripe, and because he had no sons to help him harvest it, he had had no choice but to turn around and go back home.

When I heard all this, I felt like a blind man who has recovered his sight, or as though my deceased father and mother had come to me in a dream from the palace of King Emma,[28] and in my dream I felt great joy. It is a strange and wonderful thing, but both here and in Kamakura, very few persons among my followers have died from this plague. It is as though all of us were riding in the same boat and, though it would be too much to expect that we should all survive, still, when disaster seemed to be upon us, another boat came out to rescue us. Or it is as though the dragon deities were watching over us and making it possible for us to reach the shore in safety. It is indeed wondrous to contemplate!

Concerning Ichinosawa Nyūdō,[29] please tell his wife, the nun, that I am grieved to hear of his death. But I have already told her quite clearly how matters stand with her husband, and she will no doubt recall my words. Regardless of the fact that he had a chapel dedicated to Amida Buddha in his house, Amida Buddha will not save an enemy of the Lotus Sutra. On the contrary, such a person renders himself a foe of Amida Buddha. After his death, he must have fallen into the realm of evil and be filled with deep regret. It is a great pity.

However, I am mindful that the *nyūdō* on several occasions saved my life by hiding me in the corridor of his home, and I have therefore tried to think of something that can be done for him. Will you please ask Gakujō-bō to read the Lotus Sutra regularly at his grave? Even so, I do not think that this will enable him to reach enlightenment. Please tell his wife, the nun, that I grieve at the thought of how desolate and lonely she must feel. I will write more at another time.

Nichiren

The twenty-eighth day of the seventh month

Notes

1. The pre-Lotus teachings generally hold that women cannot attain Buddhahood in their present form, because they are bound by the five obstacles and other karmic hindrances. The five obstacles are: a woman cannot become a Bonten, a Taishaku, a devil king, a wheel-turning king, or a Buddha.

2. Daṇḍaka is the name of a mountain in Gandhara in northern India, where Shakyamuni is said to have carried out the practice of almsgiving in a past existence, according to the *Rokudoshū* (T3, 9a) and other sutras. A number of secondary sources

refer to this mountain as the place where prince Siddhartha practiced austerities before attaining enlightenment as Shakyamuni Buddha, and Nichiren generally uses the name in this sense. It is not known if the mountain corresponds to an actual place.

3. Kumārāyana was the son of the chief minister of an ancient Indian kingdom in the fourth century. When the ruler's hostility toward Buddhism forced him to leave the country, he crossed the Pamir range to the north, traveling toward China. The king of Kucha gave him an official welcome and designated him as Teacher of the Nation. In compliance with a royal decree, Kumārāyana married the king's younger sister, Jīvaka, who also had deep faith in Buddhism. Their son was the famous translator, Kumārajīva, whose name combined those of his parents.

4. Śūryasoma was a prince of Yarkand in central Asia and the teacher of Kumārajīva. He is mentioned in the *Hokke Honkyō Kōki*, attributed to Seng-chao and contained in the *Hokke Denki*, where the quotation that follows in the text is to be found (T51, 54b).

5. Reference is to Yao Hsing (366–416), the second emperor of this short-lived kingdom.

6. Kimmei (509–571) was the twenty-ninth emperor of Japan, or when Empress Jingu is included in the lineage, the thirtieth. According to the *Nihon Shoki* (Chronicles of Japan), Buddhism was formally introduced during his reign.

7. Paekche, along with Silla and Koguryŏ, was one of the three ancient kingdoms of Korea that contributed greatly to the introduction of Chinese culture to Japan. King Sŏngmyŏng (d.554) was the twenty-fifth Paekche king; he had close contact with the Liang dynasty in China and was responsible for the spread of Chinese culture and Buddhism to his country and to Japan. He sent the statue of Shakyamuni Buddha and various Buddhist texts to the Yamato court in 552 (another theory says 538).

8. Prince Shōtoku (574–622), second son of the thirty-first emperor, Yōmei, is famous for his application of the spirit of Buddhism to Japan. As regent for Empress Suiko, he carried out various reforms. He revered the Lotus Sutra, Śrīmālā Sutra, and Vimalakīrti Sutra, and commentaries on these works are attributed to him.

9. In the above passage, the quotation from the *Muryōgi* Sutra is at T9, 386b; from the *Hōben* (2d) chapter, T9, 6a; from the *Hōtō* (11th) chapter, T9, 32b; and from the seventh volume (*Jinriki*, 21st chapter), T9, 52b. The long, broad tongue is one of the thirty-two distinguishing features of a Buddha.

10. These are among the ten comparisons set forth in the *Yakuō* (23d) chapter of the Lotus Sutra.

11. A reference to the three Shinto shrines located in the Kumano district of Wakayama prefecture. They are Kumano Nimasu Shrine in Hongū, enshrining the god Susanoo no Mikoto; Kumano Hayatama Shrine in Shingū, enshrining the Kumano Hayatama deity: and the Kumano Nachi Shrine in Nachi, enshrining the Kumano Fusumi deity.

12. Suzuka is a district in Ise Province (now northern Mie Prefecture), the location of an important barrier station on the route connecting Yamato and Ise. It is the site of many old temples and shrines and archaeological remains.

13. Reference is to the *Amida* Sutra (T12, no. 366). *Namu Amida Butsu* is the Nembutsu chant of Pure Land devotees.

14. *Hokke Shūku* (DDZ3, 226).

15. *Hokke Mongu* (T34, 97a).

16. The *Three Records* were works said to record the deeds of the three legendary

rulers: Fu Hsi, Shen Nung, and Huang Ti. The *Five Canons* were the writings concerning the five emperors (Shao Hao, Chuan Hsü, Ti Kao, T'ang Yao, and Yü Shun) who followed the legendary rulers. These works no longer exist. The *Classic of Filial Piety* is one of the thirteen classics, said to have been recorded by the disciples of Tseng Tzu, a disciple of Confucius.

17. Shan-tao (613–681) was the third patriarch of the Chinese Pure Land school. Eshin refers to the Eshin-in on Mount Hiei, the temple at which the Tendai priest Genshin (942–1017) lived. He is famous as the compiler of the *Ōjō Yōshū*, an early work extolling the pleasures of the Pure Land. Eikan (1032–1111), also called Yōkan, was a Sanron monk who wrote several works concerning Amida's Pure Land. Honen (1133–1212) was the founder of the Japanese Pure Land sect. All these men are frequently condemned by Nichiren.

18. Taira no Masakado (d.940) was a warrior of the Taira clan who rose to power in eastern Japan. In 939 he attacked the government headquarters in Hitachi and other provinces and installed his own men as governors. Proclaiming himself the "new emperor," he became the first of the newly emerging warrior class to rebel against the throne. His rebellion was crushed the next year by his cousin, Taira no Sadamori, aided by the forces of Fujiwara no Hidesato.

19. Abe no Sadato (1019–1062) was a warrior of the powerful Abe clan in Mutsu Province in eastern Japan. The imperial court had dispatched an army against his father, Abe no Yoritoki, for invading neighboring territories and refusing to forward tax revenues. When Yoritoki was killed in 1057, Sadatō continued his rebellion. He was finally put down by the imperial forces with the aid of the Kiyohara clan of Dewa Province.

20. In the text of the Lotus Sutra (T9, 59b) this is part of the vow made by the ten demon daughters to protect the sutra's votaries.

21. Liu Pang (247–195 B.C.) was the founder of the Former Han dynasty. He and another warlord, Hsiang Yü, contended for power, taking advantage of the confusion caused by the death of Shih Huang-ti, the first emperor of the Ch'in, to raise troops and attempt to overthrow the dynasty. A protracted struggle between the two ended in a victory for Liu Pang, who founded the Han dynasty in 202 B.C. The history of the founding of the Han dynasty, including the episode referred to in the text, appears in detail in the *Shih Chi* (Records of the Historian).

22. T9, 30c.

23. The story of Satta (Skt: Sattva), the third son of King Makarada, appears in the *Konkōmyō Saishōō* Sutra (T16, 354a-b). One day when Prince Satta was walking in a bamboo grove with his two elder brothers, he found an injured tigress that had given birth and was too weak with hunger to feed her cubs. After his elder brothers had returned to the palace, he gave his body as an offering to feed the famished tigress.

24. Shibi (Skt: Śibi) was the name of Shakyamuni when he was a king carrying out the practice of almsgiving in a previous existence. According to the *Bosatsu Honjō Manron* (T4, 333c), one day the god Bishukatsuma disguised himself as a dove and the god Taishaku changed into a hawk in order to test King Shibi. The hawk pursued the dove, which flew into Shibi's robes for protection. Shibi gave his own flesh to the hungry hawk in order to save the dove.

25. The entire Lotus Sutra, consisting of eight volumes, along with the one-volume *Muryōgi* Sutra and the one-volume *Fugen* Sutra, which serve respectively as a prologue and an epilogue to the Lotus Sutra.

26. Gakujō-bō (d.1301) was a disciple who lived at Ichinosawa on Sado Island. Originally a Shingon believer, he converted to Nichiren's teaching and devoted himself to propagating it at a temple he founded, the Jissō-ji.

27. Kō Nyūdō was a follower of Nichiren of whom little is known. *Kō* means a provincial office, and his name derives from the fact that he lived in Kō (present-day Mano-machi), at the time the provincial seat of Sado Island. Kō and his wife, Kō-no-ama, were converts who made offerings to Nichiren and helped protect him. Kō Nyūdō made the arduous journey from Sado to Minobu to visit Nichiren and make offerings to him.

28. The palace of Emma, King of Hell, according to the *Jō Agon* Sutra (T1, 126b), lies in the Great Diamond Mountains to the south of Jambudvīpa. The *Daibibasha Ron* (T27, 867b) places it 500 *yojanas* beneath Jambudvīpa.

29. Ichinosawa Nyūdō (d.1278) was the lay priest of the Pure Land sect at whose estate Nichiren lived for a large part of his exile on Sado. Ichinosawa never became a convert but made great efforts to protect Nichiren.

52 THE TREASURE OF A FILIAL CHILD

Nichiren sent this letter on the second day of the seventh month, 1280, to his follower Sennichi-ama on Sado Island. Sennichi-ama was the wife of Abutsu-bō Nittoku, who had passed away the year before. Abutsu-bō had originally been a Nembutsu believer, but soon, together with his wife, became a sincere follower of Nichiren, and helped provide him with food and supplies during his stay on the island. Abutsu-bō had, despite his advanced age, paid three visits to Nichiren at Minobu. He is said to have died on the twenty-first day of the third month, 1279, at the age of ninety-one. His son, Tōkurō Moritsuna, later that year made a pilgrimage to Mount Minobu with his father's ashes and laid them to rest there.

The title of this letter "Treasure of a Filial Child" (*Kōshi Takara Gosho*) is an alternative title. It is also referred to as *Sennichi-ama Gohenji* (Reply to Sennichi-ama).

***

I was deeply grieved to hear the news about the nun, the wife of Kō Nyūdō.[1] Please tell her that I think very fondly of her.

I have received your various gifts of one *kan* and five hundred *mon* of coins, laver, *wakame* seaweed, and dried rice, and have respectfully reported this in the presence of the Lotus Sutra.

The Lotus Sutra says, "Among those who hear of this Law, there is not one who shall not attain Buddhahood."[2] Although this passage consists of but ten characters, to read even a single phrase of the Lotus Sutra is to read without omission all the sacred teachings preached by Shakyamuni Buddha during his lifetime. Therefore, the Great Teacher Miao-lo says, "If, in propagating the Lotus Sutra, one is to interpret even one of its doctrines, he must take into consideration all the Buddha's lifetime of teachings and master them from beginning to end."[3]

By "beginning" he means the *Kegon* Sutra, and by "end" he means the Nirvana Sutra. The *Kegon* Sutra was preached at the time when the Buddha had first gained enlightenment, when the great bodhisattvas Dharma Wisdom, Forest of Merit,[4] and others, responding to the request of a bodhisattva called Moon of Emancipation, preached in the Buddha's presence. I do not know in what form this sutra may exist in India, in the dragon king's palace,[5] or in the Tuṣita Heaven,[6] but it has been brought to Japan in a sixty-volume version, an eighty-volume version, and a forty-volume version.[7] In the case of the last of the teachings, the Nirvana Sutra, I again do not know in what form it may exist in India or in the dragon king's palace, but in our country it exists in a forty-volume version, a thirty-six-volume version, a six-volume version, and a two-volume version.[8]

In addition to these sutras, there are the *Agon* sutras, the *Hōdō* sutras, and the *Hannya* sutras, which run to five thousand or seven thousand volumes. But even though we may not see or hear of any of these various sutras, if we read so much as a single word or phrase of the Lotus Sutra, it is just as though we were reading every word of all these various sutras.

It is like the two characters that compose the name for India, Gasshi,[9] or the name for Japan, Nihon. The two characters that make up the name Gasshi encompass the five regions of India,[10] the sixteen major kingdoms, the five hundred intermediate kingdoms, the ten thousand minor kingdoms,[11] and the countless smaller countries like scattered grains of millet, all with their great land areas, great mountains, their plants and trees, and their human inhabitants and domestic animals. Or it is like a mirror, which may be only one inch, two inches, three inches, four inches or five inches in size, but which can reflect the image of a person who is one foot or five feet in height, or of a great mountain that is ten feet, twenty feet, a hundred feet or a thousand feet in size.

Thus when we read the above passage from the Lotus Sutra, we know that all persons who hear of the sutra will, without a single exception, attain Buddhahood.

All the various beings in the nine worlds and the six paths differ from one another in their minds. It is like the case of two people, three people, or a hundred or a thousand people: Though all have faces about a foot in length, no two look exactly alike. Their minds differ, and therefore their faces differ, too. How much greater still is the difference between the minds of two people, of ten people, and of all the living beings in the six paths and the nine worlds! So it is that some love the blossoming cherry trees and some love the moon, some prefer sour things and some prefer bitter ones, some like little things and some like big. People have various tastes. Some prefer good and some prefer evil. People are of many kinds.

But though they differ from one another in such ways as these, when they enter into the Lotus Sutra, they all become like a single person in body and a single person in mind. This is just like the various rivers that, when they flow into the great ocean, all take on a uniformly salty flavor, or like the different kinds of birds that, when they approach Mount Sumeru, all assume the same [golden] hue.[12] Thus Devadatta, who had committed three of the five cardinal sins,[13] and Rāhula,[14] who observed all of the two hundred and fifty precepts, both alike became Buddhas. And both King Myōshōgon,[15] who held erroneous views, and Śāriputra, who held correct views, equally received predictions that they would attain Buddhahood. This is because, in the words of the passage quoted earlier, "There is not one who shall not attain Buddhahood."

In the *Amida* and other sutras expounded during the first forty and more years of the Buddha's preaching life, Śāriputra is said to have achieved great merit by reciting the name of Amida Buddha a million times in the space of seven days.[16] But since these sutras were repudiated as teachings belonging to the period when the Buddha had "not yet revealed the truth,"[17] such recitation is in fact as meaningless as if one were to boil water for seven days and then throw it into the ocean.

Lady Vaidehī,[18] by reading the *Kammuryōju* Sutra, was able to reach the stage known as the realization of nonbirth and nonextinction.[19] But since this sutra was cast aside with the Buddha's words that he would now "honestly discard the provisional teachings,"[20] unless Lady Vaidehī were to take faith in the Lotus Sutra, she must revert to her former status as an ordinary woman.

One's acts of great good are nothing to rely on. If he fails to encounter the Lotus Sutra, what can they avail? Nor should one lament that he has committed acts of great evil. For if only he practices the one vehicle, then he can follow in the footsteps of Devadatta [in attaining Buddhahood]. All this is because the sutra passage that declares, "There is not one who shall not attain Buddhahood,"[21] was not spoken in vain.

Some may wonder where the spirit of the late Abutsu-bō may be at this moment. But by using the bright mirror of the Lotus Sutra to reflect his image, I, Nichiren, can see him among the assembly on Eagle Peak, seated within the Treasure Tower of Tahō Buddha and facing toward the east.[22]

If what I say is not true, then it is no error of mine. Rather the tongue of Shakyamuni Buddha, who said, "The World-Honored One has long expounded his doctrines and now must reveal the truth";[23] along with the tongue of Tahō Buddha, who declared, "The Lotus Sutra . . . All that you [Shakyamuni Buddha] have expounded is the truth";[24] as well as the tongues of all the various Buddhas, who are seated side by side in four hundred billion *nayutas*[25] of lands, as numerous as hemp or rice plants, as stars or stalks of bamboo, lined up with never a gap between them, and who, without a single exception, extended their tongues up to the palace of Daibonten[26]—all these tongues, I say, will in one moment rot away like a whale that has died and decayed, or like a heap of sardines that have rotted. All the Buddhas in the worlds of the ten directions will be guilty of the offense of speaking great falsehoods; the earth of the pure land of Tranquil Light,[27] which is made of gold and emeralds, will suddenly split open; and all these Buddhas will, like Devadatta, plunge headlong into the great citadel of the hell of incessant suffering. Or, as happened to the nun Dharma Lotus Fragrance,[28] fierce flames will shoot out of their bodies because of the great lies they have told, and the flower garden of the Lotus Treasury World,[29] a Land of Actual Reward, will in one instant be reduced to a place of ashes. But how could such things be possible?

If the late Abutsu-bō alone were not admitted to the pure land of Tranquil Light, then all these Buddhas would fall into a realm of great suffering. Leaving all else aside, you should consider the matter in this light. On this basis, you may judge the truth or falsehood of the Buddha's words.

A man is like a pillar, a woman like a crossbeam. A man is like the legs of a person, a woman like the trunk. A man is like the wings of a bird, a woman like the body. If the wings and the body become separated, then how can the bird fly? And if the pillar topples, then the crossbeam will surely fall to the ground.

A home without a man is like a person without a soul. With whom can you discuss matters of business, and to whom can you feed good things? Merely to be separated from your husband for a day or two is cause for uneasiness. And you were parted from your husband on the twenty-first day of the third month of last year, and passed the remainder of the year without seeing his return. Now it is already the seventh month of this year. Even though he himself does not return, why does he not send you some word?

The cherry blossoms, once scattered, have again come into bloom, and the fruit, once fallen, has formed again on the trees. The spring breezes are unchanged, and the scenes of autumn are just as they were last year. How is it that, in this one matter alone, things should be so different from what they were, never to be the same again?

The moon sets and rises again; the clouds disperse and then gather once more. Even Heaven must regret and the earth lament that this man has gone away and will never come again. You yourself must feel the same. Rely upon the Lotus Sutra as provender for your journey, and quickly, quickly set out for the pure land of Eagle Peak so that you can meet him there!

There is a passage in one of the sutras that says that children are one's enemies. "People in this world commit many sins because of their children,"[30] it states. In the case of the birds known as the crested eagle and the eagle, though the parents raise their young with compassion, the young turn around and eat their parents. And the bird known as the owl, after it is hatched, invariably devours its mother. Such is the case among the lowly creatures.

Even among human beings, King Virūdhaka seized the throne from his father, whom he resented, and King Ajātaśatru murdered his father.[31] An Lu-shan killed his foster mother, and An Ch'ing-hsü killed his father, An Lu-shan. An Ch'ing-hsü was killed by Shih Shih-ming, [who was like a son to him,] and Shih Shih-ming was in turn killed by his son, Shih Ch'ao-i.[32] Thus there is good reason why children are spoken of as enemies. The monk named Sunakṣatra[33] was a son of Shakyamuni Buddha, the lord of teachings. But he conspired with the non-Buddhist teacher called Nirgrantha Jñātaputra[34] and attempted time and again to kill his father, the Buddha.

There is also a sutra passage that says that children are a treasure. Accordingly, the sutra states, "Because of the blessings their sons and daughters accumulate through religious practice, a great shining brightness appears, illuminating the realm of hell, and the parents [suffering in hell] are thereby able to awaken a believing mind."[35] But even if the Buddha had not taught [that children are a treasure], you could tell as much simply from the evidence before your eyes.

In India there was once a great ruler, the king of the country called Parthia.[36] This king was inordinately fond of horses and horse-raising. In time, he became so expert in raising them that he could not only turn a worthless horse into one of outstanding merit, but could also transform an ox into a horse. Eventually, he even turned people into horses and rode them. The citizens of his own state were so grieved at this last feat that he confined himself to turning men from other lands into horses. Thus, when a traveling merchant came to his kingdom from another country, he gave the merchant a potion to drink, transformed him into a horse, and tied him up in the royal stables.

Even under ordinary circumstances the merchant yearned for his homeland and in particular thought longingly of his wife and child. Thus he found his lot very difficult to bear. But since the king would not allow him to go home, he could not do so. Indeed, even had it been possible, what could he have done there in his present form? So all he could do was bewail his fate morning and evening.

This man had a son who, when his father failed to return at the expected time, began to wonder if he had been killed, or had perhaps fallen ill. Feeling that, as a son, he must find out what had happened to his father, he set out upon a journey. His mother lamented, protesting that her husband had already gone off to another land and failed to return, and that if she were now to be abandoned by her only son as well, she did not know how she could carry on. But the son was so deeply concerned about his father that he nevertheless set off for the country of Parthia in search of him.

[Upon his arrival,] he put up for the night at a small lodging. The master of the house said: "How sad! You are still so young, and I can see from your face and bearing that you are a person of distinction. I had a son once, but he went off to another country and perhaps has died there. At least I do not know what has become of him. When I think of the fate of my own son, I can scarcely bear to look at you. I say this because here in this country we have a cause for great sorrow. The king of this country is so inordinately fond of horses that he ventures to make use of a strange kind of plant. If he feeds one of the narrow leaves of this plant to a person, the person turns into a horse. And if he feeds one of the broad leaves of the plant to a horse, the horse turns into a person. Not long ago a merchant came here from another country. The king fed him some of this plant, turned him into a horse and is secretly keeping him confined in the first of the royal stables."

When the son heard this, he thought that his father must have been transformed into a horse, and he asked, "What color is this horse's coat?"

The master of the house replied, "The horse is chestnut, with white dappling on the shoulders."

After the son had learned all these things, he contrived to approach the royal palace, where he was able to steal some of the broad leaves of the strange plant. When he fed these to his father, who had been changed into a horse, his father changed back into his original form.

The king of the country, marveling at what had happened, handed the father over to the son, since the latter had shown himself to be such a model of filial concern, and after that he never again turned men into horses.

Who but a son would have gone to such lengths to seek out his father? The Venerable Maudgalyāyana saved his mother from the sufferings of the realm of hungry ghosts,[37] and Jōzō and Jōgen[38] persuaded their father to give up his heretical views. This is why it is said that a good child is a parent's treasure.

Now the late Abutsu-bō was an inhabitant of a wild and distant island in the northern sea of Japan. Nevertheless, he was anxious about his future existence, so he took religious vows and aspired to happiness in the next life. When he encountered me, Nichiren, an exile to the island, he embraced the Lotus Sutra, and in the spring of last year he became a Buddha. When the fox of Mount Shīta encountered the Law of the Buddha, he grew dissatisfied with life, longed for death, and was reborn as the god Taishaku.[39] In the same way, Abutsu Shonin grew weary of his existence in this impure world, and so he became a Buddha.

His son, Tōkurō Moritsuna,[40] has followed in his footsteps, becoming a wholehearted votary of the Lotus Sutra. Last year, on the second day of the seventh month, he appeared here at Mount Minobu in Hakiri in the province of Kai, having journeyed a thousand *ri* over mountains and seas with his father's ashes hung around his neck, and deposited them at the place dedicated to the practice of the Lotus Sutra. And this year, on the first day of the seventh month, he came again to Mount Minobu to pay respects at his father's grave. Surely, there is no treasure greater than a child, no treasure greater than a child! Nam-myoho-renge-kyo. Nam-myoho-renge-kyo.

Nichiren

The second day of the seventh month

I am sending a priestly robe of dyed silk. Please inform Bungo-bō.[42] The teachings of the Lotus Sutra are already spreading throughout the country of Japan. Bungo-bō should undertake to propagate them in the Hokuriku region,[43] but he cannot do so unless he becomes well learned. Tell him to make haste and come here no later than the fifteenth day of the ninth month.

Please send me the various sacred texts as soon as possible by way of Tamba-bō,[44] as you did with the diary. Please send Yamabushi-bō[45] here to me as I instructed earlier. I am delighted to hear that you have been treating him with such kindness.

Notes

1. Kō-no-ama is the wife of Kō Nyūdō. See Letter 51, note 27.

2. T9, 9a. This passage, in the Chinese text, consists of ten characters.

3. *Hokke Gengi Shakusen* (T33, 850a).

4. Dharma Wisdom (Hōe) and Forest of Merit (Kudokurin) are two of the four great bodhisattvas appearing in the *Kegon* Sutra. Dharma Wisdom expounded the doctrine of the ten stages of security at the third assembly described in the sutra, while Forest of Merit put forth the doctrine of the ten stages of practice at the fourth assembly. The third great bodhisattva Moon of Emancipation (Gedatsugatsu), mentioned subsequently, appears in the sixth assembly, where he requests a detailed explanation of the ten stages of development from a bodhisattva called Diamond Repository (Kongōzō), the fourth great bodhisattva. In some of his writings Nichiren refers to Moon of Emancipation as a bodhisattva who requested the preaching of the *Kegon* Sutra.

5. A legendary palace located under the sea, which is said to be filled with great treasures and beautiful ornaments. It is said that Nāgārjuna obtained the *Kegon* Sutra here.

6. Tuṣita Heaven, the "Heaven of Satisfaction," is the fourth of the six heavens of the world of desire. It is said that bodhisattvas are reborn there just before their last rebirth in the world when they will attain Buddhahood. This heaven consists of an inner court and an outer court; Bodhisattva Miroku was believed to reside in the inner court.

7. There are three Chinese versions of the *Kegon* Sutra, translated respectively by Buddhabhadra of the Eastern Chin dynasty, Śikṣānanda of the T'ang dynasty, and Prajñā of the T'ang dynasty.

8. There are four Chinese versions of the Mahayana Nirvana Sutra, translated respectively by Dharmakṣema (?) of the Northern Liang dynasty; by Hui-kuan, Hui-

yen, and Hsieh Ling-yün of the Liu Sung dynasty; by Fa-hsien and Buddhabhadra of the Eastern Chin dynasty; and by Jñānabhadra and Hui-ning of the T'ang dynasty.

9. Gasshi (Chin Yüeh-chih) is a name for India used in China and Japan. In the latter part of the third century B.C., a Central Asian tribe called the Yüeh-chih ruled a part of India. Since Buddhism was brought to China via this territory, the name came to be applied to India itself.

10. All of India; eastern, western, northern, southern, and central regions of India.

11. The passage relating to these various different-sized kingdoms is drawn from the *Ninnō* Sutra (T8, 832a).

12. The above similes are drawn from *Daichido Ron* (T25, 321a).

13. Devadatta fomented a schism in the Buddhist Order, luring away five hundred monk-disciples of Shakyamuni Buddha; injured the Buddha and caused him to bleed by dropping a boulder on him from atop a mountain; and killed the nun Utpalavārṇā when she reproached him for his evil deeds. *Daichido Ron*, (T25, 165a).

14. Rāhula was the son of Shakyamuni and Yaśodharā, and was one of the Buddha's ten major disciples, respected as the foremost in inconspicuous practice. He entered the Buddhist Order at the age of fifteen and devoted himself to inconspicuous practice of the precepts.

15. A king who appears in the *Myōshōgon* (27th) chapter of the Lotus Sutra. Originally a believer in Brahmanism, he was converted to Buddhism by his two sons, Jōzō and Jōgen. This story is frequently cited by Nichiren.

16. In the *Amida* Sutra, Shakyamuni Buddha, addressing Śāriputra as the representative of the assembly, taught that one can obtain the blessings of rebirth in the Pure Land by meditating single-mindedly upon the name of Amida Buddha for seven days (T12, 347b). The *Jōdo Ron* of Vasubandhu interprets this to mean reciting the name of Amida Buddha a million times in seven days (T47, 93a).

17. *Muryōgi* Sutra (T9, 386a).

18. Vaidehī was the wife of King Bimbisāra of Magadha and the mother of Ajātaśatru. According to the *Kammuryōju* Sutra (T12, 341c), when Ajātaśatru killed his father and confined Vaidehī to the interior of the palace, she faced Eagle Peak where Shakyamuni was preaching and prayed to him. Out of compassion he appeared in her chamber and taught her how to reach the Pure Land of Amida Buddha.

19. The stage at which a bodhisattva achieves unwavering stability of mind by awakening to the truth that there is neither birth nor death. One of the ten endurances described in the *Kegon* Sutra (T9, 580a).

20. Lotus Sutra (T9, 10a).

21. Lotus Sutra (T9, 9a).

22. According to ancient Indian custom, kings and high dignitaries were seated facing east. One may assume, therefore, that when Shakyamuni Buddha began to preach the Lotus Sutra on Eagle Peak, he was facing east, and his disciples were facing west, toward Shakyamuni. Later, the Treasure Tower emerged from beneath the earth, facing west in the presence of Shakyamuni, and ascended into space. Shakyamuni then seated himself beside Tahō Buddha, who was inside the tower. Thus Shakyamuni was facing west during the Ceremony in the Air, and the rest of the assembly facing east. "Facing toward the east" in the text would mean that Abutsu-bō is seated within the Treasure Tower, facing the Buddhas Shakyamuni and Tahō.

23. Lotus Sutra (T9, 6a).

24. Lotus Sutra (T9, 32a).

25. *Nayuta* is an Indian numerical unit of vast dimensions. Sources differ: some define it as one hundred billion (10^{11}); others as 10^7. According to the *Hōtō* (11th) chapter of the Lotus Sutra, Shakyamuni, to make room for the Buddhas who were his emanations, purified four hundred billion *nayuta* worlds and then summoned the Buddhas from throughout the universe before opening the Treasure Tower and beginning the Ceremony in the Air.

26. In the *Jinriki* (21st) chapter of the Lotus Sutra, all the assembled Buddhas extend their tongues upward to the Brahma Heaven in testimony to the sutra's truth. A long, broad tongue is one of the thirty-two distinguishing marks of a Buddha.

27. One of the four kinds of Buddha lands described in T'ien-t'ai's *Kammuryōju Kyō Sho* (T37, 188b) and elsewhere.

28. According to the *Shuryōgon* Sutra (T19, 143a) raging flames emanated from every part of the body of the nun Dharma Lotus Fragrance (Jap: Hōrenkō), because of the offense of speaking great falsehoods, and she fell into the hell of incessant suffering.

29. The text has been somewhat expanded here. The Lotus Treasury World is the abode of Vairocana Buddha, as described in the *Kegon* Sutra (T10, 39a ff.). The Land of Actual Reward means a land inhabited by bodhisattvas who have reached or surpassed either the first stage of development in the fifty-two stages in the practice of the specific teaching, or the first stage of security in the practice of the perfect teaching.

30. *Shinjikan* Sutra (T3, 302b).

31. Nichiren makes frequent mention of these two arch villains. Virūḍhaka was a king of Kośala in the days of Shakyamuni Buddha. His father was Presenajit. His mother was originally the servant of a lord of the Shakya tribe. Virūḍhaka was humiliated by the Shakyas because of his lowly birth and vowed to take revenge. After he seized the throne, he led an army against the Shakya kingdom, killing about five hundred people. It is said that seven days later, in accordance with Shakyamuni's prediction, he burned to death and fell into hell. His story is given in the *Binaya Zōji* (T24, 240a). Ajātaśatru was a king of Magadha who eventually was converted to Buddhism by Shakyamuni. His story appears in the Nirvana Sutra (T12, 480b-c) and elsewhere.

32. An Lu-shan (705–757) was a regional commander during the T'ang dynasty. He won power at court through the patronage of Hsüan-tsung's favorite consort, Yang Kuei-fei, who adopted him as her legal son. Later he contended with Yang Kuei-fei's brother for control of the central government and led a rebellion in 755, capturing the capital. The fleeing emperor Hsüan-tsung was forced by his discontented soldiers to order the execution of Yang Kuei-fei and her brother, who were blamed for the catastrophe. An Lu-shan was eventually killed by his own son, An Ch'ing-hsü (d.759) in the course of a succession dispute concerning the imperial family. Shih Shih-min (d.761) was one of the leaders of the An Lu-shan rebellion, and after killing An Ch'ing-hsü, was in turn killed by his own son, Shih Chao-i (d.763).

33. Sunakṣatra was one of Shakyamuni's disciples and was said to be a son whom Shakyamuni sired before renouncing the world. He entered the Buddhist Order and mastered the four stages of meditation and the twelve divisions of the scriptures. However, overcome by distorted views, he is said to have fallen into hell alive. He is known as Zenshō biku; his story is found in the Nirvana Sutra (T12, 560b).

34. Nichiren writes Kutoku gedō, Achievement through Austerities. He was one of the founders of Jainism, and was one of the six non-Buddhist teachers in Shakyamuni's day.

35. *Shinjikan* Sutra (T3, 302b).

36. An ancient kingdom extending from northwestern India to Persia. Founded in 248 B.C., it fell in A.D. 226. The story of the king who turned people into horses appears in the *Hōbutsu Shū* (A Collection of Treasures) (DBZ147, 13ff,), sometimes attributed to Taira no Yasuyori (fl.1190–1200).

37. According to the *Urabon* Sutra (T16, 779b), Maudgalyāyana perceived with his divine eye that his deceased mother was suffering in the world of Hungry Ghosts. He tried to send her food through his supernatural abilities, but it turned into flames and burned her. Accordingly he sought the advice of Shakyamuni, who urged him to make offerngs to the monks for her sake on the fifteenth day of the seventh month. Maudgalyāyana made offerings of food to the Buddhist Order as instructed, and his mother was relieved of her agony.

38. See note 15, above.

39. This story appears in the *Mizou Innen* Sutra (T17, 576c ff) and the *Maka Shikan Bugyōden Guketsu* (T46, 272b). Chased by a lion, a fox accidentally fell into a dry well and remained there for three days. On the brink of starvation, he resolved to dedicate himself to the Buddhist Law and recited a verse expressing his desire to expiate his past offenses. When the fox's voice reached the god Taishaku on the summit of Mount Sumeru, Taishaku rescued him and asked him to preach the Law to him and the other heavenly gods.

40. Son of Abutsu-bō; his dates are unknown. He became Nichiren's disciple and spread the teaching in Sado and northern Japan.

41. On the original manuscript, probably having run out of space, Nichiren inserted this postscript at the beginning of the letter. In preparing the translation, we have moved it to the end, following a more recent editing of the manuscript.

42. Bungo-bō (n.d.) was a disciple of Nichiren who seems to have instructed Abutsu-bō and other followers in the province of Sado.

43. The Hokuriku region is the area including Sado and the six mainland provinces bordering the Sea of Japan. It includes the area facing the Sea of Japan from present-day Fukui to Niigata prefectures.

44. Tamba-bō (n.d.) was a disciple of Nichiren. He is said to have taken part in Nichiren's funeral procession and was among those who served in the rotation system for attending Nichiren's grave. He lived at the Myōkō-ji in Kazusa.

45. Yamabushi-bō was one of Nichiren's disciples in Sado, probably under the patronage of Abutsu-bō.

53 A SHIP TO CROSS THE SEA OF SUFFERING

This letter was sent by Nichiren on the twenty-eighth day of the fourth month, 1261, some two weeks before Nichiren was exiled to Itō in Izu. Virtually nothing is known about the recipient of this letter, Shiiji Shirō, other than that he lived in Suruga and was acquainted with one of Nichiren's leading disciples, Shijō Kingo.

"A Ship to Cross the Sea of Suffering" (*Nyoto Tokusen Gosho*) is an alternative title and is drawn from a passage in the *Yakushi* (23d) chapter of the Lotus Sutra that speaks of "a ship to cross the sea" (*watari ni fune o etaru ga gotoshi*). The title under which the letter is also known is *Shiiji Shirō-dono Gosho* (Letter to Lord Shiiji Shirō).

❧

When I asked him about what you told me the other day, I found it to be exactly as you said. You should therefore strive in faith more than ever to receive the blessings of the Lotus Sutra. Listen with the ears of Shih K'uang and observe with the eyes of Li Lou.[1]

In the Latter Day of the Law, the votary of the Lotus Sutra will appear without fail. The greater the hardships befalling him the greater the delight he feels, because of his strong faith. Doesn't a fire burn more briskly when logs are added? All rivers run to the sea, but the sea never rejects them or forces them to flow backward. The currents of hardship pour into the sea of the Lotus Sutra and rush against its votary. The ocean does not reject the river nor does the votary reject suffering. Were it not for the flowing rivers there would be no sea. Likewise, without tribulation there would be no votary of the Lotus Sutra. As T'ien-t'ai stated, "All rivers flow to the sea, and logs make a fire roar."[2]

You must realize that it is because of a deep karmic relationship from the past that you can teach others even a sentence or phrase of the Lotus Sutra. The sutra reads, "It is extremely difficult to save those who are deaf to the True Law."[3] The "True Law" means the Lotus Sutra.

A passage from the *Hosshi* chapter reads, "If there is someone, whether man or woman, who secretly teaches to one person even a single phrase of the Lotus Sutra, let it be known that he is the envoy of the Buddha."[4] This means that anyone who teaches others even a single phrase of the Lotus Sutra is clearly the Buddha's envoy, whether he be priest or nun, lay man or woman. You are a lay believer and one of those described in the sutra. One who hears even a sentence or phrase of the Lotus Sutra and cherishes it deep in his heart may be likened to a ship which navigates the sea of suffering. The Great Teacher Miao-lo stated, "Even a single phrase cherished deep in one's heart will without fail help him reach the opposite shore. To ponder one phrase and practice it is to exercise navigation."[5]

A passage from the Lotus Sutra reads, ". . . as though one had found a ship to make the crossing."[6] This "ship" might be described as follows: The Lord Buddha, a shipbuilder of infinitely profound wisdom, gathered the lumber of the four tastes and eight teachings,[7] planed it by honestly discarding the provisional teachings, cut and assembled the planks, using both right and wrong, and completed the craft by driving home the spikes of the one, supreme teaching.[8] Thus he launched the ship upon the sea of suffering. Unfurling the sails of the three thousand conditions on the mast of the Middle Way doctrine, driven by the fair wind of "all phenomena reveal the true entity,"[9] the vessel surges ahead, carrying all believers who can enter Buddhahood by their pure faith. Shakyamuni Buddha is the helmsman, Tahō Buddha mans the sails, and the Four Bodhisattvas led by Jōgyō strain in unison at the creaking oars. This is the ship in "a ship to make the crossing," the vessel of Myōhō-renge-kyō. Those who board it are the disciples and followers of Nichiren. Believe this wholeheartedly. When you visit Shijō Kingo, please have an earnest talk with him. I will write you again.

With my deep respect,
Nichiren

The twenty-eighth day of the fourth month

Notes

1. Shih K'uang, in Chinese legend, was a blind musician who could predict good and bad fortune by hearing a tune and whose sense of hearing was so acute that he could judge the quality of a newly cast bell, where ordinary musicians could not. Li Lou's sight was so acute that he could see the tip of a hair at a hundred paces.

2. *Maka Shikan* (T46, 49a).

3. Lotus Sutra (T9, 8b).

4. Lotus Sutra (T9, 30c).

5. *Hokke Mongu Ki* (T34, 349c). In the text this quotation is followed by the passage, "Only the ship of Myōhō-renge-kyō enables one to cross the sea of suffering." This has been omitted here as a sentence to the same effect appears later in the text.

6. T9, 54b.

7. The four tastes are the first four of the five tastes: milk, cream, curdled milk, butter, and ghee. They are likened to the five periods of the teaching: Kegon, Āgamas, Hōdō, Hannya, and Lotus and Nirvana. For the eight teachings, *see* Glossary.

8. Literally: ghee, the fifth taste, the Lotus teaching.

9. T9, 5c.

54 THE IZU EXILE

On the twenty-seventh day of the eighth month, 1260, Nichiren's home in Matsubagayatsu in Kamakura was attacked by a mob angered by Nichiren's attacks on Pure Land Buddhism. Nichiren managed to escape and fled to the home of his loyal disciple Toki Jōnin in Shimōsa. In the spring of 1261, however, he returned to Kamakura and resumed his propagation efforts. The government, without any official investigation, summarily sentenced him to exile in Itō on the Izu Peninsula on the twelfth day of the fifth month, 1261. The government officials charged with escorting Nichiren by ship to Ito did not complete their journey, but simply abandoned Nichiren on the beach at Kawana, a small fishing village on the northeastern coast of Izu Peninsula. Here he was given shelter by Funamori Yasaburō and his wife, and it is to this couple that the letter is addressed. After a month, the lord of the Itō district, Itō Sukemitsu, learning of Nichiren's presence, had him summoned in order that he might offer prayers for the lord's recovery from the serious illness from which he was suffering. Lord Itō recovered and both he and Funamori and his wife became steadfast followers of Nichiren. Nichiren's exile ended on the twenty-second day of the second month, 1263, and he returned to Kamakura.

This letter is known by its alternative title "The Izu Exile" (*Izu Hairu no Koto*) as well as the title *Funamori Yasaburō Moto Gosho* (Letter to the Residence of Funamori Yasaburō).

I have received the rice-dumplings wrapped in bamboo leaves, sake, dried rice, peppers, paper, and other items from the messenger whom you took the trouble of sending. He also conveyed your message that this offering should be kept secret. I understand.

On the twelfth day of the fifth month, having been exiled, I arrived at a beach I had never even heard of before. When I left the boat, still suffering from seasickness, you kindly took me into your care. What destiny brought us together? You might have been a votary of the Lotus Sutra in times past. Now, in the Latter Day of the Law, you were born as a boat-manager named Yasaburō to take pity on me. Being a man, it was perhaps natural for you to act as you did, but your wife might have been less inclined to help me. Nevertheless, she gave me food, brought me water to wash my hands and feet, and treated me with great concern. I can only describe this as wondrous.

What caused you to believe in the Lotus Sutra and to serve me during my more than thirty-day stay there? I was hated and resented by the lord and people of the district even more than I was in Kamakura. Those who saw me scowled, while those who merely heard my name were filled with spite. And yet, though I was there in the fifth month when rice was scarce, you secretly fed me. It would almost seem as though my parents had been reborn in Kawana close to Itō in Izu Province.

The fourth volume of the Lotus Sutra states, "[I will send] pure-minded men and women to make offerings to the teacher of the Law."[1] The heavenly gods and benevolent deities will assume the form of men and women and present offerings to help one who practices the Lotus Sutra. There is no doubt that you and your wife were born as just such a "pure-minded man and woman" and now make offerings to the teacher of the Law, Nichiren.

Since I wrote to you in detail earlier, I will make this letter brief. But I would like to mention one thing in particular. When the lord of this district sent me a request to pray for his recovery from illness, I wondered if I should accept it. But since he showed some degree of faith in me, I decided I would appeal to the Lotus Sutra. If I did, I saw no reason why the Ten Goddesses[2] should not join forces to aid me. I therefore pleaded with the Lotus Sutra, Shakyamuni, Tahō, and the other Buddhas throughout the universe, the Sun Goddess, Hachiman, and the other deities, both major and minor. I was sure that they would consider my request and respond by curing the lord's illness. Certainly they would never disregard Nichiren's prayer, but would respond as naturally as a person rubs a sore or scratches an itch. And as it turned out, the lord recovered. In gratitude he presented me with a statue of the Buddha, which had appeared from the sea along with a catch of fish. He did so because his illness had finally ended, an illness which I am certain was inflicted by the Ten Goddesses. The benefits of his offering will pass on to you and your wife.

We common mortals all have dwelt in the sea of suffering since time without beginning. But now that we have become votaries of the Lotus Sutra, we will without fail become Buddhas who are enlightened to the entity of body and mind which has existed since the beginningless past. We will reveal the unchangeable nature innate within us, as well as the mystic wisdom that enables us to realize the mystic truth. We will enjoy a state of life as indestructible as a diamond. Then how can we be in any way different from the Buddha who appeared from the sea? The Lord Shakyamuni, who declared, "I alone can save them," at a time even more distant than *gohyaku-jintengō*, is none other than each of us. This is the teaching of *ichinen sanzen* expounded in the Lotus Sutra. Our behavior is a personal demonstration of "I am here always, teaching the Law."[3] Thus we are all entities embodying the supreme teaching of the Lotus Sutra and the august life of Shakyamuni Buddha, though ordinary people never realize this. This is the meaning of the passage in the *Juryō* chapter, "... the deluded people cannot see me even when I am nearby."[4] The difference between delusion and enlightenment is like the four different views of the grove of sāla trees.[5] Let it be known that the Buddha of *ichinen sanzen* is anyone in any of the Ten Worlds who manifests his inherent Buddha nature.

The demon who appeared before Sessen Dōji[6] was Taishaku in disguise. The dove which sought the protection of King Shibi was the god Bishukatsuma.[7] King Fumyō,[8] who was imprisoned in the castle of King Hanzoku, was the Lord Shakyamuni himself. The eyes of common mortals cannot see their true identities, but the eyes of the Buddha can. As the sutra states, the sky and the sea both have paths [though we cannot see them] for birds and fish to come and go. A wooden statue of the Buddha is itself a golden one, and a golden statue is a wooden one. Aniruddha's gold was seen first as a hare and then as a corpse.[9] Sand in the palm of Mahānāma's[10] hand turned into gold. These things are beyond the grasp of human reason. A common mortal is a Buddha, and a Buddha a common mortal. This is exactly what is meant by *ichinen sanzen* and by the phrase, "[The time is limitless and boundless. . .] since I in fact attained Buddhahood."[11]

Thus it is quite possible that you and your wife have appeared here as reincarnations of the Lord Buddha Shakyamuni in order to help me. Although the distance between Itō and Kawana is short, we are not allowed to communicate openly. I am writing this letter for your future reference. Do not discuss these matters with other people, but ponder them yourself. If anyone should learn anything at all about this letter, it will go hard with you. Keep this deep in your heart, and never speak about it. With my deepest regard. Nam-myoho-renge-kyo.

Nichiren

The twenty-seventh day of the sixth month in the first year of Kōchō (1261)

Notes

1. T9, 32a.

2. The Ten Goddesses are the ten demon daughters (Jūrasetsu-nyo) of Kishimojin (Skt: Hāritī), described in the *Darani* (26th) chapter of the Lotus Sutra. The mother and daughters vow to protect the votaries of the Lotus Sutra.

3. Lotus Sutra (T9, 43b).

4. Lotus Sutra (T9, 43b).

5. The grove of sāla trees was where Shakyamuni expounded his last teaching, the Nirvana Sutra, and died. The four different views represent the four kinds of land: the land of enlightened and unenlightened beings, the land of transition, the land of actual reward, and the land of eternal light. The *Zōbō Ketsugi* Sutra (T85, 1337a) defines the grove of sāla trees in four different ways, according to the capacity and life condition of people: (1) as a grove composed of earth, trees, plants, and stone walls; (2) as a place adorned with seven kinds of treasure, including silver and gold; (3) as a place where Buddhas practice Buddhism; and (4) as the eternal, enlightened land of the Buddha.

6. Reference is to the story in the Nirvana Sutra (T12, 450a) in which Sessen Dōji, Shakyamuni in a previous existence, practiced the bodhisattva way. He met a demon in the Himalaya who recited the first half of a four-line verse; he was ready to sacrifice his life to hear the second half of the verse. The story is frequently cited by Nichiren.

7. Bishukatsuma (Skt: Viśvakarman) is a god who serves Taishaku, who lives on Mount Sumeru. When Shakyamuni in a past existence practiced austerities as King Shibi (Skt: Śibi), Taishaku assumed the form of a hawk, and Bishukatsuma that of a dove, as a test of the king's sincerity. In order to save the dove, Shibi gave his life, offering his flesh to the hungry hawk. The story appears in *Daichido Ron* (T25, 314c), and is frequently cited by Nichiren.

8. Fumyō was the name of Shakyamuni when he was engaged in the practice of observing the precepts in a past existence. This is another story frequently cited by Nichiren. See Letter 8, note 24.

9. Aniruddha (Jap: Anaritsu sonja) was one of the ten major disciples of Shakyamuni and was known as "foremost in divine insight." He was a cousin of Shakyamuni. The Sanskrit, *aniruddha*, means to be unobstructed, or to gratify every wish and be without desire. Long ago, a *pratyekabuddha* named Rida engaged in the practice of begging alms, but gained nothing. Seeing this, a poor man offered him

barnyard millet. Later, when the poor man went deep into the mountains to find mil-let for Rida, a rabbit happened to jump on his back and then turned into a corpse. Frightened, he tried to shake it off, but in vain. As soon as he arrived at his house, how-ever, the corpse fell off and turned into gold. Hearing of this, wicked men came to rob him of the gold, but to them it looked like a mere corpse. To the eye of the poor man, however, it was a genuine treasure of gold, and he became wealthy. Ninety-one kalpas later he was born as Aniruddha. The story appears in the *Zōhō Zōkyō* (T4, 470c-471a) and in T'ien-t'ai's *Hokke Mongu* (T34, 15a).

10. Mahānāma was one of the five monks who were ordered by Shakyamuni's father, the king, to accompany Shakyamuni when he forsook the secular world and entered religious life. They followed and practiced asceticism with Shakyamuni, but left him when he renounced ascetic practices. However, shortly after Shakyamuni obtained enlightenment, he preached his first sermon to them at Sarnath, known as the Deer Park, and they became his first disciples. According to the *Zōichi Agon* Sutra (T2, 557a), however, Mahānama is said to have possessed occult powers. The story of "sand in his palm turning into gold" is found in Tsung-i's *Tendai Sandaibu Hochū* (ZZ1 44, 3).

11. T9, 42b.

55 ENCOURAGEMENT TO A SICK PERSON

Nichiren wrote this letter on the thirteenth day of the twelfth month, 1264, to Nanjō Hyōe Shichirō (d.1265). Nanjō was the steward of Ueno Village in the Fuji district of Suruga Province. He was also known as Lord Ueno, and sometime between 1260 and 1261, or possibly between 1263 and 1264, while on an official tour of duty in Kamakura, had met Nichiren and had been converted to his teaching. This letter was written from the province of Awa, Nichiren's native area, to which he had returned after an eleven-years absence, to attend on his ill mother. Nichiren had incurred the enmity of the steward of Tōjō village, Tōjō Kagenobu, when he first proclaimed his teaching in 1253. Tōjō was a committed Nembutsu believer and, enraged at Nichiren's pronouncements, ordered him arrested. Nichiren barely managed to escape and went at once to Kamakura, where he lived at Matsubagayatsu.

Now, having come back to Awa, and with his mother's return to good health, Nichiren resumed his active propagation efforts. At that time a believer named Kudō Yoshitaka (d.1264) invited Nichiren to visit him at his home. On the way there, on the eleventh day of the eleventh month, 1264, Nichiren and his group were ambushed by Tōjō Kagenobu and his men at a place called Komatsubara (present-day Hiroba area, Kamogawa-shi, Chiba Prefecture). Nichiren escaped with a broken hand and a cut on his forehead but two of his followers were killed. This event, known as the Komatsubara Persecution, did not keep Nichiren from continuing his teaching efforts in Awa. This letter was written to strengthen the faith of Lord Nanjō, who was suffering from a severe illness at the time.

"Encouragement to a Sick Person" (Irō Sho) is an alternative title for this letter; it is also known as Komatsubara Hōnan Sho (On the Komatsubara Persecution). The standard title is Nanjō Hyōe Shichirō-dono Gosho (Letter to Lord Nanjō Hyōe Shichirō).

I have heard that you are suffering from illness. Is this true? The uncertainty of this world is such that even the healthy cannot remain forever, let alone those who are ill. Thoughtful persons should therefore prepare their minds for the life to come. Yet one cannot prepare his mind for the next life by his own efforts alone. Only on the basis of the teachings of Shakyamuni Buddha, the original teacher of all living beings, will he be able to do so.

However, the Buddha's teachings are various, perhaps because people's minds also differ greatly. In any event, Shakyamuni taught for no more than fifty years. Among the teachings he expounded during the first forty years and more, we find the *Kegon* Sutra, which says, "The mind, the Buddha, and all living beings—these three things are without distinction";[1] the *Agon* sutras, which set forth the principles of suffering, emptiness, impermanence, and egolessness; the *Daijuku* Sutra, which asserts the interpenetration of the defiled aspect and the pure aspect;[2] the *Daibon Hannya* Sutra, which teaches mutual identification and nonduality; and the *Muryōju*, *Kammuryōju*, and *Amida* sutras, which emphasize rebirth in the Land of Perfect Bliss.[3] All these teachings were doubtless expounded in order to save all living beings in the Former, Middle, and Latter Days of the Law.

Nevertheless, for some reason of his own, the Buddha declared in the *Muryōgi* Sutra, "[Expounding the Law in various ways,] I made use of the power of expedient means. But in these more than forty years, I have not yet revealed the truth."[4] Like a parent who has second thoughts about the transfer deed he has written out earlier, he looked back with regret upon all the sutras he had expounded during the past forty years and more, including those which taught rebirth in the Land of Perfect Bliss, and declared [that no matter how earnestly one may practice them,] ". . . in the end one will never attain supreme enlightenment, even after the lapse of countless, limitless, inconceivable asōgi kalpas."[5] He reiterated this in the *Hōben* chapter of the Lotus Sutra, saying, "Honestly discarding the provisional teachings, I will expound only the supreme Way."[6] By "discarding the provisional teachings," he meant that one should discard the Nembutsu and other teachings preached during the period of those forty-some years.

Having thus obviously regretted and reversed his previous teachings, he made clear his true intention, saying, "The World-Honored One has long expounded his doctrines and now must reveal the truth,"[7] and "The Tathagata long kept silence with regard to this essential truth and was in no haste to preach it."[8] Thereupon Tahō Buddha emerged from below the earth and added his testimony, declaring what Shakyamuni had said to be true, and the Buddhas of the ten directions assembled in the eight directions,[9] extending their long, broad tongues[10] until they reached the palace in the Brahma Heaven. All the beings of the two worlds[11] and the eight kinds,[12] who were gathered at the two places and three assemblies,[13] without a single exception witnessed this.

Yet, setting aside evil persons and non-Buddhists, who do not believe in Buddhism, even among the followers of Buddhism we find those who [reject this testimony and instead] have devout faith in the provisional teachings preached before the Lotus Sutra, such as the Nembutsu. They devote themselves to reciting it ten times, a hundred times, a thousand times, ten thousand, or as many as sixty thousand times each day, but do not chant Nam-myoho-renge-kyo, not even once in ten or twenty years. [In light of the above sutra passages,] are they not like a person who clings to the transfer deed already nullified by his parent and refuses to accept its revised version? They may appear to others as well as to themselves to have faith in the Buddha's teachings, but if we go by what the Buddha actually taught, they are unfilial persons.

This is why the second volume of the Lotus Sutra states, "Now this threefold world is all my domain. The living beings in it are all my children. Yet this world has many cares and troubles from which I alone can save them. But, even though I teach and instruct them, they neither believe nor accept."[14] This passage means that to us living beings, the Tathagata Shakyamuni is our parent, teacher, and sovereign. Amida, Yakushi, and other Buddhas may be a sovereign to us living beings, but they are neither a parent nor a teacher. Shakyamuni is the one and only Buddha who is endowed with all three virtues and to whom we owe the most profound debt of gratitude. There are parents and parents, yet none of them can equal him. There are all manner of teachers and sovereigns, but none so admirable as he. Could those who disobey the teaching of the one who is their parent, teacher, and sovereign not be abandoned by both heavenly gods and earthly deities? They are the most unfilial of all children. It is for this reason that the Buddha said, "But, even though I teach and instruct them, they neither believe nor accept." Even though they may follow the sutras preached before the Lotus Sutra and practice them for a hundred, a thousand, ten thousand, or a hundred thousand kalpas, if they do not believe in the Lotus Sutra and chant Nam-myoho-renge-kyo even once, they can only be termed unfilial. They will therefore be abandoned by the sacred ones[15] of the three existences and the ten directions and hated by the deities of both heaven and earth. This represents the first [of the five guides for propagation].[16]

Even those people who commit the five cardinal sins, the ten evil acts,[17] etc., or innumerable other wrongdoings may attain the Way if only their faculties are keen. Devadatta and Aṅgulimāla[18] are representative of such people. And even those of dull faculties may attain the Way, provided they are free of misdeeds. Śuddhipanthaka is an example.[19] Our faculties are even duller than those of Śuddhipanthaka. We can discern the colors and shapes of things no better than a sheep's eye. In the vast depths of our greed, anger, and stupidity, we commit the ten evil acts every day and, although we may not commit the five cardinal sins, we perpetrate similar offenses daily.

Moreover, every single person is guilty of slander of the Law, an offense exceeding even the ten evil acts or the five cardinal sins. Although few people slander the Lotus Sutra with actual words of abuse, there is none who values it. Some appear to value the sutra, but in fact, they do not believe in it as deeply as they do in the Nembutsu or other teachings. And even those with profound faith do not reproach the enemies of the Lotus Sutra. No matter what great good deed one may perform, even if he reads and transcribes the entirety of the Lotus Sutra a thousand or ten thousand times or masters the meditation to perceive *ichinen sanzen*, should he but fail to denounce the enemies of the Lotus Sutra, he will be unable to attain the Way. To illustrate, it is like the case of someone in the service of the imperial court. Even though he may have served for a decade or two, if he knows someone to be an enemy of the emperor but neither reports him to the throne nor feels personal enmity toward him, all the merit of his past services will be thereby negated, and he will instead be charged with a crime. You must understand that people of this age are slanderers of the Law. This represents the second [of the five guides for propagation].

The thousand years beginning from the day after the Buddha's passing are called the Former Day of the Law, a period when those who upheld the precepts were many, and people attained the Way. The thousand years of the Former Day are followed by the Middle Day of the Law, which also lasts a thousand years. During this period, many people broke the precepts and few attained the Way. The Middle Day is followed by the ten thousand years of the Latter Day of the Law. During this period, people neither uphold the precepts nor break them; only those without precepts fill the country. Moreover, it is called a defiled age, an age rife with disorder. In an uncorrupted age, called a pure age, the wrong is discarded while the right is observed, just as crooked timber is planed according to the markings of a carpenter's line. During the Former and Middle Days of the Law, the five impurities[20] begin to appear, and in the Latter Day, they are rampant. They rage not only like huge waves, whipped by a strong gale, battering the shore, but also like waves crashing one against another. [Among the five impurities,] the impurity of thought is such that, as the Former and Middle Days of the Law gradually pass, people transmit an insignificant heretical teaching while destroying the unfathomable True Law. It therefore follows that more people fall into the evil paths because of errors with respect to Buddhism than because of secular misdeeds.

Now the two thousand years of the Former and Middle Days of the Law have already passed, and it has been more than two hundred years since the Latter Day began. Now is the time when, because the impurity of thought prevails, more people fall into the evil paths with the intention of creating good causes than they do by committing evil. As for evil acts, even ignorant people may recognize them for what they are, and refrain from committing them. This is like extinguishing a fire with water. But people think that good deeds are all equal in their goodness; thus they adhere to lesser good and do not realize that, in so doing, they bring about major evil. Therefore, even when they see sacred structures related to Dengyō, Jikaku, and others that are neglected and in disrepair, they leave them as they are for the simple reason that they are not halls dedicated to the Nembutsu. Instead, they build Nembutsu halls beside those sacred structures, confiscate the lands that have been donated to them, and offer them instead to the halls they have erected. According to a passage of the *Zōbō Ketsugi Sutra*,[21] such deeds will bring few benefits. You should understand from the above that even if one performs a good deed, should it be an act of lesser good that destroys great good, then it will cause one to fall into the evil paths.

The present age coincides with the beginning of the Latter Day of the Law. Gone completely are those people with the capacity to attain enlightenment through either the Hinayana or provisional Mahayana sutras. There now remain only those whose capacity is suited solely to the true Mahayana sutra. A small boat cannot carry a large rock. Those who are evil or ignorant are like a large rock, while the Hinayana and provisional Mahayana sutras as well as the Nembutsu are like a small boat. If one tries to cure virulent sores with hot-spring baths, because the ailment is so serious, such mild treatment will be to no avail. For us in this defiled age of the Latter Day, embracing the Nembutsu and other teachings is like working rice paddies in winter; it does not suit the time. This represents the third [of the five guides for propagation].

One should also have a correct understanding of the country. People's minds differ according to their land. For example, a mandarin orange tree south of the Yangtze River becomes a triple-leaved orange tree if it is transplanted to the north of the Huai River.[22] Even plants and trees, which have no mind, change with their location. How much more, then, must beings with minds differ according to the place!

A work by the Tripitaka Master Hsüan-tsang called *Daitō Saiiki Ki*, or *Record of the Western Regions*, describes many countries in India. According to the nature of the country, there are countries whose inhabitants are undutiful to their parents, and others where people observe filial piety. In some countries, anger prevails, while in others, stupidity is rampant. There are countries devoted solely to Hinayana, others devoted solely to Mahayana, and still others where both Mahayana and Hinayana are pursued. There are countries wholly given over to the killing of living creatures, countries wholly given over to thieving, countries where rice abounds, and countries which produce much millet. So great is the variety of countries [in India].

Then, what teaching should our country of Japan learn if its people are to free themselves from the sufferings of birth and death? As for this question, the Lotus Sutra states, "After the passing of the Tathagata, I will cause this sutra to spread widely throughout the continent of Jambudvīpa and never allow it to perish."[23] This passage means that the Lotus is a sutra related to the people of Jambudvīpa, the continent of the south. Bodhisattva Miroku said, "There is a small country in the eastern quarter whose people are related solely to the Mahayana."[24] According to this passage from his treatise, within Jambudvīpa, there is a small country in the eastern quarter where the capacity of the people is especially suited to the Mahayana sutra. Seng-chao,[25] in his commentary remarks, "This sutra is related to a small country in the northeast."[26] This indicates that the Lotus Sutra has a connection to a country in the northeast. The Eminent Priest Annen states, "All in my country of Japan believe in the Mahayana."[27] Eshin in his *Ichijō Yōketsu* says, "Throughout all Japan, all people share the same capacity to attain Buddhahood through the perfect teaching [of the Lotus Sutra]."[28]

Thus, according to the opinions of my virtuous predecessors, such as Shakyamuni Buddha, Bodhisattva Miroku, the Tripitaka Master Sūryasoma,[29] the Tripitaka Master Kumārajīva, the Dharma Teacher Seng-chao, the Eminent Priest Annen, and the Supervisor of Monks Eshin, people in the country of Japan have a capacity suited solely to the Lotus Sutra. Those who put into practice even a phrase or a verse of this sutra are certain to attain the Way, for it is the teaching related to them. This may be likened to iron particles drawn by a magnet or dewdrops collecting on a mirror.[30] Other good practices such as the Nembutsu are unrelated to our country. They are like a magnet that cannot attract iron or a mirror that is unable to gather dew. For this reason, Annen states in his interpretation, "If it is not the true vehicle, one is doubtless deceiving both oneself and others."[31] This passage means that one who instructs the people of Japan in a teaching other than the Lotus Sutra is deceiving not only oneself but others, too. One therefore must always consider the country when propagating the Buddhist teachings. One should not assume that a teaching suited to one country must necessarily be suited to another as well. This constitutes the fourth [of the five guides for propagation].

Furthermore, in a country where Buddhism has already spread, one must also take into account the sequence of propagation. It is the rule in propagating Buddhism that one must always learn the characteristics of the teachings that have already spread. To illustrate, when giving medicine to a sick person, one should know what kind of medicine was administered before. Otherwise, different kinds of medicine may conflict and work against one another, killing the patient. Likewise, different teachings of Buddhism may conflict and interfere with each other, destroying the practitioner. In a country where non-Buddhist teachings have already spread, one should use Buddhism to refute them. For example, the Buddha appeared in India and defeated the Brahmans; Kāśyapa Mātaṅga, and Chu-fa-lan[32] went to China and attacked the Taoists; and Prince Jōgū[33] was born in the country of Japan and put Moriya[34] to the sword.

The same principle applies in the realm of Buddhism itself. In a country where the Hinayana has spread, one must vanquish it by means of the Mahayana sutras, just as Bodhisattva Asaṅga[35] refuted the Hinayana teachings upheld by Vasubandhu. In a country where provisional Mahayana has been propagated, one must conquer it with the true Mahayana, just as the Great Teacher T'ien-t'ai Chih-che defeated the three schools of the South and the seven schools of the North in China.[36] As for the country of Japan, it has been more than four hundred years since the two sects of Tendai and Shingon have spread here. [During this period,] it has been determined that all four categories of Buddhists—priests, nuns, laymen, and laywomen—have capacities suited to the Lotus Sutra. All people, whether good or evil, wise or ignorant, are endowed with the benefit of the fiftieth hearer.[37] They are like the K'un-lun Mountains,[38] where no worthless stone is to be found, or the mountain island of P'eng-lai,[39] where no harmful potion is known.

However, within the past fifty years or so, a man of flagrant slander named Hōnen appeared. He deceived all the people by showing them a stone that resembled a jewel and persuading them to discard the jewel they already possessed in favor of it. This is what the fifth volume of the *Maka Shikan* means when it refers to "treasuring tiles and pebbles and calling them bright jewels."[40] All the people are clutching ordinary rocks in their hands, convinced that they are precious jewels. That is to say, they have discarded the Lotus Sutra to chant the name of Amida Buddha. But when I point this out, they become furious and revile the votary of the Lotus Sutra, thereby increasing all the more their karma to fall into the hell of incessant suffering. Here I have explained the fifth [of the five guides for propagation].

You, heeding my assertion, discarded the Nembutsu and embraced the Lotus Sutra. But by now you must surely have reverted to being a follower of the Nembutsu. Remember that to discard the Lotus Sutra and become a believer in the Nembutsu is to be like a rock from a mountain peak hurtling down to the valley below, or like rain in the skies falling to the ground. There is no doubt that such a person will fall into the great Avīci Hell. Those related to the sons of Daitsū Buddha had to spend the duration of *sanzen-jintengō*,[41] and those who received the seed of Buddhahood in the remote past, the length of *gohyaku-jintengō*,[42] [in the evil paths]. This was because they met with very evil companions and discarded the Lotus Sutra, falling back to the provisional teachings such as the Nembutsu. As the members of your family seem to be Nembutsu adherents, they certainly must be urging it upon you. That is understandable, since they themselves believe in it. You should consider them, however, as people deluded by the followers of the diabolical Hōnen. Arouse strong faith, and do not heed what they say. It is the way of the great devil to assume the form of a venerable monk or to take possession of one's father, mother or brother in order to obstruct one's next life. Whatever they may say, no matter how cleverly they may try to deceive you into discarding the Lotus Sutra, do not assent to it.

Stop and consider. If the passages of proof [offered to support the claim] that the Nembutsu does in truth lead to rebirth in the Pure Land were reliable, then in the past twelve years during which I have been asserting that the Nembutsu believers will fall into the hell of incessant suffering, would they consistently have failed to refute me, no matter with whom they lodged their protests? Their contention must be feeble indeed! Teachings such as those left behind by Hōnen and Shan-tao[43] have been known to me, Nichiren, since I was seventeen or eighteen. And the arguments that people put forth these days are no improvement.

Consequently, since their teachings are no match for mine, they resort to sheer force of numbers in trying to fight against me. Nembutsu believers number tens of millions, and their supporters are many. I, Nichiren, am alone, without a single ally. It is amazing that I should have survived until now. This year, too, on the eleventh day of the eleventh month, between the hours of the Monkey and the Cock (around 5:00 P.M.), on the highway called Matsubara in Tōjō in the province of Awa, I was ambushed by hundreds of Nembutsu believers.[44] I was alone except for about ten men accompanying me, only three or four of whom were capable of offering any resistance at all. Arrows fell on us like rain, and swords descended like lightning. One of my disciples was slain in a matter of a moment, and two others were gravely wounded. I myself sustained cuts and blows, and it seemed that I was doomed. Yet, for some reason, my attackers failed to kill me; thus I have survived until now.

This has only strengthened my faith in the Lotus Sutra. The fourth volume [of the sutra] says, "Since hatred and jealousy toward this sutra abound even during the lifetime of the Buddha, how much worse will it be in the world after his passing!"[45] The fifth volume states, "The people will resent [the Lotus Sutra] and find it extremely difficult to believe."[46] In the country of Japan there are many who read and study the Lotus Sutra. There are also many who are beaten in punishment for attempting to seduce other men's wives, or for theft or other offenses. Yet not one person has ever suffered injury on account of the Lotus Sutra. It is clear, therefore, that those Japanese who embrace the sutra have yet to experience the truth of the above sutra passages. I,

Nichiren, alone have read the sutra with my entire being. This is the meaning of the passage that says, "We do not hold our own lives dear. We value only the supreme Way."[47] I, Nichiren, am therefore the foremost votary of the Lotus Sutra in Japan.

Should you depart from this life before I do, you should report to Bonten, Taishaku, the Four Great Heavenly Kings. and Great King Emma. Declare yourself to be a disciple of the priest Nichiren, the foremost votary of the Lotus Sutra in Japan. Then they cannot possibly treat you discourteously. But if you should be of two minds, alternately chanting the Nembutsu and reciting the Lotus Sutra, and fear what others may say about you, then, even though you may identify yourself as Nichiren's disciple, they will never accept your word. [If that should happen,] do not resent me later. Yet, since the Lotus Sutra answers one's prayers for matters of this life as well, you may still survive your illness. In that case, I will by all means visit you as soon as possible and talk with you directly. Words cannot all be set down in a letter, and a letter will not adequately convey one's thoughts, so I will stop for now.

With my deep respect,
Nichiren

The thirteenth day of the twelfth month in the first year of Bun'ei (1264)

Notes

1. T9, 465c.

2. Miao-lo in his *Kongōbei Ron* summarizes the essence of the *Daijuku* Sutra as "the interpenetration of the defiled aspect and the pure aspect" (T46, 782b) and the essence of the *Hannya* Sutra as "mutual identification and nonduality" (T46, 782a). Both statements can be interpreted to mean that, because all phenomena have emptiness or nonsubstantiality (*kū*) as their true nature, they are without fixed substance, and thus there is no fundamental separation between delusion and enlightenment, or between the common mortal and the Buddha.

3. The Land of Perfect Bliss is the name of the land of Amida Buddha, said to be located in a region of the universe ten billion Buddha lands to the west.

4. T9, 386b.

5. *Muryōgi* Sutra (T9, 387a). In this sutra these words are spoken by the bodhisattva Daishōgon.

6. T9, 10a.

7. Lotus Sutra (T9, 6a).

8. Lotus Sutra (T9, 19c).

9. North, south, east, west, northwest, northeast, southwest, and southeast. This means that all the Buddhas assembled at the ceremony of the Lotus Sutra were in the same horizontal plane.

10. The long, broad tongue is one of the thirty-two marks of a Buddha. The scene is described in the *Jinriki* (21st) chapter of the Lotus Sutra.

11. The first two divisions of the threefold world—the world of desire and the world of form. *See also* Threefold world in Glossary.

12. Eight kinds of beings who assembled at the ceremony of the Lotus Sutra. They are: (1) the gods of the world of desire, (2) the gods of the world of form, (3) dragon kings and their followers, (4) *kimnara* (gods with beautiful voices) kings and their followers, (5) *gandharva* (gods of music) kings and their followers, (6) *asura* (fighting demons) kings and their followers, (7) *garuda* (giant birds that feed on dragons) kings and their followers, and (8) the kings of the human world.

13. A division of the events described in the Lotus Sutra in terms of location and sequence. Shakyamuni began preaching the sutra on Eagle Peak; then lifted the assembly into midair, where he continued to preach; and finally returned the assembly to Eagle Peak. Thus, the "two places" are on Eagle Peak and in the air, and the "three assemblies" are the first assembly at Eagle Peak, the Ceremony in the Air, and the second assembly on Eagle Peak.

14. T9, 14c. This passage is interpreted to refer to the Buddha's three virtues of sovereign, teacher, and parent, as mentioned below in the text. "Now this threefold world is my domain" represents the virtue of sovereign; "The living beings in it are all my children," the virtue of parent; and "Yet this world has many cares and troubles from which I alone can save them," the virtue of teacher.

15. Buddhas and bodhisattvas.

16. The five guides to propagation (Jap: *gokō*) are set forth by Nichiren in the letter known as "The Teaching, Capacity, Time, and Country" (*Kyō Ki Ji Koku Shō*), see Letter 1, and elsewhere. Briefly, they are: (1) a correct understanding of the teaching; (2) a correct understanding of the capacity of the people; (3) a correct understanding of the time; (4) a correct understanding of the country; and (5) a correct understanding of the sequence of propagation. Here they are indicated by notes at the end of each relevant passage: "this is number one, . . . number two," etc.

17. The five cardinal sins are: killing one's father, killing one's mother, killing an arhat, shedding the blood of a Buddha, and causing disunity within the community of monks. The ten evil acts are: killing, stealing, unlawful sexual intercourse, lying, flattery (or random and irresponsible speech), defaming, duplicity, greed, anger, and stupidity or the holding of mistaken views.

18. Angulimāla was a notorious murderer who became a follower of Shakyamuni. "Angulimāla" means necklace of fingers, a name said to derive from a necklace he wore made of the severed fingers of his victims. He originally studied under a teacher of Brahmanism in Śrāvastī. According to the *Okutsumara* Sutra (T2, 512b), when he spurned the advances of his teacher's wife, she slandered him to her husband. Enraged, the Brahman ordered Angulimāla to kill a thousand people and cut off their fingers. Angulimāla had already killed nine hundred and ninety-nine people and was about to kill his mother to complete the thousand, when he met Shakyamuni who converted

him to Buddhism. The *Bussetsu Okutsuma* Sutra (T2, 509b) gives the number killed at ninety-nine.

19. Śuddhipanthaka (Jap: Surihandoku) was a disciple of Shakyamuni. Accounts vary considerably according to the source. In one version Śuddhipanthaka is the slow-witted sibling of a bright elder brother (*Zōichi Agon* Sutra, T2, 601b); in another version Śuddhi Panthaka is the combined name of two brothers, both of limited intelligence (*Honyaku Myōgi Shū*, T54, 1065a). According to the *Hokku Hiyu* Sutra (T4, 588c–589a), the elderly monk Pathaka was so dull-witted that in three years he was unable to learn even a single verse of the Buddhist teachings, even with five hundred arhats to instruct him. Taking pity on him, the Buddha personally gave him a verse to learn that consisted of fourteen characters in the Chinese translation: "Guard your speech, govern your mind, do not do wrong in deed. One who practices in this way will surely attain emancipation." Touched by the Buddha's compassion, Panthaka strove earnestly to learn the verse. Through these efforts, he awakened to its meaning and reached the state of an arhat.

20. The five impurities (Jap: *gojoku*) are: (1) impurity of the age, caused by natural disasters, etc.; (2) impurity of thought; (3) impurity of desires, such as greed, anger, or stupidity; (4) impurity of the people, weakened both spiritually and physically by impurities of thought and desire; and (5) impurity of life itself. They are listed in the *Hōben* (2d) chapter of the Lotus Sutra.

21. The *Zōbō Ketsugi* Sutra (T85, no. 2870) describes the characteristics of the Middle Day of the Law and stresses the practice of almsgiving.

22. This saying appears in several Chinese classics such as the *Yen-tzu ch'un-ch'iu*. It means that a person will change according to his circumstances. The Huai River flows eastward from the southern part of Honan province north of the Yellow River into Lake Hungtse.

23. T9, 61c. These words are spoken by Bodhisattva Fugen in a vow made before Shakyamuni Buddha.

24. This passage is quoted in Annen's *Futsū Ju Bosatsukai Kōshaku* (T74, 757a) as a citation from the *Yuga Ron*; however, no such passage exists in the extant version of this text. The *Yuga Ron*, properly *Yugashiji Ron*, was traditionally regarded as the words of Bodhisattva Miroku, compiled by Asaṅga who ascended by means of his occult powers to the Tuṣita Heaven, in order to receive the bodhisattva's instruction. Recent scholarship attributes the work to Asanga or Maitreya.

25. Seng-chao (384–414) was a famous priest of the Later Ch'in dynasty and one of Kumārajīva's major disciples.

26. *Hokke Hongyō no Kōki*, contained in *Hokke Denki* (T51, 54b). This passage quotes the words of Śūryasoma, when he bequeathed the Lotus Sutra to Kumārajīva.

27. Annen (841–889?) was a Tendai priest who helped establish the doctrine and practice of Tendai esotericism. He studied the exoteric and esoteric teachings under Jikaku, and also received the doctrine of the Womb Realm from the priest Henjō (816–890) of the Genkyō-ji in Kyoto. Annen himself became chief priest of this temple in 884. The quotation is from *Futsū Ju Bosatsukai Kōshaku* (T74, 757a).

28. Eshin (942–1017) is more commonly called Genshin. He practiced at a temple called Eshin-in on Mount Hiei. His *Ichijō Yōketsu*, written around 1006, stresses the one-vehicle teaching of the Lotus Sutra. He is famed as the compiler of the *Ōjō Yōshū*,

a work that had great influence on the development of the Pure Land sect in Japan. The quotation from *Ichijō Yōketsu* is at T74, 351a.

29. Śūryasoma was a prince of Yarkand in Central Asia and the teacher of Kumārajīva.

30. Vapor will condense on a mirror placed outside at night. In the past it was said that the mirror drew this water from the moon.

31. *Futsū Ju Bosatsukai Kōshaku* (T74, 757a).

32. Kāśyapa Matanga and Chu-fu-lan (Sanskrit unknown) were Indian monks traditionally believed to have introduced Buddhism to China. They are said to have come to China at the request of Emperor Ming of the Later Han dynasty in A.D. 67. The story appears in the *Kōsō Den* (T50, 322a–323b).

33. Jōgū (574–622) is usually referred to as Prince Shōtoku, the second son of the thirty-first emperor, Yōmei, famous for his application of the spirit of Buddhism to government.

34. Moriya is Mononobe no Moriya (d.587), an official of the Yamato court who opposed the introduction of Buddhism to Japan.

35. Asaṅga was a fourth-century scholar of the Consciousness-Only doctrine. Vasubandhu was his younger brother. He initially studied the Hinayana teachings but became dissatisfied with these doctrines and made efforts to master the Mahayana teachings as well. When Vasubandhu became attached to Hinayana, Asaṅga converted him to Mahayana Buddhism.

36. *See* Three schools of the South and Seven schools of the North in Glossary.

37. Reference is to the principle of "continual propagation to the fiftieth person," described in the *Zuiki Kudoku* (18th) chapter of the Lotus Sutra. Suppose, the text says, that after Shakyamuni Buddha's death, a person were to hear the Lotus Sutra and rejoice, then preach it to a second person, who also rejoices and in turn preaches it to a third, and so on, until a fiftieth person hears the sutra. The benefit received by this person on hearing the sutra, even at fifty removes, would be countless millions of times greater than that of someone who for eighty years makes offerings to the beings of four billion *asōgi* worlds and enables them all to attain the state of arhat.

38. The name of the mountainous region including the Pamirs, Tibet, and the plateau of Mongolia. According to the *Shih Chi*, it was traditionally believed that jewels could be found here.

39. P'eng-lai is a legendary mountainous island off the eastern coast of China, where, according to the *Shih Chi* and other sources, an immortal possessing the elixir of perennial youth and eternal life dwells in a palace made of gold and gems.

40. T46, 43a.

41. According to the *Kejōyu* (7th) chapter of the Lotus Sutra Shakyamuni, in the remote past, referred to here as *sanzen jintengō*, preached the Lotus Sutra as one of the sixteen sons of a Buddha called Daitsū. Those who heard the sutra at that time originally took faith in it, but later abandoned it in favor of lesser teachings, and therefore remained for a long time in the paths of suffering. *See Sanzen jintengō* in Glossary.

42. According to the *Juryō* (16th) chapter of the Lotus Sutra, Shakyamuni, in the even more remote past, referred to here as *gohyaku jintengō*, preached the Lotus Sutra to listeners who at first took faith in the teaching, but later discarded it for lesser teachings and thus sank into the realms of suffering. *See Gohyaku jintengō* in Glossary.

43. Shan-tao (613–681) was the third patriarch of the Chinese Pure Land school.

He studied the *Kammuryōju* Sutra under Tao-ch'o and disseminated the practice of calling upon the name of Amida Buddha. In Japan Hōnen studied Shan-tao's commentary on this sutra, the *Kammuryōjubutsu Kyō Sho* and founded the Japanese Pure Land sect.

44. This refers to the Komatsubara Persecution, which occurred about a month before this letter was written.

45. Lotus Sutra (T9, 31b).

46. Lotus Sutra (T9, 39a).

47. Lotus Sutra (T9, 36c).

56 HELL IS THE LAND OF TRANQUIL LIGHT

Nichiren sent this letter to the wife of Nanjō Hyōe Shichirō, known also as Lord Ueno, who had died in 1265. She was also the mother of Nanjō Tokimitsu (1259–1322), who had succeeded his father as lord of the Ueno district in Suruga Province. Lady Ueno had raised nine children after her husband's death and was a devoted mother and sincere follower of Nichiren. On this occasion she had sent Nichiren various gifts on the occasion of the tenth anniversary of her husband's death, and Nichiren's letter, dated the eleventh day of the seventh month, 1274, is in acknowledgment of her gift. On the twelfth of the fifth month, Nichiren had left Kamakura and had retired to a small dwelling at the foot of Mount Minobu. The area was isolated and the climate severe; yet Nichiren devoted himself wholeheartedly to training disciples to carry on his teachings.

"Hell Is the Land of Tranquil Light" (*Jigoku soku Jakkō Gosho*) is an alternative title for this letter. It is more frequently referred to as *Ueno-dono Goke-ama Gohenji* (Reply to Lady Ueno, the Lay Nun).

I have received your many gifts. Nothing would please me more than to know that you have communicated with the late Lord Ueno, but I know that that is impossible. Perhaps only in a dream or a vision can you see him. Never fear, though; your late husband must certainly be in the pure land of Eagle Peak, listening and watching over this *sahā* world day and night. You, his wife, and your children have only mortal senses, so you cannot see or hear him, but be assured that you will eventually be reunited on Eagle Peak.

Counting all your previous lives, you must have shared the bonds of matrimony with as many men as there are grains of sand in the ocean.

However, the man to whom you were wed in this life is your true husband. He is the only one who brought you to practice the teachings of the Lotus Sutra. You should revere him as a Buddha. Indeed, he was a Buddha while alive, and in death, he is a Buddha still. His Buddhahood transcends both life and death. This is the meaning of the profound doctrine of *sokushin jōbutsu*, or attaining enlightenment as a common mortal. The fourth volume of the Lotus Sutra states: "One who sincerely embraces this sutra is thereby embracing Buddhahood."[1]

Neither the pure land nor hell exists outside ourselves; both lie within our own hearts. Awakened to this truth, one is called a Buddha; deluded about it, he is a common mortal. The Lotus Sutra awakens us to this reality, and one who embraces the Lotus Sutra will find that hell is itself the enlightened land.

Even though one may practice the provisional teachings for uncountable kalpas, he will only fall into hell if he turns against the Lotus Sutra. These are not my own words; they were proclaimed by Shakyamuni Buddha and confirmed by Tahō Buddha and all of Shakyamuni's emanations throughout the universe. To practice the provisional teachings is to be like a man scorched by fire who enters deeper and deeper into the flames, or like a drowning man sinking to the bottom of the deep waters. Not to embrace the Lotus Sutra is like jumping into fire or water. Those who are deluded by such evil companions as Hōnen, Kōbō, and other slanderers of the Lotus Sutra and believe in the *Amida* or *Dainichi* Sutra are falling farther and farther into the fire or sinking deeper and deeper toward the bottom of the water. How can they possibly escape from agony? They will doubtless undergo the terrible heat of the hell of regeneration, the hell of black ropes, and the hell of incessant suffering,[2] and the unbearable cold of the hell of the blood-red lotus and the hell of the great blood-red lotus.[3] The second volume of the Lotus Sutra reads, "After he dies, he will fall into the hell of incessant suffering. [After one kalpa he will be reborn only to fall back into hell, and] he will go through this cycle for countless kalpas."[4]

Your late husband has escaped such agonies, for he was a follower of Nichiren, the votary of the Lotus Sutra. A passage from the sutra reads: "Even if they fall into a great fire, they will not be burned. . . . If they are swept away by a great flood, by chanting its name they can straightaway reach shallow water."[5] Another passage reads, "The good fortune of the believer cannot be burned by fire or washed away by water."[6] How reassuring!

You may think of hell, the iron rods of the wardens of hell or the rending cries of Abōrasetsu[7] as existing way off in some faraway place, but they are not like that. This teaching is of prime importance, and yet I will impart it to you just as Bodhisattva Monju revealed to the Dragon King's daughter the secret teaching of *sokushin jōbutsu*, that one can attain Buddhahood as a common mortal. Now that you are about to receive that teaching, strive even more earnestly in your faith. One who practices still more earnestly whenever he hears the teachings of the Lotus Sutra is a true seeker of the Way. When T'ien-t'ai stated, "From the indigo, an even deeper blue,"[8] he meant that something dyed with indigo becomes even bluer than the indigo plant itself. For us the Lotus Sutra is the indigo plant, and the growing intensity of our practice is "an even deeper blue."

The word *jigoku* or "hell" can be interpreted to mean digging a hole in the ground. A hole is always dug for one who dies; this is what is called "hell." The flames that reduce his body to ashes are the fires of incessant suffering. His wife, children, and relatives hurrying the dead man to his grave are the guards of hell, called Abōrasetsu. The plaintive cries of his family are the voices of the wardens of hell. The meter-long walking stick of the dead man is the iron rod of torture in hell. The horses and oxen that carry the deceased are the horse-headed and ox-headed demons, and the grave itself is the hell of incessant suffering. The eighty-four thousand earthly desires are eighty-four thousand cauldrons for torturing the dead. The dead man leaving his home is departing on a journey to the mountain of death, while the river beside which his loving children stand in grief is the river of three crossings.[9] It is useless to look for hell anywhere else.

Those who embrace the Lotus Sutra, however, can change all this. For them, hell changes into the enlightened land, the burning fires of agony change into the torch of wisdom of the Buddha in his reward body aspect; the dead person becomes a Buddha in his Law body aspect; and the fiery inferno becomes the abode where the Buddha in his manifested body aspect[10] demonstrates his great mercy. Moreover, the walking stick is transformed into that of the true entity of the Mystic Law, the river of three crossings becomes the ocean of "sufferings are nirvana," and the mountain of death becomes the towering peak of "earthly desires are enlightenment." Please think of your husband in these terms. To realize all this is to attain enlightenment as a common mortal, and to awaken to it is to open the inner eye of the Buddha wisdom. Devadatta changed the hell of incessant suffering into the enlightened paradise, and the Dragon King's daughter also was able to attain enlightenment without changing her dragon form. The Lotus Sutra can bring enlightenment even to those who at first oppose it. Such great benefits are contained in the single character *myō*.

Bodhisattva Nāgārjuna wrote, "[The Lotus Sutra is] like a great physician who changes poison into medicine."[11] Miao-lo stated, "How can one find the eternal, enlightened land anywhere outside Buddha-gayā? This *sahā* world does not exist outside the Buddha land."[12] He also said, "The true entity is invariably revealed in all phenomena, and all phenomena invariably possess the Ten Factors. The Ten Factors invariably function within the Ten Worlds, and the Ten Worlds invariably entail both life and its environment."[13] The Lotus Sutra reads, "The true entity of all phenomena can only be understood and shared between Buddhas. This reality consists of the appearance, nature . . . and their consistency from beginning to end."[14] A passage from the *Juryō* chapter states, "The time is limitless and boundless . . . since I in fact attained Buddhahood."[15] Here, "I" means all people in the Ten Worlds. All people of the Ten Worlds inherently have in them the Buddha nature; so they dwell in the pure land. A passage from the *Hōben* chapter reads, "All phenomena are manifestations of the Law and are essentially eternal."[16] Birth and death are the constant manifestations of eternal life continuing on through past, present, and future. This is nothing to regret or be surprised at. Even all the eight phases of a Buddha's existence[17] are subject to the law of birth and death. The votaries of the Lotus Sutra are enlightened to all this, thereby attaining Buddhahood as common mortals. Since your deceased husband was a votary of this sutra, he doubtless attained enlightenment. You need not grieve so much over his passing. But to grieve is natural, as you are a common mortal. Even saints are sometimes saddened. Although Shakyamuni Buddha's greatest disciples realized the truth of life, they were human also and could not help lamenting his death.

By all means offer devoted prayers for your husband. The words of a wise priest, "Base your heart on the Ninth Consciousness and your practice on the six consciousnesses,"[18] are indeed well said. This letter contains one of Nichiren's most profound teachings. Keep it deep within your heart.

Respectfully,
Nichiren

The eleventh day of the seventh month

Notes

1. T9, 46a.

2. There are eight hot hells, each with sixteen subsidiary hells, one below the other and each successively more severe in the type of punishment inflicted and the length of time its prisoners must remain. The hell of regeneration (Jap: *tōkatsu*) is the first of the hot hells. Here victims are said to fight each other viciously with iron claws, or are tortured by hell wardens with iron staves and razor-sharp swords. The hell of black ropes (*kokujō*) is the second of the hot hells. Here the denizens are either sawed in half or slashed by red hot axes. Suffering here is said to be ten times greater than in the hell of regeneration. Those who have committed the five cardinal sins are said to undergo indescribable torture in the lowest and severest hell, the hell of incessant suffering (*muken*). This hell is frequently referred to as the Avīci Hell. These hells are described in detail in the *Shōbō Nenjo* Sutra (T17, no. 721) and elsewhere. They are also described by Genshin in the first chapter of his *Ōjō Yōshū*.

3. The hell of the blood-red lotus (Jap: *guren*) and the hell of the great blood-red lotus (*daiguren*) are two of the great cold hells. They are described in the *Kusha Ron Ki* (T41, 197b). See also Letter 67, "Letter to Niike," where Nichiren writes: "The hell of the blood-red lotus is so called because the intense cold of this hell makes one double over until his back splits open and the bloody flesh emerges like a crimson lotus flower. And there are hells even more horrible."

4. T9, 15b.

5. Lotus Sutra (T9, 56c).

6. Lotus Sutra (T9, 54c).

7. *Abōrasetsu* (Skt: *Avorakṣas*) are jailers in hell who have the head of oxen, hands of human beings, and cloven hooves. They are said to cut down evildoers with razor-sharp swords.

8. T46, 1a.

9. The river of the three crossings (Jap: *sanzu no aiga*) refers to the river of envy and hate that leads to the three realms of hell, hungry ghosts, and animals.

10. The three bodies with which the Buddha is endowed. *See* Three bodies in Glossary.

11. *Daichido Ron* (T25, 954b).

12. *Hokke Mongu Ki* (T34, 333c).

13. *Kongōbei* (T46, 785c).

14. T9, 5c. Nichiren quotes only two phrases from this passage.

15. T9, 42b.

16. T9, 9b.

17. The eight phases are: (1) descending from heaven; (2) entering the mother's body; (3) coming out of the mother's body; (4) renouncing secular life; (5) conquering devils; (6) attaining enlightenment; (7) preaching the Law; and (8) entering nirvana. They are discussed in *Tendai Shikyō Gi* (T46, 745c ff.).

18. The source of this quotation is not known. Of the nine consciousnesses, the first five relate to the five senses of sight, hearing, smell, taste, and touch. The sixth consciousness is mind, which integrates the perceptions of the first five and renders them into a coherent image. The seventh consciousness (*mano*-consciousness) is concerned with the inner spiritual world and generates awareness of the self and the ability to dis-

tinguish good from evil. The eighth, or *ālaya* consciousness, is below the level of consciousness; the experiences of the present and all previous lifetimes—karma—are stored there. The T'ien-t'ai and Hua-yen (Kegon) schools postulate a ninth consciousness, *amala*-consciousness, which lies below the *ālaya*-consciousness and remains free from all karmic impurtiy.

57 *THREE TRIPITAKA MASTERS PRAY FOR RAIN*

This letter, dated the twenty-second day of the sixth month, 1275, was sent to Nishiyama Nyūdō, who lived in Nishiyama village in the Fuji district of Suruga Province. Few details of his life are known; his name appears to have been Ōuchi Tasaburō Taira no Yasukiyo and he was at one time an adherent of the Shingon sect. A lay priest, he was a sincere believer and frequently visited Nichiren at Minobu, bringing him various offerings.

As the title indicates, this letter details the failed attempts to produce rain of three famous Shingon priests in China and goes on to discuss similar failures in Japan. The three Chinese Tripitaka Masters are: Shan-wu-wei (Skt: Śūbhakarasiṁha), 637–735, who first introduced the esoteric teachings to China from India. He arrived in 716, was welcomed by Emperor Hsüan-tsung, and translated several important esoteric works into Chinese; Chin-kang-chih (Vajrabodhi), 671–741, who arrived in Ch'ang-an in 720, translated several esoteric scriptures into Chinese and is regarded as the fifth patriarch in the esoteric tradition; Pu-k'ung (Amoghavajra), 705–774, is regarded as the sixth patriarch in this lineage. He arrived in Lo-yang in 720 and became Vajrabodhi's disciple. He traveled to India in 741 in search of esoteric scriptures, returning to China in 746. He translated texts and taught a large number of disciples, among them Hui-kuo (746–805), who was the teacher of Kōbō, the founder of Japanese Shingon.

This letter is known also by the alternative title, *Nishiyama-dono Gohenji* (Reply to Lord Nishiyama).

When a tree has been transplanted, though fierce winds may blow, it will not topple if it has a firm stake to hold it up. But even a tree that has grown up in place may fall over if its roots are weak. Even a feeble person will not stumble if those supporting him are strong, but a person of considerable strength, when alone, may lose his footing on an uneven path.

Moreover, had the Buddha not appeared in the world, then in all the major world system, with the exception of Śāriputra and Mahākāśyapa, every single person would have sunk into the three evil paths. But through the strong bonds formed by relying upon the Buddha, large numbers of people have been able to attain Buddhahood. Even wicked persons such as King Ajātaśatru or Aṅgulimāla,[1] who one would expect could never reach enlightenment but would invariably fall into the Avīci Hell, by encountering a great man, the Lord Buddha Shakyamuni, were able to attain Buddhahood.

Therefore, the best way to attain Buddhahood is to encounter a *zenchishiki*, or good friend. How far can one's own wisdom take him? If one has even enough wisdom to distinguish hot from cold, he should seek out a good friend.

But encountering a good friend is the hardest possible thing to do. Thus the Buddha likened it to the rarity of a one-eyed turtle finding a floating log with a hollow in it the right size to hold him,[2] or to the difficulty of trying to lower a thread from the Brahma Heaven and pass it through the eye of a needle on the earth.[3] Moreover, in this evil latter age, evil companions are more numerous than the dust particles that comprise the earth, while good friends are fewer than the specks of dirt one can pile on a fingernail.

Bodhisattva Kanzeon of Mount Potalaka acted as a good friend to Zenzai Dōji,[4] but though the bodhisattva taught him the two doctrines of the specific and perfect teachings,[5] he did not reveal to him the pure and perfect teaching [of the Lotus Sutra]. Bodhisattva Jōtai[6] sold himself as an offering in his quest for a good teacher, whereupon he encountered Bodhisattva Dommukatsu.[7] But from the latter he learned only the three doctrines of the connecting, specific, and perfect teachings, and did not receive instruction in the Lotus Sutra. Śāriputra acted as a good friend to a blacksmith and gave him instruction for a period of ninety days, but succeeded only in making him into an *icchantika*.[8] Pūrna[9] discoursed on the Buddhist doctrine for the space of an entire summer's retreat, but he taught Hinayana doctrines to persons who had the capacity for Mahayana doctrines, and thereby turned them into Hinayana adherents.

Thus even great sages [such as Kannon and Dommukatsu] were not permitted to preach the Lotus Sutra, and even arhats who had obtained the fruit of emancipation[10] [such as Śāriputra and Pūrna] were not always able to gauge people's capacity correctly. From these examples, you may imagine how inadequate are the scholars of this latter, evil age! It is far better to be an evil person who learns nothing [of Buddhism] at all than to put one's faith in such men, who declare that heaven is earth, east is west, or fire is water, or assert that the stars are brighter than the moon or an anthill higher than Mount Sumeru.

In judging the relative merit of Buddhist doctrines, I, Nichiren, believe that the best standards are those of reason and documentary proof. And even more valuable than reason and documentary proof is the proof of actual fact.

In the past, around the fifth year of the Bun'ei era (1268), when the Ezo barbarians[11] were rebelling in the east and the Mongol envoys arrived from the west with their demands, I surmised that these events had come about because people did not put faith in the true Buddhist doctrines. I guessed that prayer rituals would surely be performed to subdue the enemy, and that such rituals would be conducted by the priests of the Shingon sect. Of the three countries of India, China, and Japan, I will leave aside India for the moment. But I am certain that Japan, like China, will be undone by the Shingon sect.

The Tripitaka Master Shan-wu-wei journeyed to China from India in the reign of Emperor Hsüan-tsung of the T'ang. At that time there was a great drought, and Shan-wu-wei was ordered to conduct prayers for rain. He succeeded in causing a heavy rain to fall, and as a result everyone from the emperor on down to the common people was overcome with joy. Shortly thereafter, however, a great wind began to blow, wreaking havoc throughout the land, and the people's enthusiasm quickly palled.

During the same reign, the Tripitaka Master Chin-kang-chih came to China from India. He too prayed for rain, and within the space of seven days, a heavy rain fell and people rejoiced as they had earlier. But when a great wind of unprecedented violence arose, the ruler concluded that the Shingon sect was an evil and fearsome doctrine and came near to sending Chin-kang-chih back to India. The latter, however, made various excuses and contrived to remain.

Again, in the same reign, the Tripitaka Master Pu-k'ung prayed for rain. Within three days a heavy rain fell, producing the same kind of joy as before. But once more a great wind arose, this time even fiercer than on the two previous occasions, and raged for several weeks before subsiding.

How strange were these occurrences! There is not a single person in Japan, whether wise or ignorant, who knows about them. If anyone wishes to find out, he had better question me in detail and learn about these matters while I am still alive.

Turning to the case of Japan, in the second month of the first year of the Tenchō era (824), there was a great drought. The Great Teacher Kōbō was requested to pray for rain in the Shinsen-en garden.[12] But a priest named Shubin came forward and, protesting that he had been a member of the priesthood longer and ranked higher than Kōbō, asked that he be allowed to conduct the ritual. Shubin was granted permission and carried out the prayers. On the seventh day a heavy rain fell, but it fell only on the capital and not in the surrounding countryside.[13]

Kōbō was then instructed to take over the task of praying, but seven days went by without any rain falling, then another seven days, and still another seven days. Finally, the emperor himself prayed for rain and caused it to fall. But the priests of Kōbō's temple, Tō-ji, referred to it as "our teacher's rain." If one wishes for details, he need only consult the records.

This was one of the greatest frauds ever known in our nation. And in addition, there were the matters of the epidemic that broke out in the spring of the ninth year of the Kōnin era (818)[14] and of the three-pronged *vajra* implement,[15] which were also frauds of a most peculiar kind. Word of them should be transmitted verbally.

There was a great drought in China in the period of the Ch'en dynasty, but the Great Teacher T'ien-t'ai recited the Lotus Sutra, and in no time at all rain began to fall. The ruler and his ministers bowed their heads, and the common people pressed their palms together in reverence. Moreover, the rain was not torrential, nor was it accompanied by wind; it was a shower of soft rain. The Ch'en ruler sat entranced in the presence of the Great Teacher and forgot all about returning to his palace. At that time, he bowed three times [in acknowledgment to the Great Teacher].

In Japan in the spring of the ninth year of the Kōnin era, a great drought occurred. Emperor Saga ordered Fujiwara no Fuyutsugu[16] to send a lower-ranking official, Wake no Matsuna,[17] [to the Great Teacher Dengyō to ask him to offer prayers in an appeal for rain]. The Great Teacher Dengyō prayed for rain, reciting the Lotus, *Konkōmyō*, and *Ninnō* sutras, and on the third day thin clouds appeared and a gentle rain began falling softly. The emperor was so overjoyed that he gave permission for the building of a Mahayana ordination platform,[18] whose establishment had been the most difficult undertaking in Japan.

Gomyō, the teacher of the Great Teacher Dengyō, was a saintly man, the foremost priest in Nara, the southern capital. He and forty of his disciples joined together in reciting the *Ninnō* Sutra to pray for rain,[19] and five days later rain began to fall. It was certainly splendid that rain fell on the fifth day, but less impressive than if it had fallen on the third day, [as in the case of the Great Teacher Dengyō]. Moreover, the rain was very violent, which made Gomyō's performance inferior. From these examples, you may judge how much more inferior were Kōbō's efforts to produce rain.

Thus, the Lotus Sutra is superior, while Shingon is inferior. And yet, as though deliberately to bring about the ruin of Japan, people these days rely exclusively on Shingon.

Considering what had happened in the case of the Retired Emperor of Oki,[20] I believed that if the Shingon practices were used to try to subdue the Mongols and the Ezo barbarians, Japan would surely be brought to ruin. Therefore I determined to disregard my own safety and speak out in warning. When I did so, my disciples tried to restrain me, but in view of the way things have turned out, they are probably pleased at what I did. I was able to perceive what not a single wise man in China or Japan had understood in more than five hundred years!

When Shan-wu-wei, Chin-kang-chih, and Pu-k'ung prayed for rain, rain fell, but it was accompanied by violent winds. You should consider the reason for this. There are cases of people making rain fall even through the use of non-Buddhist teachings, even those of the Taoists, which are hardly worth discussion. And of course with Buddhist teachings, even though they are only those of the Hinayana, if they are correctly applied, then how could rain fail to fall? And how much more so if one uses a text such as the *Dainichi* Sutra, which, though inferior to the *Kegon* and *Hannya* sutras, is still somewhat superior to the *Agon* sutras [of the Hinayana]! Thus rain did indeed fall, but the fact that it was accompanied by violent winds is an indication that the doctrines being applied were contaminated by grievous errors. And the facts that the Great Teacher Kōbō was unable to make rain fall although he prayed for twenty-one days, and that he misappropriated the rain that the emperor had caused to fall and called it his own, are indications that he was even more gravely in error than Shan-wu-wei and the others.

But the wildest falsehood of all is that which the Great Teacher Kōbō himself recorded when he wrote: "In the spring of the ninth year of the Kōnin era (818), when I was praying for an end to the epidemic, the sun came out in the middle of the night."[21] This is the kind of lie this man was capable of! This matter is one of the most important secrets that is entrusted to my followers. They should quote this passage to drive their opponents to the wall. I will not go into the matter of doctrinal superiority here, but simply stress that the matters I have written above are of the utmost importance. They should not be lightly discussed or passed on to others. But because you have shown yourself to be so sincere, I am calling them to your attention.

And what of these admonitions of mine? Because people regard them with suspicion and refuse to heed them, disasters such as those we now face occur. If the Mongols should attack us with great force, I am sure that [the teachings of the Lotus Sutra] will spread far and wide in this present lifetime. At such a time, those persons who have treated me harshly will have reason to regret.

The Brahman teachings date from about eight hundred years before the time of the Buddha. At first they centered around the two deities[22] and the three ascetics,[23] but eventually they split into ninety-five schools. Among the Brahman leaders were many wise men and persons endowed with supernatural powers, but none of them was able to free himself from the sufferings of birth and death. Moreover, the people who gave allegiance to their teachings in one way or another all ended by falling into the three evil paths.

When the Buddha appeared in the world, these ninety-five groups of Brahmans conspired with the rulers, ministers, and common people of the sixteen major states of India,[24] some of them reviling the Buddha, others attacking him or slaying his disciples and lay supporters in incalculable numbers. But the Buddha did not slacken his resolve, for he said that, were he to cease preaching the Law because of intimidation from others, then all living beings alike would surely fall into hell. He was deeply moved by pity and had no thought of desisting.

These Brahman teachings came about through a mistaken reading of the various sutras of the Buddhas who preceded Shakyamuni Buddha.

The situation today is much the same. Though many different Buddhist doctrines are being taught in Japan, originally they all derive from the eight sects, the nine sects, or the ten sects.[25] Among the ten sects, I will set aside for the moment the Kegon sect and others. Because Kōbō, Jikaku, and Chishō were deluded as to the relative merits of the Shingon and Tendai sects, the people of Japan have in this life been attacked by a foreign country, and in their next life they will fall into the evil paths. And the downfall of China as well as the fact that its people were destined to fall into the evil paths also came about through the errors of Shan-wu-wei, Chin-kang-chih, and Pu-k'ung.

Moreover, since the time of Jikaku and Chishō, the priests of the Tendai sect have been constrained by the false wisdom of these men and developed into something quite unlike the original Tendai sect.

"Is this really true?" some of my disciples may be asking. "Does Nichiren really have an understanding superior to that of Jikaku and Chishō?" But I am only going by what the Buddha predicted in the sutras.

The Nirvana Sutra states that in the Latter Day of the Law, those persons who slander the Law of the Buddha and fall into the hell of incessant suffering as a result will be more numerous than the dust particles that comprise the earth, while those who uphold the True Law will be fewer than the specks of dirt one can pile on a fingernail.[26] And the Lotus Sutra says that even though there might be someone capable of lifting up Mount Sumeru and hurling it away, it will be hard indeed to find anyone who can preach the Lotus Sutra just as it teaches in the Latter Day of the Law of Shakyamuni Buddha.[27]

The *Daijuku, Konkōmyō, Ninnō, Shugo, Hatsunaion,* and *Saishōō* sutras[28] record that when the Latter Day of the Law begins, if there should appear a person who practices the True Law, then those who uphold false teachings will appeal to the ruler and his ministers, and the ruler and his ministers, believing their words, will revile that single person who upholds that True Law or attack him, send him into exile, or even put him to death. At that time, King Bonten, Taishaku, and all the other innumerable deities and the gods of heaven and earth will take possession of the wise rulers of neighboring countries and cause them to overthrow the nation where these things take place. Doesn't the situation we face today resemble that described in these sutras?

I wonder what good causes formed in your past lives have enabled all of you to visit me, Nichiren! But whatever you might discover in examining your past, I am sure that this time you will be able to break free from the sufferings of birth and death. Śuddhipanthaka[29] was unable to memorize a teaching of fourteen characters even in the space of three years, and yet he attained Buddhahood. Devadatta, on the other hand, had committed to memory sixty thousand sacred texts but fell into the hell of incessant suffering. These examples exactly represent the situation in the world in this present latter age. Never suppose that they pertain only to other people and not to yourselves.

There are many other things that I would like to say, but I will stop here. I do not know how to thank you for all you have done in these troubled times, so I have here outlined for you some important points in our doctrine.

Thank you for the cowpeas and green soybeans.

Nichiren

The twenty-second day of the sixth month

Notes

1. King Ajātaśatru is frequently referred to as an example of evil by Nichiren. Aṅgulimāla is noted for his cruelty. See Letter 55, "Encouragement to a Sick Person," note 18.

2. The one-eyed turtle analogy is mentioned briefly in the *Myōshōogonnō* (27th) chapter of the Lotus Sutra. The story behind it appears in the *Zō-agon* Sutra (T2, 108c). A blind turtle, whose life span is immeasurable kalpas, lives at the bottom of the sea. Once every hundred years it rises to the surface. There is only one log floating in the sea with a hollow in it suitable to the turtle's size. Since the turtle is blind and the log is tossed about by wind and waves, the likelihood of the turtle finding the log is extremely remote. This story is frequently alluded to by Nichiren.

3. A similar statement is found in the *Hōon Jurin* (T53, 455b).

4. Zenzai Dōji is a bodhisattva in the *Kegon Sutra* who visits a total of fifty-three teachers in his search for the Law. He is described in detail in both the sixty-volume *Kegon* Sutra (T9, 688a ff) and the eighty-volume text (T10, 348a ff.). The meeting with Bodhisattva Kanzeon on Mount Potalaka, said to be located on the southern coast of India, is described at T9, 718a.

5. Two of the four teachings of doctrine. The specific teaching is a higher level of provisional Mahayana taught exclusively for bodhisattvas. The perfect teaching here refers to that which was expounded before the Lotus Sutra, and which still includes elements of the provisional teachings. *See also* Eight teachings in Glossary.

6. Jōtai (Skt: Sadāprarudita) is a bodhisattva described in the *Daichido Ron* (T25, 732a) and some of the *Hannya* sutras including the *Daihannya Haramitta* Sutra (T6, 1059a). He was called Jōtai (Ever-weeping) because he wept in his efforts to seek the teaching of the perfection of wisdom.

7. Dommukatsu (Skt: Dharmōdgata) is a bodhisattva described in the *Daibon*

Hannya Sutra (T8, 417b) and the *Daichido Ron* (T25, 734b). He is said to have preached on the perfection of wisdom in his palace in the City of Fragrances. It is said that those who listened to his teaching and embraced it never fell into the evil paths.

8. According to the Nirvana Sutra (T12, 764a-b) Śāriputra attempted to instruct a blacksmith by teaching him to meditate on the vileness of the body, and a washerman, by teaching him to count his breaths in meditation. As a result, neither gained the slightest understanding of the Buddha's Law but fell into erroneous views. Later, Shakyamuni Buddha reversed the instruction, teaching the blacksmith to count his breaths and the washerman to meditate on the vileness of the body, after which they were both said to have quickly reached the state of arhat.

9. Pūrna was one of Shakyamuni Buddha's ten major disciples. He was known as the foremost in preaching the Law, and is said to have converted five hundred people of his tribe.

10. Here, the six supernatural powers that Buddhas, bodhisattvas, and arhats are said to possess. They are: (1) the power of being anywhere at will, (2) the power of seeing anything anywhere, (3) the power of hearing any sound anywhere, (4) the power of knowing the thoughts of all other minds, (5) the power of knowing past lives, and (6) the power of eradicating illusions.

11. Indigenous inhabitants of northern Japan. Sources from the Nara (710–794) and Heian (794–1185) periods refer to them as barbaric tribes who had once occupied the entire Japanese archipelago but retreated northward under military pressure from the Japanese state. Considerable disagreement exists as to whether the ancient Ezo were ancestors of the aboriginal inhabitants of Hokkaido (known as the Ainu), unpacified Japanese, or some other as yet unidentified people.

12. Shinsen-en was a garden established on the grounds of the imperial palace in Kyoto by the Emperor Kammu. It was the site of a large pond, said to be inhabited by a female dragon. Since dragons were thought to bring rain, prayers for rain were held here.

13. This story is found in *Genkō Shakusho* (DBZ 101, 152–153). Shubin (n.d.) was a Shingon priest who studied Sanron and Hossō teachings as well. In 823 he was given the Sai-ji (West Temple) by Emperor Saga, while Kōbō was given the Tō-ji (East Temple). Shubin's biography is found in *Honchō Kōsō Den* (DBZ 103, 158–159).

14. This refers to Kōbō's claim in his *Hannya Shingyō Hiken* (T57, 12c), which Nichiren cites later, that while he was praying to end an epidemic, the sun came out at night. Nichiren also questions this assertion at some length, as well as the following story concerning the *vajra* implement, in "Repaying Debts of Gratitude," *Selected Writings of Nichiren*, 296–297.

15. A ritual implement used in esoteric Buddhism, symbolizing the adamantine resolve to attain enlightenment, which can destroy all illusion. The *Kōbō Daishi Goden* (*Zoku Gunsho Ruiju*, vol. 8, part 2, 534) states: "On the day that he set out by ship from China, he voiced a prayer, stating, 'If there is a spot that is particularly suitable for the teaching of these doctrines that I have learned, may this three-pronged *vajra* implement land there.' Then he faced in the direction of Japan and threw the implement up into the air. It sailed far away and disappeared among the clouds. In the tenth month he returned to Japan. . . . He journeyed to the foot of Mount Kōya and determined to establish his place of meditation there . . . and later it was discovered that the three-pronged *vajra* implement which he had thrown over the sea was there on the mountain."

16. Fujiwara no Fuyutsugu (775–826) was a court official of the early Heian period, who eventually became minister of the left.

17. Wake no Matsuna (786–846) was a court official who supported Dengyō and was instrumental in assembling priests from the Nara temples to attend lectures by Dengyō on the Lotus Sutra. This story is found in the *Isshin kaimon* (T74, 637).

18. Up until this time, priests in Japan had been ordained exclusively in the Hinayana precepts. Dengyō had repeatedly sought imperial permission to establish a Mahayana ordination center on Mount Hiei, over the fierce objections of the Nara sects. His continued efforts in this direction, coupled with his dramatic success in the prayers for rain and with the requests of Fujiwara no Fuyutsugu and others, finally moved Emperor Saga to consent. He formally granted permission in 822, a week after Dengyō's death. The ordination center was completed in 827 by Dengyō's successor, Gishin.

19. Gomyō (758–834) was a priest of the Hossō sect. In 819 he petitioned the throne to protest Dengyō's attempt to establish a Mahayana ordination platform. The story of the prayers for rain appears in the *Isshin kaimon* (T74, 637). There is no source for the statement that Gomyō was Dengyō's teacher.

20. Reference is to the eighty-second emperor, Gotoba (1180–1239). In 1221, after having retired, he attempted to overthrow the Kamakura government, and had a great number of priests offer esoteric Shingon prayers for the victory of the imperial forces. However, the leader of the Kamakura shogunate, Regent Hōjō Yoshitoki, emerged victorious. This incident, called the Jōkyū Disturbance, in effect destroyed the political power of the imperial house and enabled the samurai government in Kamakura to consolidate its influence. As a result, Gotoba was exiled to the island of Oki.

21. *Hannya Shingyō Hiken* (T57, 12c).

22. Two Brahman deities, Śiva and Viṣṇu.

23. The three ascetics are Kapila, Ulūka, and Rṣabha. Kapila was a founder of the Samkhya school, one of the six philosophical schools in ancient India. Ulūka, also called Kānada, was a founder of the Vaiśesika school, another of the above six schools. Rṣabha's teachings are said to have paved the way for Jainism.

24. No details are known concerning the ninety-five groups of Brahmans. Their existence is mentioned in the Nirvana Sutra (T12, 668a). The sixteen states refers to the number of states into which India was divided during Shakyamuni's lifetime.

25. The eight sects are the Kusha, Jōjitsu, Ritsu, Hossō, Sanron, and Kegon sects, which flourished in the Nara period, and the Tendai and Shingon sects which rose to prominence in the Heian period. The nine sects comprise these eight plus the Zen sect, which appeared in the early part of the Kamakura period. The ten sects are these nine plus the Jōdo sect which also spread during the Kamakura period.

26. T12, 925a.

27. A rephrasing of a passage in the *Hōtō* (11th) chapter of the Lotus Sutra, which reads, "To seize Mount Sumeru and fling it far off to the measureless Buddha lands — that is not difficult . . . But in the evil times after the Buddha's passing, to be able to preach this sutra—that is difficult indeed!" (T9, 34a).

28. The *Daijuku* or *Daishutsu* Sutra (T13, no. 397) is a collection of seventeen separate works, translated into Chinese by Dharmakṣema (385–433) and others. The *Ninnō* Sutra (T8, no. 245) is considered the concluding sutra of the *Hannya*, or wisdom sutras. It was translated by Kumārajīva in the Later Ch'in dynasty. The *Shugo* or

Shugo Kokkai Shu Darani Sutra (T19, no. 997) is an esoteric sutra that expounds the benefit of protecting the sovereign. The *Hatsunaion* Sutra (T1, no. 6) is a Chinese version of the Nirvana Sutra, translated by Fa-hsien and Buddhabhadra of the Eastern Chin in 418. The *Saishōō* Sutra, an abbreviation of the *Konkōmyō Saishōō* Sutra (T16, no. 665), translated by I-ching of the T'ang dynasty. It is the most recent of three extant Chinese translations of the *Konkōmyō* Sutra.

29. See Letter 55. "Encouragement to a Sick Person," note 19.

58 THE MONGOL ENVOYS

This letter was sent to Nishiyama Nyūdō (Ōuchi Tasaburō Taira no Yasukiyo) sometime in 1275; the exact date is not indicated. Nishiyama had just returned to his estate in Nishiyama village in the Fuji district of Suruga Province after having completed a tour of duty in Kamakura. Nishiyama had reported to Nichiren the fact that five Mongol envoys who had come demanding that Japan pay tribute to the Mongol empire had been executed at the execution grounds at Tatsunokuchi. Nishiyama had further informed him that because of the imminent threat of the Mongol invasion, a hunt scheduled to be held on Nishiyama's estate in honor of the late Hōjō Tokiyori had been canceled, and that Nishiyama had not been ordered to participate in the defense of Kyushu. Nichiren's letter is in reply to the various items of information that had been included in Nishiyama's letter.

I can hardly express my joy on learning of your safe return from Kamakura. I have also received your news about the beheading of the Mongol envoys. How pitiful that they have beheaded the innocent Mongol envoys and yet failed to cut off the heads of the priests of the Nembutsu, Shingon, Zen, and Ritsu sects, who are the real enemies of our country! Those who do not understand the details of the matter will no doubt think that I say this out of conceit because my prophecy has been fulfilled.[1] Yet for more than twenty years now I have been privately lamenting to my disciples day and night that this would happen, and I have publicly remonstrated with the authorities on several occasions [to prevent it].

Among all grave matters, the ruin of the nation is the most serious. The *Saishōō* Sutra states, "Among all forms of harm, none is heavier than the loss of the ruler's authority."[2] This passage means that among all evils, the worst is to become the ruler, misgovern the country, and meet defeat at the hands of another kingdom. The *Konkōmyō* Sutra also states, "Because evil men are respected and favored and good men are subjected to punishment, ... marauders will appear from other regions and the people of the country will meet with death and disorder."[3] This passage means that when a man becomes the ruler of a state and values evil men while condemning good ones, then his country will surely be defeated by another country. The fifth volume of the Lotus Sutra states, "They will be respected and revered by the world as though they were arhats who possess the six supernatural powers."[4] This passage describes the enemies of the Lotus Sutra. It is saying that the ruler of the country will revere men who firmly uphold the two hundred and fifty precepts[5] and appear to be like Mahākāśyapa and Śāriputra, and will attempt to destroy the votary of the Lotus Sutra.

A teaching of great importance is something close at hand. One who can, according to the time, discern without the slightest error what is vital both for oneself and for the country is a person of wisdom. The Buddha is called worthy of respect because he discerns the past and knows the future. In his perception of the three existences, no wisdom surpasses his. Although they were not Buddhas, sages and worthies such as Nāgārjuna, Vasubandhu, T'ien-t'ai, and Dengyō, though unequal to the Buddha in wisdom, nevertheless generally understood matters of the three existences, and their names have therefore been handed down to posterity.

Ultimately, all phenomena are contained within one's life, down to the last particle of dust. The nine mountains and the eight seas[6] are encompassed by one's body; the sun, moon, and myriad stars are contained within one's mind. However, [common mortals do not perceive this,] just as the blind do not see images reflected in a mirror or as an infant fears neither flood nor fire. The non-Buddhist teachings set forth in the outer writings[7] and the Hinayana and provisional Mahayana teachings of the inner scriptures[8] all teach no more than fragments of the Law inherent in one's life. They do not expound it in its entirety as the Lotus Sutra does. Thus there are both superiority and inferiority among the sutras, and the people who embrace them may also be divided into sages and worthy men. There is no end to matters of doctrine, so I will stop here.

I deeply appreciate your sending a messenger so quickly after your return from Kamakura. And, in addition, you sent me various offerings, which I am very glad to have received. While all the people of

Japan lament, I, Nichiren, and my followers alone rejoice amid our grieving. Living in this country, we cannot possibly escape the Mongol attack, but since Heaven knows that we have suffered persecution for our country's sake, we can rejoice that we will surely be saved in our next life. You, moreover, have already incurred a debt of gratitude to the Mongol nation in your present life. Had the threat of invasion not arisen, since this year marks the thirteeth anniversary of the death of the lay priest Saimyō-ji,[9] the hunt commemorating that occasion would surely have been held on your estate. Furthermore, you have not been sent to Tsukushi[10] like Lord Hōjō Rokurō.[11] This turn of events may run contrary to the desires of you and your clan, but it is not a punishment being inflicted upon you. From one point of view, are you not rather being protected by the Lotus Sutra? I know you feel you have been gravely wronged [but it is in fact a cause for rejoicing]. Since so joyful a thing has befallen you, I would have liked to go and congratulate you in person, but since others might think it strange, I have refrained. I have responded to your letter without delay.

Nichiren

Notes

1. Reference is to Nichiren's prophecy, first made in 1260 in his "Risshō Ankoku Ron" (*Selected Writings of Nichiren*, pp. 11–41) that Japan would suffer foreign invasion if the people continued to put faith in mistaken teachings.

2. *Saishōō* Sutra (T16, 443c).

3. *Konkōmyō* Sutra (T16, 443a). Nichiren cites the same sutra (*Saishōō Konkōmyo Sutra*), using different parts of the title in each instance.

4. T9, 36c. This passage refers to the third group of the three groups of powerful enemies of the Lotus Sutra, who will persecute the votaries of the Lotus Sutra in the evil latter age after the Buddha's death, described in the *Kanji* (13th) chapter of the Lotus Sutra. See Letter 57, "The Three Tripitaka Masters Pray for Rain," note 10.

5. The rules of discipline to be observed by ordained monks of Hinayana Buddhism. Here Nichiren is probably referring to his enemy, the eminent priest Ryōkan of the Gokuraku-ji in Kamakura, who prided himself in upholding all the monastic precepts.

6. The nine mountains and eight seas constitute the world, according to ancient Indian cosmology. The nine mountains are Mount Sumeru, which stands in the center of the world, and the eight concentric mountain ranges that surround it. All these mountain ranges are made of gold except for the outermost, which is made of iron. Mount Sumeru and the eight mountain ranges are separated from each other by a sea.

The innermost seven seas are of perfumed water, while the eighth outermost sea, just inside the iron-wheel mountain, is salty. In this sea lie the four continents, including Jambudvīpa.

7. Non–Buddhist writings (Jap: *gaiten*).

8. Buddhist scriptures (Jap; *naiten*).

9. The lay priest Saimyō-ji is Hōjō Tokiyori (1227–1263), who became the fifth Kamakura regent in 1246. In 1256 he relinquished the regency to Hōjō Nagatoki (1229–1264) and took Buddhist vows at the Saimyō-ji, but in fact continued to rule the country. It was to Tokiyori that Nichiren submitted the *Risshō Ankoku Ron*.

10. Tsukushi is the ancient name for the southern island of Kyushu. When Kyushu was divided into nine provinces during the Nara period, the term Tsukushi came to refer specifically to the provinces of Chikuzen and Chikugo. This area formed the front line of defense against the Mongols, and many warriors were dispatched there from throughout the country.

11. Hōjō Rokurō (d.1289) refers possibly to Hōjō Tokisada, a younger brother of Hōjō Tokiyori. He was sent to Tsukushi to aid in the defense against the Mongols and is said to have participated in the defense in both the 1274 and 1281 attacks and to have remained in Kyushu until his death.

59 THE FOURTEEN SLANDERS

This letter, dated the ninth day of the twelfth month, 1276, is addressed to Matsuno Rokurō Zaemon (d.1278), a devoted follower, who lived in Matsuno village of Ihara district of Suruga Province. Lord Matsuno, through his relatives, had close connections to Nichiren. His daughter was the wife of Nanjō Hyōe Shichirō (d.1265) and the mother of Nanjō Tokimitsu (1259–1332), known also as Lord Ueno, who was a staunch supporter of Nichiren and Nichiren's disciple, Nikkō Shonin (1246–1333). Lord Matsuno's second son, Nichiji (1250–?) was active in the Matsuno village area, but at the age of forty-six he set out for Hokkaido to propagate the teaching; however, nothing further is known about him.

"The Fourteen Slanders" (*Jūshi Hibō Sho*) is the alternative title of this letter. It is also referred to as *Matsuno-dono Gohenji* (Reply to Lord Matsuno), 1276.

I received the string of coins, the horseload of polished rice, and the white kimono that you sent.

Rolling fields and hills stretch out more than a hundred *ri* to the south of this mountain. To the north stands lofty Mount Minobu, which joins the peaks of Shirane farther off. Jutting sharply up to the west is a peak called Shichimen. Snow remains on these peaks throughout the year. There is not a single dwelling other than mine in the area. My only visitors, infrequent as they are, are the monkeys that come swinging through the treetops. And to my regret, even they do not stay for long, but scurry back to where they came from. To the east run the overflowing waters of the Fuji River, which resemble the flowing sands of the desert. It is extraordinary indeed that you send letters from time to time to this place whose inaccessibility makes visitors rare.

I learned that Priest Nichigen[1] of Jissō-ji temple, upon becoming a disciple of mine, was driven out by his own disciples and parishioners and had to give up his lands, so that he now has no place of his own. Nonetheless, he still visits me and takes care of my disciples. What devotion to the Way! How saintly! Nichigen is already unrivaled as a scholar of Buddhism. Yet he has discarded all desire for fame and fortune and become my disciple. He has lived the words in the sutra, "We do not hold our own lives dear."[2] To express his gratitude to the Buddha, he has taught you and your fellow believers and inspired you, Matsuno, to make these sincere offerings. All this is truly amazing.

The Buddha stated that during the Latter Day of the Law, priests and nuns with the hearts of dogs would be as numerous as the grains of sand in the Ganges.[3] By this he meant that the priests and nuns of that day would run like dogs after fame and fortune. Because they wear robes and surplices, they look like ordinary priests and nuns. But in their hearts, they wield a sword of evil, hastening here and there among their patrons and filling them full of countless lies so as to keep them away from other priests or nuns. Thus they strive to keep their patrons to themselves and prevent other priests or nuns from coming near them, like a dog who goes to a house to be fed but who growls and springs to attack the moment another dog approaches. Each and every one of these priests and nuns is certain to fall into the evil paths. Being the scholar that he is, Nichigen must have read this passage in the sutra. His unusual consideration and frequent visits to me and my disciples are deeply appreciated.

In your letter you write, "Since I took faith in this sutra [the Lotus], I have continued to recite the *Jūnyoze*[4] and the *Jigage*[5] and chant the daimoku without the slightest neglect. But how great is the difference between the blessings received when a sage chants the daimoku and the blessings received when we chant it?" To reply, one is in no way superior to the other. The gold that a fool possesses is no different from the gold that a wise man possesses; a fire made by a fool is the same as a fire made by a wise man.

However, there is a difference if one chants the daimoku while acting against the intent of this sutra. There are many forms of slander that go against the correct practice of this sutra. Let me sum them up by quoting from the fifth volume of the *Hokke Mongu Ki*: "In defining the types of evil, the *Hokke Mongu* states briefly, 'Expound among the wise but not among the foolish.'[6] One scholar[7] enumerates the types of evil as follows: 'I will first list the evil causes and then their effects. There are fourteen evil causes: (1) arrogance, (2) negligence, (3) arbitrary, egotistical judgment, (4) shallow, self-satisfied understanding, (5) attachment to earthly desires, (6) lack of seeking spirit, (7) not believing, (8) aversion, (9) deluded doubt, (10) vilification, (11) contempt, (12) hatred, (13) jealousy, and (14) grudges.' "[8] Since these fourteen slanders apply equally to priesthood and laity, you must be on guard against them.

Bodhisattva Fukyō of old said that all people have the Buddha nature and that if they embrace the Lotus Sutra, they will never fail to attain Buddhahood. He further stated that to slight a person is to slight the Buddha himself. Thus, his practice was to revere all people. He revered even those who did not embrace the Lotus Sutra because they too had the Buddha nature and might someday believe in the sutra. Therefore, it is all the more natural to revere those priests and lay people who do embrace the sutra.

The fourth volume of the Lotus Sutra states, "The offense of uttering even a single derogatory word against the priests or laity who believe in and preach the Lotus Sutra is even graver than that of abusing Shakyamuni Buddha to his face for an entire kalpa."[9] The Lotus Sutra also states, "[If anyone shall see a person who embraces this sutra and try to expose the faults or evils of that person, he will in the present age be afflicted with white leprosy,] whether what he speaks is the truth or not."[10] Take these teachings to heart, and always remember that believers in the Lotus Sutra should absolutely be the last to abuse each other. All those who keep faith in the Lotus Sutra are most certainly Buddhas, and one who slanders a Buddha commits a grave offense.

When one chants the daimoku bearing in mind that there are no distinctions among those who embrace the Lotus Sutra, then the blessings he gains will be equal to those of Shakyamuni Buddha. In the *Kongōbei Ron*, Miao-lo writes, "Both the life and environment of Hell exist within the life of Buddha. On the other hand, the life and environment of Buddha do not transcend the lives of common mortals."[11] You can surmise the significance of the fourteen slanders in the light of the above quotations.

That you have asked me about Buddhism shows that you are sincerely concerned about your future life. The Lotus Sutra states that people who will listen to [and accept] this teaching are very rare.[12] Unless the Buddha's true envoy appears in this world, who can expound this sutra in exact accord with the Buddha's intent? And moreover, it would appear that there are very few who ask about the meaning of the sutra in an effort to resolve their doubts and thus believe in it wholeheartedly. No matter how humble a person may be, if his wisdom is the least bit greater than yours, you should ask him about the meaning of the sutra. But the people in this evil age are so arrogant, prejudiced, and attached to fame and fortune that they are afraid that, should they become the disciple of a humble person or try to learn something from him, they will be looked down upon by others. They never rid themselves of this wrong attitude, so they seem to be destined for the evil paths.

The *Hosshi* chapter states in essence, "The blessings obtained by making offerings to a priest who teaches the Lotus Sutra are even greater than the blessings obtained by offering incalculable treasures to the Buddha for eight billion kalpas. And if one can then hear him teach this sutra even for a moment, he shall experience delight at the great benefit he has obtained."[13]

Even an ignorant person can obtain blessings by serving someone who expounds the Lotus Sutra. No matter if he is a demon or an animal, if he proclaims even a single verse or phrase of the Lotus Sutra, you must respect him as you would the Buddha. This is what the sutra means when it says, "Most certainly one should rise and greet him from afar, and respect him in the same way as one does the Buddha."[14] You should respect one another as Shakyamuni Buddha and Tahō Buddha did at the ceremony[15] in the *Hōtō* chapter.

Priest Sammi-bō[16] may be lowly, but since he can explain even a little about the Lotus Sutra, you should respect him as you would the Buddha and ask him about Buddhism. "Rely on the Law and not upon persons"[17] should be your guideline.

Long, long ago there was a young man who lived in the Snow Mountains and was called Sessen Dōji.[18] He gathered ferns and nuts to keep himself alive, made garments of deerskin to clothe his body, and quietly practiced the Way. As he observed the world with care and attention, Sessen Dōji came to understand that nothing is permanent and everything changes, and that all that is born is destined to die. This weary world is as fleeting as a flash of lightning, as the morning dew that vanishes in the sun, as a lamp easily blown out by the wind, or as the fragile leaves of the plantain that are so readily broken.

No one can escape this transience. In the end, all must take the journey to the Yellow Springs, the land of death. When we imagine the trip to the other world, we sense utter darkness. There is no light from the sun, the moon, or the stars; not even so much as a torch to illuminate the way. And along that dark road, there is no one to keep you company. When one is in the *sahā* world, he is surrounded by parents and relatives, brothers and sisters, wife and children, and retainers. Fathers may show lofty compassion, and mothers, profound loving sympathy. Husband and wife may be as faithful as two shrimps of the sea who vow to share the same hole and never to part throughout life. Yet, though they push their pillows side by side and sport together under the quilts embroidered with mandarin ducks,[19] they can never be together on that journey to the land of death. As you travel alone in darkness, who will come to encourage you?

Though old and young alike dwell in the realm of uncertainty, it is part of the natural order for the elderly to die first and the young to remain awhile. Thus, even as we grieve, we can find some cause for consolation. Sometimes, however, it is the old who remain and the young who die first. No one feels more bitter resentment than a young child who dies before his parents. No one despairs more deeply than parents who see their child precede them in death. People live in this fleeting world where all is uncertainty and impermanence, yet day and night they think only of how much wealth they can amass in this life. From dawn to dusk they concentrate on worldly affairs, and neither revere the Buddha nor take faith in the Law. They ignore Buddhist practice and lack wisdom, idling their days away. And when they die and are brought before the court of Emma, the king of hell, what can they carry as provisions on the long journey through the threefold world? What can they use as a boat or raft to ferry themselves across the sea of the sufferings of birth and death to the land of Actual Reward or the land of Tranquil Light?[20] When one is deluded, it is as if he were dreaming. And when one is enlightened, it is as if he had awakened. Thinking in this way, Sessen Dōji resolved to awake from the dream of the transient world and to seek the reality of enlightenment. So he secluded himself in the mountains and devoted himself to deep meditation, sweeping away the dust of delusion in his single-minded pursuit of the Buddhist Law.

The god Taishaku looked down from heaven and observed Sessen Dōji in the distance. He thought to himself, "Though the baby fish are many, there are few that grow up to be big fish. Though the flowers of the mango tree are many, there are few that turn into fruit. In like manner, there are many people who set their hearts on enlightenment, but only a few who continue their practice and in fact attain the true

Way. The aspiration for enlightenment in common mortals is often hindered by evil influences and easily swayed by circumstances; though many warriors don armor, few go without fear into battle. Let me go test this young man's faith." So saying, Taishaku disguised himself as a demon and appeared at Sessen Dōji's side.

At that time the Buddha had not yet made his appearance in the world, and although Sessen Dōji had sought everywhere for the Mahayana teachings, he had been unable to learn anything of them. Just then he heard a faint voice saying, "All is changeable, nothing is constant. This is the law of birth and death." Sessen Dōji looked all around in amazement, but there was no one in sight except a demon standing nearby. In appearace it was fierce and horrible; the hairs on its head were like flames and the teeth in its mouth like swords, and its eyes were fixed on Sessen Dōji in a furious glare. When Sessen Dōji saw this, he was not frightened in the least. He was so overjoyed at the opportunity to hear something of the Buddhist teaching that he did not even question it. He was like a calf separated from its mother that hears the faint sound of her lowing. "Who spoke that verse? There must be more!" he thought, and once more he searched all around, but still there was no one to be seen. He wondered if it could have been the demon who recited the verse. But on second thought that seemed impossible, since the demon must have been born a demon in retribution for some evil act in the past. The verse was certainly a teaching of the Buddha, and he was sure it could never have come from the mouth of a lowly demon. But as there was no one else about, he asked, "Was it you who preached that verse?" "Don't speak to me!" replied the demon. "I've had nothing to eat for days. I'm starved, exhausted, and almost out of my mind. I may have uttered some sort of nonsense, but in my dazed condition I don't even know what it was."

"For me to hear only the first half of that verse," said Sessen Dōji, "is like seeing only half the moon or obtaining half a jewel. It must have been you who spoke, so I beg you to teach me the remaining half." The demon replied sarcastically, "You are already enlightened, so you should feel no resentment even if you don't hear the rest of the verse. I'm dying of starvation and I haven't the strength to speak—say no more to me!"

"Could you teach me if you had something to eat?" asked Sessen Dōji. "If I had something to eat, I might be able to," said the demon. Elated, Sessen Dōji said, "Well then, what kind of food would you like?" But the demon replied, "Ask no more. You will certainly be horrified when you hear what I eat. Besides, you would never be able to provide it."

Yet Sessen Dōji was insistent. "If you will just tell me what you want, I will try to find it for you." The demon answered, "I eat only the tender flesh of humans and drink only their warm blood. I fly through the air far and wide in search of food, but people are protected by the Buddhas and gods so that even though I want to kill them, I cannot. I can only kill and eat those whom the Buddhas and gods have forsaken."

Hearing this, Sessen Dōji decided to give his own body for the sake of the Law, so that he could hear the entire verse.

"Your food is right here," he said. "You need look no further. Since I am still alive, my flesh is warm, and my blood has had no time to turn cold. Therefore, I ask you to teach me the rest of the verse, and in exchange, I will offer you my body." Then the demon grew furious and demanded, "Who could believe your words? After I've taught you the rest of the verse, who can I call on as a witness to make you keep your promise?"

Sessen Dōji replied, "This body of mine is mortal. But if I give my life for the Law, casting away this vile body which would otherwise die in vain, in the next life I will certainly be able to attain enlightenment and become a Buddha. I will receive a pure and wonderful body. It will be like throwing away a piece of crockery and receiving a precious vessel in exchange. I call upon Bonten and Taishaku, the Four Heavenly Kings, and all the Buddhas and bodhisattvas in the ten directions to be my witnesses. I could not possibly deceive you before them."

The demon, somewhat mollified, said, "If what you say is true, I will teach you the rest of the verse." Sessen Dōoji was overjoyed and, removing his deerskin garment, spread it out for the demon to sit upon while he preached. Then Sessen Dōji knelt, bowed his head to the ground, and placed his palms together in reverence, saying, "All I ask is that you teach me the rest of the verse." Thus he offered his heartfelt respect to the demon. The demon, seating himself on the deerskin, then recited these words: "Extinguishing the cycle of birth and death, one enters the joy of nirvana." The moment he heard this, Sessen Dōji was filled with joy, and his reverence for the verse was boundless. Resolved to remember it even until the next life, he repeated it over and over again and etched it deep in his heart.

He pondered, thinking to himself, "I rejoice that this verse, [though it came from a demon,] is no different from the teaching of the

Buddha, but at the same time I lament that I alone have heard it and that I am unable to transmit it to others." Thereupon he inscribed the stanza on stones, cliff faces, and the trees along the road, and he prayed that those who might later pass by would see it, understand its meaning, and finally enter the true Way. This done, he climbed a tall tree and threw himself down before the demon. But before he had reached the ground, the demon quickly resumed his original form as Taishaku, caught Sessen Dōji, and gently placed him on a level spot. Bowing before him reverently, Taishaku said, "In order to test you, I held back the Buddha's holy teaching for a time, causing anguish in the heart of a bodhisattva. I hope you will forgive my fault and save me without fail in my next life."

Then all of the heavenly beings gathered around to praise Sessen Dōji, saying, "How wonderful! He is truly a bodhisattva." Thus, by casting away his body to listen to half a verse, Sessen Dōji was able to transcend the realm of birth and death for twelve kalpas. This story appears in the Nirvana Sutra.

In the past Sessen Dōji was willing to give his life in order to hear but half a verse. How much more thankful should we be to hear a chapter or even a volume of the Lotus Sutra! How can we ever repay such a blessing? Indeed, if you care about your next life, you should make Sessen Dōji your example. Even though you may be too poor to offer anything of value, if the opportunity should arise to give up your life for the sake of the Buddhist Law, you should offer your life in order to study Buddhism.

This body of ours in the end will become nothing more than the soil of the hills and fields. Therefore, it is useless to begrudge your life, for though you may wish to, you cannot cling to it forever. Even people who live a long time rarely live beyond the age of one hundred. And all the events of a lifetime are like the dream one dreams in a brief nap. Though one may have been fortunate enough to be born as a human being and may perhaps have even renounced the world in order to seek the truth, if he fails to study Buddhism and to refute its slanderers but simply spends his time in idleness and chatter, then he is no better than an animal dressed in priestly robes. He may call himself a priest and earn his livelihood as such, but in no way does he deserve to be regarded as a true priest. He is nothing but a thief who has stolen the name of priest. How shameful and frightening!

In the theoretical teaching of the Lotus Sutra there is a passage which reads, "We do not hold our own lives dear. We value only the supreme Way."[21] Another passage from the essential teaching reads, "They do not begrudge their lives."[22] The Nirvana Sutra states, "One's body is insignificant while the Law is supreme. One should give his life in order to propagate the Law."[23] Thus both the theoretical and essential teachings of the Lotus Sutra, as well as the Nirvana Sutra, all indicate that one should give one's life to spread the Law. It is a grave offense to go against these admonitions, and though one cannot see it with the eye, the error piles up until it sends one plummeting to hell. It is like heat or cold, which has no shape or form that can be seen with the eye. Yet in winter the cold comes to attack trees and grasses, men and beasts, and in summer the heat comes to torment people and animals.

As a layman, the most important thing for you is to chant Nam-myoho-renge-kyo single-mindedly and to provide support for the priests. And if we go by the words of the Lotus Sutra, you should also teach Buddhism to the best of your ability. When the world makes you feel downcast, you should chant Nam-myoho-renge-kyo, remembering that although the sufferings of this life are painful, those in the next life could be much worse. And when you are happy, you should remember that your happiness in this life is nothing but a dream within a dream, and that the only true happiness is that found in the pure land of Eagle Peak,[24] and with that thought in mind, chant Nam-myoho-renge-kyo. Continue your practice without wavering up until the final moment of your life, and when that time comes, look carefully! When you climb the mountain of wondrous enlightenment and gaze around you in all directions, then to your amazement you will see that the entire universe is the land of Tranquil Light. The ground will be of lapis lazuli, and the eight paths[25] will be set apart by golden ropes. Four kinds of flowers[26] will fall from the heavens, and music will resound in the air. All Buddhas and bodhisattvas will be present in complete joy, caressed by the breezes of eternity, happiness, true self, and purity.[27] The time is fast approaching when we too will count ourselves among their number. But if we are weak in faith, we will never reach that wonderful place. If you still have questions, I am waiting to hear them.

Respectfully,
Nichiren

The ninth day of the twelfth month in the second year of Kenji (1276)

Notes

1. Nichigen (d.1315) was the priest of the Jissō-ji, a temple that belonged to the Tendai sect. He became a disciple of Nichiren after the latter's retirement to Mount Minobu. Later, he returned to Jissō-ji, and converted other priests, and built many temples in Musashi and Suruga provinces.

2. Lotus Sutra (T9, 36c).

3. The source of this statement is not known. The sense of the following text is drawn from a passage in the *Dai Hōshaku* Sutra (T11, 504a).

4. The *jūnyoze* are the ten factors, also referred to as the ten suchnesses, the aspects common to all existence in any of the ten worlds, mentioned in the *Hōben* (2d) chapter of the Lotus Sutra. (*See* Ten Factors in Glossary.) Strictly speaking, the passage relating to these factors reads: "The true entity of all phenomena can only be understood and shared between Buddhas. This reality consists of appearance, . . . and their consistency from beginning to end." Here, however, it presumably indicates the part from the opening of the chapter: *Niji seson jū sammai anjō ni ki* (At this time the World-Honored One serenely arose from meditation) through the passage on the ten factors ending with *hommatsu kukyōtō* (consistency from beginning to end) 9T9, 5b-c.

5. The verse section which concludes the *Juryō* (16th) chapter. It begins with the phrase *ji ga toku burrai* (since I attained Buddhahood) and ends with the phrase *soku jōju busshin* (quickly attain Buddhahood), restating the teaching of the eternity of the Buddha's enlightenment revealed in the foregoing prose section of the same chapter (T9, 43b-44a).

6. This statement from T'ien-t'ai's *Hokke Mongu* (T34, 79a) is in reference to a passage in the *Hiyu* (3d) chapter of the Lotus Sutra that says that one should not expound this sutra among the foolish, in order to protect them from committing the evil of slandering the sutra (T9, 15b).

7. This "one scholar" has been identified as the Hossō scholar, Tz'u-en (632–682) by Ts'ung-i (1042–1091) in his *Hokke Sandaibu Fuchū* (ZZ1, 44, 104). The attribution, however, is dubious. Tz'u-en in his *Hokke Gensan* (T34, 765b) mentions slanders, but does not enumerate or enlarge upon them.

8. *Hokke Mongu Ki* (T34, 274a).

9. A restatement of a passage in the *Hosshi* (10th) chapter of the Lotus Sutra (T9, 31b).

10. Lotus Sutra (T9, 62a).

11. *Kongōbei Ron* (T46, 781a).

12. This is mentioned in the *Hōben* (2d) chapter of the Lotus Sutra (T9, 10a).

13. Paraphrase of a passage in the *Hosshi* (10th) chapter of the Lotus Sutra (T9, 31b).

14. T9, 62a.

15. In the *Hōtō* (11th) chapter of the Lotus Sutra, Shakyamuni assembles all the Buddhas from throughout the universe and then opens the Treasure Tower. Tahō Buddha invites him to share his seat, and the Ceremony in the Air begins.

16. Sammi-bō Nichigyō was an early disciple of Nichiren. From Shimōsa, he studied on Mount Hiei and was esteemed for his great learning and debating skills. He is said to have become arrogant about his own knowledge and eventually abandoned his faith.

17. Nirvana Sutra (T12, 642a).

18. The story of Sessen Dōji is found in the Nirvana Sutra (T12, 450a ff.).

19. Mandarin ducks are symbols of conjugal happiness. The male and female are said to remain faithful to each other throughout their lives.

20. Two of the four kinds of lands described in T'ien-t'ai's *Kammuryōju Kyō Sho* (T37, 188b) and elsewhere. The land of Actual Reward signifies a land inhabited by the bodhisattvas who have reached or surpassed either the first stage of development in the fifty-two stages of the practice of the specific teaching, or the first stage of security in the practice of the perfect teaching. The land of Tranquil Light is a land where a Buddha lives.

21. T9, 36c.

22. T9, 43c.

23. This passage actually appears in Chang-an's commentary on the Nirvana Sutra, *Nehangyo Sho* (T38, 114b).

24. Here the Buddha land or state of Buddhahood achieved by the chanting of Nam-myoho-renge-kyo.

25. The eightfold path is an early teaching of Buddhism, setting forth the principles to be observed in order to attain emancipation. They are: (1) right views, (2) right thinking, (3) right speech, (4) right actions, (5) right way of life, (6) right endeavor, (7) right mindfulness, and (8) right meditation.

26. The four kinds of flowers are: *mandārava* (white lotus), *mahāmandarava* (great white lotus), *mañjūsaka* (white heavenly flower), and *mahāmañjūṣaka* (great white heavenly flower), flowers said to bloom in heaven, according to the Indian tradition.

27. Eternity, happiness, true self, and purity are the four virtues or noble qualities of the Buddha's life expounded in the Nirvana Sutra (T12, 511b) and elsewhere.

60 THE WORKINGS OF BONTEN AND TAISHAKU

Nichiren sent this letter to Nanjō Tokimitsu (1259–1332) from Mount Minobu on the fifteenth day of the fifth month, 1277. Tokimitsu had, as a young man, succeeded his father as steward of Ueno village in the Fuji district of Suruga Province and was referred to as Lord Ueno. His father had previously governed Nanjō village in Izu Province, before moving to Ueno. Both of Tokimitsu's parents had been adherents of Nichiren's teachings, and he himself was a dedicated follower of Nichiren as well as Nichiren's disciple Nikkō Shonin (1246–1333).

"The Workings of Bonten and Taishaku (*Bon Tai Onhakarai no Koto*) is an alternative title for this letter. It is known also as *Ueno-dono Gohenji* (Reply to Lord Ueno, 1277).

I received on the fourteenth day of the fifth month the horseload of taros which you took the trouble to send me. Considering the labor involved in digging them, taros today are as precious as jewels or medicine. I will comply with the request you made in your letter.

Once there was a man named Yin Chi-fu.[1] He had an only son, whose name was Po-ch'i. The father was wise, and so was the son. One would have thought that no one would try to estrange them, but Po-ch'i's stepmother frequently slandered him to her husband. However, Chi-fu would not listen to her. Undaunted, she continued for several years to contrive a variety of plots against her stepson. In one such scheme, she put a bee into her bosom, rushed to Po-ch'i and had him remove the insect, making sure as she did so that her husband would observe the scene. Then, in an attempt to have her stepson killed, she accused him of having made advances to her.[2]

458

A king named Bimbisāra[3] was a wise ruler and the greatest patron of the Buddha within the continent of Jambudvīpa. Moreover, he reigned over Magadha, the state where the Buddha intended to preach the Lotus Sutra. Since the king and the Buddha were thus united in mind, it seemed certain that the Lotus Sutra would be expounded in Magadha. A man named Devadatta wished to prevent this by any means possible, but all his attempts ended in failure. After much thought, he spent several years befriending King Bimbisāra's son, Prince Ajātaśatru,[4] and gradually obtained his confidence. Then he set out to estrange father and son. He deceived the prince into killing his own father, King Bimbisāra.

Now that Ajātaśatru, the new king, had become of the same mind as Devadatta and the two had banded together, Brahmans and evil people from all five regions of India[5] swarmed like clouds or mist gathering into Magadha. Ajātaśatru flattered them and won them over by giving them land and treasures. Thus the king of the state became an archenemy of the Buddha.

Seeing this, the Devil of the Sixth Heaven, who dwells atop the world of desire,[6] descended with his innumerable minions to Magadha and possessed the bodies of Devadatta, Ajātaśatru, and the six ministers.[7] Therefore, although these people were human in appearance, they wielded the power of the Devil of the Sixth Heaven. They were more boisterous, frightful, and alarming than a high wind flattening the grasses and trees, a gale agitating the surface of the sea, a great temblor jolting the earth, or a conflagration devouring one house after another.

A king named Virūḍhaka,[8] incited by Ajātaśatru, put hundreds of people of Shakyamuni Buddha's clan to the sword. King Ajātaśatru unleashed a herd of drunken elephants and let them trample to death countless disciples of the Buddha. He also had many other disciples killed by concealing his soldiers in ambush at the roadsides, defiling well water with excrement, or persuading women to bring false charges[9] against them. Śāriputra and Maudgalyāyana[10] were severely persecuted. Kālodāyin[11] was buried in horse dung. The Buddha was forced to survive for ninety days, one whole summer, on horse fodder.

People thought that perhaps not even the Buddha's power could match that of those evil persons. Even those who believed in him swallowed their words and said nothing, and closed their eyes so that they might not see. They could only fold their arms helplessly, speechless with dismay. Finally, Devadatta beat to death Shakyamuni's foster mother, the nun Utpalavarṇā,[12] and then caused the Buddha's body to bleed.[13] Accordingly, there was no one who would side with the Buddha.

And yet somehow, despite all these many persecutions, the Buddha at length managed to preach the Lotus Sutra. A passage from this sutra states, "Since hatred and jealousy toward this sutra abound even during the lifetime of the Buddha, how much worse will it be in the world after his passing?"[14] This passage means that even while the Buddha was alive, the enemies of the Lotus Sutra offered fierce opposition; all the more will they harass those who, in the Latter Day of the Law, preach and believe in a single character or even a single dot in the Lotus Sutra.

In light of this passage, it would seem that no one, during the more than 2,220 years since the Buddha expounded the Lotus Sutra, has lived it as the Buddha himself did. Only when one encounters great persecutions can we know that he has truly mastered the Lotus Sutra. The Great Teachers T'ien-t'ai and Dengyō would appear to have been votaries of the Lotus Sutra, but they did not meet persecution as severe as the Buddha did in his lifetime. They encountered only minor opposition—T'ien-t'ai from the three schools of southern China and seven schools of northern China, and Dengyō from the seven major temples of Nara.[15] Neither of them was persecuted by the ruler of the state, attacked by the people brandishing swords, or abused by the entire nation. [According to the Lotus Sutra,] those who believe in the Lotus Sutra after the Buddha's passing will suffer obstacles more terrible than those of the Buddha. Yet neither T'ien-t'ai nor Dengyō met oppression as harsh as the Buddha did, let alone persecutions that were greater or more numerous.

When a tiger roars, gales blow; when a dragon intones, clouds gather.[16] Yet a hare's squeak or a donkey's bray causes neither winds nor clouds to arise. As long as the foolish read the Lotus Sutra and the wise lecture on it, the country will remain quiet and undisturbed. It seems, however, that when a sage emerges and preaches the Lotus Sutra exactly as the Buddha did, the nation will be thrown into an uproar and persecutions arise that are greater than those during the Buddha's lifetime.

Now I, Nichiren, am not a worthy, let alone a sage. I am the most perverse person in the world. However, my actions seem to be in exact accord with what the sutra teaches. Therefore, whenever I meet great difficulties, I am more delighted than if my deceased parents had returned to life, or than one who sees the person he hates meet with some mishap. I am overjoyed that I, a foolish man, should be regarded as a sage by the Buddha. There are wise persons who strictly observe the two hundred and fifty precepts and are revered by the entire nation more than Taishaku is by all heavenly beings. Yet what if, in the eyes of Shakyamuni Buddha and the Lotus Sutra, they are as sinister as Devadatta? They may appear respectworthy to others now, but what horrors await them in their next life!

If the rumor spreads that you seem to be a votary of the Lotus Sutra, both those who are close to you and those who are not will respond adversely and admonish you as if they were your true friends, saying, "If you believe in the priest Nichiren, you will surely be misled. You will also be in disfavor with your lord." Then you will certainly abandon your faith in the Lotus Sutra. What is dreadful even for those of worth are the stratagems people devise. So it is advisable that you do not carelessly let it be known that you are a believer. Those possessed by a great devil will, once they succeed in persuading a believer to recant, use him as a means for making many others abandon their faith.

Shōfu-bō, Noto-bō, and Nagoe-no-ama[17] were once Nichiren's disciples. Greedy, cowardly, and ignorant, they nonetheless let themselves pass for wise people. When persecutions befell me, they took advantage of these to convince many of my followers to drop out. If you allow yourself to be so persuaded, those in Suruga who seem to believe in the Lotus Sutra, as well as the others who are about to take faith in it, will all discard the sutra without exception. There are a few in this province of Kai who have expressed their desire to take faith. Yet I make it a rule not to permit them to join us unless they remain steadfast in their resolve. Some people, despite their shallow understanding, pretend staunch faith and speak contemptuously to their fellow believers. Thus they often disrupt the faith of others. Leave such people strictly alone. The time will certainly come when, by the workings of Bonten and Taishaku, the entire Japanese nation will simultaneously take faith in the Lotus Sutra. At that time, I am convinced, many people will insist that they too have believed since the very beginning.

If your faith is firm, then you should single-mindedly resolve: "I maintain faith not for the sake of other people but for the benefit of my deceased father. Others will not perform memorial services for him; because I am his son, I am the one who must pray for his repose. I govern one village. I will spend one half of my revenue making offerings for the sake of my deceased father, and use the other half to feed my wife, children and clansmen. Should an emergency arise, I will give my life for my lord." Speak in a mild manner, no matter what the circumstances.

If anyone should try to weaken your belief in the Lotus Sutra, consider that your faith is being tested. Say to him sardonically, "I deeply appreciate your warning. However, you should save your admonishment for yourself. I know well that our superiors do not approve of my faith. The idea of your threatening me in their name is simply absurd. I was contemplating visiting you and giving you some advice, but you came here before I could carry out my plan. You will surely join your palms together and beseech me for help when you, along with your beloved wife and children, are dragged out before Emma, the king of hell."

What you say about Niida[18] may well be true. I have also heard about the people at Okitsu.[19] Should the occasion arise, you should behave exactly as they did. When those of rank reproach you for your faith, think of them as worthy adversaries of the Lotus Sutra. Consider it an opportunity as rare as the blossoming of the *udumbara* plant or the blind turtle encountering a floating sandalwood log,[20] and reply to them firmly and resolutely.

There have been instances in which those who governed a thousand or ten thousand acres of land had their lives summarily taken and their estates confiscated over trifling matters. If you give your life now for the sake of the Lotus Sutra, what is there to regret? Bodhisattva Yakuō burnt his own body for twelve hundred years and became a Buddha. King Suzudan[21] made a bed of his own body for his master for a thousand years; as a result, he was reborn as Shakyamuni Buddha.

Do not make a mistake. If you abandon your faith in the Lotus Sutra now, you will only make yourself the laughing-stock of your foes. Shamelessly pretending friendship, they will try to maneuver you into recanting, with the intention of later laughing at you and letting others ridicule you as well. Let them say all they have to say. Then tell them, "Instead of advising me in the presence of many people, why don't you admonish yourselves first?" With this remark, abruptly rise from your seat and depart.

Please let me know in a day or two what happened since you wrote. There are so many things I want to say that I cannot write all of them here. I will do so in my future letters.

With my deep respect,
Nichiren

The fifteenth day of the fifth month in the third year of Kenji (1277)

Notes

1. Yin Chi-fu was a minister who served King Hsüan, the eleventh ruler of the Chou dynasty, who reigned from 828 to 782 B.C. He is said to have helped restore the dynasty's declining fortunes.

2. This story appears in the *Konjaku Monogatari* (Tales of Times Now Past), vol. 9. With this scheme, the stepmother succeeded in arousing the king's suspicions. Po-ch'i, distressed, left home and drowned himself.

3. Stories about King Bimbisāra appear in a great number of texts and in a variety of different versions. It is difficult to determine to which text or texts Nichiren is referring.

4. Stories about Ajātaśatru appear in the Nirvana Sutra and elsewhere and are frequently mentioned by Nichiren. Incited by Devadatta, he killed his father, King Bimbisāra (Nirvana Sutra, T12, 480b), but eventually repented and was converted to Buddhism.

5. All of India.

6. The first division of the threefold world, so called because its inhabitants are ruled by various desires, such as the desire for food and sexual desires. In the highest of the six heavens of the world of desire lives the Devil of the Sixth Heaven, who is said to have a strong desire to control others at his will and prevent them from attaining enlightenment.

7. High ministers who served King Ajātaśatru. According to the Nirvana Sutra (T12, 474b ff), when Ajātaśatru broke out in virulent sores because of guilt over his father's death, they advised him to ask six non-Buddhist teachers for counsel.

8. Virūḍhaka was a king of Kosala in the days of Shakyamuni Buddha. His father was Prasenajit and his mother served originally as a servant to a lord of the Shakya tribe. Virūḍhaka was humiliated by the Shakyas because of his lowly birth and vowed to take revenge. After he seized the throne, he led an army against the Shakya kingdom, killing about five hundred people. It is said that seven days later, in accordance with Shakyamuni's prediction, he burned to death and fell into hell. *Binaya Zōji* (T24, 240a).

9. In an attempt to disgrace the Buddha's followers, Ajātaśatru persuaded women to pretend to have been impregnated by these followers.

10. These two leading disciples of Shakyamuni, while on their travels to spread Buddhism in Rājagṛha, once refuted the master of a group of Brahmans. As a result they were attacked with staves, and Maudgalyāyana is said to have been beaten to death. *Binaya Zōji* (T24, 287c).

11. Kālodāyin was a follower of Shakyamuni Buddha. According to the *Jūju Ritsu* (T23, 121c ff) he was given offerings by a woman when he was going about begging for alms in Śrāvasti. Her jealous husband killed Kālodāyin and buried his head in horse dung.

12. According to most accounts, Shakyamuni's foster mother was his maternal aunt, Mahāprājaptī, under whose guidance the nun Utpalavarṇā is said to have attained the state of arhat. The story of Utpalavarṇā is found in *Daichido Ron* (T25, 160a).

13. This is one of the nine great ordeals (Jap: *Kuō no dainan*) that Shakyamuni Buddha underwent. They are mentioned in the *Daichido Ron* (T25, 121c) and elsewhere. Here the reference is to the attempt to kill the Buddha by Devadatta, who dropped a boulder from the top of Eagle Peak; it missed and injured only the Buddha's toe.

14. T9, 31b.

15. The seven major temples of Nara are: Tōdai-ji, Kōfuku-ji, Gangō-ji, Daian-ji, Yakushi-ji, Saidai-ji, and Hōryū-ji.

16. The saying that the roar of a tiger causes the wind to blow is found in the *Kammiroku Jōshō Tōsotsuten Gyō San* (T38, 296a). That rain is produced when a dragon chants is mentioned in the *Wen-hsüan*.

17. Disciples of Nichiren who later abandoned their faith. Shōfu-bō is said to have begun doubting Nichiren at the time of his exile to Izu in 1261. Noto-bō fought in Nichiren's defense during the attack at Matsubayatsu in 1260, and was even wounded, but is said to have lost his faith around 1271. Nagoe-no-ama, the wife of Hōjō Tomotoki, a younger brother of the third regent Yasutoki, abandoned her faith around the time that Nichiren was almost executed at Tatsunokuchi in 1271.

18. Niida Shirō Nobutsuna (n.d.), was a native of Hatake in Izu Province. He was the elder brother of Nichimoku Shonin (1260–1333) and his mother was an elder sister of Nanjō Tokimitsu. Together with Tokimitsu and others he attempted to spread Nichiren's teachings in the Ōshū area of northern Japan. What Tokimitsu reported about him is not clear.

19. Okitsu was a village located on the shore of Suruga Bay. The "people of Okitsu" possibly refers to Jōren-bō, a disciple who lived here, and to other followers.

20. The *udumbara* plant and the one-eyed turtle are frequently mentioned by Nichiren as analogies for events of extremely rare occurence.

21. Suzudan is the name of Shakyamuni when he was a king in a past life. He renounced the throne to seek the True Law and devoted himself to austerities under the sage Ashi (Asita) for a thousand years in order to learn the Lotus Sutra. The hermit was later born as Devadatta. The story appears in the *Devadatta* (12th) chapter of the Lotus Sutra, although the name Suzudan is not specifically mentioned.

61 LETTER TO MISAWA

Nichiren sent this letter to Misawa Kojirō (n.d.), although another theory holds that it was sent to Kojirō's grandson, Masahiro. Dated the twenty-third day of the second month, 1278, this is one of only two letters that Nichiren wrote to this follower. Misawa was from the island of Awaji and had apparently been assigned to a manor in the Fuji district of Suruga Province. Misawa appears to have kept his distance from Nichiren for fear of antagonizing the Kamakura government, although he seems to have been a steadfast disciple.

An alternative title for this letter is *Sazen Sago Shō* (Before and After Sado).

       ➤

Please tell the people of Suruga that they should unite firmly in faith.[1]

I have received your offerings of a hundred oranges, kelp, green laver, *ogo*,[2] and other produce that you took the trouble of sending to me in this remote mountainous place. I have also received the quilted robe made by Utsubusa-no-ama.[3]

I have read your letter most attentively. Although the people who study Buddhism outnumber the dust particles of the earth, those who actually become Buddhas are fewer than the number of dust particles one can place on his fingernail. This the Lord Buddha Shakyamuni clearly states in the Nirvana Sutra. On reading it, I wondered why it should be so difficult, but after some thought, I realized the most plausible answer. Although one studies Buddhism, it is difficult to practice it correctly because of the foolishness of his mind, or because, even though one may be wise, he follows an evil teacher and fails to realize that he is being misled.

Moreover, even though one may encounter a good teacher and the sutra of the true teaching and thereby learn the True Law, inevitably, at the time when he resolves to free himself from the sufferings of birth and death and attain Buddhahood, he will encounter the three obstacles and four devils,[4] just as surely as a shadow follows the body and rain is accompanied by clouds. Even if you should manage to overcome the first six, if you are defeated by the seventh, you will not be able to become a Buddha.

Let us leave the first six for now. The seventh is caused by the Devil of the Sixth Heaven. When a common mortal of the Latter Day of the Law is ready to attain Buddhahood, having realized the true meaning of all the Buddha's teachings and understood the profound teaching of the *Maka Shikan*, this devil is greatly surprised. He says to himself, "This is most vexing. If I allow this person to remain in my domain, he will not only free himself from the sufferings of birth and death but lead others to enlightenment as well. Moreover, he will take over my realm and change it into a pure land. What shall I do?" The devil then summons all his underlings from the threefold world of desire, form, and formlessness and tells them, "Each of you now go and harass that votary, according to your respective skills. If you should fail to make him abandon his Buddhist practice, then enter into the minds of his disciples, patrons, and the people of his land and thus try to persuade or threaten him. If these attempts are also unsuccessful, I myself will go down and enter the mind and body of his sovereign to persecute that votary. Together, how can we fail to prevent him from attaining Buddhahood?"

I, Nichiren, have long been aware of all this, and therefore know how difficult it is for a common mortal of the Latter Day to become a Buddha in this lifetime. The sutras describe in many places how Shakyamuni Buddha attained enlightenment, and the obstacles he suffered because of the Devil of the Sixth Heaven seem absolutely unbearable. The fiendish acts of Devadatta and of King Ajātaśatru[5] were due solely to the workings of that devil. The Lotus Sutra says, "Since hatred and jealousy abound even during the lifetime of the Buddha, how much worse will it be in the world after his passing?"[6] A common mortal like Nichiren would not be able to bear any of the Lord Buddha Shakyamuni's sufferings for a single day or even for a single moment, let alone all the various persecutions which befell him during a period of more than fifty years. Moreover, it is taught that in the Latter Day of the Law, persecutions will be ten billion times greater than those in Shakyamuni's day. I wondered how I could possibly withstand them. A sage, however, is said to be capable of predicting what will occur in the future. With regard to the three periods of past, present and future, an understanding of the future is the mark of a true sage. I, Nichiren, may not be a sage, but I have for some time known that Japan would in our day bring ruin upon itself [because of its attachment to heretical teachings].

I knew that if I dared to say this openly, then surely I must be the votary of the Lotus Sutra whom the Buddha prophesied would appear after his death and fulfill the Buddha's teaching, " how much worse will it be in the world after his passing?" But if, though knowing what the future holds, I remained silent, I would be condemned to be born a mute or a stutterer in lifetime after lifetime. I myself would become a great enemy of the Lord Shakyamuni and a traitor to the ruler of Japan. After death, I would fall into the great citadel of the hell of incessant suffering. For years, therefore, I have continually admonished myself that, even though I might lack food or clothing, or be rebuked by my parents, brothers, teacher and friends, or be persecuted by the ruler and all the people, if I were going to waver even in the slightest on that account, I would have done better never to have spoken out in the first place.

Since the infinite past, I may have met the Lotus Sutra several times and set my heart on attaining enlightenment. However, while I may have been able to bear one or two minor difficulties, I must have given up when faced with a succession of great obstacles. In this life, I knew that if I were truly resolved to withstand the harshest trials, then I must speak out. This I did, and I encountered major persecutions one after another, just as the sutra predicts.

My resolution is now inflexible. Determined to endure any hardship, I have fulfilled the Buddha's prediction, and I have no doubt [that I am the votary of the Lotus Sutra]. Now I am living here in these desolate mountains and forests. Even if you should abandon your faith in the Lotus Sutra, how could I regard as strangers people who, if only for a day or even for a moment, have helped me survive? Never have I cared what happens to me personally. I promised that no matter what might befall me, I would maintain my faith without regressing, and if I became a Buddha, I would lead all of you to enlightenment. You have less knowledge of Buddhism than I, and moreover, you are lay believers with lands, families and retainers. Therefore, it may be extremely difficult for you to sustain your faith throughout life. This is why I have always told you that because of your position, it would be better to feign ignorance of this teaching. No matter what may happen in the future, be assured that I will never forsake or neglect you.

As for my teachings, regard those before my exile to Sado as equivalent to the Buddha's pre-Lotus Sutra teachings. I had thought that if the ruler of this country desired to govern well, he would summon the priests of the Shingon sect for an open debate with me, and that, on that occasion, I would reveal for the first time the true teaching of supreme importance. Before my exile, I withheld this teaching even from my disciples for fear that if I should tell them, even in confidence, they might inadvertently disclose it to the Shingon priests, who would then avoid the debate. This is why I refrained from revealing the true teaching to all of you as well.

Then on the night of the twelfth day of the ninth month in the eighth year of Bun'ei (1271), I was very nearly beheaded at Tatsunokuchi. From that time, I felt pity for my followers because I had not yet revealed the true teaching to any of them. With this in mind, I secretly conveyed my teaching to my disciples from the province of Sado. After the Buddha's death, great scholars and teachers of Buddhism such as Mahākāśyapa, Ānanda, Nāgārjuna, Vasubandhu, T'ien-t'ai, Miao-lo, Dengyō, and Gishin[7] knew this teaching, but kept it in their hearts and did not express it in words. The reason was that the Buddha had forbidden them to spread it, stating, "After my death, this great Law should not be revealed until the Latter Day of the Law arrives."[8] I, Nichiren, may not be an envoy sent by the Buddha, but my appearance in this world coincides with the age of the Latter Day. Moreover, quite unexpectedly, I came to realize this teaching, which I now expound to prepare the way for a sage.

With the appearance of this teaching, all the teachings advocated by the scholars and teachers of Buddhism during the Former and Middle Days of the Law will be like stars after sunrise or an awkward apprentice beside a skilled craftsman. It is predicted that once this Law is revealed in this era, the Buddha images as well as the priests of the temples built in the Former and Middle Days will all lose their power to benefit people, and only this one great Law shall spread all over the world. Since all of you have a bond with this teaching, you should feel reassured.

Utsubusa came a long distance to visit me despite her advanced age, but since I was told that it was merely a casual visit on her way back from the shrine of her ancestors, I would not see her, although I pitied her greatly. Had I permitted her to see me, I would have been allowing her to commit slander against the Lotus Sutra. The reason is that all gods are subjects, and the Lotus Sutra is their lord. It is against even the code of society to visit one's lord on the way back from calling on one of his subjects. Moreover, Utsubusa is a nun, a follower of the Buddha. She should have the Buddha foremost in mind. Because she made this and other mistakes as well, I refused to see her. She was not the only one, however. I refused to see many others who stopped by to visit me on their return from the hot spring resort at Shimobe.[9] Utsubusa is the same age that my parents would be. I feel deeply sorry to have disappointed her, but I want her to understand this point.

After you came here to see me the year before last, I received word—true or not, I do not know—that you were ill, and I wanted to send a messenger to inquire after you. However, my disciples said that much as they understood how I felt, they advised against it, as it might embarrass you. Therefore I abandoned the idea, acknowledging that such is the way of the world. I thought that if you were really ill, you would inform me, since you have always been sincere and faithful. I did not hear from you, however, so I myself deliberately refrained from inquiring after you, although I have been anxious about you all this time. Change is the way of all things, but last year and this year too the world has changed so greatly that I feared I might not be able to see you any more. Just when I was longing to hear from you, your letter arrived. Nothing could have given me greater pleasure. Please tell the Lady Utsubusa about all that I have written here.

I would like to explain further about my teaching, but this letter is already too long. Earlier I mentioned the Zen, Nembutsu, and Ritsu sects. However, of the many sects of Buddhism, Shingon is the very teaching that brought ruin upon China and will destroy Japan as well. Not only were six priests—Shan-wu-wei, Chin-kang-chih, and Pu-k'ung of China, and Kōbō, Jikaku, and Chishō of Japan—confused as to the relative superiority of the Lotus Sutra and the three sutras of Dainichi,[10] but also the first three made false objects of worship[11] representing the two realms and misled people to believe that these mandalas had originated in India. Being so deceived, the latter three priests learned the doctrines of Shingon, brought them to Japan, and spread them throughout the land, from the ruler down to the common people. Emperor Hsüan-tsung of China lost his empire because of the Shingon doctrines, and our country is also steadily declining. The retired eighty-second emperor, Gotoba,[12] was robbed of his power by the Kamakura government despite Bodhisattva Hachiman's oath[13] to protect one hundred successive rulers. This misfortune was solely the result of the prayers offered by eminent priests who followed the three Shingon priests—Kōbō and the others—on behalf of the imperial court. These evil prayers "returned to the originators."[14]

Because the Kamakura shogunate attacked the evil doctrine of Shingon and its evil men, it might have ruled our land for eighteen generations more, in accordance with the oath of Bodhisattva Hachiman. However, it has now turned to the men of the same evil doctrine it once opposed. Therefore, as Japan no longer has a ruler worthy of protection, Bonten, Taishaku, the gods of the sun and the moon and the Four Heavenly Kings have replied to this slander by ordering a foreign country to invade Japan.[15] They have also dispatched the votary of the Lotus Sutra as their envoy. The ruler, however, does not heed his warnings. On the contrary, he sides with the evil priests, thus creating chaos in both religious and secular realms. As a result, he has become a formidable enemy of the Lotus Sutra. And as his slander has long continued, this country is on the verge of ruin.

Today's epidemic is no less than the harbinger of defeat in a great war which is to come. How pitiful! How tragic!

Nichiren

The twenty-third day of the second month

Notes

1. It is somewhat unusual for an exhortation of this kind to appear at the very beginning of a letter. It may well have been that Nichiren intended it as a postscript, but added it here because of lack of space at the end of the letter.

2. *Ogo* is a type of dark green seaweed, somewhat like long, unkempt hair.

3. Utsubusa-no-ama was a follower of Nichiren who lived at Utsubusa in the Ihara district of Suruga Province. She is said to have been a relative of Misawa.

4. *See* Three Obstacles and Four Devils in Glossary.

5. The villainies of Devadatta and King Ajātaśatru are frequently referred to by Nichiren.

6. T9, 31b.

7. Gishin (782–833) was appointed the first chief priest of the head temple of the Tendai sect, the Enrayku-ji, by imperial command. He had accompanied his teacher,

Dengyō, to China, and in 827 established a Mahayana ordination center on Mount Hiei, in accordance with his teacher's wishes.

8. The source of this quotation is not known.

9. The Shimobe hot springs are located about seven km. northeast of Minobu in present-day Yamanashi Prefecture.

10. The three basic sutras of esoteric Buddism are the *Dainichi*, *Kongōchō*, and *Soshitsuji* sutras.

11. Reference is to the Womb Realm mandala and the Diamond Realm mandala. The Diamond Realm mandala, based on the *Kongōchō* Sutra, depicts the Diamond World, which represents Dainichi Buddha's wisdom, while the Womb Realm mandala, based on the *Dainichi* Sutra, represents the fundamental principle of the universe, that is, the Dharma Body of Dainichi Buddha.

12. Ex-emperor Gotoba (1180–1239) was defeated in 1221 in his attempt to overthrow the Kamakura shogunate, despite the fact that he had Tendai and Shingon priests pray for his victory. He was exiled to the island of Oki.

13. Hachiman is the Shinto god highly esteemed by the samurai; he has been incorporated into Buddhism as the Bodhisattva Hachiman. He is said to have made an oath during the reign of Emperor Heizei (774–824) to the effect that he would protect one hundred successive rulers of Japan.

14. Lotus Sutra (T9, 58a). Nichiren is indicating that because evil, in other words esoteric prayers and exorcisms, were used against an enemy, they worked in reverse, bringing misfortune to the ex-emperor.

15. Reference is to the Mongol invasion of the tenth month of 1274 and the threat of another invasion, which materialized in 1281.

Nichiren sent this letter from Mount Minobu to Nanjō Tokimitsu, lord of the Ueno district in Suruga Province on the twenty-fifth day of the second month, 1278. The previous year had been a time of turmoil; a serious drought had devastated crops and the resulting famine brought countless hardships. In addition, from the fall of that year an epidemic had swept the area, bringing many deaths. At the same time the threat of a second invasion by Mongol forces contributed to the general feeling of unease. Tokimitsu was one of Nichiren's most loyal adherents and his efforts to defend Nichiren and his followers incurred the displeasure of the Kamakura shogunate, with the result that onerous tax burdens were imposed upon him.

"Two Kinds of Faith" (*Suika nishin Shō*), means literally, faith like fire and faith like water, as Nichiren explains in the text of the letter. The standard title of this letter is *Ueno-dono Gohenji* (Reply to Lord Ueno); some twenty-one letters bear the same title.

I have duly received your offerings of taro, skewer-dried persimmons, baked rice, chestnuts, bamboo shoots, and bamboo containers of vinegar.

There was once a king named Aśoka the Great in India. He reigned over a quarter of the world and, attended by the dragon kings,[1] controlled the rain at his will. He even used demons to do his bidding. At first he was a merciless ruler, but later he was converted to Buddhism. He made offerings to sixty thousand priests each day and erected eighty-four thousand stone stupas. In inquiring into the previous lifetime of this great sovereign, we find that in the days of Shakyamuni Buddha there were two little boys called Tokushō Dōji and Mushō Dōji, who once offered the Buddha a mudpie. Because of this act of sincerity, the elder boy Tokushō was reborn as King Aśoka within one hundred years.[2]

The Buddha is of course respectworthy, but when compared with the Lotus Sutra, he is like a firefly beside the sun or the moon. The Lotus Sutra is as superior to Shakyamuni Buddha as heaven is higher than the earth. To present offerings to the Buddha produces such great benefits as to be born a king, yet even greater benefit is obtained by making offerings to the Lotus Sutra. If such a marvelous reward was brought about by the mere offering of a mudpie, how much more will come about as a result of all your various gifts! The Buddha was far from being short of food, but now we are in a land where hunger prevails. Therefore I am certain that the Buddhas Shakyamuni and Tahō and the Ten Goddesses will never fail to protect you.

Today there are people who have faith in the Lotus Sutra. The belief of some is like a fire while that of others is like water. When the former listen to the teachings, their passion flares up like fire, but when by themselves, they are inclined to discard their faith. To have faith like water means to believe continuously without ever regressing. Since you pay frequent visits to me regardless of the difficulties, your belief is comparable to flowing water. It is worthy of great respect!

Is it true that there is illness in your family? If so, it cannot be the work of demons. The Ten Goddesses must be testing the strength of your faith. None of the demons who appeared in the Lotus Sutra would ever dare trouble a votary of the sutra and have their heads broken as punishment.[3] Persist in your faith with the firm conviction that both Shakyamuni Buddha and the Lotus Sutra are free from any falsehood.

With my deep respect,
Nichiren

The twenty-fifth day of the second month

Notes

1. Dragons are one of the eight kinds of nonhuman beings that protect Buddhism. Not only are they believed to bring rain, but they are said to have supernatural powers and the ability to produce miraculous phenomena.

2. This story appears in various sources with varying details; which ones Nichiren

used cannot be determined. When Shakyamuni was going about begging on the outskirts of the city of Rājagṛha, he came upon two boys, Tokushō Dōji and Mushō Dōji, playing in the mud. The boys, observing the so-called "thirty-two marks" that distinguish a Buddha, decided that they would make an offering to him and proceeded to shape mudpies. Tokushō Dōji placed them in Shakyamuni's begging bowl while the younger boy, Mushō, then pressed his hands together in a gesture of reverence. Shakyamuni received the gift of mudpies with a smile. His disciple Ānanda, who was accompanying him, asked him why he smiled, whereupon he replied, "I have a reason for smiling, Ānanda, and you shall know it. One hundred years after my death, this boy will become a wheel-turning king at Pāṭaliputra, who will rule over all regions. His name will be Aśoka, and he will rule through the True Law." It is said that Tokushō Dōji was born as King Aśoka and Mushō Dōji, as either his wife or his brother. This story is found in *Aikuō Den* (T50, 99b) and the *Aikuō* Sutra (T50, 131C).

3. Reference is to a verse in the *Darani* (26th) chapter of the Lotus Sutra that reads: "Whoever resists our spell / And troubles a preacher of the Dharma, / May his head split in seven pieces / Like the branches of an *arjaka* tree." It is also said that if one touches an *arjaka* flower its petals open and fall in seven pieces.

63 *THE TEACHING FOR THE LATTER DAY*

This letter, dated the first day of the fourth month, 1278, is one of the many communications Nichiren sent to Nanjō Tokimitsu, Lord of Ueno village and a loyal follower of Nichiren. Nichiren thanks Tokimitsu for the food he received and expresses his distress at the news of the death of the daughter of Ishikawa no Hyōe Nyūdō (n.d.). Ishikawa was the steward of Omosu village in the Fuji district of Suruga Province, and his wife was an elder sister of Nanjō Tokimitsu. Thus the daughter who had passed away was Tokimitsu's niece.

"The Teaching for the Latter Day" (*Mappō Yōhō Gosho*) is again an alternative title. It also bears the familiar title *Ueno-dono Gohenji* (Reply to Lord Ueno, 1278).

———

I have received a quarter-sack[1] of polished rice, a horse-load of taro, and five strips of *konnyaku*[2] that you took the trouble to send me.

First of all, regarding the daughter of Ishikawa no Hyōe Nyūdō. She often sent me letters, and in one that reached me on the night of the fourteenth or fifteenth day of the third month, she wrote, "When I observe the world around me, it seems that even healthy people will be unable to survive this year. I have been ill for a long time, but my illness has suddenly worsened, and I imagine that this will be my last letter to you." So she has already passed away!

Most people believe that those who chant Namu Amida Butsu at the moment of their death are sure to be reborn in the Pure Land, for this is what the Buddha taught. For some reason, however, the Buddha surprisingly reversed his statement and said, "[For the past more than forty years,] I have not yet revealed the truth,"[3] and "Honestly discarding the provisional teachings, [I will expound only the supreme Way.]"[4] I, Nichiren, have been teaching as the Buddha advocated, but all Japan has become enraged and denounced my words as groundless fabrications.

There were other occasions when the Buddha unexpectedly reversed an earlier teaching. In the Hinayana sutras he taught that there is no Buddha other than himself in any of the ten directions and that living beings do not possess the Buddha nature. But in the Mahayana sutras he taught that there are Buddhas throughout the ten directions and that the Buddha nature dwells in every living being. How then can there be anyone who still employs the Hinayana sutras? All people have since come to place their faith in the Mahayana sutras.

Moreover, we find that there are even more unfathomable distinctions which Shakyamuni Buddha drew between the sutras. In the Lotus Sutra, he suddenly refuted all the other sutras that he had preached, now preached, and would preach in the future, and declared that only the Lotus Sutra was true. But his disciples would not believe him. At that time, Tahō Buddha came to bear witness to what the Buddha had said, and all the Buddhas of the ten directions added their testimony to his, extending their tongues until they reached the Brahma Heaven.

After Tahō Buddha had closed the door of the Treasure Tower and the other Buddhas had returned to their original lands, not even Shakyamuni Buddha himself could have denied the Lotus Sutra, whatever other sutras he might have expounded in an effort to do so, because the other Buddhas had all joined in affirming its truth. That is why the *Fugen*[5] and Nirvana sutras, which follow the Lotus Sutra, praise it and in no way disparage it.

Nevertheless, priests like Shan-wu-wei of the Shingon sect and the founders of the Zen sect repudiate the Lotus Sutra, and the entire Japanese nation has now taken faith in their teachings, just like those who were deceived by the rebels Masakado[6] and Sadatō.[7] Japan is now on the brink of ruin because it has for many years been the archenemy of Shakyamuni, Tahō, and all the other Buddhas of the ten directions, and in addition, the person who denounces these heresies is persecuted. Because such offenses are thus accumulated one on top of another, our nation will soon incur the wrath of heaven.

Perhaps because of karma from past lives or some other reason, the daughter of Ishikawa no Hyōe Nyūdō chanted Nam-myoho-renge-kyo at the moment of her death. This is as rare as the one-eyed turtle finding a suitable hollow in a floating sandalwood log, or a thread lowered from the heavens passing through the eye of a needle on the earth.[8] How wondrous!

The sutras clearly show that those who believe in the Nembutsu are destined to fall into the hell of incessant suffering, but since people are not aware of this, they all think that it is my own fabrication. People can see neither their own eyebrows, which are so close, nor the heavens in the distance,[9] as the saying goes. Had my teaching been false, the nun, Ishikawa's daughter, could not have died with a correct and steadfast mind.

Among my disciples, those who think themselves well-versed in Buddhism are the ones who make errors. Nam-myoho-renge-kyo is the heart of the Lotus Sutra. It is like the soul of a person. To revere another teaching as its equal is to be like an empress who is married to two emperors or who secretly commits adultery with a minister or a humble subject. It can only be the cause for disaster.

This teaching was not propagated in the Former or Middle Day of the Law because the other sutras had not yet lost the power of benefit. Now in the Latter Day of the Law, neither the Lotus Sutra nor the other sutras lead to enlightenment. Only Nam-myoho-renge-kyo can do so. And this is not merely my own opinion. Shakyamuni, Tahō, and all the other Buddhas of the ten directions as well as the innumerable Bodhisattvas of the Earth have so determined. To mix other practices with this Nam-myoho-renge-kyo is a grave error. A lamp will be useless after the sun rises. How can dewdrops be beneficial once the rain falls? Should one feed a newborn baby with anything other than its mother's milk? Good medicine works by itself; there is no need to add other medicine. Somehow Ishikawa's daughter remained true to this principle and continued to uphold her faith until the last moment of her life. How admirable!

With my deep respect,
Nichiren

The first day of the fourth month in the first year of Kōan (1278)

Notes

1. A quarter-sack is about 18 liters.
2. *Konnyaku* is a kind of paste or gelatin made from the root of the *konnyaku*

(devil's root) plant. It is believed that it eliminates poisonous substances from the body.

3. T9, 386b.

4. T9, 10a.

5. The *Fugen* Sutra is regarded as a conclusion or epilogue to the Lotus Sutra. Following the *Fugen* (28th) chapter of the Lotus Sutra, this sutra describes how to meditate on Bodhisattva Fugen and explains the benefits of this practice. It also exhorts people to embrace and propagate the Lotus Sutra.

6. Taira no Masakado (d.940) led the first major rebellion by a warrior against the central government. Based in Shimōsa, near present-day Tokyo, he led a struggle to gain control of the area. He attacked government offices in Kanto and adopted the title of New Emperor. In 940 he was defeated by forces led by Fujiwara no Hidesato and his cousin Taira no Sadamori.

7. Abe no Sadatō (1019–1062) was head of a powerful family in eastern Japan. He sought independence from imperial rule but was defeated and killed in a battle with the imperial army.

8. These are both metaphors to indicate occasions of extreme rarity; Nichiren makes frequent reference to them.

9. This statement appears in the *Maka Shikan* (T46, 57b) and elsewhere, indicating the ignorance of common mortals. Nichiren first quotes the expression and then paraphrases it; the quotation is omitted here to avoid repetition.

64 *THE ONE ESSENTIAL PHRASE*

This letter was sent by Nichiren from Mount Minobu on the third day of the seventh month, 1278, to Myōhō-ama, who lived in Okamiya village in Suruga Province. Virtually nothing is known of Myōhō-ama. This letter is written in response to a letter she had sent Nichiren, asking whether one could gain enlightenment only by chanting Nam-myoho-renge-kyo. We know from another letter that Myōhō-ama's husband had died shortly after this letter was written, and that her inquiry was most likely made on his behalf. It should be noted that there were four women named Myōhō-ama, with whom Nichiren was acquainted: the present recipient of this letter, Shijō Kingo's mother, the mother of Nakaoki Nyūdō from Sado, and the grandmother of Nichimoku Shonin.

The title of this letter, "The One Essential Phrase" (*Ikku Kanjin no Koto*) is an alternative title. It is also known as *Myōhō-ama Gozen Gohenji* (Reply to Lady Myōhō-ama).

First, for you to ask a question about the Lotus Sutra is a rare source of good fortune. In this age of the Latter Day of the Law, those who ask about the meaning of even one phrase or verse of the Lotus Sutra are much fewer than those who can hurl great Mount Sumeru to another land like a stone, or those who can kick the entire galaxy away like a ball. They are even fewer than those who can embrace and teach countless other sutras, thereby enabling the priests and laymen who listen to them to obtain the six supernatural powers.[1] Equally rare is a priest who can explain the meaning of the Lotus Sutra and clearly answer questions concerning it. The *Hōtō* chapter in the fourth volume of the Lotus Sutra sets forth the important principle of six difficult and nine easy acts. Your asking a question about the Lotus Sutra is among the six difficult acts. This is a sure indication that if you

479

embrace the Lotus Sutra, you will certainly attain Buddhahood. Since the Lotus Sutra defines our body as the Law body (*hosshin*) of the Buddha, our mind as his bliss body (*hōshin*), and our actions as his manifested body (*ōjin*), all who embrace and believe in even a single phrase or verse of this sutra will be endowed with the blessings of these three bodies. Nam-myoho-renge-kyo is only one phrase, but it contains the essence of the entire sutra. You asked whether one can attain Buddhahood only by chanting Nam-myoho-renge-kyo, and this is the most important question of all. It is the heart of the entire sutra and the substance of its eight volumes.

The spirit within one's body may appear in just his face, and the spirit within his face may appear in just his eyes. Included within the word Japan is all that is within the country's sixty-six provinces: all of the people and animals, the rice paddies and other fields, those of high and low status, the nobles and the commoners, the seven kinds of gems[2] and all other treasures. Similarly, included within the title, Nam-myoho-renge-kyo, is the entire sutra consisting of all eight volumes, twenty-eight chapters, and 69,384 characters, without the omission of a single character. Concerning this, Po Chü-i[3] stated that the title is to the sutra as eyes are to the Buddha. In the eighth volume of his *Hokke Mongu Ki*, Miao-lo stated that T'ien-t'ai's *Hokke Gengi* explains only the title, but that the entire sutra is thereby included. By this he meant that, although the text was omitted, the entire sutra was contained in the title alone. Everything has its essential point, and the heart of the Lotus Sutra is its title, Nam-myoho-renge-kyo. Truly, if you chant this in the morning and evening, you are correctly reading the entire Lotus Sutra. Chanting daimoku twice is the same as reading the entire sutra twice, one hundred daimoku equal one hundred readings of the sutra, and a thousand daimoku, a thousand readings of the sutra. Thus, if you ceaselessly chant daimoku, you will be continually reading the Lotus Sutra.

The sixty volumes of the T'ien-t'ai doctrine[4] present exactly the same interpretation. A law this easy to embrace and this easy to practice was taught for the sake of all humankind in this evil age of the Latter Day of the Law. A passage from the Lotus Sutra reads,"During the Latter Day of the Law, [if one wishes to teach this sutra, he should employ the mild way of propagation.]"[5] Another reads, "In the Latter Day when the Law is about to perish, a person who embraces, reads and recites this sutra [must abandon feelings of envy and deceit.]"[6] A third states,"In the Latter Day of the Law, one who embraces this sutra [will be carrying out all forms of service to the Buddha.]"[7] A fourth reads, "In the fifth five hundred years [after my death,] accomplish worldwide *kōsen-rufu* [and never allow its flow to cease.]"[8] The intent of all these teachings is the admonition to embrace and believe in the Lotus Sutra in this Latter Day of the Law. The heretical priests in Japan, China, and India have all failed to comprehend this obvious meaning. The Nembutsu, Shingon, Zen, and Ritsu sects follow either the Hinayana or the provisional Mahayana teachings but have discarded the Lotus Sutra. They misunderstand Buddhism, but they do not realize their mistakes. Because they appear to be true priests, the people trust them without the slightest doubt. Therefore, without realizing it, both these priests and the people who follow them have become enemies of the Lotus Sutra and foes of Shakyamuni Buddha. Not only will all their wishes remain unfulfilled, but their lives will be short and, after this life, they will be doomed to the hell of incessant suffering. This is made clear in the sutra.

Even though one neither reads nor studies the sutra, chanting the title alone is the source of tremendous good fortune. The sutra teaches that women, evil men, and those in the realms of Animal and Hell—in fact, all the people of the Ten Worlds—can attain Buddhahood. We can comprehend this when we remember that fire can be produced by a stone taken from the bottom of a river, and a candle can light up a place that has been dark for billions of years. If even the most ordinary things of this world are such wonders, then how much more wondrous is the power of the Mystic Law. The lives of human beings are fettered by evil karma, earthly desires, and the inborn sufferings of life and death. But due to the three inherent potentials of Buddha nature—innate Buddhahood, the wisdom to become aware of it, and the action to manifest it—our lives can without doubt come to reveal the Buddha's three bodies or properties. The Great Teacher Dengyō declared that the power of the Lotus Sutra enables anyone to manifest Buddhahood. He stated this because even the Dragon King's daughter, who was a reptile, was able to attain Buddhahood through the power of the Lotus Sutra. Do not doubt this in the least. Let your husband know that I will explain this in detail when I see him.

Nichiren

The third day of the seventh month in the first year of Kōan (1278)

Notes

1. The six supernatural powers, also called six mystic powers, are expounded in the *Kusha Ron* (T29,142c): (1) the power to appear anywhere at will; (2) the power to observe all phenomena in the world, no matter how small, near or far; (3) the power to understand all sounds and languages; (4) the power to read minds; (5) the power to know people's past lifetimes; and (6) the power to be free form all innate desires.

2. Lists vary according to the text. The *Hōtō* (11th) chapter of the Lotus Sutra gives, gold, silver, lapis lazuli, coral, agate, pearl, and carnelian.

3. Po Chü-i (772–846) is a famed Chinese poet, much admired in Japan.

4. The three major works of T'ien-t'ai—*Hokke Gengi* (T33, no. 1716), *Hokke Mongu* (T34, no. 1718), and the *Maka Shikan* (T46, no.1911), and Miao-lo's commentaries of them—*Hokke Gengi Shakusen* (T33, no.1717), *Hokke Mongu Ki* (T33, no.1719), and *Maka Shikan Bugyōden Guketsu* (T46, no.1912).

5. In this and the following quotations, Nichiren gives only abbreviated portions of the text. The bracketed portions represent fuller translations of the passages in question, and have been added for clarity. The present passage is at T9, 37, a–b.

6. T9, 38b.

7. T9, 46b.

8. T9, 54c.

65 PERSECUTION BY SWORD AND STAFF

This letter, one of many addressed to Nanjō Tokimitsu, is dated the twentieth day of the fourth month, 1279. Nichiren's retirement to Mount Minobu was entering upon its fifth year; Nikkō Shonin was actively spreading the teaching in Atsuhara village in the Fuji district of Suruga Province. The success of Nichiren's and Nikkō's efforts was reflected in a series of persecutuions that lasted over a period of three years in the Atsuhara area. The priest of the Tendai temple in Atsuhara, angered at the defection of several young priests to Nichiren's teachings, enlisted the aid of a few prominent samurai in the area in having several local farmers, who refused to recant their allegiance to Nichiren, arrested. Eventually three farmers were beheaded and others were banished from Atsuhara.

The title "Persecution by Sword and Staff" (*Tōjōnan no Koto*) is an alternative name for this letter. It is more frequently referred to as *Ueno-dono Gohenji* (Reply to Lord Ueno, 1279).

The greatest of all the persecutions I have suffered were those at Komatsubara in Tōjō,[1] and at Tatsunokuchi.[2] where I was nearly beheaded. None of the others were direct attempts on my life. I have been reviled, denounced, exiled, falsely accused, and struck across the face, but these were all comparatively minor incidents. I, Nichiren, am the only person in Japan to be abused in both body and mind for practicing the Lotus Sutra. If anyone else has been slandered as I have, it was not because of the Lotus Sutra. One incident I especially can never forget is how Shōfu-bō[3] seized the fifth volume of the Lotus Sutra[4] and struck me across the face with it. His attack on me stemmed from the three poisons of greed, anger, and stupidity.

Once in India there was a jealous woman[5] who hated her husband so much that she smashed everything in the house. Her excessive rage completely altered her appearance; her eyes blazed like the sun and moon, and her mouth seemed to belch fire. She looked exactly like a blue or red demon.[6] She seized the fifth volume of the Lotus Sutra, which her husband had been reciting for some years, and trampled it savagely with both feet. Later she died and fell into hell, all of her except her feet. Though hell's wardens tried to force them down by beating them with iron staves, her feet remained outside of hell as a result of the relationship, albeit a reverse one, which they had formed with the Lotus Sutra by trampling on it. Shōfu-bō struck me in the face with the fifth volume of the Lotus Sutra because he hated me. Thus he too has formed a reverse relationship[7] with this sutra.

One incident occurred in India, the other in Japan; one was perpetrated by a woman, and the other by a man; in one, a pair of feet committed the violence, and in the other, a pair of hands; one happened because of jealousy, and the other because of the Lotus Sutra. However, the same fifth volume of the sutra was involved in both instances. The woman's feet did not enter hell, so why should Shōfu-bō's hands? The woman, however, hated only her husband and not the Lotus Sutra itself, whereas Shōfu-bō hated both the Lotus Sutra and me, Nichiren. Therefore his entire body will enter hell. As the sutra states, "After he dies, he will fall into the hell of incessant suffering."[8] There is no mention of his hands being spared. How pitiful! Eventually, however, he will meet me again and be able to attain Buddhahood, just as the four kinds of arrogant people were ultimately saved by Bodhisattva Fukyō.[9]

The fifth volume contains the heart of the Lotus Sutra, for it reveals that the Dragon King's daughter attained Buddhahood without changing her dragon form. Devadatta represents the spiritual aspect of enlightenment, and the Dragon King's daughter, the physical aspect. The principle of attaining Buddhahood in one's present form can be found nowhere else in Shakyamuni's teaching. The Great Teacher Dengyō enumerated ten outstanding principles in which the Lotus Sutra surpassed all others.[10] One of them is the superiority of leading people to attain Buddhahood in their present form.[11] This principle appears to have its origin in a passage in the *Hokke Mongu* that discusses the enlightenment of the Dragon King's daughter.[12] It is also a point of controversy between the Shingon and Tendai sects. The Dragon King's daughter attained enlightenment through the power of the Lotus Sutra. Bodhisattva Monju stated, "I always proclaim and teach only the Lotus Sutra."[13] The words "only" and "always" are the key to this quotation. However, the *Bodaishin Ron* reads, "[The principle of attaining Buddhahood in one's present form] is found only in the teachings of Shingon."[14] Which "only" is correct? The *Bodaishin Ron* must be mistaken. The *Muryōgi* Sutra states, ". . . in these more than forty years, I have not yet revealed the truth."[15] The Lotus Sutra reads, "The World-Honored One has long expounded his doctrines and now must reveal the truth."[16] Tahō Buddha affirmed that only the Lotus Sutra enables one to attain Buddhahood as a common mortal when he said, "All that you (Shakyamuni Buddha) have expounded is the truth."[17] No matter how repeatedly the believers in provisional doctrines may insist that one can attain enlightenment through the pre-Lotus Sutra teachings, it is as easy to refute their assertions as it is to smash a thousand pieces of earthenware with a single hammer. T'ien-t'ai states, "The practice of the Lotus Sutra is *shakubuku*, the refutation of the provisional doctrines."[18] The Lotus Sutra indeed is the most profound and secret teaching.

Ever since Jikaku, scholars of the Tendai sect have interpreted the passages of the *Hokke Gengi*, *Hokke Mongu*, and *Maka Shikan* in one way or another, and have given plausible explanations. Their views, however, are as useless to us now as last year's calendar or yesterday's meal. Even if someone should insist that, in the first five hundred years of the Latter Day of the Law, there exists a way to enlightenment apart from the daimoku of the Lotus Sutra, you should not pursue it, even if it is based on the Buddha's teachings, and even less so if it is merely some scholar's opinion. The *Devadatta* chapter of the Lotus Sutra teaches that Devadatta was Shakyamuni Buddha's master in some past existence. He who was once the master is now the disciple, and he who is now the disciple was formerly the master. On pondering this chapter, I, Nichiren, realized that it reveals the profound meaning of the Lotus Sutra through the principle of the oneness of past and present and the inseparability of the one who teaches and the one who learns. Therefore, the merciful Shakyamuni Buddha became the master of the wicked Devadatta, and the wise Monju became the master of the ignorant daughter of the Dragon King. Certainly I, Nichiren, can in no way be inferior to Monju or to Shakyamuni Buddha. The men of Japan are like Devadatta and the women are like the Dragon King's daughter. Whether by following it or opposing it, they shall attain enlightenment through the Lotus Sutra. This is the message of the *Devadatta* chapter.

Next we come to the *Kanji* chapter. Only I, Nichiren, have read with my entire being the twenty-line verse[19] from this chapter, which a vast multitude of bodhisattvas proclaimed in a single voice. Since the Buddha's death, who else in the three countries of India, China, and Japan has ever read this verse as I have? No one even claims to have done so, nor do I believe that anyone has. The *Kanji* chapter states, "[There will be many ignorant people who will] . . . attack us with swords and staves." Perhaps others have been beaten with staves, but I have never heard of any who were injured by the sword.

We know that Bodhisattva Fukyō was attacked with staves, in accordance with the words of the sutra, "They would beat him with sticks and staves, and stone him with rocks and tiles,"[20] but he was not persecuted by the sword. T'ien-t'ai, Miao-lo, Dengyō, and others also escaped persecution by sword and staff, in accordance with the words, "Swords and staves will not touch him."[21] I, Nichiren, however, have been attacked by both. As I mentioned before, I was attacked by the sword at Komatsubara in Tōjō and later at Tatsunokuchi. No one else has been thus assaulted for the sake of the Lotus Sutra even once, but I, Nichiren, have been so assaulted twice. As for being attacked with staves, I have already been struck in the face by Shōfu-bō with the scroll of the fifth volume of the Lotus Sutra. Strangely enough, it is precisely that volume which carries the prediction that the votaries of the Lotus Sutra will be attacked with staves. Shōfu-bō hit me before dozens of people, and, though I knew it was for the sake of the Lotus Sutra, being human, I felt miserable and ashamed. Had I had the strength, I would have wrested the weapon from his hand and trampled it to pieces, except that it was in fact the scroll of the fifth volume of the Lotus Sutra.

This brings to mind a story.[22] A father, anxious about his son's future, thrashed the boy with a bow made of boxwood because he refused to study. At the time, the son resented his father's action and hated the boxwood bow. However, he applied himself to his studies, disciplined his mind, and eventually achieved a great self-awakening which also benefited others. In retrospect, he saw that he owed his achievements to his father's thrashings. It is said that in gratitude he erected a stupa made of boxwood to honor his father's memory.

It is the same with me, Nichiren. When I attain Buddhahood, how will I be able to forget my obligation to Shōfu-bō? Much less can I forget the thanks I owe to the fifth volume of the Lotus Sutra with which he struck me. When I think of this, I cannot restrain my tears of gratitude.

The *Yujutsu* chapter also explains something about me, because it states that Bodhisattva Jōgyō and others will appear in the Latter Day of the Law to propagate the five characters of Nam-myoho-renge-kyo.[23] I, Nichiren, have appeared earlier than anyone else. How reassuring to think that I will surely be praised by bodhisattvas equal in number to the [grains of] sand of sixty thousand Ganges Rivers! Be that as it may, commit yourself to the Lotus Sutra and have faith in its teachings. You must not only believe in them yourself but also encourage others to do the same, so that you may save your deceased parents and ancestors.

From the time that I was born until today, I, Nichiren, have never known a moment's ease; I have thought only of propagating the daimoku of the Lotus Sutra. I do not know how long I or anyone else may live, but without fail, I will be with you at the time of your death and guide you from this life to the next. All the Buddhas of the past, present, and future attain enlightenment between the hours of the Ox and the Tiger.[24] In all three countries of India, China, and Japan, the place of Buddhist practice is located to the northeast, in the direction of the demon gate.[25] These are secret teachings of Buddhism, which are reverently transferred from master to disciple. I will explain in more detail later.

With my deep respect,

As you crave food when hungry, seek water when thirsty, long to see a lover, beg for medicine when ill, or as a beautiful woman desires powder and rouge, so should you put your faith in the Lotus Sutra. If you do not, you will regret it later.

Nichiren

The twentieth day of the fourth month in the second year of Kōan (1279)

Notes

1. Komatsubara was the name of the area in Tōjō village in Nichiren's native province of Awa where, on the eleventh day of the eleventh month, 1264, Nichiren was ambushed by Tōjō Kagenobu and his men. He received a cut on his forehead and had his hand broken.

2. Tatsunokuchi was the name of the execution grounds in Kamakura where the deputy police chief Hei no Saemon attempted to execute Nichiren on the twelfth day of the ninth month, 1271.

3. Shōfu is a title indicating the deputy or vice-chief of a government ministry. Nichiren frequently mentions a Shōfu-bō and he may well be referring to one of several individuals of the same title. Here reference is to a Shōfu-bō who was originally a follower of Nichiren's teachings but later abandoned his faith. When Hei no Saemon and his men went to arrest Nichiren on the first day of the ninth month, 1271, he accompanied them as Saemon's chief retainer.

4. The Lotus Sutra consists of twenty-eight chapters in eight volumes, or rolls, wrapped around a wooden staff. When used as a weapon, these rolls could inflict considerable damage. The fifth volume includes four chapters from the twelfth through the sixteenth. A passage in the *Kanji* (13th) chapter states that votaries of the Lotus Sutra will be attacked by sword and staff.

5. The source of this story is not known. A somewhat similar story, but involving a Chinese woman, appears in *Hokke Denki* (T51, 292c).

6. Demons that punish the denizens of hell.

7. A connection with the Lotus Sutra formed by opposing it. Although one who slanders the sutra must suffer retribution for his slander, he nevertheless forms a bond with the sutra and thus can ultimately attain Buddhahood.

8. T9, 15b.

9. This story is found in the *Fukyō* (20th) chapter of the Lotus Sutra. The four kinds of arrogant people are priests and nuns, laymen and laywomen who slandered and persecuted Bodhisattva Fukyō when he revered them for their inherent Buddha nature. What he practiced at the time was the Lotus Sutra, and because of their slander of that sutra the people fell into the hell of incessant suffering. Eventually, however, due to the reverse relationship they had formed with the Lotus Sutra, they met Bodhisattva Fukyō again and were able to attain enlightenment.

10. These are enumerated in the third volume of *Hokke Kushū* (DDZ3, 241 ff).

11. This is the eighth principle discussed in *Hokke Kushū* (DDZ3, 260–67).

12. T34, 117a.

13. T9, 35b.

14. T32, 572c.

15. T9, 386c.

16. T9, 6a.

17. T9, 32c.

18. *Hokke Gengi* (T33, 742b).

19. The verse section of the *Kanji* (13th) chapter that states that votaries of the Lotus Sutra will be attacked with swords and staves (T9, 36b).

20. T9, 32a.

21. Lotus Sutra (T9, 39b). This refers to one of the benefits that bodhisattvas gain as a result of the peaceful ways of practice set forth in the *Anrakugyō* (14th) chapter.

22. The following story appears in the *Sangoku Denki* (DNBZ 148, 361 ff), under the entry for Enshō (883–967). This work dates to about 1431; the source of Nichiren's account is not known.

23. The five characters are the title of the Lotus Sutra; the additional Nam (Namu) invokes the sutra.

24. The hours 1:00 to 5:00 A.M.

25. In correlating hours with spatial direction, the hours of the Ox-Tiger correspond to the northeast, believed to be the location of both Buddhism and demons.

66 THE DRAGON GATE

This letter was sent by Nichiren from Mount Minobu to Nanjō
Tokimitsu, Lord of the Ueno district of Suruga Province. Dated the sixth
day of the eleventh month, it is a reply to a report by Tokimitsu on the role
he was playing in assisting the followers of Nichiren's teaching in the
Atsuhara area, who were being persecuted by forces associated with the
Kamakura government. The dragon gate to which Nichiren refers cannot
be identified exactly. There are four places with extremely swift rapids and
steep waterfalls along the Yellow River that make it impossible for fish to
ascend them; should a fish succeed, legend has it that it would become a
dragon.

"The Dragon Gate" (*Ryūmon Gosho*) is again an alternative title. The
letter is also referred to as *Ueno-dono Gohenji* (Reply to Lord Ueno,
1279).

In China there is a waterfall called the Dragon Gate. Its waters plunge
a hundred feet, swifter than an arrow shot by a strong archer. It is said
that thousands of carp gather in the basin below, hoping to climb the
falls, and that any which succeeds will turn into a dragon. However,
not a single carp out of a hundred, a thousand, or even ten thousand
can climb the falls, not even after ten or twenty years. Some are swept
away by the strong currents, some fall prey to eagles, hawks, kites, and
owls, and others are netted, scooped up, or even shot with arrows by
fishermen who line either bank of the wide falls. Such is the difficulty
a carp faces in becoming a dragon.

There were once two major warrior clans in Japan, the Minamoto
and the Taira. They were like two faithful watchdogs at the gates of the

Imperial Palace. They were as eager to guard the emperor as a wood-cutter is to admire the harvest moon as it rises from behind the mountains. They marveled at the elegant parties of the court nobles and their ladies, just as monkeys in the trees are enraptured by the sight of the moon and stars glittering in the sky. Though of low rank, they longed to find some way to mingle in court circles. But even though Sadamori of the Taira clan[1] crushed the rebellion of Masakado,[2] he was still not admitted to court. Nor were any of his descendants, including the famous Masamori. Not until the time of Masamori's son, Tadamori, were any of the Taira clan granted permission to enter the court. The next in line, Kiyomori, and his son Shigemori, not only enjoyed life among court nobles but became directly related to the throne when Kiyomori's daughter married the emperor and bore him a child.

Attaining Buddhahood is no easier than for men of low status to enter court circles or for carp to climb the Dragon Gate. Śāriputra, for example, practiced bodhisattva austerities for sixty kalpas in order to attain Buddhahood, but finally could persevere no longer and slipped back into the paths of the two vehicles. Even some of those taught by Shakyamuni, when he was the sixteenth son of Daitsū Buddha, sank into the world of sufferings for the duration of *sanzen-jintengō*. Some others taught by him in the even more remote past when he first attained enlightenment suffered for the length of *gohyaku-jintengō*. All these people practiced the Lotus Sutra, but when persecuted by the Devil of the Sixth Heaven in the form of their sovereigns or other authorities, they forsook their faith and thus wandered among the six paths for countless kalpas.

Up until now these events seemed to have no bearing on us, but now we find ourselves facing the same kind of persecution. My wish is that all my disciples will cherish the great desire of attaining enlightenment. We are very fortunate to be alive after the widespread epidemics which occurred last year and the year before. But now with the impending Mongol invasion it appears that few will survive. In the end, no one can escape death. The sufferings at the time of invasion will be no worse than those we are facing now. Since death is the same in either case, you should be willing to offer your life for the Lotus Sutra. Think of this offering as a drop of dew rejoining the ocean or a speck of dust returning to the earth. A passage from the seventh chapter of the Lotus Sutra reads, "Our desire is to share this blessing equally with all people, and we, together with them, will attain Buddhahood."[3]

With my deep respect,
Nichiren

The sixth day of the eleventh month

POSTSCRIPT:
I write this letter in deep gratitude for the encouragement you are giving those involved in the Atsuhara Persecution.

Notes

1. The lineage of the Taira clan:

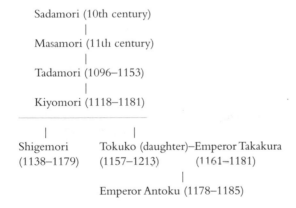

Sadamori (10th century)
|
Masamori (11th century)
|
Tadamori (1096–1153)
|
Kiyomori (1118–1181)

| |
Shigemori   Tokuko (daughter)–Emperor Takakura
(1138–1179)   (1157–1213)   (1161–1181)
|
Emperor Antoku (1178–1185)

2. Taira no Masakado (d.940) led the first major rebellion by a warrior against the central government. Based in Shimōsa, near present-day Tokyo, he led a struggle to gain control of the area. He attacked government offices in Kanto and adopted the title of New Emperor. In 940 he was defeated by forces led by his cousin, Taira no Sadamori, and Fujiwara no Hidesato.
3. T9, 24c.

67 LETTER TO NIIKE

Nichiren wrote this letter on an unspecified day of the second month of 1280 to Niike Saemon-no-jō, a samurai associated with the Kamakura regime. Niike was from Niike village in the Iwate district of Tōtōmi Province (present-day Shizuoka Prefecture). Virtually nothing is known of Niike; he and his wife maintained their faith in Nichiren's teachings despite pressures from the government.

What joy to have been born in the Latter Day of the Law and to have shared in the propagation of true Buddhism! How pitiful are those who, though born in this time, cannot believe in the Lotus Sutra!

No one can escape death once he is born as a human being, so why do you not practice in preparation for the next life? When I observe what people are doing, I realize that although they profess faith in the Lotus Sutra and clasp its scrolls, they act against the spirit of the sutra and thereby readily fall into the evil paths. To illustrate, a person has five major internal organs,[1] but should even one of them become diseased, it will infect all the others and eventually he will die. The Great Teacher Dengyō stated, "Even though one praises the Lotus Sutra, he destroys its heart."[2] He meant that even if one embraces, reads, and praises the Lotus Sutra, if he betrays its intent, he will be destroying not only Shakyamuni but all other Buddhas in the universe.

The sum of our worldly misdeeds and evil karma may pile up as high as Mount Sumeru, but once we take faith in this sutra, they will vanish like frost or dew under the sun of the Lotus Sutra. However, if one commits even one or two of the fourteen slanders[3] set forth in this sutra, his offense is almost impossible to expiate. Killing a single Buddha would be a far greater offense than destroying all living beings in the universe, and to violate the sutra's spirit is to commit the sin of destroying all Buddhas. One who commits any of these fourteen is a slanderer.

Hell is a dreadful dwelling of fire, and the realm of hungry ghosts is a pitiful state where starving people devour their own children. Asura means strife and Animality means to kill or be killed. The hell of the blood-red lotus is so called because the intense cold of this hell makes one double over until the back splits open and the bloody flesh emerges like a crimson lotus flower. And there are hells even more horrible. Once one falls into such an evil state, the fact that one was a ruler or a general means nothing. One is no different from a monkey on a string, tormented by the wardens of hell. What use are fame and fortune then? Can one still be arrogant and persist in false beliefs?

Stop and ponder! How rare is the faith that moves one to give alms to a priest who knows the heart of the Lotus Sutra! He will not stray into the evil paths if he does so even once. Still greater are the benefits arising from ten or twenty contributions, or from five years, ten years, or a lifetime of contributions. They are beyond even the measure of the Buddha's wisdom. The Buddha taught that the blessings of a single offering to the votary of this sutra are a hundred thousand myriad times greater than those of offering boundless treasure to Shakyamuni for more than eight billion kalpas. When you embrace this sutra, you will overflow with happiness and shed tears of joy. It seems impossible to repay our debt to Shakyamuni, but by your frequent offerings to me deep in these mountains you will repay the merciful kindness of both the Lotus Sutra and Shakyamuni Buddha. Strive ever harder in faith and never give in to negligence. Everyone appears to believe sincerely when he first embraces the Lotus Sutra, but as time passes, he tends to become less devout; he no longer reveres nor serves the priest and arrogantly forms distorted views. This is most frightening. Be diligent in developing your faith until the last moment of your life. Otherwise you will have regrets. For example, the journey from Kamakura to Kyoto takes twelve days. If you travel for eleven but stop on the twelfth, how can you admire the moon over the capital? No matter what, be close to the priest who knows the heart of the Lotus Sutra, keep learning from him the truth of Buddhism and continue your journey of faith.

How swiftly the days pass! It makes us realize how few are the years we have left. Friends enjoy the cherry blossoms together on spring mornings and then they are gone, carried away like the blossoms by the winds of impermanence, leaving nothing but their names. Although the blossoms have scattered, the cherry trees will bloom again with the coming of spring, but when will those people be reborn? The companions with whom we composed poems praising the moon on autumn evenings have vanished with the moon behind the shifting clouds. Only their mute images remain in our hearts. Though the moon has set behind the western mountains, we will compose poetry under it again next autumn. But where are our companions who have passed away? Even when the approaching Tiger of Death[4] roars, we do not hear. How many more days are left to the sheep bound for slaughter?

Deep in the Snow Mountains lives a bird called Kankuchō which, tortured by the numbing cold, cries that it will build a nest in the morning. Yet, when the day breaks, it sleeps away the hours in the warm light of the morning sun without building its nest. So it continues to cry vainly throughout its life. The same is true of people. When they fall into hell and suffocate in its flames, they long to be reborn as humans and vow to put everything else aside and serve the Three Treasures in order to attain enlightenment in their next life. But even on the rare occasions when they happen to be reborn in human form, the winds of fame and fortune blow violently and the lamp of Buddhist practice is easily extinguished. Without a qualm they squander their wealth on meaningless trifles but begrudge even the smallest contribution to the Buddha, the Law and the Priesthood. This is very serious, for then they are being hindered by messengers from hell. This is the meaning of "Good by the inch invites evil by the yard."

Furthermore, since this is a land whose people slander the Lotus Sutra, the gods who should be protecting them thirst for the Law and ascend to heaven, forsaking their shrines. The empty shrines are then occupied by demons who mislead the worshipers. The Buddha, his teachings completed, returned to eternal paradise. Temples and shrines were abandoned to become the dwellings of devils. These imposing structures stand in rows, built at state expense, and still the people suffer. These are not merely my own words; they are found in the sutras, so you should learn them well.

Neither Buddhas nor gods would ever accept contributions from those who slander the Law. Then how can we human beings accept them? The deity of Kasuga Shrine[5] proclaimed through an oracle that he would accept nothing from those with impure hearts, though he should have to eat the flames of burning copper; that he would refuse to set foot in their homes, though he should have to sit on redhot copper. He would rather come down to a miserable hut with weeds choking the passageway, or to a poor thatched cottage. He declared that he would never visit the unfaithful even if they hung sacred festoons for a thousand days to welcome him, but that he would go to a house where the people believe, no matter how others might shun their wretchedness. Lamenting that slanderers overrun this country, the gods abandoned it and ascended to heaven. "Those with impure hearts" means those who refuse to embrace the Lotus Sutra, as is stated in the fifth volume of the Lotus Sutra. If the gods themselves regard alms from slanderers as "flames of burning copper," how could we common mortals possibly consume them? If someone were to kill our parents and then try to offer us some gift, could we possibly accept it? Not even sages or saints can avoid the hell of incessant suffering if they accept offerings from slanderers. Nor should you associate with slanderers, for if you do, you will share the same guilt as they. This you should fear above all.

Shakyamuni is the father, sovereign, and teacher of all other Buddhas and all gods, of the whole assembly of human and heavenly beings, and of all sentient beings. What god would rejoice if Shakyamuni were killed? Today all the people of our country have proved to be enemies of Shakyamuni, but more than lay men or women, it is the priests with twisted understanding who are the Buddha's worst enemies. There are two kinds of understanding, true and perverted. No matter how learned a person may appear, if his ideas are warped you should not listen to him. Nor should you follow priests merely because they are venerable or of high rank. But if a person has the wisdom to know the spirit of the Lotus Sutra, no matter how lowly he may appear, pay respect to him and serve him as though he were a living Buddha. This is stated in the sutra. That is why the Great Teacher Dengyō said that the lay men and women who believe in this sutra, even if they lack knowledge or violate the precepts, should be seated above Hinayana priests who strictly observe all 250 commandments.[6] The priests of this Mahayana sutra should therefore be seated even higher. Ryōkan of Gokuraku-ji temple is believed to be a living Buddha, but men and women who believe in the Lotus Sutra should be seated high above him. It seems extraordinary that this Ryōkan, who observes the 250 commandments, should become angry and glower whenever he sees or hears about Nichiren. The sage, it seems, has been possessed by a devil. He is like a basically even-tempered person who, when drunk, reveals an evil side and causes trouble. The Buddha taught that giving alms to Mahākāśyapa, Śāriputra, Maudgalyāyana, and Subhūti, who did not yet know of the Lotus Sutra, would lead one to fall into the three evil paths. He said that these four great disciples were more base than wild dogs or jackals. They adamantly upheld the 250 Buddhist commandments, and their observance of the three thousand standards[7] was as perfect as the harvest moon. But until they embraced the Lotus Sutra they were still like wild dogs to the Buddha. In comparison, our priests are so base that they are beyond description.

So flagrantly do the priests of the Kenchō-ji and Engaku-ji[8] break the code of conduct that it resembles a mountain which has collapsed into rubble. Their licentious behavior is like that of monkeys. It is utterly futile to look for salvation in the next life by giving alms to such priests. There is no doubt that the protective gods have abandoned our land. Long ago the gods, bodhisattvas and *shōmon* pledged together in the presence of Shakyamuni that if there should be a land hostile to the Lotus Sutra, they would become frost and hail in summer to drive the country into famine, or turn into insects and devour the crops; or cause droughts, or floods to ruin the fields and farms; or become typhoons and sweep the people to their deaths; or transform themselves into demons and plague the people. Bodhisattva Hachiman was among those present. Does he not fear breaking the oath made at Eagle Peak? Should he break his promise, he would surely be doomed to the hell of incessant suffering—a fearful, terrible thing to contemplate. Until the envoy of the Buddha actually appeared to expound the Lotus Sutra, the rulers of the land were not hostile to it, for they revered all the sutras equally. However, now that I am spreading the Lotus Sutra as the Buddha's envoy, everyone—from ruler to the lowliest subject—has become a slanderer. So far Hachiman has done everything possible to prevent hostility toward the Lotus Sutra from developing among our people, as reluctant to abandon them as parents would be to abandon an only child, but now in fear of breaking the pledge he made at Eagle Peak, he has razed his shrine and ascended to heaven. Even so, should there be a votary of the Lotus Sutra who would give his life for it, Hachiman will watch over him. But since both Tenshō Daijin and Hachiman have gone, how could the other gods remain in their shrines? Even if they did not wish to leave, how could they stay another day if I reproach them for not keeping their promise? A person may be a thief and as long as no one knows, he can live wherever he wishes. But when denounced as a thief by someone who knows him, he is forced to flee at once. In the same way, because I know of their vow, the gods are compelled to abandon their shrines. Contrary to popular belief, the land has become inhabited by demons. How pitiful!

Many have expounded the various teachings of Shakyamuni, but until now, no one, not even T'ien-t'ai or Dengyō, has taught the most important of all. That is as it should be, for that teaching appears and spreads with the advent of Bodhisattva Jōgyō during the first five hundred years of the Latter Day of the Law.

No matter what, always keep your faith in the Lotus Sutra steadfast. Then, at the last moment of your life, you will be welcomed by a thousand Buddhas, who will take you swiftly to the pure land of Eagle Peak where you will experience the true happiness of the Law. If your faith weakens and you do not attain Buddhahood in this lifetime, do not reproach me. If you do, you would be like the patient who refuses the medicine his physician prescribes and takes the wrong medicine instead. It never occurs to him that it is his fault, and he blames the physician when he does not recover. Faith in this sutra means that you will surely attain Buddhahood if you are true to the entirety of the Lotus Sutra, adhering exactly to its teachings without adding any of your own ideas or following the arbitrary interpretations of others.

Attaining Buddhahood is nothing extraordinary. If you chant Nam-myoho-renge-kyo with your whole heart, you will naturally become endowed with the Buddha's thirty-two marks and eighty characteristics. Shakyamuni stated, "At the start I pledged to make all people perfectly equal to me, without any distinction between us."[9] Therefore, it is not difficult to become a Buddha. A bird's egg contains nothing but liquid, yet by itself this develops into a beak, two eyes, and all the other parts which form a bird, and can fly into the sky. We, too, are like the egg, ignorant and base, but when nurtured by the chanting of Nam-myoho-renge-kyo, which is like the warmth of the mother bird, we develop the beak of the Buddha's thirty-two marks and the feathers of his eighty characteristics and are free to soar into the skies of the ultimate reality. A sutra states that all people are enclosed by the shell of ignorance, lacking the beak of wisdom. The Buddha comes back to this world, just as a mother bird returns to her nest, and cracks the shell so that all people, like fledglings, may leave the nest and soar into the skies of enlightenment.[10]

"Knowledge without faith" describes those who may be knowledgeable about the Lotus Sutra but do not believe in it. These people will never attain Buddhahood. Those of "faith without knowledge" may lack knowledge but believe, and can attain Buddhahood. These are not merely my own words but are explicitly stated in the sutra. In the second volume of the Lotus Sutra, the Buddha said to Śāriputra, "It is by faith and not by your own intelligence that you can attain enlightenment."[11] This explains why even Śāriputra, unsurpassed in his intelligence, was able to attain Buddhahood only by embracing and firmly believing in the sutra. Knowledge alone could not bring him to enlightenment. If Śāriputra could not reach enlightenment through his vast knowledge, how can we, of little knowledge, dare to dream that we may attain Buddhahood if we do not have faith? The sutra explains that people in the Latter Day of the Law will be arrogant, though their knowledge of Buddhism is trifling, and will show disrespect to the Priesthood, neglect the Law and thereby fall into the evil paths. If one truly understands Buddhism, he should show this in his respect for the Priesthood, reverence for the Law and offerings to the Buddha. Shakyamuni Buddha is not among us now, so you must respect the person with enlightened wisdom as you would the Buddha himself. If you sincerely follow him, your blessings will be bountiful. If one wishes for happiness in his next existence, he should renounce his desire for fame and fortune and respect the priest who teaches the Lotus Sutra as a living Buddha, no matter how humble that priest's station. Thus it is written in the sutra.

The Zen sect today violates the five great principles of humanity[12]—benevolence, righteousness, propriety, wisdom, and faith. To honor the wise and virtuous, to respect the elderly and protect the young, are recognized universally as humane conduct in both Buddhist and secular realms. But the Zen priests were until yesterday or the day before no more than uneducated rabble, unable to distinguish black from white. But now that they have donned fancy priestly robes they have become so conceited that they belittle the learned and virtuous priests of the Tendai and Shingon sects. They observe none of the proper manners and think that they rank higher than all others, behaving worse than animals. The Great Teacher Dengyō wrote that the otter shows his respect by offering up the fish he has caught, the crow in the forest carries food to its parents and grandparents, the dove takes care to perch three branches lower than its father, wild geese keep perfect formation when they fly together, and lambs kneel to drink their mother's milk. He asks, if lowly animals conduct themselves with such propriety, how can human beings be so lacking in courtesy?[13] Judging from the words of Dengyō, it is only natural that the Zen priests should be confused about Buddhism when they are ignorant even of how men should behave. They are acting like devils.

Understand clearly what I have taught you here and practice without negligence all the teachings of the Lotus Sutra's eight volumes and twenty-eight chapters. When you long to see me, pray toward the sun and my image will at the same time be reflected there. Have the priest who is my messenger read this letter to you. Trust him as a priest with enlightened wisdom and ask him any questions you may have about Buddhism. If you do not question and resolve your doubts, you cannot dispel the dark clouds of illusion, any more than you could travel a thousand miles without legs. Have him read this letter again and again and ask whatever questions you wish. In expectation of seeing you again, I will conclude here.

Respectfully,
Nichiren

The second month in the third year of Kōan (1280)

Notes

1. The lungs, heart, spleen, liver, and kidneys.
2. *Hokke Shūku* (DDZ3, 252).
3. The fourteen slanders (Jap: *jūshi hibō*) are enumerated in Miao-lo's *Hokke Mongu Ki* (T34, 274a) on the basis of the *Hiyu* (3d) chapter of the Lotus Sutra. They consist of fourteen attitudes that believers should avoid in their practice: (1) arrogance, (2) negligence, (3) arbitrary, egotistical judgment, (4) shallow, self-satisfied understanding, (5) attachment to earthly desires, (6) lack of seeking spirit, (7) not believing, (8) aversion, (9) deluded doubt, (10) vilification, (11) contempt, (12) hatred, (13) jealousy, and (14) grudges.
4. The Tiger of Death is derived from a passage in the *Daichido Ron* (T25, 200a) that remarks that no matter how sweet the water or lush the grass, sheep will go hungry for fear of the ferocious tiger.
5. An important shrine in Nara, associated with the Fujiwara family.
6. Based on a passage in Dengyō's *Tendai Hokke Shūgaku Shōshiki Mondō* (DDZ1, 355).
7. The 250 commandments mentioned above are the precepts of discipline

Hinayana monks must observe. There were 250 commandments for each of the four cardinal acts of walking, standing, sitting, and lying, totaling 1,000 commandments. Then there are 1,000 commandments for each of three groups of people, divided according to the strength of their faith. Altogether they total 3,000. They are described in *Dai Biku Sanzen Igi* (T24, no. 1470).

8. Two of the five major Zen temples in Kamakura, founded by Regent Hōjō Tokiyori in 1253 and by Regent Hōjō Tokimune in 1278 respectively.

9. Lotus Sutra (T9, 8c).

10. The source of this quotation is not known.

11. T9, 15b.

12. The code of ethical principles deriving from Confucianism.

13. The source of this passage has not been identified.

68 *REPLY TO NICHIGON-AMA*

This brief letter was sent by Nichiren to Nichigon-ama on the twenty-ninth day of the eleventh month, 1280, to thank her for her gift and to comment on the written prayer she had sent to him. Details concerning Nichigon-ama are lacking. One theory has it that she was a relative of Takahashi Nyūdō, a prominent figure among the believers in the Fuji district of Suruga Province. Another theory describes her as the mother of Nichigen, the priest of the Jissō-ji, a Tendai temple in Suruga, who converted to Nichiren's teachings.

On the eighth day of the eleventh month in the third year of Kōan (1280), I placed before the Lotus Sutra the written petition in which you, Nichigon-ama, expressed your prayer, together with your offerings of one *kan* of coins and an unlined robe made of thread spun from bark fiber, and reported the matter to the gods of the sun and the moon. In addition, you should not presume to fathom [the blessings of the Gohonzon]. Whether or not your prayer is answered depends upon your faith; [if it is not,] the fault in no way lies with me, Nichiren.

When the water is clear, the moon will be reflected in it. When the wind blows, the trees sway. One's mind is like the water. Faith that is weak is like muddy water, but faith that is resolute is like clear water. The trees are like the principles [of all things], and the wind that sets them in motion is like the recitation of the sutra. You should understand things in this way.

With my deep respect,
Nichiren

The twenty-ninth day of the eleventh month

69 *THE PERSON AND THE LAW*

Nichiren sent this letter from Mount Minobu to Nanjō Tokimitsu on the eleventh day of the ninth month, 1281. Nanjō, known also as Lord Ueno, had succeeded his father while still in his early twenties. He was a loyal follower of Nichiren and the government officials taxed his estate heavily so that he had difficulty in maintaining his family. From just what illness he was suffering is not indicated; at any rate, he recovered and lived for some fifty years after the letter was written.

"The Person and the Law" (*Hōmyō Ninki no Koto*) is an alternative title for this letter; it is drawn from a passage in the letter that states that the Law is supreme and the person is worthy of respect. The better known title is *Nanjō-dono Gohenji* (Reply to Lord Nanjō, 1281).

I have just heard from your messenger that you are suffering from a serious illness. I hope you will recover soon and come to see me.

Also, I have received your gifts of two sacks of salt, a sack of soybeans, a bag of seaweed, and a bamboo container of sake. I have not seen you since you returned home from the province of Kōzuke, and I have been wondering how you are. I can hardly find words to say how much I appreciate your sincerity in sending me a letter and your many gifts.

As you well know, one of the sutras tells us the story of Tokushō Dōji, who offered a mud pie to the Buddha and was later reborn as King Aśoka, who ruled over most of India.[1] Since the Buddha is worthy of respect, the boy was able to receive this great reward even though the pie was only mud. However, Shakyamuni Buddha teaches that one who makes offerings to the votary of the Lotus Sutra in the Latter Day of the Law for even a single day will gain incomparably greater fortune than he would by offering countless treasures to the Buddha for one hundred thousand kalpas. How wonderful then is your heartfelt sincerity in supporting the votary of the Lotus Sutra over the years! According to the Buddha's own words, you are certain to be reborn in the pure land of Eagle Peak. What great good fortune you possess!

This is a mountainous place, remote from all human habitation. There is not a single village in any direction. Although I live in such a forsaken hovel, deep in this mortal flesh I preserve the ultimate secret Law inherited from Shakyamuni Buddha at Eagle Peak. My heart is where all Buddhas enter nirvana; my tongue, where they turn the wheel of doctrine; my throat, where they are born into this world; and my mouth, where they attain enlightenment. Because this mountain is where the wondrous votary of the Lotus Sutra dwells, how can it be any less sacred than the pure land of Eagle Peak? Since the Law is supreme, the Person is worthy of respect; since the Person is worthy of respect, the Land is sacred. The *Jinriki* chapter reads, "Whether in a grove, under a tree, or in a monastery . . . the Buddhas enter nirvana."[2] Those who visit this place can instantly expiate the sins they have committed since the infinite past and transform their illusions into wisdom, their errors into truth, and their sufferings into freedom.

A suffering traveler in central India once came to Munetchi Lake[3] to quench the fires of anguish in his heart. He proclaimed that its waters satisfied all his desires, just as a cool, clear pond quenches thirst. Although Munetchi Lake and this place are different, the principle is exactly the same. Thus, the Eagle Peak of India is now here at Mount Minobu. It has been a long time since you were last here. You should come to see me as soon as you possibly can. I am eagerly looking forward to seeing you.

How can I describe your sincerity? In truth, it is splendid!

Nichiren

Notes

1. Nichiren frequently alludes to the story of Tokushō Dōji. See Letter 62, note 2.
2. T9, 22a.
3. An imaginary lake described in the *Kusha Ron* (T29, 58a), the source of the four great rivers of Jambudvīpa. Its shores are formed of gold, silver, lapis lazuli, and crystal, and its cool waters moisten the whole continent.

This letter was sent to Nanjō Tokimitsu (Nanjō Shichirō Jirō) on the twenty-eighth day of the second month, 1282, one of several letters Nichiren sent to his beloved disciples in what was to be the last year of his life. Tokimitsu was the recipient of many letters from Nichiren and this young disciple made many sacrifices to defend Nichiren's followers in his domains in the Ueno area, which covered a vast slope of Mount Fuji.

This letter has also the alternative title *Shikatsu Sho* (On Life and Death).

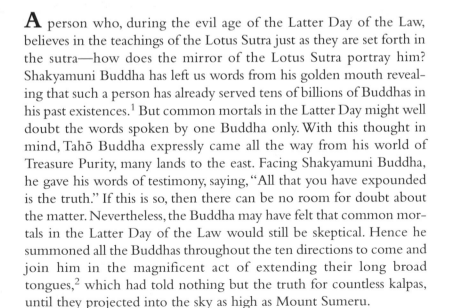

A person who, during the evil age of the Latter Day of the Law, believes in the teachings of the Lotus Sutra just as they are set forth in the sutra—how does the mirror of the Lotus Sutra portray him? Shakyamuni Buddha has left us words from his golden mouth revealing that such a person has already served tens of billions of Buddhas in his past existences.[1] But common mortals in the Latter Day might well doubt the words spoken by one Buddha only. With this thought in mind, Tahō Buddha expressly came all the way from his world of Treasure Purity, many lands to the east. Facing Shakyamuni Buddha, he gave his words of testimony, saying, "All that you have expounded is the truth." If this is so, then there can be no room for doubt about the matter. Nevertheless, the Buddha may have felt that common mortals in the Latter Day of the Law would still be skeptical. Hence he summoned all the Buddhas throughout the ten directions to come and join him in the magnificent act of extending their long broad tongues,[2] which had told nothing but the truth for countless kalpas, until they projected into the sky as high as Mount Sumeru.

Since this is the case, when a common mortal in the Latter Day believes in even one or two words of the Lotus Sutra, he is embracing the teaching to which all the Buddhas in the ten directions have given credence. I wonder what good karma I created in the past to have been born as such a person, and I am filled with joy. Shakyamuni's words which I have mentioned above indicate that the blessings that come from having served tens of billions of Buddhas are so great that, even though one may have believed in teachings other than the Lotus Sutra and as a result of this slander been born poor and lowly, he is still able to believe in this sutra during this lifetime. Miao-lo states, "One who falls to the ground rises by pushing himself up from the ground,"[3] Those who slander the Lotus Sutra will fall to the ground of the three evil paths, Humanity or Heaven, yet through the help of the Lotus Sutra they will in the end attain Buddhahood.

Now since you, Ueno Shichirō Jirō, are a common mortal in the Latter Day of the Law and were born into a warrior family, you should by rights be called an evil man, and yet your heart is that of a good man. I say this for a reason. Everyone, from the ruler on down to the common people, refuses to take faith in my teachings. They inflict harm on the few who do embrace them, heavily taxing or confiscating their estates and fields or even in some cases putting them to death. So it is a difficult thing to believe in my teachings, and yet both your mother and your deceased father dared to accept them. Now you have succeeded your father as his heir and, without any persuasion from others, you too have wholeheartedly embraced these teachings. Many people, both high and low in rank, have reprimanded or threatened you, but you have refused to give up your faith. Now that you appear certain to attain Buddhahood, the Devil of the Sixth Heaven and other demons are trying to use this illness to intimidate you. But remember that life in this world is limited. Never allow yourself to be intimidated!

And as for you demons—will you cause this disciple of mine to suffer and swallow a sword point first, or embrace a raging fire, or become the archenemy of all the Buddhas throughout the universe and in the three existences of life? How terrible this will be for you! Now, will you cure this man's illness immediately and hereafter give him your protection instead, in this way escaping from the grievous sufferings that are the lot of demons? Or do you prefer to have your heads broken into seven pieces[4] and after your death to fall into the hell of incessant suffering?

Bear what I say in mind and do not forget; if you ignore my words, you will regret it later.

The twenty-eighth day of the second month in the fifth year of Kōan (1282)

Notes

1. This is mentioned in the *Hosshi* (10th) chapter of the Lotus Sutra.

2. The long, broad tongue is one of the thirty-two marks of a Buddha.

3. *Hokke Mongu Ki* (T34, 349c). The sentence following this quotation is a restatement of the quotation and has been omitted in the translation.

4. Reference is to a verse in the *Darani* (26th) chapter of the Lotus Sutra, which reads: "Whoever resists our spell/And troubles a teacher of the Dharma,/May his head split in seven pieces/Like the branches of an *arjaka* tree." It is also said that if one touches an *arjaka* flower, its petals open and fall into seven pieces.

71 *THE KALPA OF DECREASE*

Neither the date nor the addressee of this letter is known, although it is thought to have been written sometime after 1276 at Mount Minobu. Judging from the concluding paragraph, Nichiren may have sent it via his disciple Daishin Ajari to someone in the clan of the late Takahashi Rokurō Hyōe Nyūdō, a believer who lived in Kajima in the Fuji disctrict of Suruga Province.

An alternative title for this letter is *Chie Bōkoku Sho* (Wisdom and the Destruction of the Nation).

The kalpa of decrease[1] has its origin in the human mind. As the poisons of greed, anger, and stupidity gradually intensify, the life span of human beings accordingly decreases and their stature diminishes.

In the lands of China and Japan, before the introduction of Buddhism, the outer classics[2] of the Three Rulers,[3] the Five Emperors,[4] and the Three Sages[5] were used to order the minds of the people and govern the world. However, as the people's minds gradually diminished in good and grew accomplished in evil, the wisdom of the outer classics, being shallow, could no longer restrain the people's offenses, for their evil was deep. Because it became impossible to govern the world by means of the outer classics, the Buddhist sutras were gradually introduced, and when they were used in governing, the world was restored to tranquillity. This was solely because the wisdom of Buddhism fully elucidates the nature of the people's minds.

What are called "outer writings" in the present day differ essentially from the original outer classics. When Buddhism was introduced, the outer classics and the Buddhist scriptures vied with one another. But because in time the outer classics were defeated and the ruler and the people ceased to employ them, adherents of the outer classics became followers of the inner scriptures, and their former confrontation came to an end. In the meantime, however, the adherents of the outer classics extracted the heart of the inner scriptures, thus increasing their wisdom, and incorporated it into the outer classics. Foolish rulers suppose [that such wisdom derives from] the excellence of these outer writings.

Furthermore, as good wisdom gradually diminished and evil wisdom came to dominate people's minds, though men tried to govern society by means of the Buddhist scriptures, when they employed the wisdom of the Hinayana sutras, the world was not at peace. At such times, the Mahayana sutras were spread and used in governing, and the world was somewhat restored to order. After this, because the wisdom of the Mahayana teachings in turn became inadequate, the wisdom of the sutra of the one vehicle[6] was brought forth and used to govern the world, and for a brief period, the world was at peace.

The present age is such that neither the outer classics, the Hinayana sutras, the Mahayana sutras, nor the one vehicle of the Lotus Sutra has any effect. The reason for this is that the intensity of the greed, anger, and stupidity in people's minds rivals the Greatly Enlightened World-Honored One's superiority in great good. To illustrate, a dog, in the keenness of its sense of smell, is superior to a man; in picking up the scent of birds and beasts, its nose is not inferior to a great saint's supernatural power of smell. The owl's keenness of hearing, the kite's sharpness of eye, the sparrow's lightness of tongue, and the dragon's magnificence of body—all of these surpass even the faculties of a wise man. In this way, the extremity of greed, anger, and stupidity in people's minds in the impure world of the latter age is beyond the power of any sage or worthy man to control.

This is because, although the Buddha cured greed with the medicine of the meditation on the vileness of the body, healed anger with the meditation on compassion for all, and treated stupidity with the meditation on the twelve-linked chain of dependent origination,[7] to teach these doctrines now merely makes people worse and compounds their greed, anger, and stupidity. For example, fire is extinguished by water, and evil is defeated by good. However, if water is cast on fire that has emerged from water, it will on the contrary have an effect like that of oil, producing an even greater conflagration.

Now in this latter, evil age, great evil arises less from secular wrongdoing than with respect to the doctrines of the religious world. Because people today are unaware of this and endeavor to cultivate roots of merit, the world declines all the more. To give support to the priests of the Tendai, Shingon, and other sects of today may outwardly appear to be an act of merit, but in reality it is a great evil surpassing even the five cardinal sins and the ten evil acts.[8]

For this reason, if there should be a wise man in the world with wisdom like that of the Greatly Enlightened World-Honored One, who, so as to restore the world to order, meets with a wise ruler like King Sen'yo;[9] and if together they put an end altogether to these acts of "goodness" and commit the great "evil" of censuring, banishing, cutting off alms to or even beheading those people of the eight sects[10] who are thought to be men of wisdom, then the world will surely be pacified to some extent.

This is explained in the first volume of the Lotus Sutra where it says: "The true aspect of all phenomena can only be understood and shared between Buddhas."[11] In the phrase "consistency from beginning to end," "beginning" indicates the root of evil and the root of good, while "end" indicates the outcome of evil and the outcome of good. One who is thoroughly awakened to the nature of good and evil from their roots to their branches and leaves is called a Buddha. T'ien-t'ai states, "Life at each moment is endowed with the Ten Worlds."[12] Chang-an states: "The Buddha regarded this doctrine as the ultimate reason [for his advent]. How could it ever be easy to understand?"[13] Miao-lo adds that "this is the ultimate revelation of the final and supreme truth."[14] The Lotus Sutra states: "[And whatever he preaches according to his understanding] will never contradict the truth."[15] And T'ien-t'ai interprets this to mean that "no affairs of life or work are in any way different from the ultimate reality."[16] A person of wisdom is not one who practices Buddhism apart from worldly affairs but, rather, one who thoroughly understands the principles by which the world may be governed.

When the Yin dynasty became corrupt and the people were suffering, T'ai-kung Wang[17] appeared in the world and beheaded King Chou of the Yin, bringing an end to the people's anguish. When the second ruler [of the Ch'in dynasty][18] caused the people to taste bitterness, Chang Liang appeared and restored order to the world, enabling them to know sweetness. Though these men lived before the introduction of Buddhism, they helped the people as emissaries of Lord Shakyamuni. And though the adherents of the outer classics were unaware of it, the wisdom of such men incorporated in its essence the wisdom of Buddhism.

In the world today, at the time of the great earthquake of the Shōka era[19] or at the time of the great comet of the Bun'ei era,[20] had there been a ruler of outstanding wisdom, he would surely have heeded me, Nichiren. Or, even if he did not do so then, when strife broke out within the ruling clan in the ninth year of Bun'ei (1272)[21] or when the Mongols attacked in the eleventh year of the same era (1274), he ought to have welcomed me as King Wen of the Chou dynasty welcomed T'ai-kung Wang, or sought me out as King Kao-ting[22] of the Yin dynasty sought out Fu Yüeh from seven *ri* afar. Thus it is said that the sun and moon are not treasures to one who is blind, and that a worthy man will be hated by a foolish ruler. Rather than go on at length, I will stop here. The heart of the Lotus Sutra is just as I have explained. You should not think of it as otherwise. Great evil portends the arrival of great good. If all of Jambudvīpa should be thrown into chaos, there can be no doubt that [this sutra] will "spread widely throughout the continent of Jambudvīpa."[23]

I am sending Daishin Ajari[24] to pay a visit to the grave of the late Rokurō Nyūdō.[25] In the past, I had thought that if there were people in the Kanto region[26] who had heard this teaching, I would go to their graves myself and recite the Jigage.[27] However, if I were to go there under the present circumstances, the entire province would hear of it within the day, and it would probably cause an uproar as far away as Kamakura. And, even though they may have steadfast faith, wherever I go, the people there will have to fear the eyes of others.

Because I have not yet been to visit, I had thought how greatly the late Rokurō Nyūdō must be longing to see me, and that there must be something that I could do. Therefore, I have first of all sent a disciple to recite the Jigage before the grave. I ask for your understanding on this point.

With my deep respect.

Notes

1. A kalpa of decrease is a period when the human life span diminishes. In the Kalpa of Continuance (*see* kalpa in Glossary) the life span of human beings is said to repeat a cycle of change, decreasing by a factor of one year every hundred years until it reaches ten years, and then increasing at the same rate until it reaches eighty thousand years. Then it begins to decrease again until it reaches ten years, and so on. It is

said that Shakyamuni appeared in the present Kalpa of Continuance, in the ninth kalpa of decrease, when the life span of human beings is one hundred years long.

2. The outer classics is a general term for non-Buddhist scriptures, particularly those of Confucianism and Taoism. The term is used in contrast to "inner scriptures," which denotes Buddhist writings.

3. Fu Hsi, Shen Nung, and Huang Ti, legendary rulers of ancient China said to have realized model governments. These books do not exist.

4. Shao Hao, Chuan Hsü, Ti Kao, T'ang Yao, and Yü Shun, said to have reigned after the Three Rulers. Their books do not exist.

5. Three wise men of ancient China. T'ien-t'ai in the *Maka Shikan* (T46, 78c) gives them as Lao Tzu, Confucius, and Yen Hui, Confucius' foremost disciple.

6. The Lotus Sutra.

7. These are three of the five meditations for quieting the mind and ridding it of error (Jap: *gojōshinkan*). The others are breath-counting meditation and meditation on the analysis of the six elements of which all things are composed.

8. Killing, stealing, committing adultery, lying, deceiving, defaming, engaging in duplicity, greed, anger, and stupidity.

9. King Sen'yo is a previous incarnation of Shakyamuni Buddha. According to the Nirvana Sutra (T12, 434c), King Sen'yo was the ruler in Jambudvīpa, who believed in Mahayana sutras. When Brahmans slandered these sutras he had them put to death. The sutra says that because of this he was never thereafter in danger of falling into hell.

10. Kusha, Jōjitsu, Ritsu, Hossō, Sanron, Kegon, Tendai, and Shingon.

11. Lotus Sutra (T9, 5c). The phrase "consistency from beginning to end," mentioned subsequently, concludes the passage describing "the true aspect of all phenomena."

12. *Maka Shikan* (T46, 54a).

13. *Kanjin Ron Sho* (T46, 609c).

14. *Maka Shikan Bugyōden Guketsu* (T46, 296a).

15. T9, 50a.

16. *Hokke Gengi* (T33, 683a).

17. T'ai-kung Wang was teacher and adviser to Hsi Po, the Earl of the West (later known as King Wen of the Chou dynasty). His strategies are said to have enabled Hsi Po's son, King Wu, to overthrow the Yin dynasty and establish the Chou dynasty.

18. Hu Hai (229–207 B.C.) was the second emperor of the Ch'in dynasty. A puppet ruler, he was controlled by the eunuch official Chao Kao, who eventually forced him to commit suicide to further his own ambitions. Chang Liang (d. 168 B.C.), mentioned subsequently, was a statesman and strategist who assisted Liu Pang in the overthrow of the Ch'in and the establishment of the Han dynasty.

19. Reference is to a major earthquake that leveled much of Kamakura in the eighth month, 1257.

20. This refers to a large comet that appeared in the sky from the sixth through the eighth month of 1264 and was widely interpreted as an evil omen.

21. This refers presumably to the unsuccessful coup attempt staged by Hōjō Tokisuke (1247–1272) against his half brother, the regent Hōjō Tokimune (1251–1284) in this year.

22. Kao-ting was the twenty-second ruler of the Yin dynasty. According to the *Shih Chi* (Records of the Historian), Kao-ting sought to revive the declining Yin dynasty but could find no able advisers. At length he learned of Fu Yüeh, who had been liv-

ing in retirement, and appointed him his minister. With Fu Yüeh's counsel, he was able to revive the dynasty.

23. Nichiren alludes here to a passage from the *Fugen* (28th) chapter of the Lotus Sutra that states, "After the Buddha's death, I [Bodhisattva Fugen] will spread this sutra widely throughout the entire continent of Jambudvīpa." (T9, 61c).

24. Daishin Ajari (n.d.) was a priest disciple of Nichiren's who was born in Shimōsa Province and is thought to have been a relative of the Soya family.

25. Rokurō Nyūdō is thought to be Takahashi Rokurō Hyōe Nyūdō, a disciple of Nichiren's, who was a leading figure among the lay believers in the Fuji area. He was converted to Nichiren's Buddhism by Nikkō Shonin, who was his wife's nephew.

26. The eastern part of Japan.

27. Jigage is the verse section that concludes the *Juryō* (16th) chapter of the Lotus Sutra. It states the teaching of the eternity of the Buddha's life found in the preceding prose section of the same chapter. The verse (Jap: *ge*) section begins with the words *ji ga toku burrai* ("Since I attained Buddhahood").

72 NEW YEAR'S GOSHO

This letter was written to the wife of Lord Omosu on the fifth day of the first month. The year, however, is not given. Lord Omosu derives his name from the name of the area in which his estate was located, Omosu village in the Fuji district of Suruga Province. His full name was Ishikawa Shimbei Yoshisuke (n.d.); his wife was the elder sister of Nanjō Tokimitsu.

I have received a hundred *mushimochi*[1] cakes and a basket of fruit. New Year's Day marks the first day, the first month, the beginning of the year, and the start of spring.[2] A person who celebrates this day will gain virtue and be loved by all, just as the moon becomes full gradually, moving from west to east,[3] and the sun shines more brightly traveling from east to west.

First of all, as to the question of where exactly hell and the Buddha exist, one sutra states that hell exists underground and another sutra says that the Buddha is in the west. However, closer examination reveals that both exist in our five-foot body. The reason I think so is that hell is in the heart of a man who inwardly despises his father and disregards his mother. It is like the lotus seed, which contains both flower and fruit at the same time. In the same way, the Buddha dwells inside our hearts. For example, flint has the potential to produce fire and gems possess intrinsic value. We common mortals can see neither our own eyebrows, which are so close, nor heaven in the distance. Likewise, we do not see that the Buddha exists in our own hearts. You may question how is it that the Buddha can reside within us when our bodies, originating from our parents' sperm and blood, are the source of the three poisons and the seat of carnal desires. But repeated consideration shows the validity of my claim. The pure lotus flower blooms out of the muddy pond, the fragrant sandalwood grows from the soil, the graceful cherry blossoms come forth from trees, the beautiful Yang Kuei-fei[4] was born of a maidservant, and the moon rises from behind the mountains to shed light on them. Misfortune comes from one's mouth and ruins one, but fortune comes from one's mind and makes one worthy of respect.

The sincerity of making offerings to the Lotus Sutra at the beginning of the New Year is like flowers blooming from trees, a lotus unfolding in a pond, sandalwood blossoming on the Snow Mountains, or the moon beginning to rise. Japan, in becoming an enemy of the Lotus Sutra, has now invited misfortune from a thousand miles away, whereas those who believe in the Lotus Sutra will gather fortune from a distance of ten thousand miles. The shadow is cast by the body, and just as the shadow follows the body, misfortune will befall the country whose people are hostile to the Lotus Sutra. The believers in the Lotus Sutra, on the other hand, are like the sandalwood with its fragrance. I will write you again.

Nichiren

The fifth day of the first month
In reply to the wife of Lord Omosu

Notes

1. Mushimochi is the steamed rice cake, traditionally eaten during the New Year's holiday season.

2. According to the lunar calendar, spring begins with the first month of the lunar year.

3. This refers to the fact that the new moon is first seen in the west just after sunset. On successive nights as the moon grows fuller, it appears to move a little further toward the east. Of course, the moon's movement is the same as the sun and stars, east to west, but because of its orbital motion, it appears to move slightly in retrograde, from west to east, each day.

4. Yang Kuei-fei (719–756) was the favorite of Emperor Hsüan-tsung, sixth ruler of the T'ang dynasty. Though of humble birth, she was chosen by the emperor for her extraordinary beauty.

73 *THE GIFT OF RICE*

This letter lacks the name of the addressee as well as the date of composition. The last portion of the letter has, unfortunately, been lost. The title "The Gift of Rice" derives from the opening passage of the letter, in which Nichiren gives thanks for the offerings made. Life at Mount Minobu was harsh and Nichiren was always in need of food and other provisions. Fortunately he had a loyal group of disciples who helped provide him with necessities.

This letter has an alternative title, *Jiri Kuyō Gosho* (Offerings in Principle and Actuality).

❧

I have received the sack of rice, the sack of taro, and the basket of river-plants which you were so good as to send me by your servants.

Man has two kinds of treasure: clothing and food. One sutra states, "All sentient beings live on food."[1] Man depends on food and clothing to survive in this world. For fish, water is the greatest treasure and for trees, the soil in which they grow. Man's life is sustained by what he eats. That is why food is his treasure.[2]

However, life itself is the most precious of all treasures. Nothing throughout the entire major world system matches the value of a living being.[3] Life is like a lamp, and food like oil. When the oil is gone, the flame will die out, and without food, life will cease.

People place the word "Namu" before the names of all deities and Buddhas in worshiping them. But what is the meaning of "Namu"? This word derives from Sanskrit, and means to devote one's life.[4] Ultimately it means to offer our lives to the Buddha. Some may have wives, children, retainers, estates, gold, silver, or other treasures according to their status. Others have nothing at all. Yet, whether one has wealth or not, life is still the most precious treasure. This is why the saints and sages of ancient times offered their lives to the Buddha, and were themselves able to attain Buddhahood.

Sessen Dōji offered his body to a demon to receive a teaching composed of eight characters. Bodhisattva Yakuō burned his arms as an offering to the Lotus Sutra.[5] In our own country, Prince Shōtoku peeled off the skin of his hand on which to copy the Lotus Sutra, and Emperor Tenji burned his third finger as an offering to Shakyamuni Buddha.[6] Such austere practices are for saints and sages, but not for ordinary people.

Yet even common mortals can attain Buddhahood if they cherish one thing: earnest faith. In the deepest sense, earnest faith is the will to understand and live up to the spirit, not the words, of the sutras. What does this mean? In one sense, it means that offering one's only robe to the Lotus Sutra is equivalent to tearing off one's own skin, and in a time of famine, offering the Buddha the single bowl of rice on which one's life depends is to dedicate one's life to the Buddha. The blessings of such dedication are as great as those Bodhisattva Yakuō received by burning his own elbow, or Sessen Dōji by offering his flesh to a demon.

Therefore, saints consecrated themselves by offering their own bodies, whereas common mortals may consecrate themselves by the sincerity with which they give.[7] The *pāramitā* of almsgiving[8] expounded in the seventh volume of the *Maka Shikan* in effect teaches the spirit of offering.

The true path of life lies in the affairs of this world. The *Konkōmyō* Sutra reads, "To have a profound knowledge of this world is itself Buddhism."[9] The Nirvana Sutra reads, "All scriptures or teachings, from whatever source, are ultimately the revelation of Buddhist truth. They are not non-Buddhist teachings."[10]

In contrast, the sixth volume of the Lotus Sutra reads, "No affairs of life or work are in any way different from the ultimate reality."[11] In discussing the underlying significance of these quotations, Miao-lo taught that the first two sutras are profound, but still shallow when compared to the Lotus Sutra. Whereas they relate secular matters in terms of Buddhism, the Lotus Sutra explains that secular matters ultimately are Buddhism.

The sutras that came before the Lotus Sutra taught that all phenomena derive from one's mind. The mind is like the earth, and phenomena are like the plants growing in the earth. But the Lotus Sutra teaches that the mind is one with the earth and the earth is one with its plants. The provisional sutras say that a tranquil mind is like the moon and a pure heart is like a flower, but the Lotus Sutra states that the flower and moon are themselves heart and mind. Therefore, it is obvious that rice is not merely rice but life itself.

Notes

1. The source of this quotation has not been identified.

2. This paragraph has been somewhat condensed in translation for the sake of clarity.

3. The source of this quotation is not known; however, it may well be based on a passage of similar import in the *Bommōkyō Koshakki* (T40, 703b).

4. The literal translation here is: "This word comes from Sanskrit and is translated *kuei-ming* in Chinese and *kimyō* in Japanese." *Namah* in Sanskrit, *kuei-ming* in Chinese, and *kimyō* in Japanese all have the same meaning. "Namu" is at times rendered as "reverence to," "take refuge in," etc. In intoning, "Namu" is frequently elided to form "Nam." In this passage the translation has been simplified to avoid repetition.

5. The story of Sessen Dōji offering his body to a demon in order to hear a line from a verse is found in the Nirvana Sutra (T12, 450a). The story of the Bodhisattva Yakuō burning his arms is found in the *Yakuō* (23d) chapter of the Lotus Sutra.

6. The account of Shōtoku Taishi peeling skin from his hand is found in Kenshin's (1130–1192) *Shōtoku Taishi Den Shiki* (DBZ 82, 92). The account of Emperor Tenji burning his third finger is found in *Fusō Ryakki* (*Kokushi Taikei*, vol. 12, 60).

7. The translation here is expanded to convey the meaning of the two technical terms, *ji kuyō*, to offer one's life for the Buddha or the Law, and *ri kuyō*, to offer the aspiration for a sincere faith.

8. One of the six *pāramitās*.

9. Quoted from the *Maka Shikan* (T46, 77b) and based on a passage in the *Konkōmyō* Sutra (T16, 385a).

10. Quoted from the *Maka Shikan* (T46, 77a-b) and based on a passage in the Nirvana Sutra (T12, 412–413a).

11. This passage actually appears in T'ien-t'ai's *Hokke Gengi* (T33, 683a), as an annotation to the following passage in the *Kudoku Hosshi* (19th) chapter of the Lotus Sutra: "And whatever he preaches according to his understanding will never contradict the truth. All matters that he preaches pertaining to learning, government, language, and daily living will accord with the True Law" (T9, 50a).

APPENDIX 1

SANSKRIT PERSONAL NAMES

Sanskrit Names | **Japanese Names**

Ajātaśatru | Ajase　阿闍世
Ajita | Agita　阿耆多; Aitta　阿逸多
Ajita Keśakambala | Agita Shishakimbara　阿耆多翅舍欽婆羅
Ānanda | Anan　阿難
Anavatapta | Anabadatta　阿那婆達多
Aṅgulimāla | Ōkutsumara　鴦掘摩羅
Aniruddha | Anuruda　阿兒樓駄; Anaritsu　阿那律
Āryadeva | Daiba　提婆
Āryasiṃha | Shishi Sonja　師子尊者
Asaṅga | Mujaku　無著
Asita | Ashida　阿私陀
Aśoka | Aiku　阿育; Asoka
Aśvaka | Asetsuka　阿説迦
Aśvaghoṣa | Memyō　馬鳴; Asubakusha　阿湿縛裏沙
Bhadrapāla | Baddabara　跋陀婆羅
Bhāvaviveka | Shōben　清弁
Bodhidharma | Bodaidaruma　菩提達磨
Buddhabhadra | Buddabaddara　仏陀跋陀羅; Kakugen　覺賢
Chanda | Senna　闡那
Ciñcāmāṇavikā | Senshanyo　旃遮女
Devadatta | Daibadatta　提婆達多 or Chōdatsu　調達
Dharmagupta | Darumakikuta　達摩掬多
Dharmakṣema | Dommushin　曇無讖
Dharmapāla | Gohō　護法
Dharmarakṣa | Jikuhōgo　竺法護
Dharmodgata | Dommukatsu　曇無竭
Droṇodana | Kokubon-ō　斛飯王
Gautama | Kudon　瞿曇
Guṇaprabha | Tokukō Ronji　德光論師
Hārītī | Kishimojin　鬼子母神
Jīvaka | Giba　耆婆
Kakuda Kātyāyana | Karakuda Kasennen　迦羅鳩駄迦旃延

519

Kālodāyin	Karudai 迦留陀夷
Kāṇadeva	Kanadaiba 迦那提婆
Kapila	Kabira 迦毘羅
Kaśyapa Mātaṅga	Kashōmatō 迦葉摩騰
Kātyāyana	Kasennen 迦旃延
Kokālika	Kugyari 瞿伽利
Kumārajīva	Kumarajū 鳩摩羅什
Kumārāyaṇa	Kumaraen 鳩摩羅炎
Kuntī	Kōdai-nyo 皋諦女
Mahādeva	Daiten 大天
Mahākāśyapa	Kashō 迦葉
Mahānāma	Shakumanan 釈摩男
Mahāprajāpatī	Makahajahadai 摩訶波闍波提
Maheśvara	Makeishura 摩醯首羅; Daijizai-ten 大自在天
Marīci	Marishi-ten 摩利支天
Maskarī Gośālīputra	Makkari Kusharishi 末迦利瞿舍梨子
Maudgalyāyana	Mokuren 目連
Māyā	Maya 摩耶
Nāgārjuna	Ryūju 竜樹
Nanda	Nanda 難陀
Nārāyaṇa	Naraen-ten 那羅延天
Nirgrantha Jñātaputra	Niken 尼犍
Pārśva	Kyō-biku 脇比丘
Pilindavatsa	Hitsuryō 畢陵
Prajñā	Hannya 般若
Prasenajit	Hashinoku-ō 波斯匿王
Punarvasu	Futsunabatsu 弗那跋
Puṇyayaśas	Funasha 富那奢
Pūraṇa Kāśyapa	Furanna Kashō 富蘭那迦葉
Pūrṇa	Furuna 富樓那
Puṣyamitra	Hosshamittara-ō 弗沙彌多羅王
Rāhula	Ragora 羅睺羅; Raun 羅云
Ratnamati	Rokunamadai 勒那摩提
Rṣabha	Rokushaba 勒沙婆
Sadāprarudita	Jōtai 常啼
Sañjayi Vairatīputra	Sanjaya Birateishi 刪闍耶毘羅胝子
Sāramati	Kenne 堅慧
Śāriputra	Sharihotsu 舍利弗; Shinshi 身子
Sattva	Satta 薩埵
Śibi	Shibi 尸毘
Siddhārtha	Shitta 悉達
Śuddhipanthaka	Surihandoku 須利槃特
Śuddhodana	Jōbon-ō 淨飯王
Sunakṣatra	Zenshō 善星; Shizen 四禪
Śūryasoma	Shuriyasoma 須利耶蘇摩
Suśānta	Shusenta 須扇多
Udayana	Uden 優填

Ulūka	Kuru 拘留; Urusōgya 漚樓僧佉
Upananda	Batsunanda 跋難陀
Utpalavarṇā	Rengeshiki 蓮華色; Keshiki 華色
Vaidehī	Idaike 韋提希
Vairocana	Birushana 毘盧遮那
Vasubandhu	Seshin 世親; Tenjin 天親
Vimalakīrti	Yuimakitsu 維摩詰
Vimalamitra	Muku Ronji 無垢論師
Virūḍhaka	Haruri-ō 波瑠璃王
Viṣṇu	Bichū-ten 毘紐天
Viśvakarman	Bishukatsuma 毘首羯磨
Yaśodharā	Yashutara-nyo 耶輸多羅女

APPENDIX 2

CHINESE PERSONAL NAMES

Chinese Names	Japanese names	
An Ch'ing-hsü	An Keisho	安慶緒
An Lu-shan	An Rokuzan	安禄山
Chang-an	Shōan	章安
Chang Liang	Chō Ryō	張良
Chang Wen-chien	Chō Bunken	張文堅
Ch'en Ch'en	Chin Shin	陳臣
Ch'eng, King	Sei-ō	成王
Ch'eng-kuan	Chōkan	澄觀
Chia-hsiang	Kajō	嘉祥
Chieh, King	Ketsu-ō	桀王
Chih-che	Chisha	智者
Chih-i	Chigi	智顗
Chih Po	Chi Haku	智伯
Chih-tu	Chido	智度
Chih-yen	Chigon	智儼
Ching-hsi	Keikei	荊溪
Ch'ing-liang	Shōryō	清涼
Chin-kang-chih	Kongōchi	金剛智 (Vajrabodhi)
Chi-tsang	Kichizō	吉藏
Cho-an Te-kuang	Settan Tokkō	拙菴德光
Chou, King	Chū-ō	紂王
Chuan Hsü	Sen Gyoku	顓頊
Chu-fa-lan	Jikuhōran	竺法蘭
Ch'ung Hua	Chō Ka	重華
Ch'u Shan-hsin	Cho Zenshin	褚善信
Fa-ch'üan	Hassen	法全
Fa-hsien	Hokken	法顯
Fan K'uai	Han Kai	樊噲
Fa-tao	Hōdō	法道
Fa-yün	Hōun	法雲
Fei Shu-ts'ai	Hi Shukusai	費叔才
Fu Hsi	Fukki	伏羲

Fu Ta-shih	Fu Daishi	傅大士
Fu Yüeh	Fu Etsu	傅悦
Hsiang-tzu	Jōshi	襄子
Hsiang Yü	Kō U	項羽
Hsieh Ling-yün	Sha Reiun	謝靈運
Hsing-man	Gyōman	行滿
Hsi Po	Sei Haku	西伯
Hsüan-tsung, Emperor	Gensō-tei	玄宗帝
Huang Ti	Kō Tei	黃帝
Hua T'o	Ka Da	華陀
Hui-k'o	Eka	慧可
Hui-kuan	Ekan	慧觀
Hui-kuo	Keika	惠果
Hui-neng	Enō	慧能
Hui-ssu	Eshi	慧思
Hui-tsung, Emperor	Kisō-tei	徽宗帝
Hui-yen	Egon	慧嚴
Hui-yüan	Eon	慧苑
Hung Yen	Kō En	弘演
I-hsing	Ichigyō	一行
Kan-chiang	Kanshō	干將
Kao-ting	Kōtei	高丁
Kao-tsu, Emperor	Kōso	高祖
Kao-tsung, Emperor	Kōsō-tei	高宗帝
Kuang-wu, Emperor	Kōbu-tei	光武帝
K'uei-chi	Kiki	窺基
K'ung Tzu	Kōshi	孔子 (Confucius)
Lao Tzu	Rōshi	老子
Li Kuang	Ri Kō	李廣
Li Lou	Ri Rō	離婁
Liu Pang	Ryū Hō	劉邦
Lung-p'eng	Ryūhō	竜蓬
Lü Hui-t'ung	Ryo Keitsū	呂慧通
Ma-tzu	Mashi	麻子
Miao-lo	Myōraku	妙樂
Ming, Emperor	Mei-tei	明帝
Mo Hsi	Bakki	妹喜
Mo-yeh	Bakuya	莫耶
Nan-yüeh	Nangaku	南岳
Pao Ssu	Hō Ji	褒姒
Pien Ch'üeh	Hen Jaku	扁鵲
Pien Ho	Ben Ka	卞和
Pi Kan	Hi Kan	比干
Po-ch'i	Hakuki	伯奇
Po Chü-i (Lo-tien)	Haku Kyoi	白居易 (Rakuten 樂天)
Po I	Haku I	伯夷
Pu-k'ung	Fukū	不空 (Amoghavajra)

Seng-chao	Sōjō	僧肇
Seng-ch'üan	Sōsen	僧詮
Shang Chün	Shō Kin	商均
Shan-tao	Zendō	善導
Shan-wu-wei	Zemmui	善無畏　(Śubhakarasiṃha)
Shao Hao	Shō Kō	少昊
Shen Nung	Shin Nō	神農
Shih Ch'ao-i	Shi Chōgi	史朝義
Shih K'uang	Shi Kō	師曠
Shih Shih-ming	Shi Shimei	史師明
Shu Ch'i	Shuku Sei	叔齊
Shun	Shun	舜
Ta Chi	Dakki	妲己
T'ai-kung Wang	Taikō Bō	太公望
T'ai-tsung, Emperor	Taisō-tei	太宗帝
Tan, Duke of Chou	Shūkō Tan	周公旦
Tan Chu	Tan Shu	丹朱
T'ang Yao	Tō Gyō	唐堯
T'an-luan	Donran	曇鸞
Tao-an	Dōan	道安
Tao-ch'o	Dōshaku	道綽
Tao-hsien	Dōsen	道暹
Tao-sui	Dōsui	道邃
T'ien-t'ai	Tendai	天台
Ti Kao	Tei Koku	帝嚳
Ts'ai Yin	Sai In	蔡愔
Ts'ung-i	Jūgi	從義
Tsun-shih	Junshiki	遵式
Tu-shun	Tojun	杜順
Tz'u-en	Jion	慈恩
Wang Pa	Ō Ha	王霸
Wang Tsun	Ō Jun	王遵
Wen, King	Bun-ō	文王
Wu, King	Bu-ō	武王
Wu-i	Ui	烏遺
Wu-tsung, Emperor	Busō-tei	武宗帝
Yang Kuei-fei	Yō Kihi	楊貴妃
Yang Meng	Yō Mō	陽猛
Yao	Gyō	堯
Yen Hui	Gan Kai	顏回
Yen Yüan	Gan En	顏淵
Yi, Duke	I Kō	懿公
Yin Chi-fu	In Kippo	尹吉甫
Yü	U	禹
Yüan-chung	Genjū	元重
Yü Jang	Yo Jō	予讓
Yü Shun	Gu Shun	虞舜

APPENDIX 3

JAPANESE TITLES OF LETTERS

1. The Teaching, Capacity, Time, and Country: Kyo Ki Ji Koku Shō 教機時國抄. 1262.
2. The Daimoku of the Lotus Sutra: Hoke Kyō Daimoku Shō 法華經題目抄. 1266.
3. Letter from Sado: Sado Gosho 佐渡御書. 1272. Also known as: Reply to Toki and others. Toki-dono Tō Gohenji 富木殿等御返事.
4. On Practicing the Buddha's Teachings: Nyosetsu Shugyō Shō 如説修行抄. 1273.
5. On the Buddha's Prophecy: Kembutsu Mirai Ki 顯仏未來記. 1273.
6. Teaching, Practice, and Proof: Kyō Gyō Shō Gosho 教行証御書. 1275.
7. On Persecutions Befalling the Sage: Shōnin Gonan Ji 聖人御難事. 1279.
8. The Four Debts of Gratitude: Shion Shō 四恩抄. 1262. Also known as: The Exile to Izu: Izu Gokanki Shō 伊豆御勘気抄.
9. The Tripitaka Master Shan-wu-wei: Zemmui Sanzō Shō 善無畏三藏抄. 1270.
10. Reply to Nii-ama: Nii-ama Gozen Gohenji 新尼御前御返事. 1275.
11. Letter to the Priests of Seichō-ji: Seichō-ji Daishu Chū 清澄寺大衆中. 1276.
12. Reply to a Believer: Dannotsu Bō Gohenji 檀越某御返事. 1278.
13. Great Evil and Great Good: Daiaku Daizen Gosho 大惡大善御書.
14. On Attaining Buddhahood: Isshō Jōbutsu Shō 一生成仏抄. 1255.
15. Lessening One's Karmic Retribution: Tenju Kyōju Hōmon 轉重輕受法門. 1271.
16. Letter from Teradomari: Teradomari Gosho 寺泊御書. 1271.
17. Aspiration for the Buddha Land: Ganbō Bukkoku no Koto 願望仏國事. 1271. Another name for: Reply to Toki Nyūdō: Toki Nyūdō-dono Gohenji 富木入道殿御返事.
18. The Votary of the Lotus Sutra Will Meet Persecution: Hokke Gyōja Hōnanji 法華行者逢難事. 1274.
19. The Problem to Be Pondered Night and Day: Shika Dammin Gosho 止暇斷眠御書. 1275. Another name for: Letter to Toki: Toki-dono Gosho 富木殿御書.
20. Curing Karmic Disease: Gōbyō Nōji no Koto 業病能治事. 1275. Another name for: Reply to Ōta Nyūdō: Ōta Nyūdōdono Gohenji 太田入道殿御返事.

21. A Sage Perceives the Three Existences of Life: Shōnin Chi Sanze Ji 聖人知三世事. 1275.
22. Admonitions against Slander: Jōbutsu Yōjin Shō 成仏用心抄. 1276. Another name for: Reply to Soya: Soya-dono Gohenji 曾谷殿御返事.
23. On Prolonging Life: Kaen Jōgō Sho 可延定業書. 1279.
24. A Comparison of the Lotus Sutra and Other Sutras: Shokyō to Hoke Kyō to Nan'i no Koto 諸經與法華經與難易事. 1280. Also known as: The Teaching That Is Difficult to Believe in and Difficult to Understand: Nanshin Nange Hōmon 難信難解法門.
25. The Treatment of Illness: Jibyō Daishō Gonjitsu Imoku 治病大小権実違目. 1282. Title also abbreviated to Jibyō Shō 治病抄.
26. Letter to the Brothers: Kyōdai Shō 兄弟抄. 1275.
27. The Three Obstacles and the Four Devils: Sanshō Shima no Koto 三障四魔事. 1275. Another name for: Reply to Hyōe Sakan: Hyōe Sakan-dono Gohenji 兵衞志殿御返事.
28. Recitation of the *Hōben* and *Juryō* Chapters: *Hōben Juryō* Dokuju no Koto 方便壽量誦事. 1264. Another name for: Letter on Menstruation: Gessui (Gassui) Gosho 月水御書.
29. The Essence of the *Juryō* Chapter: *Juryō-bon* Tokui Shō 壽量品得意抄. 1271.
30. The Persecution at Tatsunokuchi: Tatsunokuchi Gosho 竜口御書. 1271. Another name for: Letter to Shijō Kingo: Shijō Kingo-dono Goshōsoku 四條金吾殿御消息.
31. The Causal Law of Life: Dōshō Dōmyō Gosho 同生同名御書. 1272.
32. Letter to Nichimyō Shonin: Nichimyō Shōnin Gosho 日妙聖人御書. 1272.
33. Reply to Kyō'ō: Kyōō-dono Gohenji 經王殿御返事. 1273.
34. Rebuking Slander of the Law and Eradicating Sins: Kashaku Hōbō Metsuzai Shō 呵責謗法滅罪抄. 1273.
35. On Recommending This Teaching to Your Lord: Shukun Ni'nyū Shihōmon Men Yodōzai Ji 主君耳入此法門免與同罪事. 1274. Also known as: The Offense of Complicity: Yodōzai no Koto 與同罪事.
36. The Difficulty of Sustaining Faith: Shikyō Nanji Gosho 此經難持御書. 1275. Another name for: Reply to Shijō Kingo: Shijō Kingo-dono Gohenji 四條金吾殿御返事.
37. The Eight Winds: Happū Shō 八風抄. 1277. Another name for: Reply to Shijō Kingo: Shijō Kingo-dono Gohenji 四條金吾殿御返事.
38. The Supremacy of the Law: Shinkyō Hōjū Shō 身輕法重抄. 1275. Another name for: Letter to Oto Gozen: Oto Gozen Goshōsoku 乙御前御消息.
39. A Warning against Begrudging One's Fief: Fukashaku Shoryō no Koto 不可惜所領事. 1277. Another name for: Reply to Shijō Kingo: Shijō Kingo-dono Gohenji 四條金吾殿御返事.
40. The Real Aspect of the Gohonzon: Gohonzon Sōmyō Shō 御本尊相貌抄. 1277. Another name for: Reply to Nichinyo Gozen: Nichinyo Gozen Gohenji 日女御前御返事.
41. The Three Kinds of Treasure: Sanshu Zaihō Gosho 三種財寶御書. 1277. Another name for: The Story of Emperor Sushun: Sushun Tennō Gosho 崇峻天皇御書.

42. General Stone Tiger: Sekko Shōgun Gosho 石虎將軍御書. 1278. Another name for: Reply to Shijō Kingo: Shijō Kingo-dono Gohenji 四條金吾殿御返事.

43. The Strategy of the Lotus Sutra: Hoke Kyō Heihō no Koto 法華經兵法事. 1279. Another name for: Reply to Shijō Kingo: Shijō Kingo-dono Gohenji 四條金吾殿御返事.

44. The Meaning of Faith: Shinjin Hongi no Koto 信心本義事. 1280. Another name for: Reply to Myōichi-ama: Myōichi-ama Gozen Gohenji 妙一尼御前御返事.

45. The Swords of Good and Evil: Zennaku Nitō Gosho 善惡二刀御書. 1274. Another name for: Reply to Yagenta: Yagenta-dono Gohenji 彌源太殿御返事.

46. Heritage of the Ultimate Law of Life: Shōji Ichidaiji Kechimyaku Shō 生死一人事血脈抄. 1272.

47. On the Treasure Tower: Hōtō Gosho 寶塔御書. 1272. Another name for: Letter to Abutsu-bō: Abutsu-bō Gosho 阿仏房御書.

48. The True Entity of Life: Shohō Jissō Shō 諸法実相抄. 1273.

49. Bestowal of the Mandala of the Mystic Law: Myōhō Mandara Kuyō no Koto 妙法曼陀羅供養事. 1279.

50. Letter to Ichinosawa Nyūdō: Ichinosawa Nyūdō Gosho 一谷入道御書. 1275.

51. The Sutra of True Requital: Shinjitsu Hōon Kyō no Koto 真実報恩經事. 1278. Another name for: Reply to Sennichi-ama: Sennichi-ama Gozen Gohenji 千日尼御前御返事.

52. The Treasure of a Filial Child: Kōshi Takara Gosho 孝子財御書. 1280. Another name for: Reply to Sennichi-ama: Sennichi-ama Gohenji 千日尼御返事.

53. A Ship to Cross the Sea of Suffering: Nyoto Tokusen Gosho 如渡得船御書. 1261. Another name for: Letter to Shiiji Shirō: Shiiji Shirō-dono Gosho 椎地四郎殿御書.

54. The Izu Exile: Izu Hairu no Koto 伊豆配流事. 1261. Another name for: Letter to Funamori Yasaburō: Funamori Yasaburō Moto Gosho 船守彌三郎許御書.

55. Encouragement to a Sick Person: Irō Sho 慰勞書. 1264. Another name for: Letter to Nanjō Hyōe Shichirō: Nanjō Hyōe Shichirō-dono Gosho 南條兵衞七郎殿御書; also called: The Komatsubara Persecution: Komatsubara Hōnan Shō 小松原法難抄.

56. Hell Is the Land of Tranquil Light: Jigoku Soku Jakkō Gosho 地獄即寂光御書. 1274. Another name for: Reply to the Widow of Lord Ueno: Ueno-dono Goke-ama Gohenji 上野殿後家尼御返事.

57. Three Tripitaka Masters Pray for Rain: San Sanzō Kiu no Koto 三三藏祈雨事. 1275. Also known as Reply to Nishiyama: Nishiyama-dono Gohenji 西山殿御返事.

58. The Mogol Envoys: Mōko Tsukai Gosho 蒙古使御書. 1275.

59. The Fourteen Slanders: Jūshi Hibō Shō 十四誹謗抄. 1276. Another name for: Reply to Matsuno: Matsuno-dono Gohenji 松野殿御返事.

60. The Workings of Bonten and Taishaku: Bon Tai Onhakarai no Koto 梵帝御

計事. 1277. Another name for: Reply to Ueno: Ueno-dono Gohenji 上野殿御返事.

61. Letter to Misawa: Misawa Shō 三沢抄. 1278. Also known as: Before and after Sado: Sazen Sago Shō 佐前佐後抄.

62. Two Kinds of Faith: Sui Ka Nishin Shō 水火二信抄. 1278. Another name for: Reply to Ueno: Ueno-dono Gohenji 上野殿御返事.

63. The Teaching for the Latter Day: Mappō Yōhō Gosho 末法要法御書. 1278. Another name for: Reply to Ueno: Ueno-dono Gohenji 上野殿御返事.

64. The One Essential Phrase: Ikku Kanjin no Koto 一句肝心事. 1278. Another name for: Reply to Myōhō-ama: Myōhō-ama Gozen Gohenji 妙法尼御前御返事.

65. Persecution by Sword and Staff: Tō Jō Nan no Koto 刀杖難事. 1279. Another name for: Reply to Ueno: Ueno-dono Gohenji 上野殿御返事.

66. The Dragon Gate: Ryūmon Gosho 竜門御書. 1279. Another name for: Reply to Ueno: Ueno-dono Gohenji 上野殿御返事.

67. Letter to Niike: Niike Gosho 新池御書. 1280.

68. Reply to Nichigon-ama: Nichigon-ama Gozen Gohenji 日嚴尼御前御返事. 1280.

69. The Person and the Law: Hōmyō Ninki no Koto 法妙人貴事. 1281. Another name for: Reply to Nanjō: Nanjō-dono Gohenji 南條殿御返事.

70. The Proof of the Lotus Sutra: Hokke Shōmyō Shō 法華証明抄. 1282. Also known as: On Life and Death: Shikatsu Shō 死活抄.

71. The Kalpa of Decrease: Genkō Gosho 減劫御書. after 1276. Also known as: Wisdom and the Destruction of the Nation: Chie Bōkoku Sho 智慧亡國書.

72. New Year's Letter: Mushimochi Gosho 十字御書.

73. The Gift of Rice: Hakumai Ippyō Gosho 白米一俵御書. Also known as: Offerings in Principle and Actuality: Jiri Kuyō Gosho 事理供養御書.

GLOSSARY

NOTE: Buddhist technical terms are generally given in their translated form. Titles of texts and the names of figures who appear in sutras appear in Japanese unless otherwise indicated. Names of historical figures are given in the language of the country of their origin with the exception of Indian scholars who made their way to China.

Agon sutras: (Skt: *Āgama-sūtra*) A generic term for all Hinayana sutras. T'ien-t'ai classified Shakyamuni's teaching into five periods, according to the order of preaching. The *Agon* sutras belong to the second period. *See also* Five periods.

Ajātaśatru: (Jap: *Ajase*) The son of King Bimbisāra of Magadha, India. Incited by Devadatta, he killed his father, a follower of Shakyamuni, and ascended the throne to become the most influential ruler of his time. Later he is said to have contracted a terrible disease and, out of remorse for his evil acts, converted to Buddhism and supported the First Buddhist Council for the compilation of Shakyamuni's teachings. His story is frequently mentioned by Nichiren.

Ānanda: (Jap: Anan) One of Shakyamuni's ten major disciples. He was a cousin of the Buddha and also the younger brother of Devadatta. He accompanied Shakyamuni as his personal attendant for a great many years and, as a result, heard more of his teachings than any other disciple. Therefore, he was known as the foremost in hearing the Buddha's teachings.

Animality: (Jap: *chikushō*) The third of the Ten Worlds. *See also* Six Paths; Ten Worlds.

Annen (841–889?) A Tendai priest who studied both the exoteric and the esoteric teachings under Jikaku Daishi. He founded a temple known as the Godai-in on Mount Hiei and wrote widely on the subject of esoteric Tendai teachings.

Anryūgyō, *see* Four bodhisattvas.

Arhat: (Jap: *arakan*) The highest state of Hinayana enlightenment. Also one who has attained this state. It is the highest of the four states to which a *shōmon* can attain.

Āryasiṃha: (Jap: Shishi sonja) According to the T'ien-t'ai classification, the last of the twenty-four successors of Shakyamuni. His efforts to propagate Buddhism led to his execution by Dammira, a king who destroyed many Buddhist temples and murdered scores of monks. The Zen school holds that before his death he passed on his teaching to a twenty-fifth successor or patriarch.

Asura (Jap: ashura) A class of fighting demons in Indian mythology who clash continually with the god Indra or Taishaku. Asuras live at the bottom of the ocean surrounding Mount Sumeru. They occupy the fourth of the Ten Worlds. They represent the world of Anger. *See also* Six Paths; Ten Worlds.

Aśvaghoṣa: (Jap: Memyō) A second-century Mahayana scholar and poet of Śrāvasti, India. Listed as twelfth in the line of patriarchs or successors to Shakyamuni.

Atsuhara Persecution: A series of threats and acts of violence against Nichiren's followers in Atsuhara village in the Fuji district of Suruga Province over a period of three years, beginning in 1278. Nichiren's disciple, Nikkō Shonin (1246–1333), had successfully propagated Nichiren's teachings at Ryūsen-ji, a Tendai temple in Atsuhara, converting several of the younger priests and lay parishioners. Gyōchi, the deputy chief priest of the temple, was enraged and conducted an investigation. Eventually some twenty farmers who were believers in Nichiren's teachings were arrested for allegedly harvesting rice from fields that did not belong to them, and sent to Kamakura for trial. Their case was presided over by the deputy chief of the Office of Military and Police Affairs, Hei no Saemon (*q.v.*). Eventually three of the group were beheaded and the others sentenced to be banished from Atsuhara.

Avīci Hell, *see* Hell of incessant suffering.

Benevolent deities (Jap: *shoten zenjin*) This term is used in various contexts. Frequently it refers to the Shinto deities: the Sun Goddess (Amaterasu Ōmikami or Tenshō Daijin), the God Hachiman, and the Mountain God of Mount Hiei (Sannō). The term is used also in reference to the gods in the Lotus Sutra who assemble from throughout the universe to listen to Shakyamuni preach.

Bodhisattva: (Jap: *bosatsu*) The ninth of the Ten Worlds, a state characterized by compassion in which one dedicates one's self to saving others. The bodhisattva vows to postpone his own entrance into Buddhahood until all sentient beings have been saved. *See also* Ten Worlds.

Bodhisattvas of the Earth: (Jap: *Jiyu no bosatsu*) The *Yujutsu* (15th) chapter of the Lotus Sutra describes the appearance of an innumerable host of bodhisattvas who well up from the space below the earth and to whom Shakyamuni entrusts the propagation of the Lotus Sutra. Their leader is Jōgyō (Viśiṣṭacārita, Superior Conduct). The other leaders are Muhengyō (Anantacārita, Limitless Conduct), Jōgyō (Jyōgyō) (Viśuddhacārita, Pure Conduct), and Anryūgyō (Supratisthitacārita, Conduct of Standing Firm). (Note that the two Jōgyōs are written with different characters.) Nichiren identifies himself with the Bodhisattva Jōgyō, the leader of the four.

Bonten: (Skt: Brahmā) Also Dai-Bonten (Mahābrahman). A god said to live in the first of the four meditation heavens in the world of form above Mount Sumeru and to rule the *sahā* world. In Buddhism he was adopted as one of the two major tutelary gods, together with Taishaku. Bonten is also the Japanese name for the Brahma Heaven.

Brahma Heaven, *see* Bonten.

Buddhahood: (Jap: *butsu*) The highest of the Ten Worlds, characterized by boundless wisdom and infinite compassion. *See also* Ten Worlds.

Buddha land: (Jap: *butsudo*) The place where a Buddha dwells; there are countless Buddha lands. The term is also used in the sense of the enlightened state of a Buddha.

Ceremony in the Air: (Jap: *kokūe*) One of the three assemblies described in the Lotus Sutra. The description extends from the latter portion of the *Hōtō* (11th) chapter through the *Zokurui* (22d) chapter. In the *Yujutsu* (15th) chapter, the Bodhisattvas of the Earth make their appearance; the essential teaching (*hommon*) begins here. In the *Juryō* (16th) chapter, Shakyamuni reveals his original enlightenment in the remote past of *gohyaku-jintengō*. In the *Jinriki* (21st) chapter, he transfers the essence of the sutra to the Bodhisattvas of the Earth led by Bodhisattva Jōgyō, entrusting them with the mission of propagating it.

Chang-an (561–632): (Jap: Shōan) Also known as Kuan-ting (Jap: Kanjō). T'ien-t'ai's disciple and successor. He recorded T'ien-t'ai's lectures and later compiled them as the *Hokke Gengi*, *Hokke Mongu*, and *Maka Shikan*. His own works are the *Nehangyō Sho* (Commentary on the Nirvana Sutra) and the *Nehan Gengi* (Profound Meaning of Nirvana).

Ch'eng-kuan (738–839): (Jap: Chōkan) The fourth patriarch of the Hua-yen (Kegon) school, known also by his title Ch'ing-liang (Seiryō or Shōryō). He studied various schools under different masters but concentrated his teachings on the *Kegon* Sutra, participating in the translation of the forty-volume version of this sutra. He was greatly honored by several emperors and was awarded numerous titles and high rank.

Chia-hsiang, *see* Chi-tsang.

Chi-tsang (549–623): (Jap: Kichizō) Known also as Chia-hsiang (Kajō) after the temple at which he lived. He is often regarded as the first patriarch of San-lun (Sanron) in China. He studied the three treatises of Sanron: *Chū Ron*, *Jūnimon Ron*, and *Hyaku Ron*, and organized the teachings of this school.

Chih-che (Jap: Chisha): An honorific name given to the Great Teacher T'ien t'ai. He is also known as Chih-che ta-shih, and most commonly as Chih-i (Chigi). Nichiren on almost all occasions refers to him as T'ien-t'ai.

Chin-kang-chih (671–741): (Jap: Kongōchi; Skt: Vajrabodhi) The second, after Shan-wu-wei, famous Indian esoteric master to come to China during the T'ang dynasty. Arriving in 720, he soon gained the support of Emperor Hsüan-tsung. He translated several texts and was the teacher of Pu-k'ung.

Ch'ing-liang, *see* Ch'eng-kuan.

Chishō (814–891): Also called Enchin or Chishō Daishi. The fifth chief priest of the Enryaku-ji, the head temple of the Tendai sect on Mount Hiei. In 853 he went to T'ang China, where he studied the T'ien-t'ai and esoteric doctrines. On his return he combined esoteric doctrines with the Tendai. He also erected a hall for performing the esoteric *abhiṣeka* (Jap: *kanjō*) ceremony at the Onjō-ji (Mii-dera) in Ōtsu. Nichiren frequently condemns him for distorting the Tendai teachings.

Dai–Bonten, *see* Bonten.

Daimoku: (1) The title of a sutra, in particular the title of the Lotus Sutra, *Myōhō-renge-kyō*; (2) The invocation of Nam-myoho-renge-kyo, along with the *honzon*, the object of worship, and the *kaidan*, the high sanctuary, that, in Nichiren's teaching comprise the Three Great Secret Laws (Jap: *Sandai hihō*).

Daishi: "Great Teacher." An honorific title awarded to eminent priests in China and Japan by the imperial court, usually after their death. In 866, Saichō was given the posthumous name Dengyō Daishi (The Great Teacher Dengyō) and Kūkai, that of Kōbō Daishi. These are the first instances of the use of this honorific title in Japan.

Daishōnin: Literally, Great Sage, the title given to Nichiren, especially in the Nichiren Shōshū. Other Nichiren schools refer to him as Shōnin (sage) or Daibosatsu (Great Bodhisattva).

Daitsū: (Skt: Mahābhijñājñābhibhū) Also Daitsūchishō Buddha. According to the *Kejōyu* (7th) chapter of the Lotus Sutra, he was a king who attained Buddhahood in the remote past of *sanzen-jintengō* and expounded the Lotus Sutra at the request of his sixteen sons. Later all sixteen spread the Lotus Sutra as bodhisattvas. The sixteenth son was after many kalpas reborn in the *sahā* world as Shakyamuni.

Daitsūchishō, *see* Daitsū.

Dengyō (767–822): The founder of the Tendai sect in Japan. He is often referred to as Saichō; his honorific name and title are Dengyō Daishi (The Great Teacher Dengyō). In the fourth month of 785 he was ordained in the Hinayana precepts at the Tōdai-ji in Nara and in the sixth month established a temple on Mount Hiei near Kyoto. In 804 he went to China to study at Mount T'ien-t'ai. Returning the next year, he founded the Tendai sect in Japan. He made continued efforts to establish a Mahayana ordination center on Mount Hiei in the face of determined opposition from the older sects in Nara. Permission was finally granted shortly after his death, and his immediate successor, Gishin, completed the ordination center in 827.

Devadatta: (Jap: Daibadatta) A cousin of Shakyamuni Buddha, who followed him but later became his enemy out of jealousy. In his arrogance he sought to kill the Buddha and usurp his position. He fomented a schism in the Buddhist Order, luring away other monks. He also goaded Prince Ajātaśatru of Magadha into overthrowing his father, the king, a patron of Shakyamuni. With the new king supporting him, Devadatta made several attempts on the Buddha's life and persecuted his Order. He is said to have fallen into hell alive. However, in the *Daibadatta* (12th) chapter of the Lotus Sutra, Shakyamuni reveals that in some past existence he himself had practiced Buddhism under a hermit named Ashi (Skt: Asita) and that this hermit is the present Devadatta. He also predicts that Devadatta will attain enlightenment in the future as a Buddha called Heavenly King.

Devil of the Sixth Heaven: (Jap: Dairokuten no Maō) The king of devils, who dwells in the highest of the six heavens of the world of desire. He works to obstruct Buddhist practice and delights in sapping the life force of other beings.

Dragon king's daughter: (Jap: Ryūnyo) The daughter of Shakatsura (Skt: Sāgara), one of the eight dragon kings said to dwell in a palace at the bottom of the sea. According to the *Daibadatta* (12th) chapter of the Lotus Sutra, she began to seek enlightenment when she heard Bodhisattva Monju preach the Lotus Sutra in the dragon king's palace. Later she appeared in front of the assembly at Eagle Peak and immediately attained enlightenment without changing her dragon form. The pre-Lotus sutra teachings generally held that women could not attain Buddhahood and that even men had to practice austerities for innumerable kalpas in order to do so.

Eagle Peak: (Jap: Ryōju-sen; Skt: Gṛdhrakūta) A mountain located to the northeast of Rājagṛha, the capital of Magadha in ancient India, where Shakyamuni is said to have expounded the Lotus Sutra. In English it is often called Vulture Peak, based on its Sanskrit name. Kumārajīva, in his translation of the Lotus Sutra, referred to it as Eagle Peak, and his version has been followed here.

Eight kinds of nonhuman beings: (Jap: *hachibu-shū*) They are described in the *Hiyu* (3d) chapter of the Lotus Sutra. They are: (1) gods, (2) dragons, (3) *yasha* (Skt: *yakṣa*), demons, sometimes described as fierce, who are followers of Bishamonten, one of the Four Heavenly Kings, (4) *kendatsuba* (Skt: *gandharva*), gods of music, (5) ashura (Skt: *asura*), fighting demons, said to live at the bottom of the ocean surrounding Mount Sumeru and who inhabit the fourth of the Ten Worlds, (6) *karura* (Skt: *garuda*), birds that devour dragons, (7) *kinnara* (Skt: *kimnara*), gods with beautiful voices, and (8) *magoraka* (Skt: *mahoraga*), gods in the form of snakes.

Eight teachings: (Jap: *hakkyō*) One system by which T'ien-t'ai classified the sutras. The eight teachings are subdivided into two groups: four teachings of doctrine (*kehō no shikyō*) and four teachings of method (*kegi no shikyō*). The first is a division by content, and the second, by method of teaching,

The four teachings of doctrine are: (1) the Tripitaka teaching (*zōkyō*), which corresponds to the Hinayana texts that stress observing precepts; (2) the connecting teachings (*tsūgyō*), introductory Mahayana teachings for those in the states of *shōmon*, *engaku*, and bodhisattva; (3) the specific teaching (*bekkyō*), a higher level of provisional Mahayana taught exclusively for bodhisattvas; the three truths (*q.v.*) are discussed here, but are indicated as being separate from each other; and (4) the perfect teaching (*engyō*), or true Mahayana, which is directed to people of all capacities and holds that all can attain Buddhahood.

The four teachings of method are: (1) the sudden teaching (*tonkyō*), or those teachings that Shakyamuni expounded directly upon his own enlightenment without giving his disciples preparatory knowledge. An example is the *Kegon* Sutra, traditionally regarded as the first teaching he expounded after his enlightenment at Buddhagayā; (2) the gradual teaching (*zenkyō*), or teachings Shakyamuni expounded to his disciples in progressive stages in order to gradually elevate their capacity to understand higher doctrines; (3) the secret teaching (*himitsukyō*), or teachings from which the Buddha's listeners each unknowingly received a different benefit according to their capacity; and (4) the indeterminate teaching (*fujō-kyō*), from which the Buddha's listeners each knowingly received a different benefit.

Emanations of the Buddha: (Jap: *funjin* or *bunshin*) Buddhas who are different manifestations of a Buddha. The Buddha can divide his body an infinite number of times and appear in innumerable worlds at once in order to save the people there. In the *Hōtō* (llth) chapter of the Lotus Sutra, Shakyamuni summons the Buddhas who are emanations from throughout the universe.

Emma: (Skt: Yama) The lord of hell, who judges the dead for the deeds they did while alive and sentences them accordingly.

Enchin, *see* Chishō.

Enchō (772–837): The second chief priest of the Enryaku-ji on Mount Hiei. He became a disciple of Dengyō at twenty-seven. He received the bodhisattva precepts in 808 and lectured on various sutras. His posthumous title was Jakkō Daishi.

Engaku: (Skt: *pratyekabuddha*) Those who seek to obtain enlightenment without a teacher. Sometimes translated as Men of Realization, they represent the eighth of the Ten Worlds. *See also* Ten Worlds.

Ennin, *see* Jikaku.

Essential teaching: (Jap: *hommon*) The last fourteen chapters of the Lotus Sutra, from the *Yujutsu* (15th) through the *Fugen* (28th) chapters. In his *Hokke Mongu*, T'ien-t'ai divided the Lotus Sutra into two parts, the first fourteen chapters, or theoretical teaching, and the last fourteen chapters, or essential teaching. The essential teaching starts when the historical Shakyamuni reveals his true identity as the Buddha who gained enlightenment in the remote past of *gohyaku-jintengō*. *See also* Theoretical teaching.

Fa-tao (1086–1147): (Jap: Hōdō) Chinese priest who remonstrated with Emperor Hui-tsung of the Sung dynasty when the emperor supported Taoism and attempted to reorganize the order of Buddhist priests. Later he was branded in the face and exiled to Tao-chou, south of the Yangtze River. He is frequently referred to by Nichiren.

Fifth five-hundred-year period: (Jap: *go gohyakusai*) The last of the five five-hundred-year periods following Shakyamuni's death. It corresponds to the beginning of the Latter Day of the Law (*mappō*). According to the *Daijuku* Sutra and other works, this period is one of contention and strife in which Shakyamuni's Buddhism will perish. *See also* Three periods; Latter Day of the Law.

Fifty-two stages of bodhisattva practice: (Jap: *gojūni i*) The fifty-two ranks through which a bodhisattva progresses toward Buddhahood. They are described in the *Bosatsu Yōraku Hongō* Sutra (Sutra of the Bodhisattvas' Prior Jewel-like Acts). The fifty-two consist of ten stages of faith (*jisshin*), ten stages of security or ten abodes (*jūjū*), ten stages of practice (*jūgyō*), ten stages of devotion or merit transfer (*jū ekō*), ten stages of development (*jūji*), *tōgaku*, the stage almost equal to enlightenment, and *myōgaku*, enlightenment.

Five cardinal sins: (Jap: *go gyakuzai*) The five most serious offenses in Buddhism. Explanations vary according to different sutras and treatises. The most common version is: (1) killing one's father, (2) killing one's mother, (3) killing an arhat, (4) injuring a Buddha, and (5) causing dissension in the Buddhist Order.

Five impurities: (Jap: *gojoku*) (1) Impurity of the age caused by war, natural disasters, etc.; (2) impurity of thought, (3) impurities of desires, such as greed, anger, or stupidity; (4) impurity of the people, weakened both spiritually and physically by impurities of thought and desire; and (5) impurity of life itself. They are listed in the *Hōben* (2d) chapter of the Lotus Sutra; here it states that the Buddha appears in an evil world that is defiled by the five impurities.

Five periods: (Jap: *goji*) T'ien-t'ai's classification of Shakyamuni's teachings according to the order of preaching. They are: (1) The Kegon period, in which the Buddha expounded his first teachings (the *Kegon* Sutra) after his enlightenment, (2) the Agon period, or period of the *Agon* sutras, in which the Hinayana teachings were expounded, (3) the *Hōdō* period in which such sutras as the *Amida, Dainichi,* and Vimalakirti were preached, (4) the Hannya period in which the *Hannya*, or Wisdom sutras were taught, and (5) the Hokke Nehan period, an eight-year interval in which Shakyamuni expounded the Lotus and Nirvana sutras.

Five practices: (Jap: *goshu no myōgyō*) The five kinds of practice described in the *Hosshi* (10th) chapter of the Lotus Sutra. They are to embrace, read, recite, teach, and transcribe the Lotus Sutra.

Five types of vision: (Jap: *gogen*) (1) the eyes of common mortals that distinguish form and color, (2) the divine eye that sees things even in the darkness and at a distance, (3) the eye of wisdom, or the ability of people in the two vehicles to judge right and wrong and recognize what must be done, (4) the eye of the Dharma by which bodhisattvas see all phenomena from the viewpoint of Buddhism, and (5) the eye of the Buddha that sees the true nature of life in the past, present, and future.

Former Day of the Law: (Jap: *shōbō*) The period when the True Law was taught; the first thousand years after Shakyamuni's death. Frequently referred to as the Period of the True Law. *See also* Three periods.

Four bodhisattvas, *see* Bodhisattvas of the Earth.

Four categories of Buddhists: (Jap: *shishu*) Sometimes called the four kinds of believers. Monks, nuns, laymen, and laywomen.

Four continents: (Jap: *shishū*) The continents situated respectively to the east, west, north, and south of Mount Sumeru, according to ancient Indian cosmology. They are Tōhotsubadai (Skt: Pūrvavideha), Saikuyani (Aparagodānīya), Hokkuru (Uttarakuru), and Nanembudai (Jambudvīpa).

Four evil paths: (Jap: *shiakushu*) The first four of the Ten Worlds: Hell, Hungry Ghosts, Animals, and Asura. *See also* Ten Worlds.

Four Heavenly Kings: (Jap: *Shitennō*) The lords of the four quarters who serve Taishaku as his generals and protect the four continents. They are Jikokuten (Dhrarāṣṭra), Kōmokuten (Virūpākṣa), Bishamonten (Vaiśravaṇa), and Zōchōten (Virūḍhaka). They are said to live halfway down the four sides of Mount Sumeru. In the *Darani* (26th) chapter of the Lotus Sutra they vow to protect those who embrace the sutra.

Fourteen slanders: (Jap: *jūshi hibō*) Fourteen kinds of slanders against Buddhism described in the *Hiyu* (3d) chapter of the Lotus Sutra: (1) arrogance toward

Buddhism, (2) negligence in Buddhist practice, (3) arbitrary, egotistical judgment of Buddhist teachings, (4) shallow, self-satisfied understanding, (5) adherence to earthly desires, (6) lack of a seeking spirit, (7) lack of faith, (8) disgust toward Buddhism, (9) mistaken doubt, (10) vilification of Buddhism, (11) contempt for Buddhist believers, (12) hatred toward believers, (13) jealousy toward believers, and (14) grudges against believers. The first ten are slanders against the Law and the latter four are slanders against those who embrace the Law.

Fugen: (Skt: Samantabhadra) With Monju, one of the two bodhisattvas who attend Shakyamuni and lead the other bodhisattvas. In the *Fugen* (28th) chapter of the Lotus Sutra he vows to protect the sutra and its votaries.

Fugen Sutra: "Sutra of Meditation on Bodhisattva Fugen," a one-volume sutra said to have been preached three months before Shakyamuni's passing. Since this sutra is a continuation of the Fugen (28th) chapter of the Lotus Sutra, T'ien-t'ai regarded it as the conclusion of the Lotus Sutra.

Fukyō: (Skt: Sadāparibhūta) A bodhisattva who appears in the *Fukyō* (20th) chapter of the Lotus Sutra. After the death of Ionnō Buddha in the remote past, he propagated a teaching expressed in twenty-four Chinese characters and showed respect toward all people for their innate Buddha nature. People ridiculed him and attacked him with staves and stones, but he continued to practice in this way. Those who slandered him fell into hell, but, after expiating their offense were reborn with Fukyō and were saved by practicing the Lotus Sutra under his guidance. The name Fukyō means "never despising."

Genshin (942–1017): Tendai priest, known also as Eshin Sōzu, who established a temple, the Eshin-in, on Mount Hiei. In 985 he compiled the *Ōjō Yōshū*, a work that had considerable influence on the later development of the Pure Land sect in Japan.

Gods of the sun and moon: (Jap: *nitten gatten*) The deification of the sun and moon. Nichiren regarded them as Buddhist gods who protect the votaries of the Lotus Sutra.

Gohonzon: The mandala which forms the object of worship in Nichiren's Buddhism.

Gohyaku-jintengō: A time in the extremely remote past when Shakyamuni first attained enlightenment, derived from the *Juryō* (16th) chapter of the Lotus Sutra. Also, the length of time that has elapsed since that attainment. Not until the essential teaching (*hommon*) of the Lotus Sutra was expounded did Shakyamuni reveal that his enlightenment had originally taken place long before his lifetime in India. *Gohyaku-jintengō* is derived from a passage in the *Juryō* chapter that reads: "Suppose there is one who reduces five hundred, thousand, ten thousand, hundred thousand *nayuta* (10^{11}), *asōgi* (10^{59}) major world systems to particles of dust, and then takes them all to the east, dropping one particle each time he traverses five hundred, thousand, ten thousand, hundred thousand, *nayuta*, *asōgi* worlds. Suppose that he continues traveling eastward in this way, until he has finished dropping all the particles. . . . Suppose all these worlds, whether they received a particle or not, are once more reduced to dust. Let one particle represent one kalpa. Then the time which has passed since I attained Buddhahood surpasses this by one hundred, thousand, ten thousand, hundred thousand, *nayuta, asōgi* kalpas."

Gosho: The individual and collected writings of Nichiren, which include letters of personal encouragement, treatises on Buddhism, and recorded oral teachings.

Great Teacher, *see* Daishi.

Guketsu: The abbreviation of *Maka Shikan Bugyōden Guketsu*, Miao-lo's annotations on the *Maka Shikan*.

Hachiman: A popular Shinto deity who protects warriors. In the Nara period he was regarded as a guardian of Buddhism and is often called Hachiman Daibosatsu. Hachiman was adopted as a guardian deity by the Minamoto family; Yoritomo erected the Tsurugaoka Hachiman shrine in Kamakura in 1191. Nichiren considered him one of the gods who protect the votaries of the Lotus Sutra.

Hannya sutras: Higher provisional Mahayana sutras belonging to the fourth of the periods of Shakyamuni's teaching, according to T'ien-t'ai's classification. *See also* Five periods.

Heaven: (Jap: *ten*) The sixth of the Ten Worlds. The realm of the gods. *See also* Ten Worlds.

Hei no Saemon: (d.1293): An official of the Hōjō regency, also known as Taira no Yoritsuna. He served two successive regents, Hōjō Tokimune (1251–1284) and Hōjō Sadatoki (1271–1311) and wielded tremendous influence in political and military affairs as deputy chief (the chief being the regent himself) of the Office of Military and Police Affairs. He took an active part in persecuting Nichiren and his followers.

Hell: (Jap: *jigoku*) The first and lowest of the Ten Worlds. *See also* Ten Worlds.

Hell of incessant suffering: (Skt: Avīci; Jap: *mugen jigoku*) The most terrible of the eight hot hells. It is so called because its inhabitants are said to suffer without a moment's respite.

Hōdō sutras: Lower provisional Mahayana sutras belonging to the third of the five periods of Shakyamuni's teachings, according to T'ien-t'ai's classification. *See also* Five periods.

Hōjō Tokimune (1251–1284): Hōjō regent to whom Nichiren addressed a letter in 1268 warning of an imminent invasion by the Mongols. The letter was ignored.

Hokke Gengi: "Profound Meaning of the Lotus Sutra." One of T'ien-t'ai's three major works. It gives a detailed explanation of the meaning of the title of the Lotus Sutra, *Myōhō Renge Kyō* (T33, no. 1716).

Hokke Mongu: "Words and Phrases of the Lotus Sutra." One of T'ien-t'ai's three major works. A ten-fascicle commentary on the Lotus Sutra expounded by T'ien-t'ai and recorded by Chang-an (T33, no. 1718).

Hōnen (1133–1212): Also called Genkū. The founder of the Jōdo (Pure Land) sect in Japan; it is also referred to as the Nembutsu sect, after the calling of the name (*nembutsu*) of the Buddha Amida. Hōnen first studied Tendai doctrines, but later turned to the exclusive calling of the Buddha's name. His school and those derived from it gained immense popularity. Nichiren roundly condemns Hōnen throughout his writings.

Hossō sect: (Chin Fa-hsiang tsung) Based on the writings of Asaṅga and Vasubandhu, this school was introduced into China by Hsüan-tsang and developed by his principal disciple K'uei-chi (632–682); Nichiren frequently refers to him as Tz'u-en, the name of his temple. The Hossō teachings were highly detailed and abstruse and the school never gained a substantial following. It was introduced to Japan on four occasions during the Nara period. Dōshō (629–700) of the Gangō-ji is considered the founder of the sect in Japan.

Hsüan-tsang (602–664): (Jap: Genjō) A Chinese T'ang dynasty priest, famed for his trip to India to bring back scriptures. He left for India in 629 and studied the Consciousness-Only doctrine at the Nālandā monastery. In 645 he returned to China with many Sanskrit texts, many of which he later translated. His travels are described in the *Daitō Saiiki Ki* (Record of the Western Regions), the source for many of Nichiren's stories. He and his disciple K'uei-chi (also known as Tz'u-en) are regarded as the founders of the Fa-hsiang (Hossō) school.

Humanity: The fifth of the Ten Worlds, the world of human beings. *See also* Ten Worlds.

Hungry Ghosts: (Jap: *gaki*) The second of the Ten Worlds. *See also* Six Paths; Ten Worlds.

Icchantika: (Jap: *issendai*) Those of incorrigible disbelief, who have no faith in Buddhism, no aspiration for enlightenment, and thus no prospect for attaining Buddhahood. Some sutras say that *icchantika* are inherently incapable of attaining Buddhahood; later Mahayana texts hold that even an *icchantika* can become a Buddha.

Ichinen sanzen: "A single life-moment, or instant, possesses three thousand realms." A philosophical system established by T'ien-t'ai in the *Maka Shikan* on the basis of the Lotus Sutra. *Ichinen* (one mind or life-moment, sometimes rendered "instant of thought") is the life that is manifested at each moment by common mortals, and *sanzen* (three thousand), the varying aspects and phases it assumes. At each moment, life experiences one of the ten conditions, that is the Ten Worlds (*q.v.*). Each of these worlds possesses the potential for all ten within itself, thus making one hundred possible worlds. Each of these hundred worlds possesses the ten factors or suchnesses (*q.v.*; Jap: *jū-nyoze*), thus becoming one thousand factors. Finally each of these factors possesses the three realms of existence (*q.v.*; Jap: *sanseken*), thus equaling three thousand realms.

Ikegami brothers: Ikegami Munenaga (d.1283) and Ikegami Munenaka (d.1293) were the sons of Ikegami Saemon-no-tayū Yasumitsu, the director of the Office of Construction and Repair of the Kamakura government. The father was a devoted supporter of Ryōkan, priest of the Ritsu temple, Gokuraku-ji. The sons were followers of Nichiren and Munenaka, the elder brother, was twice disowned (in 1275 and 1277) by the father. The brothers were, in 1278, eventually able to convert their father to Nichiren's teachings.

Ionnō: (Skt: Bhiṣmagarjitavararāja) A Buddha mentioned in the *Fukyō* (20th) chapter of the Lotus Sutra. According to this chapter, in the past, two billion Buddhas appeared one after another, all having the same name, Ionnō. Bodhisattva Fukyō appeared during the Middle Day of the Law after the death of the first Ionnō Buddha and revered all people for their inherent Buddha nature.

Itai dōshin: Unity of people with a common cause. *Itai* (literally, different bodies) points to the need for many different personalities and abilities in achieving a given purpose. *Dōshin* (same mind) indicates the importance of uniting in the same spirit or maintaining a common ideal to achieve success. For Nichiren, *itai dōshin* means that people advance together to achieve the common goal of *kōsen-rufu* (*q.v.*).

Jambudvīpa: (Jap: Embudai) In Indian and Buddhist cosmology one of the four continents situated respectively in the four directions with Mount Sumeru as the center. Jambudvīpa is located to the south and is the place where Buddhism appears and spreads. It is often used in the sense of the entire world inhabited by humanity. *See also* Four continents.

Jikaku (794–866): Also called Ennin or Jikaku Daishi. Third chief priest of the Enryaku-ji. In 838 he journeyed to China where he studied both T'ien-t'ai and esoteric Buddhism. He returned to Japan in 847 and in 854 became head of the Tendai sect. He is frequently condemned by Nichiren for having introduced esoteric elements into the Tendai teachings.

Jōdo sect: Known also as Pure Land and Nembutsu. The teaching founded by Hōnen (*q.v.*) that called for recitation of the name of the Buddha Amida to obtain rebirth in his Western Paradise. This teaching achieved great popularity in Nichiren's time and is the object of frequent attacks by him.

Jōgyō: (Skt: Viśiṣṭacāritra) Leader of the four Bodhisattvas of the Earth who appear in the *Yujutsu* (15th) chapter of the Lotus Sutra. In the *Jinriki* (21st) chapter Shakyamuni transfers his teachings to Bodhisattva Jōgyō. Several of Nichiren's writings refer to his own propagation efforts as "the work of Bodhisattva Jōgyō."

Jōgyō: (Skt: Viśuddhacāritra, Pure Conduct), *see* Bodhisattvas of the Earth.

Jōjitsu sect: (Chin Ch'eng-shih tsung) A school based on Harivarman's *Jōjitsu Ron*, as translated by Kumārajīva in the fifth century. The school flourished briefly in China and was brought to Japan where it was classified as one of the Nara sects; however, it never became an independent sect and was studied in conjunction with the Sanron teachings.

Juryō chapter: "The Life Span of the Tathagata." The sixteenth chapter of the Lotus Sutra, regarded as the key chapter of the essential teaching (*hommon*). Shakyamuni reveals here that he first attained enlightenment not in this lifetime but in the remote past of *gohyaku-jintengō*, and that ever since then he has been in the *sahā*, or mundane world, teaching the Law.

Kakutoku: Priest who appears with King Utoku in the Nirvana Sutra. A considerable time after the death of the Buddha called Kangi Zōyaku Nyorai (literally, Joy Increasing Tathagata), Buddhism was about to perish. Kakutoku tried to protect the orthodox teachings and was harshly persecuted by many misguided priests and their followers. Utoku fought against these slanderous people to protect Kakutoku and died in the battle. It is said that because of their devotion to Buddhism, King Utoku was born as Shakyamuni Buddha and Priest Kakutoku as Kashō Buddha. This story is frequently alluded to by Nichiren.

Kalpa: (Jap: *kō*) Sometimes rendered as aeon. An extremely long period of time. Sutras and treatises differ in their definitions. Kalpas fall into two major categories, those of measurable and those of immeasurable duration. There are three kinds of measurable kalpas: small, medium, and major. One explanation says that a small kalpa is approximately sixteen million years long. According to Buddhist cosmology, a world repeatedly undergoes four stages: formation, continuance, decline, and disintegration. Each of these four stages lasts for twenty small kalpas and is equal to one medium kalpa. Finally, one complete cycle forms a major kalpa. Immeasurable kalpas are described in several ways. For example, a kalpa has been said to be longer than the time required to wear away a cube of stone forty *ri* (one *ri* is about 600 meters) on each side if a heavenly nymph alights on it and brushes it with a piece of cloth once every hundred years.

Kannon: (Skt: Avalokiteśvara) Also Kanzeon. A bodhisattva who appears in the *Fumon* (25th) chapter of the Lotus Sutra. According to the sutra he assumes thirty-three different forms and manifests himself everywhere in order to save people. Often Kannon appears in the form of a woman and is frequently so depicted in sculpture and painting.

Kanzeon, *see* Kannon.

Kātyāyana: (Jap: Kasennen) One of the ten major disciples of the Buddha. He was born to a Brahman family in South India. He was regarded as a skilled debater, and as foremost in the analysis and exegesis of the Buddha's teaching.

Kegon sect: (Chin Hua-yen tsung) Based on the *Kegon* Sutra, according to legend, the first sutra preached by Shakyamuni; it was so abstruse and difficult to understand that he taught next the simpler Hinayana sutras. Tu-shun (557–640) (Jap: Tojun) is the first master of the school in China, although Fa-tsang (643–712) (Jap: Hōzō) who systematized its doctrines can be considered the real founder. The founder of the Kegon sect in Japan is considered to be Shinjō (Kor: Simsang), a priest from Silla who had studied under Fa-tsang. The Tōdai-ji in Nara is the head temple of the sect.

Kōbō (774–835): The founder of the Shingon sect in Japan. He is also known as Kūkai or Kōbō Daishi. He was ordained in 793 at the age of twenty and went to China in 804, where he studied the doctrines and rituals of esoteric Buddhism. He returned to Japan in 806 and established a temple on Mount Kōya. So popular did his teachings become that many of them were later combined with those of the Tendai school. He is frequently condemned by Nichiren.

Komatsubara Persecution: An attempt by Tōjō Kagenobu, the steward of Tōjō village in Awa and a follower of Pure Land Buddhism, to assassinate Nichiren on the eleventh day of the eleventh month, 1264. Nichiren had returned to his native village to visit his mother who was seriously ill. En route to pay a call at the home of a follower, Kudō Yoshitaka, Nichiren and his party were attacked by Tōjō and his men. Nichiren escaped with a cut to his forehead and a broken hand; however, two members of his party lost their lives in the incident.

Kōsen-rufu: Literally, "To widely declare and spread [Buddhism]." The expression *kōsen-rufu* appears in the *Yakuō* (23d) chapter of the Lotus Sutra. Nichiren indicates that Nam-myoho-renge-kyo is the Law to be declared and spread widely during the Latter Day of the Law.

Kumārajīva (344–413): (Jap: Kumarajū) Famed translator of numerous Buddhist scriptures into Chinese during the Eastern Ch'in dynasty. Son of a Brahman father and a Kuchean princess, he entered the Buddhist order at the age of seven. He studied widely in all fields of Indian literature and was fully ordained at age twenty. He spent twenty years in Kucha where he studied Mahayana literature extensively. In 379 he was invited to China, but the Chinese general who had been sent to Kucha, a fervent anti-Buddhist, kept him in Kucha for seventeen years. Eventually he was able to make his way to Ch'ang-an where he and his colleagues established a translation center that produced a large number of important translations in excellent literary Chinese. Prominent among the works was the translation of the Lotus Sutra, *Myōhō Renge Kyō*.

Kusha sect: (Chin Chü-she tsung) A school based on Vasubandhu's *Abidatsuma Kusha Ron*, which was translated into Chinese by both Paramārtha and Hsüan-tsang. It flourished briefly in China during the T'ang, but later was absorbed by the Hossō (Fa-hsiang) school. It was introduced to Japan during the Nara period, when its doctrines were widely studied.

Latter Day of the Law: (Jap: *mappō*) The period beginning two thousand years after Shakyamuni's death, when his teachings lose their power. One theory holds that it lasts ten thousand years and more. Japanese Buddhists in Nichiren's day believed that the Latter Day had begun in A.D. 1052.

Mahākāśyapa: (Jap: Makakashō) One of Shakyamuni's ten major disciples. He was known as the foremost in ascetic practices. After Shakyamuni's death he presided over the First Buddhist Council for compiling the Buddha's teachings. He is counted as the first of Shakyamuni's twenty-four successors.

Major world system: (Jap: *sanzen daisen sekai*) One of the world systems in ancient Indian and Buddhist cosmology. A world consists of a Mount Sumeru, its surrounding seas and mountain ranges, a sun, a moon, and other heavenly bodies, extending upward to the first meditation heaven in the world of form and downward to the circle of wind that forms the foundation of a world. One thousand worlds make a minor world system, one thousand minor world systems comprise an intermediate world system, and one thousand intermediate world systems form a major world system. The universe was conceived of as containing countless major world systems.

Maka Shikan: "Great Concentration and Insight," one of T'ien-tai's three major works, compiled by his disciple Chang-an (*q.v.*). It elucidates, among other things, the principle of *ichinen sanzen*, based on the Lotus Sutra.

Mappō, *see* Latter Day of the Law; Three Periods.

Matsubagayatsu Persecution: An attack on Nichiren's home at Matsubagayatsu in Kamakura on the twenty-seventh day of the eighth month, 1260, by a mob of Pure Land believers, angered at Nichiren's attacks on Hōnen and his school. Several hundred Pure Land followers attacked Nichiren's home, but he managed to escape to Toki Jōnin's home in Shimōsa, where he stayed for a few months, returning to Kamakura the following spring .

Maudgalyāyana: (Jap: Mokuren) One of Shakyamuni's ten major disciples, known as the foremost in occult powers. Originally a student of Brahmanism, he is said to have become disenchanted with its teachings and to have turned eventually to Buddhism. The *Juki* (6th) chapter of the Lotus Sutra predicts his enlightenment.

Men of incorrigible disbelief, *see* Icchantika.

Miao-lo (711–782): (Jap: Myōraku) Also known as Chan-jan (Jap: Tannen). The sixth patriarch of the T'ien-t'ai school, counting from T'ien-t'ai. He is revered as the restorer of the school and wrote commentaries on T'ien-t'ai's major works, contributing to a clarification of the teaching. His principal works are: *Hokke Gengi Shakusen* (T33, no. 1717), *Hokke Mongu Ki* (T34, no. 1719), and *Maka Shikan Bugyōden Guketsu* (T46, no. 1912).

Middle Day of the Law: (Jap: *zōhō* or *zōbō*) The second thousand years after Shakyamuni's death. During this period Mahayana Buddhism spread from India to China, but the teachings gradually became formalized. Also referred to as the Period of the Simulated Law). *See also* Three periods.

Miroku: (Skt: Maitreya) A bodhisattva predicted to succeed Shakyamuni as a future Buddha. He is said to have been reborn in the Tuṣita heaven, where he is now expounding the law to the heavenly beings. It is said that he will reappear in this world 5,670 million years after the Buddha's death in order to save people. In the Lotus Sutra his persistent questions induced Shakyamuni to expound the *Juryō* (16th) chapter.

Monju: (Skt: Mañjuśrī) Also Monjushiri. Leader of the bodhisattvas of the theoretical teaching (*shakumon*). He represents wisdom and enlightenment, and with Fugen is depicted as one of the two bodhisattvas who attend Shakyamuni Buddha.

Monjushiri, *see* Monju.

Muhengyō, *see* Bodhisattvas of the Earth.

Muryōgi Sutra: "Sutra of Infinite Meaning." Serves as an introductory teaching to the Lotus Sutra and is thought of as indicating that the true teaching will be revealed in the Lotus Sutra. In this sutra Shakyamuni states that for the past more than forty years he has not yet revealed the complete truth. This is taken to mean that all the sutras preached before the Lotus Sutra represent provisional teachings.

Mutual possession of the Ten Worlds: (Jap: *jikkai gogu*) The principal that each of the Ten Worlds contains all the other ten within itself. This is taken to mean that an individual's life-condition can be changed and that all beings of the other nine worlds possess the potential for Buddhahood. *See also Ichinen sanzen;* Ten Worlds.

Myōhō-renge-kyō: (1) Japanese reading of the title of the Chinese translation of the Lotus Sutra, made by Kumārajīva in 406, consisting of eight volumes or rolls and twenty eight chapters. (2) Conceived of in terms of Nam-myoho-renge-kyo, the "entity of the Mystic Law itself."

Nāgārjuna: (Jap: Ryūju) A Mahayana scholar in southern India around the second or third century. He is counted as the fourteenth of Shakyamuni's twenty-four successors. He is the author of many important treatises on Mahayana Buddhism, such as the *Chū Ron* and the *Daichido Ron.*

Nam-myoho-renge-kyo: Regarded as the ultimate Law or absolute reality permeating all phenomena in the universe. It is also the invocation or *daimoku* in Nichiren Buddhism, one of the Three Great Secret Laws (*q.v.*). See also Myōhō-renge-kyō. (Diacritical marks are omitted and the "u" in "namu" elided to indicate the manner in which the phrase is intoned.)

Nanjō Tokimitsu (1259–1332): Also known as Lord Ueno, he was the son of Nanjō Hyōe Shichirō (d.1265), a retainer of the Hōjō clan, who had originally governed Nanjō village in Izu, and later moved to Ueno. Tokimitsu became steward of Ueno while still in his teens and was a devoted follower of Nichiren's disciple Nikkō Shonin. Tokimitsu worked to protect Nichiren's followers during the Atsuhara Persecution and he and his family, which included thirteen children, were subjected to grinding poverty because of the heavy taxation exacted from them. Nanjō received some thirty letters from Nichiren. He was one of the most loyal of followers and donated to Nikkō Shonin the land on which the temple Taiseki-ji now stands.

Nan-yüeh (515–577): (Jap: Nangaku) Known also as Hui-ssu (Jap: Eshi). T'ien-t'ai's teacher. He entered the priesthood at the age of fifteen and concentrated on the study of the Lotus Sutra. His entire life was devoted to the practice of the Lotus Sutra and the training of disciples.

Nembutsu: The calling of the Buddha's name, in particular that of the Buddha Amida. Nembutsu is practiced by the Jōdo or Pure Land sect. It was advocated by Shan-tao (613–681) (Jap: Zendō) in China, whose teachings were embraced by Hōnen (*q.v.*), the founder of the school in Japan. The term is also used to refer to the sect itself.

Nine great persecutions: (Jap: *Kuō no dainan*). Also known as the nine great ordeals. The major hardships that Shakyamuni underwent. They are listed in the *Daichido Ron* and are frequently mentioned by Nichiren.

Perfect teaching: (Jap: *engyō*). The last of the four teachings of doctrine as classified by T'ien-t'ai. The term "perfect teaching" is often used synonymously with the Lotus Sutra. *See also* Eight teachings.

Pratyekabuddha, *see Engkaku.*

Provisional teachings: (Jap: *gonkyō*) All the pre-Lotus teachings. T'ien-t'ai divided Shakyamuni's teaching into two categories: provisional and true. The provisional teachings, which include Hinayana and provisional Mahayana, were expounded during the first forty-two years after Shakyamuni's enlightenment. He taught these doctrines according to the capacity of his listeners as a temporary means to lead them to an understanding of the true teaching. The true teaching, T'ien-t'ai held, was that of the Lotus Sutra.

Pu-k'ung (705–774): (Jap: Fukū; Skt: Amoghavajra) The last of the three famous Indian esoteric masters to come to China from India during the T'ang dynasty. He arrived in China in 720 and became a disciple of Chin-kang-chih (Jap: Kongōchi; Skt: Vajrabodhi) and assisted in the translation of Shingon, or esoteric texts.

Pūrṇa: (Jap: Furuna). One of Shakyamuni's ten major disciples; he was noted as the foremost in eloquence. Born to a rich Brahman family, he is said to have practiced austerities in the Himalaya. Hearing that Shakyamuni had attained enlightenment, he became the Buddha's disciple.

Rāhula: (Jap: Ragora) Shakyamuni's son. Rāhula followed his father in renouncing the world and became one of the Buddha's ten major disciples. He was known as the "foremost in inconspicuous practice."

Ritsu sect (Chin: Lü-tsung) A Buddhist sect based on the *vinaya* or rules of monastic discipline. In China it was divided into several schools. Representative is the Nan-shan (Jap: Nanzan) school founded by Tao-hsüan (596–667) (Jap: Dōsen) that advocated a strict adherence to the precepts. In 753 Ganjin (Chin Chien-chen, 688–763) introduced the teaching to Japan. In the Kamakura period a sect that combined esoteric doctrines with a strict observance of the precepts was established; it is known as Shingon-Ritsu.

Ryōkan (1217–1303): A prominent priest of the Shingon-Ritsu sect who entered the priesthood at seventeen and received the precepts from Eizon (1202–1290), considered the restorer of the Ritsu sect. In 1261 he went to Kamakura where he was named the chief priest of the Kōsen-ji, founded by a Hōjō regent. Later he was named chief priest of the Gokuraku-ji, founded by Hōjō Shigetoki. Nichiren considered him an archenemy and writes disparagingly of his talents.

Sanron sect: (Chin: San-lun tsung) A Mādhyamika school based on the three treatises *Chū Ron*, *Jūnimon Ron*, and *Hyaku Ron*, it was systematized by Chi-tsang (Jap: Kichizō), who is often regarded as the founder of the school. There were several transmissions to Japan in the seventh century, but Ekan (Kor: Hwekwan) is generally considered the founder in Japan.

Śāriputra: (Jap: Sharihotsu) One of Shakyamuni's ten major disciples, known as the foremost in wisdom. The *Hiyu* (3d) chapter of the Lotus Sutra predicts that he will in the future become a Buddha named Kekō, Flower Light.

Shakubuku: Propagating Buddhism by refuting a person's attachment to other views and leading him to the correct teaching. The term is found in the *Maka Shikan*. It is contrasted with *shōju*, gradual propagation without refuting attachments. *See also Shōju.*

Shan-wu-wei (637–735): (Jap: Zemmui; Skt: Śubhākarasiṁha) Born as a prince in Udyāna, India, he was the first to introduce the esoteric teachings during the T'ang dynasty. He studied the esoteric teachings under Dharma-gupta at the Nālandā monastery. Arriving in China in 716, he engaged in the translation of numerous sutras, including the *Dainichi* and *Soshitsuji* sutras.

Shijō Kingo (c.1230–1300): A samurai who was a loyal follower of Nichiren. His full name was Shijō Nakatsukasa Saburō Zaemon-no-jō. Kingo served the Ema family, a branch of the Hōjō clan. Well-versed in both medicine and the martial arts, he is said to have converted to Nichiren's teachings around 1256. When Nichiren was in exile in Sado he sent messengers with various supplies and visited him there on two occasions. Shijō Kingo attended on Nichiren when he became ill, and participated in the funeral procession on Nichiren's death.

Shingon sect: (Chin: Chen-yen tsung) The school that taught the esoteric doctrines. Although esoteric texts had been brought to China at an early period, it was not until the T'ang dynasty that three famous Indian masters, Śubhākarasiṃha, Vajrabodhi, and Amoghavajra, introduced and translated the major sutras of the school. The school flourished briefly in China, but was of much greater importance in Japan. Here it was introduced by Kūkai, Kōbō Daishi, who went to Ch'ang-an in 804 and studied under Hui-kuo, a disciple of Amoghavajra. He established the Shingon sect on his return, building a temple complex on Mount Kōya. Many Shingon teachings were adopted by the Tendai sect. Nichiren condemns the Tendai priests who succeeded Dengyō Daishi for having subverted the original Tendai teachings by adding esoteric doctrines.

Shōbō, *see* Former Day of the Law; Three Periods.

Shōju: Propagating Buddhism by gradually leading a person without refuting his attachment to other teachings. The term is used in contrast to *shakubuku*. *See also Shakubuku.*

Shōmon: (Skt: *śrāvaka*) One who listens to the Buddha's teaching, and thereby gains enlightenment. The highest stage of the *shōmon* is an arhat. Sometimes translated as Man of Learning. *Shōmon* occupy the seventh of the Ten Worlds. *See also* Ten Worlds.

Six difficult and nine easy acts: (Jap: *rokunan kui*) Comparisons set forth in the *Hōtō* (11th) chapter of the Lotus Sutra. The six difficult acts are to propagate the Lotus Sutra widely, to copy it, to recite it, to teach it to even one person, to hear of the Lotus Sutra and inquire about its meaning, and to maintin faith in it. The nine easy acts are: (1) to teach innumerable sutras other than the Lotus Sutra, (2) to take up Mount Sumeru and hurl it across the universe over countless Buddha lands, (3) to kick a major world system into another quarter with one's toe, (4) to stand in the highest heaven and preach innumerable sutras other than the Lotus Sutra, (5) to grasp the sky with one hand and travel around with it, (6) to place the earth on one's toenail and ascend to Brahma heaven, (7) to walk across a burning prairie carrying a bundle of hay on one's back without being burned, (8) to preach eighty-four thousand teachings and enable one's listeners to obtain the six supernatural powers, and (9) to enable innumerable people to reach the stage of arhat and acquire the six supernatural powers.

Six non-Buddhist teachers: (Jap: *rokushi gedō*) The six most influential thinkers in central India at the time of Shakyamuni. They openly challenged the old Vedic traditions and advocated philosophical and religious concepts of their own. They are given as: (1) Purāṇa-kāśyapa, who rejected morality and denied causality and rewards and punishment for one's acts; (2) Maskari-gośāliputra, who asserted that everything was predetermined by fate; (3) Ajita-keśakambala, known as a hedonist who claimed that since the whole universe was composed of the four elements, earth, water, fire, and metal, this was true also of the human body, and therefore there was no recompense for the good or evil a man practiced; (4) Sañjaya-vairāṭīputra, a skeptic who rejected all explanations of metaphysical questions; (5) Kakuda-kātyāyana, who denied the laws of causality; and (6) Nirgranthajñātiputra, the founder of Jainism, who championed ascetic practices.

Six *pāramitā*: (Jap: *rokuharamitsu*) Six practices for Mahayana bodhisattvas in their progress toward Buddhahood: charity, observing precepts, forbearance, assiduousness, meditation, and wisdom.

Six paths: (Jap: *rokudō*) The first six of the Ten Worlds, the realms of transmigration. They are: Hell, Hungry Ghosts, Animals, Asura, Humanity, and Heaven. *See also* Ten Worlds.

Specific teaching: (Jap: *bekkyō*), *see* Eight teachings.

Subhūti: (Jap: Shubodai) One of Shakyamuni's ten major disciples. He was regarded as foremost in the understanding of the doctrine of Emptiness.

Sumeru: (Jap: Shumi-sen) In Indian and Buddhist cosmology, the mountain that stands in the center of a world system. It is 84,000 *yojana* high; the god Taishaku resides on the summit, while the Four Heavenly Kings live halfway down, one to each of its four sides. In the seas below are four continents, the one to the south being Jambudvīpa, the land where Buddhism spreads, that is, the present world.

Sun Goddess: (Jap: Amaterasu Ōmikami or Tenshō Daijin) The chief female deity in Shinto. Nichiren regarded her as a personification of the natural forces that protect those with faith in the Lotus Sutra.

Tahō: (Skt: Prabhūtaratna) A Buddha who appears seated within the Treasure Tower at the Ceremony in the Air to lend credence to Shakyamuni's teachings in the Lotus Sutra. According to the *Hōtō* (11th) chapter of the Lotus Sutra, he lives in the land of Treasure Purity in an eastern part of the universe. While still engaged in bodhisattva practice he pledged that, even after having entered nirvana, he would appear to attest to the validity of the Lotus Sutra, wherever it might be taught.

Taishaku: (Skt: Śakra devendra) Generally known as Indra, he is the god of the Trāyastrimśa Heaven (Jap: Tōriten). Originally a Hindu god, he together with Bonten are the principal tutelary gods who protect Buddhism. He is served by the Four Heavenly Kings and rules the other thirty-two gods in his heaven at the top of Mount Sumeru. According to the *Jo* (1st) chapter of the Lotus Sutra, he and twenty thousand retainers, took part in the assembly at Eagle Peak.

Tao-hsüan (596–667): (Jap: Dōsen) The founder of the Nan-shan (Nanzan) branch of the Lü (Ritsu) school that emphasized the Vinaya, or monastic rules. From 645 he assisted Hsüan-tsang in his translation work. He compiled several books, including the *Zoku Kōsō Den*, containing the biographies of five hundred eminent priests who lived between 502 and 645.

Tendai sect: (Chin: T'ien-t'ai tsung) The school was established by Chih-i (538–597) (Jap: Chigi), most frequently referred to by Nichiren by his posthumous name T'ien-t'ai ta-shih (Tendai Daishi, or the Great Teacher Tendai). The school flourished during the Sui dynasty, fell into decline during the T'ang, although it was revived somewhat by Miao-lo (Myōraku), known also as Chan-jan (Tannen). Its texts were introduced to Japan in the Nara period, but the sect was established in Japan by Saichō (Dengyō Daishi), who founded the Tendai center on Mount Hiei.

Ten demon daughters, *see* Ten Goddesses.

Ten directions: (Jap: *jippō*) The eight points of the compass as well as up and down.

Ten factors: (Jap: *jūnyoze*) Also referred to as the ten suchnesses, they are the aspects common to all existence in any of the ten worlds . They are mentioned in the *Hōben* (2d) chapter of the Lotus Sutra. They are; (1) appearance or form (*nyozesō*), (2) nature or quality (*nyozeshō*), (3) substance or entity (*nyozetai*), (4) power (*nyozeriki*), (5) activity or influence (*nyozesa*), (6) cause (*nyozein*), (7) indirect cause or relation (*nyozeen*), (8) effect (*nyozeka*), (9) reward or retribution (*nyozehō*) and (10) the unifying factor that makes the above nine consistent from outset to end (*nyoze hommatsu kukyōtō*). *See also* Ichinen sanzen.

Ten Goddesses: (Jap: Jūrasetsu-nyo) The ten daughters of Kishimojin (Skt: Hāritī), described in the *Darani* (26th) chapter of the Lotus Sutra. The mother and daughters vow to protect the votaries of the Lotus Sutra. They are known also as demon daughters (rākṣasī).

Tenshō Daijin, *see* Sun Goddess.

Ten Worlds (Jap: *jikkai*) The standard interpretation of the Ten Worlds is as physical places, each with its own inhabitants: (1) Hell (*jigoku*), (2) Hungry Ghosts (*gaki*), (3) Animals (*chikushō*), (4) Asura or Fighting demons (*asura*), (5) Humanity (*nin*), (6) Heaven (*ten*), (7) *Shōmon, śrāvaka*, one who practices the four noble truths to gain Nirvana, (8) *Engaku, pratyekabuddha*, one who gains enlightenment for himself, (9) Bodhisattva, and (10) Buddha. The Ten Worlds are also sometimes interpreted as potential conditions of life, inherent in each individual. Thus, the Ten Worlds are rendered as: (1) Hell, (2) Hunger, (3) Animality, (4) Anger, (5) Humanity or Tranquility, (6) Heaven or Rapture, (7) Learning, (8) Realization, (9) Bodhisattva, and (10) Buddhahood.

Theoretical teaching: (Jap: *shakumon*) The first fourteen chapters of the Lotus Sutra as classified by T'ien-t'ai in his *Hokke Mongu*. This portion of the sutra represents the preaching of the historical Shakyamuni who first attained enlightenment during his lifetime in India. The last fourteen chapters of the sutra are classified as the essential teaching (*hommon*). *See also* Essential teaching.

Three bodies: (*sanshin* or *sanjin*) Also called the three properties: (1) Law or Dharma body (Jap: *hosshin*; Skt: *dharmakāya*), the body of ultimate reality; (2)

the reward or bliss body (Jap: *hōjin* or *hōshin*; Skt: *sambhogakāya*), the Buddha body received for meritorious actions; and (3) the manifested body (Jap: *ōjin*; Skt: *nirmāṇakāya*), the body in which a Buddha appears to correspond to the needs and capacities of sentient beings.

Three calamities and seven disasters: (Jap: *sansai shichinan*) Calamities and disasters as described in the sutras. There are two kinds of the three calamities: the three greater calamities of fire, water, and wind that destroy a world at the end of the Kalpa of Decline, and the three lesser calamities of high grain prices or inflation (especially that caused by famine), warfare, and pestilence. The seven disasters differ with the sutra. The *Yakushi* Sutra lists them as: pestilence, foreign invasion, internal strife, unnatural changes in the heavens, solar and lunar eclipses, unseasonable storms and typhoons, and drought.

Three evil paths: (Jap: *sanakudō*) The three lowest of the Ten Worlds: Hell, Hungry Ghosts, and Animals. *See* Ten Worlds.

Three existences: (Jap: *sanze*) Also referred to as the three periods of time: past, present, and future.

Threefold world: (Jap: *sangai*) The world of unenlightened beings who transmigrate among the six paths or the first six of the Ten Worlds. The *Kusha Ron* divides this world into three: (1) the world of desire (Jap: *yokkai*), which consists of Hell, the realms of Hungry Ghosts, Animals, Asura, Humanity, and parts of Heaven; here the beings have sexual and other appetites; (2) the world of form (Jap: *shikikai*), which comprises part of Heaven; here the beings have neither sexual nor any other kind of appetite; (3) the world of nonform (Jap: *mushikikai*), also part of Heaven, where the beings are free both from desires and material elements and devote themselves to different states of meditation.

Three Great Secret Laws: (Jap: *sandai hihō*) One of the most important elements of Nichiren's teaching. The Three Great Secret Laws are the *honzon*, the sacred object of worship; the *daimoku*, the title of the Lotus Sutra itself; and the *kaidan*, the ordination platform. These three Laws are qualified by *hommon no*, indicating that they represent the essential teaching. The object of worship (*honzon*) is the Gohonzon or the eternal Buddha of the *Juryō* (16th) chapter; the *daimoku*, the title of the sutra itself as well as its invocation; and the *kaidan* is the ordination platform, although this latter term was not precisely defined by Nichiren and various interpretations of its meaning have been forwarded.

Three groups of *shōmon* disciples: (Jap: *sanshū no shōmon*). The *shōmon* whose enlightenment was prophesied in the first half of the Lotus Sutra. Shakyamuni taught that the ultimate purpose was to obtain Buddhahood rather than some lower state, but his disciples differed in their capacity to understand this teaching. Śāriputra was the first to understand, on hearing it explained in the *Hōben* (2d) chapter. He represents the first group and his enlightenment is predicted in the *Hiyu* (3d) chapter. Maudgalyāyana, Mahākāśyapa, Kātyāyana, and Subhūti through the parable of the burning house in the *Hiyu* chapter; these disciples form the second group and their enlightenment is predicted in the *Juki* (6th) chapter. Pūrṇa, Ānanda, Rāhula, and others, who finally understood the Buddha's teaching by hearing about their past relationship with Shakyamuni since the remote past of *sanzen-jin-tengō*, as explained in the *Kejōyu* (7th) chapter, comprise the third group. Their future enlightenment is predicted in the next two chapters.

Three illusions: (Jap: *sanwaku*) Also called the three categories of illusion. Classification of illusions established by T'ien-t'ai in the *Maka Shikan*: (1) illusions of thought and desire (Jap: *kenshi waku*), (2) illusions as numerous as particles of dust and sand (Jap: *jinja waku*), (3) illusions of basic ignorance (Jap: *mumyō waku*).

Three obstacles and four devils: (Jap: *sanshō shima*) Various obstacles to the practice of Buddhism. They are listed in the Nirvana Sutra and the *Daichido Ron*. The three obstacles are: (1) *bonnō-shō*, obstacles arising from the three poisons, greed, anger, and stupidity; (2) *gō-shō*, obstacles due to bad karma created by committing the five cardinal sins or the ten evil acts. They may also refer to opposition from one's spouse or children; (3) *hō-shō*, obstacles caused by retribution for actions in the three evil paths. It also may refer to obstacles caused by one's superiors, such as rulers or parents. The four devils are: (1) *bonnō-ma*, obstructions arising from the three poisons; (2) *on-ma*, the hindrance of the five components or aggregates (*go'on* or *goun*; Skt: *skandhas*): form, perception, conception, volition, and consciousness; (3) *shi-ma*, the hindrance of death, because fear of death impedes the practice of Buddhism; (4) *tenji-ma*, obstruction by the Devil of the Sixth Heaven, which usually manifests itself in oppression by men of power. This is the most difficult of all to overcome.

Three periods: (Jap: *sanji*) The three periods or stages into which the time following Shakyamuni Buddhas death is divided. These are conventionally described as *shōbō*, the age when the true law was propagated, *zōhō*, or *zōbō*, the age when the simulated law obtained, and *mappō*, the degenerate age when Buddhism fell into confusion. *The Major Writings of Nichiren Daishonin* renders these terms as the Former, Middle, and Latter Day of the Law, and this terminology has been followed here. The duration of each period differs with the text. Nichiren adopted the view that the Former and Middle Day of the Law each lasted one thousand years, and that the world had now entered the period of the Latter Day of the Law. It was generally believed that the year 1052 marked the beginning of the Latter Day of the Law.

Three poisons: (Jap: *sandoku*) Greed, anger, and stupidity.

Three realms of existence: (Jap: *sanseken*) sometimes rendered: three categories of realm. T'ien-t'ai's elaboration of a concept that appeared originally in the *Daichido Ron*: (1) the realm of the five components or aggregates — form, perception, conception, volition, and consciousness (*go'on-seken*), (2) the realm of sentient beings (*shujō-seken*), and (3) the realm of the environment of sentient beings (*kokudo-seken*). See also *Ichinen sanzen*.

Three schools of the South and seven schools of the North: (Jap: *nansan hokushichi*) T'ien-t'ai's designation for the principal systems of comparative classification of the Buddhist sutras in vogue in China during the Northern and Southern dynasties period. These systems are outlined in his *Hokke*

Gengi. All three southern schools characterized the sutras under three categories: sudden, gradual, and indeterminate. The seven northern schools had each its own classification, but they all gave precedence to the Nirvana or the *Kegon* Sutra. T'ien-t'ai disputed their conclusions with his classification of the five periods.

Three thousand conditions: (Jap: *sanzen* or *sanzeno hō*) All phenomena in the universe. *See Ichinen sanzen.*

Three Treasures: (Jap: *sambō*) The Buddha, the Law, and the Priesthood.

Three truths: (Jap: *santai*) Three related aspects of truth, developed by T'ien-t'ai in the *Hokke Gengi* and the *Maka Shikan.* They are: the truth of nonsubstantiality (*kūtai*), the truth of temporary existence (*ketai*), and the truth of the Middle Way (*chūtai*), where all phenomena are both insubstantial and temporary but yet are basically neither.

Three types of learning: (Jap: *sangaku*) Precepts, meditation, and wisdom.

Three vehicles: (Jap: *sanjō*) the states and the teachings of *shōmon, engaku,* and bodhisattva. These states were originally encouraged by Shakyamuni, but were rejected in the Lotus Sutra, where the ultimate goal is Buddhahood.

Three virtues: (Jap: *santoku*) The virtues of sovereign, teacher, and parent that are possessed by the Buddha.

T'ien-t'ai (538–597): (Jap: Tendai) Another name for Chih-i (Chigi), the founder of the T'ien-t'ai school. Nichiren most frequently refers to him as T'ien-t'ai, or the Great Teacher T'ien-t'ai. He entered the priesthood at eighteen and studied the Lotus Sutra at Mount Ta-hsien. His teacher was Nan-yüeh Hui-ssu (Nangaku Eshi, 515–577). T'ien-t'ai was the great organizer of his school's doctrines. His principal works, the *Hokke Gengi,* the *Hokke Mongu,* and the *Maka Shikan* were all compiled and edited by his immediate disciple Chang-an (*q.v.*).

Toki Jōnin (1216–1299?): A lay follower of Nichiren, he served as a retainer to a certain Lord Chiba at Wakamiya in Shimōsa Province. In 1251 he became a lay priest, taking the name Jōnin, and in 1254 became a follower of Nichiren. Jōnin was highly educated and Nichiren entrusted him with a number of his more important works. Jōnin sheltered Nichiren after the attack at Matsubagayatsu and actively supported Nichiren's followers in Shimōsa while Nichiren was in exile on Sado Island.

Treasure Tower: (Jap: *hōtō*) The tower of Tahō Buddha that appears from beneath the earth in the *Hōtō* (llth) chapter of the Lotus Sutra.

Twenty-four successors: (Jap: *Fuhōzō no nijūyonin*) The successors of Shakyamuni. They are listed in the *Fu Hōzō Innen Den* (The History of the Buddha's Successors). They are (1) Mahākāśyapa, (2) Ānanda, (3) Madhyāntika (omitted in the *Fu Hōzō Innen Den,* but included in later Tendai works), (4) Śaṇavāsa, (5) Upagupta, (6) Dhṛtaka, (7) Miccaka, (8) Buddhanandi, (9) Buddhamitra, (10) Pārśva, (11) Puṇyayaśas, (12) Aśvaghosa, (13) Kapimala, (14) Nāgārjuna, (15) Kāṇadeva or Āryadeva, (16) Rāhulata, (17) Saṅghānandi, (18) Gayaśāta or Samghayaśas, (19) Kumārata, (20) Jayata, (21) Vasubandhu, (22) Manorhita, (23) Haklenavaśas. and (24) Āryasiṁha.

Two vehicles: (Jap: *nijō*) Teachings expounded for the *shōmon* and *engaku.* The term is also used in reference to the seventh and eighth of the Ten Worlds. The *Major Writings of Nichiren Daishonin* refers to them as Learning and Realization. *See also* Ten Worlds.

Tz'u-en (632–682): (Jap: Jion) The founder of the Chinese Fa-hsiang (Hossō) school. He is also known as K'uei-chi (Kiki). One of the outstanding disciples of Hsüan-tsang, he collaborated with him on the translation of many important texts, and wrote several commentaries on the Consciousness-Only doctrine.

Vasubandhu: (Jap: Tenjin or Seshin) A Buddhist scholar of northern India, thought to have lived around the fourth or fifth century. He originally studied Hinayana and wrote the *Kusha Ron*. He is later said to have been converted to Mahayana by his elder brother Asanga and wrote numerous treatises designed to clarify the Mahayana teachings.

Votary of the Lotus Sutra: (Jap: *Hokekyō no gyōja*) One who propagates the Lotus Sutra and practices Buddhism in accordance with its teachings. Nichiren considered T'ien-t'ai and Dengyō votaries, and was convinced that he himself fulfilled the sutra's prophecies and served as its votary.

Wise Kalpa: (Jap: *kengō*) The present major kalpa in which a thousand Buddhas of great wisdom, including Shakyamuni, will appear in order to save people.

Yakuō: (Skt: Bhaiṣajyarāja) A bodhisattva said to possess the power to cure all physical and mental diseases.

Yakushi: (Skt: Bhaiṣajyaguru) The Healing Buddha or the Buddha of Medicine who dwells in the Pure Emerald World in the east. As a bodhisattva he made twelve vows to cure all illnesses and to lead all people to enlightenment.

BIBLIOGRAPHY

BUDDHIST WORKS CITED BY NICHIREN

Ahidatsuma Daihibasha Ron 阿毘達磨大毘婆沙論. T27, no. 1545.

Abidatsuma Kusha Ron. See *Kusha Ron.*

Abidatsuma Shūimonsoku Ron 阿毘達磨集異門足論. T26, no. 1536.

Agon Kyō 阿含經 Āgama Sutras. T1–2, nos. 1–151.

Aikuō Den 阿育王伝. T50, no. 2042.

Aikuō Kyō 阿育王經. T50, no. 2043.

Amida Kyō 阿彌陀經. T12, no. 366.

Anraku-shū 安樂集, by Tao-ch'o 道綽 (Dōshaku). T47, no. 1958.

Basubanzu Hosshi Den 婆藪槃豆法師伝. T50, no. 2049.

Ben Kemmitsu Nikyō Ron 弁顯密二教論, by Kūkai (Kōbō Daishi) 空海 (弘法大師).
T77, no. 2427. Also called: *Nikyō Ron.*

Binaya Zōji 毘奈耶雜事. T24, no, 1451. Full title: *Kompon Setsu Issai Ubu Binaya Zōji*
根本説一切有部毘奈耶雜事.

Bodaishin Ron 菩提心論. T32, no. 1665.

Bodai Shiryō Ron 菩提資糧論. T32, no. 1660.

Bommō Kyō 梵綱經. T24, no. 1484.

Bommō Kyō Koshakki 梵綱經古迹記. T40, no. 1815.

Bosatsu Honjō Manron 菩薩本生鬘論. T3, no. 160.

Bosatsu Yōraku Hongō Kyō 菩薩瓔珞本業經. T24, no. 1485.

Bosatsu Zenkai Kyō 菩薩善戒經. T30, no. 1583.

Bussetsu Ōkutsuma Kyō 仏説鴦崛摩經. T2, no. 118.

Busso Tōki 仏祖統紀. T49, no. 2035.

Butsujikyō Ron 仏地經論. T26, no. 1530.

Butsuzō Kyō 仏藏經. T15, no. 653.

Chōshōō Koji Kyō 頂生王故事經. T1, no. 39.

Chū Ron 中論. T30, no. 1564.

Chūhen Gikyō 中辺義鏡, by Tokuitsu (Tokuichi) 德一. Original is lost but significant
portions are cited in the *Shugo Kokkai Shō.*

Daibibasha Ron. See *Abidatsuma Daibibasha Ron.*

Dai Biku Sanzen Igi 大比丘三千威儀. T24, no. 1470.

Dai Birushana Kyō Kuyō Shidaihō Sho 大毘盧遮那經供養次第法疏. T39, no. 1797.

Daibon Hannya Kyō 大品般若經. T8, no. 223. Also known as *Maka Hannya Haramitsu*
Kyō 摩訶般若波羅蜜經.

Daichido Ron 大智度論. T25, no. 1509.

Dai Hannya Haramitta Kyō 大般若波羅蜜多經. T5–7, no. 220.

Daihatsu Nehan Gyō. See *Nehan Gyō.*

Daihi Kyō 大悲經. T12, no. 380.

Dai Hōshakkyō 大寶積經. T11, no. 310.

Daijikkyō 大集經. See *Daijuku Kyō.*

Daijō Kishin Ron 大乘起信論. T32, no. 1666, 1667.

Daijō Rishu Rokuharamitta Kyō 大乘理趣六波羅蜜多經. T9, no. 261. Also known as *Rokuharamitta Kyō.*

Daijō Shikan Hōmon 大乘止觀法門, by Hui-ssu 慧思 (Eshi). T46, no. 1924.

Daijuku Kyō 大集經. T13, no. 397, Also read: *Daijikkyō and Daishutsu Kyō.*

Dainichi Kyō 大日經. T18, no. 848. Full title: *Dai-Birushana Jōbutsu Jimben Kaji Kyō* 大毘盧遮那成仏神變加持經.

Dainichi Kyō Sho 大日經疏, by I-hsing 一行 (Ichigyō). T39, no. 1796.

Dairon. See *Daichido Ron.*

Daishutsu Kyō. See *Daijuku Kyō.*

Daitō Daijion-ji Sanzō Hosshi Den 大唐大慈恩寺三藏法師伝. T50, no. 2053.

Daitō Saiiki Ki 大唐西域記, by Hsüan-tsang 玄奘 (Genjō). T51, no. 2087.

Dentō Roku. See *Keitoku Dentō Roku.*

Eizan Daishi Den 叡山大師伝. DDZ 5, 1–48 at end.

Fu Hōzō Innen Den 付法藏因緣伝. T50, no. 2058. Also called *Fu Hōzō Kyō.*

Fushō Ki. See *Hokke Mongu Fushō Ki.*

Futsū Ju Bosatsukai Kōshaku 普通授菩薩戒廣釈, by Annen 安然. T74, no. 2381.

Gejimmikkyō 解深密經. T16, no. 676. Also called *Jimmitsu Kyō.*

Genkō Shakusho 元亨釈書. DNBZ 101.

Gensōchō Hongyō Sanzō Zemmui Zō Kōro-kyō Gyōjō 玄宗朝翻經三藏善無畏贈鴻臚卿行狀, by Li Hua 李華 (Ri Ke). T50, no. 2055.

Gobunritsu 五分律. T22, no. 1421. Full title: *Mishasokubu Wake Gobunritsu* 彌沙塞部和醯五分律.

Gonjikinyo Kyō 銀色女經. T3, no. 179.

Guketsu. See *Maka Shikan Bugyōden Guketsu.*

Hannya Shingyō 般若心經. T8, no. 251.

Hatsunaion Kyō 般泥洹經. T1. no. 6.

Himitsu Shōgon Ron 秘密莊嚴論 by Saichō (Dengyō Daishi) 最澄 (伝教大師). This work is no longer extant.

Hizō Hōyaku, 秘藏寶鑰 by Kūkai (Kōbō Daishi) 空海 (弘法大師). T77, no. 2426.

Hōbutsu Shū 寶物集. DNBZ 147.

Hoke Kyō Mongu Fushō Ki. See *Hokke Mongu Fushō Ki.*

Hoke Kyō Shogisan 法華經疏義纘. ZZ1, 45, 3. Also known as *Tōshun* 東春 and *Hokke Mongu Tōshun.*

Hokke Denki 法華伝記. T51, no. 2068.

Hokke Gengi 法華玄義, by Chih-i (T'ien-t'ai Ta-shih) 智顗 (天台大師) Chigi (Tendai Daishi). T33, no. 1716. Full title: *Myōhō Renge Kyō Gengi*

Hokke Gengi Shakusen 法華玄義釈籤, by Chan-jan (Miao-lo) 湛然 (妙樂) Tannen (Myōraku). T33, no. 1717.

Hokke Gengi Shiki 法華玄義私記, by Shōshin 証真. DNBZ 21, 1–382.

Hokke Genzan 法華玄賛, by K'uei-chi (Tz'u-en) 窺基 (慈恩) Kiki (Jion). T34, no. 1721. Also called *Myōhō Renge Kyō Genzan.*

Hokke Mongu 法華文句, by Chih-i (T'ien-t'ai) 智顗 (天台大師) Chigi (Tendai Daishi). T34, no. 1718. Full title: *Myōhō Renge Kyō Mongu*

Hokke Mongu Fushō Ki 法華文句輔正記, by Tao-hsien 道暹 Dōsen. ZZ1, 45, 1. Also known as *Hoke Kyō Mongu Fushō Ki*

Hokke Mongu Ki 法華文句記, by Chan-jan (Miao-lo) 湛然 (妙樂). Tannen (Myōraku). T34, no. 1719.

Hokke Mongu Tōshun. See *Hoke Kyō Shogisan.*

Hokke Sandaibu Fuchū 法華三大部補註, by Ts'ung-i 從義 Jūgi. ZZ1, 43, 5–44, 3.

Hokke Shūku 法華秀句, by Saichō (Dengyō Daishi) 最澄 (伝教大師). DDZ 3, 1–280.

Hokke Zammai Kyō 法華三昧經. T9, no. 269.

Hokku Hiyu Kyō 法句譬喻經. T4, no. 211.

Honchō Kōsō Den 本朝高僧伝. DNBZ 102–103.

Honyaku Myōgi Shū 翻釈名義集. T54, no. 2131.

Hōon Jurin 法苑珠林. T3, no. 2122.

Hōon Kyō 報恩經. T3, no. 156.

Hōshō Ron 寶性論. T31, no. 1611. Full title: *Kukyō Ichijō Hōshō Ron* 究竟一乘寶性論.

Hyaku Ron 百論. T30, no. 1569.

Ichijō Yōketsu 一乘要決, by Genshin 源信. T74, no. 2370.

Isshin Kaimon 一心戒文, by Kōjō 光定. T74, no. 2379.

Isshin Kongō Kaitai Hiketsu 一心金剛戒体秘決, by Saichō (Dengyō Daishi) 最澄 (伝教大師). DDZ 1, 449–496.

Jimmitsu Kyō. See *Gejimmikkyō.*

Jizō Jūō Kyō 地藏十王經 ZZ2B, 23, 4. Full title: *Jizō Bosatsu Hosshin Innen Jūō Kyō* 地藏菩薩發心因緣十王經.

Jion Den. See *Daitō Daijion-ji Sanzō Hosshi Den.*

Jōagon Gyō 長阿含經. T1, no. 1

Jōmyō Kyō 淨名經. See *Yuima Kyō.*

Jūjūbibasha Ron 十住毘婆沙論. T26, no. 1521.

Jūju Ritsu 十誦律. T23, no. 1435.

Jūjūshin Ron 十住心論, by Kūkai (Kōbō Daishi) 空海 (弘法大師).

Jūnimon Ron 十二門論. T30, no. 1568.

Kambutsu Zammai Kyō 觀仏三昧經. T15, no. 643.

Kammiroku Jōshō Tosotsuten Gyō San 觀彌勒上生兜率天經賛, by K'uei-chi (Tz'u-en) 窺基 (慈恩) Kiki (Jion). T38, no. 1772.

Kammuryōju Butsu Kyō Sho 觀無量壽仏經疏, by Chih-i (T'ien-t'ai) 智顗 (天台大師) Chigi (Tendai Daishi). T37, no. 1750.

Kammuryōju Butsu Kyō Sho 觀無量壽仏經疏, by Shan-tao 善導 Zendō. T37, no. 1753.

Kammuryōju Kyō 觀無量壽經. T12, no. 365.

Kanjin Ron Sho 觀心論疏, by Kuan-ting (Chang-an) 灌頂 (章安) Kanjō (Shōan). T46, no. 1921.

Kannen Amida Butsu Sōkai Zammai Kudoku Hōmon 觀念阿彌陀仏相海三昧功德法門, by Shan-tao 善導 Zendō. T47, no. 1959. Also known as: *Kannen Hōmon* 觀念法門.

Kannen Hōmon. See *Kannen Amida Butsu Sōkai Zammai Kudoku Hōmon.*

Kegon Gokyō Shō. See *Kegon Ichijō Kyōgi Bunzai Shō.*

Kegon Ichijō Jūgemmon 華嚴一乘十玄門, by Tu-shun 杜順 Tojun.

Kegon Ichijō Kyōgi Bunzai Shō 華嚴一乘教義分齊章, by Fa-tsang 法藏 Hōzō. T45, no. 1866. Also known as: *Kegon Gokyō Shō.*

Kegon Kyō 華嚴經. 1) old (60v.) T9, no. 278; 2) new (80v.) T10, no. 279.

Keitoku Dentō Roku 景德伝燈録. T51, no. 2076. Also known as: *Dentō Roku.*

Kengu Kyō 賢愚經. T4, no. 202.

Ken Hokke Gi Shō 顯法華義鈔, by Anne 安慧. No longer extant.

Kenkai Ron 顯戒論, by Saichō (Dengyō Daishi) 最澄 (伝教大師). T74, 2376; DDZ 1, 25–198.

Kōbō Daishi Goden 弘法大師御伝. *Zoku Gunsho Ruijū*, v.8, pt. 2, 526–562.

Kōkigyō Kyō 興起行經. T4, no. 197.

Kompon Setsu Issai Ubu Binaya 根本説一切有部毘奈耶. T23, no. 1442.

Kongōbei 金剛錍, by Chan-jan (Miao-lo) 湛然 (妙樂) Tannen (Myōraku). T46, no. 1932. Also known as *Kongōbei Ron* 金剛錍論.

Kongōbei Ron. See *Kongōbei*.

Kongōchō Kyō 金剛頂經. T18, no. 865.

Konkōmyō Kyō. See *Konkōmyō Saishōō Kyō*.

Konkōmyō Saishōō Kyō 金光明最勝王經. T16, no. 665. Also known as: *Konkōmyō Kyō*.

Kōsō Den 高僧伝. T50, no. 2059.

Kukyō Ichijō Hōshō Ron. See *Hōshō Ron*.

Kusha Ron 俱舍論. T29, no. 1558. Full title: *Abidatsuma Kusha Ron* 阿毘達磨俱舍論.

Kusha Ron Ki 俱舍論記. T41, no. 1821.

Lotus Sutra. See *Myōhō Renge Kyō*.

Maka Hannya Haramitsu Kyō 摩訶般若波羅蜜經. T8, no. 223. Also known as *Daibon Hannya Kyō*.

Maka Shikan 摩訶止觀, by Chih-i (T'ien-t'ai) 智顗 (天台大師) Chigi (Tendai Daishi). T46, no. 1911.

Maka Shikan Bugyōden Guketsu 摩訶止觀輔行伝弘決, by Chan-jan (Miao-lo) 湛然 (妙樂) Tannen (Myōraku). T46, no. 1912. Also known as *Shikan Bugyōden Guketsu* and *Guketsu*.

Maka Sōgi Ritsu 摩訶僧祇律. T22, no. 1425. Also known as: *Sōgi Ritsu*.

Maya Kyō 摩耶經. T12, no. 383.

Mizōu Innen Kyō 未曾有因緣經. T17, no. 754.

Mongu Ki. See *Hokke Mongu Ki*.

Monjushiri Hatsunehan Kyō 文殊師利般涅槃經. T14, no. 463.

Muryōgi Kyō 無量義經. T9, no. 216.

Muryōju Kyō 無量壽經. T12, no. 361.

Muryōju Kyō Gisho 無量壽經義疏, by Chi-tsang 吉藏 Kichizō. T37, no. 1746.

Myōhō Renge Kyō 妙法蓮華經. T9, no. 362. The Lotus Sutra.

Nehan Gyō 涅槃經. Full title: *Daihatsu Nehan Gyō*. T12, no. 374 (Northern 60v.); T12, no. 375 (Southern 80v.). The Nirvana Sutra.

Nehan Gyō Sho 涅槃經疏, by Kuan-ting (Chang-an) 灌頂 (章安) Kanjō (Shōan). T38, no. 1767.

Nikyō Ron. See *Ben Kemmitsu Nikyō Ron*.

Ninnō Kyō 仁王經. T8, no. 245.

Nirvana Sutra. See *Nehan Gyō*.

Ōjō Raisan 往生禮讚, by Shan-tao 善導 Zendō. T47, no. 1980.

Ōjō Yōshū 往生要集, by Genshin 源信. T80, no. 2682.

Ōkutsumara Kyō 央掘魔羅經. T2, no. 120.

Rengemen Gyō 蓮華面經. T12, no. 386.

Rokudo jikkyō 六度集經. T3, no. 152.

Rokuharamitta Kyō 六波羅蜜多經. T9, no. 261.

Saishōō Kyō. See *Konkōmyō Saishōō Kyō*.

Sangoku Denki 三國伝記. DNBZ 148, 183–506.

Sankō Sanzembutsu Engi 三劫三千仏緣起. T14, no. 446.

Senchaku Shū 選択集, by Hōnen 法然. T83, no. 2608. Full title: *Senchaku Hongan Nembutsu Shū* 選択本願念仏集.

Shakusen. See *Hokke Gengi Shakusen*.

Shakushi Keiko Ryaku 釈氏稽古略. T49, no. 2037.

Shibun Ritsu 四分律. T22, no. 1428.

Shibun Ritsu Biku Kaihon 四分律比丘戒本. T22, no. 1429.

Shibun Ritsu Gyōji Shō 四分律行事鈔, by Tao-hsüan 道宣 Dōsen. T40, no. 1804.

Shichibutsu Kyō 七仏經. T1, no. 2.

Shikan Bugyōden Guketsu. See *Maka Shikan Bugyōden Guketsu*.

Shi Nenjo 四念處, by Chih-i (T'ien-t'ai) 智顗 (天台大師) Chigi (Tendai Daishi). T46, no. 1918.

Shinji Kangyō 心地觀經. T3, no. 159.

Shōbō Nenjo Kyō 正法念處經. T17, no. 721.

Shō-hokke Kyō 正法華經. T9, no. 263.

Shohō Mugyō Kyō 諸法無行經. T15, no. 650.

Shōman Gyō 勝鬘經. T12, no. 353. *Śrīmālā Sutra*.

Shōtoku Taishi Den Shiki 聖德太子伝私記. DNBZ 112, 85–118.

Shugo Kokkai Shō 守護國界章, by Saichō (Dengyō Daishi) 最澄 (伝教大師). T84, no. 2362; DDZ 2, 151–681.

Shugo Kokkaishu Darani Kyō 守護國界主陀羅尼經. T19, no. 997.

Shuryōgon Gyō 首楞嚴經. T15, no. 642. Full title: *Shuryōgon Zammai Kyō*.

Sōgi Ritsu. See *Maka Sōgi Ritsu*.

Soshitsuji Kyō 蘇悉地經. T18, no. 893. Full title: *Soshitsuji Kara Kyō* 蘇悉地羯羅經.

Soshitsuji Kyō Ryakusho 蘇悉地經略疏, by Ennin (Jikaku Daishi) 円仁 (慈覺大師). T61, no. 2227.

Sō Kōsō Den 宋高僧伝. T50, no. 2061.

Śrīmālā Sutra. See *Shōman Gyō*.

Tembon Hoke Kyō 添品法華經. T9, no. 264. Full title: *Tembon Myōhō Renge Kyō*. 添品妙法蓮華經.

Tendai Hokkeshū Dembōge 天台法華宗伝法偈, by Saichō (Dengyō Daishi) 最澄 (伝教大師). DDZ 5, 1–30.

Tendai Hokkeshū Gakushōshiki Mondō 天台法華宗學生式問答, by Saichō (Dengyō Daishi) 最澄 (伝教大師). DDZ 1, 335–413.

Tendai Hokkeshū Gozu Hōmon Yōsan 天台法華宗牛頭法門要纂, by Saichō (Dengyō Daishi) 最澄 (伝教大師). DDZ 5, 49–68.

Tendai Sandaibu Fuchū 天台三大部補註, by Ts'ung-i 從義 (Jūgi). ZZ 1, 43, 5–44, 3.

Tendai Shikyō Gi 天台四教儀. T46, no. 1931.

Tendai Zasu Ki 天台座主記. *Zoku Gunsho Ruijū* 4, pt. 2.

Tōshun 東春, by Chih-tu 智度 (Chido). ZZ 1, 40, 3. The name by which Nichiren refers to the *Hoke Kyō Shogisan* 法華經疏義纘, also known as *Hokke Mongu Tōshun*.

Ubasokukai Kyō 優婆塞戒經. T24, no. 1488.

Vimalakīrti Sutra. See *Yuima Kyō*.

Yakushi Hongan Gyō 藥師本願經. T14, no. 449. Full title: *Yakushi Nyorai Hongan Gyō* 藥師如來本願經.

Yakushi Kyō. See *Yakushi Hongan Gyō*.

Yakushi Rurikō Nyorai Hongan Kudoku Kyō 藥師瑠璃光如來願功德經. T14, no. 450.

Yuga Ron 瑜伽論. T30, no. 1579. Full title: *Yuga Shiji Ron* 瑜伽師地論.

Yuga Shiji Ron. See *Yuga Ron*.

Yuima Kyō 維摩經. T14, no. 475. Vimalakīrti Sutra. Also known as *Jōmyō Kyō* 淨名經 and *Yuimakitsu Shosetsu Kyō* 維摩詰所説經.

Zōbō Ketsugi Kyō 像法決疑經. T85, no. 2870.

Zō Hōzō Kyō 雜寶藏經. T4, no. 203.

Zōichi Agon Gyō 增一阿含經. T2, no. 125.

Zoku Kōsō Den 續高僧伝. T50, no. 2060.

INDEX

practices, 329; and courtesy, 498–99; and Gohonzon, 326, 327–28; and Great Law, 176; and Hokke sect, 195; Hsing-man and, 292; and Mahayana Buddhism, 441n18; and Myōhō-renge-kyō, 359; opposition to, 460; persecution of, 65, 102, 486; prayer for rain, 435; prophecies of, 74; slander of, 180–81; and teachings of Buddha, 219; and Tz'u-en, 229; and ultimate law, 351

—and Lotus Sutra, 25–26, 179, 212–13, 429, 484; faith in, 495; practice of, 69; propagation of, 289

Dentō Roku, 142, 146–47n10

Devadatta, 17, 33, 39–40, 49n58, 50nn59, 60, 56, 80n25, 113n7, 181, 228, 262, 294–95, 395, 401n13, 415, 428–29, 439, 459–60, 528; in Gohonzon, 327; killing of nun, 108; Lotus Sutra and, 90, 313; as spiritual aspect of enlightenment, 484

Devadatta chapter, Lotus Sutra, 255, 485

Devil Eloquence, 184n15

Devil of the Sixth Heaven, 113n3, 153n13, 220, 230–31, 237, 240n24, 332, 372, 459, 463n6, 528; in Gohonzon, 327; nature of, 107; and persecutions of Shakyamuni, 466; and practitioners of Lotus Sutra, 490; and T'ien-t'ai, 234

Devils, 237, 242n57, 245–47, 466, 545

Dharma, slander of, 186

Dharma Lotus Fragrance, 396, 402n28

Dharmapāla, 134n3

Dharma Wisdom, Bodhisattva, 394, 400n4; *see also* Hōe, Bodhisattva

Diamond chalice, precept of, 94

Diamond Realm mandala, 128, 138n47, 471n11

Difficult acts, 479–80, 541

Difficult-to-practice way, 135nn17, 22

Disasters, 9, 22, 61n13, 62n14, 65, 71n9, 203n8, 220, 243–44, 347, 349n1, 544; civil strife, 11; drought, 10; Japan and, 221–22, 372; persecution of Nichiren and, 201, 292; predicted by Nichiren, 56, 150, 152; rejection of Lotus Sutra and, 232–33, 437; women and, 41; *see also* Mongol invasion

Doctrines: of Lotus Sutra, 383; teaching of, 529

Dōgi-bō Gishō, 131, 139n63

Dommukatsu, Bodhisattva, 114n24, 433, 439–40n7

Dōmyō (heavenly messenger), 269, 270n5, 315, 319n12, 353n7

Dōshō (heavenly messenger), 269, 270n5, 315, 319n12, 353n7

Dōshō (priest), 315, 318n9

Dōzen-bō, 8, 116, 153n15; debt of gratitude to, 130–33

Dragon Gate, 489–90

Dragon kings, 472; in Gohonzon, 327

Dragon king's daughter, 46, 90, 259n22, 275, 428, 429, 481, 528–29; Buddhahood of, 42, 484–85; in Gohonzon, 327; Lotus Sutra and, 313, 383

Dragons, 473n1

Drought, 10, 472

Eagle Peak, 44, 529

Earthly desires, 353, 428

Earthquake, as omen, 290, 291

Easy acts, 541

Easy-to-practice way, 135nn17, 22

Echi-no Rokurō Zaemon-no-jō, 182, 184n23

Eightfold path, 46n3, 457n25

Eight sufferings, 58–59

Eight teachings, 529

Eight winds, 308

Elements, 356

Ema Chikatoki, Lord, 301–2, 305, 307–8, 321, 331–34, 339

Emanations of Buddha, 128, 530

Emma, 127–28, 348, 376, 530; and votaries of Lotus Sutra, 361

Emperors: Chinese, 318n1; Japanese, assassination of, 335–36

Enchin, *see* Chishō

Enchō, 187, 190n22, 530

End of the Law (*mappō*), 4; *see also* Latter Day of the Law

Endō Tamemori, *see* Abutsu-bō Nittoku

Enemies, 71n4, 146–47n21, 170, 349n2; children as, 397; of Lotus Sutra votaries, 64–65, 69; of women, 45

—of Lotus Sutra, 26–27, 143, 166, 174n32, 444, 460; Japanese people as, 317; punishment of, 386–87

Engaku, 214, 530

Engaku-ji (temple), priests of, 496

Engyō teaching, 218

Enlightenment, 159–60, 204, 353, 451; attainment of, 82–83, 85–86, 205–7; Buddha and, 261, 272; delusion and, 409; Lotus Sutra and, 214, 226; manifestation of, 220; Nichiren and, 348; in present existence, 4; search for, 5–6, 17; of

230, 261, 262, 314, 394, 413, 536; Chinese versions, 400n7; comparisons, 117, 120, 129, 187, 213; and faith, 328; preaching of, 297n17; and women, 41
Keishin, 184n14
Kenchō-ji (temple), priests of, 496
Khubilai Khan, 10
Kiken, Bodhisattva, 370, 378n6
Kikon, 231
Killing, precepts against, 301–2
Kimbara Hokkyō, 161
Kimmei, Emperor, 25, 99n69, 221, 381, 390n6
Kishimojin, 280–81, 281n2; in Gohonzon, 327; and votaries of Lotus Sutra, 361
Kiyomaro, 169, 173n23
Kiyomori, 309, 490
Knowledge, without faith, 498
Kōbō (Kūkai), 4, 23, 87, 89, 92, 187, 196, 230, 240n28, 427, 438, 536; falsehoods by, 436; and Lotus Sutra, 213; prayer for rain, 435, 436; and Shingon sutras, 149; teachings of, 215, 469
Kōdainyo, 281
Kōjō, 187, 190n23
Kokālika, 39, 40, 50n62, 56, 62n18, 72n25, 113–14n7, 258n15, 367, 368n12; slander of Śāriputra, 108
Kokūzō, Bodhisattva, 8, 130, 138n58, 149, 150, 151; image of, 148
Komatsubara Persecution, 10, 31, 106, 412, 483, 486, 487n1, 536–37
Kongōbei Ron, Miao-lo, 449
Kongōsatta, Bodhisattva, 367, 368n11
Konkōmyō Sutra, 55, 435, 438, 444, 516
Kō Nyūdō, 388, 392n27; wife of, 393
Konzoku, King, 137n46
Korea, ancient kingdoms, 390n7
Kōsen-rufu, 73–74, 201, 352, 361, 537
Kuang-wu, Emperor, 330n19
Kudokurin, Bodhisattva, 367, 368n10
Kudō Sakan no jō Yoshitaka, 31, 106, 412
K'uei-chi, 23, 28n14; see also Tz'u-en
Kugan, 231, 240n34
Kūkai, see Kōbō
Kukkuṭārāma Monastery, 317
Kumārajīva, 169, 314, 319n15, 381, 537
Kumārāyana, 316, 319n15, 381, 390n3
Kumbhāṇḍas, 79n13
K'un-lun Mountains, 419
Kusha sect, 119, 218, 223n12, 537
Kutoku gedō, 403n34
Kyō, 35–37, 160

Kyō'ō, letter from Nichiren, 280–81
Kyoto Imperial Court, 309–10

Latter Day of the Law (mappō), 4, 22, 44, 73–76, 83–85, 95, 220, 416, 537; conflicts, 243–44; enlightenment in, 477; evil paths, 498; and Gohonzon, 143, 327; illnesses of, 366; persecutions in, 162, 466–67; practice of Buddhism, 68–69; Treasure Tower, 356
—and Lotus Sutra, 64, 170, 313, 480–81; belief in, 504–5; votaries of, 181–82, 404
—propagation: of Buddha's teachings, 292; of essential teaching, 219; of Lotus Sutra, 205, 289–90, 322, 360 61, 487
—prophecies: 438–39, 448; by Buddha, 333; fulfilled by Nichiren, 102–3
Law: causal, 268–69; debt of gratitude to, 111; secret, 544; slander of, 24–25, 186–88, 254, 283–85; supremacy of, 312–18; wheels of, 114n13
Law suits, 308
Learning, types of, 546
Lesser Vehicle (Hinayana) Buddhism, 2
Letters of Nichiren, xi–xiii
Life, human, 335, dedication to Lotus Sutra, 370; nature of, 158–60; prolonging of, 208–10; sacrifice of, 26–27, 54, 112, 490, 515–17; three existences of, 200–202; transience of, 450; true entity of, 358–63; ultimate law of, 350–53; value of, 210, 301
Life span of humans, 35, 48n33
Light Bright Buddha, 33
Li Kuang, 329, 330n20, 341
Li Lou, 406n1
Liu Pang, 387, 391n21
Local custom, 259n27
Lotus Sutra, 3, 5, 26–27, 90–92, 96n25, 116–17, 151, 195–96, 245–46, 276, 332, 336, 508; abandonment of, 227–32, 242nn41, 42, 419–20, 427, 490; belief in, 269; Buddha and, 473, 476; categories, 218–19; and change of karma, 209; characters in, 274; Chi-tsang and, 195; comparisons, 23–24, 116–18, 120, 187, 212–15, 382–83; daimoku of, 31–46; dedication to, 370; Devil of the Sixth Heaven and, 107; difficulty of sustaining faith in, 305–6; enemies of, 244–47, 386–87, 460; and enlightenment, 82–83, 85–86, 205–7, 380; essence of, 95,

protection by gods, 315; and Ritsu sect, 93; and spread of Buddhism, 77; teachings of, 429; and true entity of life, 358–59; writings of, 421*n*2
—and Lotus Sutra, 37, 43, 74, 193, 194, 251, 281, 285, 405; essence of, 480; *myō* of, 39; propagation of, 393–94;
Middle Day of the Law, 4, 22, 36, 73–75, 83, 415–16, 538
Minamoto clan, 489
Minamoto no Yoritomo, 62*n*19, 101, 144, 147*nn*24, 26, 334, 337–38*n*12, 338*nn*14, 15, 369, 377*n*1
Minamoto no Yoriyoshi, 320*n*23
Minamoto no Yoshinaka, 309, 310*n*7
Minamoto no Yoshitsune, 56, 334, 337–38*n*12
Mind, human, 516–17; Buddhism and, 507–8; illness of, 218; of women, 275
Miroku, Bodhisattva, 142, 146*n*17, 251, 287, 288, 417, 418, 538
Misawa Kojirō, 465
Mission of Nichiren, 14–15
Miura Yasumura, 61*n*10, 241*n*47
Mongol envoys, execution of, 443–45
Mongol invasion, 10, 11–12, 153*n*18, 153–54*n*27, 309–10, 314, 316, 375–76, 378*n*15, 434, 437, 472, 490; Nichiren's predictions, 151–52; Shingon practices and, 436; warriors against, 103, 232
Monju (Monjushiri), Bodhisattva, 42, 142, 192, 251, 286, 287, 288, 297–98*n*24, 298*nn*25, 34, 322, 340, 367, 428, 485, 538; in Gohonzon, 327; and votaries of Lotus Sutra, 151, 361
Monks, 122, 139*n*66
Mononobe no Moriya, 221, 225*nn*26, 27, 424*n*34
Mononobe no Ōmuraji, 221, 224*n*24
Moon, movement of, 80*n*26
Moon of Emancipation, Bodhisattva, 394, 400*n*4
Moriya, *see* Mononobe no Moriya
Mother, debt of gratitude to, 384–85
Mount Hua, 64*n*37
Mount Minobu, 141, 503; Nichiren's retirement to, 12, 82, 340–41, 426, 447, 483, 515
Mount Shang, 141
Mount Sumeru, 445–46*n*6
Mo-yeh, 349*n*5; sword of, 348
Muhengyō, Bodhisattva, 286, 363; and Myōhō-renge-kyō, 359
Munemori (Taira no Munemori), 244, 248*n*7

Munenaga (Ikegami Munenaga), 226, 235, 242*n*53, 243, 534–35
Munenaka (Ikegami Munenaka), 106, 226, 235, 242*n*53, 243, 248*n*6, 308, 310*n*4, 534–35
Munetchi Lake, 503, 503*n*3
Mūrdhagata, 297*n*16
Muryōgi Sutra, 67, 86, 88, 213, 253, 261, 382, 413, 485, 538
Muryōju Sutra, 45, 413
Musashi, former governor of, *see* Hōjō Nobutoki
Mushō Dōji, 472, 474*n*2
Myō, 37–40, 42–43, 160, 274, 350
Myōgaku stage, 220
Myōhō-ama, 479
Myōhō-renge-kyō, 6, 24, 34–40, 48*n*28, 76, 83, 91, 143, 158–60, 273–74, 286–288, 322, 539; benefits of, 94; Gohonzon of, 365–67; slander of, 185; as true entity of life, 358–60; as ultimate law, 350–53; *see also* Nam-myoho-renge-kyo
Myōichi-ama, 345
Myōji-soku, 76, 83, 162, 163*n*7
Myōjō, 208
Myōon, Bodhisattva, 340
Myōshōgon, King, 395
Myōun, 308–9, 310*n*6
Mystic Law (*myōhō*), 67, 158–60; healing power of, 197; mandala of, 365–67; propagation of, 204, 360
Mystic powers of Buddhas, 287, 359
Mystic principles, 38, 49*nn*47–49
Mystic Way, spread of, 85

Nāgārjuna, Bodhisattva, 89, 169, 429, 444, 539; *Bodai Shiryō Ron*, 186; *Dai Ron*, 340; and Gohonzon, 327; and karmic illness, 193; and Lotus Sutra, 92, 179, 181, 212; and *myō* of Lotus Sutra, 39; persecutions of, 69, 102, 162; preaching of, 176
Nagasaki Tokitsuna, 103
Nagoe-no-ama, 104, 461, 464*n*17
Naishidokoro, 123
Names, xiii–xiv
Nam-myoho-renge-kyo, 6, 8, 17, 31–46, 65–66, 70, 121, 135*n*20, 179, 205, 236, 262–63, 305–6, 348, 477, 480–81, 539; and attainment of Buddhahood, 497; chanting of, 250–51, 257, 316, 351–53, 414–15, 455; propagation of, 487; and Treasure Tower, 356
Namu, 515

Namu Amida Butsu, 5, 385
Namu Amida Butsu Sutra, 383
Namu-ichijō-myōten, 255, 257, 259n24
Nandā, 124, 136n34
Nanjō Hyōe Shichirō (Lord Ueno), 412; wife of, 426, 447
Nanjō Tokimitsu (Lord Ueno), 426, 447, 458, 472, 475, 483, 489, 504–5, 539; illness of, 502
Nan-yüeh, 178n11, 206, 288, 539
Nara, temples of, 183n12, 309, 310n11
Negations, 367–68n3; Sanron sect and, 366
Nembutsu, 5–6, 57, 58, 87, 88, 89, 92–93, 252, 269, 385, 539; discarding of, 413; and enlightenment, 417; faith in, 414; and Lotus Sutra, 481; Nichiren and, 66, 120–22, 130, 149; practitioners of, 125, 372–76, 416, 419–20, 477; women and, 45; *see also* Jōdo sect
New Year's Gosho, 513–14
Nichigaku, 369
Nichigen, 448, 456n1
Nichigen-nyo, 268, 280
Nichigon-ama, 501
Nichiji, 447
Nichimyō Shonin, 276, 312, 315; letter from Nichiren, 271–77
Nichinyo, Lady, 326
Nichiren, xi, 1, 18; and attainment of Buddhahood, 55; biography, 7–13; as Bodhisattva of the Earth, 361, 363; death of, 226; disciples of, 285, 308, 328, 334, 348, 351–52, 356, 360–61, 448, 461, 464n17; and enemies of Lotus Sutra, 26–27; and erroneous sects, 371, 373–74; family of, 62n22; and Fukyō, 291; and Gohonzon, 327; hatred of, 222; *ichinen sanzen* of, 222; illness of, 340–41; Japanese people and, 352; letters of, 13–18; mother of, 31, 412; and Mystic Law, 360; and Nembutsu, 120–22; Nembutsu followers and, 420; offerings sent to, 217; opposition to, 166–67, 169, 238; persecutions of, 59–60, 56–57, 78–79, 101–5, 108–10, 112, 149, 150, 155–56, 161, 203n9, 265–66, 290–93, 295, 314, 325n7, 376, 412, 467–68, 483–87; preaching of, 293; prophecies, 55–56, 73–79; and provisional teachings, 69; Pure Land sect and, 19; and reform of Buddhism, 6; retirement to Mount Minobu, 82, 93, 426, 447, 483; and Shan-wu-wei, 128; and Shijō Kingo, 334–35,

340; slander of, 76–77, 201, 386; sufferings of, 58–59; wisdom of, 130
—exiles of, 173n25, 323, 386–87; Izu, 10, 19, 102, 106, 173n25, 283, 296n1, 369, 407–10; Sado, 11, 53, 93, 102, 161, 165–66, 173n25, 175–77, 177n1, 179, 182, 265, 283, 295, 369, 370, 374, 387
—and Lotus Sutra, 57–59, 109, 170–71, 179–80, 317–18; propagation of, 14–15; as votary of, 27, 76–77, 143, 182, 201, 266, 362, 370, 460–61
Nichiren Buddhism, xi, 1
Nichiren Daishōnin Gosho Zenshū, xii
Nichiren Shoshu International Center (NSIC), xii
Nihon Daruma-shū, 29n29
Nihon Shoki, 142
Nii-ama Gozen, letter to, 140–45
Niida Shirō Nobutsuna, 462, 464n18
Niike Saemon-no-jō, letter from Nichiren, 492
Nikkō Shonin, 145n2, 447, 483, 526
Nikyō Ron, 148, 152n3
Nine great persecutions (ordeals), 65, 71n7, 181, 539
Ninna-ji, bishop of, 309
Ninniku, 274, 278n12
Ninnō Sutra, 55, 201, 261, 292, 435, 436, 438, 441n28
Nintoku, Prince, 234–35
Nirgrantha Jñātaputra, 397
Nirvana, 353
Nirvana Sutra, 20, 23, 26–27, 32, 57, 120, 132, 166, 185, 201, 209, 213, 231, 292, 332, 394, 455, 516; and Brahmans, 180; Chinese versions, 400–401n8; comparisons, 117, 213; and karmic illness, 192, 193; and karmic retribution, 161; and Lotus Sutra, 167, 194, 476; and persecutions of Buddha, 107; and pre-Lotus Sutra teachings, 85, 86; and priests, 206; and slander of Law, 438; and suffering, 246; and tears, 362; versions of, 36; and women, 41–42
Nishiyama Nyūdō, 432, 443
Nisshō, 243, 247n1, 305, 306n1
Nitchō, *see* Iyo-bō
Non-Buddhist teachers, 541–42
Nondualism, principle of, 16
Nonhuman beings, 51n71, 529
Nōse, Prince, 278n13
Noto-bō, 104, 461, 464n17

ment of, 498; in Gohonzon, 327;
persecution of, 459
Satta, Prince, 54, 61*n*6, 388, 391*n*23
Scholars, and Lotus Sutra, 181
Schools, 545–46; *see also* Sects
Sects, 119–22, 134*n*13, 167–68, 171–72*n*7,
190*n*20, 437–38, 441*n*25; and attainment
of Buddhahood, 67; and capacity of
understanding, 213–14; debates with,
87–95; erroneous teachings of, 89,
117–18, 366, 371; and evil paths, 237; and
Lotus Sutra, 58, 181, 386, 481; Nara
period, 29*n*26; Nichiren and, 133, 149,
150–51; at Seichō-ji (temple), 148;
support of, 509
Seichō-ji (temple), 8, 31, 116, 148; priests of,
letter to, 148–52
Selected Writings of Nichiren, Yampolsky, xi, 1,
13
Self: Buddha within, 513; Gohonzon within,
328
Senchaku Shū, 291
Seng-chao, 29*n*23, 417, 418, 423*n*25
Seng-ch'üan, 230
Sennichi-ama, 365, 366, 380, 393
Sentient beings, 329*n*5, 350–51; in
Gohonzon, 327
Sentō, King, 137*n*42
Sen'yo, King, 302, 303–4*n*7, 509, 511*n*9
Sessen Dōji, 54, 61*n*5, 111–12, 114*n*24, 232,
272–73, 277–78*n*5, 317–18, 409, 410*n*6,
450, 451–54, 516
Setaka, 309, 311*n*15
Seven Buddhas of the Past, 48–49*n*41
Seven disasters, 56, 61*n*13, 62*n*14
Seven treasures, 61*n*4
Seven Worthies of the Bamboo Grove, 145*n*6
Shabaya river, 43
Shakubuku, 54, 66, 68–69, 162, 540
Shakusen, Miao-lo, 87
Shakyamuni Buddha, 93, 122–24, 197*n*4,
207, 295, 298*n*24, 348, 405; attainment of
Buddhahood, 91; and Bodhisattva Fukyō,
290–91; Brahmans and, 437; debt of
gratitude to, 110–11; Devadatta and,
39–40, 401*n*13, 485; disciples of, 239*n*7,
288–89, 356, 411*n*10, 544–45; emanations
of, 530; enemies of, 495; enlightenment
of, 298*n*29; and Gohonzon, 142–43, 327;
as human, 336–37; images of, 137*nn*41,
42, 289; Japanese people and, 371–73; life
of, 358; manifested body of, 224*n*16;
medicine of, 367; and *Myōhō-renge-kyō*,

274, 286–88, 358–59; and Mystic Law,
205; and omens, 78; opposition to, 166;
past existences, 61*n*5, 114–15*n*24,
241*nn*41, 42, 272–74, 277*n*1, 277–78*n*5,
278*n*9–13, 302, 303–4*n*7, 304*n*8, 317,
370, 388, 391*nn*23, 24, 409, 410*nn*6–8,
462, 464*n*212, 511*n*9; persecutions of, 65,
71*n*7, 102, 107, 459–60, 466; persons
taught by, 490; preaching of, 422*n*13; as
prince, 234; prophecies of, 200–201;
protection by, 316; reincarnations of, 409;
and *sahā* world, 122–26; *shakubuku*
practice, 69; and Shijō Kingo, 322, 323;
slander of, 108, 128, 238; son of, 47*n*9;
sovereignty of, 414; statue of, 221;
successors of, 30*nn*39, 40, 546; sutras of,
3, 213; and ultimate law, 350, 351; virtues
of, 359; women and, 268
—and Lotus Sutra, 34, 66–67, 88–89, 116,
146*n*16, 151, 196, 409; belief in, 504–5;
preaching of, 424*nn*41, 42; propagation
of, 340–41; votaries of, 94, 360–61
— teachings of, 4, 19–27, 35–38, 44, 214–15,
218–19, 253, 393–94, 396, 413–14, 427;
early, 286; contradictory, 475–77; pre-
Lotus Sutra, 89–90, 260
Shang Chün, Prince, 275
Shan-tao, 87, 89, 97*n*33, 118, 120, 134*n*7,
230, 240*n*30, 378*n*9, 391*n*17, 424–25*n*43;
erroneous doctrines, 125; teachings of,
372, 420
Shan-wu-wei, 87, 89, 96*n*26, 116, 126–30,
137*n*46, 169, 181, 184*n*18, 196, 230,
240*nn*19, 28, 371, 432, 438, 540–41;
comparison of sutras, 120; erroneous
teachings, 168, 469; and Lotus Sutra, 229,
476; prayer for rain, 434, 436
Shen Nung, 194, 198*n*17, 218
Shibi, King, 232, 241*n*42, 278*n*10, 388,
391*n*24, 409, 410*n*7
Shigemori (Taira no Shigemori), 244, 248*n*7
Shigeyoshi, 334, *see also* Taguchi Shigeyoshi
Shih Ch'ao-i, 397, 402*n*32
Shih K'uang, 406*n*1
Shih Shih-ming, 397, 402*n*32
Shiiji Shirō, 404
Shijō Kingo (Saburō Zaemon-no-jō), 8, 53,
61*n*1, 106, 183*n*1, 209–10, 211*n*5, 217,
266, 268, 280, 541; attack on, 342–43;
brothers of, 337*n*11; letters from
Nichiren, 155–56, 179–82, 265–66,
283–96, 301–3, 305–6, 307–10, 321–24,
339–41; Lord Ema and, 301–2, 305, 321;

and Lord Ema's illness, 331–34, 339;
and Lotus Sutra, 321–24; transfer of,
307–8
Shi'nenjo,T'ien-t'ai, 167, 172n12
Shinga, 188, 191n32
Shingon sect, 4, 120, 125, 130, 168, 195–96,
309–10, 366, 386, 419, 438, 541;
erroneous teachings, 371, 469–70;
esoteric doctrines, 127–28; founder of,
126–27; Japanese people and, 436; and
Lotus Sutra, 129, 476, 481; and Mongol
invasion, 434; Nichiren and, 66, 121–22,
148–50; reply to, 87; support of, 509;
teachers, 314
Shinjikan Sutra, 110, 112, 234
Shinjō, 536
Shintoism, and Buddhism, 1, 3
Shinzei, 188, 191n31
Ship, Lotus Sutra as, 405
Shōbōnen Sutra, 94
Shōfu-bō, 104, 461, 464n17, 488n3;
persecution of Nichiren, 483–84, 486
Shō-hokke-kyō, 35
Shōi, 25, 29n19, 62n23, 231
Shōjari, 274, 279n14
Shōju, 54, 68, 162, 541
Shōmon, 214, 541
Shōmon disciples, 227–28, 544–45
Shōmu, Emperor, 2
Shōni Shigeyoshi, 378n17
Shōtoku, Prince, 28n16, 146n12, 221,
224n25, 225n26, 335–36, 381, 390n8,
516; see also Jōgū, Prince
Shozuiki, 76, 83
Shubin, prayer for rain, 435
Shu-ch'i, Prince, 233–34
Shudama, King, 274, 278n11; see also Fumyō,
King
Shugo Sutra, 438, 441–42n28
Shukuōke, Bodhisattva, 36
Shun, King, 123, 135n27, 275
Shusenda Buddha, 34, 47n23
Shūyō Shū, 149
Sibling relationships, 295
Sick person, encouragement to, 413–21
Siddhārtha, Prince, 230, 246; see also
Shakyamuni Buddha
Simulated Law, era of, 4; see also Middle Day
of the Law
Sincerity of offerings, 516
Sins, 283–84, 296n7; cardinal, 39–40, 136n31,
283–84, 296n7, 302, 373, 376, 385, 415,
422n17, 530; eradication of, 284–85;

killing as, 302; seriousness of, 228; see also
Offenses
Six auspicious happenings, 299n43
Six paths, 542
Six portents, 299n43
Slanders, 185–88, 448–51, 499n3, 531–32;
admonitions against, 204–7; of Lotus
Sutra, 22, 24–25, 27–28n5, 57–59, 87–95,
128–29, 143, 185, 194, 196–97, 269,
284–85, 302, 415, 448–51, 470, 492–95,
496, 505; of Mahayana sutras, 57; of
Nichiren, 76–77, 201, 386
Sō (Sō no Sukekuni), 375, 378n16
Soga no Sukune, 221, 224n23
Soga no Umako, 221, 225nn26, 27, 336,
338n19
Sōgi Ritsu, 262
Soka Gakkai, xii
Sokushin jōbutsu doctrine, 427, 428
Sŏng-myŏng, King, 381, 390n7
Sō no Sukekuni (Sō), 375, 378n16
Sovereign of country: debt of gratitude to,
110; opposition to Lotus Sutra, 233
Soya Jirō Hyōe-no-jō Kyōshin (Hōren), 204
Soya Nyūdō, 161
Śrīmālā Sutra, 214
Stupidity, 508
Subhūti, 286, 297n20, 542; alms to, 496
Subject (chi), principle of, 356
Śuddhipanthaka, 17, 415, 423n19, 438–39
Śuddhodana, King, 230, 234, 246, 279, 381
Suffering, 58–59, 216nn14, 15, 246, 231–32,
353
Suiko, Empress, 225n26
Sujin, Emperor, 220–21
Suke no Ajari, 144
Sunakṣatra, 32–33, 40, 50n66, 72n25, 102,
105n3, 397, 402n33; slander of Buddha,
238
Sundarī, 181
Sun Goddess, 122–23, 144, 177n6, 348–49,
542; and epidemics, 221; see also Tenshō
Daijin
Suri Handoku, 161, 163n1
Śūryasoma, 381, 390n4, 418
Sushun, Emperor, 225n26, 335–36, 338n19
Sutras, 20, 43–45, 507; classification of, 3,
263–64n18; comparisons, 87–91, 116–20,
128–29, 187, 195–96, 213–14, 218–19,
226–27, 313–14, 382–83; distinctions
among, 253; divisions of, 174n29; and evil
paths, 237; false, 118; interpretation of,
129; minor, and Lotus Sutra, 386;

Gohonzon, 326, 327; and Great Law, 176; and *ichinen sanzen*, 129; and intensity of practice, 428; *Maka Shikan*, 236–27; and meditation, 222; and Myōhō-renge-kyō, 359, 360; and Nirvana Sutra, 167; and omens, 78, 290; opposition to, 65, 460; persecutions of, 102, 486; practice of Buddha's teachings, 79; prayer for rain, 435; precepts of, 209; and pre-Lotus Sutra teachings, 262; prophecies of, 73, 74, 85; and Tathagata, 359; teachings of, 118–19, 480; and teachings of Buddha, 219; and Treasure Tower, 355; and ultimate law, 350–51; and wisdom of Buddhas, 204
—and Lotus Sutra, 68, 69, 169, 179, 193, 212, 229, 251, 485; essence of, 480; faith in, 306
Tiger of Death, 494
Timing of Buddhist teachings, 21–22, 24–25, 55, 68; Lotus Sutra propagation, 289–92, 416–17
Tōgaku stage, 220
Tō-ji (temple), 309, 310*n*11; bishop of, 309
Tōjō Kagenobu (Tōjō Saemon Nyūdō Renchi), 10, 131, 139*n*62, 151, 153*nn*9, 24, 412, 487*n*1, 536–37; attack on Nichiren, 31
Tōjō village, 143–44
Toki Jōnin, 8, 19, 61*n*1, 158, 183*n*1, 192, 208, 323, 325*n*15, 337*n*1, 407, 546
—letters from Nichiren, 53–63, 175–77, 179–82, 185–88, 200–202, 217–22
Tokuitsu, 180, 183*n*11
Tōkurō Moritsuna, 393, 399
Tokushō Dōji, 472–73, 474*n*2, 502
Tongues of Buddhas, 91, 274, 287, 402*n*26, 422*n*10, 504, 506*n*2; and Lotus Sutra, 396
Tōnotsuji Jūrō, 53
Tōshirō, 268
Tōshun, 149
Transfer of the essence, 287
Translations of Nichiren's letters, xii–xiv
Trāyastriṃśa Heaven, 146*n*14
Treasures, 83, 515, 546; children as, 397–99; debt of gratitude to, 110–12; three kinds, 335–37
Treasure Tower, 15–16, 146*nn*15, 16, 286, 355–57, 546; Gohonzon, 327
Treatises, 87–88
Tripitaka Masters, Chinese, 432; prayers for rain, 434–39; *see also* Fa-tao; Hsüan-tsang; Kumārāyaṇa; Sūryasoma; Shan-wu-wei

True Buddha, 359
True entity, principle of, 360
True Law, 405; blessings of, 231; slander of, 194
True Object of Worship, The (Kanjin no Honzon Shō), 53
True requital, sutra of, 380–89
True sutras, 87
True teaching, protectors of, 220
Tsukahara, 11, 175; debate at, 350, 355, 369
Tsukimaro, 280
Tsukushi, Mongol attack, 151, 375, 378*n*15
Tsun-shih, 77, 80*n*30, 176, 178*n*11
Tsushima, Mongol attack, 375
Tung Yüan, 145*n*5
Tu-shun, 181, 184*n*19, 230, 536
Tuṣita Heaven, 146*n*17, 298*n*36, 400*n*6
Twenty-five successors, 162
Twenty-four characters of Fukyō, 76
Tz'u-en, 169, 173*n*20, 229, 230, 239*n*17, 547; *see also* K'uei-chi

Udayana, King, 125, 137*n*41
Uemon no Sakan, *see* Munenaka
Ueno, Lady, 426
Ueno Shichirō Jirō, *see* Nanjō Tokimitsu
Uji, Prince, 234–35
Ulūka, 134*n*12, 223*n*9, 441*n*23
Understanding: capacity for, 20–21, 24, 55, 117, 213–15; kinds of, 495
Unfilial children, 275
Unity of existence, 15–16
Universal salvation, Lotus Sutra and, 6
Utoku, King, 302, 304*n*8, 535–36
Utpalavarṇā, 39, 108, 113*n*7; Devadatta and, 459–60
Utsubusa-no-ama, 465, 468–69, 470*n*3

Vaidehī, Lady, 193, 395, 401*n*18
Vairocana Buddha, 87, 97*n*28, 262, 286, 297*n*18
Vaiśālī, 197*n*4
Vajra implement, 435, 440*n*15
Vassals, feudal Japan, 138*n*57
Vasubandhu, Bodhisattva, 187, 189*n*10, 194, 198*n*24, 424*n*35, 444, 547; and Gohonzon, 327; and Lotus Sutra, 179, 181; persecutions of, 102; preaching of, 176
Vehicles, 79*n*10, 546–47
Vimalakīrti, 192, 194
Vimalakīrti Sutra, 192, 261
Vimalamitra, 80*n*25

OTHER WORKS IN THE COLUMBIA ASIAN STUDIES SERIES

Translations from the Asian Classics

Records of the Historian: Chapters from the Shih chi of Ssu-ma Ch'ien, tr.   1969
     Burton Watson. Paperback ed. only.

Cold Mountain: 100 Poems by the T'ang Poet Han-shan, tr. Burton Watson.   1970
     Also in paperback ed.

Twenty Plays of the Nō Theatre, ed. Donald Keene. Also in paperback ed.   1970

Chūshingura: The Treasury of Loyal Retainers, tr. Donald Keene. Also in   1971
     paperback ed.

The Zen Master Hakuin: Selected Writings, tr. Philip B. Yampolsky. Also in   1971
     paperback ed.

Chinese Rhyme-Prose: Poems in the Fu Form from the Han and Six   1971
     Dynasties Periods, tr. Burton Watson. Also in paperback ed.

Kūkai: Major Works, tr. Yoshito S. Hakeda. Also in paperback ed.   1972

The Old Man Who Does as He Pleases: Selections from the Poetry and Prose   1973
     of Lu Yu, tr. Burton Watson

The Lion's Roar of Queen Śrīmālā, tr. Alex and Hideko Wayman   1974

Courtier and Commoner in Ancient China: Selections from the History of the   1974
     Former Han by Pan Ku, tr. Burton Watson. Also in paperback ed.

Japanese Literature in Chinese, vol. 1: *Poetry and Prose in Chinese by Japanese*   1975
     Writers of the Early Period, tr. Burton Watson

Japanese Literature in Chinese, vol. 2: *Poetry and Prose in Chinese by Japanese*   1976
     Writers of the Later Period, tr. Burton Watson

Scripture of the Lotus Blossom of the Fine Dharma, tr. Leon Hurvitz. Also   1976
     in paperback ed.

Love Song of the Dark Lord: Jayadeva's Gītagovinda, tr. Barbara Stoler Miller.   1977
     Also in paperback ed. Cloth ed. includes critical text of the Sanskrit.

Ryōkan: Zen Monk-Poet of Japan, tr. Burton Watson

Calming the Mind and Discerning the Real: From the Lam rim chen mo of   1977
     Tson-kha-pa, tr. Alex Wayman

The Hermit and the Love-Thief: Sanskrit Poems of Bhartrihari and Bilhaṇa,   1978
     tr. Barbara Stoler Miller

The Lute: Kao Ming's P'i-p'a chi, tr. Jean Mulligan. Also in paperback ed.   1980

A Chronicle of Gods and Sovereigns: Jinnō Shōtōki of Kitabatake Chikafusa,   1980
     tr. H. Paul Varley.

Among the Flowers: The Hua-chien chi, tr. Lois Fusek   1982

Grass Hill: Poems and Prose by the Japanese Monk Gensei, tr. Burton Watson   1983

Doctors, Diviners, and Magicians of Ancient China: Biographies of Fang-shih,   1983
     tr. Kenneth J. DeWoskin. Also in paperback ed.

Theater of Memory: The Plays of Kālidāsa, ed. Barbara Stoler Miller. Also   1984
     in paperback ed.

The Columbia Book of Chinese Poetry: From Early Times to the Thirteenth   1984
     Century, ed. and tr. Burton Watson. Also in paperback ed.

Poems of Love and War: From the Eight Anthologies and the Ten Long Poems   1985
     of Classical Tamil, tr. A. K. Ramanujan. Also in paperback ed.

The Bhagavad Gita: Krishna's Counsel in Time of War, tr. Barbara Stoler   1986
     Miller

Studies in Asian Culture

Companions to Asian Studies

Introduction to Asian Civilizations
Wm. Theodore de Bary, Editor

Sources of Japanese Tradition, 1958; paperback ed., 2 vols., 1964
Sources of Indian Tradition, 1958; paperback ed., 2 vols., 1964; 2d ed., 2 vols., 1988
Sources of Chinese Tradition, 1960; paperback ed., 2 vols., 1964

Neo-Confucian Studies

Modern Asian Literature Series